Gender, Justice and Legal Feminism

Volume 2

Series Editors

Angela Condello, University of Messina, Messina, Italy

Anne Wagner, Law Faculty, Lille University, Lille, France

The Series Gender, Justice and Legal Feminism seeks to harness the diverse and innovative work within and across the boundaries of jurisprudence and gender studies, with a specific attention to approaches inspired both by traditional and more recent feminist movements (e.g., both by difference feminism and LGBTQ+ streams – with their different conceptualizations of identity and neutrality). Sexual difference can be considered as one of the characteristics that differentiate individuals (like for instance age, or ethnic belonging) and such difference plays a focal function in issues of equality, justice, discrimination, as the philosophical concept of "différence" as properly shown. Such difference is indeed linguistic, logica, theoretical and must be studied in all its aspects. Through the lense of the difference, the series aim to publish works engaging with the intrinsic bond between justice and gender studies (through language and psychoanalysis), encouraging perspectives that can be defined as feminist according to the various meanings attributed to such term. For example, like in the meaning attributed to the term by the project of Feminist Legal Judgments, which demonstrated that legal practice can be "rewritten" and re-imagined from a point of view that includes diverse subjectivities and does not consider the male subject as the dominant and principal subject of the law. The main objective of the series is to build on theories on gender and feminism in order to propose a different perspective on legal science and method. In pursuing these tasks, the series aims to engage with the connections between gender identity, gender relations and political systems, and with all the societal aspects interacting in the construction and depiction of gender through language and human action. Such type of inquiries challenges the positivist view of law and constitutes a privileged critical point of observation. The series welcomes proposals – be they edited collections or single-authored monographs – emphasizing the conflicts and connections between justice, gender, and law, proposing critical approaches to law and feminist studies, offering analyses in areas such as jurisprudence, legal theory, gender studies, legal semiotics, law and language.

Keywords: Justice, Law, Feminism, Gender Studies, Jurisprudence, Equality, Language, Symbolic Order, Difference Feminism, Abuse, Violence, Stereotypes, Neglection, Vulnerability, Welfare, Mental health and Social Care, Anti-Discriminatory/Affirmative Actions, Human Rights, Freedom of Expression and Choice, Resilience, Queer studies, LGBTQ+ studies

Unique Selling Points:

- Challenges traditional approaches to gender and law through the unique lense of feminist discourses
- Combines the insights from legal theory, legal feminist, semiotics of law, law and language and is strongly interdisciplinary
- Proposes a new interdisciplinary field bringing together well established and young, innovative research

Angela Condello · Anne Wagner
Editors

Gender Stereotypes

Case Studies, Policies and Theoretical Approaches

Springer

Editors
Angela Condello
University of Messina
Messina, Italy

Anne Wagner
University of Lille
Lille, France

ISSN 2948-1651 ISSN 2948-166X (electronic)
Gender, Justice and Legal Feminism
ISBN 978-3-031-63904-3 ISBN 978-3-031-63905-0 (eBook)
https://doi.org/10.1007/978-3-031-63905-0

This Springer imprint is published by the registered company Springer Nature Switzerland AG
The registered company address is: Gewerbestrasse 11, 6330 Cham, Switzerland

Acknowledgments

Angela Condello and Anne Wagner wish to express their profound appreciation to everyone who contributed to the success of this volume, *Gender Stereotypes – Case Studies, Policies, and Theoretical Approaches*, the second installment in our series following *(In)Visible Signs of Gender-Based Violence* (https://link.springer.com/book/10.1007/978-3-031-35513-4).

We extend our sincere thanks to the brilliant contributors whose expertise and perspectives from diverse cultural and academic backgrounds have enriched this publication. With voices from countries across Europe, Asia, the Americas, and beyond, their collaborative spirit has helped create an invaluable resource for researchers, educators, policy-makers, and practitioners around the world, advancing a nuanced understanding of gender dynamics in contemporary society.

A special note of gratitude is owed to Anja Trautman, our Publishing Editor at Springer. Her dedication to fostering knowledge sharing and her commitment to this project have been instrumental in making this publication a reality, launching the first volume in the newly established Law Book Series: *Gender, Justice, and Legal Feminism* (https://www.springer.com/series/17265).

We also express heartfelt thanks to the Centre de Recherche Droits et Perspectives du Droit (ULR 4487), Équipe René Demogue (https://crdp.univ-lille.fr/les-equipes/equipe-rene-demogue), and the University of Lille for their unwavering support, especially during the international congress "Combating Gender-based Violence" held in July 2023 (https://crdp.univ-lille.fr/evenement/gender-equity). Our gratitude also extends to the Région Hauts-de-France, whose support for research and innovation has greatly contributed to our efforts in this domain.

This edited volume delves into the multifaceted nature of gender stereotypes, examining their manifestations across various cultural and social contexts. By exploring theoretical frameworks and presenting diverse case studies, it offers a comprehensive analysis of how gender stereotypes are constructed, perpetuated, and challenged. The insights provided aim to inform and inspire policies and practices that promote gender equality and social justice.

Région Hauts-de-France

Faculté des sciences juridiques, politiques et sociales Université de Lille

Université de Lille

DEMOGUE
Equipe de Recherche en Droit des Contrats et Théorie du Droit
CRDP-ULR n°4487

Contents

About the Editors

Angela Condello Ph.D., JD is Associate Professor of Legal Philosophy in the Law Department, University of Messina. She held a Jean Monnet Module on human rights and critical legal thinking at the University of Torino. She published seven monographs (among which *Analogica. Il doppio legame tra diritto e analogia*, Giappichelli 2018 and *Il diritto come metodo e la scienza algoritmica. Una critica a partire da Bobbio e Scarpelli*, ETS 2022) and numerous edited journal issues (Law and Literature, Law Text Culture, Rivista di Estetica, International Journal for the Semiotics of Law), on top of volumes *–Money, Social Ontology and Law* (with J.R. Searle and M. Ferraris, 2019, Routledge 2019), *Post-Truth, Philosophy and Law* (co-edited with T. Andina, Routledge, 2019), *New Rhetorics for Contemporary Legal Discourse* (Edinburgh University Press, 2020). She writes entries for the Research Handbook for Law and Literature, the Elgar Concise Encyclopedia of Law and Literature and the Research Handbook of Legal Semiotic and sits on the board of Law and Literature, Law Text Culture, International Journal for the Semiotics of Law, Teoria e critica della regolazione sociale. She directs Labont Law and is the scientific curator of the Rapporto sullo stato dei diritti in Italia for A Buon Diritto.

- She has edited the following volumes:
  - 2022, A. Simone, I. Boiano, A. Condello (eds.), *Legal Feminism. Italian Theories and Perspectives*, Routledge (translation: E. Gainsforth).

- 2020, A. Condello (ed.), *New Rhetorics for Contemporary Legal Discourse*, Edinburgh University Press, ISBN: 9781474450560.
- 2019, T. Toracca, A. Condello (eds.), *Law, Labour and the Humanities. Contemporary European Perspectives*, Series *Discourses of Law*, Routledge, Abingdon-New York, ISBN 978-0367077174.
- 2019, A. Condello, E. Sferrazza Papa (eds.), *Burocrazia, Mobilitazione, Normatività. Un dialogo tra Maurizio Ferraris e Gianluca Cuozzo*, Rosenberg & Sellier, Torino, ISBN 9788878857872.
- 2019, A. Condello, T. Andina (eds.), *Post-Truth, Philosophy and Law*, Routledge, Abingdon- New York, ISBN: 9781138324664.
- 2019, A. Simone, I. Boiano, A. Condello (eds.), *Femminismo giuridico. Teorie e problemi*, Mondadori, Milano, ISBN: 978-88-6184-692-0.
- 2018, A. Condello (ed.), *Il denaro e i suoi inganni* [J.R. Searle, M. Ferraris], edited and with an essay by A. Condello, Einaudi, Torino, ISBN: 978-88-06-23577-2. Spanish translation, *Los engaños del dinero*, ed. Altamarea, September 2020.
- 2018, A. Condello, M. Antaki, S. Huygabaert, S. Marusek (eds.), *Sensing the Nation's Law: Historical Inquiries on the Aesthetics of Democratic Legitimacy*, Springer, Berlin, ISBN: 978-3-319-75495-6.
- 2025 (Forthcoming). A. Wagner & A. Angello (eds), *(In)Visible Signs of Gender-Based Violence*, Springer.

• Her international research responsibilities are:

Since 2023: Co-PI of the National Project (PRIN) "One Too Many Moneys. Alternative Digital Currencies and the Future of Money".
From 01/09/2017 to 31/07/2020, Jean Monnet Module "Human Rights Culture in the European Union"—Section "Teaching and Research"—code: 587184-EPP-1-2017-1-IT- EPPJMO-MODULE. Website of the project: http://www.cultureofnormativity.unito.it/.
Since November 2019, Scientific Coordination of Rapporto Diritti (A Buon Diritto, funded by Chiesa Valdese), launched June 25th 2020: https://www.rapportodiritti.it.

- Her international editorial responsibilities are:
  - She is the Series Co-Editor of *Gender, Justice and Legal Feminism* (Springer) with Anne Wagner.
  - She sits on othe board of the series in Legal Philosophy *L'Europa del pensiero*, Castelvecchi Editore.
  - She coordinates the board of "Teoria e critica della regolazione sociale".
  - She sits on the board of *Studies of Law, Art and History*, Messina University Press.
  - She is in the COLLEGIO DEI REVISORI, Journal "Arte e diritto", Giuffrè.
  - She sits on the board of "Ordines".
  - She sits on the board of the *Springer Series in Law and Visual Jurisprudence.*
  - She sits on the board of "De Europa. European and Global Studies Journal".
  - She is the managing editor of the Brill Series *Research Perspectives in Art and Law.*
  - She is a general editor of "Law and Literature".
  - She sits on the board of "Rivista di Estetica".
  - She sits on the board of "Law Text Culture".
  - She is an international advisor of the "International Journal for the Semiotics of Law".

- **Angela Condello** got the following visiting posts/ fellowships:
- Visiting Professorships: University of Southern Cape, South Africa; Cardozo Law School, New York; Australian National University, Canberra; McGill Law School, Montreal; Department of Interdisciplinary Study of Law, Private Law and Business Law, University of Ghent.
- Fellowships and Scholarships: Max Planck Reseach Fellowship, Max Planck Society, Max Planck Institute for Comparative Public Law and International Law, Heidelberg; Fellow, Department of Philosophy, UC Berkeley; Permanent Fellow, Law and Theory Lab, University of Westminster, Law School, London; Fernand Braudel Fellow [IFER-Incoming; ACTION Marie Curie, Cofund, 7e PCRD], École des hautes études en sciences sociales (EHESS), Centre d'études des normes juridiques "Yan Thomas"; Käte Hamburger Kolleg "Recht als Kultur", Center for

Advanced Study in the Humanities, Rheinische Friedrich-Wilhelms-Universität, Bonn.

DIPARTIMENTO
DI ECCELLENZA
MUR
2023 - 2027

Anne Wagner Ph.D. and holder of a Habilitation à Diriger des Recherches in Private Law, is a Research Associate Professor at Lille University, affiliated with ULR 4487-CRDP (Centre de recherche Droits et Perspectives du Droit, équipe René Demogue) in France. Her primary research interests encompass visual jurisprudence, legal semiotics, visual studies, language and law, legal culture and heritage, legal translation, legal terminology, law and the Humanities, and legal discourse studies. She has been honored with the National Research Award (Rank A) for her distinguished research career and has received the "Comenda Jurista Tobias Barreto", a prestigious recognition for outstanding contributions to legal culture, from the Instituto Brasileiro de Estudos do Direito in Recife, Brazil.

- She has extensively published in the areas of legal semiotics and legal discourse analyses with research papers or special issues in: *International Journal for the Semiotics of Law; Semiotica; Law, Culture and the Humanities; Social Sciences; Journal of Civil Law Studies; Hermes; Comparative Legilinguistics; International Journal of Legal Discourse; Law & History; Law and Literature; La Semaine Juridique: Édition Générale; LSP & Professional Communication; International Journal of Speech, Language and the Law; UNESCO ALSED-LSP Newsletter; and Humanity and Society.*

- She is the author of *La Langue de la Common Law* (L'Harmattan 2002).
- She is the General Editor of the reference 10-volume project *International Handbook on Legal Language and Communication*, authoritative work under contract with Springer.
- She edited the following volumes:
  - *Contemporary Issues in the Semiotics of Law: Cultural and Symbolic Analyses of Law in a Global Context* (Hart Publisher 2005) with Tracey Summerfield and Farid Samir Benavides Vanegas
  - *Images in Law* (Ashgate 2006) with William Pencak
  - *Legal Language and the Search for Clarity: Practice and Tools* (Peter Lang 2006) with Sophie Cacciaguidi
  - *Semiotic Interpretation of Law in Legal Theory, Judicial Reasoning and Political Practice* (Springer 2006) with Wouter Werner and Deborah Cao
  - *Obscurity and Clarity in the Law: Prospects and Challenges* (Ashgate 2008) with Sophie Cacciaguidi
  - *Diversity and Tolerance in Socio-Legal Contexts: Exploration in the Semiotics of Law* (Ashgate 2009) with Vijay K. Bhatia
  - *Prospects of Legal Semiotics* (Springer 2010) with Jan M. Broekman
  - *Explorations on Courtroom Discourse: Power and Control in and behind Language* (Ashgate 2011) with Cheng Le;
  - *Transparency, Power and Control: Perspectives on Legal Communication* (Ashgate 2012) with Vijay K. Bhatia, Christoph A. Hafner and Lindsay Miller;
  - *Law, Culture and Visual Studies* (Springer 2013) with Richard K. Sherwin;
  - *The Ashgate Handbook on Legal Translation* (Ashgate 2014) with Sin King-Kui and Cheng Le;
  - *Law, Cinema and the Ill City: Imagining Justice, Order and Morality in Real and Fictional Cities* (Routledge 2019) with Cheng Le;
  - *Flags, Color, and the Legal Narrative: Public Memory, Identity, and Critique* (Springer 2021,

Winner of the 2021 Gherardi Davis Prize of the Flag Research Center) with Sarah Marusek;
  - *Research Handbook on Jurilinguistics* (Edward Elgard Publishing, 2023) with Aleksandra Matulewska;
  - *Research Handbook on Legal Semiotics* (Edward Elgard Publishing, 2023) with Sarah Marusek.
  - *Handbook on Cyber Hate: The Modern Cyber Evil* (Springer, 2024) with Sarah Marusek.
  - *(In)Visible Signs of Gender-Based Violence* (Springer, Forthcoming 2025) with Angela Condello.

- Her international research responsibilities are:
  - She is the Editor-in-Chief of the *International Journal for the Semiotics of Law* (Springer)
  - She is the President of the *International Roundtables for the Semiotics of Law* (IRSL)
  - She is the Series Co-Editor of *Law, Language and Communication* (Routledge) with Vijay K. Bhatia
  - She is the Series Co-Editor of *Law and Visual Jurisprudence* (Springer) with Sarah Marusek
  - She is the Series Co-Editor of *Living Signs of Law* (Springer) with Sarah Marusek
  - She is the Series Co-Editor of *Gender, Justice and Legal Feminism* (Springer) with Angela Condello.

Anne Wagner has been invited as Visiting Research Fellow at Örebro University in Sweden (2018, 2019), China University of Political Science and Law in China Beijing (2018, 2016, 2015, 2014), Zhejiang University in China (2017, 2018), Shanghai Jiao Tong University (2013), Zhejiang Police College in China (2012), City University of Hong Kong (2010). She has also guest lectured for the Law and Humanities course in Rome at Università degli Studi RomaTre (2014). She was invited to give talks in Italy, Sweden, Poland, Hungary, Germany, Spain, Finland, UK, Portugal, Estonia, China, Hong Kong, Brazil, Israel, Australia, and the USA.

DEMOGUE
Equipe de Recherche en Droit des Contrats et Théorie du Droit
CRDP-ULR n°4487

Faculté des sciences juridiques, politiques et sociales
Université de Lille

Université de Lille

Deconstructing Gender Stereotypes: Mythos, Logos, and Nomos

Angela Condello and Anne Wagner

Abstract This chapter critically explores gender stereotypes through the lenses of law, culture, intersectionality, and language. It highlights the pervasive influence of stereotypes in shaping societal norms, legal practices, and individual identities, drawing on theoretical and empirical insights to expose the mechanisms of bias and inequality. The analysis situates gender stereotypes within the frameworks of mythos, logos, and nomos, illustrating their entrenchment in cultural narratives, normative systems, and language. It underscores the cognitive dimensions of stereotyping, likening the process to prototypical categorization, while addressing its socio-cultural implications. The chapter emphasizes the transformative potential of interdisciplinary approaches, advocating for reforms across legal, cultural, and educational spheres to dismantle entrenched stereotypes and promote equity.

Keywords Gender stereotypes · Law · Language · Culture · Intersectionality · Narratives

Article Note: The present chapter is the product of a joint work of collaboration and critical reflection carried on in the past three years, during which Anne Wagner organized a conference in Lille (2023) on Gender-Based Violence (https://crdp.univ-lille.fr/evenement/gender-equity) and together we launched the book series Gender, Justice and Legal Feminism (https://www.springer.com/series/17265). More specifically, the paragraphs in the chapter can be attributed to us singularly and jointly as follows: §1 (Angela Condello); § 2 (Angela Condello); §3 (Anne Wagner); § 4 (Anne Wagner); § 5–Conclusion (Anne Wagner and Angela Condello).

A. Condello
University of Messina, Messina, Italy

A. Wagner (✉)
University of Lille, Lille, France
e-mail: valwagnerfr@yahoo.com

A. Condello and A. Wagner (eds.), *Gender Stereotypes*, Gender, Justice and Legal Feminism 2, https://doi.org/10.1007/978-3-031-63905-0_1

1 Deconstructing Gender Stereotypes in Legal Discourse: *Mythos*, *Logos*, and *Nomos*

In recent years, discussions about gender have increasingly recognized the complex layers of subjective identity, social expectations, and systemic bias that influence and shape individual experiences when it comes to the imagination nourishing sexed and gendered human relations. The book we are here introducing offers a critical exploration of gender stereotypes through theoretical, cultural, social, and legal perspectives. By examining the enduring impact of these stereotypes on policy, cultural norms, and personal identity, the volume aims to provide a foundational understanding for researchers, policymakers, and anyone invested in promoting a more equitable society, starting from the way in which our legal (and non-legal) imaginaries influence gender policies in a good and in a bad manner. All the chapters, in a way or another, touch upon various aspects of the relationships between gender and language (through various phenomena falling under the category of 'stereotype') within the legal realm, be it at a normative level or at the level of lawmaking. Issues like the maleness of language and of norms (Smart 1992), the process of encoding the masculine dominating worldview in various procedures and policies, the various forms of female invisibility within institutions, and the risks of false gender-neutrality—are discussed in the three sections of the volume from the point of view of stereotyping.

Starting from the first section of the volume, focusing on the theoretical issues of stereotypes in general and of gender stereotypes in particular, the reader will realize how the organization of this collection reflects the multidimensional nature of gender stereotypes. As abovementioned, it is divided in three parts, each addressing a distinct yet interconnected aspect of gender as a social construct which originates in the public dominion and then gets fixed in our ways of thinking, speaking and understanding (Lippmann 1922): after this first theoretical section, we then find a section broadly dedicated to narratives, constructions and the instruments through which stereotypes are perpetrated, and finally a section on how other normative systems (culture, religion) work through stereotypes, hence influencing legal practices. The present introductory chapter, co-authored by the editors, should guide readers through the themes and objectives of the entire collection as well as of each section, setting the stage for a deeper engagement with the nuanced discussions that follow.

Overall, across themes and fields, a cognitive analysis of stereotypes is proposed, showing that stereotyping is a kind of categorial knowledge production subject to the general constraints of prototypical categorization, with some specific features. Such features are related to the social domain of stereotyping, as well as to its social function. In fact, at a cognitive level, there is an essential *continuum* between prototypes to stereotypes and in general across all forms of classification via models: stereotypes are indeed prototypes applied to social categorization. As it will be argued in § 2, the process of stereotyping works very similarly to that of prototyping as an optimization device (energy saving), generating explanations in the context of social interactions. The social context is not without implications, obviously, as it involves some peculiarities of stereotyping, which can be interpreted as an excessive emphasis given to prototypical aspects of categorization: indeed, gender stereotypes differ based on the socio-cultural context in which they emerge and in which they are used, and on the historical period, or on the type of subjects that use them (adults, children, teenagers).

The volume testifies of how stereotypes are not just created *ex novo* from this or that subject or institution; instead, they often reflect a worldview divided into male and female, strong and weak, dominating and dominated categories of beings. Such dichotomies are part of the fantasies on which our imaginary is based (Hillmann 1978) and these fantasies, when it comes to sexuality and gender, draw from biological attributes and are then applied to other fields: for instance, when the monthly cycle is described as being designed to produce eggs, and set a suitable place for making babies, that cycle is implicitly imagined merely as a productive enterprise and therefore menstruation is viewed as a failure (Martin 1991). Male reproductive physiology, on the contrary, is valued differently, since the maturation of sperm is often described as a heroic enterprise of magnitude, conquest and proliferation, hence the egg is portayed as passive while the sperm as active. This example shows how stereotypes are often embedded on various levels of our knowledge and communication, even in fields like biology where we would not expect them to be.

Gender stereotypes intersect at least three levels of human interactions, and it would be useful to read this entire collection starting from the crossroads of these three terms: *logos*, *mythos*, and *nomos*. Issues like the continuity between prototypes and stereotypes, as discussed for example by Hilary Putnam or, in Italy, by Marina Sbisà and Turner Ken (2013), concern the level of the *logos*: i.e., that of logic and language and of their interactions (cfr. Putnam 1994; Kosgaard 1996). This level has a direct impact on how we conceptualize the normative dimension in our society (*nomos*): the way wer think and infere and speak is indeed the code through which we collectively represent our institutions and build our human relations—for this reason, feminist approaches to legal studies cannot do without feminist approaches to linguistics and philosophy (Condello and Bottici 2024). Only from such transdisciplinary efforts can experiences like feminist jurisprudence and feminist legal judgments arise and proliferate. Yet feminist approaches to our social life, on top of the levels of *logos* and *nomos*, must also consider the level of the *mythos*: like other perspectives aimed at overturning the unjust balances of society (i.e. socialism), feminism has a lot to do with the process of *mythologein*—i.e., the production of certain ideas or convictions based on shared narratives. The contributions in the present volume invite to think about our current mythologies: what are we aiming to, in the analyses of gender stereotypes? At neutrality? At the institutionalization of equality?

2 Theoretical Foundations of Stereotypes and Prototypes

In our language, various social and cognitive experiences settle; among such experiences, gender is undoubtedly relevant. How does this happen? For Saussure (1922) this happens in ways that are to some extent obscure: sometimes, such experiences are even arbitrary and yet we follow certain inclinations because of other people's beliefs or because of entrenched traditions. Uses of certain categories and convictions become rules and thus we end up confirming the classificatory behaviors and the hierarchies between the categories through which we order the world.

When discussing gender, it is important to consider such practices that, in time, become somehow arbitrary and are hence hard to dismantle. Language can change and words can acquire new referents, but we cannot just change it through our will or desire because it is a collective enterprise. Furthermore, even if we managed to change our language, that would not entail a change in our models of thought and the majoritarian uses of words and classes of words. A brilliant thinker like Marina Sbisà underlined how gender stereotypes cannot be changed just by imposing new uses in a certain language (e.g., a duplication of terms or a neutralization of the uses of a certain language through symbols like the "schwa" in Italian)– on the contrary, she claims, changes in the language can occur because of deep societal improvements. Even if changes on some terms were imposed and made mandatory, they would not necessarily produce changes on gender relation and on the models through which we learn, we classify, we are trained to think. These are, in other words, two different dimensions that interact with each other and at the same time are independent from each other.

Gender stereotypes are thus obstacles for women's freedom, fulfillment and autonomy: when language preserves stereotypes, it is hard to interrupt their continuous reproduction and regeneration also under new forms. Stereotypes are not only explicit models of thought, but they convey implicit certainties and unspoken truths: for this reason, it is hard to dismantle them just by imposing new grammatical rules in the uses of male/female/neutral for names. There are convictions and beliefs that we communicate implicitly and that circulate through our reasoning (e.g. through inferences that we make because "things have always gone that way"): such implicit convictions and beliefs are transmitted through a gentle extortion—if you do not accept them and you ignore them, you might be excluded from certain communicative circles. Because of their power, therefore, we absorb them in our ways of thinking without really deconstructing them critically and without neutralizing them properly.

Where do these practices come from? Originally, the word *stereotype* derives from two Ancient Greek roots: στερεός 'solid' and τύπος 'impression' and originally it was used by a French printer, Firmin Didot, to describe a typographical activity. From that use it moved to everyday language to describe iterative dynamics lacking originality, innovation or spontaneity, and then it entered in the realm of social sciences to indicate pictures of possible worlds that are not necessarily complete neither adherent to reality, and yet w adapt to them, and we use them. The term indicates a stability in thought, in language, in reasoning. As it is widely known, it was

Hilary Putnam who first considered stereotypes a subject of linguistics (1970, 1975). Putnam suggested that the description of meaning for the so-called *natural kind terms* like 'water', 'lemon', 'tiger' and 'electricity' (a description which includes both grammatical and encyclopedic information about the subject) is always enriched by stereotypical components, i.e. by "a conventional (frequently malicious) idea (which may be wildly inaccurate) of what X looks like or acts like or is" (1975: 249). In other words, for Putnam stereotypes are so close to other forms of cognitive models (e.g., prototypes) in the way they function that it is very hard to distinguish them when it comes to positive/negative attributes or aspects of the things in the world. From this perspective, stereotypes participate in cognitive processes because they synthetize aspects of "linguistic obligations" (e.g., the fact that lemons have a certain colour or taste, or that water is transparent, tasteless and colorless) as well as aspects of more specific linguistic competence (e.g. the fact that chemical formula of the water is H_2O).

In the Seventies, the notion of stereotype was often discussed parallel with the notion of prototype (Rosch 1973, 1975): the notions have indeed something in common, as they emphasize the value of certain features accounting for the most typical representatives of a category (e.g., 'striped' for a tiger, 'able to fly' for a bird). Yet, while prototypicality is a linguistic-psychological notion associated to categorization and modelling in general, stereotypicality is a socio-linguistic notion associated to biases (Abbatecola and Stagi 2017), evaluations, subjective judgments.

The first section of the volume contains reflections on the various forms of stereotyping: in the norm, in the decision-making procedures, in ordinary language: to understand the interaction of these forms and of the various levels of our action on which they interfere, it is important to bear in mind also the various feminist traditions involved in the debates. In any case, the remarks made by the authors show that one of the main principles of feminist thought, i.e., difference, can still play a crucial role in conceptualizing gender relations in terms that are *just*: as a matter of fact, the risks of neutralization or of the crystallization of stereotypes are intrinsic in the modes of our communication and reasoning, particularly today with digitalization. These risks grow together with linguistic rules.

3 Part 2: Thinking, Constructing, and Narrating Gender

The study of social constructs and gender identity reveals the intricate dynamics between societal norms and individual self-perception. Judith Butler's *Gender Trouble* (2002) and Michel Foucault's *The Subject and Power* (1982) provide a foundational framework for understanding how identity is not an innate truth, but a construct shaped through cultural, institutional, and social forces. Butler's theory of performativity asserts that identity is constituted through repeated acts, highlighting that:

"There is no gender identity behind the expressions of gender; that identity is performatively constituted by the very 'expressions' that are said to be its results" (Butler 2002, p. 33).

This perspective challenges views of gender, framing it as a process continually enacted and reinforced through societal expectations. Foucault complements this with his assertion that power is not merely repressive but productive, actively shaping identities by categorizing individuals into specific roles that reinforce binary constructions of identity. Through this lens, individuals are "made subjects" by the regulatory practices that impose norms and define intelligible identities (Foucault 1982, p. 781).

Judith Butler expands these ideas in *Bodies That Matter: On the Discursive Limits of "Sex"* (1993), emphasizing that even the concept of "sex" is a regulatory ideal, materialized through processes of reiteration. Butler argues:

"'Sex' is not simply what one has, or a static description of what one is: it will be one of the norms by which the 'one' becomes viable at all, that which qualifies a body for life within the domain of cultural intelligibility" (Butler 1993, p. 2).

The repetitive nature of these norms produces the illusion of stability, obscuring their constructed nature. At the same time, this process of reiteration creates openings for contestation and rearticulation, offering possibilities to destabilize hegemonic frameworks and redefine the boundaries of intelligibility.

Cultural narratives reflect and reinforce these regulatory practices, shaping societal attitudes and maintaining gender hierarchies. Chernyak's analysis, "a hen is not a bird, a woman is not a person", illustrates how deeply embedded gender dynamics in Russia perpetuate stereotypes. These cultural artifacts align with Butler's notion of regulatory practices that naturalize exclusion by relegating certain identities to the "constitutive outside"; those that exist beyond the norms of intelligibility (Butler 1993, p. 11). Such narratives reinforce traditional norms, creating boundaries that constrain alternative expressions of identity while legitimizing existing hierarchies.

Media plays a critical role in maintaining these dynamics. Spallaccia critiques the use of anti-gender rhetoric in media as a means to delegitimize feminist and LGBTQ + movements, perpetuating systemic violence. Buiten (2022, p. 113) adds to this critique by showing how portrayals of gender-based violence depoliticize the issue, framing incidents as isolated acts rather than reflections of systemic inequality. These analyses follow the ideas developed in Butler's exploration of performative acts in media, which shape cultural perceptions of gender and reinforce dominant norms, while simultaneously offering opportunities for resistance through alternative narratives (Butler 2002, p. 176).

Educational systems further reinforce gender constructs, as shown in Hauksson-Tresch's analysis of French language textbooks in Sweden. These texts subtly teach students to internalize specific gender roles by presenting stereotyped depictions of men and women. These insights into the role of institutions in creating categories of truth reflect how education serves as a tool of power, defining norms for what is considered natural in gender expressions and identities (Zadja 2022, pp. 146–148).

This mechanism illustrates Butler's concept of the "heterosexual matrix", which naturalizes binary gender roles and constrains expressions of identity to match cultural expectations (Butler 2002, p. 45).

Language is a powerful tool for both reinforcing and challenging these constructs. Wagner and Yu (2025) explore how legal language operates as a regulatory mechanism, capable of both territorializing existing norms and opening avenues for transformation. The feminization of job titles in Quebec, contrasted with the slower adoption of similar reforms in France, highlights the cultural variability in addressing gendered language (Zarea and Wagner 2024). Wagner and Marusek (2023) argue that law itself operates as part of a "dual circuit", simultaneously preserving historical values while adapting to modern needs, stating:

> Law, as a living organism, has the ability to territorialize a concept, while also creating alternative trajectories for more modern visions (Wagner and Marusek 2023, p. 194).

Accordingly, legal frameworks regulating gender identity are deeply intertwined with cultural and social norms with "crossovers and points of connection as well as divergences and points of contention" (Browne 2014, p. 25). Additionally, Wagner, Matulewska, and Cheng describe law as a culturally constituted sign-system that reflects the broader societal values within which it operates. They note:

> Law is a living reality impacted by various global phenomena and other legal systems, thus enabling it to develop in various directions depending on wider social, political, and technological contexts (Wagner et al. 2020, p. 239).

This perspective underscores how legal norms are not static but are subject to continuous reinterpretation and resistance. Similarly, Yu's analysis of gender stereotypes in Chinese media demonstrates how media, politics, and law intersect to reinforce traditional roles while also providing opportunities for reimagining identities. Yu's findings echo Foucault's relational view of power (Foucault 1982), highlighting the dynamic interplay between repressive forces and transformative possibilities.

Spengler's research into gender-based violence further illustrates the harmful impact of societal stereotypes, revealing how they exacerbate trauma by shaping public perceptions of victims. This reflects Butler's analysis of the abject—the excluded and unintelligible identities that sustain normative boundaries by marking their limits (Butler 1993, p. 3). Spengler's work emphasizes the need to address these exclusionary norms to challenge systemic violence and create more inclusive frameworks for understanding gender.

Furthermore, economic and historical contexts also influence the construction of gender identity. Müller et al. examine how economic instability disrupts traditional gender roles, forcing individuals to renegotiate identity narratives tied to stability and privilege (Müller et al. 2023, pp. 33–55). Historical analyses, such as Whyke and Brown's study of Qing Dynasty zhiguai tales, reveal alternative understandings of gender through narratives of transformation and liminality, challenging rigid binaries and reinforcing the fluidity of identity (Whyke and Brown 2023, p. 112). These perspectives echo Butler's assertion that identity is never fixed but always in the process of becoming, shaped through repetition and resistance (Butler 1993, p. 15).

Additionally, Renkin critiques nationalist policies in Hungary, which enforce strict definitions of marriage and family, using rigid gender roles as tools to advance political narratives. This approach perpetuates a stratified global discourse that dichotomizes societies as either progressive or regressive, complicating the global understanding of gender (Renkin 2023, p. 2086). These frameworks illustrate Foucault's concept of power as a productive force that creates the very norms within which identities are regulated and constrained (Foucault 1982, p. 781).

As a consequence, the cumulative insights from these analyses underscore the complexity of gender identity as a product of cultural, linguistic, and institutional practices. Regulatory norms, while deeply entrenched, are never immutable. They are constantly being negotiated, contested, and redefined through the very acts that sustain them. This ongoing interplay between power, language, and identity highlights both the constraints imposed by existing frameworks and the potential for transformative change embedded within the systems that regulate gender (Wagner and Condello 2025). While these frameworks often uphold traditional hierarchies, they also open pathways for reimagining identities, fostering diversity, and challenging exclusionary practices (Shirley and Rodríguez 2023).

4 Part 3: Rethinking Gender Through Law, Culture, and Religion

This part delves into the intersections of law, culture, and religion to explore how these frameworks construct, perpetuate, and occasionally challenge gender stereotypes. Across diverse global contexts, the chapters reveal how entrenched societal norms and systemic biases obstruct justice, while also identifying opportunities for transformative reform. Together, they emphasize the urgent need to rethink traditional approaches to gender through intersectional and culturally sensitive perspectives that account for both structural inequalities and localized realities.

The examination begins with the challenges faced by the criminal justice system in addressing gender-based violence in Southern Africa. Despite the existence of policies aimed at combating violence, systemic weaknesses, including resource limitations, societal attitudes, and implementation gaps, highlight the inadequacy of current approaches. These findings resonate with the Italian legal system's struggles to address gender-based violence, as patriarchal biases embedded in legal reasoning obstruct justice and reinforce stereotypes. Both contexts reveal the dissonance between legal frameworks and their practical application, emphasizing the need for deeper structural change. Seal (2022, p. 6) echoes this sentiment, arguing that systemic inequities in the criminal justice system often reflect deeper patterns of marginalization:

> Gendered social marginalization increases the vulnerability to criminalization, as legal systems often reflect and perpetuate societal inequalities.

Cultural dynamics further complicate these issues. In the Indian context of post-partum psychosis, the legal system fails to account for cultural and emotional factors influencing women's actions, often leading to punitive rather than rehabilitative measures. Similarly, in South Korea, cult-based sexual violence persists due to deeply rooted gender norms and the exploitation of religious authority, leaving victims without adequate recourse. These cases underline the intersectionality of gender, culture, and societal expectations, calling for reforms that address the root causes of injustice. As Zajda (2022, p. 141) emphasizes:

> Dominant ideologies embedded in education systems normalize and perpetuate inequality, shaping societal expectations of gender roles.

Furthermore, consent and sexual violence provide another lens for examining the interplay between legal and cultural narratives. The *bildungsroman* framework critiques how consent is framed as an individualized issue, obscuring systemic power imbalances. Orthodox Christian iconology, with its dual reinforcement and challenge of gender norms through representations of Mary, mirrors this tension. Both examples highlight opportunities to reinterpret entrenched stereotypes within cultural and religious traditions. Kosmina's (2023, p. vii) study of the witch as a cultural symbol offers a parallel:

> The witch serves as a key figure in understanding how history, memory, and narrative intersect, particularly in relation to gendered power dynamics.

The digital age adds further complexity. Online spaces often amplify societal prejudices, creating new avenues for both the perpetuation and contestation of stereotypes. Farris et al. (2020, p. 75) highlight how digital platforms reproduce existing biases:

> Online platforms amplify pre-existing stereotypes, providing spaces where gender and racial biases are reconstituted through visual and textual media.

The historical perspective offered by the case of Barbados demonstrates how slavery and Christianity have historically shaped gender roles, embedding systemic inequities into societal structures. Seal (2022, p. 7) complements this analysis, noting:

> Cultural representations and institutional frameworks impose gendered attributes, interpreting identical actions differently depending on the actor's gender.

These examples collectively demonstrate how gender norms and stereotypes are deeply embedded in both historical and contemporary systems. Seal's exploration of institutionalized gender performance underscores how these constructs persist across legal, cultural, and religious frameworks:

> Gender identity is created through institutional, intersubjective, and representation levels, influencing how crime and punishment are enacted. (Seal 2022, p. 5).

A unifying theme emerges: the urgent need to critically rethink how legal, cultural, and religious frameworks intersect to shape gendered power dynamics. By exposing the limitations of existing systems and exploring avenues for resistance, these chapters advocate for transformative approaches that challenge stereotypes, promote equity, and redefine justice.

As Maruenda-Bataller et al. (2024, p. 2) emphasize, such systemic change requires addressing not only structural inequalities but also the underlying discursive mechanisms:

> Systemic change requires addressing not only the structural inequalities embedded in institutional frameworks but also the discursive mechanisms that perpetuate them.

Ultimately, the insights offered here highlight that meaningful progress requires addressing both the structural foundations of inequality and the specific cultural contexts in which they operate. This dual focus enables the possibility of reimagining justice in a way that transcends entrenched stereotypes and embraces intersectional and inclusive approaches.

5 Conclusion. Toward a Nuanced Understanding of Gender Stereotypes

This volume demonstrates that gender stereotypes are not isolated prejudices confined to individual attitudes but are deeply woven into the fabric of societal structures, cultural narratives, and institutional frameworks. They perpetuate exclusion, inequality, and injustice, while simultaneously shaping both collective and individual identities. Through its comprehensive approach—spanning theoretical foundations, empirical case studies, and critical policy analyses—*Gender Stereotypes: Case Studies, Policies, and Theoretical Approaches* illuminates the pervasive and multifaceted nature of gender bias.

The analyses presented in this collection reveal that while stereotypes are often deeply entrenched, they are not immutable. Rather, they are continuously reinforced and contested through cultural practices, legal frameworks, and social interactions. This duality underscores both the constraints imposed by existing norms and the opportunities for transformative change embedded within these very systems. The contributions in this volume collectively challenge readers to question their assumptions, recognize the insidious ways stereotypes infiltrate daily life, and actively engage in fostering environments that are inclusive, equitable, and diverse.

Central to this effort is the recognition of the intersectionality inherent in gender stereotypes. By intersecting with race, class, ethnicity, religion, and other facets of identity, gender bias operates within complex and often invisible power structures. Addressing these intersecting oppressions requires nuanced, interdisciplinary approaches that incorporate insights from law, culture, education, media, and grassroots movements. The chapters highlight the importance of such frameworks in identifying the structural and discursive mechanisms that perpetuate inequality, while also advocating for concrete reforms to dismantle these systems.

From the cultural narratives that shape societal perceptions to the legal frameworks that reinforce traditional norms, this volume sheds light on the many avenues through which stereotypes are reproduced. It also highlights the transformative potential inherent in resisting and rearticulating these norms. Examples from diverse global contexts demonstrate how regulatory norms, though deeply rooted, are subject to negotiation, reinterpretation, and resistance. Whether through legal challenges, educational reforms, or alternative cultural narratives, the possibilities for change are both real and urgent.

In practical terms, this collection calls on policymakers, educators, media practitioners, and activists to leverage this knowledge to drive systemic reform. Legal systems must evolve to reflect the diversity and fluidity of gender identities, while educational institutions need to prioritize inclusivity and deconstruct harmful stereotypes from early stages. Media and cultural industries, as powerful agents of socialization, bear a responsibility to amplify narratives that challenge traditional norms and celebrate diversity. Each of these sectors has a role to play in dismantling exclusionary practices and promoting equitable representation.

Moreover, the global relevance of these issues demands collaborative and cross-cultural engagement. Gender stereotypes operate differently across regions, shaped by unique historical, economic, and social contexts. As this volume demonstrates, addressing these stereotypes requires culturally sensitive approaches that respect localized realities while challenging systemic injustices. By fostering dialogue across disciplines, geographies, and communities, we can develop strategies that not only confront bias but also envision and implement a more equitable future.

Ultimately, this collection affirms the transformative potential of collective action and critical scholarship. It reminds us that meaningful progress requires more than superficial change—it necessitates deep structural reform, sustained advocacy, and a commitment to justice. By bridging theory with practice and offering actionable insights, this volume equips readers with the tools to actively participate in reshaping societal norms and advancing gender equity on a global scale.

The work herein serves as both a foundation and a call to action, urging us to critically reimagine the world not as it is, but as it could be—a world where gender stereotypes no longer constrain human potential, and where inclusivity and respect for all identities are the norm, not the exception.

References

Abbatecola E, Stagi L (eds) (2017) Pink is the New Black. Stereotipi di genere nella scuola dell'infanzia. Rosenberg & Sellier, Torino

Anne W, Aleksandra M, Le C (2020) Law as a culturally constituted sign-system – a space for interpretation. Int J Legal Discourse 5(2):239–267

Browne V (2014) Feminism, time, and nonlinear history. Palgrave Macmillan, New York

Buiten D (2022) Familicide, gender and the media – gendering familicide, interrogating news. Springer, Singapore

Butler J (1993) Bodies that matter: on the discursive limits of "Sex." Routledge, New York

Butler J (2002) Gender trouble: feminism and the subversion of identity. Routledge, New York & London

Condello A, Bottici C (2024) Difference feminism and anarchafeminism. Perspectives on gender justice. In: Teoria e critica della regolazione sociale, pp 145–156

de Saussure F (1922) Cours de Linguistique Générale (eds Bally C, Sechehaye A). Payot, Paris

Farris ND et al (2020) Gender, sexuality and race in the digital age. Springer, Cham, Switzerland

Foucault M (1982) The subject and power. Crit Inq 8(4):777–795

Hillman J (1978) The myth of analysis: three essays in archetypal psychology. Harper Torchbooks, New York

Kosgaard CM (1996) (with Cohen GA, Geuss R, Nagel T, Williams B, ed Onora O'Neill). *Sources of normativity*. Harvard University Press, Cambridge (MA)

Kosmina B (2023) Feminist afterlives of the witch: popular culture, memory, activism. Palgrave Macmillan, Cham, Switzerland

Lippmann W (1922) Public opinion. MacMillan, New York

Lochak D (2008) Dualité de sexe et dualité de genre dans les normes juridiques. Droit et Société 15(1):659–689

Martin E (1991) The egg and the sperm: how science has constructed a romance based on stereotypical male-female roles. Signs 16–3:485–501

Maruenda-Bataller S et al (2024) Discourse, gender, and violence: insights from news and social media texts. Peter Lang, Lausanne

Müller M, Pfeil P, Dengel U, Donath L (2023) Identity under pressure: over-indebtedness in the middle class. Springer, Wiesbaden

Putnam H (1970) Is semantics possible? Metaphilosophy 1–3:187–201

Putnam H (1994) Words and life. Harvard University Press, Cambridge (MA)

Renkin HZ (2023) "Far from the Space of Tolerance": Hungary and the biopolitical geotemporality of postsocialist homophobia. Sex Cult 27:2084–2104

Rosch E (1973) Natural categories. Cognit Psychol 4(3):328–350

Rosch E (1975) Cognitive reference points. Cogn Psychol 7(4):532–547

Sbisà M, Turner K (eds) (2013) Pragmatics of speech actions (Handbooks of Pragmatics, vol. 2). Mouton de Gruyter

Seal L (2022) Gender, crime and justice. Palgrave Macmillan, Cham, Switzerland

Smart C (1992) The woman of the legal discourse. Soc Legal Stud 1:29–44

Tate SA, Rodríguez EG (eds) (2023) The Palgrave handbook of critical race and gender. Palgrave Macmillan, Cham, Switzerland

Wagner A, Condello A (eds) (2025) (In)visible signs of gender-based violence. Springer (forthcoming), Cham

Wagner A, Marusek S (2023). From life to law: towards an evolving conception of ecocide. In Fleerackers F (ed) The reaguard of subjectivity: festschrift in honour of Jan Broekman. Springer, Cham

Wagner A, Wei Y (2025) From gender binary ♀♂ to gender diversity ⚧ + X λ: unveiling new horizons in societal transformation. In Wagner A, Condello A (eds) (In)visible signs of gender-based violence. Springer (forthcoming 2025), Cham

Whyke TW, Brown MS (2023) Queering gender, sexuality, and becoming-human in Qing Dynasty Zhiguai - querying the strange tales. Palgrave Macmillan, Singapore

Zadja J (2022) Discourses of race, ethnicity and gender in education: trends in research. In: Zadja J (ed) Discourses of race, ethnicity and gender in education – emerging paradigms. Springer, Cham, pp 141–152

Zarea R, Wagner A (2024) Advancing gender neutrality: the evolution of feminized and neutral legal terminology. Int J Semiot Law 37:1899–1912

Part I
Theoretical Approaches to Gender Stereotyping in Socio-legal Studies

Gender Stereotypes Between Commonplaces and Maxims of Experience

Silvia Niccolai

Abstract Italian legal science tends today to assimilate gender stereotypes, maxims of experience and commonplaces, on the assumption that the one (the stereotypes), like the other (the maxims and commonplaces), are general statements based on the mere inductions of a "logic of the probable;" therefore, such statements are debatable and questionable, which is to say: neither true nor certain, and rather often and easily falsifiable. After recalling the historical origins from which the assimilation between stereotypes, maxims and commonplaces stems, the article argues that it underlies the confusion between the relevance of an assertion (that has to be appreciated every single time with respect to the facts of the case) and its truth (or validity in absolute terms). This confusion entails the risk of impoverishing and sclerotizing the legal reasoning, often sacrificing, also, its autonomy with respect to general social justice purposes. With no benefit, however, for the fight against stereotypes, since a legal culture hungry for "certain" truths can only continually reconstruct new stereotypes.

Keywords Gender sterotypes · Law · Legal reasoning

1 The Maxims of Experience

In this chapter I will discuss a view, quite widespread in Italy today, which assimilates gender stereotypes to "commonplaces" and therefore to "maxims of experience". These latter are the generalizations—based on a set of known facts, or on established notions in common sense—to which a degree of certainty is assigned, such that they can provoke, in the trial, important consequences: deeming as established a fact that was not proven, credible the mere statement of a witness, plausible a certain reconstruction of events.[1]

[1] Taruffo (1970), p. 196.

S. Niccolai (✉)
University of Cagliari, Cagliari, Italy
e-mail: niccolai@unica.it

A. Condello and A. Wagner (eds.), *Gender Stereotypes*, Gender, Justice and Legal Feminism 2, https://doi.org/10.1007/978-3-031-63905-0_2

My purpose is to suggest a different parallelism: stereotypes are "maxims of experience" because the latter are not (or rather do not function as) commonplaces, but, if anything, they are norms, or, rather, are understood as such. In Italy, the maxims of experience are tools of the judge's prudent appreciation in the evaluation of evidence; on their basis, in part at least, the judge can form her free conviction (condemn or absolve, etc.). For this reason, the maxims have long been considered (and still are) as many instruments of the Court of Cassazione's control over the "logicality" of the reasoning conducted by the judge for the purposes of judgment.[2]

Italian codes do not expressly refer to maxims, but the Code of Civil Procedure (enacted in 1940) provides that the judge «can, without the need for proof, place as the basis of the decision the notions of fact which are part of common experience» (art. 115 c. 2 c.p.c.). This formulation certainly refers to the so called "notorious facts" (snow is white; cats eat mice, etc.) but according to a unanimous opinion it also refers, precisely, to the "maxims of experience." This notion, however, has been elaborated by the legal science, where the maxims of experience made their appearance as an imported product. It was the German jurist Friedrich Stein who theorized the maxims of experience in an 1893 work that has exercised an undisputed magisterium on the subject. Taking up almost literally the definition of maxims of experience that was carved by Stein,[3] and which has repeated by numbers of scholars over time[4], the Italian Court of Cassation has repeatedly affirmed that the maxims, that can be correctly used by the judge, are those that represent as many «empirical generalizations independent of the concrete case based on repeated experience and therefore valid for new cases» (Cass. Pen., IV Sez., 2021/36524). This definition contains an analogy between the maxim and norm that is evident and has been emphasized many times[5]: the maxim of experience *is made* like a norm (it is independent of the concrete case; it must be able to apply to the future; therefore, it is abstract and general); *it functions* like a norm (it allows a certain conclusion to be reached), although it does not have its source in formal volitions of the legislator, but *in social data.*[6]

---

[2] De Gasperis (2024), para 3.

[3] Stein (1893), pp. 21–22: maxims of experience are «definitions or hypothetical judgments of general content, independent of the concrete case to be decided in the trial and its individual circumstances, conquered by experience, but autonomous with respect to individual cases, from whose observation they are deduced and beyond which they must apply to new cases». («Wir können sonach ihr Wesen folgendermassen bestimmen: sie sind Definitionen oder hypothetische Urtheile allgemeinen Inhaltes, vom concreten in diesem Prozesse abzuurtheilenden Falle und seinen einzelnen Thatsachen unabhängig, aus der Erfahrung gewonnen, aber selbständig gegenüber den Einzelfällen, aus deren Beobachtung sie abgezogen sind, und über die hinaus sie für neue Fälle Geltung beanspruchen.»).

[4] See the influential definition proposed by Taruffo, (1970), p. 202, summarizing in turn the positions of Stein, Wehli and Calogero: the maxim of experience is «a proposition of general content acquired through experience and independent of the concrete case».

[5] Taruffo (1970), p. 198.

[6] See Palavera (2017), p. 22 ff.

This characteristic (being *norms stemming from a social source*) makes the maxims of experience a perfect synthesis of the ideas that characterized the German legal positivism, sociologically based and historicist.

As is well known, German historicism affirmed the positive character of law, in the sense that each people have the law it gives to itself (law, therefore, is always conventional and relative, and aiming at the ends that, through it, a given social and political order sets out to achieve). If this belief was directed against traditional conceptions of natural law, which were instead convinced of the unity of law in time and space, it also implied—and this time against the "formalistic codicism"—that law is not just a complex of written rules: instead, it is the historical product of the legal and social consciousness of an individual people, evolving synchronously with it. How? Through the work of jurists, which is a true scientific work, well equipped with the technical skills that enable to building systems, ordering syllogisms, and making correct deductions.

The "maxims of experience" are carved out to confirm these assumptions. Being as many norms that can be inductively derived from the observation of natural or social facts, and such as to guarantee the basis for exact deductions, on the one side the maxims, while postulating the separation between facts and norms, do allow a contact between the "extra-legal" and the "legal," that is, between the world of facts and the world of norms. On the other side, they ensure that this contact takes place with characters of objectivity, predictability, certainty. Therefore, leaving no room for any arbitrariness, the maxims of experience do not endanger the mechanism of law enforcement. On the contrary, they perfect it.

The appeal to factual experience allows for an interpretation of the rules of law that is appropriate to the socio-historical context but guided by the purposes and principles of the legal system, Stein emphasizes in its work, which was intended as a response to the objections of another antagonist of historicist legal positivism, namely jus-liberalism.[7] While the latter extolled the contrast between "life" and "law," in the sense that the judge would have to espouse the former, with its ever new needs and tendencies, in order to overcome the narrowness of the latter, Stein set out to show that, when handling facts, the lawman follows rigorous procedures, which he masters and which at the same time bind him. Among the multiple indications that come from the world of facts, therefore, he will not choose those, that he subjectively prefers, nor will he give weight to certain facts merely because they simply repeat or happen often. The man of law, who is also a true man of the world, and in this sense a "man of experience," will stick only to those facts, of the occurrence of which it is possible to give an objective explanation. In Stein's words: the lawman will stick only on those facts, of which he is able to explain himself, and to explain to others, «why» they happen. For example, how does one determine whether a witness had that «particular difficulty in appearing before the court because of great distance» referred to in a certain paragraph of a certain code? One must not only know that «Eberswalde is six miles from Berlin» but also not be unaware «that seven trains run between these cities every day and take a travel time of 56–81 min. Thus, the answer

[7] Taruffo (1970), p. 197.

is given by experience, which consists in the expectation that on this day, as on all previous ones, the railroad will fulfill its timetable announcements and that officials will do their duty, an expectation that has evolved in the following decades, in which the introduction of the railway system has proven its reliability, except in very few exceptional cases». All these "facts" considered, concluding that Eberswalde is not at a great distance from Berlin is a «true inductive conclusion, a proposition based on experience».[8] The lesson is clear: every expression used by the law, no matter how vague and deferring to factual conditions ("the great distance") can be applied correctly and with certainty, if facts are examined objectively.

Stein was well aware that all maxims of experience, insofar as they are anchored in facts, are likely to be outdated at some point. Rooted in changing historical and social conditions, expressions of a knowledge that is itself changing, they can easily become unsuited to changed mentalities and behaviors or be falsified by new scientific findings.[9] It goes with no saying that the changeability of the maxims of experience does not contradict their character as norms but confirms it. Every historical and positive conception of law knows well that legal norms are changeable and relative. No surprise, then, that also all the Italian scholars following Stein's doctrine, have accepted this point with no difficulty.[10]

And for that matter, it suffices to recall that, in the Italian legal system, the Court of Cassazione can review the "correct of use of the maxims" made by the judge. Given that the cassation judgment, as we say, "knows only of the law and not also of the fact "(i.e., a judgment of legitimacy only), it is easy to understand that the maxims are assimilated to as many norms that the judge must apply to facts.

[8] Stein (1893), p. 24.

[9] From the consciousness that «everything flows» and therefore «we must be prepared for the fact that our knowledge will be rejected even by future generations» Stein (1893), p. 31, drew confirmation that even the trial like every human thing, «can never be in advance of the knowledge of its time and its people» («Auch der Prozess kann nirgends der Erkenntniss seiner Zeit und seines Volkes voraus sein»). «Die Relativität unseres Wissens» seemed to him to appear clear especially in judgments concerning the "impossible", judgements that are, to him, inherently conditioned by technical and scientific developments (p. 31).

[10] On the analogy between maxims of experience and norms, argued precisely because of the common aspect of mutability, are explanatory the words of Leone (1951), p. 6 ff., referred in De Gasperis (2024), para 4 note 71. According to Leone, De Gasperis writes, «the maxims of experience, precisely because of their character of abstractness and generality, 'are approachable to the legal norm, which, insofar as it constitutes the expression of a given view of social relations at a given moment, is susceptible to change, sometimes to real reversals', just like the maxims of experience, with respect to whose variability, from people to people or from age to age, there is no doubt (think, for example, of the acceptance of the Copernican theory)».

2 The Maxims of Experience Versus Commonplaces

If Stein was fighting against the "free law movement", in Italy his "maxims of experience" were enormously successful because they provided a strategic weapon in another battle, that was at that time going on in our legal culture. It was the battle against a long-standing orientation that was rooted in the medieval law tradition of Roman Law,[11] and that in the nNineteenth century was very much alive: namely, the "*interpretatio* secondo equità".

It is not possible here to relate in detail the characteristics of this tradition, but it is sufficient perhaps to recall that it was imbued with the ideal of the "fair decision". The "fair decision" was considered the proper goal and the specific function of law; accordingly, the form of knowledge that distinguished law from other sciences consisted in mastering the techniques for achieving it.

The first and most important things that every lawman educated in this tradition was trained to learn and to put in practice, was that the fair decision (which is to say: the correct rule of judgment), can be found only on the basis of a careful examination of the fact, every single time considered in its specific circumstances. Indeed, the facts that come before a jurist, and which are always human relationships, always have the form of a dispute, which arises from an imbalance, determined by an abuse, a harm, etc. (this is the "juridical side", or the "juridical form", of common human relationships). The jurist is asked to restore the balance, remedy to the tort, repress the abuse. And it is only by carefully looking in the imbalance, that is *visible in* the fact, that one can find the right balance corresponding to it in law. If the "*interpretatio* secondo equità" is often pictured as a case-based practice of law, therefore somewhat unpredictable or "subjective", one should always remember, when talking of it, that these jurists were convinced that law is unified and made coherent by a general goal which is always the same (fairness). Consequentially: if, for is nature, this goal can lead to different decisions in different cases, the decisions are nonetheless *all equal* under the point of view of their fairness.

For example, if Caius has harmed Titius, the imbalance that the fact points to also indicates the equity with which to resolve it: Caius will have to compensate Titius or return the equivalent to him. But if, upon examination of the fact, it turns out that Titius contributed to the occurrence of the damage (e.g., by his recklessness), it would not be equitable, not fair, to compensate him in full. And this is the crucial point: if every fact, in its structure, *indicates or contains its equity* (as these jurists were used to say), fact and law are connected. Thereby, separating the one from the other prevents reaching a just decision (fair, equitable).

According to Alessandro Giuliani (1925–1997), the legal historian and philosopher who was the foremost expert of this tradition in our times, the "*interpretatio* secondo equità" conceives of interpretation as an activity aimed primarily not at investigating a text, but at investigating «the quality of a fact, the nature of a thing», assuming a natural connection between the question of law and the

[11] In Italy, we speak of this tradition as the tradition of "diritto comune", literally: common law.

question of fact (quaestio iuris and quaestio facti).[12] In this lies a crucial difference between legal positivism' conceptions and those of the *interpretatio.*

In the wake of this many-centuries-old tradition, many nineteenth-century jurists in Italy were convinced that «it is not from the law that principles are derived, but, if anything, it is from the study of the case that one must trace the principle that governs it».[13] They taught, therefore, that on the one hand «to know the fact, to understand the case, is the main task of the jurist», and that, on the other hand, «the estimation of facts is done in the manner of legal reason».[14]

In order to achieve the "correct estimation of facts," the *interpretatio* made use of a set of "commonplaces," and of a certain way of handling them ("in the manner of legal reason") that had the structure of a dialectical examination. Commonplaces could be provided by rules contained in the legal sources (the Digest of Roman Law, the medieval Glossa, the legal treaties), as well as by formulas of rhetoric, or by precepts of common sense, which were used as tools to debate the fact, highlighting its aspects relevant to judging of it, and excluding the irrelevant ones. Circularly, rules of law (the *regulae iuris*) also were used as "commonplaces" of the dialectic. Even for them it was necessary to identify the most appropriate one, the one «suited to the case», through the exclusion of those that, at a dialectical examination, had proved to be unsuitable or less suitable.[15]

All this is sufficient to say that the *interpretatio* was very familiar with the "logic of the probable," the "lesser" logic taught by Aristotle, and used it not by chance, or for ignorance of a better one. The *interpretatio* used the logic of the probable in a very precise way, that is, as Giuliani says, as «a negative logic of the relevance» (which serves to identify the rule suitable for the case, excluding those that result unsuitable, not relevant, not pertinent) and therefore as the logic proper to law.

Let me pause a moment on this latter point. As everyone knows, the logic of the probable is that form of reasoning that starts from generally accepted premises and sets out to arrive at identifying "probable" consequences; and the "probable" is what lies between the certainly true and the certainly false. The certainly false is what the dialectical analysis based on commonplaces can and should exclude; the certainly true is what the logic of the probable cannot and should not propose to reach, since the certainly true can only be reached by starting from necessary premises, namely, in the field of science.

The recourse to the logic of the probable, then, implies the awareness that law is not an exact science, and should not, nor can it aspire to be an exact science, because it pertains to human things. Giuliani's enormous commitment to the study of the logic of the probable is precisely due to this: by reevaluating and seeking to

[12] Giuliani (1968), p. 223.

[13] Lozzi (1880), p. 223.

[14] Lozzi (1880), p. 134.

[15] The *regulae iuris* as commonplaces of a *more-iuridico* logic serve, in controversy, a logical-ethical function analogous to that of the dialectical definitions, «neither entirely clear nor entirely obscure», that preside over the logic of the probable; they represent «definitions» that do not aim to determine the essence, but «the limit of a proposed definition»; their function is selective: Giuliani (1997), p. 7.

understand the logic of the probable for what it was, Giuliani seeks to defend, in our times, an important awareness, that, according to him, was at the center of the *interpretatio*. Which one? That only if it thinks of itself as a science of the probable, law remains capable to adhere to human reality for what it is (inherently debatable). In doing so, law preserves the human freedom, which is the possibility of always being "otherwise" than it has been determined it ought to be. When it becomes a science of the necessary, instead, law opens itself to dangerous authoritarian implications.

3 The Logic of Controversy

In his studies Giuliani highlights two particularly important aspects. If that of the jurists of the *interpretatio* was a logic of the probable, it was so in a sense that, in the Italian language, was still in use throughout the Nineteenth century: probable is that which is worthy of assent, of approbation, and therefore is preferable (here *probabilis* is linked to *adprobari*).

Giuliani's clarification is rather obvious, since a commonplace is an opinion that, precisely because it is shared by many, has shown to be worthy of assent, and enjoys consensus. Nonetheless, stopping here risks of overlook an aspect of the probable, which involves not only the logic, but also the practice (and links the one to the other). If the probable is what is worth of approval, then starting from a commonplace not only means to start from a certain kind of premise, that does not have the degree of certainty suitable to ground a necessary inference, but it also means *to start from a premise that has on its side the approval, the consensus of many*. Then, practicing a logic of the probable means *committing to reach conclusions that are in their turn worthy of approval*. This is the ethical component of the logic of the probable, which distinguishes it from a mere eristic.[16] Therefore, and this is the first important thing that Giuliani highlights, the logic of the probable is not content with the possible, or with what mostly happens (the statistical *id quod plerumque accidit*), nor does it authorize itself to reach no matter what conclusion, as long it is maintainable. Instead, it is committed to seeking *the preferable* (the best probability).

Under these conditions, not only was a careful circumstantial analysis of the fact required, but it became possible, and indeed indispensable, also to *problematize every single rule* proposed as a rule of judgment: was it the one that guaranteed the fairest solution, considering the case?

The treaties on which scholars of *interpretatio* were trained handed down Bulgarian teaching: there is no doubt that *pacta sunt serbanda*, and that the principle is in itself very fair. However, if from the exam of facts, it results that a certain contract is based on fraud, deception, or fear, equity dictates instead that it be rescinded.[17]

Thus, a second important thing emerges: the logic of the probable and preferable was, inherently, also a "logic of the controversy", where propositions of a general

[16] Giuliani (1971), p. 231 ff.

[17] For a reconstruction of the point Niccolai (2022), p. 399.

tone are largely used (*pacta sunt serbanda*) but they are tested each time in their ability to read a single fact adequately. In the examination of a single case (the contract based on fraud) the general rule, *pacta sunt serbanda*, will be set aside, but that does not mean that it loses its validity in general, for other cases. The dialectical examination serves therefore to rule out the relevance of a commonplace, of the general rule, with respect to that certain single case. It does not serve to ascertain, generally and in the abstract, the validity of the commonplace, of the general rule, in and of itself. In other words: on the one hand, the fact is not judged in the light of a general invariable proposition, destined to be applied to the fact; instead, it is the general proposition that is tested through the dialectical analysis, to assay whether it is suitable to read that case or not. On the other hand, the general proposition that turns out not to adequately correspond to a certain case is not considered inherently false, and therefore never again usable. Only, it is considered not useful *for that case*. Indeed, while resulting not suitable for one case, the general rule *remains suitable for another case* and also for many others.

The tradition of the *interpretatio*—to which, as we see, a logic of the exception was inherent—conveyed at least two beliefs to jurists. One was the conviction of being the experts of human relations in their legal aspect (i.e., when the human relationships assume the form of a controversy, arising from harm, fraud, abuse); the other was that «without controversy the opinion of jurists however splendid remains a personal opinion».[18] Indeed, it is the *quaestio facti* that determines the borders of the *quaestio iuris* and give sense to the principle adopted to judge it.

Educated with these ideas, the Italian jurisprudence demonstrated a certain ability to distance itself, in the name of the proper ends of the trial and of Law, from socially widespread judgments and beliefs in the field, for example, of morality. I take the case of some judgments of the late Nineteenth/early Twentieth century concerning cases of seduction damages, pronounced in Naples, Rome and Palermo.[19] Discussing whether or not compensation was due to the woman who, seduced by a married man, had become pregnant, the judges make moralistic remarks, or hear them on the mouths of the parties' advocates, such as, "a good woman should not behave like this,". In their reasoning, however, they refer to these clichés to say that they are irrelevant to the judgment, whose specific and proper object and end is not the custody of morals but is to ascertain, in each and every relationship, who, of the two parties, is most responsible for the harm produced. It is certain that the man who lied to the woman about his status is, with respect to her, in malice and must compensate.

[18] With these words the Beduschi (2017), p. 20 summarizes the lessons that the Romanist tradition has transmitted over time.

[19] For a more detailed illustration Niccolai (2022), p. 707 ff.

4 Outward Journey. From Commonplaces to Maxims of Experience

The tradition of the *interpretatio* was still alive in some authoritative components of the Italian jurisprudence of the second half of the Nineteenth century. However, the practices and ideas that inspired it, rooted in medieval jurisprudence and responding to a criterion as uncertain as the probable, became a major problem in the eyes of those who aspired to have our legal culture conform to the achievements of a truly modern science, now established elsewhere. If, because of their premodern foundation, the styles of traditional jurisprudence had long been under attack (criticism of common sense is the natural companion of the modern habitus), they now made it impossible to implant in Italy the cassation judgment, limited to law alone. But the cassation judgment was felt by some to be a necessary innovation, not least because it was deemed capable of re-educating the now *national* judiciary to new modes of reasoning, oriented to the primacy of the rule over the fact, and thereby capable of guaranteeing uniformity, predictability, certainty. As I mentioned just above, the link between fact and law, so dear to the *interpretatio*, implied that the norm to be applied was understood not as a datum from which to start, but as a result to be arrived at. This meant that *the fact problematized the rule*, the appropriateness of which to the fact had to be demonstrated each time.

Clearly, in a newly unified country like Italy was at the time, these attitudes could seem to encapsulate dangerous subversions of state legislative law, which, as such, was a novelty, and not always welcome, in many parts of the land. Our jurisprudence had given some evidence to this effect. For example, in the name of the common law principle that law must be equal, and never a disadvantage can be imposed on a single person in the interest of the community without a just reciprocation, effect was denied to laws ordering expropriations against single land-owners without a fair compensation.[20] Moreover, the principles and criteria of the *interpretatio* were accused of being too narrow, because they were individualistic, that is, too anchored only in the dimension of individual relationships between two persons, between two parties, between two individuals, whereas by now there was an emerging realization that Law, beginning with private law, has a social character, in the sense that general, social interests must prevail over individual interests, and shape them in view of given ends. Finally, the *interpretatio* was based on the idea that, in the extreme variability of human facts, *some constants* are nevertheless discernible (harm, abuse, fraud), and as many constants are discernible in the principles and practices of law (always equity requires a fair reciprocation). All this bumped against Darwinism, and also against nationalism, which were then prevailing.

The fortunes of the maxims of experience can be explained in this context of Italian legal science, which was divided between sustainers of the tradition and

---

[20] In these cases, the Courts interpreted the wording of the Statuto albertino (the written Constitution of those times), in light of the "eternal and unchanging" general principles of Law. If a legislative act, instead than as equal, i.e. general, operates selectively as an administrative act, it is not "Law". See on this point Colorni (1946), pp. 42–44.

supporters of modernity, the latter often sincerely convinced—it must be stressed—that the establishing of a "positive" law and of more scientific methods would have contributed to civil and social progress. Stein's maxims of experience were for this part of our culture a real godsend. There was finally the possibility of using the "commonplaces" properly, that is, as bases for certain and unambiguous deductions and predictions.

On the one hand, because they gave the facts their weight, the maxims of experience sheltered the new culture, the scientific and modern one, from the lashing criticism of the jurists of the tradition, who accused the modernizers, "positivists", of pretending that it was possible to judge in law without knowing the facts well, which in their eyes was not only ridiculous but also dangerous.[21] On the other hand, thanks their "rigorous" way of functioning, the maxims of experience guaranteed, in the eyes of the modernizers, emancipation from what was seen as the nonsensical and overly individualistic casuistry of equity.

5 In the Name of Progress. The Alliance Between the Legal Science and the Legislator

There was, moreover, something in Stein's theses that could reassure the traditional jurists. The opening pages of his book, devoted to asserting that law is connected to life, play out a motif that jurists have been repeating since the days of Bartulus and Baldo: in some respects, Stein's doctrine vindicated the necessary knowledge, as well as of norms, of the world and of life, which jurists had always considered quintessential to their role. Moreover, the maxim of experience relates quite transparently to the logic of presumptions, particularly the presumption of the "normal," which, as such, need not be proved. A point, the latter, which in the *interpretatio* was very firm, and not only responded to reasons of argumentative economy (avoiding the *recursum* ad infinitum) but also «to ethical reasons». If something is normal it goes without saying that it is "to be approved," that there is "assent" on it. Which, moreover, did not mean that it was not possible to deviate from the normal; it only meant that it is incumbent on those who deviate from the "normal" to prove the soundness of their assertions (to prove that they are in their turn worth of approval).[22]

To some extent, the maxims of experience reassured the traditionalist jurists that facts continued to matter for "the legal estimation" and in "the manner of reasoning" proper of jurists. After all, many of the now called "maxims of experience" were mere transpositions of commonplaces well known to the legal reasoning over centuries; not only that, but the very definitions of the maxims of experience were as many transplants of the formulas used by the jurists of the *interpretatio* to describe the nexus between fact and law. Still in 1961, and quoting Stein literally, the great Italian

[21] For examples of this disagreement see Niccolai (2022), p. 568 ff.

[22] Giuliani (1971), p. 68: «Those who deny the best probability bear the burden of proving their saying». Giuliani stresses that «this idea of the probable gives us points of reference» (p. 161).

jurist Salvatore Pugliatti, in defining the maxims of experience, makes almost a cast of the proposition dear to the jurists of the *interpretatio* (every fact has its *aequitas*) which becomes «every fact has its law».[23]

Beneath these reassuring assonances, however, the advent of the maxims of experience signaled an inexorable change in the way of reasoning in law, and of conceiving law, from that which had been dear to the jurists of the *interpretatio*. The latter were alien to any syllogistic and deductive scheme, which—argumentative and dialectical as they were—they adopted neither for interpreting facts nor for interpreting norms. The new maxims of experience, if anything extended even to facts the deductive scheme, which, according to the ways of thinking that were now becoming established, was proper to the application of norms. Indeed, the idea of the maxim of experience that Stein communicated to Italian legal culture is characterized by an extreme aspiration for certainty: Italian modernizing jurists, then, saw in the maxims of experience the guarantee of finally freeing themselves from the logic of the probable that was typical of the *interpretatio* and the highroad to fully adhere to the dictates of truly scientific legal conceptions. Furthermore, the maxims of experience made it possible, as I said, to reply to the criticism of the traditionalist jurists—who drew attention to the facts and considered arbitrary an interpretation limited to the sole norms. The maxims demonstrated that positive jurists also knew how to handle facts, indeed they knew how to handle them better (to obtain certainty from them) than it had previously been known.

Actually, it is difficult to explain the fortune of Stein's maxims of experience in the Italian legal science between the Nineteenth and Twentieth centuries if not in the context of the choice to ally with legislation against jurisprudence, made at the time by our legal science (the one that "counted" in the brand new universities of the Kingdom, and whose most prestigious exponents, professors and lawyers, were numbering more and more every day among parliamentarians and ministers).[24] The most important outcome was to banish even from memory the ancient conception of the "commonplace". As we have seen, this was considered a tool for proving, which had to be proved every time (if pun is allowed), that is, a tool for testing both fact and rule, and not at all a proof in itself. At its place it remained the "maxim of experience", which was a means of proof, which is to say: an assertion stating the certain and the true, that granted deductive logicality to the judge's reasoning and offered at the same time a way of controlling that reasoning.

Indeed, the "modern" Italian legal science praised the maxims of experience especially because they allow the Court of Cassation to scrutinize the "logicality" of the judges' ruling. As I have mentioned, the introduction of the cassation judgment as a judgment of legitimacy only was in those days a disputed matter, on the outcomes of which the maxims of experience played an important and ambiguous role. They reassured the traditional jurists that at least *something* of the fact would have had a role in the cassation judgment (thus limiting what they saw as the inevitable arbiters

[23] Pugliatti (1961), p. 357 note 56.

[24] On this aspect of Italian legal culture in the decades following the political unification see Giuliani (1992), para III.2.

of a judgement having as object the law only and not also the fact). But in concrete, the new maxims of experience were there to allow the new court of Cassazione to disengage judges from conceptions of the world, and of law, that appeared outdated and to promote the adoption, in place of the logic of the probable, of the logic of the necessary. From now on, the new Court, controlling the maxims of experience used by the judge, selecting those that were still usable and those that were not, would have taught the judges how to *use the commonplaces as norms*, from which deduct the solution of the case.

6 Return Journey. From Maxims of Experience to Commonplaces

If the initial and firm fortune of the maxims of experience in the Italian legal culture was due to the mantle of certainty with which they presented themselves clothed, in more recent times—and in the wave of the general rediscovering of the "logic of the probable" that began in the second half of the last Century—the main Italian legal scholarship has taken it upon itself to criticize the maxims of experience precisely on the point of their certainty, which is to say, of their aptitude to found necessary deductions.

Around this point Michele Taruffo (1943–2020) has engaged his magisterium.

Taruffo is one of our most prominent legal thinkers and from all points of view an heir of the purest values that feature the modernizing side of Italian legal culture. In his highly influential work, Taruffo, who considered the (civil) trial an instrument of social justice, undertook to undo the myth that procedural truth can be other than factual truth: for Taruffo, instead, a closeness between what is true in the courtrooms and what is true in society should be promoted as much as possible. His theoretical positions—a fascinating and very Italian *mixage* of ideologically oriented analytical positivism and "anti-formalist" aspirations—led him to fight against what he considered a mystifying and dangerous belief: the idea that law is a field of knowledge and experience endowed with its own principles and ideals, and therefore endowed with its own autonomy, particularly with respect to society and politics.

On this basis, Taruffo undertook, among other things, to debunk precisely Stein's thesis about the maxims of experience.

According to Taruffo, Stein's thesis is based on the *id quod plerumque accidit* and incurs the fallacy of assuming that, since something has happened many times, it can be retained for certain that it has also occurred in the instant case and will occur again.[25] Thus, the maxim of experience cloaks with deductive force, and certainty, what is nothing but *a mere induction, in this sense a "commonplace*", based on

[25] Taruffo (1970), p. 199.The accuracy of this criticism of Stein is questionable, but the point is that confusing the probable with what happens in most cases (the *id quod plerumque accidit*), as Taruffo does, is the royal road to failing to understand the distinctive aspects, qualitative and ethical, of that logic. Stein was far from being an advocate of the logic of the probable in the sense of the ancient *interpretatio*, and his Italian supporters knew it well (and that is why they appreciated his ideas). By

merely probable reasoning. It is therefore necessary to subject each maxim to careful examination, to show whether it really has justification,[26] so that it can be used in the trial. Examination will often show that, of justifications, maxims have none. It is well known that clichés border on common sense, and common sense is the bilge of prejudice, credulity, and lack of critical sense.

After Taruffo's "critical" turn, to which today «the majority of scholarship conforms»,[27] the maxims of experience have returned to be understood as the commonplaces of a logic of the probable, but in order to be all subjected to Cartesian doubt, that is, in order to be all subjected to processes of falsification. The maxims of experience have thus become the battle ground on which to operate the progressive liberation of legal and social culture from the prejudices that threaten the objectivity of judgment.

Some operations of falsifying commonplaces are very simple. To prove the falsity of a maxim, Taruffo taught, it is enough for it to be contradicted by another, or by a single fact: an only black swan invalidates the claim that swans are white.[28]

This example is sufficient to understand that Taruffo speaks of the logic of the probable but does not intend the latter as a logic of controversy, in which a general statement can be disproved with respect to a given fact but still remains valid for others. For Taruffo, the logic of the probable is a (faulty) abstract logic, producing general statements but *minus quam certae*, whose reliability can and must be disproved, once and for all, by comparison with certain data, such as those that can be provided by science or critical thinking.

The maxims of experience are thus subject to review not insofar as they have claimed to introduce into law a scientific, predictable, and objective treatment of things as inherently debatable as the human facts, but insofar as they are not really suited to guarantee that outcome, which is considered the only valid and worthwhile one.

The maxims of experience are not challenged insofar as they carry the logic of the necessary, but insofar as, and to the extent that, they are not really capable of expressing it and guaranteeing it.

---

confusing Stein's logic with that of the *interpretation,* Taruffo mystifies the latter, but, doing so, he continues the distinctive work of the Italian modernizing jurists (denigrating the *interpretatio* and condemn it to a *damnatio memoriae*).

[26] Taruffo (1970), p. 199, with proud "analytical/critical" approach. See also the p. 203 ff. No need to say that Taruffo addresses to Stein the same criticisms that, beginning with Locke and Hume's separation of facts and values, the modern thought has always conveyed against the claims of inductive reasoning to be able to provide valid generalizations, and therefore against commonplaces, innate ideas, and common sense.

[27] De Gasperis (2024), para 4.

[28] On this example see now Di Giuli (2024), p. 72.

7 From Maxims to Stereotypes

The "discovery" of the questionable, falsifiable and "only" probable character of the maxims of experience has thus been the discovery that they are nothing but trite commonplaces, in the sense of prejudices rooted in lazy and uncritical common sense.

This explains why the Italian doctrine has accomplished, and easily, the assimilation between maxims of experience and gender stereotypes: «Gender stereotypes (…) constitute a paradigmatic example of the functioning of classifications, categorizations, generalizations that contribute to the construction of that 'common sense' that we use to interpret and evaluate reality». They consist of as many «assertions about behaviors, the knowledge of which is supposedly derived from experience, which are presented as if they were endowed with a character of generality, but which have no logical status and no valid cognitive foundation», and therefore, in the legal field, «the reference notion, in this regard, is that of 'maxim of experience'».[29]

Given that maxims of experience have become, from paradigms of syllogistic certainty, true epiphanies of the (merely) probable, tracing gender stereotypes back to maxims of experience guarantees the possibility of "scrutiny" of the judge's rationality,[30] and facilitates the progress of "falsification" of prejudices in the name of a more certain and more scientific judgment.

Among the elements of the "critical scrutiny" to which a maxim of experience can and should be subjected, scholars do not fail to count the trial as such, namely the burden of proof, etc.[31] This is a path, admittedly, that could lead to a genuine rediscovery of commonplaces according to the logic of the probable as logic of the controversy.

However, one must take into account the structure of the process in which the maxims of experience operate. Ours is a process that ends with an evaluation of legitimacy alone, in which the holding of the maxim of experience is tested not in relation to the case, but as such, in abstract. This is demonstrated by the teachings that the Court of Cassazione addresses to judges, and which I have mentioned at the beginning.

The Cassazione does not recommend that judges use maxims that are relevant to the case, it does not commit them to prove that a maxim they have used offered a more adequate reading of the fact than others. Quite the opposite of that, the Cassation demands that judges use abstract and general maxims that are valid and independent of the case. In this way, the Court continues to inculcate in the minds of judges that *there are* fact-based statements capable of claiming para-scientific validity and that the judge's task is to descend from the maxim to the case, just as one descends from the norm to the fact. Meanwhile, the Court operates a continuous preemptive selection of maxims, of a "abrogative" kind, tending to exclude some of them forever from the trial (those considered "false").

---

[29] Pastore (2024), pp. 238–239.

[30] Di Giuli (2024), p. 59 ff.

[31] Pastore (2024), p. 239.

All this means that *while "rediscovering" the logic of the probable, the Italian jurisprudence remains farer than ever from rediscovering it as the logic of the controversy*. What happens, instead, is the deepening of an irreconcilable contradiction, which consists in claiming that some propositions with an uncertain logical status, which we call probable, must function as norms, as necessary propositions *or* they must be canceled. Paradoxically enough, the rediscovering of the logic of the probable ends up by confirming that the objective certainty of a statement is the unique and true "value" that counts in law. The result is that the legal doctrine, in yet another search for "purity", should hunt down all the "falsifiable" propositions in order to exclude each of them for always from the "common places/maxims of experiences" that the judge can use in reasoning.

Under these conditions, it is not much wonder that today we often find that old stereotypes are being replaced by others[32] and that, in some cases, the (criminal) trial tends to become the seat of a form of collective self-consciousness aimed at emending injustices of social and cultural origin, sometimes at the expense of the general principles of the trial, and of its purposes. This is the case, admittedly very delicate, of trials for sexual violence, where today the word of the woman (or rather of the victim, or of the woman as victim) is assigned value of proof against the defendant (arguably in reaction to other maxims of experience that Stein, for example, considered to be cast gold, namely that that women are bad witnesses because, like children, they are swayable[33]). The result is an inversion of the burden of proof that severely undermines the presumption of innocence, and which would seem to be based on the "maxim of experience" that all men are sexual predators, therefore on the accused of sexual assault there is a presumption of guilt.[34]

On the basis of the experience—which undoubtedly tells us that a victim of violence suffers a profound trauma—the Court of Cassazione also recommends to judges not to deny reliability to the victim's words, and in particular not to consider her testimony tainted, even if it is not completely coherent (as an reliable testimony is expected to be).[35] It is clear, however, that the argument: "Given that a person has been raped, you cannot expect her to remember things exactly" is a tautology (that that person has been raped is *quoad demonstrandum*) that undermines not only the equality of the parties in the trial, but the very possibility of an equal cross-examination. The tool that, in the hopes of the best doctrine, should serve to "critically evaluate" a maxim of experience.

---

[32] See Giolo (2024), p. 7 ff.

[33] Stein (1893), p. 100.

[34] On the delicate issue Mazza (2020), p. 12 ff.

[35] Reccia (2022), p. 29 ff.

8 Do Mothers Love Their Children?

Giuliani also distanced himself from the maxims of experience, but, in a manner opposite to Taruffo, he did so to note (albeit only incidentally) that they had and have *nothing to do* with the commonplaces as the *interpretatio* conceived of them.

Although Giuliani does not go to great lengths to explain why, the reason for his point is obvious: commonplaces are not maxims of experience because the latter are considered capable of ensuring certain conclusions and necessary deductions independently from the facts in question, while commonplaces serve to reach probable conclusions with respects to the facts in question. This is because the function of the commonplace in the process, according to the logic of the probable, is not that of a norm, which must be applied to every and each case and therefore must be true always and in every case. Its function is that of *an argument*, which must be screened in its usefulness for understanding a single case.

Thereby, what makes a proposition a commonplace in the sense of the logic of the probable and the controversial, is not its general tone or its ostensible grounding in the experience or consensus; what counts is the way in which that general proposition *is used*.

I am giving an example, taking it again from Giuliani, who presents it precisely to say that a commonplace (which moves in the realm of the logic of the probable) and a maxim of experience (which claims to move in the logic of the necessary) are not distinguishable in the abstract, as propositions, which is to say only considering what they assert and how they assert it. The difference, is at the level of the practical use of a proposition.

The example is offered by the *locus communis* of roman rhetoric: *Si mater est diligit filium* (If she is mother, she loves her son), handed down by Cicero and Quintilian, in which there is an echo of Solomon's famous *decisum.*[36] If we think of this proposition as a commonplace of the logic of the probable and the controversial, we should immediately think of it also as used in a context, where there is some fact in dispute, probably the custody of a child, the recognition of a filiation that has become for some reason controversial between two women. About the two women who are litigating before the judge, the examination of the facts shows that one is caring of the child, the other is not. Here *Si mater est* is relevant, can be taken into account, and helps to decide.

Si mater est diligit filius, understood in the logic of the probable means only this: if what gives evidence (presumptive, of experience) of being a mother, that is, loving the child, recurs in the facts that are before the judge, the commonplace is relevant and indicates the rule of decision, because it coincides with *the best probability* (certainly from the child's point of view). The ruling, i.e., the rule of judgment, should anchor itself in this case in the commonplace, which, in this concrete fact,

[36] The example demonstrates that the same proposition can serve as a commonplace or as a maxim of experience, depending on how it is understood and used. Cicero used *Si mater est* in the first way; Quintiliano, moralistically, "codified" it in the second. On this point and for other references see Niccolai (2022), p. 66.

indicates the preferable solution (assigning the child to the woman who loves him). But: what happens if both women, or neither of them, show that they love the child? All that will happen is that *Si mater est* will *not* be relevant in this case, and then it will be necessary, in order to go from the fact (there is a disputed child) to its rule (to whom to entrust it), to help oneself with other commonplaces, whose relevance the fact itself can signal, with its characteristics. In a logic of the probable and the controversial, «in the trial only that which is relevant must be admitted: the problem of the 'relevance' of a statement poses a problem quite distinct from that of its 'truth'», Giuliani concludes.[37] Then, it is when it is thought of as detached from a given context and a given function (that of clarifying a fact, in order to identify its rule, and the most preferable one) that a general and abstract proposition becomes a maxim of experience, which purports to the only necessary and always the same reading of a fact.

Therefore, *Si mater est* is a commonplace of the logic of the probable not because of its objective nature, but when it is used *as* a commonplace of the logic of the probable. Which is to say, when it is used in order to research, in a given conflict, to whom it is best to entrust a child *if* the relevant element signaled by the commonplace (the *affectio*) is there in the behavior of one of the two women who are litigating. But there is nothing in its formulation to distinguish it from a normative maxim, or a stereotype, and it will be whenever it is used as such. If we think *Si mater est* and we use it as a normative assertion based on "facts" that claims to fix a ought-to-be that is always true, it can easily express a gender stereotype (that of the "loving" mother), on the one hand; on the other hand, it can easily be falsified in the name of facts (how many mothers do not show love for their children!). Turning out to be falsifiable, the assertion should be thrown out (according to those who reason like Taruffo), but then we would lose a way of looking at things, which can in other cases result apt and useful. *Si mater est*, for example, can facilitate the recognition of the quality of mother to the partner of a lesbian couple who is not the biological mother but is the "social mother" of a child, that is, who has a caring and loving relationship with the child.

Therefore, overturning the hypothesis, held in doctrine, from which I started (stereotypes are commonplaces and therefore maxims of experience), I would say that a commonplace becomes a stereotype when it is used as a maxim of experience, that is, when it is treated as a norm: when it is expected to state the truth and therefore it is subjected to an analytical examination, which tends to ascertain whether the statement is false or true in absolute terms. Since it has this purpose (to ascertain the intrinsic truth or falsity of a statement), the outcome of the critical examination can only be the following: either the maxim is excluded once and for all (and thus an evaluation tool that could prove useful in other cases is lost), or it is replaced with one that seems capable of stating the truth (and thus a new stereotype is born). The result, in both cases, is to stiffen, simplify and standardize the judgment. Which means losing sight of reality.

---

[37] Giuliani (1971), p. 172.

After all—as the jurists of the *interpretatio* well knew—the presence of a black swan does not invalidate the fact that swans are usually white. It only means that the rule, according to which swans are usually white, does not help us to establish what color a black swan is. But on the other hand, the presence of a black swan does not allow us to deny the fact that (almost) all swans are white. *Exceptio firmat regulam in casibus non exceptis*. To purify the process from old and new stereotypes, it is not of help the illusion that it is possible, or useful, to enunciate maxims of experience that are always true and that infallibly lead to necessary conclusions. They only serve to defend us from the complexity, and the richness, of facts.

In conclusion, the claim to be valid always and in every case is the mark of a stereotype; then, a critique conducted against the maxims of experience insofar as they are "commonplaces" incapable of being valid always and in every case will only lead to the creation of new stereotypes. Better rethink the distrusting of the commonplaces of the logic of the probable, and rediscover them for what they really are. The most challenging, creative and liberating characteristic, though difficult, of commonplaces is that none of them can be said true or false if they are not related to a concrete a real fact, by the words of concrete and real people dialectically engaged in the common effort to seek the best way to evaluate that fact, to judge it, to give it a name and a place in our world. It is because they function like so, that the commonplaces of the logic of the probable are not maxims nor stereotypes. For the same reason, they have been and often are still now the most effective guarantors of the autonomy of the process vis-à-vis the prejudices of an era (yesterday against "seduced" women, today against "social" mothers); the guarantors of the autonomy of law, of its ideals and principles, of its ends and of its function (a fair decision) vis-à-vis the political and social goals that dominate in a historical given time.

References

Beduschi C (2017) Scritti scelti, ed Nogler L, Santucci G. University of Trento, Trento

Colorni V (1946) L'uguaglianza come limite alla legge nel diritto intermedio e moderno. Giuffré, Milan, repr. 1971

De Gasperis S (2024) Lo stato dell'arte su fatti notori e massime d'esperienza. Judicium

Di Giuli A (2024) Generalizzazioni false mascherate dal senso comune nell'argomentazione giudiziaria. In Bernardini MG, Giolo O (eds.) Giudizio e pregiudizio. Gli stereotipi di genere nel diritto. Giappichelli, Turin, pp 55–75

Giolo O (2024) La critica femminista degli stereotipi di genere nel diritto: concezioni, usi, funzioni, retoriche. In Bernardini MG, Giolo O (eds) Giudizio e pregiudizio. Gli stereotipi di genere nel diritto. Giappichelli, Turin, pp 1–13

Giuliani A (1971) Il concetto di prova. Contributo alla logica giuridica. Giuffré, Milan (reprinted unaltered).

Giuliani A (1968) La logique de la controverse et le droit chez les romanistes du XII et XIII siècle. St. et doc. Hist. et Iuris, 1968, pp 223 ff.

Giuliani A (1992) Le disposizioni sulla legge in generale. In Rescigno P (ed) Trattato di diritto privato, Utet, Turin, pp 377–502

Giuliani A (1997) Giustizia e ordine economico. Giuffré, Milan

Leone C (1951) Contributo allo studio delle massime d'esperienza e dei fatti notori. Bari

Lozzi C (1880) Introduzione al codice civile e al diritto internazionale privato, 2nd ed. Venice
Mazza O (2020) La presunzione d'innocenza messa alla prova. Dir. Pen. Contemporary, pp 1–14
Niccolai S (2022) Principi del diritto principi della convivenza. Uno studio sulle regulae iuris. Editoriale scientifica, Naples.
Palavera R (2017) Scienza e senso comune nel diritto penale. ETS, Pisa
Pastore B (2024) Postfazione. Note su stereotipi, pregiudizi e controllabilità del ragionamento probatorio. in Bernardini MG, Giolo O (eds) Giudizio e pregiudizio. Gli stereotipi di genere nel diritto. Giappichelli, Turin, pp 237–243
Pugliatti S (1961) Conoscenza e diritto. In Id., Scritti giuridici, IV. Giuffrè, Milan, pp 233 ff.
Reccia E (2022) L'attendibilità delle dichiarazioni rese dalla persona offesa da violenza sessuale. Un precedente vincolante? Iura Legal Syst 3:23–27
Stein F (1893) Das private Wissen des Richters. Unterschungen zum Beweisrecht beider Prozesse. Verlag von C.L, Hirschfeld, Leipzig
Taruffo M (1970) Studi sulla rilevanza della prova. RomaTrePress, Rome 2020 (reprinted unaltered)

Silvia Niccolai is a professor of constitutional law at the University of Cagliari. Her studies often connect issues of legal feminism with the historical paths of Italian legal culture, as is the case in her most recent book, Principi del diritto principi della convivenza. A study of the regulae iuris, Naples, 2022.

Stereotypes and Forms of Injustice. A Non-atomistic Analysis

Valeria Martino and Erica Onnis

Abstract Discrimination has been a pervasive feature of human socialisation throughout history and defies singular disciplinary framing due to its complexity. This paper approaches it from a philosophical perspective, focusing on stereotypes and considering them as generic beliefs expressed by generic statements. Among philosophers (and social psychologists alike), stereotypes have long been considered inherently false or inaccurate. These features prompted concerns about their propagation and their role in perpetuating social injustice and oppression. However, while there is no simple criterion to precisely assess the accuracy or inaccuracy of generic beliefs and utterances, apparently true or accurate stereotypes seem as harmful as blatantly false and inaccurate ones. For these reasons, this paper proposes that the biggest problem with stereotypes may not be their specific content and suggests that stereotypes, by their very nature of generic beliefs and claims, cannot be analysed *atomistically*. Instead, they should be recognized as context-dependent, functional components of wider social narratives, whose complex structures imbue them with meaning and strength. This paper also examines various forms of structural injustice, all connected to the phenomenon of stereotyping, albeit in different ways. The aim of this analysis is to elicit a deeper and multidimensional understanding of these forms of social injustice within jurisprudence, allowing for a better comprehension and regulation of phenomena related to stereotyping and social oppression.

Keywords Stereotypes · Generics · Social narratives · Injustice

The article was conceived by both authors, but Erica Onnis is primarily responsible for Sects. 2, 3, and 4, while Valeria Martino is primarily responsible for Sect. 5. Sections 1 and 6 were written jointly.

V. Martino (✉) · E. Onnis
University of Turin, Turin, Italy
e-mail: valeria.martino@unito.it

E. Onnis
e-mail: erica.onnis@unicusano.it

E. Onnis
Niccolò Cusano University, Rome, Italy

A. Condello and A. Wagner (eds.), *Gender Stereotypes*, Gender, Justice and Legal Feminism 2, https://doi.org/10.1007/978-3-031-63905-0_3

1 Introduction

Unlike many social and anthropological phenomena that are culturally, geographically, and historically situated, discrimination proves to be a common feature in the history of human socialisation.[1] Despite being globally recognised as morally wrong and therefore outlawed in most countries,[2] discrimination, like every other complex phenomenon, cannot be exhaustively defined by a single comprehensive theory developed by a particular disciplinary perspective.[3] Rather, its dynamics can be approached in various ways, from a psychological, sociological, linguistic, or philosophical point of view—to name but a few.[4]

In order to combat gender-related violence from the perspective of law and jurisprudence, it may therefore be useful to consider the different ways in which different disciplines have addressed the issue. In this paper, we approach discrimination from the point of view of philosophy, with the hope of providing some theoretical insights that may also be useful to those who engage in the subject from a different, more strictly legal perspective. We will do this by focusing on stereotypes understood as generic beliefs that are linguistically expressed by the sort of statements known as "generics".[5]

Among philosophers, stereotypes are usually considered *false* or at least *inaccurate* generic beliefs and statements—an idea defined as "the Falsity Hypothesis" by Erin Beeghly.[6] Stereotypes' falsity or inaccuracy, moreover, may be what motivates worries about their propagation and role in perpetuating the injustice and oppression associated with them. However, the philosophy of language teaches us that there is no simple criterion to establish the truth (or falsity) of generic beliefs and utterances. Generics and their meanings are notoriously difficult to analyse, and their validity does not seem to depend on statistical or empirical factors.[7] For these reasons, it may be difficult to verify the Falsity Hypothesis about stereotypes, and this indicates a

[1] See Tajfel and Turner (1979), who developed the Social Identity Theory. Social categorisation is even interspecific. See Fowers (2015), p. 252: "[...] with relatively simple cognition and no language, macaques spontaneously discriminated ingroup and outgroup members, and males demonstrated clear ingroup favoritism. Because social categorization is present across primate species, this capacity is quite evolutionarily ancient (macaque and ape lineages diverged 25–30 million years ago). It also suggests that ingroup discrimination is an automatic process whose basic functions are simple and nonlinguistic, although higher cognitive and linguistic processes could augment intergroup judgments and make them more nuanced".

[2] See, for instance, the International Covenant on Civil and Political Rights, Art. 26: "the law shall prohibit any discrimination and guarantee to all persons equal and effective protection against discrimination on any ground such as race, color, sex, language, religion, political or other opinion, national or social origin, property, birth or other status". See also Osin and Porat (2005).

[3] Vandenhole (2005), Tileagă et al. (2022b).

[4] For a review, see Nelson (2009), Altman (2020), Tileagă et al. (2022a).

[5] Blum (2004), Bosse (2022), Leslie and Lerner (2022).

[6] Beeghly (2021).

[7] Nickel (2017), Leslie and Lerner (2022).

reason why combating stereotypes by highlighting cases that do not conform to them has limited effectiveness.

Despite the current debate over the accuracy of stereotypes in describing reality,[8] the biggest problem with stereotypes may not be their falsity or inaccuracy. It may not even be their specific content. This paper develops the idea that stereotypes, for their very nature of generic beliefs or claims, cannot be analysed atomistically, but should rather be recognized as functional and powerful components of wider social narratives and contexts, whose complex structures give them meaning and strength.

These aspects of stereotypes have prompted us to consider various forms of structural injustice, namely another complex phenomenon understandable, at least in part, based on the intersection of social roles and positions, social categories, and related stereotypes. Consequently, the final part of the paper will be devoted to the analysis of three distinct types of injustice: epistemic, ontic, and categorical. All of these are connected to the phenomenon of stereotyping, albeit in different ways. We will explore their definitions and differences, with the aim of introducing unfamiliar readers to the debate. Hopefully, our endeavour may elicit a deeper and multidimensional examination of these forms of social injustice within jurisprudence—without claiming to address the difficult issue of the relationship between jurisprudence and ethics. We advocate for jurisprudence to address these types of injustice more comprehensively, allowing for a better understanding and normation of phenomena related to stereotyping and social oppression.

2 Stereotypes as Generic Beliefs

Human beings live in rich and complex environments that offer numerous stimuli. Like any other species, humans require cognitive strategies to organise and structure these stimuli and simplify the information coming from the external world. Cognitive categorization is a natural and effective way to achieve these results.[9] Thanks to categorising processes, reality is segmented into parts, such as artefacts (e.g., buildings, books, tables, spectacles), natural objects (e.g., dogs, trees, stones, mountains), or social groups (women, the elderly, Jews, Asians). Categorizing means recognizing certain properties as common and typical for each class of entities (along with their members or tokens). Categorization, therefore, organises the bewildering quantity of data emerging from human interactions with nature and other individuals, reducing the complexity of human experience, and facilitating inferences. The cognitive assistance provided by categorization, however, is not merely conceptual, but also practical. Cognitive categories do nor only offer stable epistemic structures but inform actions and behaviours, making them meaningful, comprehensible, and more predictable.[10]

---

[8] Allport (1954), McCauley et al. (1995), Jussim et al. (2009), Puddifoot (2017).

[9] McCauley et al. (1995), Fiske (2005).

[10] Smith and Medin (1981), Bodenhausen et al. (2012).

However, by emphasising typical traits and ignoring details and individual ones, categorization often leads to stereotyping. The belonging of an individual to a certain social group may become more important than their unique individuality, and the properties attributed to the group more salient than those actually possessed by the individual. This is why many authors consider social categorisation as the "basic cognitive process in stereotyping"[11]: we start by categorising and often end in stereotyping, considering social groups as homogeneous aggregates of neutral components and depriving social reality of its complexity and diversity.

The word "stereotype" comes from two Greek words. The first is the adjective στερεός (*stereos*), which means "firm", "stable" or "solid"; the second is the noun τύπος (*typos*), which can be translated as "concept", "model", "impression", "type", but also—significantly— "sketch" or "outline". A stereotype, therefore, is a stable concept or impression and, indeed, social psychologists understand stereotypes as mental images or beliefs that express generalisations about types.[12] These generalisations link certain properties (e.g., empathy) to certain groups (e.g., women)[13] and by associating traits with groups (i.e., by believing that "women are empathetic"), stereotypes create expectations that every token of the type "women" will both instantiate the property "empathy" and behave accordingly.[14] It is for these reasons that stereotypes can be understood as generic beliefs. They do not convey beliefs about the properties and features of particular individuals, but rather about the properties and features of classes of individuals.[15]

Generic beliefs, however, differ from what cognitive scientists define as "statistical beliefs".[16] While the latter are based on the perception and awareness that, *statistically*, the members of a group possess a certain feature, the former are vague and "less contingent on evidence".[17] Generic beliefs, in other words, tolerate exceptions to a considerable extent, and are usually much less accurate than statistical beliefs given that the latter, unlike the former, are based on empirical facts. Both generics and statistical beliefs are central to stereotypes, but a study conducted by Hammond and Cimpian[18] suggests that generic beliefs, which are easier to understand, use, and

---

[11] Tajfel (2001), p. 134; see also Gelman (2003) and Hirschfeld (1996). While simple categorisations such as associating an individual with just one group often elicits discrimination, multiple categorisation has prejudice-reducing effects, see Crisp et al. (2001) and Prati et al. (2016).

[12] Allport (1954), Devine (1989), Jussim et al. (2015).

[13] Fricker (2007), Haslanger (2011), Puddifoot (2017).

[14] Wheeler and Petty (2001).

[15] See also Bosse (2022), p. 2: "Generics are linguistic items that express propositions: generic propositions. Such propositions can be expressed linguistically, but we can also take a variety of attitudes towards them. We can hope for them, dread them, expect them, or, we can believe them. Such beliefs are generic beliefs. In cases in which we believe a generic proposition of a certain type concerning a social group, we hold a stereotype about that group."

[16] See Hammond and Cimpian (2017), p. 607: "Generic beliefs apply a feature to a group as a whole (e.g., men are strong), whereas statistical beliefs encode the perceived prevalence of a feature among the members of the group (e.g., how common it is for men to be strong)."

[17] Ibid., p. 607.

[18] Ibid.

remember,[19] are “more predictive of social judgement”[20] and consequently more relevant to stereotyping than statistical ones.[21] This fact makes it difficult to verify the accuracy of stereotypes because it does not depend on the actual prevalence of the stereotypical trait among the stereotyped group. This vagueness becomes equally evident when considering the linguistic aspects of stereotypes, namely how these mental representations are expressed linguistically. This will be the focus of the next section.

3 Stereotypes and Generics

Generic beliefs, which link certain traits to certain groups of objects or subjects, are beliefs in generic propositions that are linguistically expressed by statements known as “generics”.[22] Here are some examples of common generics:

(a) Ravens are black.
(b) Dogs are four-legged.
(c) Ducks lay eggs.
(d) Ticks carry Lyme disease.

The syntactic structure of these statements is always the same: the target group is expressed by a bare plural[23] (“ravens”, “dogs”, “ducks”, “ticks”) and the statement predicates one property of it using a “nonpast and nonprogressive verb”.[24] What is relevant in generics is that they do not provide explicit information about quantification, namely about the percentage of members of the group instantiating the predicated property.[25] Generics refer to entire classes of entities and predicate properties that are usually nonaccidental and “enduring”.[26] Statement (a), for instance, does not overtly say *how many ravens* are black but suggests that *all* ravens are black. This vagueness, which reflects the vagueness characterising generic beliefs, makes it difficult to analyse generics from a semantic point of view. The exact meaning conveyed by a generic is unclear: it is hard to understand precisely what I am thinking, believing, and saying about ducks when I utter statement (c). The content of generics

[19] Leslie (2008).

[20] Hammond and Cimpian (2017), p. 610.

[21] A significant result of one of the four studies is that, as regards nonsocial expectations (about properties of artefacts or animals), statistical beliefs are more relevant and predictive than generic beliefs. This may suggest that “generic beliefs are particularly influential when people make predictions about social (vs. nonsocial) targets”. Hammond and Cimpian (2017), p. 611.

[22] For a review, see Carlson and Pelletier (1995).

[23] Bare plurals can be replaced by indefinite or definite singulars (e.g., “a raven/the raven is a bird”).

[24] Gelman (2003), p. 169.

[25] About the nature of the so-called **Gen**, namely the implicit quantifier typically involved in generics, see Cohen (2012) and Sterken (2016).

[26] Carlson and Pelletier (1995).

is elusive. Let's now compare statements (a), (b), (c) and (d), which are examples of declarations that people usually accept.

Generic (a) states that ravens are black and implies that *all* or *most* ravens—except for leucistic ones—are black. Statement (b) is similar: *most* dogs are four-legged. Statement (c) is different: ducks lay eggs if mature females, so only *some* ducks (less than 50%) possess the property predicated by the generic. Generic (d), finally, is true for a small percentage of ticks, especially in certain territories where just around 1% of ticks are infected with the Lyme disease bacterium.

Given the different degrees of accuracy of commonly accepted generics, scholars have proposed various ideas about what makes them true and reliable. Before delving into this topic, however, it's important to highlight a distinction between two different forms of generics.

Generics can be understood as "kind-predications",[27] i.e., as statements about kinds. Statement (b), for instance, can be read as associating the property of being four-legged with the natural kind "dog". In this interpretation, generics directly predicate properties of kinds. Generics involving this "direct kind predication"[28] are also known as D-generics (where "D" stands for "definite").

Another way to understand generics is by saying that the properties predicated by the generics characterise the individual members of the kind at issue rather than the kind itself. In this second case, (b) would associate the property of being four-legged with the individual dogs belonging to the kind "dog". These generics are known as I-generics ("I" for "indefinite") or "characterising generics".

D-generics, by directly predicating kinds, are less vague than I-generics. Let's consider the following D-generic:

(e) Dodos are extinct.

If (e) means that the natural kind "dodo" is characterised by the property "being extinct", then all token dodos will no longer exist, and the generic will be true in that case—the discovery of *one* single dodo alive and well would falsify the generic. However, it is impossible to predicate the property "being extinct" of an individual dodo. An individual dodo may be dead, but not extinct. Only species, i.e., kinds, can be extinct.

On the contrary, I-generics such as "ravens are black" imply that the token members of the kind "raven" are black, and we are all prone to accepting these generics even if we know that there are some exceptions to the predications they express. As mentioned, not every raven is black and not every dog is four-legged, yet we still believe and confidently assert that ravens are black and dogs have four legs.

One way to understand the "robustness" of generics, which, unlike universal generalisations (e.g., "*all* ravens are black"), tolerate exceptions and non-conforming cases, is by grounding their reliability on the concept of normality.[29] It may be said

---

[27] Liebesman and Sterken (2021), p. 2.

[28] Leslie and Lerner (2022).

[29] See Asher and Morreau (1995), Pelletier and Asher (1997), Prasada (2000).

that normal ravens—i.e., non-leucistic ravens—are black. Equally, normal dogs—i.e., non-malformed/non-mutilated dogs—are four-legged. In other words, *normally*, all ravens are black, and all dogs have four legs.

These so-called "normalcy-based accounts" of generics[30] can explain statements like (a) and (b), providing reasons why it is still reasonable to believe in such generics despite the presence of exceptions. Such accounts, however, cannot explain generics like (c) and (d), because being a female duck is not "more normal" than being a male duck, just as carrying the Lyme disease bacterium cannot be reasonably considered "normal" for ticks.

Some authors solve this problem by highlighting that certain generics, despite appearances, actually refer to a salient sub-kind of the kind in question. Statement (c), for instance, pertains to the sub-kind "female ducks" of the kind "ducks" and, by restricting the domain of the generic, the latter maintains its accuracy. What should be clarified, at this juncture, is why a sub-kind is salient. There are several possible answers to this question. For instance, regarding statement (d), even if ticks do not often carry the Lyme disease bacterium, it is important to remember that ticks *can* carry it because the bacterium is dangerous, and danger prioritises attention.[31] It should be noted, therefore, that in addition to salient individuals and sub-kinds, properties can be salient as well.

But let's get back to ducks. The property of laying eggs, despite being possessed by female ducks alone, defines important features of the biological species commonly called "ducks". Modes of reproduction are important for biological classification, and this is general knowledge (just as it is commonly understood, for instance, that all birds lay eggs). The property of laying eggs, therefore, may be salient in this respect. We all know that biological properties such as "laying eggs", "flying", "having or not having the amniotic sac" or "having a certain number of legs" are particularly relevant for taxonomy, so these types of features might generally be more salient than others when describing animals.

To conclude, generics have indeterminate truthmakers, and their particular tolerance to exceptions and non-conforming cases can shed light on the dangerous robustness of stereotypes and their analogous ability to resist counterevidence.

4 The Falsity Hypothesis About Stereotypes

What has just been stated explains why verifying the accuracy of generics—and generic beliefs—is far from straightforward. This circumstance makes it difficult to take a stance about what Erin Beeghly defined as the "Falsity Hypothesis", namely the widespread idea that stereotypes are false. As Beeghly points out, the hypothesis can be read in two different ways:

---

[30] Leslie and Lerner (2022).

[31] Notebaert et al. (2011). For a social analysis of the topic see e.g. Leslie (2017).

Universal falsity hypothesis: stereotypes are always false or inaccurate.

Generic falsity hypothesis: stereotypes are (typically or usually) false or inaccurate.[32]

The first version of the Falsity Hypothesis, which, in Beeghly's opinion, is extremely widespread among psychologists and philosophers, states that falsity is a necessary condition to recognise and define stereotypes. According to this view, all stereotypes are false (or at least inaccurate), and this is the reason why stereotypes should be fought.[33] The second version of the hypothesis is weaker than the first, and states that stereotypes are *typically* or *usually* false or inaccurate, which means that *sometimes* stereotypes are true and accurate. This raises the question of how true and accurate stereotypes should be approached. Is it legitimate to express a stereotype if it is true and accurate? What is the relationship between true and accurate stereotypes and social oppression?

If stereotypes are socially harmful only because of their falsity and inaccuracy, as some authors seem to suggest, true and accurate stereotypes should be harmless. The problem, however, is that that is not the case. l This can be explained by observing that stereotypes convey a twofold message. On the one hand, they have an explicit meaning corresponding to the generalisation they express—e.g., "women are nurturing". On the other hand, they imply and suggest *a causal connection* between the trait and the group: the trait is understood as a property that the group has *by its very nature*.[34] This is one form of essentialism often recognised in stereotyping, but also in general lay theories about social groups[35]: the predicated property is seen as a stable, static and essential characteristic defining the nature of the (members of the) group. This hypothesis excludes other possibilities, such as acknowledging that these properties are rather dynamic, contingent, context-dependent, and/or socially constructed. As highlighted by Haslanger,[36] for instance, women are indeed submissive (or, at least, more submissive than men), but this may not be due to their essential nature but rather to the social context in which they grow up and live, namely "under conditions of male dominance".[37]

In the opening of *The Essential Child*, Susan Gelman provides brilliant examples of the conscious or unconscious desire for epistemic stability—something that, in her opinion, already arises in children. She reminisces:

> I was in elementary school, maybe third grade. My classmates and I were waiting to take a standardized IQ test. As we sat, with our number 2 pencils sharpened and ready, I was awed by the power of this test. As I understood it, the IQ score would reveal my intellectual capacity—immutable, fixed, and unchanging. [...] The number would not change—it would stay in our permanent records, but more important, *it would tell us who we were, and who we could become* [emphasis added].[38]

---

[32] Beeghly (2021), p. 37.

[33] Langton, Haslanger, and Anderson (2012).

[34] See Wodak and Leslie (2017) for an analysis about race and generics.

[35] Levy et al. (2001), Khalidi (2013), Haslanger (2014).

[36] Haslanger (2011).

[37] *Ibidem*, p. 4.

[38] Gelman (2003), p. 3.

Essentialism provides a stable framework for understanding reality and offers precious epistemic tools. If entities or kinds of entities have essential properties (and if those properties are recognised as essential), it becomes possible to formulate solid knowledge about them. For instance, if the property of attracting positively charged particles and repelling negatively charged particles is recognised as an essential property of electrons, it becomes possible to define electrons as "particles that attract positively charged particles and repel negatively charged particles". This definition not only provides clarity but also enables predictions about the behaviour of electrons, because these essential properties are causal properties or dispositions, as they dispose their bearers to certain typical behaviours. In the case of electrons, we would know that whenever they are near a positively charged particle, they will attract it, and whenever they are near a negatively charged particle, they will repel it.

An essentialist strategy may work with phenomena such as fundamental particles, because all particles of the same type (e.g., all electrons, all neutrinos, all muons) possess the same (essential) properties (i.e., particular mass, charge, and spin values) and consequently behave in the same way. When applied to more complex phenomena and upon analytical reflection, however, essentialism shows its limitations. Many authors suggest that essentialism often underpins knowledge about biological and social kinds. Since Darwin, though, it has been established that biological species are historical and evolving entities, so an essentialist approach cannot capture their peculiar nature.[39] Similarly, social groups are too variable and heterogeneous to be properly understood through an essentialist approach.[40] Nonetheless, essentialism remains a widespread cognitive bias, and its robustness is bolstered by the large use of generics in common language.[41] As pointed out by Gelman,[42] for instance, generics are widely used by parents, meaning that children are indirectly encouraged to consider reality from an essentialist perspective.[43]

To conclude, an *atomistic* analysis of stereotypes aimed at defining their semantic value and linking this value to the harm they cause will likely fail for at least two intertwined reasons. On the one hand, the degree of persuasiveness and legitimacy of stereotypes do not exclusively depend on their truth and accuracy in representing the world. On the other hand, the harm and oppression associated with stereotypes do not exclusively depend on their falsity or inaccuracy in representing the world. In other words, stereotypes are not believable or convincing because of their ability to reflect empirical truths, and they are not harmful because of their falsity or inaccuracy

[39] Wilson et al. (2007).

[40] Mallon (2004), Khalidi (2013).

[41] Gelman (2003), Gelman et al. (2010), Rhodes et al. (2012).

[42] Gelman (2003).

[43] About the frequency of maternal generics, see Gelman (2003), pp. 171–172. About the reason why generics are successful when parents want to explain something to their toddlers and young children (in short, explicit and detailed explanations are too complex for them), see Keil (1998). See also Leslie and Gelman (2012), p. 186, who explore and positively assess the hypothesis that "generics express cognitively default generalizations".

in describing reality.[44] Therefore, an analysis of the precise content of a stereotype, outside the context in which it is embedded, will not provide much information about its power and consequences.

We would like to conclude this paragraph with one last remark. A further factor to be considered when evaluating the usefulness of an analysis of stereotype content concerns the positivity or negativity of stereotypical traits and their harmfulness. Let's consider what follows:

(f) Blondes are stupid.
(g) Americans are hard-working.

Statements (f) and (g) associate a negative and a positive trait with two social groups, blonde women and Americans, respectively. "Blonds are stupid" is offensive, while "Americans are hard-working" is appreciative. Stereotypes are commonly understood as false or inaccurate categorisations and, according to many authors, the stereotyped feature, to be such, has to be hostile, negative or stigmatising.[45] As a result, statement (f) is easily recognisable as a stereotype, while statement (g) is not.

The positivity of the trait attributed to Americans, however, is not absolute but context-dependent.[46] Consider what follows:

(h) Indians are hard-working.

If you imagine yourself as an American, the trait that is perceived as positive when associated with your fellow citizens can be viewed as negative when associated with other social groups, such as Indians coming to your country and allegedly "stealing your jobs". The stereotyping attribute is the same, but its positivity or negativity depends on the context. Statement (h), for instance, would not be considered a harmful stereotype in India.

Another example of the non-trivial relationship between the quality of the attributes and the harmfulness of the stereotypes concerns stereotypes where the association of a positive trait to a group still produces injustices. Consider the following:

(i) Women are nurturing.
(j) Asians are good at maths.

"Being nurturing", unlike "being stupid", is a positive trait. So, statement (j) seems to be appreciative rather than offensive. Ascribing this attribute to women

[44] About this, consider stereotype threats, which "occurs when members of a stigmatized social group perform worse than they otherwise would have, because their membership in that group was made salient to them. For example, the performance of women and African-Americans on standardized tests is lowered if they are reminded first of their group membership by, e.g., being asked to report their gender or race before the exam" (Leslie and Lerner 2022; see also Steele and Aronson 1995).

[45] See Allport (1954), p. 7, who defines a stereotype as "A hostile attitude towards a person who belongs to a group, simply because he belongs to that group, and is therefore presumed to have the objectionable qualities ascribed to that group". See also Blum (2004), Beeghly (2015) and Puddifoot (2017).

[46] Brown and Pehrson (2019).

(alone), however, still produces social inequality because of the inferences that the stereotype encourages. For example, if women are seen as naturally nurturing, then the responsibility of taking care of children or the elderly will naturally fall on them.

Moving to (l), "being good at maths" is, again, a positive stereotype. Together with other stereotyped features (e.g., being hard-working, economically successful, or highly educated), it contributes to the notion of Asians as the so-called "model minority".[47] However, these positive stereotypes have been associated with significant disadvantages. For instance, Asians tend to underperform in maths tests when their group membership is made salient before their performance, because they choke "under the pressure of high expectations".[48] Also, they often feel depersonalised and undifferentiated from their peers because their group membership is considered more salient than their individual features.[49]

More generally, positive stereotypes, like negative ones, perpetuate social inequalities, albeit in a more politically correct or superficially inclusive way.[50] As highlighted by Czopp et al. (2015), historically, negative stereotypes about Blacks, Asians and gay men have shifted from being strikingly negative to being moderately positive.[51] Still, these shifts in content do not change the underlying bias that defines individuals by the social group they belong to, leading to specific expectations and differential treatment.

Again, the context and social narrative in which stereotypes are embedded are essential to understand their meaning and power, so any thorough analysis of stereotypes must consider them as parts of wider conceptual frameworks.[52] By doing so, it becomes easier to comprehend the kind of oppression and injustice that stereotyping engenders, and this enhanced understanding of discrimination can hopefully enable a more effective implementation of these analyses in the legal system.

---

[47] See Lee (2015)

[48] Cheryan and Bodenhausen (2000), p. 399. See also Gupta et al. (2011).

[49] Czopp et al. (2015), Lee (2015).

[50] Sometimes, positive stereotypes are even more detrimental than negative ones. See Czopp et al. (2015), p. 455: "women who heard benevolent sexism performed worse than did those women who heard blatant hostile sexism". This may be related to the fact that positive stereotypes are more prescriptive than negative ones (ibid., p. 456).

[51] See Czopp et al. (2015), p. 452: "As the statuses of social groups have shifted throughout history, so too have the content and valence of the corresponding stereotypes of those groups shifted. For example, Black slaves were stereotyped as animals with little intellectual capacity for whom menial physical labor was appropriate and beneficial. After slavery, stereotypes of Black moral and intellectual inferiority persisted. However, new stereotypes of athleticism and musical ability also emerged and strengthened as society permitted, acknowledged, and celebrated the participation and achievements of Black Americans within certain domains of sports and entertainment [...]. Stereotypes of Asian Americans have also evolved in a manner reflecting their shifting social status. Nineteenth century Chinese immigrant laborers were stereotyped as dirty, crude, and lazy [...], but as their academic and socioeconomic statuses improved, stereotypes reflecting more positive associations with intelligence, diligence, and competitiveness emerged [...]. Although stereotypes toward gay men (there is considerably less work on lesbians) still possess strong negative associations of psychological and moral deviance and abnormality, they have also begun to accommodate more favorable beliefs related to emotional sensitivity, style, and refinement".

[52] Ásta (2019), p. 295.

5 Epistemic, Ontic, and Categorical Injustice

As we said in Sect. 2, stereotypes have both a social and an epistemic function. They allow individuals to represent the world and enable groups to distinguish themselves from others.[53] In each case, stereotypes imply a degree of sharing. If a stereotype is believed to be true or used only by an individual, it remains a stereotype but does not have the social value we usually attribute to stereotypes. The sharing of stereotypes appears to be distributive or summative,[54] in the sense that the same stereotype is held by a majority of individuals belonging to the same group. In this sense, there is an element of common knowledge necessary to have group stereotypes about groups. By definition, stereotypes presuppose that their content is common knowledge in some groups, subgroups, or larger communities, otherwise they remain simply personal beliefs. This is a further reason to analyse stereotypes in a non-atomistic, structural way. The negative effects associated with a stereotype and, therefore, its potential for harm, however, may not be immediately apparent and may require empirical investigations,[55] or even a sustained effort of awareness, which may lead to the recognition of a form of injustice. And to understand why and how stereotypes may lead to forms of injustice, a structural analysis is required. To borrow an effective metaphor from Marilyn Frye,[56] if we focus only on one bar of a birdcage, we will not understand why the bird is not free, but if we consider all the bars and the way they are interconnected, then we will understand what a cage is.

As we stated in the previous section, indeed, the idea that women are nurturing might initially seem natural, and therefore not perceived as a stereotype; similarly, a positive feature attributed to a category may not be seen as leading to a form of injustice. Nonetheless, as we have seen, if the positive trait reinforces a standard division of labour, perpetuates a sharp distinction between "good" and "bad" people or underpins an unequal status quo, it can (and should) be recognized as a source of injustice or even oppression.

In what follows, we will analyse three forms of injustice linked to social groups, which, let us remember, are the subjects of stereotypes. These forms of injustice are ontic, epistemic, and categorical injustice. Each of these accounts involves the attribution of one or more traits to a category of people and results in a form of unjust social arrangement. However, they do it from different perspectives and by highlighting different forms of injustice that arise from *how* we attribute features to groups of people. Considering their relevance to juridical or legal perspectives, we can make a few observations. First, the concept of epistemic injustice could prove particularly

[53] Stereotypes help us make decisions in uncertain contexts and, at the same time, reinforce the contraposition between ingroup and outgroups, as the Social Identity Theory proved. See Brown and Pehrson (2019).

[54] The classic definition of what it means for an account to be summative is taken from Quinton (1975).

[55] Tripodi (2013), (2015).

[56] Frye (1983).

helpful in legal analysis insofar as it deals with people's credibility and testimonials. Ontic injustice seems to apply to very specific cases, but has an evident legal component as it translates into a social category being either entitled to, or excluded from, something by institutionally established norms. Finally, categorical injustice appears more general than the other two, even though it presupposes two different applications, one institutional and one based on common sense. Let's describe them in more detail in order to evaluate their differences and similarities and highlight why they should be taken into account if we want to combat forms of discrimination that rely, at least partly, on stereotyping and generic beliefs. We will analyse them from a chronological perspective, namely in the order in which they were formulated and developed in the literature.

5.1 *Epistemic Injustice*

Epistemic injustice, as the name suggests, is a form of injustice that directly concerns the credibility and the reliability, and thus the epistemic value, attributed to individuals as members of a certain category. Coined by Miranda Fricker,[57] the concept is widely accepted and used in contemporary feminist philosophies, for example in relation to the issue of rape or gender-based violence in general.[58] Fricker distinguishes two types of epistemic injustice, which she calls testimonial and hermeneutic injustice.[59] Hermeneutic injustice occurs when a community does not have the tools to identify a wrong suffered by an individual. In this sense, hermeneutic injustice is closely related to ontic injustice—although the two cases are distinguishable, as we will see in the next subsection. Testimonial injustice is more specific, but also particularly relevant in the debate. The attribution of credibility can be either positive or negative. Due to the proliferation of stereotypes about groups, we may be inclined to attribute less or even more credibility than is due to a person. This explains the devaluation of the testimonies of certain individuals because of their group membership, but also the uncritical acceptance of the testimonies of other individuals for the same reason.

An interesting case, in this regard, pertains to sexual abuse. As the literature highlights, it is very common to find that people are not believed, for instance black men asserting their innocence of sexual abuse charges or women asserting to be the victims Conversely, other categories are readily believed or justified because their role is valued positively in our societies, such as successful white men.[60] In this sense, being part of a social category often determines whether people are believed

---

[57] Fricker (1998), (2007).

[58] For instance, Srinivasan (2021), Chapter 1.

[59] See Tripodi (2015).

[60] Manne (2017), among others, interestingly shows how we tend to justify violent behaviour in white men, according to the phenomenon she calls "himpathy".

or not both as perpetrators and as victims of sexual abuse[61] or misogyny.[62] This has significant implications from a legal point of view, because testimonies are a crucial component of trials. Moreover, reliability is a key element throughout a judicial process, from collection by the police to potential judgement by the court.

5.2 *Ontic Injustice*

The phrasing "ontic injustice" was coined by Katherine Jenkins[63] to describe a specific form of injustice related to her account of social roles based on the so-called "Constraints and Enablements Framework" (CEF). The use of the term 'ontic' to define this form of injustice is a clear reference to "epistemic injustice": if the latter, as we saw earlier, refers to the epistemic value of people, ontic injustice applies to social categories themselves and, as a consequence, is related to the ontological component rather than the epistemological one.

According to the CEF, social roles, groups and certain social kinds (those related to groups of people) can be understood by recognizing that playing social roles entails both constraints and enablements that define what individuals are entitled to do. Ontic injustice arises when there is a mismatch between what people are morally entitled to do and what they are actually able to do based on their socially constructed identity. The examples used by Jenkins to elucidate ontic injustice are *being a slave* and *being a wife in England and Wales before 1991*. Both cases entail a form of injustice strictly dependent on an individual's group membership. Indeed, being a slave entails a reduction in the range of actions that one can perform. The same can be said for being a wife in England and Wales before 1991, the year when the crime of sexual harassment within the marriage was legally recognized. Before that date, wives could be raped by their husbands without legal consequences. What we now recognize as a crime and a morally unjust behaviour was not understood as such in the past. Consequently, simply being a member of the social kind "wife" could result in the actualization of injustice.

The concept of ontic injustice allows us to explain some cases of diminishment and a sense of impotence felt especially by certain marginalised groups. It also helps understand some of the negative implications of certain social kinds, especially gender and race, and therefore enables us to challenge them.

The cases used by Jenkins are certainly illuminating and have a markedly legal component: the issue here is not the social definition of slaves and wives, but the legal

---

[61] Interestingly, Srinivasan (2021) points out issues related to the movement "Believe women". She writes: "For many women of colour, the mainstream feminist injunction 'Believe women' and its online correlate #IBelieveHer raise more questions than they settle. Whom are we to believe, the white woman who says she was raped, or the black or brown woman who insists that her son is being set up?" (p. 9). In this sense, she further problematizes the question of credibility in relation to social categories.

[62] Manne (2017).

[63] Jenkins (2020), (2023).

one. The problem arises when something immoral is embedded in the legal definition of a category. We can of course imagine cases of ontic injustice due to norms other than legal ones, such as those stemming from patriarchal societies. Still, a reference to officially recognized norms seems necessary. For the sake of completeness, it is worth noting that according to Jenkins,[64] ontic injustice is the basis for dealing with ontic oppression, a subset of ontic injustice that arises when an individual is a victim of ontic injustice because of their membership in a social group. Oppression thus occurs when social limitation is systematic, group-based, and subordinating.[65] Here we do not want to go deeper into the analysis of oppression, but we wish to underscore the relevance of non-atomistic analysis in grasping complex social phenomena. It's also noteworthy how the very institutional definition of a social category can lead to injustices.

5.3 *Categorical Injustice*

The expression "categorial injustice" is borrowed from Ásta (2019) and is based on her theory of conferred social categories.[66] Within this framework, a property is conferred upon people when physical, relational, or social properties are taken to be relevant in a social context and determine others' behaviour in that context. According to Ásta, properties can be institutional or communal depending on the institutionality of the context and the related norms. Interestingly, in both cases the categorised individuals may not actually have the base property. For instance, consider the example examined by Ásta, involving the property of 'being married'. Imagine a party where people are curious about whether others are married or not. Alex is married but he behaves as if he is not. Thus, people confer on him the property 'not married' even though he is.[67]

Indeed, according to Ásta's account, stereotype thinking doesn't necessarily need to be conscious. Stereotypes can subconsciously determine who assumes specific social roles within a social context. Consider Ásta's example of a car stuck in the snow with four passengers, two men and two women.[68] The decision of who is going to drive and who is going to push will be based not only on institutional properties like having a driving licence, but also on stereotypes concerning physical fitness. As a consequence, it's likely that men will push and a woman will drive, even though in this specific case the best solution could be a different one. Interestingly, as Ásta

---

[64] Jenkins (2023).

[65] Ibid., p. 56.

[66] Ásta (2018).

[67] Ibid., p. 9. This specific aspect is important for the application of these forms of injustice to well-studied cases such as those of race and gender. For instance, consider Haslanger's definition of 'woman', according to which women are subordinated because of their observed or imagined features deemed relevant to reproductive function. The crucial fact is not that they have the reproductive function, but that they are assumed to have it (Haslanger 2012).

[68] Ásta (2019), p. 396.

noticed, operative stereotypes are especially widespread in contexts where people do not know each other well, so that stereotypes work as common knowledge based on which to make decisions and assign distinct roles.[69]

Categorical injustice enters the picture when an individual who is institutionally entitled to perform a certain action is prevented from doing so by their membership in a category. As a consequence, their actions are made impossible or unintelligible. Ásta provides an example of a woman engineer issuing an order to a worker, which the latter takes as a comment rather than an order precisely because the engineer is a woman. This is based on the stereotype that women do not give orders. The fundamental mismatch is between what a person is *institutionally entitled* to do (an engineer giving orders to workers) and what the person is *actually able to do* (the action not taken as an order because the engineer is a woman). According to Ásta, this is a source of injustice that ought to be distinguished from both epistemic and ontic injustice. From our perspective, categorical injustice is interesting because it directly stems from our tendency towards stereotyping. It vividly shows how apparently innocuous beliefs about groups of people can yield harmful results.

6 Conclusive Remarks

The analysis of these three forms of injustice, all rooted in the categorization of an individual within a certain category, demonstrates how stereotypes, as generalisations about groups of people, carry a normative value that can lead to injustice. We do not mean to imply that generalisations should be eliminated from knowledge and common language. Rather, we wish to underscore the importance of recognising such strategies and forms of injustice and assessing their possible impact within the legal sphere. This awareness is doubly important for the law: it can prompt jurists to reflect on the types of injustice they may perpetuate in their daily practice and, at a more general level, it can encourage questioning about the corrective measures jurisprudence could or should enact. While in the present work we were unable to address all the complexities of this issue, including the nuanced relationship between ethics and law, as well as the tension between liberal and interventionist societal perspectives, we believe it's crucial to foster awareness as a crucial step toward fostering a fairer society.

References

Allport GW (1954) The nature of prejudice. Perseus Books, Cambridge MA
Altman A (2020) Discrimination. In Zalta EN (ed) The Stanford Encyclopedia of Philosophy. https://plato.stanford.edu/archives/win2020/entries/discrimination/

---

[69] Ibid., p. 397.

Asher N, Morreau M (1995) What some generic sentences mean. In: Carlson GN, Pelletier FJ (eds) The generic book. University of Chicago Press, Chicago, pp 300–339
Ásta (2019) Categorical injustice. J Soc Philos 50:392–406
Ásta (2018) Categories we live by. MIT Press, Cambridge MA
Beeghly E (2015) What is a stereotype? What is stereotyping? Hypatia 30(4):675–691
Beeghly E (2021) What's wrong with stereotypes? The falsity hypothesis. Soc Theory Pract 33–61
Blum L (2004) Stereotypes and stereotyping: a moral analysis. Philos Pap 33(3):251–289
Bodenhausen GV, Kang SK, Peery D (2012) Social categorization and the perception of social groups. In: Fiske ST, Macrae CN (eds) The SAGE handbook of social cognition. Sage, New York, pp 311–329
Bosse A (2022) Stereotyping and generics. Inquiry 1–17
Brown R, Pehrson S (2019) Group processes: dynamics within and between groups. Wiley, Hoboken
Carlson GN, Pelletier FJ (eds) (1995) The generic book. University of Chicago Press, Chicago
Cheryan S, Bodenhausen GV (2000) When positive stereotypes threaten intellectual performance: the psychological hazards of "Model Minority" status. Psychol Sci 11(5):399–402
Cohen A (2012) No quantification without reinterpretation. In Mari A, Beyssade C, Prete FD (eds) Genericity. Oxford University Press, Oxford
Crisp RJ, Hewstone M, Rubin M (2001) Does multiple categorization reduce intergroup bias? Pers Soc Psychol Bull 27:76–89
Czopp AM, Kay AC, Cheryan S (2015) Positive stereotypes are pervasive and powerful. Perspect Psychol Sci 10(4):451–463
Devine PG (1989) Stereotypes and prejudice: their automatic and controlled components. J Pers Soc Psychol 56:5–18
Fiske ST (2005) Social cognition and the normality of prejudgment. In: Dovidio JF, Glick P, Rudman LA (eds) On the nature of prejudice: 50 years after allport. Wiley-Blackwell, Oxford, pp 36–53
Fricker M (2007) Epistemic injustice: power and the ethics of knowing. Oxford University Press, Oxford
Fricker M (1998) Rational authority and social power: towards a truly social epistemology. Proc Aristot Soc 98(2):159–177
Fowers B (2015) The evolution of ethics: human sociality and the emergence of ethical mindedness. Springer, Berlin
Frye M (1983) Oppression. In The politics of reality. Crossing, Berkeley (CA), pp 1–16
Gelman SA (2003) The essential child: origins of essentialism in everyday thought. Oxford University Press, Oxford
Gelman SA, Ware EA, Kleinberg F (2010) Effects of generic language on category content and structure. Cogn Psychol 61(3):273–301
Gupta A, Szymanski DM, Leong FTL (2011) The "Model Minority Myth": internalized racialism of positive stereotypes as correlates of psychological distress, and attitudes toward help-seeking. Asian Am J Psychol 2(2):101–114
Hammond MD, Cimpian A (2017) Investigating the cognitive structure of stereotypes: generic beliefs about groups predict social judgments better than statistical beliefs. J Exp Psychol Gen 146(5):607–614
Haslanger S (2014) The normal, the natural and the good: generics and ideology. Politica & Società 3:365–392
Haslanger S (2012) Resisting reality. Oxford University Press, Oxford, Social Construction and Social Critique
Haslanger S (2011) Ideology, generics, and common ground. In: Witt C (ed) Feminist metaphysics: explorations in the ontology of sex, gender, and the self. Springer, Dordrecht, pp 179–209
Hirschfeld LA (1996) Race in the making: cognition, culture, and the child's construction of human kinds. The MIT Press, Cambridge (MA)
Jenkins K (2023) Ontology and oppression. Race, gender, and social reality. Oxford University Press, Oxford
Jenkins K (2020) Ontic injustice. J Am Philos Assoc 6(2):188–205

Jussim L, Cain TR, Crawford JT, Harber K, Cohen F (2009) The unbearable accuracy of stereotypes. In Nelson TD (ed) Handbook of prejudice, stereotyping, and discrimination, pp 199–227
Jussim L, Crawford JT, Rubinstein RS (2015) Stereotype (In)accuracy in perceptions of groups and individuals. Curr Dir Psychol Sci 24:490–497
Keil FC (1998) Words, moms, and things: language as a road map to reality. Monogr Soc Res Child Dev 63(1):149–157
Khalidi MA (2013) Natural categories and human kinds. Cambridge University Press, Cambridge
Langton R, Haslanger S, Anderson L (2012) Language and race. In: Russell G, Graff Fara D (eds) The Routledge companion to philosophy of language. Routledge, New York, pp 753–767
Lee SJ (2015) Unraveling the "Model Minority" stereotype: listening to asian american youth. Teachers College Press, New York
Leslie SJ (2008) Generics: cognition and acquisition. The Philos Rev 117:1–47
Leslie SJ (2017) The original sin of cognition: fear, prejudice, and generalization. J Philos 114(8):393–342
Leslie SJ, Lerner A (2022) Generic generalizations. In Zalta EN, Nodelman U (eds) The Stanford Encyclopedia of philosophy. https://plato.stanford.edu/archives/fall2022/entries/generics/
Leslie SJ, Gelman SA (2012) Quantified statements are recalled as generics: evidence from preschool children and adults. Cogn Psychol 64(3):186–214
Levy SR, Plaks JE, Hong YY, Chiu CY, Dweck CS (2001) Static versus dynamic theories and the perception of groups: different routes to different destinations. Pers Soc Psychol Rev 5:156–168
Liebesman D, Sterken RK (2021) Generics and the metaphysics of kinds. Philos Compass 16(7):1–14
Mallon R (2004) Passing, traveling and reality: social constructionism and the metaphysics of race. Noûs 38(4):644–673
Manne K (2017) Down girl. Oxford University Press, Oxford, The logic of misogyny
McCauley CR, Jussim LJ, Lee YT (eds) (1995) Stereotype accuracy: toward appreciating group differences. American Psychological Association, Washington
Nelson TD (2009) Handbook of prejudice, stereotyping, and discrimination. Psychology Press
Nickel B (2017) Generics. In: Hale B, Wright C, Miller A (eds) A companion to the philosophy of language. Wiley, Hoboken, pp 437–462
Notebaert L, Crombez G, Van Damme S, De Houwer J, Theeuwes J (2011) Signals of threat do not capture, but prioritize, attention: a conditioning approach. Emotion 11(1):81–89
Osin N, Porat D (eds) (2005) Legislating against discrimination: an international survey of anti-discrimination norms. Martinus Nijhoff, Leiden
Pelletier FJ, Asher N (1997) Generics and defaults. In: van Benthem J, ter Meulen AGB (eds) Handbook of logic and language. The MIT Press, Cambridge (MA), pp 1125–1177
Prasada S (2000) Acquiring generic knowledge. Trends Cogn Sci 4:66–72
Prati F, Crisp RJ, Meleady R, Rubini M (2016) Humanizing outgroups through multiple categorization: the roles of individuation and threat. Pers Soc Psychol Bull 42(4):526–539
Puddifoot K (2017) Stereotyping: the multifactorial view. Philos Top 45(1):137–156
Quinton A (1975) Social objects. Proc Aristot Soc 76:1–27
Rhodes M, Leslie SJ, Tworek CM (2012) Cultural transmission of social essentialism. Proc Natl Acad Sci 109(34):13526–13531
Smith EE, Medin DL (1981) Categories and concepts. Harvard University Press, Cambridge (MA)
Srinivasan A (2021) The right to sex. Oxford University Press, Oxford, Feminism the twenty-first century
Steele CM, Aronson J (1995) Stereotype threat and the intellectual test performance of African Americans. J Pers Soc Psychol 69(5):797–811
Sterken RK (2016) Generics, covert structure and logical form. Mind Lang 31(5):503–529
Tajfel H (2001) Social stereotypes and social groups. In: Hogg MA, Abrams D (eds) Intergroup relations: essential readings. Psychology Press, London, pp 132–145
Tajfel H, Turner JC (1979) An integrative theory of intergroup conflict. In Austin WG, Worchel S (eds) The social psychology of intergroup relations. Brooks/Cole, Monterey (CA), pp 33–37

Tileagă C, Augoustinos M, Durrheim K (eds) (2022a) The Routledge international handbook of discrimination, prejudice and stereotyping. Routledge, London.

Tileagă C, Augoustinos M, Durrheim K (2022) Towards a new sociological social psychology of prejudice, stereotyping and discrimination. In: Tileagă C, Augoustinos M, Durrheim K (eds) The Routledge international handbook of discrimination, prejudice and stereotyping. Routledge, London, pp 3–9

Tripodi V (2015) Filosofie di genere. Differenza sessuale e ingiustizie sociali. Carocci, Roma

Tripodi V (2013) Stereotipi. In Turri MG (ed) Manifesto per un nuovo femminismo. Mimesis, Milano-Udine, pp 209–224

Vandenhole W (2005) Non-discrimination and equality in the view of the UN human rights treaty bodies. Intersentia, Oxford

Wheeler SC, Petty RE (2001) The effects of stereotype activation on behavior: a review of possible mechanisms. Psychol Bull 127:797–826

Wilson RA, Barker MJ, Brigandt I (2007) When traditional essentialism fails: biological natural kinds. Philos Top 35(1/2):189–215

Wodak D, Leslie SJ (2017) The mark of the plural: generic generalizations and race. In: Taylor P, Alcoff L, Anderson L (eds) The Routledge companion to the philosophy of race. Routledge, London, pp 277–289

Valeria Martino is a Postdoctoral Research Fellow at the Department of Philosophy and Education Sciences of the University of Turin and a member of the Labont—Center for Ontology. Her research interests lie in social ontology and in theories concerning social groups.

Erica Onnis is an Associate Professor in Theoretical Philosophy at Cusano University, Rome, and a member of the Labont—Center for Ontology. Her research interests lie in metaphysics and philosophy of science.

Gender Stereotypes in the City: A Socio-Normative Approach

Valerio Nitrato Izzo and Patrícia Branco

Abstract Urban space has long been associated with a unique, homogenous point of view that has overlooked the representation of gender in the city. Building on recent literature that has uncovered the potentialities of using a gendered lens for addressing the city and urban space, we offer a socio-normative approach that brings law, rights and legal stereotypes in conversation with such literature. In order to do so we will first look briefly at the reciprocal constitution of law, space and stereotypes. Then we will address examples and specific characteristics of urban space and norm/rights enjoyment, exploring different kinds of urban spaces and their theorization where gender issues and normative elements are at stake. We conclude by arguing that law, gender and urban space suffer from a reciprocal invisibilization that has greatly limited the detection of discriminatory attitudes in the urban domain as well as of practices of resistance.

Keywords Gender stereotypes · Urban public space · Just cities · Law and gender

1 Introduction[1]

Even if it has been seldom explicitly admitted, abstract urban space in urbanism and urban studies, since their very first inception, have long been associated with a unique, homogenous point of view, that of a male (and often white, middle-class) subject as the urban dweller. Especially in the twentieth century and in Western

[1] While the authors share the overall argument and research findings of the chapter, the parts must be attributed individually as follows: paragraphs 1,2,3 should be attributed to Valerio Nitrato Izzo and paragraphs 3.1,3.2,3.3, 4 to Patrícia Branco; paragraph 5 jointly by the two authors.

V. Nitrato Izzo (✉)
University of Naples Federico II, Naples, Italy
e-mail: valerio.nitratoizzo@unina.it

P. Branco
University of Coimbra, Coimbra, Portugal
e-mail: patriciab@ces.uc.pt

A. Condello and A. Wagner (eds.), *Gender Stereotypes*, Gender, Justice and Legal Feminism 2, https://doi.org/10.1007/978-3-031-63905-0_4

urbanism, the organization of the urban space has been overall an organization that strived for uniformization and functionalism. The making of the city has historically been the making of a universal space but aimed at a very specific kind of subject. Interestingly, critical thinkers were aware of this aspect. Henri Lefebvre, the French philosopher associated with the social production of space and the right to the city, distinguished in his critique of abstract space a dominant masculine principle and a dominated feminine one. On the point, Lefebvre highlighted, among the formants he identified as pertaining to abstract space (geometrical and visual), a *phallic* one, metaphorically symbolizing force, male fertility, masculine violence. In his critique of abstract space as inherently aiming for homogeneity and a mere reflection as opposed to spatial practice, namely a space constructed for desire and social matters, he argued that *the space of a (social) order is hidden in the order of space.*[2] What was hidden was a feminine principle, present in ancient times and lost in association with modernity.

Gender has also been at the core of preoccupations of more contemporary thinkers about space. For Doreen Massey "The limitation of women's mobility, in terms both of identity and space, has been in some cultural contexts a crucial means of subordination. Moreover, the two things—the limitation on mobility in space, the attempted consignment/confinement to particular places on the one hand, and the limitation on identity on the other—have been crucially related".[3]

Interestingly, while these hidden peculiarities of our conception of space were—not universally—remarked, the seeing like a city literature[4] made a convincing argument that cities could offer a different point of view for pretty much everything with respect to seeing like a state.[5] This was also related to the role law played in shaping such a dialectics between city and states[6] and how a politics based in urbanism could move away from state embedment of belonging and provide an open space for the creation and practice of different citizenships.[7]

Nevertheless, only recently was possible to say that *seeing like a gender in the city* has become the primer concern for much discussion. While contemporary awareness of the issue has certainly arisen, as demonstrated by recent influential scholarly work,[8] the invisibility of women's lives in and uses of the urban space is the most common condition when we take a closer look. In her work, Perez demonstrated with a vast array of examples how the dominance of a male subject of a certain kind simply obscures other gender representations. From snow cleaning services to kitchen utensils in India, from gloves design to sidewalk dimensions, most apparently neutral topics and practices are, when better scrutinized, oriented towards a universal masculine subject. When project managers disregard feminine needs, spaces become

[2] Lefebvre (1991), p. 289.

[3] Massey (1994), p. 179.

[4] Amin and Thrift (2017), Sassen (2008).

[5] Scott (1998).

[6] Valverde (2011), Frug (1980).

[7] Magnusson (2012), Sassen (2006).

[8] Kern and Criado-Perez (2019), Granata (2023).

masculine by default, simply omitting that half of the world's population has a female body. While the domination of a certain gender was by no means just a matter of chance, the neutral view of the urban space as a space equal for all can be described itself as an *urban stereotype*, an image of the urban that in the end rests more over a simplification rather than the real experience of the city.[9] In a certain way this is similar to what happened at the intersection of urban theory and law. Interestingly, while much scholarship built around a critical conception of space led to a spatial turn in social sciences as well as in law, the emergence of cities as an object of study for both law and social sciences has not been immediately associated with gender issues.

The relationship between law, gender and urban spaces is a story of what we could call a *double invisibilization*. On the one hand, while gender studies currently have a considerable amplitude of scholarship, gender issues are still often overlooked in general doctrinal studies of law that are oriented towards gender sensitive topics in urban law. On the other hand, the actual reevaluation of the connections between law, space and the city comes after a long overlooking of the theoretical and epistemological connections between these elements. Notwithstanding a growing literature on the relationship between law, geography and space[10] and consequently the affirmation of a *spatial turn* that law, among other social sciences, has finally embraced,[11] critical approaches to the topic have outlined that the concept of law has remained essentially indifferent to spatiality, often limiting itself to a kind of formula in which the word space is added and 'mixed' to see what comes out. This means, on the one hand, a re-proposition of a kind of paradoxical fetishization of space, already denounced by Lefebvre, in that it would be enough to add the spatial element to law to rebalance its characteristics, and on the other hand, the denial of the role that law plays in any spatial process. Radicalizing the relationship of co-constitutivity between law and space, in this order of ideas, the characteristics of space as representation, text, abstraction, system and closure would in fact be dependent on a legal understanding of space in which it is the legal discourse that guides the ways in which other disciplines relate to space.[12] Thus, the presence of the normative relation would be mutually original and constitutive of the spatial one. Considering law as an integral and unavoidable part of spatial thinking has profound consequences for both law and space: 1. space should necessarily be described as open and closed both at the same time because of the different legal instruments that allow or ensure closure; 2. consequently, law helps to explain why space can be closed/textual/negative etc., helping to offer reasons (ownership, community, national jurisdiction etc.) for the desirability of certain spatial formations; 3. law allows for a deeper understanding of the power structures that emerge when bodies move towards or into a certain space, generating different spaces and norms while in motion.[13]

---

[9] Burgess (1974), p. 168.

[10] Blomley et al. (2001).

[11] Blomley (2008), Blank and Rosen-Zvi (2010).

[12] Philippopoulos-Mihalopoulos (2021), p. 627.

[13] Philippopoulos-Mihalopoulos (2021), p. 637.

This theoretical alternative framework proposed by Philippopoulos-Mihalopoulos is based on the concept of *lawscape* that is that dense network of normative relations in which each body is constantly immersed, every spatial positioning becomes legally relevant by being controlled or potentially controllable through law.[14] In the author's own definition, this is a kind of tautology, since it would not be possible, as we have seen, for law or space to exist without mutual reference. Through this complete rethinking of the relationship between law and space in a radically material and constitutive sense at the same time, an intellectual project aimed at overcoming a generic rethinking in a normative and spatial sense that has almost always underestimated or completely neglected the contribution of law to questions of spatial justice is placed at the center. This perspective thus moves towards the declared aim of rethinking the concept of spatial justice in a legal context,[15] considered as a theoretical platform to redefine not only the connection between law and geography, but above all the conceptual bases of law and space.[16] Spatial justice thus becomes the expression of a legal and at the same time spatial claim to a single position that is destined to conflict: "spatial justice emerges from the fact that only one body can occupy a specific space at any specific time", being defined as "[...] the struggle between bodies to be in a specific space at a specific time".[17] Spatial justice, in this sense, will then always be contingent, mobile, and not determinable a priori insofar as it is open to the ethical dimension of spatial withdrawal on the part of those occupying a space; and the possibility that it is precisely through movement and the desire for a new spatial location that new social formations open.

The spatial justice approach also allows the merging of the two elements that actually constitute a city, the physical space and the experience of living in the city. According to Sennett, building and dwelling are two constitutive dimensions of our understanding of cities that remind us of the differences between *ville* and *cité,* as expressed in French language. From this perspective "how people want to live should be expressed in how cities are built"[18] and this is the exact challenge a gendered city poses to traditional ways of seeing the urban form inspired by a spatial justice approach. As we are now aware, the configuration of space is not just a matter of physical space only, but also of how this space is normatively organized, regulated, segregated, forbidden, allowed, and to whom and when. The very definition of any ideas of a "public space" and how and if a subject acts into it, appears in it or is separated from it rests on these terms.

In this chapter we consider that issues of spatial justice arise when urban spaces are normatively questioned through the lens of gender and other perspectives that put into question a single point of view and a mono-subjectual practice of the city. This connects to the idea of a just city in urban studies, often developed in critical terms relying on a philosophical appreciation for the protection of difference in the urban

---

[14] Philippopoulos-Mihalopoulos (2015), p. 175.

[15] Philippopoulos-Mihalopoulos (2010), p. 203.

[16] Philippopoulos-Mihalopoulos (2010), p. 201.

[17] Philippopoulos-Mihalopoulos (2015), p. 176.

[18] Sennett (2018), p. 2.

realm but often developed without a direct reference to gender.[19] But what could a gendered concept of just city mean? According to Kern, "Feminist urbanism would be one that recognizes and remunerates unpaid care, and where women's needs are taken into account in both design and budgetary decisions".[20]

2 Rights and Gender in the City Space

As there is no spatial justice without taking into consideration the law and the normative element, a further look is needed on the connections between rights in the urban space. As a corollary to the recovery of the legal significance of the urban, in the wake of what in the social sciences has been called the spatial turn, legal scholars have also become aware of a kind of "urbanization of fundamental rights",[21] and engaged in an interdisciplinary interest for the question of the relationship between the city and human/fundamental rights. Cities and/or urban spaces are powerful points of observation for the practice of rights claiming as well as their infringements.[22] The directions along which the question of rights in the city has unraveled can be, at least as a first approximation, oriented towards two fundamental theoretical directions, one inspired by the theoretical platform of the right to the city and another resting on the institutional and social practice of the human rights cities.[23]

Regarding the first strand, we highlight the rediscovery of the French Marxist philosopher Henri Lefebvre, who first theorized the idea of a right to the city and made it a fortunate concept, also thanks to the appeal of a formula vague enough to be interpreted in many, and sometimes contradictory, ways. Defined by Lefebvre in a 1968 text, "the right to the city cannot be conceived of as a return to traditional cities. It can only be formulated as a transformed and renewed right to urban life".[24] Over the years, the right to the city has become a concept sometimes referred to too emphatically, to the point of significantly diminishing its original emancipatory scope and force. This has not prevented the concept from playing a crucial role as a theoretical catalyst for many urban movements. From a legal point of view, the difficulties of translating it into more immediately applicable terms have been numerous, even though the expression has also managed to make its way into various national legal systems (particularly in South America).

The second strand refers to the phenomenon and movement of Human Rights Cities (HRCs) and its various social and institutional configurations. Although this is a relatively recent field of study, we share Grigolo's definition: "[…] a city that

---

[19] Fanstein (2010).

[20] Kern (2019).

[21] Auby (2013), p. 20.

[22] Nitrato Izzo (2017).

[23] Auby (2022), pp. 29–33, Chueca (2016).

[24] Lefebvre (1996), p. 158.

is organized according to human rights norms and principles".[25] Cities are increasingly asserting themselves as the main actors in the local implementation of human rights, placing themselves on a ridge that is sometimes openly conflicting with state legal systems. It is now a matter of acknowledging that the local dimension of the implementation of human rights is to all intents and purposes recognized within the framework of global international law.

Both approaches can prove crucial for a critical look at gender issues in the city. A Lefebvrian inspired right to the city approach has been used to look at the practice of everyday life as "an important but undertheorized space outside feminist scholarship. Here the multiple temporalities of space are revealed as contested sites for identity and rights."[26]

The practice of human rights cities is also relevant as many cities and municipalities that made human rights a principle of their local politics are also at the edge of this stance, as is the case of the City of Vienna, one of the most active cities in implementing both human rights and gender equality in its institutional ray of action.[27] The city's council has developed an extensive monitoring report mechanism that serves as a constant data base where different sources of information are gathered according to several indicators, such as political participation or access to public space, in which Vienna has been at the forefront of enhancing gender equality in access to parks and green areas, mobility and transportation issues, sport and other elements. Recent research focused on Milan city has also addressed a variety of ways in which gender urban planning lens can be a different way to rethink urbanism. Other experiences highlight that a more inclusive city from a gender perspective encourages women's participatory empowerment on topics like street lighting and transportation, making improvements that are in the end positive for all city users.[28] And these social and institutional mechanisms should not be confined only to Western or European contexts, as these dialectics are now recognized in other cultures and geographies as well.

These bottom-up exercises of city protagonism in collecting data at a local level seem to confirm Perez's argument regarding the urgent need for elaborating data that is aimed at representing women's needs, uses and placements in city life. At the same time, from the point of view of normative and institutional practices locally implemented, they also offer a concrete initial start for rights-based practices in the urban space inspired by gender urbanism. A gender-based approach has been a longstanding preoccupation for institutions such as the UN and its bodies, especially

[25] Grigolo (2016), p. 277.

[26] Beebeejaun (2016), p. 328. In a more critical sense see also Fenster (2005).

[27] Vienna City Council has developed a detailed Gender Equality Monitoring Report since 2013 (https://www.wien.gv.at/english/social/women/gender-equality-monitor.html) as well as hosting, since 2015, a Human Rights Office working on the basis of the declaration "Vienna—city of human rights" https://www.wien.gv.at/english/social/integration/human-rights/office.html.

[28] It is the case of the Glasgow City Council declaration as the first UK feminist city regarding city development. See https://www.mayeast.co.uk/blog/diary-of-a-feminist-city.

regarding matters of safety, particularly for young women in the city.[29] Having often to do with physical as well lived and built space in many aspects, they could also be read through new spatial justices approaches that are now emerging, especially in administrative and urban law, as in European legal culture.[30]

These approaches reinforce the idea of a correlation between urban space and rights enjoyment, a nexus that could be further explored in a gender sensitive direction, which is the aim of this chapter. In order to do so we will first look briefly at the reciprocal constitution of law, space and stereotypes. Then we will address examples and specific characteristics of urban space and norm / rights enjoyment, exploring different kinds of urban spaces and its theorization where gender issues and normative elements are at stake.

3 Gender Stereotyping

Abstraction and generalization are typical characteristics of modern law. From this derives that law inevitably heavily relies on generalizations, profiles and stereotypes.[31] From a legally informed perspective stereotypes can be defined as 'a generalized view or preconception of attributes or characteristics possessed by, or the roles that should be performed by, members of a particular group' or more briefly as "widely accepted beliefs about groups of people".[32] Stereotyping is now a form of discrimination increasingly recognized by judicial discourse. In human rights law, identifying harmful stereotyping requires identifying whether the application of a stereotype constitutes a human rights violation, and/or whether the application of a stereotype is a contributing factor in a human rights violation.[33] As for the variety of possible discriminations that are relevant for the law, identifying harmful stereotypes requires a form of contextual analysis, as the problem is not the use of the generalization but that of its justification. This is even more challenging regarding gender stereotypes, as they are pervasive and operate subtly in various contexts. One such peculiar context is public urban space, where a dual ambiguity exists regarding the visibility and invisibility of female bodies. As Mubi Brighenti argued, "The visible is the field in which city and subject mutually interpenetrate and constitute each other".[34] Understanding these dynamics is crucial for promoting gender equality and

---

[29] See for example the Safer Cities for Girl Program in https://sdgs.un.org/partnerships/safer-cities-girls-programme.

[30] For an overview see the special issue of Istituzioni del Federalismo *La giustizia tra i territori: teorie e modelli*, edited by J B Auby and M De Donno, available online at https://www.regione.emilia-romagna.it/idf/numeri/2023/speciale-2023.

[31] Schauer (2003).

[32] Timmer (2011), p. 708.

[33] Brems and Timmer (2016), p. 4.

[34] Mubi Brighenti (2010), p. 134.

challenging harmful stereotypes. By acknowledging both visibility and invisibility, we can work toward a more equitable society.

Visibility manifests itself through instances like sexual harassment on city streets, which disproportionately affects girls and women. Shocking statistics highlight the prevalence of such mistreatment. Additionally, discrimination against women who breastfeed in public further underscores the visibility aspect. On the other hand, invisibility becomes apparent in several ways. For instance, street names: a scarcity of streets named after women perpetuates their invisibility in public discourse. Monuments: the absence of monuments dedicated to women (excluding allegorical representations) reinforces this dichotomy. The visibility/invisibility dichotomy is also notorious in the justice spaces, like the courthouse: even within legal professions, women encounter stereotypes and biases, highlighting their struggle for visibility and recognition. In this context, the term 'stereotype' pertains to the perception of women's bodies as deviating from societal norms. These non-conforming bodies challenge established expectations, leading to labels such as 'sluts,' 'tramps,' or 'attention seekers.' Such derogatory terms imply sexual availability and a lack of self-respect. The prevailing expectation, conversely, is for women to exhibit discretion and docility. And to keep out of public space.

In the next subsections, we will explore three critical topics: street harassment and breastfeeding in public; toponymy and monuments; and women in the courthouse spaces. In public urban spaces, we are thus confronted with practices that perpetuate stereotypes, but also with spatial practices that materialise resistances and activisms.

3.1 Street Harassment and Breastfeeding[35] in Public: Sluts and Tramps, or the Importance of Being Discreet

Despite the legal enshrinement of the principle of equality before the law, in national and international documents, women are, as a social group, more severely affected by sexist myths, prejudices and stereotypes. These are fed by social imaginaries that construct an idea about who people are and how they should act and behave.[36] Gender stereotypes thus contain both a descriptive character (they describe what gender groups are like) and a prescriptive character (they indicate what these groups should be like).[37] There is thus always something that sends women a message: to get back to their place—the domestic one. The condition of being 'out of place' is hence socially constructed based on visuality, language and lived interactions.[38]

[35] We are aware that people who identify as transmasculine and non-binary may prefer the term chestfeeding. See https://www.lllc.ca/chestfeeding.

[36] Duarte (2022), p. 32.

[37] Castillo-Mayén and Montes-Berges (2014).

[38] Mathews (2019).

According to many international reports, like Metropolis,[39] troubling levels of violence against women and girls are experienced daily.[40] And much of this violence takes place in public urban spaces. International research conducted by Hollaback! (currently known as Right to Be) and Cornell University, in which 16,607 women from 22 countries around the world participated, found that the majority of these women had experienced street harassment during puberty, more than 50% had been touched or groped in public, and 71% of them had been stalked.[41] Other reports detail such statistics: for example, 97% of young women in the UK have experienced sexual harassment in public; also, in Belgium 91% of women between the ages of 15 to 24 have experienced sexual intimidation in the public space, compared to 28% of young men.[42]

Another report, ARUP,[43] also reveals that many women feel that buildings, infrastructure and public urban spaces do not take their needs into account. Moreover, the key issues identified regard unsafe streets and other public spaces, and reduced mobility due to safety concerns. Like Beebeejaun asserts, how rights are experienced or not has a spatial dimension,[44] which means that urban public space is a site where many inequalities are reflected and felt. It is important to refer to the French legislation implemented in August 2018, the so-called "Loi Schiappa", aiming to improve the repression of sexist and sexual violence, which created the sexist contempt offence to punish street harassment.[45] As we know, however, one thing is to create the law, another thing is how it comes to be implemented. For example, Ribeiro's study,[46] regarding the Portuguese context and the crime of *importunação sexual* (art. 170 of the Penal Code), concluded that the implementation of the law, made difficult by the characteristics inherent to this type of harassment, appears to occur in an environment marked by the prevalence of a masculine culture, with signs of adherence to sexist myths, and devaluation of the seriousness of the offense.

But if men can dare more in the public context, women are taught from early childhood to be afraid, to adopt self-protective attitudes and behaviours that limit their movements, and the place they occupy in the cities.[47] Not surprisingly, the

---

[39] Metropolis (2018).

[40] It important to acknowledge that fear of and actual attack and harassment is not equal across different groups of women. It thus intersects with racism, homophobia and transphobia, ableism, ageism, religion (e.g., Islamophobia). See URBACT (2022), Kern (2019).

[41] Calabresi (2023).

[42] ARUP (2022), Marinucci and Wiersum (2023).

[43] ARUP (2022).

[44] Beebeejaun (2016).

[45] https://www.vie-publique.fr/loi/20794-loi-schiappa-3-aout-2018-lutte-contre-atteintes-sexuelles-et-sexistes. There are other examples of legislation to prevent sexual harassment in public spaces, like Manila's City Ordinance, in the Philippines. Contrary to France's legislation, it has a city-level application, whereas the French law has a nation-wide application.

[46] Ribeiro (2021).

[47] Kern (2019) warns us that to adopt a feminist stance in relation to urban public space means adopting an intersectional lens as well, and ask ourselves if women's desire of security, for example, could determine a higher police control over other communities, like people of colour.

frequency of the incidents involving street harassment also makes women accustomed to being harassed. Additionally, street harassment—catcalling, being leered at, unwanted remarks, or touching—still takes on expressions of a "natural" manifestation of the normative references of hegemonic masculinity,[48] a power system that constantly denigrates women by sexualizing and objectifying them without their consent. Therefore, Shaw is right when she claims that it is often the apparently minor and overlooked oppressions which, by being an integral part of human relations, reinforce women's subordination to structures of male power and domination.[49] As Marinucci and Wiersum explain, in criminology studies the concept of 'fear of crime' refers to the fear women experience in anticipation of an incident taking place and is often used to discredit women's anxieties, further perpetuating the normalisation of street harassment.[50]

In addition to the normalisation of street harassment, women victims of violence and abuse are frequently accused of bringing it upon themselves because of their behaviour or the way they present themselves, often enduring remarks like "It's the fault of how they dress", "They're provocative and then they play the victim", "Why were you alone at the bus stop?".[51] As a result, women internalize the idea that their safety is exclusively their responsibility, and that urban public space is not suitable for them.[52]

The unsuitability of urban public space is also manifested through physical, social and legal barriers to breastfeeding. In the US, for example, it is interesting to note that thirty-one states, the District of Columbia, Puerto Rico and the Virgin Islands have exempted breastfeeding from public indecency laws[53]—which means it required legislation to create a legal exception, otherwise it would be considered as an indecent act. Decorum as a regulative criterion for creating urban spaces where each body is specifically allowed to certain portions of it according to specific subjective qualities is rising in cities worldwide. Such a concept acts as a justification for regulating "deviant" behaviours that while often not illegally per se (sleeping on benches; consuming alcohol in the streets, eating on public space) can be seen as attempts to create a clean space where most interactions are regulated by market—consumer-oriented mechanisms.

This idea of the indecent act or of a deviant behaviour is thus not uncommon. A study conducted by Grant in the UK revealed that women who breastfed in public were seen as atypical, exhibitionists, lacking in "pride" or "self-respect", or as bad citizens, and therefore deviant—all this even though the Equality Act 2010 (Sections 17 and 18) states that to treat a woman unfavourably if she is breastfeeding

[48] See Oliveira (2014), Marinucci and Wiersum (2023), Calabresi (2023).

[49] Shaw (2010), p. 38.

[50] Marinucci and Wiersum (2023).

[51] See, for example, https://www.theguardian.com/global-development/2023/jul/16/any-victim-is-a-liar-sexual-violence-scandals-in-italy-expose-deep-seated-sexism. Also Kern (2019).

[52] ARUP (2022), Kern (2019), Duarte (2022), Pitch (2001), p. 49.

[53] See https://www.ncsl.org/health/breastfeeding-state-laws#:~:text=All%20fifty%20states%2C%20the%20District,breastfeeding%20from%20public%20indecency%20laws.

is sex discrimination and an offense, punishable with a fine.[54] Moreover, breasts, and the act of breastfeeding, were considered distasteful, and as something that should only be carried out in private.[55] The idea that breasts may function in modes other than at the service of male sexual desire disrupts public comfort and is seen as vulgar,[56] or indecent. In a recent article by CNN Portugal addressing the topic of breastfeeding in public, a disturbing comment was highlighted.[57] A mother, while breastfeeding on a terrace, was subjected to derogatory remarks from another woman, who stated, "They are all shameless," and further added, "and afterward they don't understand why they get beaten by their husbands." This incident underscores a troubling societal perception that women who breastfeed in public are not engaged in the nurturing act of feeding their children, but rather in acts of sexual exhibitionism. Such views erroneously suggest that these women are provocative and, consequently, bear responsibility for gender-based violence, including domestic violence. This narrative perpetuates harmful stereotypes and victim-blaming, which are detrimental to efforts aimed at promoting gender equality and protecting women's rights.

Thus, women are encouraged to be discrete or to seek out designated lactation rooms, which are frequently difficult to locate and user-unfriendly. Boyer further contends that the establishment of such spaces perpetuates the notion that breastfeeding should be conducted away from public view.[58]

This regulation of the female body's presence in public spaces, and the definition of appropriate behaviour, is highly controlled across different times and locations. Misogynistic behaviours and educational deficiencies continue to persist. Additionally, Kern emphasizes that the underlying cause of much social hostility is the design and function of urban environments, which have historically been structured to complicate women's lives.[59]

3.2 *The Bodies that (Do not) Count: Public Monuments and Street Toponymy*

The critical issues of street harassment and public breastfeeding highlight the hypervisibility that women's bodies, or specific parts thereof, experience while navigating,

[54] https://www.citizensadvice.org.uk/scotland/law-and-courts/civil-rights/breastfeeding/breastfeeding-s/#:~:text=A%20woman%20has%20the%20right,basis%20of%20having%20become%20mothers.

[55] Grant (2016).

[56] Boyer (2012).

[57] https://cnnportugal.iol.pt/amamentacao/gravidez/sao-todas-umas-descaradas-depois-nao-percebem-porque-e-que-levam-porrada-dos-maridos-amamentar-em-publico-e-um-problema-para-muitas-mulheres/20240805/66a107d2d34e049892238599.

[58] Boyer (2012), p. 559.

[59] Kern (2019), p. 45.

sitting, or otherwise utilising urban public spaces. Paradoxically, despite this heightened visibility, women are often conspicuously absent from representations within these public spaces.

Belotti contends that urban public spaces exhibit a pronounced gender imbalance, as evidenced by statues, monuments, and toponymy. In numerous cities, the preponderance of statues and street names[60] honour men, whereas female representation is predominantly allegorical, such as figures of Lady Justice,[61] or limited to women who were saints, queens, or handmaidens.[62] A survey carried out by the Italian organisation *Mi Riconosci* between 2021 and 2022,[63] which surveyed Italian public statues dedicated to real women, anonymous collective figures or literary ones, confirmed very low numbers (245!), pigeonholing the women represented in roles of mother/wife/saint or seductress. Vega hence highlights that the paucity of statues or monuments dedicated to notable women/real women—apart from queens or saints—and the limited number of women chosen for public commemoration by monument commissioners, merely reflect the underrepresentation of women within the patriarchal framework of "eminences" deemed worthy of public recognition.[64] To the patriarchal framework we can add racism and/or ableism (and other isms) and ask: how many statues/streets do we know that homage coloured or disabled women?[65] The hostility of the urban art form reflects societal hostility to these bodies.

Moreover, the female body is often hypersexualised. The portrayal of women in urban public spaces continues to perpetuate stereotypes that reduce them to mere (naked) bodies, primarily existing to satisfy male desires. For that reason, a statue caused a sensation in Italy, especially because it wanted to represent a denunciation against gender violence. In 2013, the *Violata* statue[66] by sculptor Floriano Ippoliti was inaugurated in Ancona, a monument that wanted to be a statement in memory of "all women victims of violence", sponsored by the Equal Opportunities Commission of the Marche Region. The statue represents a woman with ragged clothes that reveal her breasts and bottom in full evidence—such representation was judged by many feminist organisations as inappropriate and offensive to the dignity of women victims of violence. A petition has collected the signatures of thousands of people, but the statue remains. In 2021, to give it a different meaning, the organisation *Non Una di*

---

[60] As pointed out by the Osservatorio Balcani e Caucaso Transeuropa, in 30 of Europe's biggest cities, streets named after women make up only 9 per cent of the streets dedicated to individuals. See https://www.balcanicaucaso.org/eng/Areas/Italy/The-gender-gap-in-Europe-s-street-names-is-here-to-stay-223794.

[61] For an analysis of Lady-Justice, see Resnik and Curtis (2011), Branco (2017).

[62] URBACT (2022).

[63] See https://www.miriconosci.it/mappa-dei-monumenti-femminili-italiani/. And https://www.theartnewspaper.com/2024/05/03/italys-statues-have-a-gender-bias-new-research-reveals.

[64] Vega (2016).

[65] See https://journal.voca.network/ableist-space-disabled-body/. For a critical relation between feminist and disabilities studies, see Bernardini (2024), in: https://www.ais-sociologia.it/wp-content/uploads/2024/06/Bernardini_corpi-muti.pdf.

[66] See https://www.nazioneindiana.com/2014/11/24/violata/.

Meno hung the purple scarf around its neck, issuing a statement that read they thus made it a feminist statue, a sister in the struggle against violence.[67]

Such public representations contribute to a culture that views women as objects rather than as individuals with their own agency and aspirations. This phenomenon is not only a reflection of deep-seated societal biases but also a reinforcement of gender inequality. In addition, the lack of female monuments or of female-named streets sends the message that female accomplishments are not significant enough to respect or recognize,[68] and thus do not deserve to occupy a place in public space.

3.3 Women in the Justice Spaces

A prominent public environment characterized by the predominance of allegorical female representation is the courthouse. Statues of Lady Justice and her Virtue-Sisters are ubiquitous in these settings. Additionally, courthouse buildings, such as the United States Supreme Court, employ a masculine architectural grammar, exemplified by their columns and stairs. As Kern asserts, the gender symbolism inherent in the built urban environment serves as a reminder of the city's creators, symbolizing the separate spheres[69] and the societal roles assigned to women. This observation is equally applicable to the sphere of justice.

The initial foray of women into the legal profession, by the end of the nineteenth century, was met with significant resistance, as societal norms and prejudices of the time dictated that the practice of law was inherently a male domain. It was argued that the courtroom was a "gladiatorial arena" unsuitable for the perceived gentleness and emotional nature of women. Critics contended that women lacked basic legal intelligence and that their inherent qualities, such as grace, purity, delicacy, and emotional impulses, were incompatible with the rigors of legal practice.[70] In 1894, Anna Kuliscioff highlighted the challenges faced by the first female lawyers in Italy and Belgium, noting that they were often dismissed with derisive excuses related to pregnancy, lactation, and even the impracticality of their attire, such as the beret and gown. Victims of caricature, women lawyers were portrayed in skimpy clothes, more concerned with makeup than on the debate in the courtroom, skilled seducers of those poor judges who were victims of female coaxing.[71] What emerges from these pictures is a strong sense of anxiety about women who were conceived of as being out of place in the courthouse.[72]

---

[67] See https://www.cronacheancona.it/2021/09/28/18-lo-stesso-blitz-nella-notte-abbiamo-reso-la-violata-femminista/325415/.

[68] Solnit (2019).

[69] Kern (2019).

[70] Tacchi (2009).

[71] Kuliscioff (2011), p. 55, Tacchi (2009), p. 54.

[72] Mulcahy (2015).

Despite progress, contemporary female lawyers continue to encounter denigration rooted in traditional beliefs about women's social roles. This includes derogatory remarks from judges and colleagues about their appearance[73] and dress, which undermine their professional standing. Moreover, women in the legal profession face systemic discrimination, manifesting in salary disparities, limited career advancement opportunities, underrepresentation in leadership positions, and confinement to less lucrative areas of practice.[74]

Furthermore, as previously discussed in relation to monuments in general, women who have made significant contributions to the field of law are frequently overlooked or marginalized within legal monuments. Godden-Rasul's analysis of portraits of women in law at UK universities and law schools reveals a predominance of male depictions, which associate the legal profession with masculine attributes. This visual representation contributes to the marginalization of women in legal history.[75] Similarly, Kari's investigation into the historic Osgoode Hall in downtown Toronto, Canada, demonstrates how courthouse architecture perpetuates stereotypes. The male changing rooms are opulent and spacious, featuring a comfortable lounge area with a sofa and a large wooden table and chairs for last-minute preparations before court appearances. In contrast, the female changing room is small, furnished with mismatched items and an old desk. Additionally, the sign on the entrance door reads "Lady Barristers", which, as the author argues, conveys a message: "we don't think you are staying long".[76] Meaning: this is not your place.

4 Spaces of Resistance

But if urban public spaces can be hostile to women, they can also be privileged sites for resistance and awareness raising. Just as Kern asserts, cities offer the right mix of resources to make each protest visible and effective.[77]

SlutWalks are one good example.[78] These marches have taken place around the world after one Toronto police officer said to York University students in 2011 that women should avoid dressing like "sluts" to prevent being sexually assaulted. SlutWalks can be seen as a manifesto against the social control of female bodies, as they fight against the idea that sexual violence is almost inevitable in certain environments and that people should take precautions such as dressing discreetly.[79] Nevertheless,

[73] For an account on this, read Amanda's Byrd personal essay: https://www.cbc.ca/radio/sunday/the-sunday-edition-june-3-2018-1.4685998/i-spent-hundreds-of-hours-preparing-for-moot-court-when-i-got-there-i-was-told-to-smile-more-1.4687442.

[74] Branco (2017).

[75] Godden-Rasul (2019).

[76] See https://www.canadianlawyermag.com/practice-areas/criminal/a-womans-place/275239.

[77] Kern (2019), p. 147.

[78] See https://wgrc.arizona.edu/slutwalk.

[79] Oliveira (2014), Kern (2019), p. 158.

it is important to acknowledge that these marches have also been criticised for not being diverse enough or because the word *slut* cannot have a positive connotation. Still, these marches use urban public space to call attention to the stereotypes women must endure.

Another international movement is the one called Chalk Back, which provides a platform for sharing personal stories of sexual harassment and promote cultural change through art, using bright, pastel-coloured chalk, writing phrases on city sidewalks to bring awareness to street harassment.[80]

Art has also been the answer when it comes to unfriendly environments encountered by mothers who breastfeed in public. In 2011, American artist Jill Miller conceived a performative and humorous response called the *Milk Truck*: a truck topped by a huge breast with a flashing nipple riding around town in Pittsburgh, US. It raised awareness to the fact that women are tired of breasts being sexualized all the time, underscoring the absurdity that breastfeeding in public is seen as a problem.[81] Public awareness campaigns have also been promoted in other countries, such as the giant breast that was placed on top of a building in the Shoreditch area of London, in March 2017.[82]

Many cities are also taking action to bring visibility to the contributions of women through street names and monuments. Such was the case in the city of Naples, with the adoption, in 2012, of a Municipal Regulation for Toponyms and City Numbering. In accordance with article 11, letter d), and in compliance with the principle of equal opportunities, the following criteria must be observed when naming circulation areas and places: to find new female names to be assigned from Neapolitan or Campania citizens or of Italian or foreign women who had a privileged relationship with the city, and that were women of scientific, literary or cultural social relevance. These types of actions can lead to an awareness of the over-representation of (wealthy white) men across urban public space, but data suggests that this awareness has not yet led to a significant change in street naming.[83]

A significant action occurred recently, during the opening ceremony of the Olympic Games in Paris (2024). Under the idea of Sorority, as a counteract to Fraternity, we saw the unveiling of 10 statues paying tribute to historical Frenchwomen philosophers, lawyers, sportswomen, politicians, feminists. It can be seen as a nationalistic demonstration of pride, but it is also a powerful way of calling attention to the absence of women in urban public space and the inequality it underscores, particularly because Paris, like so many other cities, has many male statues (about 260 statues) and no more than 40 statues of women.[84]

---

[80] See https://nbcuacademy.com/street-harassment-nyc/. In Italy you can find the *CatCalls of Turin*, promoting several initiatives in the city of Turin: see https://www.facebook.com/catcallsofturin/.

[81] Buller (2013). See https://www.facebook.com/TheMilkTruck/.

[82] See https://www.publico.pt/2017/03/29/sociedade/noticia/uma-mama-gigante-para-lembrar-que-amamentar-em-publico-e-natural-1766989.

[83] See https://www.balcanicaucaso.org/eng/Areas/Italy/The-gender-gap-in-Europe-s-street-names-is-here-to-stay-223794.

[84] See https://www.theguardian.com/sport/article/2024/jul/26/singing-spectacle-and-subplots-on-the-seine-in-the-rain. And https://www.sortiraparis.com/en/news/olympic-games-paris-2024/articles/317893-opening-ceremony-statues-who-are-the-10-women-honored-on-the-seine#:~:text=Close%20to%20the%20National%20Assembly,Alice%20Guy%20and%20Louise%20Michel.

Another interesting project occurred in Naples, Italy, also in 2024, with the creation of the *Vico delle donne resilienti*, a botton-up initiative where street art artists (Trisha Palma and Giulia Pagano) have painted female personalities seen as examples of struggle and courage. One of the notable figures selected was Artemisia Gentileschi. She holds the distinction of being the first woman admitted to the Accademia di Arte del Disegno in Florence. Additionally, she was a central figure in a highly publicized judicial trial concerning sexual violence.[85]

Increasing the visual representation of women in law was also the aim of the *In Plain Sight* initiative, in Ireland, created in response to a notable under-representation of female subjects displayed in the collections of The Bar of Ireland and The Honorable Society of King's Inns.[86]

The examples we provide here can be seen as a materialisation of Gender Equality and Sustainable Cities and Communities, two of the SDGs of the 2030 Agenda. They take place and shape in urban public spaces and call attention to the importance of fighting stereotypes.

5 Concluding Remarks

In this chapter we made an initial attempt at identifying possible relationships between law, gender and urban spaces relating to stereotypes or a stereotyped use of space. The theoretical connections and implications suffer from a reciprocal invisibilization that has greatly limited the detection of discriminatory attitudes in the urban domain. As we tried to show, an analysis of legal and normative mechanisms is in need for a more in-depth comprehension of how regulation plays a role in shaping both the physical enjoyment of space and the lived experience of the city. This has proven fruitful for taking into account how stereotypes develop in different urban spaces with a discreet but present legal background, often overlooked in urban and gender urbanism studies. These regulations operate in different forms and degrees of legality, in a porous way where the boundaries are not clearly or easily established, as is the case with breastfeeding in public. In other areas, for example that of the appearance of female bodies in the public space or what emerges from issues like mobility justice, the implication of the law is apparently more evident but nonetheless subtle as the ideals of urban decorum show, relying on a mixture of implicit social and normative regulation.

In every respect, using a strategy that values *making gender visible in the city*, this approach shows how regulation takes place in all aspects of urban life. Making these issues visible both in the epistemological presuppositions and in its actual

[85] See https://www.fridakahlo.it/en/scheda-news.php?id=268. See as well https://www.britannica.com/biography/Artemisia-Gentileschi.

[86] See https://www.lawlibrary.ie/inplainsight/.

connections to examples of urban life, was the principal aim of the chapter. But the law can also be seen as an indicator of where and how practices of resistance can be put into place. The variety of initiatives taken forward by many cities worldwide heavily recur to a diversity of institutional and legal mechanism as the right to the city and human rights cities movements prove. As we have seen, a different municipal regulation can make the difference in making women visible in street toponymy. From this point of view gender in the city raises demands for spatial justice to which the law would be called to play a role. As further studies are needed, we advocate for a fruitful meeting of gender urbanism and law from a critical spatial justice perspective aimed at making both law and gender visible as a precondition for the endless quest for a just city for everyone.

References

Amin A, Thrift NJ (2017) Seeing like a city. Polity, Cambridge

Arena FJ (2016) Los estereotipos normativos en la decisi6n judicial. Una exploraci6n conceptual. Revista de Derecho XXIX 51–75

ARUP (2022) Cities alive. University of Liverpool, Designing cities that work for women

Auby JB (2013) Droit de la Ville. Lexis Nexis, Paris

Auby JB (2022) Droit à la ville et droit de la ville. Constructif 63:29–33

Beebeejaun Y (2016) Gender, urban space, and the right to everyday life. J Urban Aff 39:323–334

Blank Y, Rosen-Zvi I (2010) The spatial turn in legal theory. HAGAR: Stud Cult, Polity Identities 10:37–60

Blomley N (2008) Making space for law. In: Cox KR, Low M, Robinson J (eds) The SAGE handbook of political geography. Sage, London, pp 155–168

Blomley N, Delaney D, Ford R (2001) The legal geographies reader: law, power and space. Wiley-Blackwell

Boyer K (2012) Affect, corporeality and the limits of belonging: breastfeeding in public in the contemporary UK. Health Place 18:552–560

Branco P (2017) Exploring justitia through éowyn and niobe: on gender, race and the legal. Liverpool Law Rev 38:63–82

Brems E, Timmer A (2016) Stereotypes and human rights law. Intersentia, Antwerp

Burgess JA (1974) Stereotypes and urban images. Area 6:167–171

Calabresi G (2023) Spazi molesti. InGenere. https://www.ingenere.it/articoli/spazi-molesti

Castillo-Mayén R, Montes-Berges B (2014) Análisis de los estereotipos de género actuales. Anales De Psicología 30:1044–1060

Chueca EG (2016) Human rights in the city and the right to the city. Two paradigms confronting urbanization. In: Davis MF, Grigolo M (eds) Oomen B. Global Urban Justice. The Rise of Human Rights Cities. Cambridge University Press, New York, pp 103–120

Cook R, Cusack S (2011) Gender stereotyping: transnational legal perspectives. University of Pennsylvania Press, Philadelphia

Duarte M (2022) Uma boa mulher é difícil de encontrar? Reflexões sobre a "vítima ideal" no direito penal. Revista Ex Aequo 45:31–43

Fainstein S (2010) The just city. Cornell University Press, Ithaca and London

Fenster T (2005) The right to the gendered city: different formations of belonging in everyday life. J Gend Stud 14:217–231

Frug G (1980) The city as a legal concept. Harv Law Rev 93:1057–1154

Godden-Rasul N (2019) Portraits of women of the law: re-envisioning gender, law and the legal professions in law schools. Leg Stud 39:415–431. https://doi.org/10.1017/lst.2018.41
Granata E (2023) Il senso delle donne per la città. Curiosità, ingegno, apertura. Einaudi, Torino
Grant A (2016) "I… don't want to see you flashing your bits around": exhibitionism, othering and good motherhood in perceptions of public breastfeeding. Geoforum 71:52–61
Grigolo M (2016) Towards a sociology of the human rights city. Focusing on practice. In: Davis MF, Grigolo M (eds) Oomen B. Global Urban Justice. The Rise of Human Rights Cities. Cambridge University Press, New York, pp 276–293
Kern L (2019 [2024]) La città femminista. La lotta per lo spazio in un mondo disegnato da uomini. Trad. Pennacchietti N. Treccani, Rome
Kuliscioff A (2011) Il Monopolio dell'Uomo. Ortica Editrice, Aprilia
Lefebvre H (1991) The production of space. Blackwell, Oxford
Lefebvre H (1996) Writings on cities. Blackwell, Oxford
Magnusson W (2012) Politics of urbanism: seeing like a city. Routledge, London
Marinucci N, Wiersum L (2023) Women navigating the city. How to negotiate public spaces for safety, European Urban Knowledge Network, Belgium
Massey D (1994) Space, place. University of Minnesota Press, Minneapolis, Gender
Mathews V (2019) Reconfiguring the breastfeeding body in urban public spaces. Soc Cult Geogr 20:1266–1284. https://doi.org/10.1080/14649365.2018.1433867
Metropolis (2018) Safety and public space: mapping metropolitan gender policies. Metropolis
Mubi Brighenti A (2010) Visibility in social theory and social research. Palgrave Macmillan, Basingstoke
Mulcahy L (2015) Watching women: what illustrations of courtroom scenes tell us about women and the public sphere in the nineteenth century. J Law Soc 42:53–73
Nitrato Izzo V (2017) Gli spazi giuridici della città contemporanea. Rappresentazioni e pratiche. Editoriale Scientifica, Napoli.
Oliveira A (2014) O assédio sexual nos espaços públicos. Cabo dos trabalhos 10
Perez C (2019) Invisible women: exposing data bias in a world designed for men. Chatto & Windus, Abrams
Philippopoulos-Mihalopoulos A (2010) Spatial justice: law and the geography of withdrawal. Int J Law Context 6:201–216
Philippopoulos-Mihalopoulos A (2015) Spatial justice. Body, lawscape, atmosphere. Routledge London.
Philippopoulos-Mihalopoulos A (2021) And for law: why space cannot be understood without law. Law, Cult Humanit 17:620–639
Pitch T (2001) La città delle donne. In Pitch T, Ventimiglia C (eds) Che genere di sicurezza. Donne e uomini in città. FrancoAngeli, pp 49–83
Resnik J, Curtis D (2011) Representing justice: invention, controversy, and rights in city-states and democratic courtrooms. Yale University Press, Yale
Ribeiro B (2021) Assédio Sexual em Espaço Público em Portugal: Obstáculos à Implementação do Artigo 170.º do Código Penal ao Nível dos Burocratas de Rua da PSP. Master Thesis, NovaFCSH, Lisbon
Sassen S (2006) Territory, authority, rights: from medieval to global assemblages. Princeton University Press, Princeton
Sassen S (2008) Seeing like a city. In: Burdett R, Sudjic D (eds) The endless city. Phaidon, London, pp 276–289
Schauer F (2003) Profiles, probabilities, and stereotypes. Harvard University Press, Cambridge
Scott JC (1998) Seeing like a state: how certain schemes to improve the human condition have failed. Yale University Press, New Haven
Sennett R (2018) Building and dwelling. Ethics for the city. Penguin, London
Shaw J (2010) Against myths and traditions that emasculate women: language, literature, law and female empowerment. Liverpool Law Rev 31:29–49. https://doi.org/10.1007/s10991-010-9071-z

Solnit R (2019) Across America, racist and sexist monuments give way to a new future. The Guardian. https://www.theguardian.com/commentisfree/2019/jan/02/racist-sexist-confederate-monuments-new-future

Tacchi F (2009) Eva Togata. Donne e professioni giuridiche in Italia dall'Unità ad oggi. UTET Libreria, Turin

Timmer A (2011) Toward an anti-stereotyping approach for the european court of human rights. Hum Rights Law Rev 11:707–738

URBACT (2022) Gender equal cities 2022. Urbact

Valverde M (2011) Seeing like a city: the dialectic of modern and premodern ways of seeing in urban governance: seeing like a city. Law Soc Rev 45:277–312

Vega E (2016) Una violencia invisible? Las mujeres en los monumentos públicos. Boletín De Arte 37:213–225

Valerio Nitrato Izzo is Associate Professor at the Department of Law, University of Naples Federico II, Italy, where he teaches Philosophy of Law and Philosophy of Human Rights. His main research interests lie in philosophy of law, legal reasoning, and law and humanities.

Patrícia Branco is a researcher at the Centre for Social Studies of the University of Coimbra (CES-UC), Portugal. Her research interests and publications reflect her enthusiasm for understanding the complex and dynamic relationships between law, society and culture. Some of the topics investigated are courthouse architecture and spaces of justice; changes in family, child and youth law, and their connection to gender and juvenile delinquency and crime; sociolegal studies and the humanities.

What Is the Genus of Genders? On Semio-Cognitive and Legal Tools for Prospectively Defusing Gender-Based Violence

Mario Ricca

Abstract In this essay, I will try to propose a semiotic strategy geared toward defusing the triggers of both GBV epistemic and physical violence. The methodology adopted will be interdisciplinary and will involve law, anthropology, semiotics, biology, cognitive psychology, ethology and literature. My overall goal coincides with the determination of the genus of genders through its identification with a meta-categorical criterion of structuring social relations: and this irrespectively of any naturalistic determinism or nature/culture dualism. The final part of the essay will address the legal implications of this approach and the reconfiguration of law, beyond the 'is/ought' divide, as a means of planning/producing social facts.

Keywords Gender/sex · Categorization · Semiotics · Violence · Feminism · Post-human

1 Prologue

The decades-long debate on 'gender' has produced the pluralization of this category through a dialectical critical approach to its relationship with 'sex.'[1] Despite the proliferation of emancipatory distinctions and rearticulations, it seems to me that one question has become crucial but has still remained unanswered (if ever explicitly

[1] In a huge literature, see at least, Stoller (1968), MacKinnon (1989), Witt (1995), Haslanger (1995, 2003, 2005) Butler (1990), Fausto-Sterling (2012, 2021), Stone (2004), Àsta (2018), Mikkola (2006, 2016) Barnes (2020). For a useful linguistic-normative analysis of the use of the term 'gender' in European institutional practice see Scotto di Carlo (2023).

M. Ricca (✉)
University of Roma Tre, Rome, Italy
e-mail: mario.ricca@icloud.com

A. Condello and A. Wagner (eds.), *Gender Stereotypes*, Gender, Justice and Legal Feminism 2, https://doi.org/10.1007/978-3-031-63905-0_5

raised): What is the genus of genders? In my view, all attempts to critically reformulate and/or reshape gender and 'gender discourse' can be meta-categorized as classification/reclassification activities. In this regard, however, it should be noted that cognitive categorization/classification is itself an act of violence. Epistemic violence,[2] in other words, is inherent in cognition, namely the same cognitive activity that is the source of what—ex post—is considered as 'semantic order.'

Critical feminist theory has developed an intersectional genealogical reading of the cultural/social determinants of gender discrimination, making visible—so to speak—how the lexicon of gender functions as a collection of metonymic epitomes of widespread social habits in human conduct. In this respect, it could be said that 'words have consequences' but in the sense that they embody pragmatic implications that radially spread through the materialized space–time of people's experience.[3] Fruitful as they are, intersectional analyses seem to limit the semiotic-radial (or, omnidirectional) understanding of the gender lexicon mainly to the past. In other words, they appear critically reconstructive but not equally projective.[4] At the opposite theoretical pole, on the other hand, the recipe of performativity and its alleged tautological/ontological assertiveness/effectiveness shows the same blindness to the future in a striking way.[5]

In my view, gender-based violence is intermingled with, if not even continuous to, the violence of categorization. However, precisely because categorization is value-laden, it is vulnerable to semiotic analysis of the invisible/implicit radial components inherent in each resulting category and its socio-communicative reification.[6] Dis-composing the semiotic fabric of categories can pluralize—as it were—the horizon

---

[2] On epistemic violence and injustice see the collection of essays edited by Kidd et al. (2017), Boncompagni and Coliva (2024), Pérez (2019); as for a post-colonial perspective, see Brunner (2021).

[3] As will become evident later, the statement just proposed in the text does not imply that I advocate a constructivist view. It is so because I adopt a semiotic-relational rather than representationalist or referentialist approach, which is partly close to contemporary enactivism of both categories and meaning: see Ricca (2023a) and there for further bibliographical references. Constructivism, on the other hand, maintains at least operationally an epistemological distance between culture and nature, between symbolic-social and empirical-factual dimensions, relying on a referential approach to language and meaning. See, in this regard, Ásta (2015).

[4] For a more detailed critical analysis of the intersectionalist approach, albeit in the most genuine appreciation of its theoretical and pragmatic goals, see Ricca (2025) and the related bibliographical references. My criticism, in any case, is not at all dissimilar to Lutz's (2014) observations on the use of the international approach on a global scale and, therefore, detached from the specific domain in which and for which it was developed. However, this author's overall position seems to be not without ambiguity: see, for example, Lutz (2015).

[5] For a more general critique of the category 'performative' in language and communication, even beyond the use proposed by feminist thought as regards 'gender performativity,' I refer to Ricca (2022a, b). With specific regard to gender issues, see Schep (2012), Padron (2021) and their critical observation about the approach to gender performativity proposed by Butler (1988, 1990, 1993, 2004).

[6] On this topic, I think two extraordinarily relevant readings, though for different reasons, are Lohman (2018) and Cohen (2000), respectively.

of values/ends relevant to the categorical construction and, in this way, open the floodgates for a relativization of the categorical structures, the relationships between what is assumed as denotative and connotative, and so on. But this is but a consequence of the collapse of categorical spectrums on their ubiquitous, though often hidden, internal inconsistencies and contradictions. In my view, this relativization is the main remedy human beings have to mitigate the violence inevitably inherent to all cognitive effort and adaptive behavior. The ability to shift the axis of salience at the base of categorical structures—including those related to gender and sex—is ultimately what makes human beings human and, as such, responsible for the making of the world that, in one way or another, overdetermines their lives—as paradoxical as this may seem. I think, on the other hand, that the inclusion of gender critique in legal discourse and its idiomatic dynamics makes the rigidity of the 'natural/commonsense' lexicon and its pragmatic/reifying implications even more vulnerable. This is also due—I would like to suggest—to the explicitness of the axiological yardstick underlain by the use of words in law. All this, however, only on the condition that legal experience is approached and managed with semiotic awareness.

What should be taken as crucial is that the recipe for both performativity and analytical-classificatory efforts (both nominalist, realist, normative and constructionist) to critically reshape gender categories and their intersectional determinants will, in turn, have radial or even magmatic implications, both social and (over the medium and long term) and biological. These implications, however, elude any attempt to make any prognosis of effectiveness on their unfolding through space and time. To overcome the semantic and emotional blindness that the metonymic assumption of sex and/or gender induces in social habits and mindsets, humans should polyphonically and multivocally try to grasp and handle all the radial/magmatic implications that the activity of recategorization can produce. Actually, unveiling the value component of categorization does not mean radically unmooring value options from the factual world. On the contrary, precisely this unveiled continuity should make attempts to recategorize the lexicon of gender and sex reflexive.

To lay the cards on the table and avoid misunderstandings, I make it clear from the outset that I assume the above work of recategorization, in which law is an absolutely involved 'agency,' to be a post-human work. But, in my eyes, it is 'naturally' legitimized to the extent that 'humanity' has always been the '*post*,' the consequence of itself.[7] In the same vein, I will try to investigate the ways in which the strategy to prevent gender-based violence, to be carried out also through law, has to

[7] In this regard, I want to clarify that my posthumanism does not overlap with postmodern approaches to posthumanism. While I disagree with nothing of the possible declination in Promethean terms of the posthuman or transhuman, I do not espouse the Deleuzian-inspired logic of nomadic and anarchically transversal thinking. I am not at all sure that the human species can renounce categorization. Rather than claiming to do away with it, I think instead that it is a matter of using it modestly—an undoubtedly more difficult task—in a world of phenomena that is interwoven with magmatic and semiotically dynamic relations, today as always. My chorological (Ricca 2023a, b) and relational-magmatic approach Ricca (2025) to the semiosis of experience is not in tune with the idea of post-human transversal subjectivities that some well-known scholars–such as, for example, Braidotti (2019)–propose.

include an analysis of the psycho-cognitive attitudes and the related methods available to activate/de-activate violence. However, this is not to downplay the significance of freedom and self-determination in the context of the gender/sex debate and related efforts to overcome experiential asymmetries. Rather, my genuine goal is to improve the use of cognitive resources to prevent the violence of categorization and its subsequent reification from making the voice of freedom a mere *flatus vocis*.

2 The Violence of Categorization: Why Is Sex/gender Discourse Unable to Unmoor Itself from the Sex-Gender Binarism?

My analysis of gender discourse starts from a pragmatic concern. It focuses on epistemic and physical violence. The conjunction 'and' between them does not imply any assimilation, but it does not exclude that they are closely related. The last co-implication depends, as mentioned, on the force and, in many cases, the violence inherent in the categorization activity.

The link between violence as denial of Otherness, on the one hand, and categorization, on the other, came on the stage early in human consciousness. In Semitic-Christian-Islamic cultures it finds its first recognition in the Bible and, specifically, in the Edenic story.[8] The distinction between good and evil, between being and non-being, was in a sense already inscribed in the power, given by Yahweh to Adam, to name what inhabited Eden. To limit the comparison to Greek culture, something similar can be found in the Odyssey and the original sin of Odysseus, master of words. His damnation to wandering the seas stems from the pretension to 'make the world with words,' to enclose and petrify it in the form and practical implications encapsulated in names and their categorizing use. The hybris of language consists, throughout the Homeric narrative, in the assumption that the human word can make itself the law of experience and thereby deny its insurmountable exceedance, its being always more than the sign/symbol human language would aspire to encage.[9]

The force/violence inherent in categorization is not limited to the pigeonholing of language and its use. Categories are always the epitome and, at the same time, the prospective anticipation of human activities—be they mental, bodily, or both. What to include and what to exclude from each category is the result of choices driven by values and ends. Ascribing something to one category rather than another, as well as making analytical distinctions, is by no means 'harmless' or purely virtual behavior. To exclude or include an object from a category is to inhibit or allow its inclusion in one or more axiological-teleological pragmatic paths. The same applies to creating new categories or shaping them. However, subtracting something from an axio-teleological path is equivalent to not involving it in a possible process of engendering experience and the facts that can thus stem from it. To put it roughly,

[8] In this regard, see Ricca (2022a).

[9] For an anthropological-semiotic reading of Odyssey I refer to Ricca (2015).

to say of something "this doesn't fit" or "it is beside the point" is to say that it cannot 'enter' a possible frame of experience. It is outside the game. And this being outside is tantamount to preventing it from translating itself into what can happen, into the dynamics of events, and taking part in them, so as to contribute to the production of the space-world. Similarly, to de-categorize or de-classify someone or something is to deprive them of possible avenues of existence. This 'offense' often goes unnoticed. This happens because categories are presented as 'portraits' of the nature of things, of how the world is. Although they are always the result of axiological-teleological activity, endowed with both biological and cultural import, they are somehow 'naturalized.' This is precisely the 'unheard-of' force or violence inherent in categorization. Its inherent perlocutory performativity disguises the fact that it does not merely determine what should or should not be; rather, categorization determines what is and what is not. It is the product of a cultural gaze that, by superimposing itself on experience, tends to obfuscate, to render implausible, invisible, and almost inconceivable that which does not fit into its patterns of compartmentalization. Unfortunately, this reifying absolutization of categorization is often totally embodied in human thought.

Many philosophers, linguists, epistemologists are influenced by the above categorical absolutization. As a consequence, they distinguish between the structural meaning of something and its ends. The former is thought of as semantically intrinsic, the latter as functional and thereby 'external.'[10] In so doing, however, human beings end up hiding in the background, when they themselves have not already and definitively lost sight of it, that values and ends are genetically intrinsic to the determination of categories, to their assumed structure. And this simply because they are underlying and prompting the choice of what to include and what to exclude from them. Any proposed change in categorization patterns is thus perceived as cognitive violence; when, on the contrary, the primary (…*Edenic*) violence is inherent in the abstraction of categorization from the ends genetically embedded in it.

The human brain is much more intelligent than human beings, their conscious portion. Resistance to categorical change is not just a matter of symbolic classifications. The struggle for categories is always for praxis and spaces. The mind knows this perfectly, even when the conscious thinking of human beings induces them to demonstrate exactly the opposite. Often, however, the apparent striving for the integrity of categorial formal/linguistic morphologies turns into a conduct endowed with reflexive and molding implications. Unconscious or disguised acting eventually cages human thinking, sabotaging the very capacity for carrying out adaptive categorization. The main implication of this attitude is the production of a heterogenesis of ends. In other words, categories become counterproductive to the very values/ends that genetically and constitutively shaped and carved out them from the denotatively indetermined stream of experience. The alienation of human beings in their language, their becoming overdetermined by it, by its ossified patterns, thus reaches its full expression.

[10] See, for example, an expert in linguistic issues such as Searle (1995). In the legal area, see Coleman (2003)—although he self-identified as a pragmatist.

I believe that no one in the Western tradition has ever explained this phenomenon with more poetic force and historical poignancy than Giambattista Vico. The topic "human beings alienating themselves in the normativity of their own language" is one of the Neapolitan philosopher's most powerful philosophical and literary-cognitive loci.[11] Actually, both Daoism and Zen thought have perfectly identified the alienating potential of language, of human words. However, the insistence of these traditions of thought on emptiness or nothingness/absolute indeterminacy as the source of being and its distinctions tends to turn into an underestimation of the relationship between language and praxis. This underestimation, in turn, gives rise to a kind of acquiescence to extant cultural and pragmatic patterns. Truth, in other words, is held by them to dwell beyond the appearances of reality, so that those appearances are left to reproduce themselves in the phenomenal dimension.

I think that the discourse on sex and gender is dramatically plagued by the naturalistic resilience/ossification of categories. And yet, I am fully aware that this is not a discovery. Feminist thought, in its many and very rich manifestations, has long dwelt on this anthropological and linguistic issue. What I would like to point out, however, as the main implication of the considerations made so far regarding categorization, is the inability (or perhaps the disguised refusal) of all emancipatory discourses hinging on gender to break free from the anchoring to the male/female dichotomy of biological origin. I am fully aware that this statement may sound provocative or even superficial. However, the distinction between the biological and psycho-cultural character of sex and gender respectively does not seem to me to have succeeded in erasing that link and thereby the reifying scope of the 'empirical naturalistic' categorization coextensive with sexual binarism.[12] In this regard, let me take the example of the currently established gender fluidity.[13] Until not so long ago, this expression was used mainly in reference to the changing tendencies of individuals in choosing partners they wanted to involve in sexual activities. Data on this phenomenon have been documented by empirical research and, among other things, used to argue that gay or lesbian behaviors have no biological or organic determinants. This conclusion may seem like a kind of anti-deterministic achievement. And to a certain extent it actually is. However, excluding that a law of biological necessity causes sexual choices that fall outside 'heterosexual normality' only partially unmoors their categorization from a reference to biological-sexual binarism.[14] The reasons for this observation can be made explicit in a few lines.

To fulfill my task, I would like to propose a challenge that is semiotic and, in that sense, more than linguistic. I ask readers to venture into a thought experiment. More specifically, I propose that the reader try to ponder the discourse involving gender and its categorical articulations/variations—man, woman, male, female, queer, gay,

[11] Vico (1999, 2000), Danesi (1993, 2012), Heritier (2020).

[12] Among countless other works, see in this regard, Alcoff (2006). By using the term 'erase' with even an indirect reference to sexual binarism, however, I do not intend-as will be seen below-to endorse any of the many declinations of the so-called eliminativist approach.

[13] See, among many others, Diamond (2008).

[14] On this point I am unable to agree with Butler (2004: 65).

lesbian, non-male, non-cis, non-heterosexual, gender fluid, etc.—independent of any underlying reference to the dualistic-biological distinction between male and female sex. Are we sure it is possible to find a clear way through this forest of increasing distinctions? In other words, if taken in and of themselves, do these terms have the semantic self-sufficiency to claim effective ontological and semantic autonomy?[15]

In this regard, if I were to identify with the reader, I must say that my answer could only be negative. In general terms, I must confess that I do not believe in ontologisms[16] and nor even their usefulness on the political level—though ontologizing discourse is very fashionable today.[17] In my view, nothing exists outside relationships and their dynamics. I am inclined to think that ontological assumptions have only a heuristic value. Actually, they help produce meaning precisely by virtue of their rigidity. In this sense, they function as dams in the flow of experience and its transformations. However, they do not pre-exist and/or resist the transformations of the relational dynamics on which they float and sometimes claim to be able to hover. In a sense—I have to admit—asking if any word and/or category is semantically self-sufficient already includes the negative answer within. Nonetheless, the question of whether the—in any case—relative semantic self-sufficiency of a category rests on a potentially open but, at least at that moment, relatively stable semiotic-relational network is different. In this regard, I think it can be argued that the increasing mobility of categories used in gender discourse gushes out from a polarized and tendentially ossified relationality, which is thus far from being open. For example, unfortunately, even the protean formula 'gender-fluidity' roots its alleged inherent semantic indeterminacy on the supposed, albeit denied, underlying semantic cornerstone co-extensive with male–female biological binarism. More in general, I surmise that its polarization is pervasive and even overdetermines the overall 'gender discursivity.'

I am fully aware that the last assertion may seem provocative and perhaps baseless in the eyes of many people engaged in gender discourse. From a political and even emotional point of view I fully understand this kind of reaction. Yet, if deprived of its dialectical counter-axis—coinciding with bio-sexual dualism and its psychic, social, cultural, etc. projections—no term of the critical discourse on gender, and even the word 'gender' itself, I fear would turn out to be decipherable. In a way, it is as if the word 'gender' cannot wriggle free from being gendered male and female first. From my point of view—just to be clear—this is a semiotic, and therefore unfortunately also a practical, vicious cycle that demeans the cognitive and behavioral potentialities of the human species. In this sense, to claim that standards currently extant in nature

---

[15] As Mikkola (2016) argues, both Frye (1996) and Young (1997) can be taken as paradigmatic cases of failure in this direction. More specifically, their approaches fail to define independently (and apart from dialectical opposition to the male/male category) what "a gender" is (in their case the female gender, woman; but the argument also applies to all instances of gender.

[16] In this sense I agree with Mikkola, although our approaches to non-ontologism are not coextensive because of her analytical theoretical-methodological background. As for the genetic and processive relationship between values and categorical structures see above.

[17] My referral is to the so-called 'ontological turn' in anthropology. For a bird's-eye view of this approach, including its implications regarding gender issues, see Heywood (2017).

or in history embody by the very fact of their existence unquestionable ontological evidence is merely tautological and thus ideological discourse.

My belief—which I will try to articulate below—is that human beings are 'naturally unnatural,' at least if by 'natural' one means the biological status quo at a given evolutionary stage. The assumption that a current stage and its phenomenal components is 'not surmountable' would equal to a mere and eventually inhuman surrender to the way 'things happen.' In other words, I think that even in male–female binary categorization there is a coefficient of semiotic violence—as occurs, after all, in all categorizations. However, the polarized reaction to that semiotic and epistemic violence through the multiplication of gender categorizations does not seem to me useful towards emancipating human beings from it. On the contrary, such an approach runs the risk of multiplying the dimensions and channels of dialectical polarization and, in this way, reinforcing the ubiquitous influence of the binary distinction of 'biological' origin. I think, moreover, this is a paradigmatic case of linguistic alienation. Its source lies in having neglected that the word is first and foremost a sign, a *means* that is open to the production of *meaning*. Words must—to put it differently—be used in an 'in-conceptual' way, just as categories must be employed with humility in facing experience. Otherwise, the human being will eventually be dominated by experience, alienating himself—the same maker of words. Likewise, I do not think that the dismantling-deconstruction—so pervasive in gender studies and their varied strains—of the inherent masculinity of public language implies an immediate and self-produced emancipation of all non-cis-het-males from the stereotypes of binary discourses rooted in the sex/gender nexus. Even the semantic compartmentalization of the words 'sex' and 'gender'—obtained by referring the former to the biological domain and the latter to the cultural domain—seems to me self-defeating and ultimately ineffective, if not even harmful.

In any case, I am not sure that this just mentioned distinction between nature and culture is viable. Who can exclude that in the categorization of sex there is no coefficient of culture? Are we sure that the body, taken in its morphology, is semantically and categorically self-evident—even when it is ambiguous, hybrid, inter-categorical, as in the case of hermaphrodites? To put the question differently: Why should genitalia really be the salient element to be considered in distinguishing the different sexes? Or, while willing to admit that genital and sex are quasi-synonymous or strictly co-implicated, are we sure that this co-defining relationship is so very relevant for the 'natural' distinction between human bodies? In other words, can we exclude the possibility that the definition of what is 'nature' is a cultural issue? That is to say, that natural categorization is a consequence of value/ends-laden choices regarding what is to be included in each category and what is to be selected as an axis of semantic salience of it? And, even before this, are we sure that culture does not contribute to defining human nature at large?[18]

[18] In this regard, I must make a clarification. The overcoming or semantic relativity of the distinction between nature and culture can be considered an established fact: see, in an immense literature, Strathern (1980) Deschola (2014). In many cases, however, the above overcoming is observed and argued by taking the perspective axis of classifications elaborated by different cultures and their

Consider, with regard to the above questions, the historical and transformative relationship between the bow and human bodies. The bow is an instrument, apparently an object neatly distinct and distinguishable from the human body. And yet, if the human body is, today, the thing that it is, the way it is, this is at least partially due to its invention of the bow and its use as a kind of body prosthesis. Human bodily morphology, from an evolutive point of view, is closely tied to the use of bow. By virtue of it, killing an animal, even those by far heavier and bigger than a human being, is a task that can be carried out by a skinny little boy or girl, as long as they have good aim. The invention of the bow changed the relationship between the human organism and its environment, as well as the history of its bodily evolution. And yet, the bow is undoubtedly a product of culture. Can it be excluded that for the genitals/sex relationship it is the same? My answer is 'yes and no' at the same time. But let me propose, with respect to this issue, another series of issues.

Is the morphology of genitals an outcome of the recent evolutionary development of human beings? That is to say, from the stage when the culture and its effects began to influence and mold the course of human evolution and, consequentially, the morphology of the human body? I think it is. Sexual preferences have changed as a result of the impact of culture's products in the adaptive success of individuals. Consequentially, even the morphological aspects of genitals and their dynamic functioning were altered. And besides, what genitalia may become in the future with respect to human evolution remains an open question. I am not at all sure that reproduction through the sexual act will remain the preferred and most adaptive one; nor do I have any confidence that organic genetic make-up alone will be able to ensure human survival in an evolving terrestrial environment or in space. The use of biotechnology may prove indispensable to ensure the survival of the human species. However, I will not unduly dwell on these aspects of historical or evolutionary anthropology here except to emphasize that a sharp distinction between culture and nature is almost impossible—at least, if we do not deliberately decide to fall prey to the temptation, always lurking in human mind, to eternalize what coincides with the present situation and its current categorizations.

The above little detour through relationships between culture and nature, however, allows me to underscore that in contemporary times the distinction between the element of the trinomial 'culture and nature, creative options, and sex/genital morphology' relies upon an epistemologically false pre-assumption. And this not

---

variability. My understanding of the nature-culture continuum extends and is engrained instead in the semiotic-material interpenetrative implication between nature and culture involved the evolutionary process and epitomized by its interlocutory steps. In the anthropological field, again in an immense literature, my view is similar to that used in the sympathetic approach provided by Ingold (2022). More in general, however, see Dewey (1958) and Peirce (1892), non-representationalism and enactivism. My approach to categorization thus makes my considerations of gender distinct and not commensurable with either gender nominalism (e.g. Frye Young, Stoljar), realism (Alcoff 2006; Bach (2012), Haslangher 2003, 2006, 2012), constructivism (Hacking 1999; Wendell 1990; Haslanger 2012; Mallon 2018; Àsta 2012, 2015, 2018, but again Alcoff 2006) or 'performativism' (Butler 1990, 1993).

only because there is a kind of semiotic ideology rooted in the aprioristic conception of human freedom, but rather because the possibility of culturally or artificially changing the bodily features of human beings is not a novelty—including the morphology of sexual organs according to their relevance in evolution and the adaptive challenge. Such a dynamic, on the contrary, has long accompanied homo sapiens' evolution. On the other hand, the interpenetrative relationship between culture and nature shows how much what is external to the body is internalized in its morphology through bodily life, to the extent that this ongoing process results in morphological modifications. This entails that even the distinction between the 'body,' on one side, and the environment, on the other, is undermined.

What applies to the body when considered in its entirety, is to be considered relevant/pertinent also with regard to the meaning of the alleged ontological/natural synonymic binomial genitals/sex. To put it more explicitly: sex, its categorization, its meaning, depends on its environmental dynamic surroundings, that is, its material effects and semantic implications. Genitals/sex, insofar as they consist of an act of categorization, are an epitome of their implications, their semiotic omnidirectional experiential projections that reflexively determine what is to be included and what is to be excluded from the correspondent category—up to the point of putting into question the configurability itself of their current categorization.

The final outcome of the above arguments is that if we assume, following some gender discourse strands of thought, a parallel divide between nature and culture, on one hand, and sex and gender, on the other, this analogical correspondence becomes anthropologically groundless. The body (taken in its morphological fixity) and its dynamic interplay with the environment are two wings of the same phenomenon. They are only heuristically and contingently distinguishable but have no ultimate ontological separateness. Does this mean, then, that gender claims must resign themselves to the insuperable and pervasive overdetermination inherent in biological sexual binarism? Quite the opposite, at least in my opinion.

The pivotal implication of the last interlocutory conclusion is that the choice of gender does not pertain to an alleged domain of freedom and/or unbounded cultural creativity utterly secluded in the symbolic realm. On the contrary, determinations about gender should be assumed as possible factors of an ongoing remolding of bodily morphology.[19] This is because there is no material shape that is not the result of a progressive morphing in the elaboration of biological information. And, in turn, the biological domain is a semiotic circuit that is not immune from the communicative inputs stemming from the behavioral and cultural domain. Life, if considered as a whole, does not recognize unsurmountable semiotic frontiers between its 'biological' and 'cultural' aspects. Human history is the most overwhelming evidence of this communicative and horizontal continuity. We can distinguish these two domains

[19] Consider in this regard the process of transformation that biologists and ethologists have traced in the transition from estrus, common to most mammals, to human menstruation. The physiological transformations of sex organs and mating rhythms, as well as the physical invisibility of the fertile period in females, are closely related to behavioral and cultural changes (e.g., the invention of fire, tools, and construction techniques), which in turn have enabled the human species to adapt to the environment relatively independently of climatic and seasonal variations.

only for the present, in view of specific ends, but not in absolute or ontological terms. The body and its implications are separable only contingently. If observed according to its evolutionary projections, this relationship is reflexive and interpenetrative: the living body is the result of its own consequences, and these are projections of the bodily activity. What appears to be permanent, even if through its ongoing change, is the relationship between the body/organism and what is assumed to be external to it.

Freedom in gender variations is by no means without implications for body morphology and sex. In my view, we should abandon the idea that the personal choice about gender will have 'only' social, psychological, political, etc. implications. The same applies to the related claim that freedom can be lightheartedly and generously exerted while the 'hated' nature fixity lies out there, in some forgotten place, waiting to receive and ready to host our mental changes while remaining *ontically* immune to them. Human beings (and their nature) *are the changes* that cultural activity allows them to give to their life experience. Just as no ontology can be ideologically posed in opposition—by virtue of false epistemologies—to the cultural ability of human beings to reshape their own nature, similarly no natural condition can be considered unaffected by the effects of cultural choices. The body's surroundings and its own 'substance' must be thought of as intertwined by transient and relational conditions of continuity. We, the humans, are responsible for what becomes of both of them. Any change, any recategorization in one of these domains reverberates sooner or later in the other, and vice versa. Hence the question: if gender and sex, culture and nature, the social and the biological, are two sides of a single ongoing transformative *semiosic* phenomenal process, what is the genus of genders? What is the axis of salience to be assumed to categorize genders and their variations? What is the ultimate nub of gender choice?

If we consider the reticular and unlimited implications of that choice in light of the above observations, then any claim to the absolute power of gender performativity immediately appears as a *flatus vocis*: however much it is fully justified by millennia of discrimination arising from sexual difference and alleged normality. I think that it is not enough to redefine one's identity by symbolic-linguistic means. The performativity of 'linguistic gestures' must necessarily reckon with the silent and almost inconceivably powerful performativity inherent in categorization, which in turn constitutes the scaffolding of constative language and thus of its interpenetrative relation between individual imagination and the experiential world. Unfortunately, the language of experience is filled with wide-ranging relational implications, distributed far more than intersectionally with innumerable and ever-changing circuits of practical life. Symbolic-cultural activity, over time, has become pervasively embedded in these practical domains and their co-implications with often essentialized, ontologized categorical schemes. There is nothing wrong with this, at least in abstract terms. These are simply communicative patterns that stem from the fixation of behavioral and cognitive habits learned by humans through cultural transmission. And besides, habits are essential to conducting practical life. They also facilitate reactions to environmental challenges because, once learned, they tend to be managed by the mind/body unit in an irreflexive and thus swift, automatic, hyper-efficient manner. However, this efficiency has a side-implication. The more unreflectively habits are activated, the more difficult it is to gain awareness of them and, therefore, to succeed in adaptively modifying the cognitive and pragmatic scripts they encapsulate. As if to say that learning to change habits is one of the most difficult abilities for any living being to acquire. And yet, were I to identify an eminently human faculty, the tendency to change one's own habits is undoubtedly primary. Nonetheless, I must reiterate that it is difficult to acquire and even more difficult to practice assiduously.

Sex/gender is radially—or, even better, magmatically—ubiquitous. It is everywhere. It gives rhythm to urban spaces and topographies, economic dynamics, commodity production, the compartmentalization of individuals' lifetimes, etc. In the same vein, if someone were to ask me where the womb is, I would answer: almost everywhere out there, just as that 'out there' is nested in the womb and in the way human cultures experience it. What I would like to make explicit is that changing sex/gender categorization and corresponding social habits is also a bodily issue. As with the bow example, if we mutate behavioral habits, we will also change bodies as relational entities. The semiotic continuity between bodily interactions and symbolic communication, between mind and matter, makes this omnidirectionality of sexual and gender choices inevitable. But human bodies are nothing but epitomes of adaptive relations with the environment. Changing them through noetic and symbolic activity is inherently and inexorably human. The human species has always done so, and its supposed current 'nature' is the consequence of these mutations. There is no human nature, no 'ontological truth,' that self-guarantees its worthiness or can claim a right to immutability. To be outraged at the post-human or trans-human that would lurk in the changes concerning the management of the morphological structure of bodies is pure hypocrisy, if not also cowardice, a refusal to take responsibility for the human species itself, for what it has made of itself and its surroundings. What the human species is today is the "post" of what it once was. A "post" that it has itself produced and for which it is responsible. Moreover, this is kind of responsibility that not only concerns the past but, inescapably, stretches into the future.

Gender creativity has to deal with endless social and material implications. If it stems from an exercise of freedom, then it would better to grasp how much freedom is to be understood in cognitive terms. Without looking at the consequences, claims for freedom risk transmuting into instruments of self-alienation, the source of which are only presumptuous aprioristic absolutizations. In sexual matters, no Kantianism will lead far. On the other hand, in rejecting it as an eleutheristic recipe, I am not proposing a form of ethical naturalism either. And this is precisely because between nature and culture I think there is a semiotic *continuum.* As I observed above, humans are 'naturally unnatural' or, if the reader prefers, 'naturally cultural.' I think nature and culture should be approached transactionally and approached as relational circuits. Any assumptions about them and their components must be adopted and managed with cognitive and pragmatic modesty by remaining adaptively responsive as any of their implications come to the fore. This is a task that needs to be undertaken as soon as possible regarding gender discourse. Sexual binarism has discriminatory implications that are too obvious and radically at odds with the entire scaffolding of ends/values that steer contemporary experience. The suffering of many people who perceive themselves as victims of sex or gender discrimination is a consequence of the contradiction just underscored. In other words, the sexual binarism inherited from the past causes the collapse of the overall cultural landscape upon itself. The mentioned widespread suffering of individuals is its epiphenomenon and, at the same time, a symptom of the urgent need for adaptive change.

In the face of the just stressed necessity to change the habits of categorization, what puzzles me most is precisely the resilience of the sexual binarism in the background of all attempts to overcome it. Even the merely 'eliminativist' approach, which proposes to stop talking about men and women, fails to escape this resilience (earning, on the other hand, rejection by many feminists). And this is for the very reason that it is not enough to eliminate reference to sex or gender in public language to almost magically erase the relational/pragmatic patterns that are co-extensive with the projections of sexual binarism in the space of experience. As I tried to stress, the womb (as well as the penis) is (also) out there, spread throughout the surroundings of individual organisms. Even if one stopped naming them, they would continue to exist and operate as a tacit category: no doubt diluted, but no less ubiquitous in social practice. What should be done to overcome the inconsistencies engrained in binary sex/gender traditional categorizations is to simultaneously change the language and overall relationships that engrain and weave sexual binarism in and through daily practices. However, this goal I do not think can be achieved by inventing new gender categories or by relying on the supposed performativity of linguistic/identitarian freedom to come up with new formulas of sexual self-representation. As long as we continue to speak the language of sex or gender, we cannot avoid producing semantic entities dialectically related to traditional binarism, keeping in this way—however much unintentionally—its centrality and all-pervasiveness alive.

Lest I be misunderstood: I find nothing inherently wrong with any of the gender critical movements. I respect and even sincerely understand the emancipatory instance looming on the teleological horizon of each of them. But I do not believe that they can free themselves from the dialectical trap that is triggered as soon as they attempt—as virtually all of them do—to overcome sexual or gender binarism by talking, even if in an innovative and critical way, about sex or gender.

At this point, I am sure the reader will ask: but then how is it possible to overcome sex-gender patterns without talking about sex-gender, that is, without trying to propose new ones or new categorizations of them? Actually, it is exactly in this regard that I pose again the question embedded in the title of this essay: what is the genus of genders?

3 In Search of the Genus of Genders: Stories of Retrospective and Prospective Semiotic Peripheralization

The answer to the question raised at the end of the previous paragraph is based on a semiotic and axiological assumption. It depends on fixing the axis of salience of the hybrid sex/gender category. For the sake of clarity, I provide the answer at once. Moving from there, as in a flashback sequence, I will try to provide the underlying reasons for it and, in particular, for the selection of the axis of semiotic salience from which it emerges.

In my view, the genus of genders coincides with 'criterium for the regulation/organization of intersubjective relations.'[20] I fully realize that, at first glance, this answer may appear unsatisfactory. Above all, it may seem to overlook the bio-morphological feature that serves as the semantic pivot, in common thinking, in the use of the terms sex and gender.

However, let me begin my flashbacks.

I do not want to dissimulate that the starting point of my analysis of the 'gender issue' and its legal implications coincides with the phenomena of violence, both epistemic and material, related to it and the suffering that results from it. The connection of it with the biological dimension—as already pointed out—was the first ground for consideration. In the background, of course, operates the distinction elaborated by contemporary critical thought regarding the biological and cultural domains with respect to which each of the two terms would, at least preferentially, have semantic relevance. The first stumbling block—to put it that way—in my assessment of the tripartite relationship between violence, sex and gender took shape with reference to human sexuality.

In the animal world, gender violence is strongly connected to the reproductive process. This also applies to mammals like human beings. It is so preeminently because sexuality and reproduction are synchronous phenomena. Mating—usually—occurs only in conjunction with female estrus. Some species are obviously exceptions—as is the case in the well-known example of the bonobo. However, in most cases, female estrus is accompanied by obvious changes in the sexual organs and the emission of pheromones. This emanation, in turn, produces in males an olfactory reaction that arouses an intense production of testosterone. Such hormone causes both sexual appetite and a high coefficient of aggression, which stimulates fights between males in order to acquire primacy in mating. Visible physical modifications—the most varied depend on the species—and odor function as triggers of

[20] In some respects, my position does not move along a different line from those proposed, in different ways, by Haslanger (2000, 2003, 2006), Barnes (2020, 2022), Mikkola (2016), who respectively, alongside gender understood as a category moreover of problematic and perhaps only asymptotically determinable definition, place attention on 'social positionality,' 'social role,' and 'de-humanization.' I will seek to proceed further along a path of peripheralization of gender with respect to a different axis of salience of the determination of relations between subjects of different genders.

the sexual relationship. On average, the whole process occurs seasonally, but again with variations from species to species. However, it appears strictly functional to reproduction and its rhythms of adaptation to environmental conditions. All this is almost absent, or at any rate modified, in the human species.[21] First and foremost, the menstrual cycle is hidden.[22] With the exception of blood loss, human females have no physical changes during the fertile period that are visible to human males. The menstrual cycle is continuous, that is, it has no seasonality. It stops during pregnancy but has no connection with the readiness of either sex to mate, i.e., sexual appetite. Of course, here I do not want to dwell unduly on the analysis of the evolutionary processes underlying the distancing of the human species from others, and specifically other mammals. Theories are many and multifarious. Common to all, however, is the recognition of the impact of cultural transformations primarily on the enfranchisement from the seasonality of estrus and the morphologically almost 'invisible' character of the female fertility period. In turn, these physiological changes have involved further cultural adaptations, such as the ways in which couple relationships are constructed, the rearing of offspring and its timing, and the distribution of social roles associated with the disengagement of sexual relations from the rhythms of reproduction.

Body morphology and culture, once again, prove to be mutually interpenetrating factors that co-determine human development. Through the brief bio-anthropological excursus just outlined, I only intend to point out that the dissociation between sex and reproduction, also achieved through bodily modifications, is a transformative path that human beings have already undertaken in history. However, the separation of sexuality and reproduction demonstrates a tendency peculiar to the human species to reshape bio-ethological structures. In this wake, humans have repositioned the salience axis of sexuality and related social relations, making it independent of both morphological changes related to estrus and the perception of pheromones emanating from females. This is a semiotic remodeling carried out simultaneously on the biological and behavioral-cultural dimension. Undoubtedly, the above dissociation has not led to the overcoming of the binary categorization between the sexes, nor the undermining of its salience within the structure of social relations. Conversely, however, it cannot be denied that there has been a 'culturalization'—as it were—of sex/gender relations and their meaning.

It can be hypothesized that the culturalization of sexual appetite and its satisfaction, as well as their simultaneous disconnection from reproduction, on the one hand,

[21] There are other species, especially among primates, that have monthly estrus: see Emera et al. (2012), Jarrell (2018), Gangestadt et al. (2023), Thornhill and Gangestad (2023). However, zoologists and ethologist generally reserve the term 'menstruation' only for the human species. There are many reasons for this. There is a heated debate among anthropologists. In general, in this regard, it should be noted that beyond the difference in positions, there is a progressive convergence on the synergy of biological and cultural/environmental factors in determining the transition from estrus to menstruation in the human species and related behavioral habits. In other words, mono-causal or mono-factorial explanations of evolutionary change are implausible. In this regard, see Pawłowski (1999) and the debate among various scholars that finds space at the end of the article.

[22] See, for example, Claassen (2011), Faust and Katz (2016).

have given way over time to the emergence of relational channels of sexual attraction that are asymmetrical with respect to heterosexual relationships. On the other hand, conversely, that same culturalization has undoubtedly intensified male–female relationships by placing reproduction within a broader relational script characterized by continuity over time and diversification of social roles. Family relationships—even the so-called nuclear ones—as we know them today are probably a consequence of those ancestral bio-cultural transformations. It is not easy to assert whether this has alleviated or intensified the violence implicit in many sexual relationships among, for example, nonhuman mammals. A violence that is precisely a direct consequence of testosterone production aroused by female pheromones emitted during estrus. Actually, outside of fertile periods, females are not subject to violence—at least of a sexual nature—from males. Among humans, on the other hand, the unremitting sequence of women's menstrual cyclicity seems to have given rise to couple relationships strongly marked by dominance-control over women for the purpose of satisfying male sexual appetite and, hence, the need for genetic reproductive continuity. The 'brand of testosterone' somehow seems to have escaped the script of the seasonality of female estrus and reproduction cycles, morphing into a behavioral habit in gender relations. Perhaps, this is also the reason why in many cultural and religious traditions the role of women with respect to sexual appetite and satisfaction is in most cases characterized in terms of passivity. The culturalization and generalization of 'testosterone' and its behavioral implications was perhaps not a direction compelled by developmental-adaptive factors. It is difficult to determine whether the greater physical fitness of human males compared to females is a prerequisite or a consequence of the structure of male testosterone-based social bonds. According to many anthropologists, the dominance of males over females within stable couple relationships is also an indirect implication of the combination of two factors, namely, respectively: the need for males to control the genetic descent of females' descent and the tendency toward neoteny in the human species, that is, the expanding duration of the ontogenetic process and the increasingly crucial role assumed by parental education and transmission of cultural knowledge. This is undeniably not a unique and exclusive anthropological path. Other directions have been taken. However, their overall incidence in human culture is a minority, and this, in all likelihood, is also due to the processes of colonization that have accompanied the belligerent history of humankind to the present day.

The subjugation of women in the economy of family relations, on the one hand, and the decoupling of sexual activity from reproduction seasonal rhythms, on the other, are in any case potentially harbingers of contradictions and inconsistencies. In this regard, it should be considered that the fading of a biunivocal link between sexual appetite and reproduction relativizes the importance of the binary nature of the sexes and sexual dimorphism of bio-ethological origin. In other words, the trigger for this relativization is bio-evolutionary and not exclusively cultural. Unless one wants to pursue creationist fantasies, one must recognize that nature and not culture has decreed for the human species the decoupling of sexual pleasure from reproduction, and thus the aforementioned relativization of sexual binarism in erotic interaction. However, the sexual pleasure associated with the non-seasonality of women's fertility cycles seems to be the ground on which the asymmetrical structure of the human pair bond and the dominant role of the male within it takes shape. In short, the pursuit of sexual pleasure seems to acquire an ambiguous, two-faced meaning. On the one hand, it seems to escape the anthropological normativity of the heterosexual couple bond; on the other hand, it seems to underpin it. Perhaps, however, it is precisely because of this dual valence that it has proved throughout human history to be a source of polarization between homosexuality and heterosexuality. The former, in part because of its obvious unrelatedness of its inherent erotic/affective component from reproduction, has threatened heterosexuality as the exclusive axis for family structures, as well as the social implications and power dynamics that came with it. Thus, as absurd as it may seem, in the history of human culture the primacy of the heterosexual couple relationship over the homosexual one has been argued on the basis of exactly what it is evolutionarily disengaged from, namely reproduction. This, in turn, reinforced the thesis of the primacy of both heterosexuality in the erotic sphere and the binary division between the sexes as a biologically, and therefore naturally, indispensable element for the continuation of the human species through a stable pair bond. But paradoxically—it should be stressed again—this stability is the result of the detachment, pregnant with organic-body evolutionary modifications, of the experience of sexual intercourse from the rhythms of reproduction.

In light of these latest considerations, is it really shocking that even today issues of gender and both physical and epistemic violence within heterosexual couples and in the broader social arena seem irresolvable? My answer is that the ambivalence of the common evolutionary determinant placed at the base of both horns of dialectical-conflictual relations works as a generator of polarization. As provocative as it may seem, my idea is that humankind has not yet succeeded in going all the way down the road it has already taken in the past: namely, the complete disengagement of the erotic-affective dimension from the biological-reproductive one. In my view, the fundamental reason for the incompleteness of this path and all its inconsistent and conflicting implications lies in the circumstance that reproduction is an existentially and evolutionarily crucial node. Sexual binarism persists because human beings have not yet invented a viable method to become capable of disregarding sex dimorphism in order to perpetuate their species over time. This latent contradiction is a source of symbolic and pragmatic chaos. And as is peculiar and even intrinsic to their anthropological function, it is by no means a coincidence that religions have attempted to remedy it. A remedy, as usual, based on the sacralization of practices deemed indispensable for the orderly and possibly safe interest of communities and, therefore, of the human species. Hence the normative naturalization, covered with divine significance, of all processes and practices revolving around the reproduction and the perpetuation of the species: from marriage, to sexual binarism, to heterosexuality in erotic relationships with the consequent criminalization of homosexuality as counter-nature, the creation of rites of passage for the placement of individuals within the epistemic and social order that sex binarism entails, etc.

Religious authorities' obsession with reproduction and their compulsive struggling against the far-reaching subversive consequences of the general pursuit of eroticism-affectivity outside sexual binarism are two sides of the same coin. The not easily predictable and controllable dynamics of an eros and affectivity accompanied by bodily pleasure are perceived by religious thought as a threat to the entire social order—in one way or another made the object of sacralization—that revolves around the necessity and constraints of reproduction. The very fact, however, that reproduction is embedded in social figures based on the increased and continuous practice of sexuality/affectivity ends up opening a chasm of contradictions in religious thought itself. Many religions are filled with myths in which deities reproduce—as it were—by parthenogenesis with the most imaginative generation processes. In this regard, even the best-known monotheistic religions, among the most 'committed' to the stigmatization of the practice of sexuality outside the social structures that are passed off as hinging on reproduction, are no exception. In Judaism, Eve is begotten by God through a process of separation/extraction and certainly not as a result of an impossible—in the narrative economy of Genesis–sexual coupling. In the Christian perspective, the Trinitarian approach to monotheism, as such foreign to Judaism, envisions the Son, the second person of the Trinity, as begotten and not created but, again, not through a form of ontological-sexual binarism. But there is more. The very conception of Jesus Christ by Mary does not transit through a sexual relationship but occurs by divine infusion (today we would say a kind of 'heterologous fertilization'). And again, although Christianity, in its various projections, has progressively identified the genetic family as the derivative of the so-called Holy Family, the Gospel narrative proffers an entirely different story. Joseph is not the father of Jesus and, as it were not enough, the latter calls himself "Son of Man": an expression that in Aramaic meant "Son of Adam before the Fall" or "Son of Mankind." Actually, Jesus is both Joseph's adopted son and, as he is God himself, Joseph's father. Being father and son, in short, seems to have nothing to do with genetic derivation conveyed by sex or sexual binarism. On the contrary, the deeper meaning of the Immaculate Conception seems identifiable with a precise message: there is no need for heterosexual coupling for there to be familiarity between human beings. The Immaculate Conception seems, in this, to be a kind of foreshadowing of the discovery of common human DNA. Hence, the circumstance that the first family, the prototypical family of Christianity, is an adoptive one, seems accordingly to propose the message that any child on earth (and perhaps tomorrow in space) is simultaneously the child of any living adult.[23]

Needless to say, the above relativization, if not outright marginalization, of the family based on genetic reproduction has not been embraced by Christianity and its various strains. On the other hand, it clashed and clashes with all anthropological-social patterns based on the centrality of reproduction and the certification of it by religious knowledge. Any attempt to convert humanity to the idea that all were sons and simultaneously fathers to all I fear remains even today a more revolutionary undertaking than the current evolution of human culture can allow. It is a message in a bottle launched through time. However, its trace seems to be recognizable in the practice of adoption, which is increasingly widespread on a transnational scale and

[23] On this topic I refer to Ricca (2019) for more detailed considerations and bibliographical references.

contradictorily supported and promoted by Christian denominations themselves. In this contradiction there is nothing but the re-proposition of the basic evolutionary ambiguity coinciding with the ambivalence of the enfranchisement of the erotic-affective dimension from the heterosexual reproductive one. The idea of co-belonging to the same universal family, regardless of blood ties, is also found—even if, again, shrouded in a quagmire of contradictions—in Islamic culture. Actually, according to Islamic law, adoption is unlawful. The child is only the one who is genetically descended from the parents. Nonetheless, universal brotherhood and omnidirectional duty of brotherhood/solidarity constitute the pillars of Islamic thought and social practice and finds a place in some institutions directed to remedy the unfortunate condition of the orphan, such as the *kafalah.*

Generation by parthenogenesis or separation/extraction combined with unitary descent from divinity, Immaculate Conception and the prototypicality of the adoptive model, as well as general brotherhood/solidarity provide a not insignificant clue. Within the same religions and cultural traditions seems to be the idea that genetic reproduction is not a diriment element with respect to mutual love and affectivity. In this regard, it could be argued that the feeling of familiarity, parental love and brotherhood are not coextensive to eros or 'natural' sexual instinct. It may be so. However, they are not totally distinguishable from it. And they would be even less so if the minds of human beings were educated to dissociate mutual love from binary sexual reproduction, that is, from mating understood in zoological-biological terms. Unexpected as it may seem, the ancestors of homo sapiens succeeded in doing so, though not completely. Today's humans, on the other hand, face a dramatic difficulty in making the last leg of the journey in the direction traced by those who came before them. The centrality of adoption in Christian thought, for example, demonstrates a total distinction between social structures co-extensive with 'reproduction-oriented couples' and the loving, affective care of the Other human being as such: namely who is considered as a target of love just for being human. In a sense, religions, precisely through their internal contradictions, seem to point, albeit intermittently, to a way out of the original ambiguity arising from the human disengagement of sexual experience and seasonal reproduction rhythms.

In any case, the contradictions associated with the incompleteness of the anthropic path towards the separation of sexual relations from reproduction remain. As the reader may have observed, I have progressively introduced in conjunction with the term 'sexual' the adjective 'affective.' According to experience, the stability of the couple is not only the result of the culturalization of male testosterone, that is, it is not only a relationship based on the power, control, and strength exerted by the male. The affective determinant and inter-personal bonding play an equally important role, especially as a function of the progressive prolongation of the function of raising and sustaining offspring. Actually, affectivity has undertaken, in many cultures, a path of semantic-pragmatic symbolization and structuring. The outcome of this process is the moral icon of 'conjugal fidelity.' Although the language often betrays a male chauvinist bias by qualifying fidelity as 'marital,' nevertheless it is in principle reciprocal: that is, it is required of both partners. In this reciprocity we can see, once again, a progressive distancing of the couple bond based on sexual relationship and affectivity from the purposes of reproduction and genetic offspring.

It is certainly true that, in practice and also in legal experience both secular and of religious origin, in many cultures the breaking of fidelity by women is still stigmatized much more fiercely. However, the moral icon of commitment to fidelity retains in principle the imperative of a reciprocal duty. And this is to the point that cultures and ethical-legal systems in which polygyny is legitimized, as in the case of Islam, the inclusion of multiple partners in the family unit is more or less surreptitiously justified by complementarily qualifying it as a 'remedy' for male infidelity. Family unity and its maintenance are among the triggering determinants that undergird polyandric relationships. Nevertheless, fidelity and the anthropic inclination to non-reproductive sexual relationship turn out to be—as it were—twin-enemies, especially if their interplay is considered against the backdrop of intersubjective affectivity.

The gradual spreading of the imperative of fidelity as an essential requirement of the couple regime placed at the foundation of the family has generated a series of binary divisions between licit and illicit behavior. These dualisms were then accompanied by the elaboration of taboos, the function of which is to serve as tools to buttress the family-based social organization and surrounding power relations. Needless to say, couple regimes and the constellation of taboos vary from culture to culture, and this is certainly not the place to dwell on an anthropological analysis of their differences. In my view, however, the 'gravitational pull' exerted by the ethical iconization of conjugal fidelity with respect to intersubjective affectivity however connected to sexual relations has ended up producing at least two contradictory and psycho-socially negative implications. On the one hand, conjugal fidelity and its constant countering of the urge toward sexual relations outside the marriage has obscured the prominence and social care of affectivity in non-marital intersubjective relations that are also sexually connoted. As a counterbalance to this overshadowing, sex outside of marriage or heterosexual relationships at least potentially culminating in it has come to be the object of de-skilling and dis-valorization. The stigma on extra-marital sexual relationships has equally fallen on homosexual and heterosexual relationships, albeit in different ways. In the case of homosexual relationships, even when characterized by stability, it has ended up making the affective component inherent in them psycho-socially and ethically-legally irrelevant, stigmatizing them instead as an expression of perverse sexual longing. As regards extra-marital sexual relationships, as potential ruptures of a taboo coinciding with the sexual exclusivity of the marriage model, they ended up being equated with pure and selfish erotic satisfaction. But these are epistemic-axiological postures by no means coincident with the generality of intersubjective experience. Their communicative function, however, is not scientific-cognitive but strategic. Both serve to bestow stability and uniqueness to the trinomial fidelity, reproduction, sexuality embodied by marriage and family. The untruthfulness of the content of the above postures is nothing more than the flip side of the coin of the inherent anthropological vulnerability of the 'sex-marriage binomial.' A vulnerability that stems, precisely, from the contradictions related to the evolutionary-cultural incompleteness of the anthropic path towards the disengagement of sexual interaction from reproduction.

Instinctual drives, taboos, and violence are always intertwined. In my opinion, the inconsistencies just illustrated are at least among the factors favoring the conflation in the individual imagination of sex and power. Anything that undermines the uniqueness of the family model is stigmatized precisely because it undermines the control of sexuality and behavioral structuring that revolves broadly around marriage-family. At the same time, precisely because marital-familial stability is covered with connotations of power and social stability, its violation, namely the satisfaction of sexual appetite outside of or even in direct violation of its inherent obligations of fidelity, transmutes into an exercise of counter-power. Violence finds in all this a kind of generative habitat. In saying this, I am of course referring not only to physical violence but also to the epistemic violence that accompanies sexual binarism and consequent discrimination. The tendency to exclude women from the public sphere or to empower them only within the private sphere, which still characterize many contemporary societies—in my opinion, also as a result of Western colonization of the world—undoubtedly have a connection with the attempt to rarefy their opportunities for extra-conjugal sexual relations. All this, when considered from an evolutionary point of view, is so inconsistent as to be almost grotesque. The attitude of many human males seems in this very close to that of other mammals struggling to acquire the power to mate coinciding with the seasonality of female estrus. Yet the shift away from seasonal fertility biologically embodied by the continuous cyclicity of menstruation of human females has gone in the exact opposite direction to the exclusivity of sexual practice by the dominant male of the pride, pack or herd. Sexual and genetic pluralism—to put it that way—and thus social roles springing from the substitution of monthly menstruation for seasonal estrus will never receive sufficient consideration. It is a patent demonstration of the inseparability of nature and culture in human experience, as well as of the 'relational' significance, ubiquitously projected in the space of experience, of the body.[24]

The relational-spatial ubiquity of the body and sexuality is to be considered the receptacle that hosts the evolutionary-cultural contradictions of the relationship between social structures and sex. In a sense, it is as if its components belong to different biological-cultural eras. For that matter, this is also true of the human brain. And besides, evolution builds on itself, progressively and at the same time randomly. The task of culture, of knowledge, should be precisely to become aware of the 'anachronistic compound' that characterizes human habits and their biological ground. If epistemic and physical violence still exists today in sex-gender relations, its origin, in my opinion, can be traced to a cognitive cause, better still to a cognitive under-commitment. Among its causes, unfortunately, is also the dogmatic hardening of certain habits of behavior inherited from more recent evolutionary/cultural history and nurtured by the institutional agencies of both secular ethics and religions (not always in line, as we have seen, with the authentic message of the very faiths they

---

[24] In this regard, I agree with Stone (2004) on adopting a genealogical perspective as a remedy to essentialism in gender issues. I believe that this genealogical approach, however, should have a scope and basis of analysis that is not only socio-historical, but also anthropological-evolutionary, placing nature and culture along a semiotic-transformative *continuum*.

purport to represent). Of course, I do not mean to deny by this that the causes of gender-based violence, especially physically perpetrated violence, can have the most varied contributing factors—including ideological, emotional, mental or organic-neurological inclinations or even disorders.[25] Nonetheless, nature and culture are not separable. The semio-cognitive environment in which humans 'breathe' has an importance that I do not hesitate to qualify as overdetermining.

I am fully aware that for human beings the satisfaction of sexual appetite is extremely important. I do not diminish this 'fact' at all. However, even religions, precisely because of their internal semantic inconsistencies, show how human affectivity/sexuality and reproduction are not inseparable and that separating them can cause suffering, lack of solidarity and intersubjective aggression. The very adoption or filiation they legitimize, if not also encourage, can also be understood as a strategy to ensure 'intersubjective affective and material caregiving' and to relativize the genetic management of reproduction. Despite the opposition of many religious faiths—those belonging to the Christian strain first—to both contraception and the artificial management of reproduction, the relativization of the latter with respect to the moral commitment to human affectivity is undeniable. From this perspective, I believe that the adoption and artificial management of conception and gestation are both evolutionary lanes of human transformation. For this very reason, in my view, adoption and in vitro procreation—when it becomes safe and viable—are to be regarded as denoted by the same 'unnatural naturalness' that characterized the bio-cultural transition from estrus to menstruation. Like it or not, human beings are always, even in biological terms, the 'post-' or 'trans-' of themselves. Any dogmatic ontologizing of the 'natural past' is contradictory to the dynamic character of the 'cultural nature' of human beings. And this inherent inconsistency is the first and inevitable cause of violence or social destructiveness, which are in most cases the effect of the lack of intelligence in managing the relations between the organism and its environment.

However, I do not wish to be misunderstood. I do not intend to infer immediate value implications from the transformative character of human evolution (particularly with regard to sexual morphology). And this is not because I think that in the abstract 'is' and 'ought' belong to different and incommensurable domains. On the contrary, precisely because I assume that nature and culture, objective and subjective, etc., are involved in a dynamic semiotic-relational *continuum*, I do not ultimately intend to ontologize or fix any 'nature.' 'Human nature,' in my perspective, is the consequence of what human beings will make of themselves and their relations with the environment. The 'being' of the human species, or its nature, lies in the future. Any ontologizing of the past is nothing more than the result of pathological *idolatrous iconism* that sacralizes and ossifies what has already been or is already known.

---

[25] For a recent overview of sex-assault and gender-based violence see O'Donohue and Schewe (2019), Ali and Rogers (2023). An interesting philosophical analysis of the semantic-etiological ambiguity underlying sexual violence/assault can be found in Maung (2021). In this essay, I cannot dwell on the multiple theories developed to understand the causes/motivations of gender-based violence and sexual violence (clinical, psychopathological, psychoanalytic, developmental, sociocultural, quadripartite and so on).

In my opinion, human beings are at a historical developmental crossroads—even if I believe this has been the case for some time. They are faced with the alternative of whether to structure intersubjective and social relations by emphasizing affectivity or, alternatively, sexual or gender difference, insofar as the latter are both related directly or dialectically to biological sexual binarism. My idea is that affectivity is endowed with a 'trans-sexual' and 'trans-gender' scope and significance. Its preeminent and increasing anthropological salience—as already observed—is a side-effect of the relativization of the role of reproduction in the organization of sexual and intersubjective relations at large. The fading exclusivity of binary heterosexual relationships as a channel for the satisfaction of sexual appetites is also linked to the anthropologically central acquisition of intersubjective affectivity. From its origin as a complementary component to sexual instinct it has acquired increasing salience. This inversion is also related to the circumstance that eroticism has been drawn into the symbolic and imaginary sphere, multiplying its possibilities for implementation practice. In a sense, it can be said that it has become culturalized and, therefore, 'artificialized'—but this, in my perspective, means precisely that it has become more and more peculiarly *human*. A very lucid understanding of this transformative dynamic can be found in Plato's distinction between the aesthetic plasticity of erotic practice and the latent violence and behavioral stiffness of the sexual act oriented to reproduction (see Plato's *Symposium*). But the same also applies to Hindu tradition (e.g.: Kamasutra) as well as the Jewish one (e.g.: Solomon Song or Canticle of Canticles). I think that culturally/artificially unmooring biological reproductive affectivity and sexual pleasure from heterosexual-binary mating practices are not at all strategies to be stigmatized as post-human, qualifying the latter as perversely contrary to authentic human nature. In this sense, I do not exclude the liberating possibility that scientific and technological knowledge can devise artificial methods to procure erotic satisfaction more effectively and deeply than can be derived from organic intercourse with other human bodies. And all this not to the detriment of intersubjective affectivity but, on the contrary, as a means of supporting its centralization in the construction of relationships between individuals (of whatever sex or gender they may be). I am aware that such considerations may sound like 'ethical-naturalistic blasphemy' to many conservative thinkers and others. On the contrary, however, I believe such strategies towards the artificializing of sexual/erotic practices might help to peripheralize their role in determining the criteria of social organization. Those same criteria that today, precisely because of their contradictory link with the ancestral and not completely set aside sex/reproduction binomial, continue to engender inconsistencies and, therefore, epistemic and physical violence.

With respect to the attribution of centrality to affectivity and the implications in terms of the possibilities for coexistence and human advancement that could stem from it, I believe that the distinction between sexes and genders—however pluralistic and differentiated the latter may be—shows its semantic pertinence to nothing but the genus of the criteria for organizing social relations. A categorical relevance that, however, also makes understandable its fungibility with other criteria, especially in light of its internal inconsistencies and the anti-social implications arising from them. Differently from the *eliminativist* approach to sex or gender distinctions or the façade blindness to the sex/gender of public discourse of liberal/democratic legal systems, I suggest that a fruitful strategy to defuse epistemic and physical sex/gender-based violence and discrimination is not to ignore sex/gender distinctions but rather to semiotically peripheralize them. I fully realize that in the eyes of many this may seem a hopeless undertaking, a mere rambling utopia. In the following section, however, I will try to illustrate why it is not so different from other anthropological semiotic repositioning already successfully achieved by the human species. At the same time, I will try to show how law can play a decisive role in producing a cultural metamorphosis endowed with implications for the 'relational nature' of anthropic experience and, over time, for human morphology as well.

4 Smell/Stink, Sex and the Law: The Cultural Reworking of Sensory Attitudes and Their Anthropo-Poietic and Political Import in Social Past and Future Experience

The sundering of the cultural intertwining of sex/gender, on the one hand, and respectively reproduction and erotic relationship with each other's bodies, on the other, will no doubt be considered by traditionalists and non-traditionalists, clergymen and publicists, filmmakers and perfumers, politicians and psychologists, and so on, the foreshadowing of a nightmare. "Insult to human nature" is perhaps the most sober definition the majority would use to label the proposal presented at the end of the previous paragraph. Heedless of the danger, however, I intend to continue in proffering the idea that the peripheralization of reproduction and erotic pleasure in social organization in favor of affectivity could defuse the explosive mixture of sexuality, power and individual identitarian self-assertion that underlies and triggers, in my view, the epistemic and physical violence associated with sexual domain and gender difference. As a result of such a semiotic/anthropological shift within the categorical landscape, the conflict over 'sexual relations' could probably be considered something not worth spending too much energy on. The decrease in conflict would benefit freedom—as everyone knows, where there is no interest, freedom can germinate without too many obstacles. Arguably, if reproduction became an artificially managed medical matter that could be controlled in a sanitary and aseptic way from A to Z, even the difference between the sexes would no longer matter much. The whole structuring of society, its relational cartography, would change accordingly. All this could be marked down as a possibility—for many, perhaps, not even too desirable—destined, if anything, to take shape in the more than distant future. I think, instead, that it lives in the contradictions of the present and, in part, has already happened, albeit peripherally and insufficiently heeded. The field—so to speak—of this 'neglected occurrence' is organic human body odor turned into stink.

The relationship between sexual relations and odor is extraordinarily important in nonhuman animals. In mammals, as mentioned, it is crucial precisely because of the eliciting power of the female pheromones, which function as sexual-reproductive vectors precisely by virtue of the males' aptitude to smell them. After all, anyone who has had some experience with domestic animals knows that inter-individual recognition among animals and even the way they elaborate environmental-relational maps depends on the odors emitted by their sexual organs, as well as those deputed to the elimination of food residues. Human beings would feel disgusted to see other human beings adopt the same behavior. As some anthropological and historical investigations have shown, the dualism of scent/smell, good smells/bad smells, is a tool for the spatial, relational, and thus categorical cartography of experience.[26] What is judged to be a 'bad smell' is, at the same time, that from which many socio-spatial subdivisions originate, both the dialectical pole against which they are defined, maintained and dialectically reinforced. The semantics of 'foul odor,' in other words, is endowed with an inherent cognitive-pragmatic force and, for that very reason, also serves as a device of power. With regard specifically to odors related to the reproductive ritual processes of other animals, humans seem to have proceeded over time to gradually neutralize/expel them from their sensory landscape. Odors emanating from genital organs and, more generally, odor of organic origin emanating from bodies have been made the target of stigmatizing and concealing practices. To their own body odor, in an attempt to supersede and/or neutralize it, humans have superimposed other fragrances, most often obtained through the processing and modulation of odorous substances of vegetable (or, at least, non-human: e.g., white musk—and its cruel process of production) origin. In a sense, it is as if humans aim to present themselves as endowed with olfactorily transparent bodies, which as such emanate the smell of something other-than-human.

The neutralization of organic odor, which is crucially involved in the dynamics of other animals' reproductive processes, has produced a radical semiotic re-cartography of the cognitive and behavioral habits associated with sexual relationships. Setting aside the smell of female pheromones as the eliciting vector of mating constitutes a revolution of enormous scope and extraordinarily far-reaching ethological-cultural consequences. Humans have done all this and, I believe, are proceeding evolutionarily on the transformative path that denotes it.[27]

In my view, the importance of the above evolutionary data cannot be overstated. The contradiction inherent in the behavioral 'co-occurrence' within the human behavioral patterns of intersubjective affectivity and sexual/reproductive appetites/needs, respectively, could be interpreted as the clue to an interlocutory step in a broader anthropological transformative process that is already underway. Imagining the relativization of sexual relations and inter-corporeal eroticism itself in the construction of social relations does not seem to me to be an anthropological revolution of greater magnitude than that already accomplished and related to the peripheralization/neutralization of organic odor and its semantic conversion into stench, and thereby a source of psycho-social disgust and revulsion. In the same vein, I do not

[26] Bubandt (1998). See also Drobnick (2006), Bradley (2015), Classen et al. (1994), Majid (2021), Reinarz (2014) and Ramšak (2024).

[27] On sex and smell/odor in human experience see Reinarz (2014: esp. ch. 4) and Ramšak (2024: esp. ch. 9).

think the artificial management of conception and gestation is without semantic continuity with adoption. It is a question of categorization habits. Many artificial things, which belong to the mode of artifacts invented by the human species, are now considered an integral part of a natural existence. Who would say that using a hoe is post-human or trans-human? However, between the hoe and gestation entrusted to technological apparatuses, rather than women's bodies, there is no categorical discontinuity. Someday—perhaps not too far away—that too might be perceived as 'natural,' namely, befitting 'human nature.'

I realize that the above perspective may be disquieting. In that case, however, one would have to conclude that the same evolutionary process, which in the experience of human beings is further enhanced by the use of symbols, is inherently frightening and uncertain, as it leads toward 'unknown waters'—as Machiavelli would have put it. However, there is no ontological stiffening that can serve as medicine to the uncertainty, the indeterminacy of becoming in experience. Absolutizing the past, ontologizing or eternalizing the present by passing it off as 'sacred and immutable nature,' is only a self-deceiving oneiric-palliative exercise and the source of a tragic heterogenesis of ends. The inclination not to oppose or encourage change is more often than not stigmatized as a Promethean attitude. In my view, however, if Prometheanism is there, it should be recognized in the ontologizations of the past, which turn at the pragmatic level into an apriorism that serves presumption and irresponsible ignorance more than genuine freedom. Responsiveness to experience requires that freedom/creativity and cognitive modesty go hand in hand: one, without the other, would be equally pernicious.

The rush to unbridled and compulsive satisfaction of sexual appetites as well as an artificialization of reproduction for its own sake, pursued for the mere sake of technologizing it without any regard to both the physical and psychological health of the human being, would be in open conflict with the very core of intersubjective affectivity. On the other hand, shifting the axis of salience toward affectivity in the criteria overarching social/intersubjective, regardless of sex/gender differences, could not be accomplished without an anthropological/emotional categorical reshaping and translation of the attitudes usually ascribed aesthetically and morally by various cultures to 'masculinity' and 'femininity,' respectively. In this regard, I believe that opportunities for individuals of different sexes/genders to experience human potentialities could only benefit from such a shift toward affectivity. The polarity between the qualities prototypically ascribed to men and women is a kind of transcultural constant. Although semantically varied, the cognitive and behavioral habits of all peoples show traces of dialectical differentiation. For example, in Western culture, the feminine is identified with gentleness, meekness, predisposition to generosity, fragility, emotionality, a certain amount of passivity, and so on. The masculine, conversely, is coupled with qualities such as resourcefulness, courage, aggressiveness, rationality (sigh!), inclination to exercise power and violence, and all that feminist thought has labeled 'phallocentric.' And this is to say nothing of the 'biologisms' with which the psychological literature, and others as well, appears to be filled: especially when they trace the presence of the above qualities to parallel organic morphological and hormonal differences between males and females. From my point of view, these are stereotypes that the usual culture/nature dualism attempts to ontologize relying on the implicit idea of the non-modifiability, or only relative changeability, of nature by culture. As already observed, the nature/stability and culture/variability coupled dualisms are not supported by the analysis of the evolutionary process of the human species. The palette of human qualities distributed by current traditional law between males and females is—it almost goes without saying—an encyclopedia of pragmatic-relational metonymies. These qualities embody and stand for cognitive and behavioral dispositions. For this reason, they are like pantographs: the lexicon of psychic qualities draws and, at the same time, encapsulates the map of social interactions and its axiological-normative patterns. Beyond cultural patterns and expectations, however, everyone knows from personal experience that the exclusivity of the pertinence of those qualities to either sex (or gender) is constantly belied by concrete human conduct.

I believe that every individual, regardless of sex or gender, would have much to gain from embedding the supposed other sex's quality in their own habits.[28] The promotion of those qualities in either sex/gender depends on circumstances and environmental challenges: namely, something that can change over time. And there is nothing biological that can prove the 'naturalness' and thus the 'non-translatability/transferability' of those qualities between different sexes/genders. If the biological level influences culture, the reverse is also true. In the biological, in other words, there is no evidence either of the unchangeability of human features or of the objective (natural) legitimacy of attempts to oppose their modification. What the relationship between the biological and cultural dimensions—assuming they can ever be entirely distinguished—imposes is only a prudent and constantly updated assessment of the actual possibilities for change in relation to their respective 'evolutionary times.' This is not to be understood as limiting change but as an integral part of the cognitive process that human beings can activate in attempting to self-reflexively orient it (at least in part).

These latter considerations place me on a line of only relative attunement with feminist positions, particularly those of contemporary ecofeminism. The ecofeminist critique of what they characterize as phallocentrism has many undoubtedly shareable aspects. The identification between the anthropocene and the related ecological disasters, on the one hand, and the dominance of phallocentric thinking in the multi-millennial exploitation of the environment by humans, on the other, seems to me sincerely as reifying and dialectically polarizing as the overall attitude they reproach the 'other half of heaven' (the masculine domain). After all, there is no lack of binary bipartition between masculine and feminine qualities in their discourse. Needless to say, all the masculine ones correspond to the factors that have led to the alteration of the ecological balance: in their view, of course, 'capitalism' or 'capitalocene' is all masculine. In contrast, the list they provide of feminine qualities

[28] In this regard, I must make a caveat. The qualities I refer to are distinct from the classificatory properties sometimes proposed, albeit with different approaches, by feminist thought in an attempt to shape a definition of the meaning of the category "woman." More recently, see Àsta (2018).

is presented as an anti-anthropocene recipe. In short, if the feminine had predominantly informed human culture … there would probably have been no steam engine (assumed by some, needless to say, as mimicked in its operating structure on the male pelvic motion during mating, complete with piston as dynamic embodiment of the phallic morphology). Such semantic polarizations once again bring out the difficulty of elaborating non-masculinist discourses that manage to disregard the implicit reference to underlying sexual binarism. A difficulty that can and must, on the other hand, necessarily be overcome. This is so if only because the critique of sexual binarism through a discourse, however pluralistic, pivoted upon sex fails to evade the self-referential implications that, in turn, end up reinforcing that binarism and its discriminatory effects rather than enfranchising human beings from its discrimination-laden inconsistencies. I think the direction to be taken is one of translation-metaphorization between masculine and feminine, to be achieved through a process of mutual learning and metamorphosis based on the already 'trans-sex/gender' significance and experience of affectivity.

Law can accompany and underpin the semiotic transformations of cognitive and behavioral habits necessary to defuse the epistemic and physical violence that is engrained (at least, in my view) in the semantic/pragmatic ossification of sex/gender difference. I will move almost immediately to illustrate what this entails. First, however, I would like to proffer a literary detour that is remarkably explanatory of what I have tried to argue so far.

In 1971, the imagination of the great Polish science fiction writer Stanislaw Lem gave birth to a very short text, a kind of bonsai story in the guise of a review of another nonexistent text written by the ghostly author Simon Merrill. The title is "Sexplosion."[29] The protagonist of the story is a chemical substance: Nosex. This substance, which according to the narrative had been synthesized since the early 1960s in the United States, had the property of breaking down all sexual urges and perceptions in humans. It resulted in a terrifying weapon, capable of eliminating the reproductive capabilities of a population in a very short time. Its lethality had discouraged its use. The consequences could have been fatal for the whole of mankind. Needless to say, around the year 2000 a massive gas leak occurred—even if the causes could not be ascertained. The planet, hitherto in the grip of a kind of planetary erotic obsession fueled by the endless financial greed of the capitalist porn industry, plunged into the deepest revulsion for sex.

Since that time, any sexual intercourse is experienced as pure drudgery and rejected in the name of freedom of self-determination. Progressively, the idea of sex begins to provoke desire to escape, repulsion. The human species is at risk. The whole economy wobbles. The overall constellation of businesses—innumerable—orbiting around sex collapses: from jewelry to fashion stores, from restaurants to hotels, from hairdressers to cosmetics and perfume factories, and so on, all are miserably bankrupt. The sex-porn multinationals, up to that point capable of making stellar profits through the invention of the most abstruse contrivances to create the desire and need to consume sex, suddenly record zero sales. The sexual capacities of the

[29] Lem (1979).

human body become permanently extinct. The most erotic attributes become mere 'body parts' strictly and exclusively functional for vital needs and locomotion. The eternal fascination with sex and eroticism, ancestrally assumed as naturally coeval with human existence, with the species itself, is only a troublesome memory.

The risk of extinction spurs the governments of the world and even the authorities of all religions to urge the enjoyment of sex, to exercise the duty of mating. Penalties are even enacted for those who do not have sex. At the same time, according to the dictates of penal reward legislation, fornication contests are even instituted. Mating becomes a humiliating effort, an intolerable slavery. Anti-sexual corruption runs rampant. Anyone who can pays to evade the duties of the world's citizen-erotic. After many failures, an alternative path is finally chosen: the de-sexualization and dis-embodiment of reproduction. Insemination of female eggs is artificialized and managed by health technology. Gestation of new human beings is carried out by machines. Humanity is saved; sex/eros can evolutionarily be set aside forever.

At this point, however, the author-reviewer introduces a twist. He conveys it through a kind of anthropological aphorism. He states peremptorily that culture does not admit of voids. Thus, the giddy void opened by the implosion of sex was soon filled by the compulsive obsession with food. In a kind of 'structuralist transposition à la Lèvi-Strauss,'[30] food consumption, just like 'ancient sex,' was also bifurcated: permitted/normal and forbidden/wrong. Before long, food taboos sprout and multiply out of all proportion. Food pornography gives breath to capitalist industry. Food pornography boosts the world economy. Sexual differences, with their underlying binary dualism, vanish from the most diverse areas of culture. Clothes are unisex. Beauty is focused on plumpness rather than morphological-sexual prerogatives. Digestion becomes a taboo, an itchy affair about which children should not be told. The biological sciences are charged, pro-future, to take charge of the elimination of any organic substratum of sex, an unbearable prehistoric remnant. The horizon, the hope, is to use genetic engineering to bring forth sexless individuals. The 'Asexual' is the coveted protagonist of a new dawn of humanity and its gastronomy-based anthropological-social organization.

The above genius literary work can be upsetting. The shift from sex to food, as a criterion for the differentiation and social organization of humanity, is homologous, however, to the processes of enfranchisement from the seasonality of estrus and the relativization of organic smell with its recategorization as stench. The profound irony of the text—which among other things mocks Macluhan's "The Mechanical Bride: Folklore of Industrial Man" and its oracular urges—has something Kafkaesque about it. It appears absurd, artificial in that it is caused by Nosex, something that is profoundly human. That is the capacity for 'semiotic re-positioning,' to be understood in both noetic and biological-material terms according to a semiotic-global approach à la Sebeok. Lem refers to 'semiotic/categorical re-positioning', namely the shifting of the categorical axis of salience, and not of 'elimination or semiotic vacuum.'

I do not agree theoretically with the metaphysical-structural transposition thesis inspired by Lévi-Strauss and adopted by some anthropologists even after him to

[30] Friedman (1994).

explain/illustrate cultural changes. However, by asserting that culture does not tolerate a void, Lem seems to indicate how the possibility of enfranchisement from pre-existing cultural or biological patterns is possible not through simple erasure but, rather, through shifting the axis of salience of pre-existent categorizations.[31] A shift that can also be triggered by sudden traumatic events, but which can only be progressive, since every meaning, every cognitive or behavioral habit, every entity, is relational and potentially, often invisibly, omnidirectional. Lem's masterpiece seems to suggest that mere linguistic performativity is unsuccessful and ultimately impractical to trigger and achieve effective change; at the same time, however, it tells us that semiotic and thus experiential repositioning is possible.

The story also contains rhapsodic forays into the philosophy of law. Lem ironically lays bare the inability of any legal authority (whether secular or religious) to achieve its goals through sanctions when faced with semiotic conflicts: that is, when the conditions of the semantic, even before the political, social contract have changed. In short, law cannot disregard meaning and the experience of 'sense' (a word that, in this case, must be interpreted in all its polysemous projections).

In Lem's account, nature and culture are situated along a transformative *continuum*. It is with them, through understanding in cognitive terms their internal semiotic-transformational dynamics, that law must come to terms in order to reflexively and openly achieve its purposes.

I think that the semiotic strategy embedded in Lem's science fiction narrative provides a metaphorical indication in line with the considerations made in the text so far. I refer, in particular, to the shift of the axis of categorical salience in the elaboration of the criteria of social organization from the difference between sexes or genders—in one way or another inescapably even if dialectically anchored in biological sexual-binarism—to another category and its axiotelic scope. Lem provocatively proposes 'food.' I think that it could be 'intersubjective affectivity' even because it already part and parcel of the evolutionary disengagement from the 'sex/seasonal reproduction' binomial and its functioning as a cornerstone for intersubjective relationships.

In my view, law will be able to help defuse epistemic and physical violence related to sexual and gender difference only by promoting the semio-pragmatic relativization of sex-gender difference and shifting the semiotic axis of salience in structuring social structures and the individual roles. This goal, however, cannot be achieved simply by stopping talking about sex or by adopting a neutral or morphologically sex-blind politics of legal discourse. The sex/gender and the surrounding categorizations do not dwell only in people's bodies, nor in their possible representations of it, but also in the whole relational/experiential apparatus that gravitates around it, to

[31] Lem is the author of another short story, entitled 'The Mask,' of great speculative depth and regarding the relationship between sex/gender paradigms and the self-determination of individuals, even in cases where the individual is a 'female robot.' On this text see Parker's (1992) very valuable essay. I think this text by Lem is an interesting background against which to evaluate the theoretical and pragmatic implications of the attempts of Hanslanger (2003, 2006), Mikkola (2016), and Barnes (2020, 2022); at the same time, it could serve as a critical doppelgänger of the eliminativist approach: see, for example, Dembroff (2021)—although this author's position is far more nuanced than might be inferred from the label 'eliminativist.'

its adoption as the axis of construction of criteria for mapping social relations. It is not possible to neutralize sex without simultaneously reshaping the whole constellation of semantic ramifications that move from it and return to it. Actually, even Lem's Nosex destroys the surrounding anthropic landscape at large. Fear of this possible upheaval of their established interests accompanies all those who exercise their political-communicative power conservatively to preserve patriarchal patterns linked to family logics and to oppose gender freedom and women's emancipation endowed with radical anthropological significance. The real struggle, as happens in all wars over symbols, is not over the formal/official bone of contention, in this case the stability of the sex category, as much as it is over the maintenance of the whole experiential landscape that that category epitomizes. On the other hand, that in spite of the importance of sexual pleasure and reproductive needs biological sex matters not so much, is already relativized, is—as repeated many times—an acquired achievement-means of human evolution. The artificialization of sexual pleasure and its communicative compulsive emphasis for speculative-commercial purposes are not only narrative elements of possible science fiction tales, but also well-nestled phenomena in current experience. I think that the worldwide increase in sexually based physical violence on women and children is closely related to the economic exploitation of sexual appetites and the multinational sex market. And besides, that the competitiveness inherent in capitalism and the contemporary 'market religion' is strongly connected to the stereotypical list of so-called masculine anthropic qualities I think is one of the most compelling assumptions of feminist thought. I am by no means convinced, however, that flesh-and-blood female human individuals are immune to the desire for accumulation, any more than I think that all human males are subjugated by it as a result of some sort of bio-archetypical determinism. The family structure based on the control of sexual relations and genetic offspring, in my view, contributes greatly to enhance the competitiveness on which the capitalist behavioral habits rely by providing a kind of species-specific teleological horizon. The family or group logic contains within itself a triggering factor of the clash for power and accumulation for the benefit of offspring. This triggering agent may have different projections in male and female behavior respectively with respect to the sphere outside the family. However, competition, power and accumulation for the familiar group and its descent are recognizable in both female and male attitudes, although they tend to have different nuances with respect to the articulation of social power. Traditionally, in women it appears more individualistically and affectively oriented to the protection of the family group and its members; in men it takes on the more generalizing and constitutive implications of asserting one's social role and power. These are, however—and it must be strongly emphasized—only tendential data, resoundingly belied by individual cases that depend on each person's life contexts and prerogatives. In Western societies, for example, the gradual opening of the public sphere to the presence of women has produced in women a strong inclination to embody the same power-based competitive appearances practiced by men. Many women in power appear more macho than the men themselves. That underlying these attitudes is the factor of discrimination, chauvinist prejudice, and the difficulty of making room for oneself in a world dominated by men and their patterns of behavior may be true but, at same time, reveals itself as an anthropologically meaningless circumstance. I believe that despite their sex/gender each human being is endowed with the predisposition to fluidly embody the qualities that traditional culture bestows to the two halves of heaven—so to speak. I am convinced that this is essential for human development toward at least less conflictual and discriminating styles of coexistence. The shift from sex/reproduction toward affectivity as a criterion for the construction of social relations seems to have occurred already in the evolutionary past in precisely this direction. Gauging on it to carry out a shift in the axis of salience of the criteria for organizing social relations involves a reworking of the qualities stereotypically attributed to the respective sexes. And it is precisely this recombination that can provide law with a decisive role in defusing the epistemic and physical violence associated with sex/gender difference. I will immediately try to illustrate the reasons underlying these assertions.

Affectivity is both a metaphorical ground and a relational pattern. As such, it is remarkably functional in serving as a metaphorical/translational interface between the qualities traditionally attributed to the two sexes/genders and their respective pragmatic projections. Let me illustrate further.

Consider, for example, courage and sensitivity. When semantized according to the relational dynamic of affectivity, it is not difficult to see how one is a means of the other and vice versa. The impulse to enact courageous behavior in defense or aid of the other is oriented and by sensitivity toward him or her and finds in it its own semantic ingredient. Symmetrically, the inability to 'sense the Other' will often turn into indifference, disengagement, selfish attitude and even cowardice. In Christian tradition there is a resounding and even scandalous example in this regard. I refer to the presence of Mary Magdalene at the tomb of Christ and the circumstance that, according to the Gospel narrative, she was the first to meet Jesus after his resurrection. At the tomb there was only her and no apostle. Jesus' execution on the cross had frightened all the disciples. A fear that in Peter's triple denial of his discipleship finds its paradigmatic exemplification. Mary Magdalene, a woman outcast by society because she was a prostitute but redeemed by Christ, overcomes all fear because she does not resist the affective imperative, empathic pity for her beloved master. The Fathers of the Church, who tended to be patriarchal and masculinist, showed a hermeneutical attitude toward Magdalene prone to her masculinization. Her courage, faith and dedication to Jesus made her 'manly' in their eyes.[32]

In my view, Mary Magdalene should be categorized with regard to her courageous conduct neither as a man nor a woman, but simply as a human being who manages life by choosing affectivity as the driving force and drawing on the full range of human qualities to select the tools to achieve it. Taking the semiotic shift underlying the Augustinian metaphor as an illustrative axis, it really succeeds in asserting that Mary Magdalene's behavior is masculine or feminine. It is trans-categorical. However, this trans-categoriality is nothing but the sema/sign of an incipient or possible thirdness,

[32] On the ambiguous and simultaneous masculinization/feminization of women in early Christian experience see Mattioli (1992), Cobb (2008) and there for further bibliographical references on this topic.

that is, of a new categorization of human beings pivoted on affectivity and, simultaneously, on the relativization of gender differences in the semantization of social roles. The social implications of such a recategorization are potentially enormous and profoundly renew the domain of empirical-pragmatic tokens onto which it projects and which in turn define its semantic structure. All this, needless to say, provided that the metaphorical/translative transposition takes place in a symmetrical, open and non-domesticating way.

What, then, does law have to do with the story of Mary Magdalene? Legal language belongs to the deontic domain. As such, it is steeped in axiotelic determinants. The semantic scope of the categorizations included in descriptive/phrastic parts of legal rules is strongly determined by their functionality with respect to the ends/values that undergird their legitimacy. Especially in multilevel legal systems, the inconsistency of these categorizations with hierarchically superordinate principles and/or end/values gives rise to rulings of illegitimacy that result in the reshaping of the categorical scope. This implies that the legal rule will have to include what it had originally excluded from its qualifying/applicative scope or, conversely, exclude what it had originally included. A typical device for achieving this effect in legal systems that include the judicial review of legislation are rulings of partial unconstitutionality.[33]

At this point, it is to be emphasized that the emotional dispositions that substantiate human qualities are the basis of values. There would be no qualities without the capacity for emotional appreciation (meaning the category 'emotion' as broadly as possible and not only with reference to the so-called primary emotions). In turn, emotional/qualitative appreciation is the 'marrow' of values and ends, These, symmetrically, could be defined as the semantic 'dress,' the linguistic envelope, of the results of the qualitative-emotional appreciation activity. The Gospel narrative of Mary Magdalene and the 'categorical scandal' that triggered Augustine's metaphorization demonstrate how shifting the axis of salience from sex/gender to affectivity allows for a rearticulation of the lexicon of masculine and feminine qualities capable of producing omnidirectional effects on the semantic landscape of social practices. If applied on a large scale, this semiotic device could relativize the incidence of divisions based on 'sex-gender' and circumvent the overdetermining influence of sexual binarism self-referentially impinging on any critical discourse on it. On the other hand, it is perhaps useful to point out that focusing on emotions and qualities does not at all mean dealing with something relegated to the realm of the subjective, the merely psychic, and only indirectly related to 'social facts.' Just as in the relationship between culture and nature, emotions and qualitative perception are tools for articulating relationships with the environment. They are not simply or causally aroused by environmental conditions, nor do they correspond to factual situations phenomenally independent of them. On the contrary, emotions and qualitative perceptions are means, dynamic tools for directing the organism's action, which often operate unconsciously and enactively. External situations are the result

[33] The methodological-theoretical framework underlying the translational/transactional legal solutions proposed in the text can be found in Ricca (2023a, b). They were specifically developed with reference to the cross-cultural use of law.

of the organism's action oriented by emotions and qualitative perceptions. In other words, emotions and qualities are embedded in the process of producing 'phenomenal reality' and its unremitting unfolding. They are dynamic ingredients of what gives rise to human phenomenal experience, namely what we term 'reality.' As such, they play a constitutive role in determining what is to be included or excluded from categories if only because they substantiate the values/ends that steer the categorization activity. Working toward a renewal of the emotions/qualities ascribed to the masculine and feminine by cultural discourse can thus have immediate consequences for the values/ends of the legal system with respect to which they are semantically and pragmatically continuous. As a cascade, the resulting reshaping of inter-categorial relations between emotions and between values can produce further effects on the categorizations of behaviors and 'items of the world' included in legal rules and therefore on the social relational landscape.

Consider, for example, freedom, human dignity and solidarity. The role of emotions and values in determining the semantic scope of these categories is extraordinarily incisive and, I would argue, unavoidable. Metaphorically reshaping the relationships between feminine and masculine 'qualities/emotional dispositions' with regard to the relational ground of affectivity can have extraordinary implications on the interpretation of legal utterances referring to freedom, dignity and solidarity. The grammar of emotions—as it were—is decisive in determining what it means to 'behave and feel treated with dignity'. The same applies to 'being/feeling free' in relation to Others since the universal measure of freedom–without which it would only be power–rests on the elaboration of an anthropology of the subject and the semantics of its qualities. As for solidarity, I think it is not difficult to realize that deprived of any reference to the affective, and therefore emotional/qualitative dimension, the expression solidarity would lose its source of 'meaning/sense.'

Here, I do not have the opportunity to expand by providing a list of examples. However, giving one further illustration of the implications between law and affectivity, taken as an axis of semiotic-relational salience, I think may be fruitful. To this end, I would like to refer to adoption, about which I have anticipated some remarks. The cultural legitimization of adoption represents a form of artificialization of reproduction. It has an affective kernel, and extra-genetic affectivity—so to speak—and its unmooring from the reproductive-sexual semiotic axis seems to be its most prominent feature. Despite a vague trend toward the 'naturalization' of adopted children, still found in some national legislations, nevertheless the affective pivot of adoption remains unquestionable. For that matter, other legal collateral figures such as 'temporary foster care,' by definition at odds with any 'naturalizing temptation,' fully demonstrate the prominence of affectivity in and of itself. However, if affectivity is to be recognized as the generative source of the adoptive family, the resistance of many lawmakers to adoption by singles or same-sex couples turns out to be grounded on sex-gender based relational models that are incompatible with the very cornerstone of affective-adoptive acting. In the Christian tradition, as noted, the emphasis on the family based on sex/reproduction appears opposed to the most revolutionary message that brightly flows from the icon of the so-called holy family. Immaculate conception and adoption of Jesus—the son of humankind—disclose to human beings that every adult, regardless of their sex, should feel like a parent to any child living on Earth. I think this visionary anthropological framework is in perfect continuity with the evolutionary path taken by the human species. If taken seriously and developed consistently, it would recognize the adoptive imperative as a paradigm for measuring relational affectivity and, therefore, for redetermining the entire range of social values and their categorical implications accordingly. I believe that all structures orbiting around sexual binarism would be affected. Probably the entire scaffolding of socio-economic competitiveness would have to come to terms with a semiotic shift of this huge anthropological scope: beginning with employer-employee relations, if only because the worker's children would also be the employer's children, to the socio-economic appreciation of each parent's educational work that would acquire the significance of the fulfillment of a duty proper to every other living adult, and so on.[34]

Adoption, moreover, is a perfect framework for testing the aptitude of affectivity to function as an interface in the dynamic interrelationship between qualitative emotions/dispositions, on the one hand, and values/ends included in the legal system, on the other. If we start from the use of affectivity as a metaphorical-translational ground among the qualities traditionally ascribed to the two genders within the adoption framework we find, in sequence, at least two pairs: hospitality, sensitivity/prematurity (feminine) and dutifulness, responsibility (masculine). The adoptive parent and his or her actions are a blend of those qualities mediated/interfaced metaphorically by affectivity. However, the metaphorical overlap between these pairs of qualities gives rise to a blend of ingredients that are able to orchestrate quite adequately the synthesis of solidarity, freedom, and dignity/doingness that adoption embodies. After all, there could be no genuine solidarity without freedom, just as there could be no authentic solidarity without the respect and duty to the other that rhythms the experience of being an adoptive parent day in and day out.

Of course, I am under no illusion that shifting the axis of salience can act as effectively on both epistemic and physical sexual violence (which must be defused and combated by every possible means). In this case, we have to deal with sexual pleasure and its instinctual component. Education to respect the other sex or gender of others may not be enough. And, in fact, experience shows their failure. On the contrary, precisely because that educational pattern emphasizes gender difference, I fear that the more sexual satisfaction-oriented violence is stigmatized, the more it becomes a target of individual self-affirmation, wrapped in the allure of power that always accompanies the violation of a taboo.

Comparison with the animal world and, once again, stink management may prove useful. Some species have developed strategic devices to evade violence from the would-be partner. Skunks, for example, use the weapon of disgust. Their ability to give off chemical-organic compounds with a repulsive odor succeeds in inhibiting the aggressive behavior of unwanted males. I think that the processing of olfactory disgust, which has played such an important part in enfranchising human sexual relations from the rhythms of seasonal reproduction, should be taken into account as

---

[34] Ricca (2019).

a bio-cultural channel against inter-sex violence. Research in this direction should be promoted rather than insisting on equipping women with cell phone sprays, tasers and other such pseudo-weapons. And this also because the effect of behavioral modifications induced on the bio-organic level in the human circuit are amenable to be transferred to the symbolic-categorical level. All this, however, provided that no one sees this as a 'local' and compartmentalized remedy to sexual violence that can work by leaving unchanged the semantic universe that is co-extensive with existing social structures hinged on sexual binarism rather than intersubjective affectivity.

Undoubtedly, sexual appetite and disgust are mutually exclusive on both ethological and anthropological levels. It should not be overlooked, however, that the processing of disgust is a total social fact, affecting the entire cartography of intersubjective and environmental relations—as demonstrated by the spatial semiotics of smell/stench.

I think that the role of law cannot be separated from a work of recategorization pivoted on shifting the constructive axis of intersubjective relations so as to relativize the still current semio-pragmatic centrality of sex/gender, or more specifically of the sexual/reproductive binarism couple. From my perspective—which of course is only mine—if the world of law and public institutions, at least in most cases, really aim—as the latter officially declare—at defusing epistemic and physical sexually based violence, as well as the marginalization and discrimination of those who are not 'male,' then the centralization of affectivity and the peripheralization of the sex/gender and reproduction binomial cannot be dismissed. Employing legal instruments in a performative-deontic way rather than in a semiotic-recategorizing one I fear will be ineffective, if not also counterproductive. Stigmatizing violence, of any kind, vis-à-vis a dialectically polarized Other will only build up motivations to motivate it, sometimes even turning perpetrators into mirror victims. Sanctions and educational initiatives aimed at triggering respect for people of the other gender, but without including the recategorization of sexual binarism and the whole constellation of social habits engrained in it, may perhaps address some symptoms but will fail to disactivate the overall social causes and practices of which that violence is imbued. On the contrary, I believe that law should promote pedagogical efforts that focus on training individuals in the use of affectivity as a metaphorical ground for translation between the qualities traditionally attributed to the male and female genders, so as to produce a wide-ranging recategorization of social practices untethered from sexual binarism. Simultaneously, the resulting new emotional/qualitative lexicon and its related tokens coinciding with the figures of daily life practice should be used by courts and legal interpreters in order to redefine the mutual relationships and thereby the semantic scope of legal values/ends like freedom, dignity, solidarity, etc. This activity, on the other hand, would be somewhat channeled and conveyed by the circumstance that emotions and qualitative dispositions are generative ingredients of both the determination of values/ends and their meaning, on the one side, and the categorization of social roles and experiential/pragmatic objects, on the other. Both the educational and hermeneutical/applicative functions of legal action, as just described, are to be ascribed to a conception of law to be intended no longer as a deontic superstructure with respect to the world of socio-empirical phenomena but, rather, as a means of translation/production of social facts straddling the present and the future.[35] As for the general coordinates of this approach, however, I must necessarily refer to the considerations made elsewhere.

Currently, things are not going at all—I will not hide it—in the direction I foreshadow here. The reader only has to take a look, in the ocean of existing regulatory and planning measures at the planetary level, at the following two institutional texts to find evidence of my assertion:

The International Rescue Committee proposes the following remedies angainst gender based violence.[36]

Our 10 ways to help end violence against women and girls feature outlines several steps those in power can take to help end GBV in crisis settings, including:

Increasing relevant funding
Keeping girls in school
Empowering women economically
Giving women cash support
Engaging male allies
Including women in decision-making at leadership level

Unhcr Prevention Strategies[37]

> Operations will plan and implement context-appropriate programming that aims to transform the systems and social norms that perpetuate gender inequality and discrimination. Programming must address the root causes of GBV in order to effectively change behaviour and social norms, including through long-term approaches, and will require the engagement of men and boys as well as programming that empowers women and girls. Programme design should therefore contribute to dismantle, not reinforce, abusive and unequal power relations. UNHCR will also advocate for and support the inclusion of PoC in related national prevention programming, and through targeted interventions, as appropriate.
>
> Response refers to immediate interventions that address survivors' physical safety, health concerns, psychosocial needs, and access to justice, in line with the survivor-centred approach. The provision of multi-sectoral services and assistance to all survivors of GBV contributes to ensuring people's safety, improving physical, mental, sexual and reproductive health, and facilitating access to justice. All survivors of GBV, including survivors of SEA perpetrated by humanitarian workers, have the right to immediate life-saving protection and GBV services. Survivors of SEA should be treated equally as survivors of other forms of GBV. Working with perpetrators of GBV is not the responsibility of GBV response programming.

Despite the apparent understanding that the so-called GBV stems from holistic systemic-cultural factors, the suggested remedial pathways in the quotes above do not stray an inch from the logic of categorical bias. If everything remains as it is, however, I fear that legal language and action will inevitably remain entangled in an insuperable irresponsibility to the needs of those who experience epistemic and

[35] See Ricca (2020).

[36] See at https://www.rescue.org/article/what-gender-based-violence-and-how-do-we-prevent-it.

[37] See at https://www.unhcr.org/media/unhcr-policy-prevention-risk-mitigation-and-response-gender-based-violence-2020; but also https://www.unhcr.org/what-we-do/protect-human-rights/protection/gender-based-violence.

physical gender violence. No claim based on the valorization of the 'feminine' and a feminine 'semantics,' as well as the performativity of gender in the name of the right to its fluid management by individuals, will be able to erase the overdetermining imprint of sexual binarism. It is not possible to engender equality except as an effect of the invention of a common semantic universe, for the simple reason that it is not possible to unify for pluralistic and libertarian purposes what each persists in keeping ontologically divided. Overcoming gender violence by emphasizing gender difference—the Chinese would say—is like climbing a tree to catch fish. My work in cross-cultural relations has sadly taught me that equal can be born and… reborn as a result of reinventing a new world, but never become one in a universe, both discursive and practical, previously generated by Others.

5 Conclusion

If the proposals that I ventured to proffer in this essay do not find followers—as I am almost sure they will not—this means that I shall resign myself to waiting for someone to invent and disseminate something equivalent to Lem's Nosex. Even if, in truth, that sci-fi vision already seems somewhat embedded in the present. While global porn-capitalism rages on in our real world, in many Western countries politicians and religious leaders are inciting the population to remedy the growing—as some say—'demographic winter.' Meanwhile, a kind of planetary obsession with food seems to have taken over worldly communication and action. This obsession increasingly transmutes in a parallel 'food-visual' pathology. People are constantly eating and constantly posting online on social media the image of what they are about to eat: as if it were a supreme device of identity self-assertion and personal power. The time does not seem far off when food can supplant sex in the ranking of icons of power and intersubjective prevarication.

Just as an example, media accounts of major international meetings among the world's powerful are increasingly punctuated by the meticulous listing of the delicacies they consume on the sidelines of farcical work sessions allegedly designed to solve the problems of the world's population. Thus, they show themselves intent on devouring like tentacled cannibals what thousands of human bodies have produced all over the world for their own pleasure, simultaneously ignoring with arrogance and contemptuous indifference the hunger of many others. Many others, whose number grows tragically and paradoxically the more the amount of food produced at the planetary level exceeds any precedent. I do not think I am exaggerating in labelling these media shows as gastro-pornographic kermesses. Unfortunately, or instead fortunately, I do not believe that gastro-porn serves to undermine or supersede gender violence. Between the two, however, it is extremely difficult to choose the lesser of two evils.

In spite of everything, however, I do not resign myself to abandoning faith in the evolutionary and *semiosic* action of affectivity. My hope is that someday everyone will be free to "act out their gender" as they have been able to become free to manage their scent (…today).

References

Alcoff LM (2006) Visible identities: race, gender, and the self. OUP, New York

Ali P, Rogers MM (eds) (2023) Gender-based violence: a comprehensive guide. Springer, Cham.

Ásta SK (2012) The social construction of human kinds. Hypatia 2013, 28(4):716–732. https://doi.org/10.1111/j.1527-2001.2012.01317.x

Ásta SK (2015) Social construction. Philos Compass 2015:1–9. https://doi.org/10.1111/phc3.12265

Ásta SK (2018) Categories we live by: the construction of sex, gender, race, and other social categories. Oxford University Press, New York

Bach T (2012) Gender is a natural kind with a historical essence. Ethics 122:231–272

Barnes E (2020) Gender and gender terms1. Noûs 54:704–730. https://doi.org/10.1111/nous.12279

Barnes E (2022) Gender without gender identity: the case of cognitive disability. Mind 131(523):838–864. https://doi.org/10.1093/mind/fzab086

Boncompagni A, Coliva A (2024) Liminal identities and epistemic injustice: introduction to the special issue, social epistemology. https://doi.org/10.1080/02691728.2024.2403631

Bradley M (ed) (2015) Smell and the ancient senses. Routledge, London, New York.

Braidotti R (2019) Transversal posthumanities. Philos Today 63(4):1181–1195. https://doi.org/10.5840/philtoday2020128318

Brunner C (2021) Conceptualizing epistemic violence: an interdisciplinary assemblage for IR. International Politics Review 9:193–212

Bubandt N (1998) The odour of things: smell and the cultural elaboration of disgust in Eastern Indonesia. Ethnos 63(1):48–80

Butler J (1988) Performative acts and gender constitution: An essay in phenomenology and feminist theory. Theatr J 40(4):519–531

Butler J (1990) Gender trouble: feminism and the subversion of identity. Routledge, New York, London

Butler J (1993) Bodies that matter. Routledge, New York, London

Butler J (2004) Undoing gender. Routledge: New York, London

Claassen C (2011) Rock shelters as women's retreats: understanding Newt Kash. Am Antiq 76(4):628–641. https://doi.org/10.7183/0002-7316.76.4.628

Classen C, Howes D, Synnott A (1994) Aroma: the cultural history of smell. Routledge, London

Cobb LS (2008) Putting women in their place: Masculinizing and feminizing the female martyr In: Id. Dying to be men: gender and language in early christian martyr texts. Columbia University Press, New York, Chichester, West Sussex, pp 92–123

Cohen S (2000) States of denial: knowing about atrocities and suffering. Blackwell, Malden (MA)

Coleman J (2003) The practice of principle: in defense of a pragmatist approach to legal theory. OUP, New York

Danesi M (1993) Vico, metaphor and the origin of language. Indiana University Press, Bloomington

Danesi M (2012) The languages of the law. An integrated view from Vico and conceptual metaphor theory. Int J Semiot Law 25(1):95. https://doi.org/10.1007/s11196-011-9250-9

Dembroff R (2021) Escaping the natural attitude about gender. Philos Stud 178:983–1003

Deschola P (2014) Beyond nature and culture. Chicago University Press, Chicago

Dewey J (1958) Experience and nature (1925). Dover Publications, New York

Diamond LM (2008) Sexual fluidity: understanding women's love and desire. Harvard University Press, Cambridge (MA), London

Drobnick J (ed) (2006) The smell culture reader. Berg, Oxford, New York

Emera D, Romero R, Wagner G (2012) The evolution of menstruation: a new model for genetic assimilation: explaining molecular origins of maternal responses to fetal invasiveness. Bioessays 34(1):26–35. https://doi.org/10.1002/bies.201100099. Epub 2011 Nov 7. PMID: 22057551; PMCID: PMC3528014

Faust A, Katz H (2016) The archaeology of purity and impurity: a case-study from Tel ʿEton, Isrel. Camb Archaeol J 27(1):1–27. https://doi.org/10.1017/S0959774316000494

Fausto-Sterling A (2012) Sex/gender: biology in a social world. Routledge, London, New York

Fausto-Sterling A (2021) A dynamic systems framework for gender/sex development: from sensory input in infancy to subjective certainty in toddlerhood. Front Hum Neurosci 15. https://doi.org/10.3389/fnhum.2021.613789

Friedman J (1994) Cultural identity & global process. Sage, London

Frye M (1996) The Necessity of Differences: Constructing a Positive Category of Women. Signs 21: 991–1010.

Gangestad, S W et al (2023) Understanding women's estrus and extended sexuality: The dual sexuality framework. In: Buss DM (ed) The oxford handbook of human mating. Oxford University Press, Oxford, pp 700–738. https://doi.org/10.1093/oxfordhb/9780197536438.013.9

Hacking I (1999) The social construction of what? Harvard University Press, Cambridge (MA)

Haslanger S (1995) Ontology and Social Construction. Philosophical Topics 23 (2): 95–125.

Haslanger S (2000) Gender and race: (what) are they? (what) do we want them to be? Noûs 34:31–55

Haslanger S (2003) Social construction: the 'debunking' project. In: Schmitt FF et al (eds) Socializing metaphysics: the nature of social reality. Rowman & Littlefield, Lanham, pp 321–325

Haslanger S (2005) What are we talking about? the semantics and politics of social kinds. Hypatia 20(4):10–26

Haslanger S (2006) What good are our intuitions*? Proceedings of the Aristotelian society.* Supplementary Volume 80, pp 89–118

Haslanger S (2012) Resisting reality: social construction and social critique. Oxford University Press, Oxford

Heritier P (2020) Vico's "Scienza Nuova": sematology and thirdness in the law. Inter J Semiot Law 33:1125–1142

Heywood P (2017) 2023. Ontological turn, the. In Stein F (ed) The open encyclopedia of anthropology. Facsimile of the first edition in The Cambridge Encyclopedia of Anthropology. https://doi.org/10.29164/17ontology

Ingold T (2022) Imagining for real: essays on creation, attention and correspondence. Routledge, London, New York

Jarrell J (2018) The significance and evolution of menstruation. Best Pract Res Clin Obstet Gynaecol 50:18–26. https://doi.org/10.1016/j.bpobgyn.2018.01.007

Kidd IJ, Medina J, Pohlhaus Jr. G (eds) (2017) The routledge handbook of epistemic injustice. Routledge, Abingdon, Oxon, New York

Lem S (1979) Sexbomb. In Id. A perfect vacuum: perfect reviews of nonexistent books. Harcourt Brace Jovanovich, London, New York, pp 41–48

Lohmann G (2018) The ambivalence of indifference in modern society. Dissonância: Revista de Teoria Crítica 2(2):23–55

Lutz H (2014) Intersectionality's (brilliant) career—how to understand the attraction of the concept? Working Paper Series "Gender, Diversity and Migration", No. 1. https://www.make-way.org/wp-content/uploads/2023/02/34.pdf

Lutz H (2015) Intersectionality as method. J Diversity Gend Stud 2(1–2):39–44

MacKinnon C (1989) Toward a feminist theory of state. Harvard University Press, Cambridge, MA

Majid A (2021) Human olfaction at the intersection of language, culture, and biology. Trends Cogn Sci 25(2):111–123

Mallon R (2018) The construction of human kinds. OPU, Oxford

Mattioli U (1992) Donne nel Vangelo: linee di esegesi in Mattioli U (ed) La donna nel pensiero cristiano antico. Marietti, Genova, pp 51–78

Maung HH (2021) A dilemma in rape crisis and a contribution from philosophy. Humanities and Social Sciences Communication 8:93. https://doi.org/10.1057/s41599-021-00769-y
Mikkola M (2006) Elizabeth Spelman, gender realism, and women. Hypatia 21:79–96
Mikkola M (2016) The wrong of injustice: dehumanization and its role in feminist theory. OUP, Oxford
O'Donohue WT, Schewe PA (eds) (2019) Handbook of sexual assault and sexual assault prevention. Springer, Cham.
Padron M (2021) Gender theory vs. pragmatism: A point of diversion between Judith Butler's gender performativity and the psychosocial limitations of gender construction. Inq J 13(04). http://www.inquiriesjournal.com/a?id=1897
Parker JA (1992) Gendering the robot: Stanislaw Lem's "the mask" (Le Sexe et le robot: "Le Masque" de Stanislaw Lem). Sci Fict Stud 19(2):178–191
Pawłowski B (1999) Loss of oestrus and concealed ovulation in human evolution: the case against the sexual-selection hypothesis. Curr Anthropol 40(3):257–275
Peirce CS (1892) The law of mind. Monist 2(4):533–559
Pérez M (2019) Epistemic violence: reflections between the invisible and the ignorable. El Lugar Sin Límites 1(1):81–98
Ramšak M (2024) The anthropology of smell. Springer, Cham
Reinarz J (2014) Past scents: historical perspective on smell. University of Illinois Press, Urbana, Chicago, and Springfield
Ricca M (2015) Polifemo. La cecità dello straniero. Torri del Vento, Palermo
Ricca M (2019) Children in tatters across the earth: intercountry adoptions, intercultural discriminations. Calumet–Intercultural Law Hum Rev 9:62–104. https://calumet-review.com/index.php/2019/10/11/children-in-tatters-across-the-earth-intercountry-adoptions-intercultural-discriminations/
Ricca M (2020) Planning facts through law: legal reasonableness as creative indexicality and trans-categorical re-configuration. Int J Semiot Law 33:1089–1123
Ricca M (2022a) Perpetually Astride Eden's boundaries: the limits to the 'limits of law' and the semiotic inconsistency of 'legal enclosures.' Int J Semiot Law 35:179–229
Ricca M (2022b) The 'spaghettification' of performativity across cultural boundaries: the trans-culturality/trans-spatiality of digital communication as an event horizon for speech acts. Int J Semiot Law 35:2435–2479
Ricca M (2023a) Intercultural spaces of law: translating invisibilities. Springer, Cham
Ricca M (2023b) How to undo (and redo) words with facts: a semio-enactivist approach to law, space and experience. Int J Semiot of Law 36:313–367
Ricca M (2025) The Fluid Ubiquity of Food: Why Human Beings are Space–Time Cannibals. Int J Semiot Law 38: 197–279. https://doi.org/10.1007/s11196-024-10237-w
Schep D (2012) The limits of performativity: a critique of hegemony in gender theory. Hypatia 27(4):864–880
Scotto di Carlo G (2023) Defining 'gender' across europe: a linguistic analysis of the definition, translation, and interpretation of the word 'gender' from the Beijing declaration to the Istanbul convention. Int J Semiot Law 36:1217–1238
Searle JR (1995) The construction of social reality. Free Press, New York
Stoller RJ (1968) Sex and gender: on the development of masculinity and femininity. Science House, New York
Stone A (2004) Essentialism and anti-essentialism in feminist philosophy. J Moral Philos 1:135–153
Strathern M (1980) No nature; no culture. In: MacCormack C, Strathern M (eds) Nature, culture, gender. CUP, Cambridge
Thornhill R, Gangestad SW (2023) 'Estrus', The evolutionary biology of human female sexuality online edn, Oxford Academic https://doi.org/10.1093/oso/9780195340983.003.0008. Accessed 28 Oct 2024

Vico G (1999) The new science of Giambattista Vico: unabridged translation of the third edition (1744) with the addition of "Practic of the New Science." Cornell University Press, Ithaca, London
Vico G (2000) The Universal right (or. De universis iuris 1720/21). Rodopi, Amsterdam, Atlanta.
Wendell S (1990) The rejected body: feminist philosophical reflections on disability. Routledge, New York
Witt C (1995) Anti-essentialism in feminist theory. Philos Top 23(2):321–344
Young I M (1997) Gender as Seriality: Thinking about Women as a Social Collective. In Iris Marion Young, Intersecting Voices, 12–37. Princeton, NJ: Princeton University Press.

Mario Ricca is full professor in Intercultural Law at University of Roma Tre, Italy. He is managing director of the online journal 'Calumet—Intercultural Law and Humanities Review.' He has published several books on intercultural law. His research areas interplay among law, anthropology, semiotics, and geography. Among his latest publications: Intercultural Spaces of Law: Translating Invisibilities. Springer, Cham (2023).

Still Inessential—Women with Disabilities, (Gender) Stereotypes, and Law

Maria Giulia Bernardini

Abstract Although women with disabilities have gained greater visibility in more recent years, it is not unreasonable to argue that they are still *inessential* and are among the most at risk of having their rights violated. After briefly recalling the theoretical and political reasons behind their historical inessentiality, the essay identifies the most prevalent sexist and ableist stereotypes and analyzes how they interact. To this aim, it examines two areas where the most serious violations of these women's rights occur, namely violence and sexual and reproductive health, with particular attention to forced sterilization.

Keywords Gender · Disability · Women with disabilities · Stereotypes · Violence · Forced sterilization

1 Women with Disabilities as (Political and Legal) Subjects

In the 1990s, in *Inessential Woman*,[1] Elisabeth Spelman challenged the partiality that characterized feminist thought. By referring solely to the reality of middle-class white women, it reproduced the widespread social hierarchies that saw some women as *more equal* than others. According to the philosopher, for feminism to truly represent all women, it was necessary to include considerations of race and class in the feminist discourse.

In her book, Spelman made no reference to disability, in line with a widespread trend of those years and beyond: the silence on disability—and consequently on the

[1] Spelman (1990, 1997).

M. G. Bernardini (✉)
Maria Giulia Bernardini, University of Ferrara, Ferrara, Italy
e-mail: mariagiulia.bernardini@unife.it

A. Condello and A. Wagner (eds.), *Gender Stereotypes*, Gender, Justice and Legal Feminism 2, https://doi.org/10.1007/978-3-031-63905-0_6

condition of women with disabilities[2]—long characterized both mainstream theoretical reflection and feminist thought, for reasons that feminist disability studies (FDS) have extensively explored.[3] A consequence of this silence was the prolonged failure to recognize the subjectivity of these women, who were even more marginalized than the other subjectivities identified by Spelman, and to whom we now refer by invoking the notion of intersectionality.[4]

Therefore, it is not surprising that NGOs, public institutions and feminist disabilities studies scholars and activists referred in the past to women with disabilities as 'invisible subjects' or 'missing voices.' Even today, women with disabilities are described as 'silent victims', 'silent tears', or 'missing bodies.' For this reason, when we think of women with disabilities, we mostly have a non-image, due to a lack of recognition that stems from their invisibility. Women with disabilities have long been forgotten in public discourse and relegated—both symbolically and physically—to private spaces (mainly homes and social care facilities).

In line with what has happened with other excluded and discriminated subjects, the confinement of women with disabilities in the private sphere has primarily taken on political significance, which has had important legal consequences as well: while in the public space a person becomes visible, being confined in the private leads to invisibility, which in turn results in social irrelevance. Clearly, this invisibility also has legal implications: critical theory has extensively highlighted how ascribing individuals to the private sphere is a technique that creates a boundary, delineating the threshold between what counts as legally cognizable and what is regarded as significant solely within the moral domain. Critical theory has also emphasized that this operation is not at all neutral but rather aimed at concealing important issues, mainly affecting people who do not embody the liberal subject. In Joan Tronto's words, the distinction between private and public is not at all natural, but rather political in nature,[5] since issues concerning rights and their violations also arise in the private sphere.

In this respect, with reference to the intersection between gender and disability, one might consider issues like the recognition of the rights of both the caregiver and the cared-for, as well as violence against women with disabilities, which has even

---

[2] In their advocacy, disability organizations are very careful to include not only women, but also girls with disabilities in their analyses on the intersection between gender and disability. In this way, age, which still is a 'Cinderella' for law—and particularly for anti-discrimination law—becomes one of the relevant elements in the multiple discrimination of women with disabilities. The same approach is found within the UN Convention on the Rights of Persons with Disabilities, whose Article 6(1) begins with a reference to women *and girls* with disabilities. More recently, the issue of elderly women with disabilities has also been raised, as they are even more *inessential* both within theoretical reflection and in the society. For reasons of clarity, throughout this essay we will refer almost exclusively to women with disabilities, without disregarding that importance of adopting an intersectional perspective which considers the interaction among disability, gender and other discrimination factors, starting from age.

[3] On FDS, see Garland Thomson (2005), Hall (2011, 2015), Bê (2019), Stienstra (2019). The possible reasons for this exclusion are outlined in paragraph 2 below.

[4] Cf. Crenshaw (1989, 2017).

[5] On the political nature of the boundaries between public and private, cf. Tronto (1993).

more alarming incidence rates compared to that against women without disabilities.[6] After all, it is important to remember that people with disabilities have long been considered *objects*—rather than *subjects*—of law, and women with disabilities have been depicted as *defective objects* of no value.[7]

After briefly recalling the theoretical and political reasons behind the perceived *inessentiality* of women with disabilities (para. 2), we will identify the most widespread sexist and ableist stereotypes against them and their interaction (para. 3). Thereafter, to analyse how these intersectional stereotypes function in practice, we will consider two areas where the most severe violations of these women's rights occur: violence (para. 3.1) and sexual and reproductive health (para. 3.2). Finally, we will conclude by explaining why, in our opinion, women with disabilities should still be considered *inessential* subjects (para 4).

2 Possible Theoretical and Political Reasons for *Inessentiality*

Disability has long been a challenge for modern legal and political thought, which has elevated autonomy, independence, rationality, and productivity as characteristics of (neo)liberal subjectivity. With 'able-bodied normality' as the standard, the network of beliefs, processes, and practices known as 'ableism'[8] has contributed to treating disability as a reduced state of humanity.

Until the turn introduced theoretically with the 'social model' of disability and culminating, on the legal level, with the entry in force of the Convention on the Rights of Persons with Disabilities (CRPD, 2008), in the history of Western thought disability was *necessarily* and unavoidably associated with characteristics such as dependence, passivity, irrationality, incapacity, and unproductivity. The anthropological model assumed by Lockean, Kantian, and Cartesian philosophy—the conceptions underlying the theory of the legal subject—inevitably viewed disability as a 'lack' that led to incapacity. Therefore, the 'stakes' of recognition as full subjects and, as such, rights holders, hinged on not being disabled.[9]

Within this cultural framework, the inessentiality of women with disabilities has been even more radical: on the one hand, disability has long been removed from the

---

[6] In this area, official data is scarce and largely unavailable. However, available estimates show that women with disabilities are two to five times more likely to experience violence. This issue, explored in more detail in para. 3.1, can be further examined in the European Disability Forum (EDF) report (2021).

[7] According to the Women's NGOs who wrote the Italian shadow report on the implementation of the Istanbul Convention, "sexism does not spare women with disabilities and in fact renders them victims twice over. Disabled women are not only viewed as 'objects,' but being disabled renders them defective objects of no value". Cf. Biaggioni and Pirrone (2018), p. 15.

[8] Campbell (2001).

[9] Bernardini (2023).

feminist agenda; on the other hand, reflections on gender in Disability Studies have appeared only later and have long been of marginal importance.

The reasons for this exclusion may be various. Regarding feminist thought, one possible explanation for the silence is the pervasiveness of ableism, which may have also claimed feminism among its victims, causing it, due to the socio-cultural context, to adopt the stereotypes that depict people with disabilities as inevitably "unfortunate, useless, different, oppressed, and sick."[10]

Moreover, feminism has long referred to disability as a metaphor to describe the exclusion experienced by women, who *were disabled* by a patriarchal system that considered them weak, irrational, physically and morally fragile (thus 'disabled', from an ableist perspective) and, on this basis, removed or limited their legal agency, due to the relationship, assumed as necessary, between disability and incapacity.

Finally, it can be reasonably assumed that feminist silence on disability has been due to strategic considerations. In a socio-cultural context where both women and people with disabilities were relegated to the domestic sphere and associated with care, disability could have been perceived as an obstacle to the feminist emancipation project. Indeed, while the feminist struggle for liberation from the caregiving role and the private sphere had already begun at least since the nineteenth century, the situation for disability was very different: until the 1980s,[11] disability was considered a personal condition to be cared for and looked after, one that could and should be 'managed' only within the private sphere.

For this reason, among feminists, attention to disability was probably seen as somehow 'dangerous,' as it risked reasserting the centrality of women in their roles as caregivers within the private sphere. Through this route, silence on disability led to women with disabilities being considered inessential, contributing to their non-recognition as subjects, their exclusion from the roles from which feminists were striving to break free (such as the roles of mothers and wives), and the violation of their rights, sometimes even supported by feminists without disabilities. It is well known, for example, that in the 1930s, American reformists advocated the nonconsensual sterilization of women with disabilities.[12]

In the case of the disability rights movement, the invisibility of women with disabilities can be attributed both to political dynamics and theoretical reasons. On the political front, even though women with disabilities have been involved in the movement and its struggles from the very beginning, its leadership was for a long time exclusively in the hands of men. By leaving women with disabilities 'on the margins,' men were thus able to maintain their power.[13]

---

[10] Hunt (1966).

[11] Here we refer to the historical period when the 'social model' of disability was developed. On the level of rights advocacy, the new perspective on disability became public at the end of the 1960s. On the phases of the theoretical elaboration within disability studies, see Ralston and Ho (2009).

[12] Carlson (2001, 2010).

[13] Among the few exceptions is Judy Heumann, remembered as the 'mother' of the disability rights movement.

On the theoretical level, at least until the 1990s, Disability Studies deliberately omitted any reference to the body in order to overcome the reductionist view that equates disability with impairment, and thereby promoting the opposite perspective, according to which disability is more correctly to be understood as disablement—that is, a form of social oppression. For this reason, there was a widespread belief that the body could function as a Trojan horse that would lead again to consider disability from a medical perspective. Again, the outcomes for women with disabilities are clear: if the *disabled body* is not included in the theoretical reflection, it follows that *'other' bodies*, such as those of women with disabilities, will remain invisible and be perceived as *inessential.*

3 Stereotypes and Prejudices About Women with Disabilities: A Brief Taxonomy

Inessentiality has historically provided fertile ground for the spread and entrenchment of stereotypes and prejudices against women with disabilities, which in turn have fostered their social exclusion, discrimination and violation of rights. Even today, the same stereotypes continue to significantly influence the lives of these women.

Like the other women, also those with disabilities are subject to those cultural pressures related to their bodies that can be summarized in the expression "tyranny of perfection,"[14] according to which the female body must be beautiful, harmonious, healthy, and sexually desirable. Being disabled, the bodies of these women are perceived as 'non-conforming'—therefore anomalous and deviant—both with respect to 'normal and abled' body and to the aesthetic standards to which the female one is deemed to respond. As such, they cannot ascend to either the rank of 'normal' or 'desirable' bodies, to the point that there is a widespread tendency to consider women with disabilities as 'angelic' and asexual individuals. Contributing to this image is also the stereotype of infantilization, where people with disabilities are seen as eternal children who are incapable of making decisions for themselves.

Sometimes, by a process only seemingly opposite, the failure to meet the standard of able-bodied femininity results in the stereotype of hyper-sexuality, according to which women with disabilities –especially those with intellectual ones—use their sexuality improperly and are too exuberant.

The above-mentioned stereotypes are connected to those related to the presumption of incompetence of people with disabilities, which involve both the (in)ability to meet role expectations and the presumed incapacity for decision-making that is believed to be inherent in the presence of a disability, especially when it is intellectual. When framed in terms of gender, the most relevant stereotypes regarding role expectations are those suggesting that women with disabilities are incapable of being either romantic partners or 'good mothers.'

[14] Morris (1992).

The stereotypes that heavily influence this perception include both the belief that women with disabilities are asexual and the idea of their incapacity for conscious self-determination, particularly in the sexual sphere. In the first case, it is even conceptually unimaginable that they might aspire to romantic relationships; thus, the very possibility of forming a family is denied to them. In the second case, reasons of opportunity and Foucauldian defence—both of society and potential offspring that might result from an excessive exercise of sexuality—suggest that such women should not be granted any freedom in this area and should not be recognized as capable of any responsibility within the family sphere. They are seen as incapable of making such important life decisions and, if they chose to have children, would be unsuitable to properly fulfil the duties associated with the role of parenting.

Also weighing on the latter aspect is the stereotype of infantilization evoked earlier, namely the belief that people with disabilities are eternal children, and as such, are incapable of self-determination. Thus, this alleged immaturity not only *justifies*, but rather *requires* others to make decisions for them, according to their (alleged) best interests.

These stereotypes clearly have relevant legal consequences as well. In particular, the idea that people with disabilities are incapable of meeting role expectations, are unable to self-determine, or to take responsibility for their choices, has led to their long-standing exclusion from the recognition and exercise of rights related to these areas, through limitations on their legal capacity.

To deconstruct this imagery, the UN Convention on the Rights of Persons with Disabilities—where attention to gender, in addition to being expressed in Article 6, is cross-cutting—reaffirms the legal capacity of persons with disabilities on an equal basis with individuals without disabilities, and the entitlement to numerous rights, starting with those related to self-determination. Regarding women with disabilities, among the rights that take on greater significance, considering the pervasiveness of their violations, are the right not to be subjected to exploitation, violence, and abuse, and the rights to sexual and reproductive health.

3.1 Violence Against Women with Disabilities

To date, women with disabilities are among the most vulnerable to gender-based violence, domestic violence, and sexual exploitation. On one hand, the lack of an intersectional approach has long prevented recognition of how the interaction between gender and disability significantly increases the risk of being exposed to such an acute form of discrimination. On the other hand, the scarcity of data, the gaps in those which are available, and the peculiarities of the violence against these women make it difficult to raise awareness of the significance of the phenomenon.[15]

[15] Cf. World Health Organization (2024); for an overview of the most relevant international literature on the subject, see García-Cuéllar et al. (2023). The topic has been the subject of systematic reflection for several years: Ortoleva and Lewis (2012). Within the context of international human rights, both

The violence experienced by women with disabilities indeed has several specific aspects, starting with the perpetrators (who are often family members and professional caregivers) and the locations where it occurs (not only the 'traditional' ones, such homes, but also social care facilities). The degree of proximity often held by the perpetrator and the isolation that typically characterizes the daily life of these women significantly facilitate the commission of abuse and the related impunity.

The forms of violence experienced by women with disabilities also have unique characteristics. Women with disabilities are exposed to the more 'canonical' forms of violence, such as physical, sexual, economic, and psychological. However, these forms can take on specific modes due to the presence of a disability. For example, psychological violence can also include the denial of adulthood, that is, seeing women with disabilities as eternal children. On another front, the killing of a support animal (such as a guide dog) can be interpreted not only as a case of psychological violence but also of a physical violence, as it is often used to limit the mobility of women with sensory disabilities. Furthermore, mobility may also be impeded by removing or threatening to remove modes of access, such as communication aids, wheelchairs, or canes. Finally, perpetrators may financially abuse women with disabilities by reducing or controlling their access of funds, as well as their use, while caregivers may manipulate the women for whom they are supposed to be caring by threatening to stop performing their care work.[16]

There are also forms of violence that women with disabilities are victims of much more frequently than others, and which can therefore be considered in some way 'specific.' These include drug abuse, the denial of essential healthcare, and non-consensual sterilization, which—besides being one of the forms of violence against women with disabilities that raises the most concern today—also constitutes a violation of their sexual and reproductive rights.[17]

Furthermore, women with disabilities are particularly exposed to so-called 'institutional violence,' a phenomenon that is receiving increasing attention from international institutions.[18] In relation to this form of violence, the pervasiveness of the interaction between sexist and ableist stereotypes is particularly evident, especially regarding secondary victimization, namely the victimization that occurs not as a direct result of the criminal act but through the response of institutions and individuals to the victim.

As noted earlier, in the collective imagination women with disabilities are seen as either angelic or hyper-sexual beings. This false belief leads to the assumption that

---

the UN Convention on the Rights of Persons with Disabilities and the Istanbul Convention recognize that women with disabilities are more exposed to violence than other women.

[16] In relation to all these aspects, the picture is further complicated by the fact that the 'nature' of violent acts is often linked to the kind of disability. For example, while women with intellectual disabilities are generally victims of psychological violence, women with physical and sensory disabilities are typically subjected to forms of violence that impact their freedom.

[17] On forced sterilisation cf *infra*, para 3.2.

[18] Amongst others, mention may be made of the work done by the Office of the High Commissioner for Human Rights, specifically in relation to stereotypes related to sexual and reproductive health and rights. See Office of the High Commissioner for Human Rights—OHCHR (2017).

it is highly unlikely they could experience violence, because in the first case, it is presumed that these women cannot be the object of male desire, while in the second, it is believed that they must have provoked their sexual partner by not exercising their sexuality appropriately. In both cases, it is difficult for violence to emerge, partly because women with disabilities often do not receive education that enables them to recognize the violence directed at them.

When women with disabilities come to report the violence, they face the well-known problem of epistemic injustice,[19] which, in their case, takes on even more alarming connotations compared to the experiences of women without disabilities. Indeed, in addition to sexist stereotypes, which cause women to be considered non-believable subjects par excellence, there is also the condition of disability, which can also affect the way in which the fact is told, making it much more difficult for them to be believed. It is very likely, for example, that women with intellectual, psychosocial, or deaf-blind disabilities who assert to have been victims of violence do not tell the story in a straightforward manner. While in such cases the presence of properly trained personnel is necessary to understand the content of the narrative and provide appropriate protection, what often happens in practice is quite the opposite. As a rule, in fact, inconsistencies are assessed by reference to the logicality, coherence and congruence of a narrative that would be made by a person without a disability, in adherence to the parameter of the 'reasonable subject,'[20] with the effect of leading to such women's statements being considered unreliable. Even at this stage, access to justice for women with disabilities seems to be hindered by a barrier that appears almost insurmountable.[21]

However, women with disabilities encounter many barriers also in the subsequent phases of their access to justice. It often happens that the mere fact that a woman has a psychosocial or intellectual disability, or requires assisted communication, leads judges to *exclude* her testimony or, alternatively, to request further evidence to support the narrative made. Moreover, if a woman has undergone psychiatric treatment throughout her life, her testimony can easily be discredited.

---

[19] Fricker (2007), Anderson (2012), Kidd et al. (2019).

[20] The same applies in other intersectional cases, for example, when it comes to assessing the credibility of migrants with disabilities. In the case of an asylum seeker with cognitive or psychosocial disabilities, the assessment of their communicative capacity, as well as the overall strength of their narrative, becomes problematic: it may be difficult for these individuals to properly articulate their claim or to develop a coherent, 'rational' narrative. On this point, Behrman (2014).

[21] Women with disabilities face numerous barriers to accessing justice even beforehand. For example, only in recent years, following the increasing public attention to disability and the fact that women with disabilities are no longer as marginalized as in the past, have anti-violence centers begun to question whether they are really accessible to these women. Relevant accessibility, of course, is not only about the absence of architectural barriers, but also about providing proper reception, which requires adequate skills among staff, accessible communication, and the adoption of various 'reasonable accommodations,', to be intended, in accordance with Art. 2 of the CRPD, as "necessary and appropriate modification and adjustments not imposing a disproportionate or undue burden, where needed in a particular case, to ensure to persons with disabilities the enjoyment or exercise on an equal basis with others of all human rights and fundamental freedoms."

In short, the interplay between sexist and ableist stereotypes continues to render women with disabilities largely *inessential* subjects when placed on the plate of a hypothetical scales of justice where protection from any form of violence must be ensured.

3.2 Sexual and Reproductive Health for Women with Disabilities

Another area where the inessentiality is very evident is that of sexual and reproductive health rights of women with disabilities. Stereotypes regarding the non-conforming sexuality of women with disabilities also have a major impact on the recognition and/or effectiveness of sexual and reproductive rights, which include both being able to make decisions over sexuality and reproduction, as well as accessing facilities and services related to these decisions.[22]

First, stereotypes concerning disabled women's asexuality and lack of training mean providers are less likely to offer women with disabilities information about contraceptive methods, prevention of sexually transmitted infections (including HIV), or to screen for domestic or sexual violence or reproductive cancers.[23] Little—if any—sexuality education and health counselling is available for these women. However, discrimination does not stop at the level of missing and incorrect information, which is already significant in itself, but also concerns the physical accessibility of obstetrics and gynaecology clinics. Since the latter, as a rule, are still mostly inaccessible to women with disabilities, their right to health—when not openly violated—is structurally at risk.

Furthermore, in the event of becoming pregnant, the stereotype of the 'bad mother' becomes operational: women with disabilities will likely face a very high pressure to end their pregnancy, particularly if they live in social care facilities. The documents where international institutions and non-governmental organizations deal with the issue agree in recognizing its relevance from a human rights perspective. They argue that misleading information related to pregnancy and *post-partum* care—aimed at persuading women with disabilities to terminate their pregnancy—is not only an expression of the false common assumptions spread in society, but also a clear violation of their sexual and reproductive rights, as it undermines their freedom of choice in this field.[24]

---

[22] See Committee on Economic, Social and Cultural Rights, General comment No. 22 (2016) on the right to sexual and reproductive health, E/CN.4/2004/49, para. 5. For the European Disability Forum (2019), p. 3, "[M]enstrual management, forced sterilisation and contraception, female genital mutilation and coerced abortion are just some examples of denial of rights that many women and adolescents with disabilities suffer, without giving their consent or fully understanding the intentions."

[23] Matin et al. (2021).

[24] Cf. Special Rapporteur on the rights of persons with disabilities (2017).

Among the violations of sexual and reproductive rights that have received increasing attention in recent years from international institutions and in public debate is non-consensual and forced sterilization.

At the cultural level, forced sterilization finds its source of legitimacy in both the entrenched stereotype regarding the hyper-sexuality of women with disabilities and the myth of the 'bad mother,' which interact with the more general lack of recognition of the right to legal capacity, due to the stereotype regarding the inability of persons with disabilities. Frequently, decisions about the sexual and reproductive health and rights of women with disabilities are made, on their behalf, by guardians, health professionals and other actors.

Non-consensual sterilization of women with disabilities is a long-standing phenomenon: one of the leading cases on the subject is the well-known *Buck vs. Bell* decision, handed down in 1927 by the U.S. Supreme Court.[25] By eight out of nine votes, the Court ruled that the 1924 Virginia Statute, which at the time considered the sterilization of 'feebleminded'[26] persons lawful, did not violate the equal protection and due process clauses of the U.S. Constitution. On this basis, it allowed the sterilization of Carrie Buck. The ruling was entirely in line with the socio-cultural context of the time, which was heavily influenced by eugenics. As Justice Holmes famously remarked in a now-iconic passage, "It is better for all the world if, instead of waiting to execute degenerate offspring for crime or to let them starve for their imbecility, society can prevent those who are manifestly unfit from continuing their kind [...]. Three generations of imbeciles are enough."[27]

Far from being relegated to the past, forced sterilization is still widely practiced today.[28] To stay within the European context, whereas only 9 EU Member States explicitly criminalize forced sterilization as a distinct offense, at least 13 EU Member States allow some forms of forced sterilization in their legislation, where a guardian, a legal representative, an administrator, or a doctor can authorize the sterilization of a person—usually a woman—with disabilities. In some States, sterilization is even *required* as a condition to access institutions, like social care homes.[29] Clear in this regard is the desire to prevent the occurrence of unwanted pregnancies: the peculiarity

---

[25] For detailed commentary and analysis of the case, see Cohen (2016), Leuchtenburg (1995), Lombardo (2008).

[26] This term was used to refer to all those who were not considered 'normal;' they included people with intellectual disabilities.

[27] Supreme Court of United States, *Buck v. Bell*, 274 U.S. 200 (1927). Although over time the jurisprudential approach in this matter has lost the radical character evident in the case at hand, it has never been explicitly overruled, even though, starting from *Skinner v. Oklahoma*, 316 U.S. 535 (1942), the practice of non-consensual sterilizations has significantly contracted. During the heyday of the eugenics movement, nearly 70000 people were sterilized against their will. They were mostly people who were disabled or perceived as such, and disproportionately Black and brown women.

[28] Non-consensual sterilization is still practiced in various parts of the world, such as Germany, Denmark, Finland, Switzerland, Sweden, England, Norway, Belgium, Austria, India, China, Japan, as well as in some areas of Australia. For further details, see: Open Society Foundation (2011); CERMI and European Disability Forum (2017), CRPD Committee (2016), General Comment n. 3—Article 6: Women and girls with disabilities.

[29] An updated overview is provided in European Disability Forum (2024).

of these settings, which are often isolated and removed from external control, exposes women with disabilities to violence by people around them, whether they were health, service or care workers.[30]

Moreover, the spread of the phenomenon is also influenced by the fact that, even where it is formally prohibited, forced sterilization is often practiced de facto: it is usually hidden behind the removal of uterine fibroids or performed in conjunction with appendectomies, for supposed medical reasons. The situation of particular vulnerability of these women—who often discover they have been subjected to non-consensual sterilization only after many years—means that cases rarely come to the attention of the courts.[31] When this does happen, it is usually possible to identify the persistence of stereotypes about women with disabilities, which often influence not only the legal actors but also the judging bodies.[32]

Among the arguments of those who request or authorize the non-consensual sterilization of a woman with disabilities, the notion of best interest often appears. The reasoning followed is essentially this: unwanted sterilization can be a valid tool for pregnancy prevention and to manage the further medical complications associated with it. It thus primarily serves a medical purpose, protecting the woman's health. Furthermore, it is not uncommon to read considerations regarding the fact that, if a woman with disabilities were to be the victim of sexual assault and become pregnant, this would create a very complicated ethical and medical situation. Therefore, the judging bodies or the other legal actors argue that resorting to a hysterectomy allows for better protection, as it preserves her, given that she is unable to protect herself from potential abuse. Sterilization not only prevents conception but also makes a woman with disabilities "less appealing."[33]

Further best interests are also highlighted. First, sterilization seems to serve the best interests of the caregiver, who will not be burdened with the 'management' of the health of the woman with disabilities (especially regarding menstrual management and personal care), which would become even more complex in the case of a pregnancy. In this way, the caregiver will not even have to take care of the newborn. Finally, sterilization also serves the best interests of the child whose conception is prevented, because, if born, the child would have a mother who is not capable of adequately fulfilling the parental role.

---

[30] Vadysinghe et al. (2017).

[31] The situation of vulnerability is contextual: it is primarily caused by the barriers to access to justice and the degree of proximity that often exists between the person who is the victim of forced sterilization, and the individual recognized as having the power to consent (such as a guardian, who is usually a family member).

[32] An analysis of the arguments of some judges who are in favour of this practice can be found in Powell and Stein (2016), which are summarized here. The role of the judiciary in addressing the harmful gender and intersectional stereotypes related to sexual and reproductive health and rights was analysed in Office of the High Commissioner for Human Rights—OHCHR (2017).

[33] This is how the treating physician and the guardian of an Italian girl with a disability expressed themselves, requesting her sterilization even against her will. In this case, which in Italy has become very well known among those involved in the rights of people with disabilities, the judge rejected the request, considering the proposed solution "completely aberrant." Cf. Trib. Catanzaro, Sez. Civ., decree 18 November 2013 (Judge De Lorenzo).

Upon critical analysis, it is evident how these arguments are based on the stereotypes repeatedly mentioned, such as the need to regulate the sexual activity of women with disabilities by neutralizing its effects, their inability to make conscious self-determined choices, and the myth of the 'bad mother.' Although these stereotypes portray women with disabilities in different ways (too assertive and sexually active, defenceless against violence and therefore in need of protection, or unfit to assume parental responsibility because of their incapacity of understanding its meaning), they converge in justifying the performance of irreversible interventions on their bodies.

From a performative perspective, these arguments even *create* the reality in which sterilization would be functional in *preventing* sexual abuse, where it would even be able to affect the desirability of a body, and in any case could avert the occurrence of pregnancy. It is clear, in fact, how this argument is entirely specious, not only because it is unclear how sterilization could affect a person's external appearance by making her less desirable, but especially because, through it, the cause is confused with the effect: the circumstance that a sexual assault cannot result in pregnancy because the victim has been sterilized does not mean that the act is no longer a violation of human rights and a form of discrimination. Rather, in such cases, sterilization seems aimed at compensating for the gaps in protection and the lack of real and effective support from family and institutions. In short, stereotypes on women with disabilities contribute to devaluing their subjectivity, culturally and legally endorsing the violation of their sexual and reproductive rights. Women with disabilities therefore become bodies that 'do not matter' and, as such, are *inessential.*

4 Women with Disabilities as *Essential* Subjects? Current Situation and Future Perspectives

Although nowadays women with disabilities are expressly recognized by the UN Convention on the rights of persons with disabilities as human rights holders, the analyses conducted in this context have shown that in practice this recognition is largely ineffective. Indeed, the interplay between sexist and ableist stereotypes—sometimes combined with additional stereotypes, primarily related to age—fosters the continuation of structural discrimination, which often has dramatic consequences, particularly in the areas of violence and sexual and reproductive health. Therefore, it seems justified to assume that women with disabilities are *still inessential* subjects.

However, this inessentiality is very different from the one that led Elizabeth Spelman to overlook women with disabilities in the 1990s, inadvertently contributing to their invisibility. Although very slowly, something is changing today, thanks to the advocacy work of women with disabilities, whose legal and political subjectivity can no longer be denied.[34] In addition, multilevel institutions are showing increasing

[34] One need only consider the importance of the three Manifestos on the rights of women and girls with disabilities, adopted by the General Assembly of the European Disability Forum (EDF)

awareness regarding the importance of promoting radical cultural and legal change in relation to women with disabilities. For instance, following the adoption of General Comment No. 3 on Article 6 of the CRPD by the UN Committee on the Rights of Persons with Disabilities, in 2018 the European Economic and Social Committee (EESC) issued a document, prompted by the European Parliament, calling on EU institutions and Member States to take greater action on the protection of women and girls with disabilities. In the same year, the European Parliament adopted Resolution 29 November 2018 on the situation of women with disabilities, highlighting the multiple forms of intersectional discrimination faced by them across all sectors covered by the Istanbul Convention. On July 13, 2021, the Human Rights Council adopted Resolution 47/15 with the aim of accelerating efforts to eliminate all forms of violence against women and girls, also by preventing them. More in general, there is a growing trend to consider also women with disabilities in legal acts that are not specifically dedicated to them (amongst them is the EU Directive 2024/1385 on combating violence against women and domestic violence).

However, this attention remains overly episodic and insufficient. After the formal recognition of women with disabilities as legal subjects, further steps must be taken. In particular, it is crucial to continue deconstructing the stereotypes that remain so stubbornly prevalent in order to eradicate sexism and ableism, which even today interact to obscure the violations of their rights, even going so far as to justify them, as seen in the case of non-consensual sterilization. To this end, it is necessary also to amend the existing regulations that incorporate these stereotypes.

The progress made so far regarding the rights of women with disabilities, although extremely slow and difficult, warrants cautious optimism about the possibility of achieving further results in a not-too-distant future. However, the pervasiveness of rights violations and the widespread lack of social awareness on the condition of these women suggest that they continue to be regarded as *inessential*, with the hope that the moment when they can be considered truly *essential* subjects is nearby.

References

Anderson E (2012) Epistemic justice as a virtue of social institutions. Soc Epistemol 26(2):163–173

Bê A (2019) Feminism and disability. A cartography of multiplicity. In: Watson N et al (eds) Routledge handbook of disability studies. Routledge, London, pp 363–375

Behrman S (2014) Accidents, agency and asylum: Constructing the refugee subject. Law Critique 25:249–270

---

following a proposal from the EDF Women's Committee, for the recognition of these women's rights. Among these documents, particular significance is given to the Second Manifesto (2011), where the rights recognized in the UN Convention on the rights of persons with disabilities are framed specifically for women with disabilities. Through this operation, women with disabilities ideally inherited the teaching of Olympe de Gouges and succeeded in bringing to the attention of the public debate, with a force perhaps hitherto unseen, the importance of their recognition as legal subject and of providing an effective protection to their rights.

Bernardini MG (2023) Vulnerable capacity. Notes on a quiet legal revolution. Int J Semiot Law 36(4):1415–1442
Biaggioni E, Pirrone M (eds) (2018) Shadow report 'Implementation of the Istanbul Convention in Italy: Report of Women's NGOs'
Campbell FK (2001) Inciting legal fictions: disability's date with the ontology and the ableist body of law. Griffith Law Review 10(1):42–62
Carlson L (2001) Cognitive ableism and disability studies: Feminist reflections on the history of mental retardation. Hypatia 16(4):124–146
Carlson L (2010) Philosophers of intellectual disability: a taxonomy. In: Kittay E, Carlson L (eds) Cognitive disability and its challenge to moral philosophy. Wiley-Blackwell, Hoboken (NJ), pp 315–329
CERMI Women's Foundation & European Disability Forum (2017) Joint report ending forced sterilization of women and girls with disabilities. Madrid. https://www.edf-feph.org/publications/ending-forced-sterilisation-of-women-and-girls-with-disabilities/
Cohen A (2016) Imbeciles: the supreme court, American eugenics, and the sterilization of Carrie Buck. Penguin Books, London
Crenshaw K (1989) Demarginalizing the intersection of race and sex. Univ Chic Leg Forum 4:139–167
Crenshaw K (2017) On intersectionality: essential writings. The New Press, New York
CRPD Committee (2016) General Comment n. 3 – Article 6: Women and girls with disabilities. https://www.ohchr.org/en/documents/general-comments-and-recommendations/general-comment-no3-article-6-women-and-girls
European Disability Forum (2019) Sexual and reproductive health and rights of women and girls with disabilities. https://www.edf-feph.org/publications/sexual-and-reproductive-health-and-rights-of-women-and-girls-with-disabilities/
European Disability Forum (2021) Violence against women with disabilities in the European Union—position paper. https://www.edf-feph.org/publications/edf-position-paper-on-violence-against-women-and-girls-with-disabilities-in-the-european-union/
European Disability Forum (2024) EDF Human rights report 2024—legal capacity: personal choice and control, https://www.edf-feph.org/publications/human-rights-report-2024-legal-capacity/
Fricker M (2007) Epistemic injustice: power and the ethics of knowing. Oxford University Press, Oxford
García-Cuéllar MM et al (2023) The prevalence of intimate partner violence against women with disabilities: a systematic review of the literature. Disabil Rehabil 45(1):1–8. https://doi.org/10.1080/09638288.2022.2025927
Garland-Thomson R (2005) Feminist disability studies. Signs 30(2):1557–1587. https://doi.org/10.1086/423352
Hall K (ed) (2011) Feminist disability studies. Indiana University Press, Indiana
Hall K (ed) (2015) New conversations in feminist disability studies. Hypatia 30:1–12
Hunt P (1966) A critical condition. In: Hunt P (ed) Stigma: the experience of disability. Geoffrey Chapman, London, pp 145–159
Kidd J et al (eds) (2019) The Routledge handbook of epistemic injustice. Routledge, New York
Leuchtenburg WE (1995) Mr. Justice Holmes and three generations of imbeciles. In: Leuchtenburg WE (ed) The Supreme Court reborn: The constitutional revolution in the age of Roosevelt. Oxford University Press, Oxford, pp 3–25
Lombardo P (2008) Three generations, no imbeciles: Eugenics, the Supreme Court, and Buck v. Bell. Johns Hopkins University Press, Baltimora,
Matin BK et al (2021) Barriers in access to healthcare for women with disabilities: a systematic review in qualitative studies. BMC Women's Health 21(44). https://doi.org/10.1186/s12905-021-01189-5
Morris J (1992) Tyrannies of perfection. New Int 233:16–17

Office of the High Commissioner for Human Rights—OHCHR (2017) Background paper on the role of the judiciary in addressing the harmful gender stereotypes related to sexual and reproductive health and rights. A review of case law. https://www.ohchr.org/en/women/gender-stereotyping
Open Society Foundation (2011) Against her will: Forced sterilization of women worldwide. https://www.opensocietyfoundations.org/publications/against-her-will-forced-and-coerced-sterilization-women-worldwide
Ortoleva S, Lewis H (2012) Forgotten sisters—a report on violence against women with disabilities: an overview of its nature, scope, causes and consequences. Northeastern University School of Law Research Paper No. 104-2012. https://ssrn.com/abstract=2133332
Powell RM, Stein MA (2016) Persons with disabilities and their sexual, reproductive, and parenting rights: an international and comparative analysis. Frontiers of Law in China 11(1):53–85
Ralston DC, Ho J (2009) Introduction: philosophical reflections on disability. In: Ralston DC, Ho J (eds) Philosophical reflections on disability. Springer, Dordrecht, pp 1–16
Special Rapporteur on the rights of persons with disabilities (2017) Sexual and reproductive health and rights of girls and young women with disabilities. New York. https://www.ohchr.org/en/documents/thematic-reports/a72133-sexual-and-reproductive-health-and-rights-girls-and-young-women
Spelman E (1990) Inessential woman. The Women's Press, London
Spelman E (1997) Fruits of sorrow: framing our attention to suffering. Beacon Press, Boston
Stienstra D (2019) Race/ethnicity and disability studies. Towards an explicitly intersectional approach. In: Watson N et al (eds) Routledge handbook of disability studies. Routledge, London, pp 376–389
Tronto J (1993) Moral boundaries: a political argument for an ethics of care. Routledge, New York
Vadysinghe AN et al (2017) A study on sexual violence inflicted on individuals with intellectual developmental disorder. Disabil Health J 10(3):451–454
World Health Organization (2024) Measuring violence against women with disability: data availability, methodological issues and recommendations for good practice. https://www.who.int/publications/i/item/9789240089563

Maria Giulia Bernardini (Ph.D. in Human Rights, University of Palermo) is Associate Professor of Philosophy of Law in the Department of Law at the University of Ferrara, where she teaches Law and Gender and Legal Clinic on Disability and Human Rights. Her work focuses on critical theory, with particular reference to Feminist & Gender Studies, Disability Studies, and Elder Studies, also from an intersectional perspective (with a particular focus on women with disabilities). Together with Orsetta Giolo and Javier Ansuategui Roig, she founded the permanent inter-university seminar Gender Justice & Feminist Jurisprudence, where the role of stereotypes in judicial reasoning is analysed.

Gender Stereotypes in Law and Women's Work

Orsetta Giolo

Abstract The issue of gender stereotypes in contemporary law is not a novel question and may be addressed following the approach of feminist legal critique. This process requires examining the persistence of discriminatory structures within legal practices and engaging in further reflection in order to deconstruct the sexist forms and methods embedded in the law. This essay will first summarize the feminist legal critique of stereotypes, focusing on their discriminatory function. It will then explore the invisibilization of women's work as a case study, examining how gender stereotypes have historically influenced and continue to influence law broadly—not merely in judicial decisions or jurisprudential practices—and how they are constantly repositioned and redefined.

Keywords Stereotypes · Gender · Work · Subjectivity · Feminist legal theory

1 The Critique of Gender Stereotypes in Feminist Legal Theory

The critique of gender stereotypes in law has a long history, dating back to the early reflections of feminist legal thought.[1]

The feminist critique of law has primarily focused on deconstructing the masculine canon that law historically embodies. This critique has revealed the stereotyped and homogenizing representation of women perpetuated by the patriarchal system

[1] An earlier version of this essay was published in Giolo (2024a, 2024b). Regarding the early origins of the critique of gender stereotypes, see, for example, the renowned statement by Carol Smart on male, sexist, and gendered law, cf. Smart (1992) and Scales (1992). Cf. Htun and Weldon (2018); Macduff and Gozdecka (2020). For a recent analysis, with reference to the Italian debate, cf. Morondo Taramundi (2022), Simone et al. (a cura di) (2019), Casadei (2015).

O. Giolo (✉)
Orsetta Giolo, University of Ferrara, Ferrara, Italy
e-mail: glirtt@unife.it

A. Condello and A. Wagner (eds.), *Gender Stereotypes*, Gender, Justice and Legal Feminism 2, https://doi.org/10.1007/978-3-031-63905-0_7

through norms and practices.[2] It has made evident the presence of notions, concepts, expressions, and beliefs that are deeply discriminatory toward women and rooted in culturally constructed and ideologically justified imaginaries.

The issue of gender stereotypes in contemporary law is therefore not a novel question and may be addressed following the approach of feminist legal critique. This process requires examining the persistence of discriminatory structures within legal practices and engaging in further reflection in order to deconstruct the sexist forms and methods embedded in the law. In this context, the critique of stereotypes, particularly gender stereotypes, serves as an essential tool for exploring the subtler mechanisms within the legal framework that manipulate and suppress women's subjectivity. These mechanisms confine women to predefined categories aimed at their hierarchical subordination through misrecognition and subjugation.

A notable example of this can be seen in the growing focus on feminist analyses of legal language: the problematization of expressions and terms used in legal documents, particularly in judgments,[3] has highlighted the link between linguistic practices and discriminatory practices. This connection has become so evident that it has led to judicial rulings, sanctions, and recommendations urging states to combat the use of stereotypes in law.[4]

The increasing attention to this issue—at both a theoretical and institutional level and in public debate- could effectively aid in dismantling the discriminatory practices persisting within the law. However, alongside this valuable and collective reflection, it is also crucial to question the reasons behind such growing attention. This helps to understand why new rhetoric on the subject is emerging and to remain vigilant against a potential distortion of the debate.

This essay will first summarize the feminist legal critique of stereotypes, focusing on their discriminatory function. It will then explore the invisibilization of women's work as a case study, examining how gender stereotypes have historically influenced and continue to influence law broadly—not merely in judicial decisions or jurisprudential practices—and how they are constantly repositioned and redefined.

---

[2] On this point, I would also like to refer to Facchi and Giolo (2023).

[3] See, for example, the work of analysis and rewriting described in Hunter et al. (2010).

[4] Some examples in this regard, with exclusive reference to Italy, can be found in the judgment of the European Court of Human Rights in the case *J.L. v. Italy* (application no. 5671/16) in 2021 and the decision of the CEDAW Committee in the case *F. v. Italy* (148/2019) dated June 20, 2022.

2 Challenging the Neutrality of Stereotypes in Law: Conceptions and Uses

The literature on stereotypes is interdisciplinary and extensive, though not always rooted in feminist perspectives. It is important to emphasize this because the viewpoints of women or non-paradigmatic subjects[5] do not necessarily enjoy a privileged position within these discussions. Legal studies on stereotypes, although abundant and referencing various national, European, and supranational legal systems, appear more attuned to feminist legal approaches to some extent.[6]

This wealth of material and diversity of approaches has inevitably led to significant confusion, particularly as regards attempts to integrate cognitive science theories into legal reflection without sufficiently considering the peculiarities of law. For instance, there is no clear consensus on the distinction between stereotypes and prejudices in legal contexts.[7] The two terms are sometimes used synonymously in legal texts and legal doctrine,[8] while at other times they are treated as distinct elements of a discriminatory belief system.[9]

There is also uncertainty about whether stereotypes should be considered neutral, positive, or negative, whether their nature is descriptive or prescriptive, and whether their functions are relevant on a cognitive level or specifically tied to discrimination.[10] These ambiguities complicate the analysis further, especially given the frequent conflation of stereotypes and generalizations within legal discourse.[11] Generalizations, being common in law, often appear to incorporate stereotypes, thereby neutralizing them or making it difficult for the law to function without reference to groups and categories or collective traits.

Despite these challenges, it may be possible to clarify the role of stereotypes within legal discourse by distinguishing between different fields of analysis and maintaining clear perspectives. Doing so could aid in understanding not only what a stereotype is but also how it operates within legal discourse, its effects, and its functions.

---

[5] By the term 'non-paradigmatic subjects' I mean individuals who have traditionally not held positions of dominance within society and who have therefore been, and continue to be, marginalized in legal and political theory. See Bernardini and Giolo (a cura di) (2017).

[6] See, for example, the well-known work by Rebecca Cook and Simone Cusack in Cook and Cusack (2010), and, among others, the studies by Alexandra Timmer, particularly Brems and Timmer (2016), Timmer (2011, 2016).

[7] On the indeterminacy and uncertainty with which the concept of stereotypes is addressed in the literature, see Ghidoni and Morondo Taramundi (2022). See also Timmer (2015).

[8] See, for instance, the recent observations by Costanza Nardocci on the lack of a unanimous consensus in the literature regarding the relationship between stereotypes and prejudices, in Nardocci (2023), at p. 2.

[9] For further analysis, see De Giuli (2023a). See also, among others, Dovidio et al. (2010), and Stangor (2000).

[10] Arena (coordinador) (2022).

[11] Arena (2016).

In this regard, it is perhaps possible to argue, in agreement with part of the legal-philosophical literature and from a feminist perspective,[12] that stereotypes in law never possess a neutral value and always assume a negative connotation, because their use in law invariably has negative effects on individuals. Stereotypes stigmatize, serialize, and homogenize by attributing to an individual characteristics and qualities that neither naturally nor personally belong to them. This prevents the judiciary from reaching an "individualized"[13] decision, one built upon the specific needs and circumstances of the individual to whom the stereotype is applied.

When one analyzes the use of stereotypes in law as a whole—within legislative processes, application practices, legal interpretation, and judicial decisions—their negative connotation becomes even more evident. However, the confusion stereotypes generate among the various layers of legal language is probably the most important aspect of their usage. A stereotype can be characterized as a proposition or descriptive statement regarding dominant traits of certain social groups. Indeed, the qualification of a stereotype often relies on the true/false dichotomy inherent to such statements.[14] Nevertheless, upon closer inspection, stereotypes—while purporting to function as propositions (empirical or analytical[15])—inevitably operate as norms directed at the legal community as a whole.

In legal and judicial practices, stereotypes converge insofar as their "normative"[16] usage is concerned: even when they are presumed to facilitate understanding by providing standardized information about the individual to whom they refer, they still serve functions of orientation/determination in shaping subjectivity, leading to discrimination and subjugation. Stereotypes define the characteristics to be attributed to a subject but also impose corresponding behaviors to be adopted toward that subject.[17]

Therefore, when stereotypes enter the legal domain, they assume a normative value by virtue of the specific use made of them by legal actors (legislators, judges, lawyers, etc.).

---

[12] See Ghidoni and Morondo Taramundi (2022).

[13] Arena (2024).

[14] In this perspective, the distinction between simple stereotypes and 'statistical-based' stereotypes is also problematic. The latter are thought to carry a descriptive value because they purportedly reflect characteristics that, statistically, are significantly associated with a group of individuals. However, one must question whether statistics can accurately represent these characteristics without themselves reinforcing stereotypes or prejudices (e.g., statistics showing that women are still predominantly engaged in caregiving work cannot assert anything about whether women are naturally inclined to perform such tasks). See the arguments made by Federico Arena in Arena (2023) and the critiques contained in Poggi (2023), and in De Giuli (2023b). See also, on the precariousness of statistical foundations, Moschel (2015 at p. 446).

[15] On the distinction between empirical and analytical propositions, see Barberis (2008, p. 65 ff).

[16] Baratta (1968, p. 17 ff).

[17] Ghidoni and Morondo Taramundi (2024).

3 The Functions of Stereotypes: Between Traditional and New Stereotyping

As if in a game of mirrors, the conceptions, uses and functions of stereotypes tend to mutually define each other, with each one influencing the others. To investigate the conceptions of stereotypes in law, one must necessarily inquire not only (or primarily) into their nature, but also and above all into the functions they perform—functions that are specifically connected to the different phases of legal experience.

Given their multifaceted operation (stereotypes may intervene in the creation of norms, their interpretation, the reconstruction of facts in litigation, and the reasoning process leading to decisions[18]), it is possible to argue that their "classic" function pertains to the need for hierarchization inherent in certain legal contexts where it becomes necessary to reaffirm the subordination of certain social groups and subjects. In this sense, stereotypes—which always have a negative connotation—function as vehicles of misrecognition and subjugation of so-called non-paradigmatic subjectivities.

This "classic" function has long pervaded the entire legal experience. Many principles, concepts, and notions in law (such as *infirmitas sexus* or "racial hierarchy", to name a few) have been developed for this purpose, contributing to the construction of discriminatory legal systems. It is no coincidence that what we today qualify as a stereotype was, for centuries, sanctioned in law as legitimate, well-founded, natural, and *just*.

Thus, the use of stereotypes is never random, accidental, or unconscious; it is always connected to the intention of reaffirming a specific hierarchy of humanity, situating the individuals to whom it applies in a defined position and condition.

This becomes particularly evident in the judicial process, indeed many stances taken by supranational bodies and institutions have been expressed through the drafting of judgments. In litigation, stereotypes allow outdated notions (such as the emotionality or irrationality of women) to re-enter the legal discourse through erroneous interpretation or reasoning. Furthermore, stereotypes are used to undermine the credibility of non-paradigmatic subjects, who consequently face greater difficulty in having their claims recognized. So-called "testimonial injustice"[19] seems directly linked to such critical issues.

Alongside this "classic" function, however, new functions that stereotypes seem to perform in the contemporary legal domain must also be considered.

The current reliance on stereotypes also appears to respond to new demands aligned with the imperatives of the neoliberal paradigm. In the current transitional phase, the reconfiguration of subjectivity is leading to the emergence of new

---

[18] On this latter point, see Ghidoni (2022, at p. 304).

[19] The expression was famously coined by Miranda Fricker, who defined it as the primary manifestation of so-called epistemic injustice, in Fricker (2009). On testimonial injustice, see Munroe (2016).

forms of stereotyping, primarily linked to the neoliberal rules of performance and competitiveness.[20]

For instance, those in a condition of subjugation, discrimination, or exploitation are classified as 'vulnerable'.[21] Similarly, those who do not conform to the model of the 'achievement-subject' are labeled as risks, dangers, or threats to society.[22] Likewise, those who reject the rule of competitiveness are portrayed as indolent or incapable.[23]

The new function expressed by these emergent stereotypes in the legal field thus appears as an additional version or contingent specification of the classical hierarchizing function of stereotypes. By redefining subjectivity through a neoliberal lens, these new stereotypes introduce new criteria, still aimed at inferiorizing and serializing individuals based on their condition, identity, or will.

4 The Ambiguities of Institutional Critiques of Stereotypes

Attention towards stereotypes on the part of institutions, courts and political actors, as noted, has undoubtedly increased in recent years at both national and international levels. Numerous official documents, public statements, and legal acts denounce the widespread persistence of stereotypes and call for overcoming and removing them.

While this new stance is certainly significant and marks a historical shift in the deconstruction of stereotypical representations of historically oppressed groups, some problematic aspects should not be overlooked because of excessive enthusiasm.

It is first necessary to clarify the type of stereotypes to which such criticism is directed. The impression is that these denunciations are focused exclusively on stereotypes that perpetuate "classic" categories of discrimination.

In contrast, new stereotypes—those reflecting the increasing prominence of neoliberal subjectivity—seem entirely neglected. While they are the subject of academic analysis (as evidenced by the extensive literature on vulnerability), there appears to be little in them among political and judicial actors. In fact, public policies over the past decades seem to embrace the (neoliberal) figure of the "achievement-subject", as demonstrated by the pervasive adoption of procedures aimed at measuring productivity and individual performance.

---

[20] The late-modern achievement-subject, as emphasized by Byung-Chul Han, is not subjected to anyone but instead becomes positive, even liberated, as a project. However, the shift from subject to project, according to Han, does not eliminate constraints but rather leads to self-discipline, culminating in self-exploitation; see Han (2015). See also, among others, Vida (2022).

[21] On the uses (and ambiguous outcomes) of the notion of vulnerability, see for example Peroni and Timmer (2013); I would refer also to Giolo and Pastore (2018), and more recently, Bernardini and Lorubbio (2023).

[22] Simon (1988, at p. 790 ff) Cf. Beck (1992).

[23] On the consequences of 'absolute competition', see also Han (2024).

On an institutional level, therefore, criticism is directed at the classic stereotypes, while the rise of new stereotyping—equally hierarchizing, discriminatory, and subordinating—remains unaddressed. Moreover, the exclusive focus on traditional stereotypes seems to align (consistently with neoliberal ideology) with the reduction of the political to the psychological sphere, through a process of "psychologization" of discrimination. From this perspective, discriminatory actions are seen as deriving from individual attitudes rather than being rooted in socially entrenched structures of domination.[24] Discriminatory feelings or ideas are thus expressed through stereotypes as the actions of individuals who, individually and erroneously, choose to rely on them.[25]

This widespread understanding of stereotypes makes any reference to the social structures producing discrimination disappear—particularly when they are structural and systemic—along with references to the cultural and ideological apparatus legitimizing them.

A rigorous analysis of the contemporary function of stereotypes must necessarily avoid falling into neoliberal rhetoric and remain vigilant about the ongoing transformation of the categories of domination.

5 The Specificities of Gender Stereotypes in Law

The general discourse on stereotypes in law outlined thus far must be examined in light of the specific category of gender stereotypes, which remain present in the legal field.

Institutional criticism has been predominantly directed at these stereotypes, making them perhaps the most scrutinized category in contemporary investigations and deconstruction efforts.

An analysis of existing literature reveals the complexity of the subject and its resistance to the "sanitized" analysis—occasionally proposed by cognitive sciences—that isolates concepts and notions from the contexts in which they were and continue to be produced. This complexity arises for several reasons.

First, the term 'gender stereotypes' refers, through the concept of gender, to the cultural and social construct that has, for centuries, constrained the identity, subjectivity, and agency of women.[26] Gender stereotypes, understood in this way, cannot be regarded as neutral or positive, as they often directly caused the severe

---

[24] A different approach is taken in the analysis of stereotypes as part of 'a system of beliefs that perpetuates a discriminatory culture and serves to justify and legitimize it' (thus avoiding the neutralization of the social, ideological, and political dimensions of discrimination), as discussed in De Giuli (2023b), pp. 285–304.

[25] Errors in law (so-called biases) are deemed ultimately to depend on subjective attitudes and behaviors that convey discrimination, primarily due to 'unintentional prejudices, ignorance, or superficiality' on the part of individuals. See Furedi (2003, at p. 24 ff).

[26] Consider, for example, Judith Butler's insights in her deconstruction of gender as a 'natural' category, as discussed in Butler (2004).

discrimination women faced until the advent of equality. It should be emphasized that gender stereotypes clearly illustrate the confusion arising between the descriptive and prescriptive dimensions that generally characterize stereotypes, due to a constant shift from the normative plane of culturally imposed expectations to the descriptive plane of natural attributes. In gender stereotypes, nature and culture (being and ought to be) clearly overlap, to the advantage of the former: this confusion, as is well known, allowed ideologically determined cultural attributions (from irrationality to caregiving obligations) to be classified as natural characteristics of women for centuries.

Second, the language of law, like language in general, is neither neutral nor unbiased; rather, it is deeply gendered and sexist. Letizia Gianformaggio, quoting Adriana Cavarero, wrote: "[l]anguage is indeed one of the institutions within which women operate—institutions ostensibly neutral but which instead are the result of a male, masculinist, and patriarchal construction."[27] The use of gender stereotypes in law takes place through this very language, thereby negating any hypothetical neutral or positive value they might otherwise hold.

Third, the issue of gender stereotypes demonstrates that the critique of stereotypes, as a whole, cannot be confined to an analysis of specific expressions or statements. Instead, the critique must directly investigate the forms (both historical and contemporary) of domination, discrimination, and oppression, which also means engaging in an analysis of the themes underlying the complex and rich feminist critique of law.

Critiquing stereotypes, particularly gender stereotypes, requires recognizing their complexity and avoiding an overly narrow or neutralizing focus. A stereotype is essentially *a practice* that participate —confusedly, contradictorily, and rhetorically—in the subordination of women.

As Carla Lonzi wrote, women are "complete individuals." Thus, transformation should not be imposed upon women themselves but rather on how women perceive themselves "within the universe" and how "others perceive them".[28]

6 Case Study: Stereotypes About Women's Work as Tools of Invisibilization of Legal and Political Subjectivity

The invisibility of women's work is a central—not incidental—element of the centuries-long marginalization of women's legal and political subjectivity.[29]

The invisibility of subjectivity has found a key mechanism in the concealment of women's work, which has enabled the erasure of the female presence in various public spheres while consolidating their roles in the domestic domain. The definition of women's work has consistently relied on "external parameters", detached from women's experiences as working subjects, and instead rooted in presumed natural

[27] Gianformaggio (2005, at p. 109).

[28] Lonzi (1974, p. 56).

[29] An earlier version of the following paragraphs was published in Giolo (2023).

aptitudes and socially constructed roles. These roles, defined across eras, have been used to facilitate, limit, or outright prevent women's access to certain professions.[30] The issue of labor is therefore tied to the history of women's invisibility and is closely connected to their very absence from history.[31]

The constant *diminution* of women's participation in various professions has been achieved through the use of specific stereotypes, which, when legally codified, have facilitated the systematic reduction of women's work to a mere activity in support of the family.[32] This stereotypical construction of women's presence in the workforce reflects many of the reasons behind the current challenges women continue to face, both in asserting their subjectivity and in professional contexts. Stereotypical narratives, representations, and rhetoric about women's roles and functions have, for centuries, obscured the actual relevance of women's productive work while entirely devaluing—and rendering unpaid—the reproductive labor traditionally assigned to them.[33]

Despite women's constant contributions in the private and public spheres, their efforts and labor have often been treated as "secondary" in legislative and representational terms. Women's work has been characterized as optional, part-time or full-time, temporary or otherwise, depending on life stages.

This leads to two key considerations. The first consideration concerns the marginalization of work in defining women's subjectivity, in contrast with its classic role as foundational for male subjectivity, particularly since the liberal and capitalist notions of society and markets displaced feudal structures.[34] The second consideration pertains to the power of stereotypes in creating distorted representations of reality, resulting in deeply entrenched beliefs that lack correspondence with actual experience.

6.1 *Stereotypes as Techniques of Invisibilization: Exclusion, Protection, Confinement, and Expropriation*

Four primary techniques of invisibilizing women's labor have been systematically employed, facilitated by stereotypes that have been absorbed and reinforced in various ways within the legal sphere: exclusion, protection, confinement, and expropriation.

Exclusion has perhaps most radically embodied the link between labor and gender stereotypes, using the latter as a foundation for the formal expulsion of women from productive work. This was achieved through legally sanctioned barriers preventing women from accessing certain roles and professions. For instance, the prohibition on

---

[30] Stolzi (2019, at p. 254).

[31] The difference of women is millennia of absence from history, writes Lonzi (1974, p. 15).

[32] Groppi (2004, at p. 269 ff.).

[33] On this point, see generally Federici (2021a, b).

[34] Pescarolo (2019, p. 17 ff.).

access to *virilia officia*[35] was originally based on the *infirmitas sexus* criterion, closely tied to the stereotype that women were incapable, irrational, and non-autonomous subjects.[36] This technique was particularly prevalent in the past, as most of these prohibitions and their corresponding legal norms have been eliminated—though some exceptions persist[37]—thus enabling women to formally access all types of productive work.

However, other techniques have not been entirely dispensed with and seem to persist, perpetuated by the law itself and the stereotypes it continues to convey. The stereotype of the female subject as inherently in need of protection, based on her presumed incapacity, has long resulted in the suppression of women's presence in certain sectors, and was often used in the past to justify their exclusion from the public sphere and their confinement to the domestic realm. Protection and confinement (sometimes difficult to discern) once relegated women to the domestic sphere, deemed the "safest" space where their "natural functions" could be fulfilled. Under liberal conceptions, the domestic sphere became *private*, further solidifying its role as a space of concealment and *deprivation* for women,[38] reducing their labor to family caregiving.[39]

Protection and confinement remain evident today in stereotypes and rhetoric that continue to attribute a natural predisposition for caregiving to women. These narratives support laws that fail to promote the redistribution of domestic workloads. Domestic labor is often obscured and neutralized by framing it within caregiving practices, predominantly interpreted as feminine rather than from a feminist standpoint.[40] This creates a trap—evident in debates on the work-life balance—which overwhelmingly burdens women in contemporary societies, perpetuating the invisibilization of their labor.[41] This is achieved by avoiding work-related language and prioritizing rhetoric centered on affectivity and familial bonds.

Similarly, the technique of expropriation seems to remain the primary method for neutralizing women's labor and subjectivity in contemporary contexts, supported by a legal discourse ambiguously invoking themes of freedom and autonomy. Historically, expropriation involved stripping women of ownership over their labor and resources, allowing men to exclusively benefit from women's work. A notable example is the

[35] Luminoso (1984, p. 1184); see also Morelli (2016).

[36] See Graziosi (1993), D'Amico and Leone (a cura di) (2017).

[37] However, even in the most resistant contexts, use of this technique seems to be gradually declining: consider that even in Saudi Arabia, a country known for imposing major restrictions on women's rights, a plan has been underway for years (the *Saudi Vision 2030* Program) to promote women's participation in the workforce.

[38] Gianformaggio (2005, p. 165 ff.).

[39] Nancy Fraser recently wrote about a 'crisis of care', which can be interpreted as an expression of the contradictions of financial capitalism regarding social reproduction, in Fraser (2021).

[40] See Carol Gilligan in Gilligan (2011, at pp. 319–320).

[41] Federici (2020, at p. 43).

case of "bailiffs"—husbands of wet nurses who were legally recognized, in 15th-century Florence, as the proprietors of their wives' work and even their milk.[42] Today, expropriation again manifests itself in practices that exploit women's bodies, perpetuating male appropriation of women's lives under the guise of "free choice". This rhetoric risks becoming a new stereotype, legitimizing practices of self-exploitation.

Women have always performed work, but their participation in the realm of labor (productive and reproductive) has consistently been subject to misrepresentation and erasure, perpetuated by powerful gender stereotypes legally established over time.

From an intersectional perspective, it becomes clear that exclusion, protection, confinement, and expropriation affect all women but with particularly devastating consequences for those who do not conform to the paradigm of the (legally and politically dominant) white, affluent individual. Historically, enslaved and servile women, and today, women who are victims of trafficking and sexual and labor exploitation, represent the most pervasive iterations of these techniques. These phenomena reveal the dangerous intersection of multiple stereotypes (concerning race, class, migration, victimhood, and others), which extend beyond the dispossession of subjectivity to its total objectification.[43]

The invisibilization of their labor can thus be interpreted as a consequence of the male monopoly over narrative frameworks. Through gender stereotypes, men have rhetorically neutralized the specific techniques aimed at disempowering and hollowing out female subjectivity.

References

Arena FJ (2016) Los estereotipos normativos en la decisión judicial. Una exploración conceptual. Revista de Derecho XXIX(1):51–75

Arena FJ (coord) (2022) Manual sobre los effectos de los estereotipos en la impartición de justicia. Suprema Corte de Justicia de la Nación, Ciudad de Mexico

Arena FJ (2023) I due volti degli stereotipi nel diritto. Notizie di Politeia 149(39):5–25

Arena FJ (2024) Stereotipi e il dovere di trattare le altre persone come individui. In: Bernardini MG, Giolo O (a cura di) Giudizio e pregiudizio. Gli stereotipi di genere nel diritto. Giappichelli, Torino, pp 35-50.

Baratta A (1968) Ricerche su "essere" e "dover essere". Nell'esperienza normativa e nella scienza del diritto. Giuffrè, Milano

Barberis M (2008) Filosofia del diritto. Un'introduzione teorica. Giappichelli, Torino

Beck U (1992) Risk society. Towards a new modernity. Sage Publications, London

---

[42] Pescarolo (2019, p. 14). The author writes that the work of wives, whether at home or outside, was therefore inseparable from the figure of the husband, and women were even deprived of control over their earnings. In that context, necessity drove wives and children from poor families to work in external and highly visible environments; these behaviors, tied to widespread poverty, were tolerated and considered inevitable. However, the female contribution was concealed by a veil that rendered it invisible, and husbands aspiring to respectability regarded women's activities as an affront when carried out in public, even though such activities were well accepted when carried out discreetly.

[43] For a recent analysis of the interaction between labor, social reproduction, gender, and race, with specific reference to the context of migration, see Rigo (2022, particularly p. 29 ff).

Bernardini MG, Giolo O (a cura di) (2017) Le teorie critiche del diritto. Pacini, Pisa
Bernardini MG, Lorubbio V (eds) (2023) Diritti umani e condizioni di vulnerabilità. Erickson, Trento
Brems E, Timmer A (eds) (2016) Stereotypes and human rights law. Intersentia
Butler J (2004) Undoing gender. Taylor & Francis Ltd, Milton Park
Casadei Th (a cura di) (2015) Donne, diritto, diritti. Prospettive del giusfemminismo. Giappichelli, Torino
Cook R, Cusack S (2010) Gender stereotyping: transnational legal perspectives. University of Pennsylvania, Philadelphia
D'Amico M, Leone S (a cura di) (2017). Dalla fragilitas sexus alla pienezza dei diritti? Un percorso non ancora concluso. Giuffrè, Milano
De Giuli A (2023a) Igualdad y creencias discriminatorias: de las ciencias psicológicas al ámbito jurídico. Revista Internacional De Pensamiento Político" 18(18):285–304
De Giuli A (2023b) Gli stereotipi e la tensione tra vulnerabilità e autonomia. Notizie di Politeia 149(39):35–39
Dovidio JF, Hewstone M, Glick P, Esses VM (eds) (2010) The SAGE handbook of prejudice, stereotyping and discrimination. Sage Publications, London
Facchi A, Giolo O (2023) Una storia dei diritti delle donne. il Mulino, Bologna
Federici S (2021a) Gréve du travail reproductif et constructions de communs reproductifs. In: Federici S, Simonet M, Morteuil M, Kaehni M (eds) Travail gratuit et grèves feminists. Entremonde, Génève-Paris, pp 26–47
Federici S (2021b) Caliban and the witch: women, the body and primitive accumulation. Penguin Classics, London
Fraser N (2021) Gender, capital, and care. In: Browne J (ed) Why Gender? Cambridge University Press, Cambridge, pp 144–169
Fricker M (2009) Epistemic injustice: power and the ethics of knowing. Oxford University Press, Oxford
Furedi F (2003) Therapy culture: cultivating vulnerability in an uncertain age. Routledge, New York
Gianformaggio L (2005) Politica delle identità (o delle differenze). In: EAD., Eguaglianza, donne, diritto. il Mulino, Bologna, pp. 107–124
Ghidoni E (2022) Aproximación a los estereotipos como elementos del razonamiento judicial a través de las presunciones. In: Arena FJ (coordinador) Manual sobre los efectos de los estereotipos en la impartición de justicia. Suprema Corte de Justicia de la Nación, Ciudad de Mexico, pp 299–325
Ghidoni E, Morondo Taramundi D (2022) El papel de los estereotipos en las formas de la desigualdad compleja: algunos apuntes desde la teoría feminista del derecho antidiscriminatorio. Discusiones 28(1):37–70
Ghidoni E, Morondo Taramundi D (2024) Contro la neutralità dello stereotipo: una lettura critica a partire dal giusfemminismo. In Bernardini MG, Giolo O (a cura di) Giudizio e pregiudizio. Gli stereotipi di genere nel diritto. Giappichelli, Torino, pp 13–33
Gilligan C (2011) La resistenza all'ingiustizia: un'etica femminista della cura. Iride 24:315–330
Giolo O (2023) L'invisibilità (giuridica?) del lavoro delle donne. Esclusione, protezione, confinamento ed espropriazione. Materiali per una storia della cultura giuridica 1:67–78
Giolo O (2024a) La critica femminista degli stereotipi di genere nel diritto: concezioni, usi, funzioni, retoriche. In Bernardini MG, Giolo O (a cura di) Giudizio e pregiudizio. Gli stereotipi di genere nel diritto. Giappichelli, Torino, pp 1–11
Giolo O (2024b) Accesso alla giustizia e funzioni degli stereotipi nel paradigma neoliberale. In: Ansuategui Roig FJ, Barranco MC (Editores) Cultura juridica y barreras en el acceso a la j ustìcia. Tirant lo blanc, Valencia pp 97–122
Giolo O, Pastore B (eds) (2018) Vulnerabilità. Analisi multidisciplinare di un concetto. Carocci, Roma
Graziosi M (1993) Infirmitas sexus. La donna nell'immaginario penalistico. Democrazia e Diritto 2:99–143

Groppi A (2004) Ottica di genere e lavoro in età moderna. In: Calvi G (a cura di) Innesti. Donne e genere nella storia sociale. Viella, Roma, pp 259–275
Han BC (2015) The burnout society. Stanford University Press, Stanford
Han BC (2024) Vita Contemplativa. Polity Press, New York, In Praise of Inactivity
Htun M, Weldon SL (eds) (2018) The logics of gender justice: state action on women's rights around the world. Cambridge University Press, Cambridge
Hunter RM, McGlynn C, Rackley E (eds) (2010) Feminist judgments: from theory to practice. Hart Publishing, London
Lonzi C (1974) Sputiamo su Hegel, Scritti di Rivolta femminile. Milano, Et. Al edizioni
Luminoso A (1984) La condizione giuridica delle donne in Italia, tra passato, presente e avvenire. Il Diritto di Famiglia e Delle Persone 13:1184
Macduff A, Gozdecka D (eds) (2020) Feminism, postfeminism and legal theory: beyond the gendered subject. Routledge, London
Morondo Taramundi D (2022) Il contributo degli studi di genere al diritto. Orizzontale, obliquo o tangenziale?. In: Casadei Th, Giolo O, Pozzolo S, Re L, (a cura di) Tra società e diritto. L'impatto degli studi di genere. Filosofia del diritto 2:305–317
Moschel M (2015) La tutela giuridica contro gli stereotipi di genere. Rivista Critica Del Diritto Privato 33:443–466
Munroe W (2016) Testimonial injustice and prescriptive credibility deficits. Can J Philos 46(6):924–947
Nardocci C (2023) La generalizzazione irragionevolmente discriminatoria: lo stereotipo di genere tra diritto e corti. GenIus—Rivista di studi giuridici sull'orientamento sessuale e l'identità di genere 20:1–30
Peroni L, Timmer A (2013) Vulnerable groups: the promise of an emerging concept in European human rights convention law. International Journal of Constitutional Law 11(4):1056–1085
Pescarolo A (2019) Il lavoro delle donne nell'Italia contemporanea. Viella, Roma
Poggi F (2023) Contro gli stereotipi nel diritto. Note a margine della teoria di F.J. Arena. Notizie di Politeia 39(149):26–31
Rigo E (2022) La straniera. Migrazioni, asilo, sfruttamento in una prospettiva di genere. Carocci, Roma
Scales A (1992) Feminist legal method: not so scary. 2 UCLA Women's Law J 1:1–34
Simon J (1988) The ideological effects of actuarial practices. Law Soc Rev 22(4):771–800
Simone A, Boiano I, Condello A (a cura di) (2019) Femminismo giuridico. Teorie e problem. Mondadori, Milano
Smart C (1992) The woman of legal discourse. Soc Leg Stud 1:22–44
Stangor C (2000) Stereotypes and prejudice: essential readings. Psychology Press, Philadelphia
Stolzi I (2019) La parità ineguale. Il lavoro delle donne in Italia fra storia e diritto. Stud Stor 2:253–287
Timmer A (2011) Toward an anti-stereotyping approach for the European court of human rights. Hum Rights Law Rev 11(4):707–738
Timmer A (2015) Judging stereotypes: what the European Court of human rights can borrow from American and Canadian equal protection law. The American Journal of Comparative Law 63:239–284
Timmer A (2016) Gender stereotyping in the case law of the EU court of justice. European Equality Law Review 1:37–46
Vida S (2022) Neoliberismo, biopolitica e schiavitù. Il capitale umano in tempo di crisi. Cosmopolis. Rivista di Filosofia e teoria politica 1

Orsetta Giolo is Associate Professor in Philosophy of Law at the Department of Law of the University of Ferrara. She is a member of the Board of Directors of Macrocrimes – European Legal Studies Centre on Major Crime (http://www.macrocrimes.eu/it/). Since 2010, she has co-coordinated, together with Lucia Re, il Gruppo di lavoro interuniversitario sulla soggettività politica delle donne She is also a member of the coordinating body of the GIFTS Network – Gender Studies (https://retegifts.wordpress.com) and one of the founding members of ASGGE – Association for Legal Gender Studies. With Maria Giulia Bernardini, she founded the permanent inter-university seminar Gender Justice & Feminist Jurisprudence, where the role of stereotypes in judicial reasoning is analyzed.

Part II
Thinking, Constructing, and Narrating Gender: Practices and Policies

Breastification: Performativity, Presumption, Possibility

Sarah Marusek and Anne Wagner

Abstract The breast is an aspect of anatomy that both female and male bodies share. The size, shape, age, and perceived use of the breast leads to stereotyping about gender fluidity and the disconnect between one's self-identity and how that identity is received or interpreted. The bosom, underboob, overboob, breasts, however they are called, become a visual of perceived identity; yet, often that identity is itself an objectification of the body to whom they belong. This chapter will examine the many aspects of 'the breast' from those bodies born female, to those born male, and those bodies transitioning in-between. The aesthetic, use, stereotype, form and function of the breast as either a productive, inoperative, or simply artistic mammary gland with attached pectoral muscle reveals much about how law and society objectify the gendering of the body and the embodied identities that materialize through the breast and its breastification in the public sphere. Additionally, this chapter will examine the womb, body hair, and the nipple as part of the larger conceptualization of power and control that breastification represents.

Keywords Breast · Womb · Nipple · Objectification · Bodily integrity · Body hair · Identity · Power · Cultural norms

1 Beyond Objectification: Unveiling the Complexities of the Breast

Breastification, within its expanded scope, incorporates the intricate dynamics of self-objectification (Gervais 2013) and addresses the roles of self-objectifiers (Puvia and Vaes 2012, pp. 487–491), whilst framing a comprehensive narrative that focuses on

S. Marusek
University of Hawai'I Hilo, Hilo, USA
e-mail: marusek@hawaii.edu

A. Wagner (✉)
University of Lille, Lille, France
e-mail: valwagnerfr@yahoo.com

A. Condello and A. Wagner (eds.), *Gender Stereotypes*, Gender, Justice and Legal Feminism 2, https://doi.org/10.1007/978-3-031-63905-0_8

female attributes such as the bosom, boobs, breasts. The breast is visible as a luscious mound underneath a shirt, or as under-boob, cleavage that shows the overboob and between boob, or as the outline of the nipple on top of the boob. Yet even as the breastification of the chest seems uniquely female, male bodies are also breastified to the degree that the presence, size, and normativity of these mammary appendages serve as the basis for the performativity of gender. The spectrum of sexual identity creates the possibility for viewing the breast as the site of gendered presumption even as the human body is mapped through the breast's size and positionality. This holistic approach of seeing the breast as a bosom, as a body, even as a beast represents a profound exploration of the ways in which bodies are perceived, experienced, and materialized through the multifaceted implications of breastification that persist within societal, legal, and visual discourses.

The bosom, emblematic of nurturing and maternal qualities, also becomes a pivotal site for self-objectification. Calogero (2012, p. 574) defines self-objectification as "a self-perspective that involves taking a primary view of the self as an object". In the landscape of breastification, the bosom is not just a symbol of femininity but also a focal point where women, men, and those beyond the binary, may internalize societal views, often viewing themselves through the lens of external valuation. This self-objectification can lead to a fragmented self-view, where the bosom is disproportionately focused upon, sometimes overshadowing the person's holistic identity. For transgendered individuals, the bosom may serve as the perceived site for the external qualification and judgment of successful transition from male to female.[1] Yet as Sonia Katyal (2017) discusses, the ascriptive versus the allocative functions of assigned sex challenge the binary stabilities of sex that presume the enlarged, potentially lactating breast to be female rather than male. Through the performativity of gender, whether as transgender or cisgender women, the breast invokes a visual terrain for expressions of identity and stereotyped characterizations of sexuality.

Integrating the concept of "bodies" within breastification emphasizes the full spectrum of the female form's representation and its susceptibility of the breast to self-objectification. In this way, the breast is attributed to female bodies even as male bodies have also breasts. The male breast, whether on transgendered bodies or on cisgendered bodies, can be enlarged in what is known as gynaecomastia, or simply appearing as larger on individuals who have a greater composition of body fat that would make for 'man-boobs'.[2] This broader perspective expands the piecemeal view often propagated by societal standards, where parts of the body are isolated and objectified. Self-objectifiers, in this context, may navigate complex social landscapes, contending with the internalization of external gazes that dissect their bodily autonomy and agency, as "viewing oneself from a third-person perspective as opposed to a first-person perspective" (Calogero, 2012, p. 574). Whether large or small, the female-ness of the boob may be tantamount to its ultimate lactating

[1] Think of Bruce Jenner's unveiling as Caitlyn Jenner on the cover of the July 2015 *Vanity Fair*.

[2] The man-boob, with the accompanying 'mansiere' are discussed on the American comedy sitcom, *Seinfeld* Season 6, Episode 18 "The Doorman" (first aired February 23, 1995 on NBC).

potentiality as the beast-fication of the boob is the breastification of the nipple that produces milk.

The inclusion of "beasts" in our discussion about breastification can be seen as a powerful metaphor for the raw, untamed aspects of femininity that challenge and resist the confines of objectification (Lameiras-Fernández et al. 2018, p. 191). This metaphor aligns with Calogero's analysis of sexual objectification, which describes a scenario where an individual is reduced to, or treated as, merely a body or a set of body parts intended for sexual use, effectively dissociating their sexuality from their personhood. Indeed, "it is the prerogative of the male sex to observe, evaluate, and use the female body for their own purposes" (Calogero 2013, p. 107). The breast itself seems to be rooted as one pivotal location of sexual attraction for straight men, lesbian and queer women as well as for the breast-owner. For Jain (2007, p. 505), cancer of the breast leads to the conceding of gender according to Eve Sedgwick's assertion that "at least one aspect of the shame of breast cancer for those who inhabit nonnormative genders lies in the seeming destiny of biological gender". Yet we know that male bodies, of course to a much lesser degree, also succumb to breast cancer. In this way, the breast is linked to the beast as a bodily site for femininity, but also as a disease of the mammary tissue.

By invoking "beasts", we draw a clear evocation of a fierce, autonomous essence of femininity that opposes the commodification and fragmentation imposed by societal views, highlighting a fight against the external control and reduction of the female body to mere objects of desire or scrutiny. The ability to sustain life is the biologically based presumption of the breast as female in the sense of beasts and bodies.

This beast metaphor extends beyond mere resistance. Indeed, it encapsulates a struggle for reclamation and wholeness, challenging the dehumanizing and objectifying narratives that society often imposes on women's bodies. It suggests a form of empowerment, where the intrinsic, untamed power of femininity confronts and defies the attempts to control, define, or limit it through objectification. The imagery of beasts in this context embodies a reclaiming of agency, asserting a presence that refuses to be simplified to an objectified state, and instead, embraces a fuller, undomesticated identity that transcends societal constraints, as exposed by Outshoorn when she underlines that:

> the control of women's bodies in the family, workplace, and public spaces undermines their abilities to participate as 'independent citizens' in the polity, which in turn affects their capacities to demand and use social rights (Outshoorn 2015, p. 3)

Accordingly, the symbolization of "beast" is pivotal in our discourse over breastification, highlighting the dynamic interplay between autonomy, objectification, and the societal narratives imposed on female bodies. The beast metaphor also imposes reproductivity as a norm associated with the female breast. Yet, the lactating breast may actually be perceived as sexually unavailable but for the child feeding from this body. This beastly breast is "the antithesis of hegemonic male-oriented female sexuality" as noted by Meredith (2003, p. 15) in "But What are Tits Really For, and Whose Are They Anyway?". The biologically male beast has mammary glands that are non-functioning in contrast to the female beast who may sustain life through mammary production; yet, the functionality of the breast presents possibilities that presumably are beyond just functionality and reveal a range of performative ascriptions to the breast as signifier of a female breasted identity. In other words, the male-boob is not the same as the female-boob for reasons attributed to presumption about play, positioning, authenticity, and identity.

The expanded scope of breastification can also consider the management of body hair, particularly underarm hair, as a significant aspect of this discourse. The choice to maintain or remove underarm hair transcends aesthetic preferences, embodying a stance against conventional beauty standards and a manifestation of autonomy and resistance. This act is imbued with political and personal significance, challenging the norms that dictate femininity and beauty, particularly around the concept of hairlessness (Smolak and Murnen 2011).

Embracing natural body hair stands as a bold counter-narrative to societal expectations, intertwining with the visibility of the bosom to make a statement about autonomy, power, and independence. This defiance against traditional beauty standards not only questions the societal norms but also redefines breastification as a symbol of personal strength, moving beyond its sexualized or maternal interpretations.

This narrative critically explores autonomy, empowerment, and women's nuanced identities in a society marked by widespread objectification. It intertwines the personal and societal aspects, highlighting breastification as both a shared and individual experience. This concept influences and is influenced by the cultural, legal, and visual narratives surrounding femininity and body politics. Fahs (2011, p. 452) speaks of "heteronormative patrolling" that would insist on the "social maintenance of heterosexuality", its appearance, and its "accompanying body practices" through the removal of body hair. Removing hair is akin to the amplification of the breast as a visual marker of female-ness for both cisgender and transgender individuals.

This narrative of presumed visual normativity draws upon the scholarship of Outshoorn (2015), Puvia and Vaes (2013), Gervais (2013), and Calogero (2012, 2013), among others, to explore the impact of societal, visual, and legal narratives on women's perceptions and experiences of their bodies. These works underscore the significance of self-objectification and self-objectifiers within the discourse on female body representation.

By examining the complex dynamics between how women's breasts and bodies are symbolized and subjectivized in society, the discussion encourages a deeper consideration of the effects of these representations on individual self-concept and societal treatment of the female form. It prompts a critical conversation about women's autonomy, empowerment, and identity amidst pervasive objectification, framing breastification as a phenomenon that both reflects and shapes the broader narratives of female-ness, femininity and body politics.

2 The Semiotics of Empowerment and Identity Through Breastification

Our exploration of breastification seeks to transcend mere biological attributes and unveils a complex reflection of societal values, cultural narratives, and gender dynamics. This multifaceted concept is vividly expressed through the aesthetics, symbolism, and visual representation of breastification, shaping societal perceptions and individual identities in significant ways.

Breastification embodies a rich tapestry of meanings, far beyond notions of femininity or sexuality, reflecting deep societal attitudes towards gender, power, and autonomy. Its portrayal across various media platforms (art, advertising, social media, etc.) acts as a mirror to prevailing cultural norms and values, showcasing how societal constructs of beauty and propriety are projected onto bodies. These portrayals can either reinforce traditional stereotypes or challenge them, providing a powerful canvas for expressions of resistance, empowerment, and individuality.

At the core of understanding breastification is the application of Charles Sanders Peirce's semiotic theory (1935a, 1935b), which can be instrumental in dissecting the complex layers of meaning embedded in the visual representations of breastification. Indeed, according to Peirce, signs are categorized into icons, indices, and symbols, each offering distinct insights into the semiotics of breastification:

Icons: These are signs that represent their objects through resemblance. Breastification, when viewed as an icon, can symbolize various cultural and personal attributes like femininity, motherhood, or sensuality, depending on the context of their representation. The iconic nature of breastification can evoke a range of aesthetic and emotional responses, resonating with the observer's preconceived notions and cultural conditioning.

Indices: These signs have a direct correlation with their objects. In the context of breastification, indices can signify deeper socio-cultural connections, pointing towards broader themes, such as gender norms, sexual objectification, or societal power structures. The indexical signification of breastification may reveal underlying societal attitudes or shifts in cultural paradigms, reflecting real-world conditions or changes.

Symbols: Symbolic signs are those where the relationship between the sign and its object is governed by convention or learned associations. Breastification, as a symbol, can carry myriad connotations, from empowerment to commodification, varying widely with cultural, historical, and social contexts. The symbolic interpretation of breastification invites a more profound contemplation of its role and significance in shaping gender discourse and influencing identity politics.

Through these semiotic lenses, the visual dynamics of breastification transform into a domain for challenging and reshaping societal norms. Artists, activists, and individuals engage with these representations to critique power structures, question cultural norms, and construct new identities that defy traditional gender categorizations. The imagery of breastification becomes a potent tool in socio-cultural discourse, facilitating the critique of existing norms and fostering new paradigms of empowerment, identity, and resistance.

Therefore, the discourse surrounding breastification is intricately connected to broader cultural reflections and societal debates. The breast is power. It is this framework of breastification that offers a nuanced perspective on how visual representations are influenced by and in turn influence the intricacies of gender, power, and identity, thereby enriching our understanding of the societal fabric and the pervasive impact of visual culture.

2.1 *Allegories of Breastification*

The concept of breastification extends beyond mere physicality, encapsulating a broader narrative that includes the aesthetics of bosoms, the totality of bodies, and the symbolic potency of beasts. This narrative is vividly reflected in art and media, where the depiction of these signs ranges from expressions of nurturing and strength to objectification. The critical examination of these portrayals reveals their power to either perpetuate traditional views or to challenge and redefine societal norms, offering fresh interpretations of gender, power, and autonomy.

In the advertisement (see Fig. 1), the French symbol Marianne is reimagined with an emphasis on maternal grace, gesturing towards the nurturing role traditionally associated with femininity. This portrayal resonates with the concept of breastification aesthetics. Rather than indulging in sexualization, the image invokes the strength and sustenance that breasts metaphorically represent, positioning them within a narrative of care and investment in societal progression. The visual rhetoric employs the bosom's iconography as an emblem of national growth and future potential, transcending conventional objectification to celebrate the nurturing essence as a catalyst for empowerment and national pride. The maternal embodiment of Marianne in this context is a deliberate departure from motherhood, recasting gender roles to connote a powerful intersection of femininity and governance, where the act of nurturing becomes a public statement of intent to foster development across pivotal sectors like education, research, and industry. This nuanced depiction engages breastification aesthetics to challenge and redefine societal norms, advocating a modern interpretation of gender, power, and autonomy within the realm of national identity and public policy.

Marianne (see Fig. 2), the personification of the French Republic, has been portrayed in myriad forms, each narrating a story of cultural and national identity through the symbolically charged aesthetics of breastification. In our chapter, the three images of Marianne offer a profound mediation on the iconography of the French Republic, demonstrating how the female form is mobilized to symbolize the nation's ideals.

In the first image on the left, Marianne is presented with dignity and vibrancy, her figure robed and the tricolor flag clasped firmly—a depiction void of explicit exposure, but still resonant with the themes of nurturing and defense through her posture

Fig. 1 La France Investit dans son avenir—February 2010[3]

Fig. 2 French symbolic aesthetics of breastification[4]

and association with the flag. The image conveys the Republic's protective embrace

[3] See https://www.gouvernement.fr/organisation/service-d-information-du-gouvernement-sig. Freely accessible and useable.

[4] Anne Wagner's personal collection.

and its revolutionary spirit without the literal interpretation of breastification, instead using symbolism to evoke the strength and nurturing qualities often associated with the feminine.

Moving to the second portrayal (see Fig. 2), Marianne appears in sculpted armor, a fortified representation in contrast to traditional maternal imagery. Her breast is not exposed but rather covered by a breastplate bearing the Gallic rooster, a martial symbol that emphasizes readiness and the protective spirit. The sculpted cuirass reshapes the concept of breastification into a metaphor for resilience and national defense during the harrowing times of World War I. The cover of "L'Illustration" from 1916 continues this martial theme, reinforcing the image of Marianne as a warrior. Her stern gaze and the defiant placement of the rooster atop her head suggest a country united under the banner of vigilance and resistance, prepared to withstand the challenges of war.

In the third image on the right titled "L'Attentat & Le Remède" (Index 1872), Marianne is depicted with her breast exposed, a powerful instance of breastification (see Fig. 2). This exposure is not gratuitous but deeply symbolic, representing a dual message of vulnerability and strength. Marianne's partial nudity serves as a critical commentary on the state of the nation, while the tricolor of France subtly wraps around her, a reminder of her unyielding role as the protector of the nation's conscience. In this image, Marianne is not just a static symbol but an active force embodying the Republic's enlightenment, standing firm against adversity and upholding democratic values at a pivotal historical juncture.

Through these images, the concept of breastification is elevated from a physical attribute to a symbol of the nurturing and protective roles that the Republic fulfills. It transcends the reductionist view of the female form, instead becoming a nuanced dialogue on empowerment, resilience, and enlightenment; values that Marianne has come to represent. Her portrayal encapsulates not only the nation's revolutionary heritage and protective might but also its commitment to liberty, equality, and fraternity, making her figure a dynamic intersection of womanhood and national identity.

2.2 *Body Hair as a Symbol of Resistance, Rebellion Against the Hijab Law Mandates in Iran*

In the context of Iran, women's hair emerges not just as a personal attribute but as a symbol laden with profound legal, social, and cultural significance, particularly in relation to the compulsory hijab law mandates.[5] These mandates, which require women to cover their hair (rather than to remove it), serve as a focal point in a broader discourse femininity and public behavior, underpinning a system of control

[5] https://iranprimer.usip.org/blog/2023/sep/06/protests-anniversary-resistance-hijab.

Fig. 3 Women. Life. Freedom

over women's bodies and autonomy,[6] "criminalizing and punishing women in breach of hijab laws".[7] The hijab transcends its physicality to embody a complex array of implications, making the act of covering or uncovering one's hair a potent form of expression and resistance.[8] The decision by Iranian women to abandon the hijab in protest is a powerful declaration of dissent.[9] This act transcends mere physical alteration. Indeed, this signifies a rejection of the constraints imposed upon them, embodying a cry for personal and civic freedoms (see Fig. 3). Gestures of defiance like these articulate a narrative centered around autonomy, rights, and resistance,[10] which the Iranian judicial authorities consider to be psychiatric disorders.[11]

The advertising campaign of 8 March 2023 in Lille (France) transcends a mere exhibition of women's postures.[12] Through its impactful imagery, the campaign contributes to a broader awareness of the ongoing struggle for women's rights in Iran, underscoring the importance of global support seeking justice and equality. It transforms public spaces into arenas of solidarity, where the act of viewing these images becomes an act of participation in the broader movement for gender equality.[13] The

---

[6] https://theconversation.com/hijab-law-in-iran-over-the-decades-the-continuing-battle-for-reform-192037.

[7] https://time.com/6305813/iran-hijab-laws-stricter/.

[8] https://www.vidc.org/en/detail/women-life-freedom-A-new-revolutionary-era-in-iran.

[9] https://www.mei.edu/blog/iranian-youth-and-protest-movement-2023-drivers-and-limitations.

[10] https://www.washingtoninstitute.org/policy-analysis/tenacity-young-iranians-protest-movement.

[11] https://www.france24.com/en/asia-pacific/20230806-iran-forces-women-defying-hijab-laws-into-psychiatric-treatment.

[12] The Figs. 3, 4, 5, 6 taken of the portrayals in Lille are Anne Wagner's personal collection.

[13] https://www.japantimes.co.jp/news/2023/02/26/world/iran-hijab-law-protest/.

Fig. 4 Incarcerated woman

campaign leverages art and public engagement as tools for advocacy to support Iranian women's rights.[14]

Red hair, with its vivid hue, symbolizes a myriad of potent emotions and traits across cultures and artistic portrayals. This distinctive color often embodies passion, anger, and a fiery spirit, marking individuals with red hair as figures of intensity and defiance (Ayres and Maier 2021, see also Fig. 3 and 4). Such symbolism takes on deeper significance in the context of resisting male dominance, where red hair represents a fierce desire for freedom and a bold rejection of societal constraints, particularly those that confine and define women's roles and appearances (see Fig. 3).

Characters adorned with red hair are often depicted as embodying resilience, independence, and a refusal to conform to restrictive norms. This portrayal (see Fig. 4) aligns with a broader cultural narrative, where red hair is not merely a physical trait but a potent symbol of opposition against systemic control and the metaphorical and visual 'incarceration' by prescribed roles. Through this perspective, red hair transcends aesthetic appeal, becoming a beacon of rebellion and a call to challenge and overcome the figurative chains of societal expectations, particularly the confinement of women to the private sphere. This visual representation stands as a powerful statement against oppression and conformity, encapsulating and imprisoning the spirit of protest and the struggle for freedom of expression. The depiction makes it clear that

---

[14] https://www.ldh-france.org/wp-content/uploads/2023/02/DL200-Monde-1.-Femme-vie-liberte.pdf.

Fig. 5 Fight for liberation and peace

their hair symbolizes a prison, embodying restrictions on their minds, thoughts, and freedom of expression (see Fig. 4).

The narrative of resistance and transformation is encapsulated in the imagery of a woman arming her right arm with a bow and a dove above (see Fig. 5). The bow symbolizes the fight for liberation, while the dove represents the hope for peace, intertwining the struggle for freedom with a universal desire for a world free from oppression and discrimination. This image (see Fig. 5) serves as a poignant reminder of the courage and resilience of women standing against restrictive laws and societal norms, demanding recognition of their rights and autonomy.

Hijab law mandates enforcing hair coverage often serve as tools of control over women's bodies and autonomy, making hair a focal point of resistance and personal expression. Within this context, cutting hair goes beyond a simple act; it becomes a powerful statement of defiance and rebellion.[15] This gesture signals a rejection of imposed restrictions and a plea for individual and collective freedoms. Such acts of defiance do not merely challenge existing norms but also weave a story of self-determination, rights, and revolt. In this light, the choice to cut one's hair becomes a symbol of liberation, symbolizing the fight for women's rights and independence. It represents a battle against forces, the morality police, that seek to control women's appearances and behaviors, casting hair as both a site of contestation and a means of asserting one's identity and autonomy (see Fig. 6).

In visual arts, women cutting their hair typically heralds a transformative phase, a severance from past constraints, moving towards a newly embraced identity free from

[15] https://www.euronews.com/culture/2022/10/06/iran-protests-why-is-cutting-hair-an-act-of-rebellion.

Fig. 6 Women break free

male governance or societal expectations. It can signify a gesture of self-preservation, rebellion, or emancipation, marking a pivotal change in life or ideology.

The emancipation of men who dress as woman is the pinnacle of rebellion, as described by RuPaul Andre Charles, American drag queen known as RuPaul. Ru Paul, who considers himself a shape-shifter in terms of gender fluidity, sees drag as the "most political you can get. It has politics at its core, because it deals with: how do you see yourself on this planet? That's highly political" (Aitkenhead 2018). For RuPaul, drag is a "celebration of people who have taken the opportunity to express themselves" (Lumsden 2024).[16] Men who dress up as women are performing the hyper-feminine by donning gowns, make-up, ultrafeminine costuming, and body enhancers. As RuPaul notes, "I don't have breasts, but when I do my push-up bra, I have the biggest boobies in the world!" (as quoted in Lumsden 2024). The ability for men to assume the visual of a hyper-feminine woman through drag is the ability to assume the breastified identity, cleavage and all.

3 Political Actions and Demonstrations Over Breastification

But breastification may go even further than cleavage to the entirety of the breast available for public viewing. In 2015, the Free the Nipple Movement captured the attention of municipalities across the United States, as noted by *New York Times.*[17] Calling attention to the censorship of the female nipple in contrast to the normativity of the exposed male nipple by shirtless men in public spaces was the primary push of the movement. Public nudity ordinances that considered the exposed female nipple indecent and obscene were based in notions of eroticism expressed through laws that discriminated against the female breast rather than the breast in general. In a

[16] See RuPaul as featured by *Cosmopolitan UK*: https://www.cosmopolitan.com/uk/entertainment/a34434708/rupaul-cosmopolitan-uk-december-january-cover/.

[17] https://www.nytimes.com/video/fashion/100000004162595/free-the-nipple.html.

2019 case, *Free the Nipple Fort Collins* v. *City of Fort Collins* (17-1103, Colorado), the courts call attention to the "erotic potential of female breasts [and] their public exposure [that] will induce misconduct".[18] In this case, the language of the court discussed the objectification of women as sex objects as a reality that is imposed on women by society with the solution being the compulsory covering of the female breast. Women's control over the bodies in spaces public and private is the ongoing breastification struggle around the world.

3.1 Defending Women's Autonomy Over Their Bodies in France

Simone Veil and Gisèle Halimi stand as monumental figures in the history of women's rights in France, particularly in their fight for the legalization of abortion, culminating in the enactment of the "Veil Law" in 1975,[19] highlighted by the landmark Bobigny trial in 1972.[20] Their advocacy transcended legal battles, delving into the broader societal and cultural challenges women faced, underscored by their resilience and determination, a concept reflected through our concept of breastification.

Leaning into the profound impact and the pivotal moments in the history of women's rights advocacy by Simone Veil and Gisèle Halimi in France, another significant milestone in this journey was the publication of "Le Manifeste des 343 salopes" (The Manifesto of the 343 sluts) on 15 April 1971 (see Fig. 7). This manifesto was a revolutionary petition signed by 343 French women, admitting to having had an abortion, which at the time was illegal under French law and subject to criminal penalties. Among the signatories were prominent figures, including Simone de Beauvoir, who played a crucial role in intellectual and feminist circles. This act of collective defiance and public confession was designed to challenge and protest the existing laws that criminalized abortion, aiming to protect women's autonomy over their own bodies and their right to make decisions regarding their own reproductive health.

Following the publication of the manifesto, Gisèle Halimi, together with Simone de Beauvoir and other feminists, organized a public demonstration in July 1971 to defend women accused of having abortions. This demonstration was not only a protest against the restrictive abortion laws but also a call to action for the government and society to acknowledge and address the unsafe conditions and legal risks

[18] For the case in its entirety, please see further https://caselaw.findlaw.com/court/us-10th-circuit/1980726.html.

[19] https://www.legifrance.gouv.fr/loda/id/JORFTEXT000000700230/.

[20] https://www.vie-publique.fr/parole-dexpert/287131-les-proces-de-bobigny-1972-pour-avortement-gisele-halimi#:~:text=Le%20jugement%20du%20second%20procès,Avortement%2C%20une%20loi%20en%20procès%20%3A.

Fig. 7 The manifesto of the 343 sluts[21]

women faced when seeking abortions. The demonstration served as a powerful catalyst for public and legislative discussions around the need for legal reforms regarding women's reproductive rights.

These actions, both the manifesto and the subsequent public demonstration, were critical in shaping the discourse around abortion in France. They paved the way for legislative changes, including the eventual enactment of the "Veil Law" in 1975, which legalized abortion in France, and underscored the importance of public advocacy and feminist solidarity in the fight for women's rights and autonomy.

At the same period of time (1973), a French poster advocating for the legalization and subsidization of abortion, dating from a period of intense activism on this issue in France appeared. The text at the top reads "Avortement libre et remboursé pour toutes", which translates to "Free and reimbursed abortion for all". The image depicts a group of women marching toward the entrance of a hospital, signifying the demand for accessible and safe abortion services within the healthcare system. The illustration style, with its stark red and black colors, conveys a sense of urgency and the critical nature of the issue at hand. The text at the bottom "MLAC" refers to the "Mouvement pour la Liberté de l'Avortement et de la Contraception" (Movement for the Freedom of Abortion and Contraception),[22] which was an activist group that played a significant role in the struggle to legalize abortion in France.[23] This poster is representative of the feminist and pro-choice movements during the time of the fierce debates over the "Veil Law" (see Fig. 8), which legalized abortion in France.

Simone Veil, facing a predominantly male National Assembly on 26 November 1974, took a stance rooted in ethical and moral considerations surrounding abortion. She emphasized the gravity with which women approach the decision to terminate a

[21] https://www.france-memoire.fr/manifeste-des-343/ (Anne Wagner's personal collection).

[22] https://www.vivamagazine.fr/il-Y-A-50-ans-le-mlac-ouvrait-la-voie-A-livg/.

[23] https://www.ina.fr/ina-eclaire-actu/mlac-luttes-droit-avortement-annie-colere.

Fig. 8 Free abortion[24]

pregnancy, challenging societal norms and illustrating her unwavering commitment to women's autonomy and rights:

> I would like to share with you a conviction of women, and I apologize for doing so in front of an Assembly made up almost exclusively of men: no woman resorts to abortion lightheartedly.[25,26]

Simone Veil's journey, marked by severe backlash, including abhorrent comparisons to Nazi actions and accusations of promoting genocide, showcased not only the sexism within the political system but also the societal resistance to changing entrenched views on women's autonomy. Despite such hostility, Veil's resilience and dedication to advancing women's rights and public health in France were unwavering.

The Bobigny trial in 1972, led by Gisèle Halimi's defense of Marie-Claire Chevalier, a 17-year-old girl prosecuted for terminating a pregnancy resulting from rape, became a pivotal moment in advocating for abortion law reform. Gisèle Halimi's strategic defense aimed not only at acquitting Marie-Claire but also at challenging

---

[24] https://www2.assemblee-nationale.fr/14/evenements/2015/anniversaire-loi-veil/la-marche-vers-la-loi#node_9802. The poster is part of the documentation and historical records maintained by family planning centers, such as the "centre de documentation du planning familial", which would collect and preserve materials related to the history of reproductive rights activism. Freely accessible and useable.

[25] https://www.lesechos.fr/2017/06/ivg-en-1974-lapre-combat-de-simone-veil-A-lassemblee-175011.

[26] https://www.youtube.com/watch?v=105PFS0cUlo.

societal and legal norms that criminalized women's rights to make decisions about their bodies. This approach extended beyond the courtroom, engaging the public and shifting the discourse on women's autonomy, sexual violence, and the need for safe abortion services. Gisèle Halimi's fierce dedication to transforming the legal and societal landscape regarding women's bodies and rights highlighted breastification in her legal and public advocacy.

The enactment of the "Veil Law" marked a significant victory for women's rights, a crucial step forward after the legalization of contraceptive pills through the Neuwirth Law of 1967.[27] This legal change was fueled by the fervent demands of feminist movements and family planning advocates in the 1970s, who saw the right to abortion as essential to bodily autonomy. Despite the accessibility of contraception, the persistence of unsafe, clandestine abortions underscored a critical public health crisis, further emphasizing the need for legal reform.

The contributions of Simone Veil and Gisèle Halimi were instrumental in advancing gender equality and the respect for women's autonomy over their bodies in France. Through their legal, theoretical, and practical endeavors, they not only secured legal victories but also inspired a broader movement for women's rights and autonomy. Their efforts showcase the power of resilience, courage, and the relentless pursuit of justice in the face of societal and political opposition, embodying the concept of breastification through their fierce and unwavering determination to challenge and dismantle patriarchal structures and norms.

This analysis reveals the complex interplay between the achievements of Simone Veil and Gisèle Halimi and the broader discourse on women's rights, providing a nuanced view of the progress and ongoing challenges in the representation and treatment of women's bodies. Their legacy bears witness to significant advances towards gender equality and the empowerment of women to make decisions about their bodies, now enshrined in the constitutional law of 8 March 2024,[28] being the first country in the world to guarantee freedom of abortion.[29]

3.2 Defending Women's Autonomy Over Their Bodies in the United States

In 2022, the United State Supreme Court overruled the longstanding precedents of *Roe v. Wade*[30] and *Planned Parenthood of Pennsylvania v. Casey*[31] in *Dobbs v. Jackson Women's Health Organization.*[32] Fifty years of legalized abortion available to women in every state of the United States was overturned by the *Dobbs* decision.

---

[27] https://www.assemblee-nationale.fr/13/evenements/1967_legalisation_pilule/.

[28] https://www.legifrance.gouv.fr/jorf/id/JORFTEXT000049251463.

[29] https://edition.cnn.com/2024/03/04/europe/france-abortion-constitution-intl/index.html.

[30] 410 U.S. 113 (1973).

[31] 505 U.S. 833 (1992).

[32] 597 U.S.___ (2022).

The rationale of the majority of the Court hinged on the absence of liberty for the mother's body, specifically of the woman seeking abortion, in favor of protecting "fetal life" or the "unborn human being". Additionally, concurring justices determined that women, who lived in states that restricted reproductive freedoms, were free to go to the ballot box to vote in change. However, the dissenting justices Kagan, Breyer and Sotomayor asserted that the without reproductive freedom over their own bodies, that women could not equally participated in the economic and social life of the Nation. They remind the Court that "Everyone, including women, owns their own bodies".

In this case, the breastification of the womb is the reality that since *Dobbs*, states across the United States no longer allow women to control their own bodies as the womb now comes under the direction of particular state legislators who often value the fetus over the mother. For the Majority and Concurring Opinions in *Dobbs*, the womb is objectified in ways that prioritize the potential viability of fetal life outside mother's womb over the mother herself whose bodily integrity is taken away. With this decision, the womb is no longer fully controlled by the woman herself, but becomes the property of various states to determine the outcome of her pregnancy. As the Dissent asserts in contrast to this newly established power, "a woman, not the government should choose whether she will bear the burdens of pregnancy, childbirth, and parenting."

4 Conclusion

The objectification of the body separates the parts from the whole. These parts include breasts, hair, nipples, and wombs in ways that represent cultural and political contests over personal identity and self-empowered claims to bodily integrity. However, because the whole is fluid in its rejection of the binary that once was so firmly engrained, the process of breastification that includes parts previously mentioned invites continued debate into how the body plays a role in public life. Performativities of power, presumptions of normativity, and possibilities of positioning destabilize hegemonic outcomes and expectations while opening up new frameworks of how we can be.

By understanding the profound impact of breastification on societal perceptions and individual identities, we see significant cultural and political phenomena that reflect and reinforce power dynamics, gender norms, and societal values. This recognition is crucial for activism, policy-making, and personal introspection, offering practical pathways for challenging entrenched gender stereotypes and broader societal norms.

Recognizing the role of breastification in perpetuating objectification provides a foundation for societal change, advocating for a view of individuals that is holistic rather than fragmented. This expanded discourse also emphasizes the fluidity of identity, challenging traditional binary classifications and encouraging a more inclusive understanding of gender and sexuality (see also Wagner and Yu 2025).

Movements that advocate for bodily autonomy and integrity underscore the larger struggle against the public and patriarchal gaze. They highlight the need for a society that values personal autonomy and respects individual rights to self-definition. By continuing to question and critique the dynamics of breastification, we contribute to a movement towards body de-objectification and reclaiming.

Breastification as a concept and practice invites ongoing debate and exploration into how bodies are politicized, sexualized, and represented. It calls for a continued commitment to understanding the complexities of body politics and the transformative potential of reclaiming identity from the confines of objectification. This dialogue is essential for empowering individuals to navigate and reshape the cultural landscapes they inhabit, promoting a society that values diversity, autonomy, and respect for all bodies.

References

Aitkenhead D. (2018) RuPaul: ‘drag is a big F-you to male-dominated culture’. In: The Guardian, March 3, 2018. https://www.theguardian.com/tv-and-radio/2018/mar/03/rupaul-drag-race-big-f-you-to-male-dominated-culture

Ayres B, Maier SE (2021) A vindication of the readhead: the typology of red hair throughout the literary and visual Arts. Palgrave Macmillan, London

Calogero RM (2013) On objects and actions: situating self-objectification in a system justification context. In: Gervais Sarah J (ed) Objectification and (De)humanization. Springer, New York, pp 97–126

Calogero RM (2012) Objectification theory, self-objectification, and body image. In: Cash TF (ed) Encyclopedia of body image and human appearance, vol 2. Academic Press, San Diego, pp 574–580.

Fahs B (2011) Dreaded ‘otherness’: heteronormative patrolling in women’s body hair rebellions. Gen Soc 25(4):451–472

Gervais SJ (2013) Objectification and (De)humanization. Springer, New York

Jain SL (2007) Cancer butch. Cult Anthropol 22(4):501–538

Katyal SK (2017) The ‘Numerus Clausus’ of sex. Univ Chicago Law Rev 84(1):389–494

Lameiras-Fernández M, Fiske ST, González Fernández A, Lopez JF (2018) Objectifying women’s bodies is acceptable from an intimate perpetrator, at least for female sexists. Sex Roles 79:190–205

Lumsden L (2024) RuPaul gets real about body confidence and being yourself. In: Cosmopolitan. February 2, 2024. https://www.cosmopolitan.com/uk/entertainment/a34434708/rupaul-cosmopolitan-uk-december-january-cover/

Meredith F (2003) But what are tits really for, and whose are they anyway?. Fortnight 410:14–15

Outshoorn J (2015) European women’s movements and body politics: the struggle for autonomy. Palgrave Macmillan, London

Peirce CS (1935a) The collected papers of Charles S. Peirce, vol 2. Harvard University Press, Cambridge

Peirce CS (1935b) The collected papers of Charles S. Peirce, vol 3. Harvard University Press, Cambridge

Puvia E, Vaes J. (2013) Being a *Body:* women’s appearance related self-views and their dehumanization of sexually objectified female targets. Sex Roles 68:484–495

Smolak L, Murnen SK (2011) Gender, self-objectification and public hair removal. Sex Roles 65:506–517

Wagner A, Yu W (2025) From gender binary ♀♂ to gender diversity ⚥ + X λ: unveiling new horizons in societal transformation. In: Wagner A, Condello A (eds) (In)Visible signs of gender-based violence. Gender, justice and legal feminism, vol 1. Springer, Cham, pp 23–40. https://doi.org/10.1007/978-3-031-35513-4_3

Sarah Marusek (PhD, UMass Amherst, Political Science 2008) is Professor of Public Law at the University of Hawai 'i Hilo (USA). Her research examines how law happens in everyday life through the fields of visual jurisprudence, legal semiotics, legal landscapes, socio-legal cultural aesthetics, and the constitutive approach to law and society. She has published widely in the areas of legal semiotics, legal geography, everyday jurisprudence, constitutive legal theory, and law and society. She is Book Series Co-Editor of _Law and Visual Jurisprudence_ (Springer) and _Living Signs of Law_ (Springer) with Anne Wagner. She is the 2011 Recipient of the University of Hawai 'i Frances Davis Award for Excellence in Undergraduate Teaching and teaches courses in law and culture, environments of law, everyday jurisprudence, visual politics, and constitutional law.

Anne Wagner , Ph.D. and holder of a Habilitation à Diriger des Recherches in Private Law, is a Research Associate Professor at Lille University, affiliated with ULR 4487-CRDP (Centre de recherche Droits et Perspectives du Droit, équipe René Demogue) in France. She is the Editor-in-Chief of the International Journal for the Semiotics of Law (Springer) and the General Editor of the Encyclopedic project titled "International Handbook of Legal Language and Communication: From Text to Semiotics" (Springer). She is the Book Series Co-Editor of Law and Visual Jurisprudence (Springer) and Living Signs of Law (Springer) with Sarah Marusek. She is the Book Series Co-Editor of Gender, Justice and Legal Feminism (Springer) with Angela Condello, and the Book Series Co-Editor of Law, Language and Communication (Routledge) with Vijay K. Bhatia. Her primary research interests encompass visual jurisprudence, legal semiotics, visual studies, language and law, legal culture and heritage, legal translation, legal terminology, law and the Humanities, and legal discourse studies. She has been honored with the National Research Award (Rank A) for her distinguished research career and has received the "Comenda Jurista Tobias Barreto", a prestigious recognition for outstanding contributions to legal culture, from the Instituto Brasileiro de Estudos do Direito in Recife, Brazil.

A Hen is not a Bird, a Woman is not a Person: Gender Stereotypes in Contemporary Russia

Elena Chernyak

Abstract Gender stereotypes are deeply ingrained in societies around the world, shaping and influencing individual behaviors, expectations, and opportunities. Historically, Russia's gender roles have been deeply influenced by Orthodox Christian traditions, rural agrarian culture, and egalitarian Soviet ideology. These historical transformations have left a lasting impact on the gender dynamics in contemporary Russia, which is experiencing the reassertion of conservative patriarchal values and norms. This chapter aims to delineate the gender dynamics in Russia, analyze the predetermining factors of gender roles in contemporary Russia, and explore how gender roles and stereotypes have evolved and continue to influence Russian society's social, economic, and political arenas. It is based on autoethnographic and ethnographic studies, content analysis of historical documents, religious texts, literature, and media, and a series of interviews with Russian men and women.

Keywords Gender · Stereotypes · Russia · Family · Society · Law · Religion

1 Introduction

Gender stereotypes are deeply ingrained in societies around the world, shaping and influencing individual behaviors, expectations, and opportunities. While progress has been made in challenging traditional gender norms in many societies, significant challenges persist, with implications for gender equality, individual well-being, and societal development. Gender stereotypes in Russia, like in many other countries, have evolved over time and are influenced by multiple cultural, historical, political, economic, and societal factors. From the Soviet era's promotion of gender equality in the workforce to the post-Soviet revival of traditional gender roles, Russia presents a unique case for examining the dynamics of gender stereotypes. While it is important to note that not all individuals in Russia conform to these stereotypes, many common

E. Chernyak (✉)
Elena Chernyak, Hartwick College, Oneonta, USA
e-mail: chernyake@hartwick.edu

A. Condello and A. Wagner (eds.), *Gender Stereotypes*, Gender, Justice and Legal Feminism 2, https://doi.org/10.1007/978-3-031-63905-0_9

expectations, norms, and roles are guided by gender-based perceptions that have existed and been observed in Russian society.

This chapter, which is based on autoethnography and ethnography, content analysis of historical documents, religious texts, literature, and media and includes interviews with Russian men and women, provides a comprehensive analysis of gender roles, norms, and expectations in the country. It discusses the historical context of gender roles and the pervasive nature of gender stereotypes in contemporary Russia, where these stereotypes continue to exert a profound influence on various aspects of people's lives, explores. Russia's history has been marked by distinct periods of gender norms, from the traditional patriarchal system of the Tsarist era to the Soviet Union's gender egalitarianism to the reassertion of conservative values in post-Soviet Russia. These historical shifts have left a lasting impact on the gender dynamics in the country.

2 Historical Roots of Gender-Based Stereotypes

Gender dynamics in contemporary Russia are characterized by a complex interplay of historical legacy, state policy, cultural narratives, societal attitudes, and global influences, which together shape the experiences and perceptions of gender and gender roles. Historically, Russia's gender roles have been deeply influenced by the Orthodox Christian traditions, rural agrarian culture, and the Soviet ideology of gender equality. Before the seventeenth century, gender-based stereotypes were significantly shaped by the confluence of various cultural, religious, and social influences of Orthodox Christianity, Byzantine legacy, and Mongol rule. The adoption of Christianity in 988 under Vladimir the Great introduced Byzantine cultural and religious norms into Russian society, reinforcing distinct roles for men and women. The official doctrine of the Russian Orthodox Church was the cornerstone on which Russia was built as a state and a nation. The Church actually shared many powers with the state until Peter the Great, and even after being officially separated from the state in the early eighteenth century, it still played a major role in the ideological control of Russia. Nowadays, the Russian Orthodox Church is the dominant state religion and influences and interferes in every part of life: economics, politics, social institutes, literature, and mass media, longing to revive the patriarchal stereotypes and principles of previous epochs.

One of the most significant works reflecting gender-based expectations and norms and providing specific rules to regulate people's lives and behavior per the Russian Orthodox faith was *Domostroi*—a book written in the sixteenth century by the monk Silvestr. This book had an enormous effect on the formation of the perception of women in Russia and established strong stereotypes about women and men, their abilities, roles, and responsibilities. *It also determined and regulated all relationships between women and men for the next several centuries. Domostroi* addressed the need to establish a definite set of rules for everyday life, which people had to follow, and a transparent punishment system for breaking these rules. For instance, the author explained in detail how husbands and wives should treat their servants, raise their children, pray in a church and at home, keep houses, cook, sew clothes, dress, treat guests, etc. Although *Domostroi described the life of a medieval patriarchal family,* the *Domostroi* model was dominant in most Russian families, especially peasant families, for several centuries. According to this model, a family's principal person or 'head' *is one person—a master of the house—a husband, a father, and an owner (Domostroi, 1994, pp. 97–112). He is a king in his family who is responsible for almost every sphere of life: economics, finance, morality, and education; he controls everything and makes decisions regarding everyone in the family: wife, children, and servants who have to ask his advice and permission for their actions (Domostroi, 1994, p. 108).*

The image of a woman, described in Domosroi, was based on the various religious books written in monasteries by male monks and the pagan image of a woman as a witch, which the Church was fighting against. Women's primary (and to a certain extent the only) role is to be a wife and a mother with the primary duty to care for her children and the house. While her status in the family and society, in general, was regarded as a 'helper' to her husband, she had certain rights, duties, and obligations. Yet, she had to obey her husband and carry out his advice: "A wife should satisfy God and her husband and maintain her house well, and submit to her husband in everything; everything, what a husband says, a wife has to listen carefully to with love and fear and do each of his precepts" (Domostroi, 1994, p. 105). A husband had the right to punish not only his children and servants but also his wife. And when a woman broke the rules or did not obey her husband, a penalty was imposed upon her: either verbal or corporal. As a result, a husband's authority as a 'family god' became an essential part of Russian folk life and culture. The influence of Domostroi, the outlook of a medieval monk, and the vision of family and women, represented in this book, is very stable and firm and has a tremendous effect on Russian men and women even today.

Most stereotypes, as well as multiple customs, laws, rules, and practices, are rooted in pagan prejudices and traditions that had tremendous influence on Russian Orthodox Christianity. According to the historical traditions based on religious roots, there is a persistent suspicious and negative attitude towards women as a symbol of original sin. The teaching of the Russian Orthodox Church "condemned women as sinful—wanton, deceitful, instigator of lust and pollution to encourage men to fear and distrust women and to control their sexuality in order to protect the family from dishonor and society from disorder" (Engel 2010, p. 8). It emphasizes conservative attitudes towards women and supports gender stereotypes according to which women are placed in an inferior position to men, being given the roles of man's servant within the family and society, and whose primary duty is being obedient to her husband. This position of not recognizing women as equal human beings was typical for the Russian Orthodox Church from the beginning of its history and is observed today (Chernyak 2016). As a result, women's experiences, knowledge, and views are ignored and often characterized "as marginal, frightening, or dangerous, or as superstition rather than real religion" (Franzmann 2000, p. 72).

Christianity and, more specifically, Russian Orthodox doctrine emphasized the virtue of female modesty, the sanctity of marriage, and the importance of motherhood, casting women primarily in the roles of wives, mothers, and caretakers (Chernyak 2016). Meanwhile, men were valorized for leadership, bravery, and their roles as protectors and providers. Saints' lives and religious texts propagated ideals of femininity and masculinity, contributing to the early codification of gender stereotypes. The *Russkaya Pravda* (the Russia Truth), the legal code of Kievan Rus, illustrates early legal distinctions between genders, particularly in matters of inheritance, marriage, and family law. While afforded certain legal protections, women were also subject to stricter controls over their behavior and social interactions. These legal distinctions were both a reflection of and a reinforcement of societal expectations regarding gender roles.

The period of Mongol dominance in Russia, which took place between the thirteenth and fifteenth centuries, had a significant and enduring effect on Russians and introduced additional complexities into the fabric of Russian social life. The Mongol rule itself did not radically alter the gender stereotypes established in ancient Russia, but the socio-economic upheaval and the militarization of society under Mongol oppression had indirect effects. The emphasis on male martial prowess and leadership was intensified, further entrenching male-dominated structures. However, the disruption also necessitated more significant roles for women in managing estates and family resources, subtly challenging traditional stereotypes of female passivity and domestic confinement.

The status and roles of women in Russia have undergone significant transformations from the 17th to the nineteenth century, reflecting broader socio-political changes in the country. This period, spanning from the reign of the Romanov dynasty to the end of the Russian Empire, was marked by profound shifts in governance, social structures, and ideologies, all of which impacted women's lives in various ways. The seventeenth century could be identified as a period of patriarchal society within the state's autocratic structure but also as a time of emerging opportunity. Women's roles were primarily confined to the domestic sphere, with marriage being their main social function. However, this period was also the period of beginning of gradual shifts. The establishment of the Romanov dynasty and subsequent social reforms slowly expanded the social and economic roles available to women, especially those from the nobility. Noblewomen began to exert influence in court politics and cultural patronage, albeit within a limited scope. However, religion still played a crucial role in the education and socialization of women during this period. The Orthodox Church's teachings reinforced women's subordinate status but also offered some the opportunity to gain literacy and education, primarily through convents. Some women, particularly from the nobility, received education in reading, writing, and languages, reflecting the early signs of changing attitudes toward women's capabilities.

The struggle for women's 'freedom' and for regaining social rights began with the ascension to the throne of Peter I the Great at the end of the seventeenth century. Overall, the eighteenth century was an era of reforms and enlightenment in Europe and Russia. This period represented a turning point in the status of Russian women, significantly caused by borrowing European traditions. Peter the Great's modernization efforts included the introduction of the Table of Ranks, which, while primarily affecting men, indirectly influenced women by emphasizing merit and service to the state over noble birth. Catherine the Great's reign further exemplified this era's contradictions. On one hand, she was a powerful ruler who contributed significantly to the spread of the Enlightenment in Russia. On the other, her policies did little to advance women's rights. Nevertheless, under Catherine's reign, women's education was significantly advanced. In particular, the establishment of the *Smolny Institute* for Noble Maidens in 1764 marked the first state-funded educational institution for women in Russia, focusing on providing a comprehensive education that included the arts, languages, and sciences. During this time, women's participation in intellectual and cultural life increased—Princess Catherine Dashkova, a close associate of Catherine the Great, exemplified women's potential for intellectual and political leadership.

The nineteenth century continued the trends of gradual change in the status and roles of women in Russia. This century was marked by the rise of the 'intelligentsia' and a growing public discourse on social issues, including the "woman question," and debates centered around women's rights, education, and participation in the workforce and politics. The legal status of women was incrementally improving throughout the century. Reforms in family law slightly expanded women's rights in marriage and property. However, these changes were limited and reflected broader societal ambivalence towards women's emancipation. The latter part of the century was characterized by increased activism among women, particularly in connection to the revolutionary and feminist movements of the end of the 19-beginning of the twentieth century. Women played active roles and were highly engaged in political and social movements, challenging their traditional roles and advocating for greater rights and freedoms.

After the Bolshevik Revolution in 1917, the position of women in Russia, renamed the USSR (the Union of Soviet Socialist Republics), was changed. The Soviet Union aimed to establish a society where men and women would enjoy equal rights and opportunities. The Marxist-Leninist ideology underlying the Soviet state posited that the liberation of women was essential for the construction of a socialist society. Gender was used by the Bolsheviks to organize the Soviet system according to their 'new view' and understanding of the roles of men and women in the new society and to achieve the primary purpose of the new authority: "transform traditional patterns of gender relations in order to consolidate its rule" (Ashwin 2000, p. 1). Immediately following the Bolshevik Revolution, the Soviet government introduced sweeping reforms aimed at dismantling the patriarchal structures of the Tsarist regime. During the next several years, the new Bolshevik government passed some new decrees (Decrees of Advice of National Commissioners), according to which women got all civic rights and freedoms and became equal to men. Laws granting women equal rights with men in marriage, the workplace, and the political sphere were enacted. All limitations for women regarding children and property that existed before were eliminated. Women were allowed to choose their profession, place of employment, place of living, and to get an education, which they were restricted before. Women also received the right to have the same salary as men. Furthermore, in 1919, a special women's department within the Communist Party—*The Zhenotdel*—was established to promote women's active participation in building socialism. However, despite all these changes and receiving all visible freedom, despite all new decrees and rules, in reality, the status of women was still different from the status of men, and traditional gender stereotypes remained. Women were encouraged to participate in the workforce and political life, yet the burden of domestic responsibilities remained predominantly on their shoulders, reflecting a disconnect between legal changes and societal attitudes. Thus, de-jury, women had equal rights with men, but de-facto, women were still discriminated against and subordinated to men in the various spheres of life: political, social, economic, and family.

The 1930s and the Second World War period highlighted the complexity of gender roles in the Soviet Union. Stalin's industrialization and collectivization campaigns required the mobilization of the entire population, including women, who entered the workforce in unprecedented numbers. During the war, women not only worked in factories but also served in the military, which challenged traditional gender norms. However, the state's narrative continued emphasizing women's roles as mothers and caretakers, essential for raising the next generation of Soviet citizens. Furthermore, after World War II, the government encouraged women to return to more traditional roles, even as the state continued to rely on their labor participation. Throughout the post-war period, Soviet women carried the 'double burden' of full-time employment and primary responsibility for household duties. State propaganda celebrated the Soviet woman as a worker, mother, and active citizen yet offered little in the way of alleviating the pressures of domestic labor.

The Soviet educational system also promoted gender equality, encouraging girls to pursue careers in science, technology, engineering, and mathematics fields. Yet, certain professions remained gendered, with women overrepresented in sectors like healthcare, education, and retail and underrepresented in leadership positions across all sectors. This segregation reflected lingering stereotypes about 'appropriate' careers for men and women. In the 1970s and 1980s, the Soviet Union experienced social and economic stagnation, which impacted the evolution of gender stereotypes. The government's efforts to promote women's participation in higher education and professional spheres continued; however, the narrative around women's roles remained focused on their dual identities as workers and mothers. At the same time, some informal discussions and movements that questioned the official narratives on gender equality laid the groundwork for more open discussions in the post-Soviet era. Overall, the Soviet era, compared to the tsarism of previous centuries, introduced radical changes in gendered social norms by promoting women's participation in the workforce and politics, allegedly eradicating the traditional gender division of labor, and claiming gender quality. However, this period also entrenched certain disparities, as women experienced the double burden of full-time employment and domestic responsibilities, highlighting a gap between official ideology and reality.

The Soviet era represents a complex picture of progress and multiple contradictions regarding gender stereotypes. It is characterized by strengthening the stereotype that women's primary sphere remained at home despite their professional achievements. While the state pursued ambitious reforms to achieve gender equality, deep-rooted societal attitudes and the practical realities of women's lives often undermined these efforts. The legacy of Soviet gender policies and stereotypes continues to influence perspectives on gender roles in post-Soviet states, highlighting the challenges of reconciling ideological aspirations with societal change.

The Restructuring and Post-Restructuring (*Perestroika* and *Post-Perestroika*) period of 1985–1992 had contradictory sequences and effects on Russian society. On the one side, *glasnost'*, which accompanied *perestroika*, allowed people to discuss many problems, including women's issues publicly. Predominant topics for discussion during this time included women's health, reproduction, birth control, abortions, medical assistance, women's diseases, and sexually transmitted diseases. Nevertheless, some problems undoubtedly were important but silenced or ignored. In particular, the issues regarding alcoholism, gender-based violence, and domestic abuse were among those that were either avoided or discussed unwillingly. Overall, the discussion of women's issues and the reactivation of the 'woman question' did not noticeably change gender stereotypes and did not significantly affect the social norms and status of women in Russia.

Following the collapse of the Soviet Union in 1991, Russia underwent significant socio-economic transformations that had profound implications for gender roles and impacted gender relations, leading to a complex interplay of traditionalism and modernity. The transition to a market economy, coupled with the resurgence of nationalist and traditionalist sentiments, led to a reassertion of conventional gender norms, valorizing women's roles as mothers and caretakers while simultaneously limiting their access to political and economic power. The post-Soviet era, particularly, witnessed significant shifts in gender norms, influenced by both—a resurgence of traditional values and the impact of global gender discourses. This shift has been accompanied by a rise in gender-based disparities, with women facing increased discrimination in the labor market, a widening gender pay gap, and underrepresentation in leadership positions across various sectors.

By the end of the twentieth century, the image of women as partners and equal to men propagandized in the USSR was replaced by the image of women as mothers/wives who devoted themselves to children and domesticity. Men, meanwhile, work and support their families financially: "…the image of women and men as partners in the building of socialism began to be replaced by that of the traditional functionalist family in which men and women have different but supposedly complementary roles: a single breadwinner battle with the world of work, and comes home to the loving care of a wife who devotes herself to home and children". Professional women are perceived as a risk and a danger to social order and the traditional and natural movements of life, as they can destroy social order. This stereotype and overall attitude towards a woman's professionalism result in doubting their professional skills and deriding women.

In recent years, the Russian state has continued reinforcing and actively promoting traditional family values, often at the expense of gender equality and LGBTQ +

rights. Legislation such as the 'gay propaganda' law and restrictions on the activities of non-governmental organizations advocating for gender and sexual rights reflect a conservative stance towards gender and sexuality. These policies reinforce traditional gender roles and heteronormativity, aligning with the Orthodox Church's dogmas and principles, which have grown significantly in post-Soviet Russia. Thus, the Soviet era's legacy of formal gender equality contrasts sharply with the resurgence of traditional gender norms in post-Soviet contemporary Russia.

3 Gender in Contemporary Russia

The economic upheavals of the 1990s and the subsequent economic and political stabilization under Putin have had complex effects on gender dynamics in post-Soviet Russia. Contemporary Russia is characterized by a paradoxical coexistence of formal gender equality, as enshrined in the Constitution, and persistent gender stereotypes and practices that reinforce male dominance and traditional gender roles. Today's Russia experiences significant transformations in its social, economic, and political spheres that have profound effects on gender, with the resurgence of traditional stereotypes juxtaposed against global movements for gender equality. In particular, globalization and internet advances have exposed Russian society to international debates on gender equality. Among younger Russians, especially urban and educated groups, there is a growing awareness of gender issues and a questioning of traditional stereotypes. Social media platforms have become important spaces for discussing gender equality, LGBTQ + rights, and feminist ideas, although these discussions often face backlash from conservative segments of society. However, while feminist activists in Russia have gained momentum, with groups advocating for women's rights, combating domestic violence, and challenging gender stereotypes, they face significant challenges, including legal restrictions on their activities and public hostility fueled by nationalist and conservative rhetoric. The controversial 'foreign agents' law implemented in 2012 in response to protest against Putin's governance has been used to target NGOs, including those working on gender issues, further complicating the efforts to address gender inequalities.

The phenomenon known as the 'double burden' continues in post-Soviet Russia. Many women have entered the workforce, yet they continue to bear the primary responsibility for household chores and child-rearing. Furthermore, under Vladimir Putin's leadership, the Russian state has increasingly promoted traditional family values, often in partnership with the Russian Orthodox Church, which reestablished its strong dominant position. This alliance has reinforced conservative attitudes towards gender roles, emphasizing women's roles as mothers and caretakers. Initiatives like the 'Mother Heroine' award, utilized by the Soviet State and reintroduced in 2022, celebrate women with many children, highlighting the state's emphasis on traditional family structures and families with three or more children. However, while the government of Russia attempts to revive the traditional family, it has made the family solely responsible for every part of a family's life: "While during the Soviet era, women tended to see having children as a useful and valued service to society, now… they are being taught that 'only you need your child'" (Ashwin 2000, p. 19).

Thus, gender in contemporary Russia is marked by a tension between traditional norms and the forces of modernization and globalization, which introduce alternative models and discourses on gender roles and identities. While the state's promotion of traditional values seeks to anchor gender norms in conservative ideals, there is some evident resistance and negotiation from various segments of society. The state's approach to gender policies has been ambivalent, oscillating between efforts to support family values and the need to address gender inequalities. This ambivalence is evident in the state's policies on parental leave, childcare, and protection against domestic violence, which reflect broader societal debates on gender and family norms. Whereas there are formal commitments to gender equality, contemporary Russia is characterized by persistent and pervasive gender stereotypes that affect individuals across various spheres of life and contribute to gender discrimination in employment, political representation, and social norms, undermining efforts to achieve gender equality. In particular, despite high levels of education and professional qualifications among Russian women, gender disparities in the workforce remain pronounced. Women often face discrimination in the workplace, are usually concentrated in lower-paying sectors, and face significant wage gaps compared to their male counterparts. Moreover, women's representation in leadership positions remains low, reflecting broader gender inequalities within the professional sphere. The challenging economic conditions have also spurred women to become entrepreneurs and engage in the informal economy. While this shift offers opportunities for independence and financial success, it also reflects the necessity driven by limited employment opportunities and the desire to balance work and family commitments. These disparities are underpinned by enduring stereotypes about women's roles and capabilities, which also manifest in higher unemployment rates and precarious employment conditions for women.

Another consequence of the Soviet system and its collapse relates to the role of men and fathers. Contemporary Russian men want to restore their dominant position in the family and society and revive their status as a 'head' of the family, often referring to the practices described in *Domostroi*. More men believe that women must be housekeepers, care for their husbands and children, and do all home duties alone. However, women's visions of the modern family and the role of men differ from those of men. Women want to have 'strong shoulders,' which means that they want men's support, involvement in family life, and participation in domestic decision-making and activities, such as spending more time with their wives and children, being more involved in household chores, etc. Women expect that men will be the breadwinner, defenders, and helpers and are looking for two things from men: financial security and emotional and practical support within the family. However, men do not want to take a 'woman's job' and assume that housekeeping and childcare are not their 'business,' regardless of whether they can provide for their family financially or not.

As one of the interview participants stated: "To be a man means to be a husband, father, master in a man's own home, family and destiny" (Maxim).[1]

This disagreement between men's and women's perceptions of their roles in the modern family often causes conflicts that sometimes spouses cannot or do not want to solve, which further may lead to divorce. While traditionally, a large percentage of divorces in Russia is caused by the alcoholism of men, relatively recently, women began initiating a divorce due to the misunderstanding and rejection of traditional notions of family and the roles of men and women in the family. This situation is further aggravated by the ability of women to be financially independent. However, the process of women's emancipation in Russia is prolonged and mainly affects big cities. For Russia, in general, the patriarchal views on family and traditions are the norm as these have been considered stable and robust: a woman must be dependent on a man, has to be married despite the circumstances, and listen to her man as he is a God and a tsar. The ex-President of Russia, Boris Yeltsin (1992–1999), clearly described the actual perception of Russian men toward women when he answered the question about whether or not he discussed the most critical issues with his wife. Yeltsin responded quickly and precisely: "Never, I am the boss." Vladimir Putin continues a similar rant by emphasizing that a woman's destiny is motherhood and that family and childbirth are a woman's highest purpose. Unsurprisingly, 72% of Russians believe that a woman's main duty is to be a mother and a good housewife (Vasenina et al. 2020, p. 10). For the majority of Russian women (67% of women vs. 75% of men, family is understood as their primary mission and obligation, and it takes top priority over having a job, especially outside of the home, and an even greater priority over building a career. According to data, 87% of men and 89% of women agreed with the statement that it is a man's duty to provide for the family, while 45% of women and only 28% of men agreed with the statement that a woman has to provide for herself" (Vasenina et al. 2020, p. 57). In addition to that, 32% believe that women have to choose between family and work (Vasenina et al. 2020, p. 51). Recent research indicates that women in Russia exist within the context of motherhood but not as independent subjects who can have concerns, problems, and personal interests unrelated to a family (Kalachikova & Gruzdeva 2019, p. 72).

> Aleksandr: "The home is a place where a man, who works hard, must find calmness, peace and repose. His wife must be a gentle, fond, and loving woman. She must understand his husband and all his needs very well. He provides for his family financially, and his wife makes their home comfortable, warm, and nice. After all, a woman's main role is to be a 'fire-keeper' (a housekeeper)".
>
> Georgiy: "I got married five years ago. I have a son at the age of 3. I am positive: my responsibility is to get money. My wife's business is to keep the house and watch the kids. I work all day, and sometimes I come home after 10 pm. My wife does not work; she is at home with our kid. However, there is always a mess at home - she does not have time to do everything. And she repeats again and again that she is tired. But I am not good at housekeeping, and this is not my concern. I think girls must be taught to domesticate by their mothers, to keep the home to avoid breaking up the marriage in the future because of a clumsy and lazy wife".

[1] This and the statements below are from the translated interviews with Russian men and women conducted by the author of this chapter between 2006 and 2023.

These interviews correspond with the recent research, according to which 89% of Russians said that men must provide for their families. This perception is typical not only for men but for women as well. It is pretty typical for women and men to think that building a career is the destiny of lonely, fortuneless, and unhappy women and that women without children are defective. Also, they believe that the majority of women who are independent, all-sufficient, and successful as professionals are single, their social status is not high enough in comparison with the married women's status, and their position is not very stable because they do not have husbands (Kotovskaja 2004, p. 214). According to recent statistics (Vasenina et al. 2020, p. 70), parents generally expect their daughters to "become a parent" (50% vs. 35% for sons) and sons to "build a career" (49% vs. 43% for daughters).

> Marina: "A woman who leaves her baby because she wants to make a career shouldn't be named a mother."
>
> Diana: "I think there is only one reason for a mother to leave her child to get money: when there are serious problems with her husband's health, which does not allow him to get money by himself. But in this case, he cannot be with a child, too. All other reasons are merely laziness, parasitism, and infantilism."
>
> Elena: "The roles of a wife and a husband must be traditional, where the wife's duty is housekeeping and raising her children and the husband's duty is a job and 'breadwinning.' It is abnormal for a father to stay home with a child while a mother works since the business of men is to earn money. In my opinion, and many Russians would agree with me, that fathers can stay at home with a child only as the exception, for instance, if he is handicapped".
>
> Svetlana: "What I can tell about a woman in a family. This is a hard job: to be at home or 'sit at home.' This is the only responsibility for women and only for women, regardless of any circumstances. Who is responsible for family leisure? Who is responsible for everyday routines? Who prepares a family for weekends, holidays, or vacations? Nobody can do this but a woman. Women must control the psychological atmosphere at home, take care of everyone's comfort, prevent any conflict, and solve any problems. There are many tiny things that make a family more solid. What words do we say when we are waking up our family? Do we see or welcome our relatives by the door or not? Do we make plans for weekends and holidays together? These are the decisions that we, as women, mothers, and wives, make for our families because this is our first and chief responsibility and job!"

Thus, it is evident that contemporary Russian society sees the woman's central role as a wife and a mother and only then as a worker: "…the workplace for a woman is with her children. She is not without work—children are her work" (Attwood 1996, p. 257). Furthermore, this attitude is determined by the stereotypical gender notions, according to which a woman must be kind, caring, fond, modest, loyal, honest, sensitive, friendly, pretty, sexy, and sacrificial. By contrast, social engagement, career-building, independence, and self-sufficiency are characteristics that are seen as unattractive for women. While 79% of Russians believe that a woman should always look good, 35% of men and 28% of women agreed with the statement that a professionally successful woman becomes less physically attractive (Vasenina et al. 2020, p. 56). The man's characteristics that are valued in society emphasize masculinity and include characteristics such as being strong and persistent, being a 'knight,' a guard or a warrior, a leader, a breadwinner, and a father (Kalachikova &

Gruzdeva 2019, p. 73). 76% of Russians said that a man should be physically strong (Vasenina et al. 2020, p. 73)

> Michael: "I think that the intellect is not very important for women. A woman must be a lady first of all, but not a man wearing a skirt".
>
> Sergei: "The vocation of women is a home and children. Therefore, I want to see womanly, carefulness, chariness, tractability, and frugality as the main characteristics of my wife".

The traditional perception of women extends to sexual relationships as well. Approximately 25% of young people stated that sexual satisfaction during marriage is more important for men than for women, while more than 35% of young women and 45% of young men believe that a woman has to satisfy the man's sexual needs regardless of a woman's desire, feelings, and mood (Kotovskaja 2004, p. 231). Furthermore, for a large number of people, the word 'woman' means sexual pleasure first of all, but not a human being: "…the woman was reduced to nothing but her sexual parts" (Attwood 1996, p. 259). Nevertheless, although in Russian society, in general, traditional patriarchal family values still dominate, the younger generation is prone to have more equal relationships and shared responsibilities. There is a discrepancy between existing stereotypes about women and reality when a woman, even though she still performs more or all house chores, more often becomes the head of the family and a breadwinner. This leads to not only a double burden for women but also discomfort caused by the effect of traditional stereotypes and leads to questioning of femininity as women carry out both masculine and feminine characteristics (Kalachikova and Gruzdeva 2019, p. 65). Interestingly, at the same time, men, while sharing financial responsibility with their wives, do not take 'female' duties.

Along with the transformation of the family as a social institution, gender stereotypes are slowly modifying as well. Some characteristics considered before as only men's or women's are now becoming more and more genderless, for example, ambition, vanity, aspiration for success, striving for power, and harshness. The authority of men/fathers, which traditionally was undeniable, in the contemporary family is questioned while more women become more financially and socially independent. Thus, gender stereotypes in contemporary Russia are marked by a complex interplay of traditional patriarchal values, economic realities, and the influence of global feminist movements. While the state promotes conservative family ideals and gender roles, economic challenges and international influences are fostering a gradual shift in public attitudes, particularly among younger generations.

4 Media and Gender in Russia: Representation, Influence, and Evolving Narratives

When discussing gender stereotypes, it is necessary to pay special attention to cultural narratives, which include folklore, literature, and media (i.e., print and news media, photography, cinema, radio and television, advertisement, digital media, and the internet).

In contemporary Russia, media plays a pivotal role in shaping and reflecting societal attitudes towards gender roles and identities, may reinforce or contest traditional stereotypes, and both reflect and shape public attitudes towards masculinity and femininity. Cultural narratives and media representations in Russia tend to perpetuate traditional gender stereotypes, portraying women primarily in roles associated with family and domesticity while emphasizing strength and authority as male attributes. It has deep roots grounded in Russian folklore and classical literature. Many Russian writers and poets, such as Tolstoy, Dostoevskij, Ostrovskij, Bunin, Leskov, and others, described the dependence of women on men and their subordinated position. In Russian literature, the image of a woman is represented as a sacrificial woman, a woman who is always ready to be a self-sacrifice or a victim, who is always ready to stand up for her children, family, relatives, and country. Virtue and patience have always been understood as synonyms for subordination and sacrifice. Mainly, this understanding spreads to women and affects women's character. Voluntary obedience to any power, unjust suffering, and even the desire to suffer are considered the only ways to live and reach the Heaven of God.

The attitudes towards women and their status in society are shown in numerous expressions and folk sayings, where women are presented as second-class people or even not a human being and where their subordinate position is emphasized. For example, "A hen is not a bird, a woman is not a person"; "If a woman is not beaten, she rots from inside"; "A woman driving a car is worse than a monkey with a hand grenade"; "Who needs to bring water?—A woman.—Who will be beaten?—A woman.—What for?—Because she is a woman"; "A wife is a bandage for her husband and a husband is a pastor for his wife"; "A wife is good when she is with her husband"; "A wife is not a female-goat, you will not feed her with grass only"; "A woman is inside of the house, flies are outside of the house"; "The brain of a woman is as a woman's shoulder yoke: curved, notched, and works both ways"; "If a woman falls from a carriage, it becomes easier for a horse."

Russian media and popular culture also often perpetuate traditional gender stereotypes. Women are frequently portrayed in roles that emphasize beauty, domesticity, and dependency on men, while men are depicted as breadwinners and protectors. These images are strongly emphasized, for example, in movie productions (e.g., "Different fortunes," "Moscow does not believe in tears," "Office romance," "Offered for singles," "Love by request," "Once upon a time 20 later," "Once upon a time there lived a simple woman," and many others). The images depicted in media reinforce the notion that women's primary value lies in their ability to maintain a household and raise children. In contrast, men's value is tied to their financial success and physical strength. One reason for reinforcing traditional gender norms and perceptions is the attempt of the Russian government 'to return women back to families' and the revival of the religious, particularly Russian Orthodox, traditions that support the image of women as a mother and a wife. Russian media often portray women in limited roles and emphasize male dominance. For example, in modern Russia, success is strongly associated with men—83% of successful people mentioned by Russians are men, while male respondents mentioned 92% of successful men versus 8% of successful women (Vasenina et al. 2020, pp. 36–37). Men hold the predominant positions in all areas, especially in business (only 1% mentioned were women), the digital economy (1% are women), and politics (4% are women), and 67% of showbusiness celebrities mentioned by Russians are men (Vasenina et al. 2020, p. 38).

The domination of successful men and the lack of successful women depicted in mass media results in the justification, reinforcement, and perpetuation of gender stereotypes. It is evident while watching Russian news, TV shows, and programs that despite women's participation in various sectors of society, men still dominate Russian politics and many high-ranking positions in businesses. While 22% of seats in parliament worldwide are occupied by women, in Russia, this number comprises 14.5%. Men are especially predominant in business, the digital economy, and politics (Vasenina et al. 2020, p. 85). Thus, gender disparity in leadership roles remains a challenge, and women continue to be underrepresented in top positions in the economy and politics. The scarcity of female voices in political and economic discourse in the media mirrors broader societal trends of gender inequality in these spheres. Russian television and cinema often perpetuate traditional gender stereotypes by portraying women primarily in roles related to beauty, domesticity, and dependency on men. Conversely, men are depicted as strong, decisive, and the primary breadwinners. Such portrayals reinforce conventional notions of masculinity and femininity, contributing to the normalization of gender roles that prioritize women's roles within the family over their professional achievements.

The representation of women in Russian news further illustrates the entrenchment of gender stereotypes. Women are underrepresented in news coverage, except in contexts that emphasize their roles as mothers-wives or that highlight their physical appearance. Indeed, Russian society places a strong emphasis on physical appearance and beauty. Women, in particular, are often expected to conform to certain beauty standards, which may include wearing makeup, dressing in a feminine manner, and maintaining a slim figure. There is also pressure on men to maintain a certain level of physical shape and grooming. Modern Russian media, especially advertisements, multiple TV shows, and music clips, frequently objectify women, reinforcing harmful beauty standards and promoting sexualization. Sex is used as a way to humiliate women, put them in their subordinate place, and make women be viewed as sex objects whose primary goal is to satisfy men's sexual desire in exchange for financial well-being. As a result, women are seen as 1less than fully human, less intelligent and knowledgeable, incapable of making decisions, and less deserving of the moral and equal to men's treatment and attitudes. At the same time, mass media also creates another image of women as passive victims of male violence: "Attempts to return women to a domestic mode of life, and the proliferation of images of violence against women which abound on cinema screens and in the press, can be seen as two sides of the same coin: this could be termed the aggressive re-masculinization of post-Soviet Russia" (Attwood 1996, p. 259).

It is important to note that the Russian state under Putin's authority significantly influences media content through direct ownership, censorship, and regulatory measures. State-controlled media promote narratives that strongly align with official and desired views on family and gender roles, emphasizing traditional values and the importance of national identity. This promotion of traditional gender norms and reinforcing gender stereotypes through media serves to strengthen the state's conservative agenda, limiting the visibility of alternative gender narratives and feminist perspectives in mainstream media. The globalization of media has introduced Russian audiences to international perspectives on gender, including feminist ideas and LGBTQ + rights. Exposure to global media content and the advent of digital media has introduced new spaces for expressing and discussing gender issues in Russia and contributed to changing attitudes among some segments of the Russian population, particularly the younger generation. However, while new social media platforms, blogs, and online news have become important venues for social justice and feminist activists and communities to share their experiences, challenge stereotypes, and advocate for gender equality, this exposure triggers backlash from conservative groups, leading to a polarized public discourse on gender roles and rights. Also, these digital spaces offer opportunities for the visibility of diverse gender identities and narratives that challenge the mainstream media's portrayal and go against the state gender politics agenda. This is why, although digital platforms provide a venue for alternative gender narratives, they are not free from challenges—online activists and feminist groups often face harassment, trolling, and state and public censorship. Additionally, the Russian government has increased regulation of the internet, including laws targeting "extremist" content, and posed significant challenges and even restrictions to the free expression of gender-related issues online.

5 Conclusion

The study of gender in Russia presents a complex and multifaceted inquiry into the interplay between tradition and modernity, shaped by historical legacies, socio-political and economic transformations, and global influences. In contemporary Russia, gender stereotypes are deeply woven into the social structure, influenced by religious and cultural traditions as well as contemporary challenges caused by globalization and advanced technology. While traditional gender roles remain deeply entrenched, there is also evidence of resistance and negotiation by individuals and groups. This chapter aims to delineate the gender dynamics in Russia, analyze the predetermining factors of gender roles in modern Russia, and explore how gender roles have evolved and continue to influence Russian society's social, economic, and political arenas.

Russia has a history of traditional gender roles, where men are often expected to be the primary breadwinners, and women are expected to take on the role of homemakers and caregivers. This expectation of women as caretakers is deeply ingrained in Russian culture, and many women still face pressure to prioritize family over career. Traditionally, the responsibility for raising children falls heavily on women. While there is a growing awareness of the importance of shared parenting responsibilities, many Russian families still follow traditional gender roles when it comes to childcare. Despite some changes and some advancements in challenging traditional norms, significant barriers remain, and traditional patriarchal gender roles remain prevalent, with men often seen as breadwinners and women as homemakers. This persists despite women's increased participation in the workforce and gaining independence.

Before the seventeenth century, Russian society was characterized by deeply entrenched gender stereotypes that defined the lives and opportunities of men and women. These stereotypes, rooted in religious doctrine, legal codes, and social practices, reinforced a patriarchal order that valued male authority while confining women to roles of domesticity and obedience. However, historical nuances and the resilience of women in navigating these constraints also highlight the complexity of gender dynamics in early Russian history. The period from the 17th to the nineteenth century was a period of significant transformation for women in Russia. While deeply rooted patriarchal norms persisted, this era witnessed gradual shifts in the social, legal, and political landscapes that expanded the roles and opportunities available to women. These changes laid the groundwork for the more radical transformations of the twentieth century, reflecting the complex interplay of continuity and change in the history of Russian women. The examination of this period highlights the importance of historical context in understanding the evolving status of women and offers valuable insights into the challenges and achievements that have shaped their current position in Russian society. The Soviet Union's collapse led to profound social and economic changes in Russia, significantly impacting gender relations. Despite the Soviet regime's emphasis on gender equality—promoting women's participation in the workforce and education—the reality was a dual burden for many women, who balanced professional responsibilities with traditional domestic roles. This legacy persists, affecting contemporary gender norms and expectations. The post-Soviet economic turmoil and the transition to a market economy further exacerbated gender disparities, with women often bearing the brunt of financial hardships. The post-Soviet era has seen significant shifts in gender dynamics, with the revival of traditional values, changing economic conditions, and the influence of global feminism shaping attitudes towards gender roles.

Nowadays, gender norms in Russia have undergone significant transformations, influenced by the country's tumultuous history, from the Tsarist era to Soviet rule and its post-Soviet evolution. It is also important to note that attitudes and perceptions regarding gender and gender expectations and stereotypes can vary widely within Russia. While there is a significant number of individuals and organizations willing and fighting to reinforce patriarchal approaches to gender and strengthen traditional gender norms, there are individuals and organizations actively working to challenge and change these stereotypes. The younger generation, in particular, tends to be more open to breaking away from traditional gender roles and expectations. Additionally, Russia has seen some progress in addressing gender-related issues and promoting gender equality, but there is still work to be done to achieve greater gender equity in various aspects of society. Addressing gender stereotypes is vital for promoting gender equality, fostering individual well-being, and advancing Russian society. Efforts to combat these stereotypes must involve policy changes, media reform, and educational initiatives, all working towards a more inclusive and equitable future for all Russian citizens. The struggle against entrenched gender stereotypes and for greater gender equality in Russia must be ongoing, reflecting broader debates about the country's identity and future direction in the twenty-first century.

References

Ashwin S (2000) Gender, state and society in soviet and post-soviet Russia. Routledge, London & New York

Attwood L (1996) The post-Soviet woman in the move to the market: a return to domesticity and dependence? In: Marsh R (ed) Women in Russia and Ukraine. University Press, Cambridge, pp 255–266

Chernyak E (2016) What is a woman created for? The image of women in Russia through the lens of the Russian Orthodox church. Fem Theol 24(3):299–313. https://doi.org/10.1177/0966735015627953

Engel BA (2010) Women in Russia 1700–2000. University Press, Cambridge

Franzmann M (2000) Women and religion. University Press, New York, Oxford

Kalachikova ON, Gruzdeva MA (2019) Gender stereotypes in the modern family: women and men. Women Russ Soc 1:64–76. https://doi.org/10.21064/WinRS.2019.1.6

Kotovskaja M (2004). Gendernye Issledovaniia: Istoriia, sovremennost', facty [Gender studies: history, the present, facts]. RAN, Moscow, Russia

Silvestr (1994) Domostroi. Saint-Petersburg. Nauka, Russia

Vasenina AS, Imaeva GR, Nikishova EV (2020) Stereotypes about women and their consequences: On the path to equal opportunities in the digital economy. NAFI Publishing House, Moscow, Russia

Elena Chernyak received her Ph.D. in Sociology from the Department of Sociology at the University of Windsor (Canada). She also holds a Master's degree in Journalism from Saint Petersburg State University (Russia), a Master of Religious Education from Assumption University (Canada), and an MSW from the University of Windsor (Canada). Elena is currently a Professor of Sociology in the Department of Sociology, Criminology and Human Services at Hartwick College, NY, USA. Her research interests encompass gender-related topics such as gender-based violence, gender ideology, gendered discourses and social institutions, family relations, cultural and religious influence on behavior and identity, and Soviet/post-Soviet societies. Elena's individual and collaborative studies have been disseminated through a number of American and international scholar conferences and publications in scholarly journals.

Anti-gender Narratives as a Discursive Form of Gender-Based Violence: A Comparative Study Between Italy, UK, and the US

Beatrice Spallaccia

Abstract Anti-gender movements have recently mobilized in many Western countries against gender equality and sexual diversity, thwarting the implementation of anti-discrimination policies and gender mainstreaming approaches. These groups use a deceptive narrative based on terms like *gender ideology*, i.e., a rhetorical device which demonizes feminist stances and LGBTQ+ rights. This contribution considers anti-gender rhetoric as a discursive form of gender-based violence. Joining the tenets of gender and critical discourse studies, it investigates qualitatively the discursive strategies and tropes found in some online newspapers articles from three selected countries: Italy, the UK, and the US. The comparative analysis follows the Discourse Historical Approach and shows similarities and differences in the use of anti-gender discourse to attack LGBTQ+ social citizenship. The contribution also offers insights on the transcultural circulation of this rhetoric, on the role it plays in legitimizing misogynistic and homotransphobic sentiments, and the challenges it poses to combating gender-based violence.

Keywords Gender stereotypes · Law · Gender ideology · Anti-gender discourse · Media discourse · Gender-based violence

1 Introduction

In the last two decades, conservative and ultra-conservative actors have made extensive use of the terms *gender ideology*, *gender theory* and *ideology of gender* in media discourse to frame and highjack debates on policies and issues related to gender, such as women's sexual and reproductive health and rights (SRHR), misogynistic

B. Spallaccia (✉)
University of Bologna, Bologna, Italy
e-mail: beatrice.spallaccia@unibo.it

A. Condello and A. Wagner (eds.), *Gender Stereotypes*, Gender, Justice and Legal Feminism 2, https://doi.org/10.1007/978-3-031-63905-0_10

and homotransphobic violence, and LGBTQ+ rights.[1] As pointed out by Rodrigo Borba,[2] the above-mentioned expressions have become not only ubiquitous but also gradually and purposely obscure, in the European bubble and beyond.[3] As a result, the strategic use of these elusive terms in the anti-gender discourse poses several challenges to its understanding and analysis. It is therefore helpful to begin by retracing the birth and evolution of anti-genderism.

In general terms, the phenomenon of anti-genderism can be understood as a "resentful mobilization against pluralism," gender equality and so-called "political correctness."[4] A thriving body of international research[5] suggests interpreting it as a strategy forged by the Vatican in the 1990s, to counter the institutionalization of a gender mainstreaming approach at international level.[6] As reviewed by several authors,[7] the first appearance of anti-gender language and sentiments followed two conferences where the term *gender* was introduced with the aim to foster more progressive policies on SRHR, i.e., the 1994 UN International Conference on Population and Development held in Cairo, and the Fourth World Conference on Women held in Beijing in 1995. In those occasions, the Vatican started condemning the very use of *gender* "as a strategic means to attack and destabilize the natural family."[8] Since then, the Vatican's discursive counterstrategy has depicted *gender* as an "ideological colonization" and turned it into a "new rhetorical device",[9] and it has worked steadily to demonize women's SRHR and LGBTQ+ people's rights alike.

Although this attack originated within Vatican boundaries, it has travelled transnationally, also thanks to the publication, translation, and dissemination of ultraconservative essays and encyclopedic dictionaries.[10] These texts contributed to the transformation of anti-genderism into a "symbolic glue"[11] which brought local actors to form a well-organized, international movement, bankrolled by religious extremist

---

[1] Here and throughout the contribution, the acronym LGBTQ+ designates all sexual minorities, that is, all people who do not conform to the standards of gender binarism and of the "heterosexual matrix" (Butler 1990), because of their sexual orientation, gender identity and/or expression, and anatomical characteristics (see Bernini 2021a).

[2] Borba (2022).

[3] "European bubble" is a term used by Datta and Paternotte (2023), p. 43 to indicate "the universe of policy makers, civil servants, lobbyists, and civil society organizations that gravitate around the EU and other European institutions centered around Brussels and Strasbourg."

[4] Von Redecker (2016), p. 2.

[5] See Garbagnoli (2016), Kuhar and Paternotte (2017), Garbagnoli and Prearo (2018).

[6] Gender mainstreaming approach—or simply *gender mainstreaming*—is "the (re)organisation, improvement, development and evaluation of policy processes, so that a gender equality perspective is incorporated in all policies at all levels and at all stages, by the actors normally involved in policy-making" (Council of Europe 2004), p. 12.

[7] E.g., Corredor (2019), Graff and Korolczuk (2022).

[8] Paternotte and Kuhar (2017), p. 9.

[9] Garbagnoli (2017), p. 191.

[10] See, among others, O'Leary's (1997), Anatrella (2011), Kuby (2016), as well as Pontificio Consiglio per la Famiglia (2003).

[11] Kováts and Põim (2015).

funders.[12] It does not come as a surprise, then, that today anti-gender sentiments are shared among conservative populist parties that have gained power in many Western countries and that have expressed homotransphobic beliefs. As Stefanie Mayer and Birgit Sauer write, "[t]he term 'gender ideology' can be defined primarily as a right-wing populist discourse, which typically aims at establishing antagonistic relations. Populism is based on the creation of a frontier within the social, the creation of antagonism."[13] This exclusionary rhetoric, based on the reconfiguration of *gender*, is strategic for the new-right agenda, which "attempt[s] to enforce a transcendent view of gender, one that is immutable, biology-driven, based on sexual dimorphism," and fixed, stereotyped, hierarchical roles for women and men, a view "in which there is not place for gay, lesbian, queer and trans folks."[14]

The anti-gender discourse has been instrumental for the current ideological backlash which has already put a brake on the implementation of gender-inclusive policies. For this reason, the present contribution suggests interpreting anti-gender narratives as a discursive form of gender-based violence against sexual minorities, aimed at reaffirming gender stereotypes and hegemonic patriarchal and heterosexist orders in contemporary society. To do so, it focuses on media discourse to critically investigate some discursive strategies and tropes which are recurring in the anti-gender rhetoric. More specifically, this paper investigates the language used by some conservative newspapers in the debate on gender-related issues and laws in three selected countries, i.e., Italy, the UK, and the USA, to offer a comparative sociolinguistic analysis of the contemporary anti-gender backlash.

2 Methodology and Theoretical Approach

In the three countries selected for this study, the status of LGBTQ+ rights varies strongly. The U.S. is often considered one of the most advanced countries when it comes to queer people's rights, and yet states lead by Republicans have recently passed a record amount of homotransphobic laws,[15] which have negatively affected the mental health of American LGBTQ + youth.[16] Italy and the UK have a different history in terms of LGBTQ+ rights but they currently show similar regressive trends regarding gender inclusion. In 2025 the Rainbow Europe report[17] attested an increase

[12] For more information on the funding system of anti-gender religious extremists and their efforts to roll back human rights in Europe, see Datta (2021).

[13] Mayer and Sauer (2017), p. 23.

[14] Balirano and Borba (2020), p. 1.

[15] See § 2.1.

[16] See The Trevor Project (2023).

[17] The Rainbow Europe report is drafted annually by the International Lesbian, Gay, Bisexual, Trans and Intersex Association (ILGA). The report rates 49 countries of the European continent, examining their laws and policies according to a set of criteria, i.e., equality and non-discrimination, family, hate crime and hate speech, legal gender recognition, intersex bodily integrity, civil society space, and asylum. See Rainbow Europe report (2025).

in homotransphobic attitudes across Europe. Italy ranks 35th out of the 49 countries investigated, also because it still lacks a law which criminalizes bias-motivated violence against LGBTQ+ people. Conversely, the UK is the country with the most dramatic drop in the Rainbow Europe ranking, dropping six places between 2024 and 2025. In particular, this comes at a time of widespread political and media anti-trans sentiment, during which the latest British governments have hindered reforms on gender recognition.

The present chapter takes into consideration the differences among these socio-cultural contexts and attempts to provide a comparative analysis of anti-gender discourse, by focusing on media discourse, more specifically journalistic discourse.

2.1 Database

The study focuses on the anti-gender discourse of three conservative news outlets in their online edition. These are the Italian *Il Resto del Carlino* (RdC), the British *The Daily Telegraph* (The Telegraph), and the American *The Daily Wire*.[18] While RdC and The Telegraph are long-established daily newspapers which circulate widely also online, the Daily Wire is a news website, founded in 2015 by Republican political commentator Ben Shapiro. The archives of the selected Italian and British newspapers were accessed via academic search engine Nexis Uni, which enables to read and download articles. Conversely, the Daily Wire articles were collected via private subscription, as it is not accessible via Nexis Uni. The archive of each platform was searched with the keywords *gender ideology* and *gender theory* for Anglophone articles, *ideologia gender* and *teoria gender* for RdC. The research was conducted for a timeframe comprised between June 2020 and June 2023. This date range was selected to cover the media report on different legal measures on LGBTQ+ rights.

More specifically, for Italy it includes the debate on bill S. 2005, known as Zan bill,[19] named after its first signatory Alessandro Zan, MP from the Democratic Party and LGBTQ+ activist. The Zan bill was proposed in 2020 with the intent to criminalize discrimination and violence on the grounds of sex, gender, sexual orientation, gender identity, and disability, but it was voted down in October 2021, after receiving a strong anti-gender backlash.[20]

For the UK and the US, the selected timeframe covers heated debates over LGBTQ+ rights, especially the so-called bathroom bills limiting transgender access to public facilities.[21] In the UK, the same period also saw the polarized discussion of the Gender Recognition Reform (Scotland) Bill, that is, a proposal passed by the Scottish Parliament in 2022 to make it simpler for trans individual to change

[18] For a classification of newspapers' political alignment see Media Bias/Fact Check [n.d.] and WorldPress [n.d.].

[19] Senato della Repubblica italiana (2020).

[20] See Bernini (2021b).

[21] See Dick (2021).

their legal gender, but later vetoed by the UK government.[22] Over the same period, LGBTQ+ rights have been endangered in many American states, especially those led by Republican governors. Probably the most notable cases are those from Florida, i.e., the 2022 Florida Parental Rights in Education Act, commonly referred to as the "Don't Say Gay" law,[23] and the so-called "Let Kids Be Kids" package, signed by governor Ron DeSantis to ban children from undergoing transgender medical treatments and to restrict the use of pronouns in schools.[24]

The search with the just-described criteria resulted in a database of 50 articles (20 IT, 16 UK, 14 US) which mention topics related to inclusive bills and policies. The discourse of the texts was investigated qualitatively following the Discourse Historical Approach.

2.2 *Discourse Historical Approach (DHA)*

The Discourse Historical Approach (DHA) is one of the major approaches developed in the research field of Critical Discourse Studies (CDS).[25] This was introduced by Ruth Wodak and her colleagues from the Department of Linguistics of Vienna University, to investigate the rhetoric of far-right populism. Since then, the DHA has been used extensively to investigate conservative discourse in politics and media representations, and the supremacist narratives of the "politics of fear" which has spread throughout Europe and beyond.[26]

The DHA focuses mainly on five discursive strategies which are summarized and defined in Table 1.

Although a complete study should include an extensive analysis of all five types of strategies, for constraints of space, this chapter focuses on those strategies whose investigation seems more suitable to show the discursive mechanism of anti-gender rhetoric, that is, nomination, predication, argumentation, and predication. Thus, the following sections present some key preliminary findings supported by examples in English and Italian, to show similarities and differences among the selected newspapers and socio-cultural contexts.[27]

---

[22] The bill intended to amend the Gender Recognition Act 2004 of the Parliament of the United Kingdom. In January 2023, it was blocked by the UK government, which used Section 35 of the Scotland Act 1998 for the first time, thus preventing the bill from proceeding to royal assent. See Walker and Brooks (2023).

[23] Florida Senate (2022).

[24] See Drenon (2023).

[25] For an overview on CDS and their major approaches, see Wodak and Meyer (2016).

[26] Wodak (2021).

[27] To help understanding, excerpts from the Italian articles come with a service translation in note, indicated as "my transl." (my translation).

Table 1 DHA Discursive strategies[28]

Nomination	Discursive construction of social actors, objects, phenomena, events, processes and actions
Predication	Discursive qualification of social actors, objects, phenomena, events, processes and actions (positively or negatively)
Argumentation	Justification and questioning of claims of truth and normative rightness
Perspectivation	Positioning the speaker's or writer's point of view and expressing involvement or distance
Intensification or mitigation	Modifying the illocutionary force of utterances

Table 2 Nomination strategies

IT	UK & US
Ideologia gender	Transgender ideology
Ideologia gender e Lgbt	Ideology of transgenderism
ideologia Lgbtq + e teoria gender	Ideology of LGBT and gender
Il gender	Gender-identity ideology

3 Comparative Analysis and Discussion

3.1 Nomination and Predication

The analysis of the nomination strategies shows that the terms searched for are used in different combinations, shown in Table 2.

These expressions are employed extensively and interchangeably in the texts. Excerpt (1) below serves as an example from the Italian context:

> (1) La giornata contro l'omotransfobia è stata una passerella pubblicitaria del pensiero unico per l'approvazione del ddl Zan. […] Il ddl Zan definisce il gender e vorrebbe introdurne i principi in Italia. L'Ideologia gender distingue il genere dal sesso, che non sarebbe più determinato dai cormosomi [sic], ma dalla scelta di una persona, che può cambiare nel tempo.[29]

This result confirms the findings of recent interdisciplinary research according to which anti-gender rhetoric mixes terms like *gender*, *ideology*, and *theory* and repeats

[28] Adapted from Reisigl and Wodak (2016), p. 33.

[29] RdC (2021a). "The day against homotransphobia was a parade aimed at promoting *pensée unique* and at approving the Zan bill. […] Zan bill establishes gender and would like to introduce its principles in Italy. Gender Ideology distinguishes gender from sex, which would no longer be determined by cormosomes [sic], but by a person's choice, which can change over time." [my transl.]

them in different combinations.[30] I therefore agree with Borba in interpreting the anti-gender rhetoric as a register, that is, "a conventionalized aggregate of co-occurring expressive forms and enactable person-types, of which 'gender ideology' is the most famous shibboleth."[31]

These combinations, however, show a major difference between Italian and Anglophone articles. On the one hand, in the Italian texts, they are employed to comment gender-related issues at large (i.e., rights of women and of all identities which fall under the acronym LGBTQ+). Conversely, in the British and American articles the terms are used to refer almost exclusively to the debate over gender-identity policies and visibility. This is confirmed by the fact that articles from The Telegraph and The Daily Wire mainly discuss trans rights, while the Italian ones also cover issues like same-sex unions and parenting. This is probably because, like in many other non-Anglophone countries, the Italian anti-gender narrative is based on the strategic use of a foreign word, i.e., the English *gender*, as an exotic term which helps conceptualize gender theory as a colonizing discipline imposed from the outside on Italian culture and tradition.[32]

Furthermore, the analysis of the predication strategies shows that gender ideology is qualified negatively in the articles. In the British and American texts, this discursive qualification relies on pejorative adjectives such as *pernicious*, *imposed*, *radical*, *restrictive*, *corrosive*, *extreme*, *dangerous*, as exemplified in excerpts (2) and (3) taken from The Telegraph:

(2) Trans-gender ideology is having a "corrosive impact" on society, according to a new study.[33]

(3) Extreme gender ideology is deeply embedded within the Scottish Government, and promoted at the highest levels including the First Minister.[34]

Similarly, in many Italian articles, gender ideology is qualified negatively with predications such as *liberticida* (i.e., oppressing freedom of speech and thought). In many articles published by RdC, the anti-gender discourse is used to attack the Zan bill. Excerpt (4) below shows another example of the use of the anti-gender rhetoric to qualify the bill as a dangerous and repressive legislation:

(4) Il gravissimo pericolo che il disegno di legge contiene è la limitazione della libertà di pensiero [...]. Non si potrà più ad esempio affermare [...] che ogni bimbo ha diritto a mamma e papà e neppure dichiarare personale dissenso all'ideologia Gender.[35]

These results confirm that anti-genderism uses a well-established rights vocabulary to delegitimize gender equality and discursively reaffirm their ultra-conservative

---

[30] See, for instance, Righetti (2021).

[31] Borba (2022), p. 60.

[32] See Manera (2018).

[33] Tominey (2020).

[34] Sanderson (2021).

[35] RdC (2020). "The greatest danger that the [Zan] bill contains is the restriction of freedom of thought [...]. It will no longer be possible, for example, to say [...] that every child has the right to have a mom and dad, nor to disagree with the Gender ideology." [my transl.]

ideology. In fact, gender detractors employ "the language of human rights and citizenship and the democratic tenets of the free circulation of ideas and nondiscrimination to justify their opposition to gender equality and sexual freedom and to embed religious morals within politics and policymaking."[36]

The demonization of gender-progressive policies and ideas is shown not only in this highly negative adjectival characterization, but also in the argumentation strategies employed in the anti-gender rhetoric.

3.2 *Argumentation and Perspectivation*

Anti-gender argumentations found in the Italian, British, and American articles show similarities to the far-right rhetoric of "the politics of fear" investigated by Ruth Wodak.[37] More specifically, the anti-gender rhetoric reveals a general frame of war and struggle that resembles racist and xenophobic discourses which have been used extensively by populist conservative politicians, commentators, and activists. The struggle frame works in discourse to systematically divide the world into two groups, i.e., "Us" and "Them". In this simplistic dichotomy, the former (*Us*) are depicted as the saviors of the nation, traditional values, and ultimately freedom, while the latter (*Them*) are represented as aggressive and dangerous ideological enemies who are discursively excluded and othered.[38]

An interesting example of this mechanism is the discursive infrastructure of an article published by the Italian newspaper RdC in May 2021. The article contains a press release written by the ultra-Catholic party Popolo della Famiglia (PdF)[39] to attack the Zan Bill and the celebrations held in the town of Bertinoro during the international day against homo-transphobia, i.e., 17th May. Excerpt (5) below quotes some passages of the article:

> (5) A Bertinoro si sono viste le prime prove di quello che diventerà il 17 maggio se passa il Ddl Zan: un'imposizione di regime sul modello del sabato fascista, con la precisa volontà di entrare nelle scuole e orientare i bambini. Col pretesto di presunti muri ideologici da abbattere, infatti, si è fatta propaganda a una vera e propria ideologia, il gender, proponendo una visione di lettura e di comprensione della realtà totalmente antiscientifica che impone accanto al sesso biologico, una nozione di 'sesso socioculturale'. [...] Con l'istituzione della giornata nazionale del 17 maggio contro l'omotransfobia [...], le scuole di ogni ordine e grado (articolo 7 ddl Zan) finiscono in prima linea nella costruzione dei nuovi balilla del politicamente corretto. [...] il Popolo della Famiglia invita i genitori a una resistenza Civile: non manderemo i nostri figli a scuola. Non li faremo indottrinare. Il 17 maggio, resteranno a

---

36 Borba (2022), pp. 59–60.

37 Wodak (2021).

38 Wodak (2020), p. 237.

39 Literally, People of the Family. The Global Project Against Hate and Extremism classifies PdF among Italian far-right hate and extremist groups, and describes it as an anti-LGBTQ+, religious nationalist party, vehemently anti-abortion, anti-trans, against same-sex couples parenting and adopting. See GPAHE (2021).

> casa e ricorderanno piuttosto Luigi Calabresi, commissario cattolico ucciso dall'odio anche di tanti che oggi sono in prima fila a favore del ddl Zan.[40]

As exemplified in (5), the text heavily relies on the discursive dichotomy which is typical of the struggle frame. Perspectivation strategies are used to place PdF, their traditional values, children, and their families in the "Us" ingroup. Conversely, the Zan bill, the alleged gender ideology, and their supporters are discursively relegated in the "Them" outgroup. The struggle frame here outlined is also based on the victim/perpetrator reversal strategy, which is often used to misrepresent marginalized communities as powerful and aggressive.[41] As pointed out by Hannah Dick in her analysis of American conservatist rhetoric, this is what Alyson Cole calls the "cult of true victimhood,"[42] that is, a rhetorical project of victimization in which "the suffering of minority groups is called out as performative, while the backlash received by those who discriminate against those groups is understood to circumscribe authentic suffering."[43] This discourse also exploits several propaganda techniques, especially logical fallacies such as the straw man fallacy (i.e., "misrepresenting someone's opinion"), the black-and-white fallacy (i.e., "presenting two alternatives as the only possibilities"), and whataboutism (i.e., "charging an opponent with hypocrisy").[44]

In the text quoted in (5), the straw man fallacy is used to compare the Zan bill to a totalitarian regime aimed at entering the school system and contaminating children with its supposedly sinister agenda, which lacks scientific rigor.[45] Indeed, children are presented as the ultimate victims of the indoctrination brought on by the bill/gender ideology, which will turn them into the "new *balillas* of political correctness."[46] As studied by Kerry Robinson,[47] the strategic use of childhood innocence is a common political mechanism to trigger moral panic which is instrumental to the maintenance of a certain status quo. As Paternotte and Kuhar note, anti-gender narratives across

---

[40] RdC (2021b). "In the town of Bertinoro we saw the first signs of what May 17th will become if the Zan bill passes: a regime imposition modelled on the Fascist Saturday, with the precise intention to enter schools and instruct children. With the pretext of alleged ideological walls to be torn down, in fact, there has been propaganda to an actual ideology, i.e., the gender ideology, proposing a totally antiscientific vision of reality that imposes a notion of 'sociocultural sex' next to biological sex. [...] By turning May 17th into the national day against homotransphobia [...], schools of all orders (Article 7, Zan bill) land at the forefront of the construction of the new balillas of political correctness. [...] Popolo della Famiglia calls on parents for Civil resistance: we will not send our children to school. We will not have them indoctrinated. On May 17th, they will stay home and rather remember Luigi Calabresi, the Catholic police chief killed by the hatred of those who today lead the way in favor of the Zan bill." [my transl.]

[41] Wodak (2020), p. 240.

[42] Cole (2007), p. 5.

[43] Dick (2021), p. 379.

[44] Da San Martino et al. (2020).

[45] The term "Sabato fascista" (Fascist Saturday) refers to the fact that, during Mussolini's dictatorship, Italians were expected to use Saturday afternoons to engage in cultural, sporting, paramilitary and political activities. It was established to further consolidate a fascist identity in Italy.

[46] *Balillas* refers to Opera Nazionale Balilla, that is, the school-grade scouting-paramilitary youth organization, established by Mussolini, to train youths as 'the fascists of tomorrow.'

[47] Robinson (2008).

Europe have used extensively the victim/perpetrator reversal to construct a conspiracy theory based on the trope of the endangered child. While, as a matter of fact, queer people have long been persecuted and discriminated against, in this narrative they become the persecutors of traditional values and children. As stressed by Graff and Korolczuk (2022: 4), gender detractors tend to use a "morally heightened militant rhetoric [...] depicting themselves as peaceful yet besieged, and warning against the alleged violence of genderists." In the text at issue, in fact, the movement calls on parents to protect their kids by opposing "a civil resistance.[48] This reminds the "savior of the nation" trope that, according to Wodak, is commonly found in populistic rhetoric and is employed in the struggle-frame.[49]

The press release ends with another dichotomy, this time between the Zan bill and Luigi Calabresi, a former Catholic police officer. On 17 May 1972, Calabresi was murdered by members of Lotta Continua, a far-left armed group which operated in Italy during the so-called Anni di piombo (lit. Years of Lead), that is, a period between the late 1960s and the late 1980s, marked by a wave of both far-right and far-left incidents of political terrorism. The reference to—and the exploitation of—Calabresi's death is highly symbolic and ideologically charged, because it establishes a connection between the heated debate on the Zan bill and the violent atmosphere of a dark period in the Italian history. The text, thus, ends with a fallacious argumentation, that is, the purposeful confusion between Calabresi's murderers and the supporters of the Zan bill.

Overall, the trope of the child groomed by genderists can be found in all the three selected newspapers. Two more examples are provided below in excerpts (6) and (7), which come from The Telegraph and The Daily Wire, respectively.

> (6) "Disney is now pushing woke gender ideology on five-year-old children."[50]
>
> (7) "My daughter was murdered by a gender ideology," Martinez told the California Judiciary Senate. "Child Protective Services took my daughter when she was 16 years old. It was helped by her public school counselor and LGBTQ group and another trans-identified girl. My daughter was taken from her loving home because the state of California claims I was abusive for not affirming her trans identity. I lost my daughter over a name and pronouns."[51]

Both excerpts show that gender ideology is attacked discursively in relation to childhood. Again, thanks to the victim/perpetrator reversal, queer groups are implicitly presented as hegemonic, in terms of institutional power, influence, and material resources. In the excerpts quoted above, this is done through the fallacious argumentation that large corporations and the state, such as Disney in (6) and social services in (7), serve the alleged gender ideology.

Moreover, in excerpt (6) gender ideology is qualified negatively with the adjective *woke*. This witnesses the interdiscursivity between the discourse here under

---

[48] The term *resistenza* (resistance) is another reference to the Fascist period, as it traditionally designates the Italian resistance groups who fought against the Nazi troops that had occupied the country and the fascist collaborationists of the Italian Social Republic in the 1940s.

[49] Wodak (2020), p. 236.

[50] Oliver (2022).

[51] Berrien (2023a).

analysis and the anti-woke discourse. According to the Merriam Webster dictionary, the adjective *woke* originates in US slang, more specifically in African American Vernacular English (AAVE), where *awake* is often rendered as *woke*, as in "I was sleeping, but now I'm woke."[52] More recently, the term gained widespread use beginning in 2014 as part of the Black Lives Matter movement, especially after the shooting of Michael Brown in Ferguson, Missouri, and the murder of George Floyd in Minneapolis, Minnesota. Thus, *woke* has gained a new popularity as a byword for social awareness. Indeed, the Oxford English Dictionary currently defines it as "Originally: well-informed, up-to-date. Now chiefly: alert to racial or social discrimination and injustice."[53] However, in most recent years, the adjective has undergone a process of discursive weaponization: along with the noun *wokeism*, it has been reframed as a disparaging label, especially by Conservative political and media discourse. Similarly to *cancel culture* and *politically correct*, these terms have been used in English-speaking countries and beyond, to downplay and attack the most recent forms of anti-discrimination campaigns, such as Black Lives Matters and rallies for the removal of confederate leaders' statues in the USA.[54] These weaponized labels, in fact, are used to misrepresent progressive youth movements and to reframe social justice struggles "as extreme deviant political positions."[55]

3.2.1 Transphobic Tropes

Finally, British and American articles recur to another trope which hints at the alleged violence of genderists, namely, the dangerous trans individual. Interestingly, this is one of the transphobic tropes that were popularized also by Hollywood representations from earlier decades, as examined recently in Netflix documentary *Disclosure*. More specifically, the trans psychopath trope abounds in the Daily Wire, which often focuses on crimes perpetrated by offenders who happen to be trans. An example is quoted in excerpt (8):

> (8) In late March, a woman claiming to be a man murdered three 9-year-old children and three adults at Covenant School in Nashville, Tennessee. [...] TikTok creator Tara Jay, who claims he is a woman, posted a video (later deleted) threatening to use guns.[56]

First, this except shows that the narrative under analysis questions the very existence of trans identities, by misgendering them. Second, the misleading link between trans people and violence is a recurring trope in American conservatist ideology. As journalist Fenit Nirappil writes on the Washington Post,

> The attempts on the right to connect violence to transgender people come even though transgender people are rarely the perpetrators of mass shootings, which are overwhelmingly

---

[52] Merriam Webster [n.d.]

[53] Oxford English Dictionary [n.d.]

[54] See Cannito et al. (2022).

[55] Cammaerts (2022), p. 730.

[56] Berrien (2023b).

> carried out by cisgender men, according to criminal justice experts. And trans people are more likely to be victims of violence than cisgender people, multiple studies have shown.[57]

This is just an example of how Conservative commentators and Republican politicians have recently exploited massive tragedies like the 2023 Nashville school shooting to escalate anti-trans rhetoric and to oppose the rising visibility of transgender people in American public life.

4 By Way of Conclusion

This contribution has shown how the anti-gender rhetoric works to victimize LGBTQ + people, and to sabotage laws and proposals that are guided by principles of respect and equality in contemporary societies. As outlined above in the literature review, this discourse has succeeded in turning the very concept of gender into an ideological bogeyman and triggered a trend of cultural and legal backsliding, which implies "reversals in transitions to liberal democracy."[58] Hence, I suggest interpreting anti-gender narratives as a discursive form of gender-based violence, because it attacks the rights of LGBTQ+ people, and thwarts the implementation of gender-sensitive policies at national and international levels. The contribution has offered insights on the transcultural circulation of anti-gender discourse, on the role it plays in legitimizing misogynistic and homotransphobic sentiments, and the challenges it poses today to combating discrimination on the ground of sex, gender, and sexual orientation.

Despite the differences pointed out in this chapter, the analysis has highlighted that anti-gender rhetoric is based on a discursive and ideological reconfiguration of the demands which come from a marginalized community as an aggressive and dangerous agenda. Given the transnational success of this discourse, a question arises: how did the galaxy of reactionary forces known as the anti-gender movement succeed in passing historically marginalized groups as hegemonic, violent, and intolerant, to stop the difficult journey toward gender equality? Clearly, a comprehensive answer to this question goes beyond the scope of this contribution and will need further academic investigation. In conclusion, however, I would like to suggest interpreting the anti-gender backlash against LGBTQ+ people as a form of discursive injustice. Several feminist linguists and philosophers of language have studied discursive injustice as a phenomenon which works to reaffirm misogynistic prejudice and stereotypes.[59] In the words of philosopher Rebecca Kukla, "members of any disadvantaged groups suffer a discursive injustice" when:

> [they] face a systematic inability to produce certain kinds of speech acts that they ought to be able to produce – and in particular when their attempts result in their actually producing a different kind of speech act that further weakens or problematizes their social position.[60]

---

[57] Nirappil (2023).

[58] Sitter et al. (2017), p. 36.

[59] See Kukla (2014), Langton (1993), and Bianchi (2021).

[60] Kukla (2014), p. 441.

I argue that anti-genderism creates a discursive injustice, as in its rhetoric the demands of an historically disadvantaged group like the queer community get confused, distorted as ultimately reframed as aggressive and dangerous, by recurring to the discursive strategies analyzed in this contribution. This discursive injustice has been used strategically by anti-gender actors in politics and in the media, to gain popularity and to exacerbate the hostility toward oppressed communities. This strategy is found especially in those countries whose current governments have capitalized on fear of diversity by exploiting a register that is strongly homotransphobic and anti-feminist, as well as nationalistic and xenophobic. An example comes from Italy, where the incumbent Prime Minister Giorgia Meloni leads the most far-right government since Mussolini's fascist dictatorship, which is explicitly anti-gender and is waging a cultural and legal war on LGBTQ+ rights, especially on same-sex parenting.[61] Therefore, further scholarly research on this transcultural phenomenon is needed, because academia should not refrain from playing its part and debunking misrepresentations of LGBTQ+ people and their demands, that are, above all, the right to exist, to be respected and valued as equal citizens.

References

Literature

Anatrella T (2011) La théorie du genre comme un cheval de Troie. In: Counseil Pontifical pour la Famille (ed) Gender. La controverse. Pierre Téqui, Paris. 3–26

Balirano G, Borba R (2020) The (anti)gender discourse of the global far-right a way of introducing. Angl AION 24(1):1–7

Bernini L (2021a) LGBTQIA+. Con un'eco di Porpora Marcasciano. Istituto della Enciclopedia Italiana fondata da Giovanni Treccani. Online edition

Bernini L (2021b) Much ado about nothing? Ddl zan, eternal fascism and the ghosts of sexuality. Soft Power: Rev Euro-Am Teoría Hist Política 8(2):279–286

Bianchi C (2021) Hate Speech. Il lato oscuro del linguaggio. Laterza, Bari

Butler J (1990) Gender trouble. In: Feminism and the subversion of identity. Routledge, New York

Cammaerts B (2022) The abnormalisation of social justice: The 'anti-woke culture war' discourse in the UK. Discourse Soc 33(6):730–743

Cannito M et al (2022) Cancel culture e ideologia gender. In: Fenomenologia di un dibattito pubblico. Rosenberg & Sellier, Turin

Cole AM (2007) The cult of true victimhood: from the war on welfare to the war on terror. Stanford University Press, Stanford

Corredor ES (2019) Unpacking "gender ideology" and the global right's antigender countermovement. Signs: J Women Cult Soc 44(3):613–638

Council of Europe (2004) Gender mainstreaming. Conceptual framework, methodology and presentation of good practices. Directorate General of Human Rights, Strasbourg

Da San Martino G et al (2020) A survey on computational propaganda detection. IJCAI. https://arxiv.org/abs/2007.08024

[61] Kassam (2023).

Datta N (2021) Tip of the iceberg: Religious extremist funders against human rights for sexuality and reproductive health in Europe 2009–2018. European Parliamentary Forum for Sexual and Reproductive Rights, Brussels
Datta N, Paternotte D (2023) "Gender ideology" battles in the European bubble. In: Lo Mascolo G (ed) The Christian right in Europe: movements, networks, and denominations. Transcript Verlag, Bielefeld, pp 43–59
Dick H (2021) Advocating for the right: alliance defending freedom and the rhetoric of Christian persecution. Feminist Legal Stud 29:375–397
Drenon B (2023) DeSantis limits trans treatments, drag shows, pronoun use in Florida. BBC. https://www.bbc.com/news/world-us-canada-65627756
Florida Senate (2022) Parental rights in education act – HB 1557. https://www.flsenate.gov/Session/Bill/2022/1557/Analyses/h1557z.EEC.PDF
Garbagnoli S (2016) Against the heresy of immanence: Vatican's "gender" as a new rhetorical device against the denaturalization of the sexual order. Relig Gend 6(2):187–204
Garbagnoli S (2017) Italy as a lighthouse: anti-gender protests between the "anthropological question" and the national identity. In: Kuhar and Paternotte (eds) Anti-gender campaigns in Europe. Lanham, Rowman & Littlefield International, pp 151–173
Garbagnoli S, Prearo M (2018) La crociata "anti-gender". Dal Vaticano alle manif pour tous. Kaplan, Turin
Global Project Against Hate and Extremism – GPAHE (2021) Far-right hate and extremist groups, Italy. https://globalextremism.org/italy/
Graff A, Korolczuk E (2022) Anti-gender politics in the populist moment. Palgrave, Abingdon & New York
Kassam A (2023) 'Orphaned by decree': Italy's same-sex parents react to losing their rights. The Guardian. https://www.theguardian.com/world/2023/aug/21/orphaned-by-decree-italy-same-sex-parents-react-losing-rights
Kováts E, Põim M (eds) (2015) Gender as symbolic glue. FEPS-FES. https://library.fes.de/pdf-files/bueros/budapest/11382.pdf
Kuby G (2016) The global revolution. In: Destruction of freedom in the name of freedom. Angelico Press, Kettering
Kuhar R, Paternotte D (eds) (2017) Anti-gender campaigns in Europe. Rowman & Littlefield Internation, Lanahm
Kukla R (2014) Performative force, convention, and discursive injustice. Hypatia 29(2):440–457
Langton R (1993) Speech acts and unspeakable acts. Philos Public Aff 22(4):293–330
Manera M (2018) Narrazioni tossiche: le parole per raccontare l'"ideologia del gender". Paper presented at the international conference "LIGHTS– LInguaggio, parità di Genere e parole d'Odio / Language, Gender, and HaTe Speech". Ca' Foscari University, Venice, 18–19 Oct 2018
Mayer S, Sauer B (2017) "Gender Ideology" in Austria: Coalitions around an empty signifier. In: Kuhar and Paternotte (eds) Anti-gender campaigns in Europe. Lanham, Rowman & Littlefield International, pp 23–40
Media Bias/Fact Check [n.d.] https://mediabiasfactcheck.com/
Merriam Webster [n.d.] Woke. https://www.merriam-webster.com/wordplay/woke-meaning-origin
Nirappil F (2023) The right exploits Nashville shooting to escalate antitrans rhetoric. The Washington Post. https://www.washingtonpost.com/health/2023/03/30/nashville-shooting-transgender-shooter/
O'Leary D (1997) The gender agenda: redefining equality. Vital Issues Press, Lafayette
Oxford English Dictionary [n.d.] Woke. https://www.oed.com/dictionary/woke_adj2?tab=meaning_and_use#1216700250
Pontificio Consiglio per la Famiglia (2003) Lexicon. Termini ambigui e discussi su famiglia, vita e questioni etiche. EDB, Bologna
Rainbow Europe report (2025) https://rainbowmap.ilga-europe.org/

Reisigl M, Wodak R (2016) The discourse-historical approach (DHA). In: Wodak & Meyer (eds) Methods of critical discourse studies. SAGE, London, pp 23–61
Righetti N (2021) The anti-gender debate on social media. A computational communication science analysis of networks, activism, and misinformation. Comun Polit 2:223–250
Robinson KH (2008) In the name of "childhood innocence": a discursive exploration of the moral panic associated with childhood and sexuality. Cult Stud Rev 2:113–129
Senato della Repubblica Italiana (2020) DDL S. 2005. Misure di prevenzione e contrasto della discriminazione e della violenza per motivi fondati sul sesso, sul genere, sull'orientamento sessuale, sull'identità di genere e sulla disabilità. https://www.senato.it/leg/18/BGT/Schede/FascicoloSchedeDDL/ebook/53457.pdf
Sitter N et al (2017) Backsliding in area of constitutional safeguards and independent institutions, corruption control, and general equality and minorities. Central European University. http://www.transcrisis.eu/wp-content/uploads/2017/05/D6.2-Backsliding-in-area-of-constitutional-safeguards-and-independent-institutionscorruption-control-and-general-equality-and-minorities-1.pdf
The Trevor Project (2023) 2023 U.S. National survey on the mental health of LGBTQ young people. https://www.thetrevorproject.org/survey-2023/#anti-lgbtq-policies
von Redecker E (2016) Anti-genderismus and right wing hegemony. Radic Philos 198:2–7
Walker P, Brooks L (2023) Court battle looms as UK ministers block Scottish gender recognition law. The Guardian. https://www.theguardian.com/uk-news/2023/jan/17/uk-government-formally-blocks-scotlands-gender-recognition-legislation
Wodak R (2020) The boundaries of what can be said have shifted. Discourse Soc 31(2):235–244
Wodak R (2021) The politics of fear: the shameless normalization of far-right discourse, 2nd edn. SAGE, London
Wodak R, Meyer M (eds) (2016) Methods of critical discourse analysis, 3rd edn. SAGE, London, pp 87–121
WorldPress [n.d.] https://www.worldpress.org/newspapers/EUROPE/italy.cfm

Newspapers Articles Quoted

Berrien H (2023a) 'Murdered by gender ideology': mother whose daughter committed suicide blasts child protective services. The Daily Wire, 22 Jun 2023. https://www.dailywire.com/news/murdered-by-gender-ideology-mother-whose-daughter-committed-suicide-blasts-child-protective-services
Berrien H (2023b) UN official warns of the 'increasing trend' toward trans activist violence. The Daily Wire, 12 Jun 2023. https://www.dailywire.com/news/un-official-warns-of-the-increasing-trend-toward-trans-activist-violence
Oliver M (2022) The mouse trap: Disney faces calls to cancel Mickey over gay law stance; Republicans turn on Magic Kingdom with threats to revoke rights over theme park. The Daily Telegraph. 18 April 2022, p 5
RdC (2020) Oggi le Sentinelle in piedi: "No alla legge sull'omotransfobia". 11 Jul 2020, p 17
RdC (2021a) La giornata contro l'omotransfobia. Il Resto del Carlino. 19 May 2021, p 13
RdC (2021b) "Bertinoro, propaganda al Ddl Zan"; Il Popolo della Famiglia invita i genitori ad opporre "resistenza civile". Il Resto del Carlino. 18 May 2021, p 14
Sanderson D (2021) Legal challenge over move to allow gender selection in census. The Daily Telegraph. 6 Dec 2021, p 14
Tominey C (2020) Transgender ideology can have a 'corrosive impact', study claims. The Daily Telegraph. 1 Ju 2020, p 11

Beatrice Spallaccia is Junior assistant professor (RTDa) in English Language and Translation at the Department of Interpreting and Translation of the University of Bologna (UNIBO). She holds a degree in Innovation and Organization of Culture and the Arts (UNIBO), and a Dual Award International Ph.D. in Translation and Intercultural Studies, between Italy and Australia (UNIBO and Monash University, Melbourne). After completing her Ph.D., she published It's a Man's World (Wide Web), which investigates online misogynistic hate speech in Italy, Australia, and the US. She has held courses on gender, language, media, and communication, as well as seminars on translation, diversity, and inclusion. Her current research focuses on representations of gender identities in American and Italian media discourse, translation of LGBTQ+ themed literature, and anti-genderism in contemporary societies.

Gender Stereotypes in Textbooks—A Critical Discourse Analysis of French Language Textbooks in Sweden

Nathalie Hauksson-Tresch

Abstract This study investigates the presence of gender stereotypes in the *Chez nous* textbook series utilized for the instruction of French at the middle school level in Sweden. Using Critical Discourse Analysis, the study examines how language reinforces social power dynamics and stereotypes. Findings reveal a quantitative dominance of female characters, but with no representation of non-binary individuals. In historical references, male figures are predominant, and gender roles are often traditional, particularly in professions where women are often portrayed as nurses and men as policemen. While sports and hobbies are presented more progressively, behavior analysis shows women are more passive, caring, and vulnerable, while men exhibit leadership and aggression. Linguistic analysis indicates an androcentric use of language, with the persistence of gender-biased linguistic structures. Despite noticeable efforts to mitigate sexism, *Chez nous* continues to reflect some entrenched gender stereotypes, influenced by the broader social context and is not wholly successful in promoting gender equality in education.

Keywords Critical discourse analysis · Gender stereotypes · Textbooks · Sweden · Curriculum

1 Introduction

School bears significant responsibility for influencing the perspectives and beliefs of young people, which in turn shape the broader social landscape.[1] In this context, textbooks are of great importance due to their prolonged use and diverse applications in the educational process. This is particularly true for books used for teaching foreign languages, as they not only impart linguistic skills but also convey cultural, social, and

[1] See for example Ballantine et al. (2021) and Lapaquellerie (2023)

N. Hauksson-Tresch (✉)
Faculty of Arts and Humanities, Department of Languages, Nathalie Hauksson-Tresch, Linnaeus University, Växjö, Sweden
e-mail: nathalie.hauksontresch@lnu.se

A. Condello and A. Wagner (eds.), *Gender Stereotypes*, Gender, Justice and Legal Feminism 2, https://doi.org/10.1007/978-3-031-63905-0_11

gender norms young learners are likely to internalize. Indeed, the values conveyed in textbooks will inevitably have an impact on the image pupils have of themselves and the world, on their behavior, their social interactions and their professional or personal projects. In this regard, the representation of gender in educational materials is a subject of significant interest, as it has the potential to either reinforce or challenge existing stereotypes. Bringing these to light can aid to eradicate inequality between men, women, and non-binary individuals, particularly in terms of career orientation.[2] The present study is an investigation of possible gender stereotypes in textbooks used in Swedish middle schools for the instruction of French as a foreign language. The aim is to apply a critical discourse analysis approach to investigate the use of signs and symbols as a means of conveying meaning in order to examine the construction and representation of gender roles and identities in these books. The semiotic lens is an invaluable tool for identifying the often subtle and implicit ways in which gendered messages are conveyed, whether through images or texts. Moreover, this research is of particular relevance in the context of Sweden, a country that is regarded as the foremost champion of gender equality in Europe.[3]

1.1 Methodology

The research encompasses a corpus of four books selected by numerous educational institutions for the teaching of French at the middle school level, the *Chez nous* series, of which only the most recent edition, published between 2022 and 2024, is subjected to analysis. The series consists of four books, one for each school year between the Swedish sixth and ninth grades, for students aged 11 to 16.[4] The publishing company is Sanoma Utbildning, which is a member of Läromedelsföretagen, a trade organization comprising eighteen member companies, collectively responsible for the publication of the majority of school teaching materials and a significant proportion of university course literature in Sweden. It should be pointed out that textbooks are teaching aids that apply general programs developed by the government, but that are subsequently entrusted to private publishers for their production.

In order to gain a comprehensive understanding of a particular issue, it is vital to analyze the entire series of textbooks. A single book might indeed present a limited or isolated perspective, while studying the whole series allows for a more comprehensive understanding of patterns and trends, providing a broader and more accurate insight into the educational material's overall impact on students. The books comprise 58 principal/main texts and some secondary texts of varying lengths. Each text is accompanied by illustrations in the form of colorful drawings or photographs

---

[2] Mosconi (2008), pp. 117–140.

[3] Courrier international (2024).

[4] For the sake of convenience, they will be referred to by the following designations: *Chez nous 6, Chez nous 7, Chez nous 8, and Chez nous 9.* The authors are: Hermansson D., Hirsch C., Norén G., Wilhelmsson L., and Winblad M.

that serve several important pedagogical and cognitive functions. They can make textbooks more engaging and can sustain interest, particularly for younger learners; they can offer cultural context and situational cues, helping learners understand not just language but also social norms and behaviors; and they can simplify complex concepts, making them more accessible by providing visual representations that support textual explanations. Consequently, it is not only the textual content of a book that is expected to embody the principles of gender equality; the illustrations must also portray individuals in a non-stereotypical manner. As a result, the illustrations in all four textbooks are analyzed to examine the representation of characters, their distribution, and how these depictions align with gender equality standards.

The manuals are subjected to both qualitative and quantitative analysis. The qualitative analysis entails a study of the situations, contexts and manner in which individuals are portrayed, while the quantitative analysis involves a counting of occurrences for an objective comparison of the visibility of each gender. In order to preclude the possibility of subjectivity on the part of the observer, the characterization of stereotypes has consistently been based on data supported by scientific research.

1.2 Background: The Swedish Model

One of the general missions of the Swedish school, as presented by the 2022 curriculum for compulsory schooling is to instill in students respect for democratic principles and human rights that encompass Swedish society.[5] According to the curriculum, teachers have a responsibility not only to teach their subject, but also to "actively and consciously promote the equal rights and opportunities of pupils, regardless of gender affiliation."[6]

Schools are also responsible for calling attention to and combating gender patterns that limit pupils' learning, choices and development. How the school organizes education, how pupils are treated and what demands and expectations are placed on them are all contributing factors that shape their perceptions of what is feminine and what is masculine. Schools shall therefore organize education in a way that enables pupils meet and work together and test and develop their abilities and interests with equal opportunities and on equal terms regardless of gender affiliation.[7]

The majority of educational establishments attach significant importance to this mission, with some even adopting a neutral pedagogical approach and banning the use of terms such as *girl* and *boy* and referring to children solely by their first name or the neutral pronoun *hen.*[8]

[5] Skolverket (2022), p. 5.

[6] Skolverket (2022), p. 5.

[7] Skolverket (2022), pp. 6–7.

[8] See for example Hussonnois-Alaya (2017).

1.3 General Theoretical Framework

The present research is situated within the field of critical discourse analysis (CDA), engaging deeply with the intricate interplay between language, power, and social structures. It draws on the critical examination of discourse to illuminate how language can shape, reinforce and challenge societal hierarchies and ideological constructs. Rooted in linguistics, social theory and critical theory, CDA is based on the premise that language is not a neutral medium of communication. As Norman Fairclough, a seminal figure in the field, has argued, language serves both to reflect and to construct the social world.[9] This implies that the utilization of language (discourse) is shaped by social structures and, in turn, serves to inform and influence those structures. It is crucial to note that power, as seen through the CDA lens, is not merely about overt domination but includes the subtle forms of control that manifest through everyday language use.[10] A key goal of CDA is then to expose and critique the ways in which discourse reinforces inequality and oppression. Scholars such as Ruth Wodak and Michael Meyer have emphasized the political nature of CDA, which aims to reveal the underlying power relations embedded in discourse, especially as they pertain to marginalized or oppressed groups.[11] It is also noteworthy that CDA facilitates a multimodal approach, as evidenced by the research conducted by Theo van Leeuwen and Gunther Kress on the manner in which visual elements, alongside verbal language, play a role in discursive power dynamics.[12]

1.4 Gender Stereotypes

Gender stereotypes are pervasive beliefs and generalizations about the characteristics, behaviors, and roles deemed appropriate for individuals based on their perceived gender. These stereotypes frequently reflect traditional, binary views of gender, ascribing specific traits and expectations to men and women.[13] While stereotypes may vary across cultures, they can be broadly classified into several categories, including those pertaining to personality traits. The prevailing stereotypes of men and women are that men are dominant, rational, and aggressive, while women are emotional, nurturing, and passive.[14] Another area of consideration is that of occupational roles. Historically, men have been associated with leadership and high-status positions, such as CEOs, politicians or engineers, whereas women have been expected

---

[9] Fairclough (1995).

[10] Van Dijk (1993).

[11] Wodak and Meyer (2009).

[12] Kress and Van Leeuwen (2001).

[13] Eagly and Wood (2012), pp. 458–476.

[14] Prentice and Carranza (2002), pp. 269–281.

Table 1 Male and female characteristics

Men and boys	Women and girls
Strong	Beautiful
Violent	Peacefull
Unemotional, harsh	Emotional, mild
Aggressive	Obedient
Competitive	Self-sacrificing
Predatory	Caring, nurturing
Protective	Vulnerable
Independent	Dependent
Active	Passive
Analyzing	Synthesizing
Thinking quantitatively	Thinking qualitatively
Rational	Intuitive
Stable	Sensitive
Powerful	Cautious
Persistent	Shy
Self-confident	Easily irritable
	Sentimental

to occupy caregiving roles, such as early childhood educators or nurses.[15] Additionally, gender stereotypes influence perceptions of physical appearance, associating masculinity with strength and femininity with beauty or thinness.[16] In her book *Barnbokens byggklossar*, Maria Nikolajeva provides a summary of these aspects in tabular form, which serves as a useful tool for analysis (see Table 1).[17]

Numerous studies have demonstrated the deleterious effects of gender stereotypes or stereotype threat when individuals are at risk of confirming negative stereotypes about their group. To illustrate, they influence the formation of educational preferences. Boys are frequently directed towards STEM (science, technology, engineering, and mathematics) disciplines, whereas girls may encounter discouragement from pursuing these prestigious fields, despite evidence indicating that they are equally capable.[18] This has resulted in the continued existence of a gender disparity in STEM careers.[19] Furthermore, gender stereotypes exert a considerable influence on leadership roles, as the assumption that men are inherently more suited to leadership responsibilities contributes to the underrepresentation of women in managerial and executive positions.[20] This stereotype is further reinforced by the "role congruity

[15] Heilman (2012), pp. 113–135.

[16] Fredrickson and Roberts (1997), pp.173–206.

[17] Nikolajeva (2017), p. 193 (My translation).

[18] Organisation for Economic Co-operation and Development (OECD) (2015).

[19] Charlesworth and Banaji (2022), pp. 538–549 and Piloto (2023).

[20] Heilman (2012), pp. 113–135.

theory", which posits that women are penalized when they assume leadership roles that are perceived as incongruent with their expected nurturing nature.[21] The presence of gender stereotypes has also been demonstrated to impede the full and authentic expression of emotions, which can in turn give rise to a range of mental health concerns. For example, societal expectations often dictate that men should suppress their emotions and adopt a stoic demeanor, which can contribute to the development of depression and anxiety.[22] Moreover, the perpetuation of stereotypes associating masculinity with aggression and dominance contributes to the higher rates of violence and sexual harassment experienced by women and serves to perpetuate a culture that tolerates or excuses such behavior.[23] Similarly, women may be subjected to social pressure to conform to ideals of emotional availability, which can contribute to elevated stress levels and the development of self-esteem issues.[24] As for individuals who identify as non-binary, they frequently encounter stereotypes and social obstacles due to the fact that their gender identities do not align with the conventional norms associated with traditional gender roles. At times, their gender identity is dismissed or perceived as non-existent. Such forms of minority stress can result in feelings of confusion, self-doubt, and emotional exhaustion.[25] Gender neutral individuals are often stereotyped as confused or mentally ill, leading to further stigmatization. This stereotype contrasts with binary transgender people, who are more likely to be recognized if they conform to societal expectations of gender transitions.[26]

A number of studies have highlighted the continued prevalence of gender stereotypes and inequality in educational resources, underscoring the necessity for sustained reforms to guarantee equitable representation.[27] Inequitable representation constitutes a form of sexism which can be said to exist when texts and illustrations in schoolbooks depict men and women in stereotyped roles "without criticizing it or presenting alternatives. This can be seen as an implicit acceptance of existing inequalities and discrimination".[28]

The examination of gender stereotypes (if any) in the *Chez nous* series is conducted through three principal avenues: the analysis of the characters' activities, the investigation of their conduct, and the examination of the language used by the authors. But prior to an analysis of these aspects it is first necessary to consider the visibility of each gender.

---

[21] Eagly and Karau (2002), pp. 573–598.

[22] Mahalik et al. (2007), pp. 2201–2209.

[23] Flood and Pease (2009), pp. 125–142.

[24] Fredrickson and Roberts (1997), pp.173–206.

[25] Johnson et al. (2020), pp. 222–233.

[26] Howansky et al. (2019), pp. 478–495.

[27] Nowak (2021), pp. 424–433.

[28] Lelièvre and Lelièvre (2014), p. 198.

2 Visibility of Male, Female and Non-binary Characters

2.1 A Strong Quantitative Representation of Women and Girls

Many studies indicate that, despite efforts to achieve gender balance, women and girls remain underrepresented and less visible in a considerable number of textbooks across the globe. This phenomenon is indicative of the pervasive stereotype that women are inherently passive, shy, less significant, and contribute less to society. Consequently, it can hinder the potential to provide a diverse array of positive female role models, not to mention the fact that the condition of invisibility is inextricably linked with a sense of powerlessness.

In contrast to the aforementioned persistent trend, the *Chez nous* series features a strong quantitative representation of female characters. Indeed, of the 160 character designations (first or last names such as "Madame Martin" or "Monsieur Morel"), 73 are male and 87 are female. Furthermore, the iconographic representations accentuate the prevalence of female characters, with a ratio of 342 to 291. With regard to the covers, there is a precise equality in representation, with two depicting girls (*Chez nous 6* and *8*) and two portraying boys (*Chez nous 7* and *9*). It is however unfortunate that there is no non-binary character represented, which precludes the possibility of direct identification for students in this group. This total exclusion may be attributed to a lack of awareness regarding the matter, despite the growing importance of this issue in the media and the willingness of the Swedish parliament to debate a bill recognizing the existence of a third gender.[29] Furthermore, it can be attributed to the fact that a considerable proportion of educational materials is based on traditional gender norms that have historically recognized only male and female identities. Consequently, they are often slow to adapt to new social realities.

Quantitative observation of the illustrations also allows us to determine the scarcity of stereotyped clothing (the majority of garments are gender-neutral if we exclude four images of veiled Muslim women) and the moderate use of the color pink, which is the color traditionally associated with femininity.[30] A total of 31 girls are depicted wearing pink, while only six boys are shown in this color, which may be interpreted as a (modest) contribution to the idea that pink is also a suitable choice for boys. Gender-stereotyped clothing perpetuates the idea that people should adhere to predefined roles based on their gender and reinforces the notion that certain behaviors, or characteristics are only appropriate for one gender, limiting opportunities for both women and men to express themselves freely.

[29] Renman (2018)

[30] Cunningham and Macrae (2011), pp. 598–614.

An observation of the dialogues in the books can also provide insight into the visibility of different genders, in so far as they play an essential role from a pedagogical perspective. Direct exchanges between characters present invaluable opportunities for language practice and proficiency development in addition to demonstrating appropriate language usage. Dialogues are regarded as an effective means of representing the proper usage of the language and they convey a social pattern by categorizing people and distributing occupational and social roles.[31] The *Chez Nous* series features a plethora of dialogues, predominantly comprising characters of both genders. In instances where this is not the case, numerical parity is observed, with ten dialogues featuring exclusively male characters and an equal number centering on female figures.

While the authors have taken great care to ensure a good quantitative representation of women and girls, the same cannot be said for the qualitative representation.

2.2 A Lower Qualitative Representation of Women and Girls

In order to gain a more nuanced understanding of the concept of visibility, I have identified and categorized the recurring characters in each of the books, as opposed to those who make a single appearance. The outcome was a discernible male predominance in the first two books (the only ones to include recurring characters), wherein the most frequently appearing protagonists are Karim and Alexandre, who collectively appear on 11 occasions within the primary texts. Moreover, each of them has a dedicated text: "La journée de Karim"[32] and "Mes copains".[33]

The selection of a recurring character's gender is not arbitrary because recurring characters can provide a sense of familiarity, creating a bond between the pupils and the world of the narrative. Such characters are frequently regarded as more significant due to the opportunity they afford readers to form emotional connections with them and to vicariously experience their diverse narratives.

2.3 An Under-Representation of Female Historical Figures

Upon examining the corpus for references to historical characters we find that women are greatly underrepresented in *Chez Nous*, as evidenced by the fact that a total of 26 historical figures are referred to (across all texts included), with only six of these being women. For example, the two books read by the pupils in the fictional classes are *Le petit prince* and *Le tour du monde en 80 jours*, both by male authors, and

[31] Jones et al. (1997), pp. 469–490.

[32] *Chez nous* 6, pp. 78–79.

[33] *Chez nous* 6, pp. 134–135.

the people that are honored by having schools and streets named after them are all male,[34] as is the stereotype of intelligence, Einstein.[35]

A more focused examination of the material presented at the end of some chapters, which can be described as quasi-authentic because it draws on resources derived from authentic real-life sources, as opposed to material created with the explicit intention of facilitating language learning or teaching, offers a slightly different perspective. Indeed, when these sources are taken into account, the imbalance between male and female representation is less pronounced but has not disappeared. Among the few characters who deserve more in-depth treatment and longer texts, we find four women: Rachel Mwanza, Queen Marie Antoinette, Camille Claudel and Hedwig Kiesler (in much shorter form) and five men: Vincent Van Gogh, Gustave Eiffel, Jules Vernes, Axel von Fersen and Alfred Dreyfus.

Such content, found in many language textbooks, facilitate cultural understanding by enabling learners to gain insights into the context in which the language is used. Furthermore, when they are devoted to the presentation of historical figures, they can foster positive role modelling, allowing readers to identify with these individuals. This illustrates the necessity of offering a range of identification options. The underrepresentation of women in historically significant roles in educational materials represents a significant issue that affects how future generations understand the past. It is of course not uncommon as even history textbooks prioritise often the achievements and perspectives of men, while omitting the crucial contributions and experiences of women. This omission can perpetuate the misconception that women have played a lesser role in shaping history.

The inclusion of Hedwig Kiesler, an inventor and scientist, on page 46 in *Chez nous 9* deserves special mention because it has the potential to positively influence the engagement of female readers in scientific pursuits. Indeed, a study published in 2008 demonstrated the positive effect of a female role model in mathematics on female students' academic performance. When such a model is presented as having worked assiduously to achieve success, it can motivate girls to believe that they, too, can succeed with hard work. The results of this study support the notion that gendered representations are significant in the context of academic success.[36] It would have been reasonable to anticipate a more prominent representation of notable women in the books, particularly in the context of scientific achievements.

---

[34] Streets and places: Emile Zola, Picasso, Réaumur, Victor Hugo, Juste Fontaine. Schools: René Descartes, Henri Matisse, Saint Exupéry, Pasteur, Chateaubriand.

[35] *Chez nous* 9, p. 31.

[36] Bagès et al. (2008), pp. 3–11.

Table 2 Presentation of professions by gender from all sources, textual and graphic

Professions	Male characters	Female characters
Neutral professions	18	15
Female-dominated professions	6	10
Male-dominated professions or those in positions of power	23	15

3 Activities Portrayed

Professional occupations and other activities exert a considerable influence on how individuals define themselves and are perceived by others.[37] It is therefore imperative to provide both girls and boys with a plethora of opportunities, exemplifying a diverse array of models that challenge traditional conventions and stereotypes and facilitate the realization of their full potential.

3.1 Traditional Presentation of Professional Roles

The first observation that can be made from studying the corpus, is that the authors have adopted a rather traditional perspective on the distribution of professional roles between genders, as illustrated in the table below (see Table 2).

The categorization of a profession within a specific category is informed by a multitude of studies that demonstrate, for instance, that certain professions are historically associated with women, such as nursing, retail sales, early childhood education, and other professions are often perceived as masculine, such as law enforcement, firefighting, and those linked to positions of authority, such as company CEOs. Teacher, which is the profession most frequently referenced in the corpus (given that the pupils depicted interact with their teachers on a daily basis), has been classified as neutral.

A review of the results indicates that each professional category is predominantly occupied by the gender that historically characterizes it. This would be even more the case if we had excluded the examples from pages 45 to 47 in *Chez nous 9*, which discuss job names and list professions with their masculine and feminine genders where possible (these are the sole occurrences of the words *policière* (policewoman) or *infirmier* (male nurse), for example).

When the focus is solely on the characters present in the various narratives, with whom students can more readily identify, certain stereotypes tend to be accentuated. To illustrate, the profession of police officer is referenced on five occasions and is assumed by only male characters. It is noteworthy that none of the male characters are nurses, while three female figures occupy this role. Furthermore, the role of au pair is exclusively assumed by a female character. In terms of the most esteemed role, that of President of the Republic, it is held by a man who is referenced in a

[37] Christiansen (1999), pp. 547–58.

fictitious press headline, similarly to the role of mayor of a city who is depicted in a portrait as a portly gentleman with a big beard.[38]

The archetypal role of housewife is implicitly present in the text "Au boulot" in the context of a recently unemployed father and a reunited family facing financial difficulties due to the loss of their principal source of income. The narrative ultimately concludes with the family's decision to operate a café, the mother will then assume the responsibility for assisting in the kitchen.[39]

3.2 *Scarcity of Counter Stereotypes in Professional Roles*

In the search for potential representations that challenge traditional gender roles, we encounter a male hairdresser, a man selling women's clothing, a young girl aspiring to become a professional soccer player or a plumber like her father, and, Mrs. Richard, a woman occupying the esteemed position of CEO of a company. Nevertheless, it is difficult to categorize this final example as a counter-stereotype, given that the position of Mrs. Richard is called into question.[40] Indeed, she is the proprietor of the Rimeca automobile garage, an enterprise that is typically associated with masculine environments. She inherited the company from her late husband and the employees do not hold her in high regard, perceiving her as lacking competence and as a person who is harsh in her dealings with others. This is evidenced by the account presented.

It is unfortunate that no woman was included as a role model for successful and accomplished entrepreneurship, given that the promotion of women in high-ranking job positions is pivotal in combating gender stereotypes and fostering gender equality. The visibility of women in leadership roles challenges the long-held assumption that men are inherently suited for high-status positions. This, in turn, makes it easier for other women to be perceived as capable leaders.[41]

The tendency towards a stereotypical portrayal of professions observed in the *Chez nous* series may not be a conscious decision on the part of the authors. Rather, it may be attributed to the prototype theory, which posits that a prototype is internalized through social interaction, thereby exemplifying a given profession in this instance.[42] Consequently, despite the current existence of male nurses, the prototype remains the female nurse, as evidenced in English by the frequent addition of the adjective *male* to the word *nurse*. In *Chez nous*, some of the female characters in the narratives are nurses, and all the nurses are women.

---

[38] *Chez nous 6*, p. 6 and *Chez nous 8*, p. 77.

[39] *Chez nous 9*, pp. 42–43.

[40] Chez nous 9, pp. 38–39.

[41] Heilman (2012), pp.113–135.

[42] Yule (1996), p. 119.

3.3 *Hobbies and Other Activities*

Promoting the visibility of girls in masculine activities and boys in feminine activities not only fosters gender equality but also enhances their confidence and mental well-being. It provides essential role models and helps to reshape societal perceptions regarding gender roles in athletics for example. These changes are vital for creating an environment where all children can pursue their interests freely, regardless of gender.

It is unsurprising that a plethora of activities are described in teaching manuals, and in order to ascertain whether gender stereotypes have infiltrated the material, we concentrate our examination on activities that are perceived to be particularly gendered.

3.3.1 A Relatively Nuanced Representation of Sports Activities

The sports traditionally associated with boys in the series have been identified as soccer, motorcycling, ice hockey and judo. With regard to these activities, the authors evince a notably progressive vision. With the exception of soccer, which is played by five boys and three girls (the latter not appearing in the main texts), ice hockey is only played by a girl, and motorcycling is solely practised by a woman.[43] The only characters engaged in combat sports are two maternal figures, namely Madame Hussein (Karim's mother) and Madame Saidi, their North African origin serving to reinforce the counter-stereotype.[44]

The practice of dancing is the sole sport traditionally associated with femininity that has been identified within the corpus. In accordance with the reputation of the practice, it is performed by two female and only one male character.

3.3.2 Hobbies and Informal Tasks

The activities of reading books,[45] playing the flute, shopping and babysitting have been identified as typically feminine, whereas activities such as drumming and online gaming are more commonly associated with a masculine identity.

The corpus reveals that shopping and reading books are the only activities that can be considered to be displayed in a stereotypical manner. This is exemplified by the trope of three girls reading books and eight girls going shopping, as well as the stereotypical nature of their purchases, such as clothes. In this domain, there is a dearth of counter-stereotypes, even if there is an instance where two male characters

---

43 *Chez nous 6*, p. 52.

44 *Chez nous 6*, p. 114 and *Chez nous* 7, p. 85.

45 Data from surveys has shown that women read more than men, and fiction reading is especially associated with women: Tepper (2000), pp. 255–275 and Pew Research Center (2016).

are observed loitering in a flea market with their female companions,[46] another one where two boys are shopping for Christmas presents,[47] and finally a boy stating that he is going shopping with his mother.[48] No male characters are depicted engaging in the act of reading a book.

In the remaining cases, both drummers are women, online games are played by a girl and a boy, and the sole character who plays the flute is Pierre Bonpain,[49] who is presented as a family man. It is also noteworthy that the act of babysitting, which is mentioned/depicted on only two occasions, is performed on each occasion by male characters.[50]

In contrast to the findings regarding professions, extra-professional activities are depicted in a more nuanced manner from a gender perspective, with the exception of soccer, which continues to be portrayed as a domain that is predominantly male dominated.

4 The Behavior of Male and Female Characters

The various categories used to analyze character behavior are principally derived from those established as stereotypes by Nikolajeva, provided that they could be identified in the corpus. This analysis will concentrate on the principal texts and their illustrations, as well as the longer texts that suggest additional reading material. Exercise pages, which may also include illustrations, are excluded from the analysis, as well as passages relating to historical figures.

4.1 Women are Presented as Being More Caring and Nurturing

The caring attitude is analyzed in relation to the character's role in caring for children and managing the family (for example, cooking for the family, doing housework, etc.). The results demonstrate that a greater proportion of these responsibilities is assumed by women in comparison to their male counterparts. In these contexts, 12 female characters are presented against six male characters. However, it would be an error to assume that all six examples can be considered counter-stereotypes. It is for example evident that, although Alexandre's father is responsible for caring for him, waking him up, and preparing his breakfast, there is no woman who could assume

[46] *Chez nous 6*, p. 51–52.
[47] *Chez nous 7*, p. 36.
[48] *Chez nous 6*, p. 124.
[49] *Chez nous* 7, p.84.
[50] *Chez nous 6*, p. 124 and 145.

this role, as Alexandre has two fathers.[51] Two further instances in which fathers assume childcare responsibilities are those of divorced fathers who find themselves alone with their children during periods of vacation. Nevertheless, three examples may be regarded as counter-stereotypes. First the initial dialogue of *Chez nous 6* features a visual representation of a father embracing his daughter. Additionally, the portrayal of Clara's father in a restaurant setting provides an example of contrasting dynamics. While he attempts to caution her about potential stains on her clothes and looks sorry once her trousers are soiled, her mother observes with a detached and somewhat ironic demeanor.[52] As a final example, we may consider the case of young Eric, who assists his mother in preparing the family meal.[53]

It is also noteworthy that when men assume childcare responsibilities, they do so in isolation, whereas women sometimes bear the burden of family caregiving, which may entail preparing meals, for example.

Social spaces, especially kitchens are also of significance on the ground that historically, the kitchen has served as a focal point for family life, where the act of preparing and sharing meals is tied to cultural associations of warmth and nurture. This emotional connection remains strong even in modern homes, symbolizing the nurturing role often attributed to the kitchen.[54] It is perhaps unsurprising, then, that two out of three kitchen scenes feature female characters.

4.2 Active Versus Passive

The traditional view is that men are more active, and women are more passive. From a semiotic perspective, it can be argued that in narratives, men are more frequently assigned the role of the subject according to Greimas' actantial model, a framework used to analyze the structure of stories by breaking them down into key actants (or roles) that drive the narrative forward. The six core actants are as follows: subject, object, sender, receiver, helper, and opponent. Each actant fulfills a particular function within the narrative and the subject is the central figure whose actions or quest the story revolves around.[55] In instances where a central character could be identified (as opposed to when the narrative features multiple characters of both genders in a relatively equal capacity), a distinct male predominance was observed, with 31 instances, in comparison to 23 stories in which female characters assume the role of main protagonist, out of a total of 85 occurrences. A typical example of this role distribution can be found in Chap. 3, section C of *Chez nous* 6, entitled "Tu aimes les animaux?" In this section, the subject, a boy, displays proudly the animals he owns

[51] *Chez nous 7*, p. 12. Although it's not really a challenge to the gender stereotype, it is noteworthy that the authors challenge here the conventional notion of the traditional nuclear family unit.

[52] *Chez nous 6*, p. 91.

[53] *Chez nous 9*, p. 42.

[54] Cooper (1987), pp. 328 - 332.

[55] Greimas (1966).

to a girl. Initially, the girl is amazed by the array of creatures, but her initial awe soon gives way to terror when she notices a snake in the boy's pocket.

To exemplify the function of the subject or hero, the theme of love and the experience of falling in love can be contemplated as well. This is a pervasive theme in literature designed for teenage readers, whether in textbooks or not. A total of ten instances of this theme can be identified, comprising either simple references to a character's romantic feelings or more elaborate narratives.[56] In the ten cases under consideration, there are only two instances in which it is explicitly stated that a female protagonist is in love.[57]

Finally, to examine the stereotypical opposition between the active man and the passive woman, it is interesting to observe the dialogues between characters who are initially unfamiliar with each other and whose objective is to get to know each other. For example, an initial exchange such as "Comment tu t'appelles" (What's your name?) may be analyzed in this context. It is notable that in all three instances, it is the male characters who assume the initiative, thereby substantiating the hypothesis that the analysis of the passive/active opposition demonstrates a distinct inclination towards substantiating the stereotype.

4.3 Violent, Aggressive, Illegal Behaviors

Given that there are more men than women incarcerated globally,[58] it can be inferred that there are more violent men than violent women. This observation contributes to the persistence of a pervasive stereotype suggesting that men are in general more violent and aggressive than women, who are perceived to be more peaceful. This stereotype is reinforced by a complex interplay of cultural, historical, and societal factors, including perceptions shaped by media portrayals and sometimes interpretations of biological differences.[59] The perpetuation of stereotypes pertaining to gender and violence can serve to reinforce harmful expectations, thereby impeding the ability of men to express vulnerability and hindering the recognition and addressing of instances of female violence in specific contexts.

The *Chez nous* manuals corroborate, to a certain extent, this stereotyped representation, as illustrated in Table 3, which depicts the distribution of male and female characters with regard to aggressive and illegal behaviors, with a predominance of males.

---

[56] In *Chez nous 6* Karim is in love with Nathalie (p. 79), in *Chez nous* 7, François is in love with Mathilde (p. 16) and Arthur is in love with Alice (p. 41), in *Chez nous* 8, Patrick recounts his first love (p.42-43), Samir declares that he is in love with Antoine (p. 40), and Antoine tells the long story of how he fell in love with Juliette (p. 94-101). In *Chez nous 9* we learn that Thomas is in love with Charlotte (p.23) and that Sabir is in love with Léa (p. 31).

[57] When Sandrine declares her love for Julien (p. 35 of *Chez nous 8*) and when Chadia confesses her love for Thomas (p. 40 of the same book).

[58] Who (2020).

[59] Ainsworth and Maner (2012), pp. 819–29.

Table 3 Illegal and aggressive behaviors according to gender

Illegal and aggressive behaviors	Male characters	Female characters
Theft	Car theft Theft of goods from a shop Burglary of telephones in a shop	Theft of a pair of trousers
Fraud		Corporate fraud
False testimony to the police		As the author of an accident As a witness
Drug sales	A dealer	
Physical aggression	Attack against a tagger	
Traffic violation	A man drives at over 100 km/h where the speed limit is 80 km/h	
Total number of illegal actions	6	4

It is worthy of note that one of the offenses exemplifies the authors' intention to challenge conventional stereotypes. The case in question concerns the fraud committed by Laurence Hammond, a female character who attempts to flee to Brazil after embezzling three million euros from her place of employment. A similar criminal act was committed by a male perpetrator, Laurent Hammond, in the preceding edition of the book, published in 2016.[60]

4.4 *Girls are not as Obedient as They are Supposed to Be*

Nikolajeva posits that obedience represents a stereotypically feminine quality. However, when this aspect is present in the corpus, the authors choose to challenge it, as evidenced by the story of Chadia, whose family wishes for her to marry Samir, yet she has no intention of obeying. In fact, she is secretly in love with a French boy named Thomas. She discusses this openly with Samir, who also refuses the arranged marriage on the grounds that he is in love with Antoine.[61] It is important to note, however, that this is a unique instance and that portraying an arranged marriage in a positive light would have been unthinkable in a publication intended for Swedish schoolchildren.

---

[60] Hirsch et al. (2016), pp. 46–48.

[61] *Chez nous 8*, p. 38–40.

4.5 A Somewhat Stereotypical View of Competence and Performance

4.5.1 More Women are Presented as Professionally Incompetent

As previously stated, there are long-standing stereotypes that women are less competent than men, particularly in domains such as STEM, as well as in leadership roles.[62]

The sole character who exemplifies this type of incompetence is the aforementioned female character, Mrs. Richard, who serves as the CEO of a car garage (see 3.2). There is not example of a woman operating a business in a competent manner, regardless of whether the environment is traditionally masculine or not.

Another instance of gross incompetence involves a much lower position and concerns the au pair, Emilie, who is responsible for failing to supervise the child in her care. While Emilie was engaged in conversation with another au pair in a park in Washington, DC, the child disappeared but was fortunately subsequently located by a male figure who could be considered the hero of the situation.[63]

Only one male character can be described as "professionally incompetent", a police officer who, rather than taking immediate action to prevent a vehicle theft, delays by absurdly questioning a witness who alerts him to the incident.[64]

4.5.2 The Educational Performance of Boys is Inferior to that of Girls

Studies show that girls tend to perform better academically than boys, particularly in areas such as reading and writing. A meta-analysis of school grades from over 500,000 students revealed that, over a period of several decades, girls consistently scored higher than boys in all subjects, and this trend was particularly strong in literary subjects. This led to the perception that boys would be less academically competent, even if these differences in performance were not present in all contexts or disciplines.[65]

The corpus does not contain any references to girls experiencing difficulties at school. However, two boys are mentioned as facing challenges in this area. Kevin is reported to have difficulties with English, while Samuel is repeating the sixth grade.[66]

---

[62] Moss-Racusin et al. (2012), pp. 16,474–16,479, and Eagly and Karau (2002), pp. 573–598.

[63] *Chez nous 9*, p. 49.

[64] *Chez nous 8*, p. 92–93.

[65] Voyer and Voyer (2014), pp.1174–1204.

[66] *Chez nous 7*, p. 27.

4.5.3 Girls are Vulnerable

In general, it is evident that girls are depicted as more vulnerable than boys. To illustrate, the sole episode in which fear is depicted is the one in which a female character is afraid of a snake, which is a male character's pet.[67]

Similarly, three female figures are observed in situations where they display a certain degree of clumsiness or mention such situations (staining trousers with ice cream,[68] dropping a mobile phone,[69] hitting a passerby on the head with a mini golf ball,[70] falling while ice skating[71]) whereas none of the masculine characters exhibit this trait. It is also notable that two of the girls are unwell,[72] whereas none of the boys are similarly affected. This final point is consistent with the stereotype highlighted by Nikolajeva, which suggests that boys are typically stronger than girls. The sole vulnerability exhibited by male protagonists is fatigue (see 5.1).

In summary, it can be posited that the various characters' behaviors largely adhere to the stereotypes associated with their respective genders.

5 Stereotyped Language

Linguistic analysis can also be employed to identify gender stereotypes, whether through a semantic or grammatical approach.

5.1 Adjectives Collocating with Male and Female Characters

An observation of adjectives indicates that there is a tendency for certain adjectives to be more frequently associated with one gender than another. The sentence *Cet homme est joli* (This man is pretty) would be regarded as semantically unusual (in French and English), as the adjective *joli* is not typically used to describe an adult male. In accordance with prevailing social norms, a male individual is typically described as *beau* (handsome) rather than *joli*.[73] Consequently, although the sentence is grammatically correct, it would appear unusual to readers, the term *joli* being typically used to describe women, children, or animals. A review of the corpus reveals an absence of instances of unconventional adjective collocation with a potential to challenge gender stereotypes.

---

67 *Chez nous 6*, p. 101.

68 *Chez nous 6*, p. 91.

69 *Chez nous 6*, p. 31.

70 *Chez nous 6*, p. 19.

71 *Chez nous 7*, p. 64.

72 *Chez nous 7*, p. 20 and *Chez nous 9*, p. 6.

73 Barczewska and Agata (2018), pp.193–213.

A review of the textbooks shows that the number of adjectives used to describe characters is relatively limited. Furthermore, the number of tokens for male and female characters is equal. (27). Two adjectives are worthy of particular mention in terms of their frequency of occurrence: the adjectives *fatigué* (tired) and *gentil* (nice) appear each on six occasions. The use of the term *tired* to describe five boys (with only one girl exhibiting fatigue) can be seen as a challenge to the stereotype that men are inherently strong. However, this interpretation must be mitigated given that the characters in question are all adolescents, who are commonly associated with feelings of fatigue (being tired is almost a stereotype of adolescence).

The most frequently used adjective to describe female characters is *gentille*, which appears six times. This aligns with the conventional portrayal of women and girls as benevolent and nurturing.

Numerous studies show that female characters are typically portrayed in terms of their appearance[74] but our corpus presents a discrepancy with these findings, as the second most prevalent adjective used to describe boys is *beau*, which is employed on three occasions, whereas adjectives pertaining to physical appearance are utilized only twice to describe girls. On one occasion, the term *belle* (beautiful) is used, and on another, *mignone* (cute) is employed.

5.2 An Androcentric Standard

In accordance with the prevailing norms observed in French-language texts, the authors of *Chez nous* have elected to adopt an androcentric standard, even though it has been argued that French, like many other languages, reflects and reinforces stereotypic gender roles through its grammatical rules and structures, which systematically prioritize the masculine over the feminine.[75] Textbook authors can hardly be expected to challenge the grammatical norm, but a few minor adaptations could have been contemplated.

Inclusive writing (or *écriture inclusive*) in French is often presented as a way to challenge and reduce gender stereotypes by promoting gender equality through language. Praised by some and criticized by others who view it as overly complicated or artificial and even ineffective in reducing gender stereotypes,[76] it aims to make women and non-binary individuals more visible. The practice includes various strategies such as using both masculine and feminine forms (e.g., *étudiant.e.s* for students), neutralizing gendered terms, or creating new words. From a cognitive perspective, studies in psycholinguistics suggest that the use of masculine generic forms can reinforce mental associations between gender and certain roles or traits. For example, a study by Gygax et al. found that when people read sentences using

---

[74] Baker and Freebody (1989) and Gouvias and Alexopoulos (2018), pp. 642–662.

[75] Baudino (2001) Politique de la langue et différence sexuelle – La politisation du genre des noms de métier.

[76] Abbou (2023).

masculine generics (e.g., *les étudiants*), they tended to visualize male individuals, even when the text theoretically referred to both genders. In contrast, when both masculine and feminine forms were explicitly mentioned, readers were more likely to imagine a mixed-gender group.[77] This indicates that inclusive writing can have a tangible effect on how people think about gender, making it a potential tool for combating stereotypes.

Notwithstanding the potential advantages previously outlined, the corpus reveals that the inhabitants of a country are invariably referred to as *les habitants*, never *les habitantes* or *les habitant.e.s*. Furthermore, an evident opportunity to utilize inclusive language was not seized when a French girl bidding farewell wrote a letter entitled "Adieu, mes chers amis!" instead of *Adieu, mes chers ami.e.s!* which could have been feasible as she corresponded with both boys and girls.

In accordance with the noted generic masculine bias, it can be observed that all animals are male. Notably, even on a page specifically dedicated to the learning of animal names, the names of the females of each breed (where applicable) are absent. The students will then learn the word *lion*, but not the feminine *lionne*, the word *chien* (dog), not *chienne*, and so forth. This finding is consistent with the results of other studies that have demonstrated the prevalence of gender-biased representations in the portrayal of animals.[78]

5.3 The Absence of a Neutral Pronoun

The pronoun *iel* is a gender-neutral personal pronoun in French, created as a combination of the masculine pronoun *il* (he) and the feminine pronoun *elle* (she). It is intended to provide a non-binary alternative for people who do not identify exclusively as male or female and can be employed in instances where the gender of the individual in question is unknown or unimportant. A comparison can be drawn between the Swedish pronoun *hen*, which has been created by the merger of the pronouns *han* (he) and *hon* (she).[79] The pronoun *iel* is used in French, primarily within non-binary, LGBTQ + communities, and it has gained increased visibility through its inclusion in dictionaries like Le Petit Robert's online edition. While its usage is still very limited and faces both linguistic and social resistance, academic discussions suggest that *iel* represents a step toward greater gender inclusivity and the recognition of non-binary identities in the French-speaking world.[80]

---

[77] Gygax et al. (2008), pp. 464–485.

[78] Norberg and Nordlund (2022), pp. 186–208.

[79] Le Bouteillec (2020), pp. 9.

[80] De Beaumont (2023).

6 Conclusion

The aim of this study was to identify any stereotypical representations of gender that may be present in textbooks, given the assumption that these vehicles of education and socialization play a role in shaping students' norms and opinions. The objective was to ascertain whether the *Chez nous* series fosters the propagation of simplistic and generalized beliefs or assumptions regarding the characteristics, roles, behaviors, or abilities deemed appropriate for individuals based on their gender. These aspects were examined from the perspective of critical discourse analysis, a theoretical approach that considers language as a tool shaped by social structures, such as institutions and power relationships, which in turn help to shape and influence those same structures. The objective of CDA is to identify the implicit power relationships embedded in language, with a particular focus on the ways in which marginalized or oppressed groups are affected. In contrast with the findings of numerous other researchers who have utilized school textbooks as their source material, our analysis shows a quantitative prevalence of female fictional characters in texts as well as in the iconic representations. Conversely, there is a notable absence of representation of non-binary individuals, depriving students who identify as such of any potential for identifying role models within the textbooks. With regard to texts that feature historical figures or make passing references to them in fictional discourses, there is a discernible imbalance in favor of male characters. This is an unsurprising outcome and reflects a fairly pervasive trend in a field that is still frequently overshadowed by male-dominated narratives. A critical examination of the professions depicted in the textbooks indicated a relatively traditional and stereotyped representation of the roles associated with each gender, despite the presence of a few counter-stereotypes. This is confirmed by the frequent depiction of women as nurses and men as policemen, However, this trend is reversed with regard to sports and hobbies, which are predominantly described in a non-stereotypical manner. An analysis of the behavior of male and female characters discloses again that traditional conceptions of gender roles are resistant to change. The caring and nurturing role is indeed assumed twice as often by female characters as by male characters. Furthermore, female protagonists are more passive than their male counterparts and less likely to occupy the position of central character or hero in the stories and even less likely to take the initiative for a new encounter.

In alignment with the stereotype that women are more peaceful, female protagonists perpetrate a reduced number of offenses, though they are not absent from this lexical field and can be seen as disobedient to their family. Female figures are also more vulnerable and weaker and less capable in managerial roles, whereas the educational performance of boys is sometimes inferior. The study concludes with an analysis of the linguistic aspect, which reveals that language is employed in a traditional and androcentric manner in the corpus.

The findings of the present study indicate that, despite the absence of overtly stereotypical gendered representations and the incorporation of strategies to mitigate sexism, the *Chez nous* manuals perpetuate some internalized gender-biased structures. This is evidenced by the relative confinement of males and females to traditional gender roles and the scarcity of gender-challenging themes and illustrations. This phenomenon can be attributed, at least in part, to a desire to reflect faithfully a certain social reality for the students, a reality in which gender stereotypes persist. However, it also reflects an inability to fully implement the curriculum's requirement that schools "actively and consciously promote the equal rights and opportunities of pupils, regardless of gender affiliation".[81]

References

Abbou J (2023) Inclusive writing. Gend Lang. https://doi.org/10.1558/genl.20021

Ainsworth S, Maner J (2012) Sex begets violence: mating motives, social dominance, and physical aggression in men. J Pers Soc Psychol 103(5):819–829

Bagès C, Martinot D, Toczek MC (2008) Le rôle modérateur de l'explication donnée à la réussite d'un modèle féminin sur la performance des filles en mathématiques: une étude exploratoire. Les Cah Int Psychol Soc 4:3–11

Baker CD, Freebody P (1989) Children's first school books. Introductions to the culture of literacy. Basil Blackwell, Cambridge

Ballantine J, Stuber J, Everitt J (2021) The sociology of education: a systematic analysis. Routledge, London

Barczewska S, Agata, A (2018) Good or marvelous? Pretty, cute or lovely? Male and female adjective use in MICASE. Suvremena lingvistika, pp 193–213

Charlesworth TE, Banaji MR (2022) Patterns of implicit and explicit stereotypes III: long-term change in gender stereotypes. Soc Psychol Pers Sci 10(4):538–549

Christiansen C (1999) The 1999 Eleanor Clarke Slagle Lecture. Defining lives: occupation as identity: an essay on competence, coherence, and the creation of meaning. Am J Occup Ther: Off Publ Am Occup Ther Assoc 53(6):547–558. https://doi.org/10.5014/AJOT.53.6.547

Cooper C (1987) The Ghost in the Kitchen: household technology at the Brattleboro Museum, Vermont. Technol Cult 28:328–332. https://doi.org/10.2307/3105571

Courrier international (2024) Infographie. La Suède, championne européenne de l'égalité de genre. https://www.courrierinternational.com/grand-format/infographie-la-suede-championne-europeenne-de-l-egalite-de-genre

Cunningham S, Macrae C (2011) The colour of gender stereotyping. Br J Psychol 102(3):598–614

De Beaumont E (2023) Vers une prise en compte de la non-binarité dans l'enseignement du FLE. Propositions pour un réagencement des pratiques pédagogiques. In: Recherches en didactique des langues et des cultures. Les cahiers de l'Acedle, pp 21–1

Eagly AH, Karau SJ (2002) Role congruity theory of prejudice toward female leaders. Psychol Rev 109(3):573–598

Eagly AH, Wood W (2012) Social role theory. In: Van Lange PAM, Kruglanski AW, Higgins ET (eds) Handbook of theories of social psychology. Sage, Thousand Oaks, pp 458–476

Fairclough N (1995) Critical discourse analysis: the critical study of language. Longman, Harlow

Flood M, Pease B (2009) Factors influencing attitudes to violence against women. Trauma Violence Abus 10(2):125–142

Fredrickson BL, Roberts TA (1997) Objectification theory: toward understanding women's lived experiences and mental health risks. Psychol Women Q 21(2):173–206

[81] Skolverket (2022), p. 5.

Gouvias D, Alexopoulos C (2018) Sexist stereotypes in the language textbooks of the Greek primary school: a multidimensional approach. Gend Educ 30(5):642–662
Greimas AJ (1966) Sémantique structurale: recherche de méthode. Larousse, Paris
Gygax P, Gabriel U, Sarrasin O, Oakhill J, Garnham A (2008) Generically intended, but specifically interpreted: when beauticians, musicians, and mechanics are all men. Lang Cognit Process 23(3):464–485
Heilman ME (2012) Gender stereotypes and workplace bias. Res Organ Behav 32:113–135
Hermansson C, Wilhemsson, L, Winblad M (2022a) Chez nous Allt-i-ett åk 6. Sanoma utbildning, Stockholm
Hermansson D, Hirsch C, Wilhemsson L, Winblad M (2022b) Chez nous Textbok åk 7. Sanoma utbildning, Stockholm
Hermansson D, Hirsch C, Norén G, Wilhemsson L, Winblad M (2023) Chez nous Textbok åk 8. Sanoma utbildning, Stockholm
Hermansson D, Hirsch C, Norén G, Wilhemsson L, Winblad M (2024) Chez nous Textbok åk 9. Sanoma utbildning, Stockholm
Hirsch C, Winblad M, Norén G (2016) Chez nous Franska 4. Sanoma utbildning, Stockholm
Howansky K, Wilton L, Young D, Abrams S, Clapham R (2019) (Trans)gender stereotypes and the self: content and consequences of gender identity stereotypes. Self Identity 20:478–495
Hussonnois-Alaya C (2017) Stéréotypes: deux écoles suéses bannissent les termes "fille" et "garçon". BFMTV. https://www.bfmtv.com/international/europe/stereotypes-deux-ecoles-suesses-bannissent-les-termes-fille-et-garcon_AN-201709280059.html
Johnson K, LeBlanc A, Deardorff J, Bockting W (2020) Invalidation experiences among non-binary adolescents. J Sex Res 57:222–233
Jones MA, Kitetu C, Sunderland J (1997) Discourse roles, gender and language textbook dialogues: who learns what from John and Sally? Gend Educ 9(4):469–490
Kress G, Van Leeuwen T (2001) Multimodal discourse: the modes and media of contemporary communication. Arnold, London
Lapaquellerie M (2023) Stéréotypes de genre dans les manuels face aux représentations des élèves: étude d'un corpus de manuels et mise en perspective dans une classe de CE2. Sciences de l'Homme et Société. dumas-04338749
Le Bouteillec N (2020) *Hen* et la quête de l'égalité en Suède. Cah Genre 2:205–229
Lelièvre F, Lelièvre C (2014) L'histoire des femmes publiques contée aux enfants. Presses universitaires de France, Paris
Mahalik JR, Burns SM, Syzdek M (2007) Masculinity and perceived normative health behaviors as predictors of men's health behaviors. Soc Sci Med 64(11):2201–2209
Mosconi N (2008) Mai 68: le féminisme de la « deuxième vague » et l'analyse du sexisme en éducation. Les Sci l'éducation-Pour L'ère Nouvelle 41(3):117–140
Moss-Racusin CA, Dovidio JF, Brescoll VL, Graham MJ, Handelsman J (2012) Science faculty's subtle gender biases favor male students. Proc Natl Acad Sci 109(41):16474–16479
Nikolajeva M (2017) Barnbokens byggklossar. Studentlitteratur, Lund
Norberg C, Nordlund M (2022) Why are all dogs male? Gender in Swedish EFL textbooks. Educare 3:186–208
Nowak JK (2021) Gender inequality in education. In: Daniela L (ed) Human, technologies and quality of education, pp 424–433
Organisation for Economic Co-operation and Development (OECD) (2015) The ABC of gender equality in education: aptitude, behaviour, confidence. OECD Publishing, Paris
Pew Research Center (2016) Book reading 2016. https://www.pewresearch.org/internet/2016/09/01/book-reading-2016/
Piloto C (2023) The gender gap in STEM: still gaping in 2023. Professional Education, Massachusetts Institute of Technology. https://professionalprograms.mit.edu/blog/leadership/the-gender-gap-in-stem/

Prentice DA, Carranza E (2002) What women and men should be, shouldn't be, are allowed to be, and don't have to be: the contents of prescriptive gender stereotypes. Psychol Women Q 26(4):269–281
Renman F (2018) En majoritet i riksdagen vill utreda frågan om ett tredje juridiskt kön. SVT Nyheter. https://www.svt.se/nyheter/inrikes/en-majoritet-vill-infora-ett-tredje-juridiskt-kon
Skolverket (2022) Curriculum for compulsory school, preschool class and school-age educare. https://www.skolverket.se/getFile?file=13128
Tepper S (2000) Fiction reading in America: explaining the gender gap. Poetics 27:255–275
Van Dijk TA (1993) Elite discourse and racism. Sage, Thousand Oaks
Voyer D, Voyer SD (2014) Gender differences in scholastic achievement: a meta-analysis. Psychol Bull 140(4):1174–1204
Who (2020) Workshop: women and prison: vulnerability and overlapping health needs of women in prison worldwide. Eur J Public Health 30.
Wodak R, Meyer M (2009) Methods of critical discourse analysis. Sage, Thousand Oaks
Yule G (1996) The study of language. Cambridge University Press

Nathalie Hauksson-Tresch is a senior lecturer at Linnaeus University (Sweden), Faculty of Arts and Humanities, Department of Languages and Program coordinator for Language and Politics. She holds a Ph.D. in law from the University Robert Shuman in Strasbourg and a Ph.D. in roman languages from the University of Gothenburg. She also has a bachelor's degree in Icelandic from the University of Iceland. She teaches various courses at all levels, especially orientated towards linguistics, and the translation of non-fictional texts. Her field of research is legal semiotics, text linguistics, discourse analysis and the interdisciplinary connection between law and literature. She is a member of the editorial board of the International Journal for the Semiotics of Law—Revue internationale de Sémiotique juridique.

Challenging Gender Stereotypes in China: The Discursive Interaction Among Media, Political and Legal Discourse Regarding Gender Roles

Wei Yu

Abstract This chapter investigates the discursive interaction among media discourse, political discourse and legal frameworks concerning gender roles and stereotypes in China, prompted by ongoing critiques of gender inequality in the country. Through an analysis of international media narratives and Chinese legal amendments, this study reveals how international media often perpetuates stereotypical views about gender roles in China. By applying rhizomatization theory, the chapter demonstrates how media discourse distorts legal and political meanings, exacerbating gender tensions. It also explores how Chinese laws, such as the *Law of the People's Republic of China on the Protection of Rights and Interests of Women* (PRIW), have evolved to address gender equity and equality. By mapping changes in both legislation and media representation, this chapter uncovers the complexities of gender inequality in China and offers insights for mitigating these tensions. The analysis underscores the need to balance gender equality and equity within legal discourse while challenging media misrepresentations.

Keywords Gender stereotypes · Chinese law · Media discourse · Rhizomatization · Gender equity and equality · Gender tensions

1 Contextualizing the Discursive Interaction of Gender Stereotypes in China's Legal and Media Landscape

The year 2022 witnessed the third amendment, the latest version, of the *Law of the People's Republic of China on the Protection of Rights and Interests of Women* (hereafter PRIW). PRIW was first adopted in 1992 and has undergone three amendments, respectively in 2005, 2018, and 2022. Following this third amendment, the

I would like to thank Professor Anne Wagner for reviewing the chapter and offering invaluable feedback and comments. Any remaining errors are my own.

W. Yu (✉)
The University of Melbourne, Melbourne, Australia
e-mail: wei.yu.1@unimelb.edu.au

A. Condello and A. Wagner (eds.), *Gender Stereotypes*, Gender, Justice and Legal Feminism 2, https://doi.org/10.1007/978-3-031-63905-0_12

13th National Women's Congress was held in 2023, with the Politburo Standing Committee attending and delivering speeches at the congress. Since then, international mainstream social media, such as *BBC* and *The New York Times*, have criticized the current Chinese government's stance on gender roles in China.

On November 3rd, 2023, *The New York Times* reporter Alexandra Stevenson wrote:

> What was notable was how officials downplayed gender equality. They focused instead on using the gathering to press Mr. Xi's goal for Chinese women: get married and have babies. In the past, officials had touched on the role women play at home as well as in the work force. But in this year's address, Mr. Xi made no mention of women at work.[1]

She criticizes the role assigned to women in contemporary China by the officials—*"get married and have babies"*. By using the evaluative verb—*"to downplay"*, this excerpt suggests that the gender roles of Chinese women in the past were more balanced than they are now. In contemporary China, this excerpt implies that women's contributions and roles in the workforce have been deemphasized, while their roles as wives and mothers have been promoted in response to the current low birth rate.

Such commentary on contemporary gender roles in China is echoed in an article by *Bloomberg*, published on November 3, 2022, titled *"China Tells Women to 'Respect Family Values' in Revised Law"*.[2] This article argues that the PRIW amendment highlights the domestic role of women within the family. These news articles uniformly suggest that gender roles in China have shifted, based on both legal and governmental perspectives. However, do these mainstream media outlets accurately represent the truth and fully understand the current situation?

In the following sections, Sect. 2 introduces the theoretical framework for analyzing social media, political discourse and legal discourse in this chapter. Following that, I will first present the common arguments made in mainstream social media discourse and uncover the reality of recent changes in China through an analysis of political speeches and the latest legal amendments in Sect. 3. Then, in Sect. 4, I will consolidate the changes in gender roles in China based on a policy and legal analysis, including *the Constitution*, PRIW, and relevant articles on marriage and family in the *Civil Code of the People's Republic of China*. Section 5 integrates legal, media, and political discourse, demystifying the stereotypical views held by international social media. While acknowledging the current gender inequality issues in contemporary China, I will also provide some suggestions for addressing these challenges in Sect. 6.

[1] See Stevenson and Ai (2023).

[2] See Xiao (2022).

2 Rhizomatization and Meaning Remaking in Discourse Dissemination

Through reposting and quoting practices, each piece of information, whether visual, textual, or auditory, evolves rapidly on online communication platforms. After multiple rounds of reposting, the original source of the information can become difficult to trace. As a result, the accuracy of the information is often a concern. In some cases, the original source is unknown, which further calls into question the reliability of the content.

Rhizomatization theory unravels the evolving nature of societal shifts and social movements, such as those in the dynamic digital healthcare setting in France.[3] On the one hand, the rhizomatic nature of this digital landscape has helped patients overcome geographical barriers. On the other hand, this evolution has raised new concerns about patient privacy, particularly with the adoption of new technologies in medical settings.[4] Rhizomatization theory has also been applied to the transmission of Internet memes, where existing images or famous sayings are modified and disseminated by anonymous Internet users with aggressive intentions, leading to misinformation and Machiavellian messaging.[5] Furthermore, this theory has been used to explain the evolving language around gender expressions, including changes in pronoun usage and the coining of occupation titles—such as replacing the gendered term "chairman" with the gender-neutral "chairperson".[6]

This book chapter will apply this theory to three genres of discourse, revealing how facts have been distorted through citing and quoting practices. The theory helps demonstrate how meaning has been remade across different types of discourse and languages, particularly Chinese and English. The rapid creation and reproduction of online content often leads to misunderstandings in the information dissemination process. In this context, meaning remaking within the rhizomatic nature of discourse can be classified into three categories: first, the selection of information; second, the addition of information; and third, the misinterpretation of meaning.

This process is paralleled by the concept of "legal formants."[7] Legal formants represent the multiple sources and interpretations within legal systems, from statutes to judicial rulings, which, like rhizomatic networks, contribute to the diversification and evolution of legal meaning. Just as the flow of information in rhizomatization leads to various interpretations and representations, legal formants create layers of legal understanding that evolve as they interact with different legal and social contexts. Legal concepts is de-territorialized in the new context in terms of language, culture and legal frameworks.[8] In the Chinese legislative contexts, the term

---

[3] See Wagner (2024a, b).

[4] See Wagner (2024a, b).

[5] See Wagner and Yu (2021); Wanger et al. (2024).

[6] See Wagner and Yu (2024, forthcoming).

[7] See Barnett (2024).

[8] See Uliasz (2024).

妇女 (*funv*) has been translated as "women" in the official translation of the Chinese law, which shows the contextualisation of the Chinese legal terminologies into the broad discussion of the women's issue at home and abroad.

Verbal language, as a type of sign, is inherently subjective to the contexts in which it is used. When it shifts from one context to another, such as from direct discourse to indirect discourse in news reporting, it undergoes a process of "deterritorialization and reterritorialization".[9] Signs not only convey information but also reflect the intentions of their users:

> Newspapers, news, proceed by redundancy, in that they tell us what we "must" think, retain, expect, etc. Language is neither informational nor communica-tional. It is not the communication of information but something quite different: the transmission of order-words, either from one statement to another or within each statement, insofar as each statement accomplishes an act and the act is accomplished in the statement.[10]

In this context, "order-words" refer to "explicit statements" or "implicit presuppositions" used to accomplish actions.[11] In mainstream newspapers, the selection of information carries its own news value and holds the potential to mislead the public, especially when the audience is global. During the process of "deterritorialization and reterritorialization", the transfer between different languages and discourse genres influences the meaning-making process. Rhizomatization theory explains the evolution of semiotic resources within dynamic societal changes, encompassing both visual and textual channels:

> This rhizomatic perspective, which views social systems and knowledge as non-hierarchical, interconnected networks, akin to the sprawling root systems of plants, offers a profound lens through which to understand the dynamic shifts in healthcare.[12]

Through an analogy between the fluid nature of knowledge change and the extensive root system of plants, the theory describes and explains the flow of information in the process of online knowledge dissemination. However, the rhizomatic nature of this information flow has both advantages and drawbacks:

> The interconnected nature of the rhizomatic structure, while beneficial for information flow and accessibility, also makes the system more vulnerable to cyber threats.[13]

Sometimes, the harm is not as severe as cyber threats but remains detrimental to social cohesion. In the discussion of gender issues in China, the flow of information exacerbates the tension between the two major gender categories in China, male and female.[14]

I propose three key characteristics in the rhizomatization process of information and knowledge flow when the downsides become prominent:

---

[9] See Deleuze and Guattari (1987).

[10] See Deleuze and Guattari (1987), p.79.

[11] See Deleuze and Guattari (1987), p.79.

[12] See Wagner (2024a, b), p.81.

[13] See Wagner (2024a, b).

[14] In this chapter, I concentrate on the two major gender categories. Other diverse gender identities in China warrant further exploration in the future.

- First, the transmission of information inevitably involves partial representation, which can occur both intentionally and unintentionally. Whether through the deliberate selection of knowledge or the unintentional omission of information, this leads to the re-making of meaning, resulting in a biased and distorted representation of the original narrative.
- Second, in this meaning-remaking process, adding extra information that was not present in the original context is a common practice. This additional information may stem from malicious intent to harm the subject or from unconscious misunderstandings due to cultural differences. Individuals who actively engage in spreading rumors or hate speech contribute to disrupting public order and exacerbating societal fragmentation.[15]
- Third, misinterpretation of the original meaning is another form of discursive meaning-remaking. Unlike the previous two characteristics, misinterpretation can completely alter the story's direction by shifting the platform, language, and genre over time. Misinterpretation occurs within discursive interactions and is often a more noticeable change than simply adding or omitting content. However, it is also more powerful in reshaping the narrative and embedding the misinterpreted information deeply within a new context. This process makes the distorted story fit the existing narrative and enhances its perceived reliability.

The next section will examine the interaction of the three discourse genres and the fluidity of meaning as it travels across contexts and cultures.

3 Mainstream Media Narratives on the Chinese Women's Movement[16]

Mainstream social media plays a crucial role in helping the public learn about and understand events happening around the world. They not only provide news articles to report stories but also opinion pieces to comment on social events. However, as previously mentioned, during the storytelling process, these stories are often rhizomatized into different versions. What's more concerning is that these mainstream news outlets have a large number of readers and subscribers. Any misinformation or disinformation they spread can lead to significant consequences due to the butterfly effect. Additionally, these news reports often intertwine policies and laws with distorted facts to legitimize their arguments.

This section will examine how Chinese domestic mainstream news media, such as *People's Daily*, and international mainstream media, such as *BBC News* and *The New York Times*, construct narratives around the Chinese Women's Movement and depict changes in the social status of women.

---

[15] See Wagner and Marusek (2023).

[16] This chapter prefers the expression "the Chinese Women's Movement" than "Feminism in China" to maintain the neutral stance. "Feminism in China" is criticised as radical.

3.1 International Media Portrayals of Gender Roles in China

An article from the *BBC News Chinese* provides a detailed account of the development of the Chinese Women's Movement over the years. This news report is presented in Chinese in the *BBC News Chinese* section, written by a BBC Chinese reporter, rather than in the English version found in the standard *BBC News* section. A similar pattern of language choice can be observed in other mainstream media outlets, such as *The New York Times*. This suggests that readers of such articles need to have a good command of Chinese literacy.

For the *BBC News Chinese* article published in July 2021, the title consists of two parts: the main title and the subtitle. The former highlights a landmark event related to the ruling party in China, focusing on the political aspect, while the latter describes the transformation of gender roles for women in China. It is evident that this news article incorporates a political perspective into the discussion of gender roles in China.

> 中共建党百年:女性从“能顶半边天”到回归家庭建设和谐社会.[17]
>
> At the centennial of the founding of the Communist Party of China: the gender role of women changes from 'holding up half the sky' to returning to the family for building a harmonious society (my translation)

The timeframe referenced in this article uses the establishment of the Communist Party of China as a benchmark. As a result, the discussion of gender issues in this news article inevitably involves the policies and political preferences regarding the role of women in China. According to the subtitle, the status of Chinese women has shifted from modern roles, where they shared equal responsibilities with men in society and took on various occupations, back to more traditional domestic roles, such as raising children and managing the household.

A news report from *The New York Times* in November 2023 holds a similar view. This news report is represented in a bilingual version and is titled "China's Male Leaders Signal to Women That Their Place Is in the Home" in English and "习近平为中国女性设立的目标:结婚生子、照顾家庭" in Chinese, rendering as "Xi Jingping setting up the goal for Chinese women: getting married, raising offsprings, and taking care of the family".[18] A close reading of this bilingual title in this report from *The New York Times* unravels that the two titles express two different meanings. The Chinese title is more explicit in blaming the current president of PRC who specifies the domestic tasks for Chinese women, taking care of the family. However, in the English title, the expressions used is relatively implicit, without specifying a particular Chinese leader or the gender roles of Chinese women. The English title uses the verb "signal" to indicate the political inclination and tendency for women to be back to the domestic roles, rather than applying their expertise in the workplace. Whichever title is consumed by the audience, the main idea of the news article is that

---

[17] See Zi (2021).

[18] See Stevenson and Ai (2023).

the party leaders in China wants to urge women to give birth to babies. The article[19] concludes that:

> "If the party could sacrifice women's body and birth rights for its one-child policy," said Mr. Su, "they could impose their will on women again.

By presenting the perspective of political science professor Mr. Fubing Su, this news article argues that leaders from China's ruling party manipulate the willingness of Chinese women to have children, either by strictly limiting the number of children or by unscrupulously encouraging them to have more. Throughout the article, President Xi's speech at the opening of the National Women's Congress is cited as evidence to support this argument. The article begins with a picture of the congress, showing male leaders at the forefront and female delegates seated behind them. The criticism extends beyond the manipulation of women's reproductive choices to the lack of female representation in the Standing Committee of the Politburo. Regarding fertility, the article states that:

> …, the party has chosen to push women back into the home, calling on them to **rear the young and care for the old**. The work, in the words of Mr. Xi, is essential for "China's path to modernization." (emphasis added)

The article assigns tasks—"rear the young and care for the old"—to Chinese women by manipulating or misinterpreting the meaning of Xi's speech. However, the original speech does not mention these roles at all. The full text of this political speech will be presented in Sect. 5. Regarding the lack of female representation in the committee, a survey from the *BBC News Chinese* has already revealed that the underrepresentation of women in political leadership groups is a widespread issue, not unique to China. The survey[20] concludes that:

> 共产党领导的中国,女性参政议政比例确实偏低;不过,这样的"女性问题"并不是中国共产党独有。
>
> Women's political engagement in China, under the leadership of the Communist Party, is indeed relatively low. However, this "women's issue" is not exclusive to the Communist Party of China. (my translation)

Overall, female participation in politics is relatively low across all countries. According to global data on national parliaments as of January 1, 2024, 26.5% of participants in China are women, ranking the country 89th on the list, while 29.1% of participants in the U.S. are women, ranking 72nd.[21] Comparatively, female political engagement in China is quite similar to that in the U.S. According to the Internal Statistical Report of the Communist Party of China, 30.4% of its members are women. Therefore, the criticism from *The New York Times* is not convincing but rather partial. Gender parity in political life is a goal for all the countries to achieve, not China alone. In this rhizomatization process, information has been fragmented, leaving out key details during the recontextualization.

---

[19] See Stevenson and Ai (2023).

[20] See The BBC News Chinese (2017).

[21] See Global Data on National Parliaments (2024).

3.2 Domestic Media Portrayals of Gender Roles in China

The quoted expression "holding up half the sky" in the title is adapted from a famous folk saying, which first appeared in an article from *People's Daily* in 1956 as "women hold up half the sky".[22] The purpose of this expression was to acknowledge the domestic work that women performed at home. Prior to this, the efforts made by women in the household were not considered contributions to society at all; rather, they were taken for granted. However, since 1956, women's domestic work has been recognized, and more importantly, women were seen as capable of performing the same work as men. In this sense, women "hold up half the sky." Furthermore, from this *People's Daily* article, the initial distinction between gender equity and gender equality began to take shape in China.

The difference between the two lies in the approach to achieving the same outcome.[23] The former (equity) values individualized accommodations and offers privileges to the disadvantaged, whereas the latter (equality) emphasizes identical treatment for everyone, regardless of background. The article acknowledges these considerations for women and criticizes the notion of equality without context, as quoted below. The idea of absolute equality is regarded as "extremely wrong". This kind of criticism has contributed to further reforms aimed at improving the status of women and protecting women's rights from an equity perspective.

> 有些人用一种极端错误的思想对待妇女劳动。他们说,妇女既然要求同工同酬,男女平等,就应该和男人做一样的活。男人揽二百斤,女人也应该揽二百斤。[24]
>
> Some people have an **extremely wrong idea** about women's labor. They argue that since women asked equal pay for equal work and gender equality, women should do the same tasks as men. If a man can carry 200 pounds, a woman should carry 200 pounds as well. (my translation, emphasis added)

Afterwards, this folk saying was repeatedly used in political speeches by key government figures. Gradually, the expression became institutionalized as part of the national discourse, and the social status of women was officially elevated through its inscription in law.[25] It marked a significant moment in the emancipation of women in Chinese history.[26]

The status of women in China has evolved over time. The rhizomatization of female gender roles in China can be seen in two aspects: (1) spatiality and (2) temporality. Spatiality refers to the transition between different social media platforms, while temporality reflects the changes occurring over time. The aforementioned BBC news article highlighted key stages in the evolution of Chinese women's roles, based on political milestones.

---

[22] See People's Daily (1956).

[23] See Minow (2021).

[24] See People's Daily (1956).

[25] See Ma (2003).

[26] See Ma (2003).

The first stage began with the establishment of the Communist Party in 1921, when the importance of women was acknowledged, leading to a significant improvement in their status compared to the traditional feudal society. In the feudal era, women held a much lower position than men due to the belief that men were superior. The fundamental reason was that men, not women, were considered the labor force in a society dominated by agricultural civilization. This reflects the fact that giving birth to baby boys was always prioritized in family planning, driven by the deeply ingrained notion that males were more valuable than females in terms of productivity. Additionally, a series of issues, such as inheritance of property and employment, were influenced by this belief prior to the founding of the PRC.

With the rise of women's status in society, there was a trend toward degenderization to combat gender stereotypes. Previously, women were confined to the home, handling all domestic work, which was not even considered labor by society. This degenderization trend enabled women to step outside their homes and take on the same work as men. From 1968 to 1978, the Sent-Down Youth Movement mobilized educated women and men from the cities to rural areas, allowing women to cultivate farmland as men had done and giving them a sense of spiritual freedom.[27]

Following the reform and opening up in 1978, people from rural areas returned to the cities, which posed new challenges for women. Due to the country's large population, the one-child policy was implemented from 1980 to 2006 to curb rapid population growth. Related legislation will be analyzed in detail in Sect. 4. During that period, women had to compromise between career planning and family planning, particularly those working in enterprises and public institutions. This strict family planning policy, along with the long-standing preference for male superiority, resulted in more baby boys being born, as families, limited by the policy, prioritized having sons.

In recent years, due to an aging population, the government has tried to boost the fertility rate to prepare for future economic growth. The one-child policy ended in 2006, and family planning restrictions were fully lifted in 2021, allowing each family to have three or more children. However, due to the immense pressure of making a living, many young people have no intention of having even one child, let alone two or three. As a result, the government has taken further steps to address this issue.

The gender roles of women have experienced fluctuations throughout Chinese history, which illustrates the temporality of rhizomatization. The criticism of the government's further actions was highlighted in a news report from *The New York Times*, as discussed in Sect. 1. Returning to this criticism, Sect. 4 will present the legislation related to the analysis in Sect. 3 and uncover the misinterpretation and misrepresentation in news media narratives. It will also unpack the spatiality of rhizomatization through the discursive transfer across different discourses.

---

[27] See Zi (2021).

4 Legislative Amendments on Gender and Gender Roles

The discussion of gender roles in this section will be structured around relevant legislation, including various amendments to *the Constitution of the People's Republic of China*, articles related to family and marriage in *the Civil Code of the People's Republic of China* as well as four versions of *the Law of the People's Republic of China on the Protection of Rights and Interests of Women*. By examining these laws and their amendments, I argue that the representation of the status of Chinese women in international news media has distorted the facts and the original meaning. International news outlets hold a biased view of the roles of Chinese women at work and at home due to law and politics.

4.1 The Constitution

The first instance of gender equality being incorporating into law was in *the Constitution of the People's Republic of China* in 1954,[28] following the establishment of the People's Republic of China in 1949. *The 1954 Constitution* was the first in China's history, though it is no longer in effect. Article 96 of *the 1954 Constitution* states that:

> 中华人民共和国妇女在政治的、经济的、文化的、社会的和家庭的生活各方面享有同男子平等的权利。
>
> 婚姻、家庭、母亲和儿童受国家的保护。
>
> Women in the People's Republic of China shall enjoy equal rights with men in all spheres of life: political, economic, cultural, social and familial.
>
> Marriage, family, mothers, and children are protected by the state. (my translation)

In this version of the Constitution, women are entitled to enjoy equal rights with men. It covers all aspects of social life, including both socio-political roles at work and domestic roles in the family. From this point on, the equal status of men and women became enshrined in the constitution, demonstrating China's commitment to gender equality. The article embodies two key clauses: one addressing equality between men and women across various aspects of life, and the other focusing on the protection of vulnerable groups, such as women and children. Thus, this article emphasizes not only gender equality but also gender equity, providing protections for women. In *the 1978 Constitution*, an additional clause was incorporated into this article.

Article 53 of *the 1978 Constitution*[29] states:

> 妇女在政治的、经济的、文化的、社会的和家庭的生活各方面享有同男子平等的权利。男女同工同酬。

---

[28] See Article 96 *The Constitution of the People's Republic of China* (1954).

[29] See Article 53 *The Constitution of the People's Republic of China* (1978).

男女婚姻自主。婚姻、家庭、母亲和儿童受国家的保护。

国家提倡和推行计划生育。

Women shall enjoy equal rights with men in all spheres of life: political, economic, cultural, social and familial. Men and women get equal pay for equal work.

Both men and women have the freedom to choose their marriage partners. Marriage, family, mothers, and children are protected by the state.

The state promotes and implements family planning. (my translation)

In the first clause, "equal pay for equal work" between men and women was added. This addition emphasized equality in the labor market, aligning with the economic focus during the period of reform and opening up. In the second clause, freedom of marriage was included to prevent arranged marriages. The third clause concerns family planning, as mentioned in Sect. 3. Family planning was established as a basic state policy, but this was removed in *the 2018 Constitution.*

Article 48 of *the 2018 Constitution*[30] stipulates:

中华人民共和国妇女在政治的、经济的、文化的、社会的和家庭的生活等各方面享有同男子平等的权利。

国家保护妇女的权利和利益,实行男女同工同酬,培养和选拔妇女干部。

Women in the People's Republic of China shall enjoy equal rights with men in all spheres of life: political, economic, cultural, social and familial.

The state shall protect the rights and interests of women, implement a system of equal pay for equal work, and train and select female officials. (official translation[31])

There are two clauses in this article. The first remains unchanged, while the expression related to pay and work in the labor market has been merged into the second clause. In the second clause, emphasis is placed on protecting the rights and interests of women, as well as on the cultivation and promotion of female officials in the workplace. Comparing *the 2018 Constitution* with *the 1978 Constitution*, the second clause shows a clear shift from focusing on domestic roles to public roles in society. The opportunities for workplace promotion reflect an improvement in the social status of women. Work, pay, and career advancement have been enshrined in the constitution to protect the rights and interests of women. Notably, gender equity has remained a key component of this clause over the years. Since women are more likely to face unfair treatment in society, the constitution guarantees their rights.

4.2 The Civil Code

Apart from *the Constitution*, Book Five: Marriage and Family in *the Civil Code* also guarantees special rights for women in marital life in China. *The Civil Code* has been

---

[30] See Article 48 *The Constitution of the People's Republic of China* (2018).

[31] See Article 48, *The Constitution of the People's Republic of China* (Official English Version, 2021). https://english.www.gov.cn/archive/lawsregulations/201911/20/content_WS5ed8856ec6d0b3f0e9499913.html For the Chinese law, the English translation does not have legal force but is only for reference, even it is official.

in effect since January 1, 2021, and has not undergone any amendments. However, this new Civil Code also demonstrates improvements in addressing family and marriage issues compared to the past. Thus, the rhizomatization process is reflected in these advancements. According to Article 1050,[32]

> 登记结婚后,按照男女双方约定,女方可以成为男方家庭的成员,男方可以成为女方家庭的成员。
>
> After a marriage has been registered, by mutual consent, the woman may become a member of the man's family or vice versa. (official translation[33])

Within the *hukou* system, a household registration system in China, patrilocality was quite common in the past. Traditionally, women would be removed from their original family's registration booklet and added to their husband's family's booklet, implying that the wife's original family "lost" a member. However, the codification of matrilocality reflects the equalization of social status between men and women. This suggests that it is now equally common for a husband to be added to his wife's household registration booklet, provided both remain connected to their original families. Such provisions remove the subordinate status traditionally associated with women in families. The freedom and flexibility in household registration show an initial step in protecting women when they enter marriage. This challenges the conventional model, which placed women in an affiliated, subordinate role.

The Civil Code also restricts a man's right to file for divorce during a specific period. During marriage, women are protected by the code in terms of marital continuity during and after pregnancy. This means that the husband is not allowed to divorce his wife within a certain period, although the wife can still initiate a divorce. Article 1082[34] requires that:

> 女方在怀孕期间、分娩后一年内或者终止妊娠后六个月内,男方不得提出离婚;但是,女方提出离婚或者人民法院认为确有必要受理男方离婚请求的除外。
>
> A husband may not file for divorce during his wife's pregnancy, within one year after his wife delivers, or within six months after termination of her pregnancy, unless the wife applies for divorce, or the people's court deems it necessary to hear the divorce request made by the husband. (official translation[35])

Prima facie, this article favours women. It shows a difference in terms of filing for divorce between the husband and the wife. However, it demonstrates gender equity between the two. During pregnancy, women invest more physical and emotional labor in the unborn child. After delivery, they also devote more time and energy to raising the baby, such as through breastfeeding and providing 24 hours care. While the continuation of the marriage may not resolve the couple's relationship issues, maintaining the marriage for a certain period during and immediately after pregnancy

[32] See Article 1050, *The Civil Code of the People's Republic of China* (2021).

[33] See Article 1050, *The Civil Code of the People's Republic of China* (Official English Version, 2020). http://en.npc.gov.cn.cdurl.cn/pdf/civilcodeofthepeoplesrepublicofchina.pdf.

[34] See Article 1082, *The Civil Code of the People's Republic of China* (2021).

[35] See Article 1082, *The Civil Code of the People's Republic of China* (Official English Version, 2020). http://en.npc.gov.cn.cdurl.cn/pdf/civilcodeofthepeoplesrepublicofchina.pdf.

provides women with a stable environment, allowing them to regain strength after the physical toll of pregnancy or its termination. If the continuation of the marriage does not bring stability and the wife does not require the continuation of the marriage, she can still apply for divorce immediately without the time constraint.

In addition to the time factor, if the wife has spent more time and energy caring for the family—whether for children or the elderly—she is entitled to financial compensation in the divorce, as stipulated in Article 1088[36] below.

> 夫妻一方因抚育子女、照料老年人、协助另一方工作等负担较多义务的,离婚时有权向另一方请求补偿,另一方应当给予补偿。
>
> Where one spouse is burdened with additional duties for raising children, looking after the elderly, or assisting the other spouse in his work, the said spouse has the right to request for compensation upon divorce against the other party, and the other party shall make due compensation. (official translation[37])

The subject discussed here can refer to either the husband or the wife, as the term used is "夫妻一方" (*fuqi yifang*, one spouse). Domestic work, whether done by the husband or the wife, is recognized as labor under the law, echoing the language used in *People's Daily* as mentioned in Sect. 3.2. The following section will provide a more detailed analysis of the special rights and interests of women in general, not just within the context of marriage.

4.3 PRIW

The Law of the People's Republic of China on the Protection of Rights and Interests of Women (PRIW in short) specifically addresses the rights and interests of women. The elimination of gender discrimination and the promotion of gender equality are the main themes of the law. The term "平等" (*pingdeng*, equality) has increased from 21 occurrences in the 1992 version to 29 in the 2022 amendment. Additionally, the law also enhances the privileges afforded to women, reflecting the concept of gender equity mentioned in Sect. 3. Gender equity in this law is realized in two ways: the elimination of stereotypical views of women and the expansion of rights for disadvantaged women.

Significant attention has been given to women's health in the latest version. In the 1992 version, the term "健康" (*jiankang*, health) appears only four times; five times in both the 2005 and 2018 versions. However, in the 2022 version, enacted in 2023, this term appears 18 times. In addition to the increased focus on health in general, the specific focus on women's health has evolved from general well-being in physical and mental aspects to reproductive health, and ultimately to health and safety during the reproductive process. The 2022 version places more emphasis on

---

[36] See Article 1088, *The Civil Code of the People's Republic of China* (2021).

[37] See Article 1088, *The Civil Code of the People's Republic of China* (Official English Version, 2020). http://en.npc.gov.cn.cdurl.cn/pdf/civilcodeofthepeoplesrepublicofchina.pdf.

the safety and health of women, moving beyond the reproductive value that was prioritized in earlier versions.

Article 51 in the 2018 version:

> 妇女有按照国家有关规定生育子女的权利,也有不生育的自由。
>
> 育龄夫妻双方按照国家有关规定计划生育,有关部门应当提供安全、有效的避孕药具和技术,保障实施节育手术的妇女的健康和安全。
>
> 国家实行婚前保健、孕产期保健制度,发展母婴保健事业。各级人民政府应当采取措施,保障妇女享有计划生育技术服务,提高妇女的生殖健康水平。
>
> In accordance with relevant national regulations, women have the right to bear children and the freedom not to bear children.
>
> Couples of the reproductive age are required to follow national family planning regulations, and relevant departments must provide safe and effective contraceptives and techniques to ensure **the health and safety of women undergoing sterilization procedures**.
>
> The state implements a system of premarital healthcare and maternal healthcare during pregnancy, and promotes the development of maternal and child healthcare. All levels of people's governments should take measures to ensure that women have access to family planning services and improve conditions for their **reproductive health**. (my translation, emphasis added)

The first clause entitles women to rights and freedoms related to reproduction. The second clause limits the scope of these rights and freedoms. Couples are required to abide by the national family planning policy, and women's health is addressed in terms of sterilization procedures, in line with this policy. Although the one-child policy was phased out in 2016, birth control was still entrenched in the 2018 amendment of PRIW. This highlights an inconsistency between different laws, particularly across various amendments over time. In the rhizomatization process, inconsistency functions like nodes in the spread of rhizomes—both hindering their development and creating opportunities for new growth.

In the second clause, if family planning is a national policy that every family must follow, then the protection of women's health during surgeries for family planning purposes is reasonable, as such procedures could pose potential risks. However, in the third clause of Article 51, the phrase "提高妇女的生殖健康水平" (*tigao funv de shengzhi jiankang shuiping*, improving the conditions for their reproductive health) places excessive emphasis on the reproductive value of women. This emphasis has been removed in the latest version of PRIW.

Article 51 in the 2018 version was divided into two articles in the 2022 version, specifically Articles 32 and 33,[38] which state:

> 第三十二条 妇女依法享有生育子女的权利,也有不生育子女的自由。
>
> 第三十三条　国家实行婚前、孕前、孕产期和产后保健制度,逐步建立妇女全生育周期系统保健制度。医疗保健机构应当提供安全、有效的医疗保健服务,保障妇女生育安全和健康。
>
> 有关部门应当提供安全、有效的避孕药具和技术,保障妇女的健康和安全。

[38] See Articles 32 and 33. *The Law of the People's Republic of China on the Protection of Rights and Interests of Women* (2022).

> Article 32 In accordance with the law, women have the right to bear children and the freedom not to bear children.
>
> Article 33 The state shall implement a healthcare system covering premarital, pre-pregnancy, perinatal and postpartum periods, and gradually establish a systematic healthcare system for women throughout such periods.
>
> Medical and healthcare institutions shall provide safe and effective medical and healthcare services to ensure **women's reproductive safety and health**.
>
> The relevant departments shall provide safe and effective contraceptives and relative technologies to guarantee **women's health and safety**.
>
> (official translation,[39] emphasis added)

The Chinese version of this legislation uses the expression "保障妇女的健康和安全" (*baozhang funv de jiankang he anquan*, ensuring the health and safety of women), indicating that the focus on women's health has shifted from improving reproductive capacity to ensuring overall health and safety. The emphasis is no longer on how capable women are in terms of reproduction, but rather on the risks they may face. The purpose of PRIW is to eliminate potential risks and guarantee the safety and health of women. Focusing on reproductive health itself is not wrong; however, the emphasis on women's reproductive value in the 2018 version seems inappropriate and may reflect discriminatory attitudes toward women. The removal of such expressions in the 2022 version affirms the value of women as whole individuals, rather than merely as childbearing machines. The focus on women's general health is further underscored by the significant rise in the use of the term "健康" (*jiankang*, health). Additionally, compared to the 2018 version, the latest version removed the family planning policy, aligning with changes in the constitution and resolving the inconsistency that arose during the rhizomatization process.

As mentioned earlier, in addition to eliminating stereotypical expressions, another representation of gender equity in this law is the entitlement of additional rights for disadvantaged women. In the 2022 amendment, Article 47[40] has been amended to further protect the special need of women:

> 用人单位应当根据妇女的特点,依法保护妇女在工作和劳动时的安全、健康以及休息的权利。
>
> 妇女在经期、孕期、产期、哺乳期受特殊保护。
>
> An employer shall, in accordance with the law, protect women's safety, health and **the right to rest at work** based on the characteristics of women.
>
> Women shall be **under special protection** during menstrual period, pregnancy, confinement period and lactation period. (official translation,[41] emphasis added)

---

[39] See Articles 32 and 33. *The Law of the People's Republic of China on the Protection of Rights and Interests of Women* (Official English Version, 2022) http://en.npc.gov.cn.cdurl.cn/2022-10/30/c_891562.htm.

[40] See Article 47, *The Law of the People's Republic of China on the Protection of Rights and Interests of Women* (2022).

[41] See Article 47. *The Law of the People's Republic of China on the Protection of Rights and Interests of Women* (Official English Version, 2022) http://en.npc.gov.cn.cdurl.cn/2022-10/30/c_891562.htm.

The characteristics of women refer to the various stages of the reproductive cycle. During these times, women endure additional physical and mental strains from carrying a child. As a result, women are entitled to "special protection" to alleviate the impact of reproduction, including the right to rest at work. This concept is also reflected in Article 7 of *the Special Provisions for the Work Protection of Female Employees,*[42] enforced since 2012, which stipulates that women are entitled to different lengths of leave depending on whether they give birth or experience a miscarriage. However, it has been argued that extending maternity leave poses a threat to the career paths of female workers in the private sector.[43] When women return from extended maternity leave, their original roles are often replaced by men, leading to a subtle escalation in tensions between men and women.

One potential solution to alleviate this tension is to equalize the length of parental leave for both men and women, as is applied in France.[44] Currently, Chinese law does not provide special provisions for reproductive health leave. However, the Queensland Government recently introduced a policy granting all public sector workers an additional 10 days of reproductive health leave annually, regardless of gender, for examinations or treatments related to reproductive health. Moving forward, further protection for women could include special consideration for reproductive health.[45] Overall, the rights and protections afforded to women due to their biological characteristics have increased, covering both the decision to give birth and additional protection during pregnancy.

Upon reviewing several laws and comparing different versions, it becomes clear that what is portrayed in international media discourse is not reflected in the legislation and its amendments. Section 5 will further explore the interaction between the two, using political discourse as a bridge.

5 Responding to Criticism: Discursive Interactions Among Law, Politics, and Society

After reviewing all these related laws, let us now turn to the criticisms from *The New York Times* mentioned in Sect. 1, which argues that Chinese women have been forced to return to traditional domestic roles. The most striking language that led to this criticism regarding the shift in Chinese women's roles comes from President Xi's speech during his conversation with the newly appointed leadership team of the All-China Women's Federation in 2023. This news article highlights the intersection between social media discourse and political discourse. In this conversation,[46] President Xi emphasizes that:

---

[42] See Article 7, *Special Provisions for the Work Protection of Female Employees* (2012).

[43] See The BBC News Chinese (2021).

[44] See The BBC News Chinese (2021).

[45] See Queensland Government (2024).

[46] See Xinhua News Agency (2023).

家庭和睦、家教良好、家风端正,子女才能健康成长,社会才能健康发展。做好妇女工作,不仅关系妇女自身发展,而且关系家庭和睦、社会和谐,关系国家发展、民族进步。要讲好家风故事,引导广大妇女发挥在弘扬中华民族传统美德、树立良好家风方面的独特作用,营造家庭文明新风尚。要积极培育新型婚育文化,加强对年轻人婚恋观、生育观、家庭观的引导,促进完善和落实生育支持政策,提高人口发展质量,积极应对人口老龄化。

Only with harmonious families, proper upbringing, and upright family values can children grow up healthy and society develop positively. Dealing with women's work well is not only essential for the development of women themselves but also for family harmony, social stability, national development, and the progress of the nation. We must tell the stories of good family values, **guiding women to play their unique role in promoting traditional virtues of the Chinese nation and fostering positive family values**, thereby **creating a new wave of family civility**. It is crucial to cultivate new marriage and childbirth cultures actively, strengthen guidance on **young people's views on marriage, childbirth, and family**, and promote the improvement and implementation of childbirth support policies. This will enhance the quality of population development and positively address population aging. (my translation, emphasis added)

In this excerpt, the themes are (1) improving the quality of the population by enhancing the cultural and moral values of families, such as fostering good family values and upbringing, and (2) addressing population decline and combating aging by implementing childbirth support policies. The former relates more to the spirit and morality of the people, while the latter focuses on boosting population growth. The first two sentences in this excerpt emphasize the importance of women's contributions to themselves, their families, society, and the country. The last two sentences specify actions for doing women's work well, such as promoting traditional values. However, it does not suggest that women must stay at home to manage domestic work. Promoting a good family climate does not imply that women cannot showcase their talents in the workplace.

The misunderstanding of "traditional virtues of the Chinese nation" leads international media to focus on domestic roles. The original text emphasizes that women should do their best to foster a good family atmosphere, but this does not diminish the importance of men's roles in families. The term "traditional virtues" aligns with "family values", which pertain to spirit and morality, rather than assigning household tasks specifically to women. Furthermore, the mention of views on marriage, childbirth, and family applies to all young people, not just women. Establishing families requires the involvement of both genders. Therefore, the criticism in *The New York Times* stems from a misinterpretation of the political speech. However, the influence of such international media is significant due to its wide audience.

The interpretation of the expression "营造家庭文明新风尚" (*yingzao jiating wenming xin fengshang*, creating a new wave of family civility) has been explained in an article from *People's Daily*,[47] which states that:

今天,女性自尊自信、自立自强的时代风采,坚韧从容的性格品德,在千行百业里闪光,也是促进家庭和睦、社会和谐不可或缺的特质。广大妇女将这些美好特质注入家庭建设…

[47] See Zhou (2023).

> Today, women's sense of self-esteem, self-confidence, and self-reliance, along with their resilient and composed character, shine in all walks of life. These qualities are also indispensable in promoting harmony in a family and cohesion in a society. Women can **bring** these admirable traits **into** family building... (my translation, emphasis added)

The good virtues, such as resilience and confidence, of contemporary Chinese women are acknowledged across various fields in the workplace. To create a new wave of family civility, Chinese women do not need to leave the workplace permanently. Instead, they bring these positive qualities into family building. Overall, in President Xi's speech, the emphasis on the role of Chinese women is placed on spirit and morality. The ruling party does not assign traditional domestic roles to women, nor does it require them to leave the workplace or focus solely on family building. Regarding the criticism that Xi did not mention women in the workplace, he actually highlights the role of women in comprehensively contributing to high-quality development, from technological advancements to rural revitalization, by stating that[48]:

> 要激励广大妇女在贯彻新发展理念、构建新发展格局、推动高质量发展、实现高水平科技自立自强、全面推进乡村振兴中发挥自身优势和积极作用。

> We must encourage women to leverage their strengths and play an active role in implementing new development concepts, shaping the new development landscape, promoting high-quality development, achieving high-level technological self-reliance, and advancing rural revitalization. (my translation)

Women are not confined to playing an important role in family building. Instead, they are encouraged to leverage their strengths and contribute in their own ways, regardless of the fields they are in.

By revisiting the political discourse, the criticisms and misunderstandings in the news media discourse can be demystified. Social media distorts the original meaning by interpreting out of context and twisting the logic. The engagement between these two types of discourse demonstrates the rhizomatization process of meaning across different genres of texts. Social media plays a malicious role in recreating meaning and disseminating misinformation. To resolve the misunderstanding between social media discourse and political discourse, legal discourse can be used as evidence to clear up misinterpretations. By reviewing various versions and types of laws, Sect. 4 demonstrates that gender equality and gender equity are balanced in Chinese legislation. The examination of laws related to women's rights also shows that Chinese society currently has strong legal provisions to protect women and children.

Law, politics, and social media are closely interconnected. Social media serves as a platform that brings these three together: politics is often the target of criticism and influences lawmaking and amendments, while the law acts as a defense mechanism to correct the distorted narratives spread on social media. The current media practice shapes people's understanding of the events and affects gender justice via its narratives.[49] Therefore, social media should take more responsibility when they disseminate information, either facts or ideas.

---

[48] See Xinhua News Agency (2023).

[49] See Wagner (2024a, b).

6 Resolving Gender Tension and Media Misrepresentations in China

The growing tension between men and women in China, particularly concerning workplace inequality and societal expectations, remains a critical issue. While legal frameworks have made strides in embedding gender equity alongside gender equality, these advancements are often overshadowed by media misrepresentations—especially in international outlets. Such portrayals can exacerbate the situation by distorting the efforts made by the Chinese government to address gender roles through policy and legislation.

This chapter has highlighted how Chinese law has evolved to balance the need for gender equality with equity, offering protections for women in both the workplace and domestic spheres. *The Law of the People's Republic of China on the Protection of Rights and Interests of Women* (PRIW), among other legislative measures, demonstrates the state's commitment to gender justice. However, the disconnect between legal frameworks and media narratives, particularly in international coverage, continues to fuel misconceptions about gender roles in China.

Moving forward, it is crucial for both domestic and international media to engage more responsibly in representing gender issues. Media outlets must avoid perpetuating stereotypes and instead focus on accurate depictions of China's complex gender landscape. Furthermore, China's legal system must continue advancing policies that not only encourage population growth but also provide significant support for women in balancing their professional and family roles.

To truly address gender tensions in China, more comprehensive policies are needed. Equal parental leave, improved childcare services, and greater recognition of domestic labor could alleviate pressures on women juggling multiple responsibilities. Moreover, public education and awareness campaigns should be implemented to challenge deeply ingrained gender stereotypes.

In conclusion, while Chinese law offers a balanced approach to gender equity and equality, much work remains to be done. Media discourse must evolve to reflect the nuances of gender relations in modern China, moving beyond simplified stereotypes. Only through such efforts can a more equitable and just portrayal of gender roles be achieved, fostering better understanding and cooperation between both domestic and international perspectives.

References

Barnett K (2024) Reflections on the principles of remoteness in contract in comparative law. *International Journal for the Semiotics of Law* 37:1587–1616. https://doi.org/10.1007/s11196-023-10053-8

Deleuze G, Guattari F (1987) *A thousand plateaus - capitalism and schizophrenia*. University of Minnesota Press, Minneapolis

Global Data on National Parliaments (2024) Monthly ranking of women in national parliaments. https://data.ipu.org/women-ranking/?date_month=1&date_year=2024
Ma S (2003) *A historical testimony of a female revolutionary*. Communist Party History Press, Beijing, pp 317–318.
Minow M (2021) Equality vs. equity. Am J Law Equal 1:167–193.
People's Daily (1956) Protecting the health of women and children in rural areas.
Queensland Government (2024) Reproductive health leave frequently asked questions. https://www.forgov.qld.gov.au/__data/assets/pdf_file/0019/524206/reproductive-health-leave-frequently-asked-questions.pdf
Stevenson A, Sha A (2023) China's male leaders signal to women that their place is in the home. *The New York Times*. https://cn.nytimes.com/china/20231103/china-communist-party-xi-women/dual/
The BBC News Chinese (2017) The BBC's fact-checking on whether the Chinese Communist Party (CCP) has a "women's issue". https://www.bbc.com/zhongwen/simp/chinese-news-41680427
The BBC News Chinese (2021) Many regions in China extend maternity leave to six months, potentially exacerbating workplace discrimination against women. https://www.bbc.com/zhongwen/simp/chinese-news-59504451
Uliasz R (2024) Cross-cultural and linguistic dynamics in the deterritorialization of legal concepts through international commercial contracts. *International Journal for the Semiotics of Law* 38(4):1291–1313. https://doi.org/10.1007/s11196-024-10207-2
Wagner A (2024a) Rhizomatic healthcare: The digital transformation of France's medical landscape. *International Journal of Digital Law and Governance* 1(1):81–90. https://doi.org/10.1515/ijdlg-2024-0006
Wagner A (2024b) Sergio Maruenda-Bataller, Laura Mercé and Elena Castellano-Ortolà: Discourse, Gender, and Violence: Insights from News and Social Media Texts. *International Journal of Digital Law and Governance* 1(2): 439–443. https://doi.org/10.1515/ijdlg-2024-0014
Wagner A, Marusek S (2023) Rumors on the net: a brackish suspension of speech and hate. *Law, Culture and the Humanities* 19(1):167–181. https://doi.org/10.1177/1743872119880121
Wagner A, Yu W (2021) Machiavellian apparatus of cyberbullying: its triggers igniting fury with legal impacts. *International Journal for the Semiotics of Law* 34(4): 945-963.
Wagner A, Yu W (2025) From gender binary ♀♂ to gender diversity ☿ + X λ: Unveiling New Horizons in societal transformation. In *(In)Visible Signs of Gender-Based Violence*. (Anne Wagner and Angela Condello ed., Vol. 1, pp. 23–40). Springer. https://link.springer.com/chapter/10.1007/978-3-031-35513-4_3
Wagner A, Yu W, Marusek S (2024) Abuse of Rhizomatic internet memes: disruptive non-verbal discourse. In *Handbook on Cyber Hate: The Modern Cyber Evil*. (Anne Wagner and Sarah Marusek ed., Vol. 13, pp. 495–515). Springer. https://doi.org/10.1007/978-3-031-51248-3_24
Xiao J (2022) China tells women to 'respect family values' in revised law. *Bloomberg*. https://www.bloomberg.com/news/articles/2022-11-03/china-tells-women-to-respect-family-values-in-revised-law
Xinhua News Agency (2023) President Xi's discussion with the new leadership team of the All-China Women's Federation. https://www.gov.cn/yaowen/liebiao/202310/content_6912723.htm
Zhou N (2023) Creating a new trend of family civilization. *People's Daily*. http://www.qstheory.cn/qshyjx/2023-11/01/c_1129951747.htm
Zi P (2021) At the centennial of the founding of the communist party of China: the gender role of women changes from 'holding up half the sky' to returning to the family for building a harmonious society. *The BBC News Chinese*. https://www.bbc.com/zhongwen/simp/chinese-news-57649035

Wei Yu is a Ph.D. candidate (near completion) at the University of Melbourne, whose research interests focus on the interdisciplinary field of law, language, and society. Her research articles have been published in *Social Semiotics* (Taylor & Francis, 2020), the *International Journal* *for the Semiotics of Law* (Springer, 2020; 2021; 2025), *Flags, Color, and the Legal Narrative: Public Memory, Identity, and Critique* (Springer, 2021), *Research Handbook on Legal Semiotics* (Edward Elgar, 2023), *Research Handbook on Jurilinguistics* (Edward Elgar, 2023), the *International Journal of Legal Discourse* (Walter de Gruyter, 2023), *Handbook on Cyber Hate, the Modern Cyber-Evil* (Springer, 2024), and (In)Visible Signs of Gender-Based Violence (Springer, 2025). She serves as an international advisor with the *International Journal for the Semiotics of Law* (Springer, since 2022) and also a book review editor with the *International Journal of Digital Law and Governance* (Walter de Gruyter, since 2023).

Researching Sexualized Violence: An Affected-Centered Approach

Jördis Spengler

Abstract This chapter focuses on the development of ethical research guidelines for qualitative interviews with individuals affected by sexualized violence. It addresses the marginalization of sexualized violence in academic curricula and research funding, emphasizing the need for standardized quality and ethical standards in research practices. Drawing on principles from critical educational sciences, trauma-informed care, and ethical research guidelines, the chapter proposes a protocol aimed at creating a safe and supportive research environment for participants. Key principles include understanding the prevalence and effects of sexualized violence, prioritizing participant autonomy and choice, and fostering self-reflection and empowerment within the research process. By integrating these principles, researchers can conduct ethical and impactful research while respecting the experiences and voices of survivors of sexualized violence.

Keywords Sexualized violence · Gender · Research · Ethical guidelines

The article is based on two preliminary set assumptions:

- Sexualized violence is a gendered form of power distribution that is interconnected with other forms of oppression and violence, Sexualized violence has pervasive and long-lasting effects for the affected. Sexualized violence is "any connection of sexuality, power and violence that violates or impairs human integrity" (Reh et al. 2012, p. 15; Hagemann-White et al. 2025).
- Contemporary research on sexualized misses best practice models that adhere to standardize quality and ethical standards, without failing the paradigms of qualitative research.

Research on sexualized violence in educational sciences and social pedagogics have been marginalized and underrepresented in the last decades (Andresen and Tippelt

J. Spengler (✉)
Hochschule Rhein Main, Wiesbasen, Germany
e-mail: joerdis.spengler@googlemail.com

Social Work, Hochschule Rhein Main, Wiesbaden, Germany

A. Condello and A. Wagner (eds.), *Gender Stereotypes*, Gender, Justice and Legal Feminism 2, https://doi.org/10.1007/978-3-031-63905-0_13

2018, p. 11). This underrepresentation is even less understandable considering that prevention and intervention of sexualized violence make up for a great part of social work and social pedagogical services. Critical educational sciences therefor must be interested examine the grounds on which sexualized violence keeps on happening (Mehrick 2021, p. 27).

The revelations of the systematic abuse of minors and teenagers by the hands of educators and pedagogues in their institutions, such as the Odenwaldschule in Germany in 2010 or the clerical institutions, have ignited wider discussions about the intrinsically problem that sexualized violence poses in social pedagogy and beyond (Baader 2022, p. 6).

However, sexualized violence is still marginalized in German university curricula's, not mandatory in the educational sciences and research projects on sexualized violence often get dismissed or little to no funding (Andresen and Demant 2017, p. 42; Baader et al. 2020, p. 6 ff).

Additionally, ethical guidelines and research practices on sexualized violence that include those affected are missing (Andresen and Tippelt 2018; Wazlawik and Dekker 2016).

This chapter wants to contribute to the discussion and development of ethical research guidelines for qualitative interviews with affected of sexualized violence. The goal was to develop a protocol to conduct qualitative interviews with affected centered principles which adhere to the openness of social sciences while offering iterative ethical considerations as well as reflexive elements. I hereby focused on ethical principles of research and guidelines developed within social work and pedagogy such as the Bonner Ethik Erklärung. Poelchau et al. (2015), principles of Trauma Informed Care in the health care system as conceptualized by Elliot and Anderson. Anderson et al. (2022), Elliott et al. (2005) and principles of researching in the field of sexualized violence (Helfferich et al. 2016; Hagemann-White et al. 2016).

1 Researching Gendered Sexualized Violence

While sexualized violence is deeply bound into the social construct of society, it was long considered a niche topic of Women- and Gender Studies. Brought to the attention by second wave feminists of the 60s and 70s which centered gendered (sexualized) violence as a social fact rather than individual fate, making the personal political and showing the devastating impact of violence. Those debates translated over into action, subsequently, the recognition of women and children rights as human rights and the development of women shelters and other specific assistance institutions in West Germany Hagemann-White (1992), Helfferich et al. (2016), followed. Women* worldwide have a higher prevalence of experiencing sexualized violence García-Moreno (2013). In a German study from 2021 on the "Lifetime prevalence of nonconsensual sexual intercourse and touch and associations with health-related factors. Results from the German Health and Sexuality Survey (GeSiD)" showed that "For women, the lifetime prevalence of (attempted/completed) nonconsensual intercourse was 14.9% and in the form of (attempted/completed) nonconsensual sexual touching was 40.8%; for men the prevalence were 3.1% and 13.2% (Brunner et al. 2021). A German wide study from 2004 by Monika Schröttle and Ursula Müller, 40% had experienced physical and sexual violence in their life. 13%, every seventh women, had experienced sexualized violence, that was relevant under German criminal law (Schröttle et al. 2004)

Schröttle and Müller also found a significant distinction within their own numbers, depending on how they asked for past experiences of sexualized violence, that are not relevant under criminal law but signify transgressions of sexual boundaries. In comparison to 13% of criminal relevant cases 34%, reported unwanted and coerced sexual experiences in their life.

Schröttle and Müllers results show the importance of research design and wording when it comes to sexualized violence and its individual and subjective understanding of it.

When considering the impact on those who have experienced sexualized violence, it becomes imperative to emphasize the distinct ways in which for example gendered and heteronormative practices unfold. Sexualized violence is thereby seen as the modality, through which different powers operate. These gendered practices manifest themselves through juridical and legislative mandates, fundings, mainstream discourse and institutional practices Martin (2004).

The systematic neglect of sexualized violence in academia can be seen as evidence of such institutional practices. Through its absence in curricula's throughput the pedagogical spectrum, one of the key issues and work fields of social work is eliminated. Educators or professionals within pedagogy / social work do not learn systematically about the prevalence, the intervention or structural components of sexualized violence or how to research those. Interested students or researchers, are thus confronted with a multitude of legal and ethical problems, with little to no guideline (Baader and Sager 2020).

Additionally, research environments such as grant reviewers or institutions predominantly prefer known, often used and considered low-risk methods. Thereby they inadvertently cut innovative ways of knowledge generation and methodological development in the field of sexualized violence, leading to low impact studies. In conjunction with confirmation bias and publication tendency, as well scholastic pressure to quantify output fast in order to succeed in ones career, Hamby (2014, p. 115). research on sexualized violence stays in the margins.

While there is no specific method to research sexualized violence, the topic bears an emotional and ethical specificality. As Kollinger et al. (2023, p. 5) discussed, the fundamentals of research and activism, differ. Research aims to clarify the factors contributing to suffering of the affected without diminishing their seriousness. Research on violence must be always done in consideration of the vulnerability, safety and dignity of the affected. There is no "Impartial" or objective when researching violence (Hagemann-White et al. 2016, p. 13).

The specificality of researching sexualized violence and doing first-person interview is visible in the ethical considerations and guidelines such as "Bonner Ethik Erklärung". A great stress if on the welfare and rights of participants that must be protected. Researchers must be aware of their ethical responsibilities and be appropriately qualified to conduct ethical and safe research aims and methods of the research must be precisely formulated and documented. It should be clear how the research results can be fed back into practice. Suitable measures should be taken to ensure that the participants are exposed to as little stress as possible. This includes avoiding replications that are not absolutely necessary, selecting suitable research instruments and limiting questions to what is necessary. Participation in the research must be voluntary and with informed consent, it must be clear that not-participating is free of consequences and harm. Further, personal data must be anonymized or pseudonymized to protect the privacy of the participants. Anonymity should also be guaranteed after publication of the research results. Conclusive, researchers should be prepared for potentially distressing situations and be informed about appropriate self-care measures and support for participants Poelchau et al. (2015). These abstract recommendations however, have to be adapted to practical situations case by case.

2 Trauma-Informed-Care

To work trauma informed, recognizes the devastating impact sexualized violence can have on the affected while simultaneously respecting the autonomy an agency of the co-producing participant in research processes. Trauma-informed principles argue that affected should have a say in how treatment services are structured and should be actively involved in providing feedback to improve these services. This involvement can take various forms, such as serving on advisory boards, participating in focus groups, or being employed as consumer specialists Elliot et al. (2005, p. 474). Trauma-informed care has been not yet been transferred to other disciplines, albeit calls for implementation in other settings such as research Elliot et al. (2005, p. 475). By creating trauma-informed research environments, researchers can enhance the experiences of participating in research, not only improving participation rates but also enhances research quality and contributing to the advancement of knowledge on sexual violence Anderson et al. (2022, p. 22). These methods aim to create a safe and supportive environment for survivors of trauma, such as sexual violence, throughout the research process. Some key principles and practices of trauma-informed research methods include establishing research environments where participants feel physically and emotionally safe. This may involve selecting neutral and comfortable locations for interviews and ensuring confidentiality and privacy. Developing trust between researchers and participants is crucial. Researchers should communicate openly, listen actively, and respect participants' autonomy and boundaries. Providing clear information about the research process, potential risks, and available support services and adherence to non-malefizenz.

For trauma-informed care respecting participants' autonomy is fundamental. This includes obtaining informed consent in a manner that is understandable and empowering for participants. Researchers should also allow participants to withdraw from the study at any time without consequences. Researchers should take proactive steps to minimize the risk of retraumatization during data collection. This may involve using trauma-informed interviewing techniques, such as avoiding triggering language, providing breaks, and allowing participants to control the pace and content of discussions. Offering access to support services, such as counseling or advocacy, can help participants cope with any emotional distress that may arise during or after participation. Researchers should be prepared to provide referrals to appropriate resources if needed When analyzing data, researchers should approach the interpretation of findings with sensitivity to the experiences and perspectives of trauma survivors. This may involve recognizing the complexities of trauma responses and avoiding reductive or stigmatizing interpretations. While specific principles may vary depending on the context and focus of the research, safety, choice, empowerment, agency, respect for diversity and informed consent are core principles Elliot et al. (2005) and Anderson et al. (2022)

3 Affected-Centered-Protocol

Concepts of understanding sexualized violence often act in binary constructions of victim or survivor. Those concepts do not do justice to the complexity of sexualized violence and its impact. Survivor and victim represent sides of the same coin in the discursive construction of rape and sexualized violence. Those terms subject the affected to a culturally normed way of reacting to the transgression and connects those with credibility and legitimacy in narrative and behavior Andrews (2014). Recognizing the multiple forms and ways in which traumatic sexualized violence alters our narrative stands in opposition to the cultural frameworks on sexualized violence that are offered so far. Concepts, like the collapsible women (Veselka 2006) or the cathartic element of trauma theories like Hermann (1998) or Tov (2009). For the affected subjects, the choice is limited. Thus, what can not be narrated, creates a void. This void is not the absence of voice, it the non-accessibility to the public sphere.

Affected centered approaches prioritize the analysis of the needs and experiences of those affected by a particular issue or situation.

Based on qualitative research ethical guidelines and trauma-informed-principles, the following protocol was drafted. Combining the recommendations from Poelchau et al. with trauma-informed-principles as seen in Elliot et al. (2005) and Anderson et al. (2022).

The protocol was aimed to be used throughout the research process. This includes planning, designing, recruiting, interviewing and analyzing of the interview. For this reason, the protocol offers guidelines for each phase of the research process.

Four key principles have been identified:

1. Understanding sexualized violence: prevalence, vulnerabilities and blind spots

Understanding the consequences and workings of sexualized violence is necessary to reflect upon study design. Firstly, researchers should strive to sample a population that reflects the full spectrum of experiences with sexualized violence, avoiding limitations to one particular demographic or type of violence. This may involve using multiple languages, employing easy-to-understand language, and considering the use of visual aids to enhance accessibility. Additionally, researchers should prioritize explaining data security measures and obtaining informed consent from participants before proceeding with any research activities. Providing reimbursement for participation and considering potential hardships that participants may face in engaging with the research are also important aspects of ensuring fairness, dignity and inclusivity. If we want to hear stories, we need to go there and make participation in research accessible. That's why essential to conduct thorough research on the prevalence of sexualized violence, the groups most vulnerable to such violence, and design research calls appropriately. Being knowledgeable and sexualized violence includes offering available support options for the participants, and understanding the functioning of the care system. This knowledge can inform the design and implementation of research protocols and ensure that appropriate support services are available to participants depending on their needs.

2. Understanding sexualized violence: effects

In acknowledging the profound impact that sexualized violence can have on survivors and their coping mechanisms, it is imperative for researchers to adopt a supportive and empathetic approach throughout the research process. Here are several strategies to apply this knowledge within research design. Engage in preliminary discussions with participants to establish rapport, set expectations, and create a safe space for dialogue. Further, providing anonymous channels for participants to express interest in participating can mitigate concerns about privacy and confidentiality, creating a sense of safety. Transparency should be prioritized throughout the research process, ensuring that participants fully understand the purpose, procedures, and potential risks involved. During the interviews, practicing careful, active listening validates experiences. Furthermore, researchers should prioritize using language that is respectful, non-judgmental, and inclusive of participants' experiences and identities. Here are additional strategies for effectively communicating with participants:

3. Choice and control

The third principle is choice and control. In order to offer a research design based on the need of the participant this key principle revolves around oddering choice.

Implementation of choice and control prioritizes the participants choices and their needs over those of the study design. Transparency should be maintained regarding the elements and goals of the study, including the provision of regular check-ins on interview transcripts and information on the possibility of resigning or withdrawing from participation. Participants should be prioritized over data collection, with efforts made to ensure their comfort and safety during interviews. This may involve interviews being conducted in a safe and familiar environment chosen by the participants and relevant materials being prepared beforehand. Preference should be given to the participants' choices regarding contact methods, and regular check-ins should be conducted during interviews to ensure that participants feel comfortable. Options should be provided to participants throughout the research process, and basic guidelines should be reiterated to reassure them of their autonomy and agency, such as the ability to pause or stop the interview at any time. Validation of participants' narratives, experiences, and feelings, both verbally and non-verbally, should be integrated into the interview process, without probing or pressuring participants for explicit explanations. Furthermore, participants should be offered information about the trajectory of the study, including the option to re-read transcripts or engage in a second interview. Additionally, feedback on the interview process should be sought from participants to ensure that their needs and preferences are being met effectively.

4. Self-)Reflection

The fourth principle aims on the realm of (self-)reflection and empowerment within the research process, several practices are integral: Materials should be reviewed by competent individuals from advocacy, care, and research backgrounds to ensure relevance and appropriateness beforehand. Additionally, iterative check-ins on the structures of the research should be conducted, allowing for adjustments based on feedback and emerging insights.

Further, the iterative process of sel-reflection is implemented here. Questions to consider include: How am I engaging in the study, and what messages am I conveying? Am I truly able to listen to and comprehend these narratives? As researcher and participant co-produce their interview, it is imperative, so self-reflect upon feeling and emotions in the interview process. It can be helpful to take field notes and create memos to document observations and reflections or make notes on personal feelings and reactions during interviews, fostering awareness of one's own emotional responses and potential biases (Table 1).

4 Discussion

The chapter has shown what a reflective, standardized guideline, that none-the less adheres to qualitative standards can look like. The explicitly incorporated trauma informed practices throughout the research process create a safe and supportive environment that allows choice for the participants. The affected centered research protocol aims to take into account power imbalances in research as well as subjectivity bias. A trauma informed environment also limits risks of re-traumatization.

Questions and fears of re-traumatization lead to disengagement of research. But there are ample examples of, when research designs are met, that engagement in research can be beneficial.

> Additionally, given the diversity of survivor experiences, risks and perceived risks may be variable among participants. Particularly, the difficulties of participating and the risk of retraumatization may not outweigh the perceived benefit of contribution for a given participant. As such, it is the imperative for the researcher to allow for individual choice in research

Table 1 Interview behavior

Principle	Application: before	During	After
1. Understanding sexualized violence: prevalence, vulnerabilities, blind spots	• A call for sampling population that is not limited to one way of experiencing sexualized violence and addresses more than group: more than one language, easy language, picture sensibility (also in data security etc.) • Take time to explain DS and Consent beforehand • Offer reimbursement • Think of possible hardships to engage • Research on prevalence, vulnerable groups, options and the care system and how it works	• Being prepared to hear all forms of testimonials • No pressing	• Refer to fitting services after
2. Understanding sexualized violence: effects	• Preliminary talks • Anonymous ways to contact researcher or signal interest • Offer maximum transparency (informed consent) • Discuss possible outcomes of participation in research with interviewee and offer options	• Careful, active listening • Using the language the interviewee uses	• Refer to fitting services • Ask if a second talk is wished • End interview with "good plays" (see Hancock 2007)

(continued)

Table 1 (continued)

Principle	Application: before	During	After
3. Choice and control	• Transparency on elements and goal of study, offer check up on transcripts, provide information on possibility of resigning and withdrawal • Participants first not data collection • Check for a safe place to conduct interview, go where the participants are comfortable • Prepare material • Ask for preferences of contact	• Check in regularly if a pause is needed and if the course of the interview is going ok • Offer options • Reassure basic guidelines ("we can stop at any time" "I am only asking to reassure I understood you right") • Integrate validation of narrative/ experiences/feeling (verbal/non verbal) • Don't probe of ask for explicit explanations	• *Offer information on course of study* • *Offer to re-read transcripts of interview* • *Offer to engage in second interview* • *Ask for evaluation of the interview process*
4. (Self-)reflection/ empowerment	• Check materials with reviewers who are competent in fields of advocacy, care and research • Considering ways to involve participants • Iterative check-in on the structures • Pre-test and case-to-case adjustments	• Employ tactics of active listening, self-reflection: How do I engage in the study, what do I convey? Can I listen to these narratives? • Field notes and memos	• *Notes on interview feelings*

participation, in which each potential participant conducts their own perceived risk-benefit assessment. (Anderson et al. 2022)

By conducting research according to best practices, researchers demonstrate a commitment to respecting the experiences and voices of survivors of sexualized violence. Empowering survivors to participate in research processes can contribute and promote community engagement. However, there are limitations to standardized protocols implementing affected-centered approaches. These methods often require significant time, resources, and expertise. Researchers may need specialized training in trauma-informed methods, and the process can be more labor-intensive.

The iterative and repeated engagement with the research process may lead to participants exhaustion or can feel triggering for some participants and thereby backfire. This can impact the quality of data collected and may strain the researcher-participant relationship. Understanding the intersecting identities of people having experienced sexualized violence may be challenging, and oversimplification of complex identities may occur. This can lead to overlooking unique challenges faced by individuals with multiple marginalized identities in favor of standardized workings.

References

Anderson KM, Karris MY, DeSoto AF, Carr SG, Stockman JK (2022) Engagement of sexual violence survivors in research: trauma-informed research in the THRIVE study. In: Violence against women. https://doi.org/10.1177/10778012221125501 (Original work published 2023).

Anderson RE, Siegel JA, Silver KE, Mitchell TL (2020) Yes, (most) men know what rape is: a mixed-methods investigation into college men's definitions of rape. https://doi.org/10.31234/osf.io/m3qnj

Andresen S, Tippelt R (2018) Sexuelle Gewalt in Kindheit und Jugend. Theoretische, empirische und konzeptionelle Erkenntnisse und Herausforderungen erziehungswissenschaftlicher Forschung. Weinheim; Basel: Beltz Juventa, 222 S. (Zeitschrift für Pädagogik, Beiheft; 64). URN: urn:nbn:de:0111-pedocs-223043. https://doi.org/10.25656/01:22304

Andresen S, Demant D (2017) Worin liegt die Verantwortung der Erziehungswissenschaft? Ein Diskussionsbeitrag zur Aufarbeitung sexualisierter Gewalt in der Erziehungswissenschaft Erziehungswissenschaft 28(1):39–50. https://doi.org/10.3224/ezw.v28i1.06

Andrews M (2014) Beyond narrative: the shape of traumatic testimony. In: Jensen M, Jolly M (Hg.) We shall bear witness. Life narratives and human rights. The University of Wisconsin Press (Wisconsin studies in autobiography), Madison, Wisconsin, SS 147–166

Baader MS (2022) Involviertheit und Verantwortung Legitimation durch Wissenschaft Aufarbeitung als Herausforderung. Sexualisierte Gewalt und erziehungswissenschaftliche Disziplin Erziehungswissenschaft 32(2):29–40. https://doi.org/10.3224/ezw.v32i2.04

Baader MS, Sager C (2020) Pädagogische Professionalität und Reflexivität im Umgang mit Gewalt und sexualisierter Gewalt in Macht-, Geschlechter- und Sorgeverhältnissen. Universitätsverlag Hildesheim, Hildesheim.

Brunner F, Tozdan S, Klein V, Dekker A, Briken P (2021) Lebenszeitprävalenz des Erlebens von Sex und sexueller Berührung gegen den eigenen Willen sowie Zusammenhänge mit gesundheitsbezogenen Faktoren. Bundesgesundheitsblatt - Gesundheitsforschung - Gesundheitsschutz 64(11):1339–1354. https://doi.org/10.1007/s00103-021-03434-6

Elliott DE, Bjelajac P, Fallot RD, Markoff LS, Reed BG (2005) Trauma-informed or trauma-denied: Principles and implementation of trauma-informed services for women. J Community Psychol 33(4):461–477. https://doi.org/10.1002/jcop.20063

García-Moreno C (2013) Global and regional estimates of violence against women. Prevalence and health effects of intimate partner violence and non-partner sexual violence. In World Health Organization (Nonserial Publications), Geneva, Switzerland. Online verfügbar unter https://ebookcentral.proquest.com/lib/kxp/detail.action?docID=1681144

Hancock AM (2007) Intersectionality as a Normative and Empirical Paradigm. Politics Gend 3(02). https://doi.org/10.1017/S1743923X07000062

Hagemann-White C, Helfferich C, Kavemann B, Kindler H (2016) Forschungsmanual Gewalt Grundlagen der empirischen Erhebung von Gewalt in Paarbeziehungen und sexualisierter Gewalt Grundbegriffe und Fragen der Ethik bei der Forschung über Gewalt im Geschlechterverhältnis Springer Fachmedien Wiesbaden Wiesbaden, pp 13–31.

Hagemann-White C, Spengler J, Stövesand S (2025) Why is StoP needed? Explanations. In: StoP EU – Community Matters! A EU-CERV program. stop-eu. Hamburg. https://stop-toolbox.eu/chapters/why-is-stop-needed/descriptions

Hamby S (2014) Intimate partner and sexual violence research: scientific progress, scientific challenges, and gender. Trauma Violence Abuse 15(3):149–158. https://doi.org/10.1177/1524838014520723

Helfferich C, Kavemann B, Kindler H (2016) Forschungsmanual Gewalt. Grundlagen der empirischen Erhebung von Gewalt in Paarbeziehungen und sexualisierter Gewalt. Springer VS, Wiesbaden. Online verfügbar unter https://ebookcentral.proquest.com/lib/kxp/detail.action?docID=3568260.

Herman JL (1998) Die Narben der Gewalt: Traumatische Erfahrungen verstehen und überwinden (3. Aufl.). Kindler, Hamburg

Kollinger B, Buchholz V, Windheuser J (2023) Konzeption und Quellen- und Literaturliste: Die Bedeutung von sexualpädagogischen Vorstellungen für die strukturelle Begünstigung von sexualisierter Gewalt im Raum der evangelischen Kirche. Humboldt-Universität zu Berlin. https://doi.org/10.18452/27014

Martin PY (2004) Rape work. Victims, gender & emotions in organization & community context. Routledge, New York (Perspectives on gender)

Mehrick M (2021) Betroffene können Zeugen sein, wenn Systeme versagt haben. In: Erziehungswissenschaft 32(63):21–28. URN: urn:nbn:de:0111-pedocs-241316. https://doi.org/10.25656/01:24131

Poelchau HW, Briken P, Wazlawik M, Bauer U, Fegert J, Kavemann B (2015) Bonner Ethik-Erklärung. Zeitschrift für Sexualforschung, 28(02):153–160. https://doi.org/10.1055/s-0035-1553220

Reh S, Baader MS, Helsper W, Kappeler M, Leuzinger-Bohleber M, Sielert U, Thole W, Thompson C (2012) Sexualisierte Gewalt in pädagogischen Institutionen – Eine Einleitung. Sondierungen und Verständigungen zu einem bislang vernachlässigten Thema. In: Thole W, Baader MS, Helsper W, Kappeler M, Leuzinger-Bohleber M, Reh S, Sielert U, Thole W, Thompson C (Hrsg.) Sexualisierte Gewalt, Macht und Pädagogik, Opladen/Berlin/Toronto, SS 13–23

Tov E (2009) Leben mit der Vergewaltigung. Narrative Identitätskonstruktionen bei Frauen mit sexualisierter Gewalterfahrung. Verlag Barbara Budrich GmbH (Opladen, Berlin, Toronto), 445 Seiten. ISBN 978-3-86649-244-8

Veselka V (2006) The collapsible woman. Cultural responses to rape and sexual abuse. In: Jervis L, Zeisler A (Hg.) BITCHfest. Ten years of cultural criticism from the pages of bitch magazine. Farrar/Straus/Giroux, New York, SS 56–61.

Wazlawik M, Dekker A (2016) Ethik in der Forschung zu sexualisierter Gewalt Zeitschrift für Sexualforschung 28(04):311–317. https://doi.org/10.1055/s-00000103 https://doi.org/10.1055/s-005-30798 https://doi.org/10.1055/s-0041-110237

Jördis Spengler is a sociologist and doctoral candidate at Hochschule Rhein Main. Their primary fields of research and teaching concern survivor centered approaches towards sexualized violence and gendered violence, intersectional perspectives of social injustice, as well as anti-bias and anti-discrimination pedagogy.

Part III
Rethinking Gender through Law, Culture, and Religion: Paradigmatic Case Studies

The Impediments to the Criminal Justice Response on Gender-Based Violence in Southern Africa: Mapping the Way Forward

Emeka E. Obioha and Ishmael Mugari

Abstract Gender-based violence continues to be one of the most pressing challenges that confronts most African nations, with some African governments labelling the scourge as a national crisis that warrants immediate redress. Notwithstanding the various measures that are available to deal with gender-based violence, the criminal justice system is perhaps the most formidable institution for dealing with the scourge. However, the criminal justice response to the scourge has been marred by a myriad of challenges. This chapter explored the challenges of the criminal justice response to gender-based violence in the Southern African region, with a particular focus on South Africa and Zimbabwe. The chapter also proffers prescriptive measures for dealing with the challenges. The chapter is based on secondary data that were collected from research articles, policy reports, civil society reports and online news articles.

Keywords Gender · Gender-based violence · Law · Criminal justice · South Africa · Zimbabwe

1 Introduction

Gender-based violence is among the most common forms of violence in most countries across the globe, with serious effects on the lives, health and wellbeing of millions of women, girls, men and boys worldwide. While gender-based violence affects all genders, global statistics reveal that women and girls are affected by gender-based violence more than their male counterparts (Ndlovu et al. 2022). Violence against women and girls is one of the most widespread violations of human rights worldwide, affecting one-third of all women during their lifetime (Oyewale 2021). It is the leading cause of death and disability of women of all ages and has many other health consequences (Jewkes et al. 2015). Notwithstanding the significance of

E. E. Obioha (✉) · I. Mugari
Department of Social Sciences, Walter Sisulu University, Mthatha, South Africa
e-mail: eobioha@wsu.ac.za

A. Condello and A. Wagner (eds.), *Gender Stereotypes*, Gender, Justice and Legal Feminism 2, https://doi.org/10.1007/978-3-031-63905-0_14

a multi-sectorial response to gender-based violence across the globe, the criminal justice response plays an instrumental role in ensuring that the victims of gender-based violence get justice. For instance, the police, being the frontline social institution to deal with incidents of gender-based violence, have a vital role in assisting victims of domestic abuse to follow through on their decision to seek recourse for the abuse (Retief and Green 2015). On the other hand, by presiding over gender-based violence cases during trial proceedings, the Court delivers justice to survivors of gender-based violence.

In this chapter, we explore the criminal justice response to gender-based violence on the African continent, with a particular emphasis on the challenges that impede the effectiveness of the criminal justice response to gender-based violence. Whilst the chapter adopts a regional approach, much emphasis will be on South Africa and Zimbabwe, two Southern African nations that have had to contend with rising incidents of gender-based violence. The chapter, which is based on secondary data sources from research articles, policy reports, civil society reports and online news articles, illuminates the obstacles that are impeding the response to one of the perennial global challenges. A clear articulation of the challenges faced by the criminal justice system's response to gender-based violence will help the relevant police departments and players in the judiciary in coming up with informed strategies for dealing with these challenges. With data gathered from a variety of secondary sources, the chapter has a rich literature grounding, which also increases the credibility of the issues that are articulated by the paper. Importantly, the chapter also proffers some prescriptive measures to the challenges that are being faced by the criminal justice system in fighting gender-based violence. We begin by giving an overview of gender-based violence, before exploring the criminal justice response to the scourge.

2 Magnitude of Gender-Based Violence

Gender-based violence has been touted by several researchers as one of the most pressing social issues affecting the Africa continent (Roy et al. 2022; Oparinde and Matsha 2021; Raditloaneng 2013). South Africa is perhaps the worst affected country on the African continent, with Matzopoulos et al (2019) averring that the nation has one of the world's highest rates of gender-based violence, including femicide, rape, and intimate partner violence. Statistics that were revealed by the South African Police Service (SAPS) in 2020 revealed that 146 women are raped in South Africa every day (SAPS 2020). Research has also shown that one in every four South African women will experience intimate partner violence in their lifetimes, while a woman is murdered every three hours in the country (Dryding and Mpako 2021; Centre for the Study of Violence and Reconciliation 2019). It is also reported that the country's intimate partner violence statistics are five times higher than the global average (Mlaba 2022). Statistics also reveal a significant rise in gender-based violence in Zimbabwe. A leading non-governmental organisation which deals with gender-based violence issues- Musasa Project, reported that gender-based violence cases doubled in 2020 compared to 2019 figures, with about 20,000 cases in 2019 and over 40,000 cases in 2020 (Zimfact 2021). In regard to rape, statistics reveal that at least 22 women are raped in the country every day, with an average of 646 women being sexually abused monthly (Dube 2022). Statistics from the police, as reported by the media, reveal that 959 sexual violence cases and 1038 domestic violence cases were reported between January and September 2022 (Mutingwende 2022), with 60% of murder cases in Zimbabwe emanating from domestic violence (Women's Coalition of Zimbabwe 2020). Sexual abuse of children has also been on the rise in Zimbabwe and 58% of all the reported sexual abuse cases in Zimbabwe involved child victims (Mutingwende 2022).

Amidst the frightening statistics on gender-based violence, there has been a general consensus that the actual number of cases could be higher, as a significant number of gender-based violence goes unreported (Moyo-Nyede 2022; Mhishi 2021; Centre for the Study of Violence and Reconciliation 2017). With one in three women and girls experiencing gender-based violence in their lifetime globally, only 4% of these women/girls will report this violation to the police due to stigma and fear (Oyewale 2021). This none reporting of gender-based violence, as well as other challenges within the prosecution and trial proceedings, are among some of the factors that militate against the criminal justice system's response to gender-based violence. As will be highlighted in the proceeding sections, the criminal justice system is also partly to blame for non-reporting of gender-based violence.

3 The Criminal Justice Response to Gender-Based Violence

The criminal justice system, comprising the police and courts, is perhaps the most formidable institution for dealing with gender-based violence. A functioning criminal justice system plays an instrumental role in ensuring that the victims of gender-based violence are able to get justice (Tracey-Temba 2020). The police, as the frontline players responsible for reacting to the incidents of gender-based violence, have a crucial role to play in the fight against the scourge. As the first responders in most of the gender-based violence cases, the police are responsible for gathering evidence and ensuring survivors obtain medical treatment. They also act as an important link to both the prosecution process and the provision of services to victims in a community (Retief and Green 2015). Being the gatekeepers to the criminal justice system, the police play a significant role in shaping the gender-based violence victims' experiences of the whole system. Apart from scene attendance and evidence gathering, the police are also responsible for protecting the victim from further harm, referring for medical treatment and suitable accommodation, and ensuring compliance with protection orders (Legalwise 2022). The courts play a role through interpreting the various anti-gender-based violence laws, presiding over cases, issuing protection orders, and importantly, delivering justice. In the proceeding section, we discuss the challenges that are being faced by the criminal justice system in dealing with gender-based violence.

3.1 Challenges of the Criminal Justice System's Response to Gender-Based Violence

Notwithstanding the efforts by the criminal justice system in both countries to deal with the scourge of gender-based violence, the system has been riddled by a myriad of challenges. We discuss these challenges under seven themes, namely, the compounding effect of public health emergencies, inadequate skills to handle gender-based violence, attitude towards gender-based violence by some police officers, limited resources for investigations and victim support, high rates of withdrawal of cases, lower conviction rates and lenient sentences, secondary victimisation, and delays in the finalisation of gender-based violence cases. It is important to also highlight that most of these challenges have the effect of promoting non-reporting of gender-based violence for processing through the formal criminal justice system.

3.1.1 Compounding Effect of Public Health Emergencies

Research has shown that challenges of the criminal justice response to gender-based violence are compounded during public health emergencies, with COVID-19 pandemic posing the most significant challenge. Given the security-centric approach to fighting the pandemic, police officers had to shift focus from receiving reports to patrolling the streets and enforcing lockdown restrictive regulations (Obioha and Mugari 2022), leaving a few police officers to attend to calls. The movement restrictions also made it difficult for survivors of gender-based violence to report their cases (UNOCHA 2020). In Zimbabwe, citizens had to move around with exemption letters so that they would be allowed to pass security checkpoints (Mugari and Obioha 2021). Given the challenges to get exemption letters for gender-based violence victims to report their abuse to the police, the victims had no option but to endure continued violence by their intimate partners and abusive relatives (Chiweshe and Bhatasara 2022). Importantly, law enforcement officials and other gender-based violence service providers were also prone to the COVID-19 virus infection just like any other ordinary citizens. In South Africa, 36 police officers had died, while over 5000 had been infected with COVID-19 by July 2020, with several police stations having to be closed to curtail the spread of the virus among police officers (Tracey-Temba 2020). The prosecution and court services were also put under serious strain during the lockdown, as judicial proceedings were either postponed or suspended. This hampered judicial protection of gender-based violence victims, as issuance of restraining and protection orders was also affected (UNODC 2021). There was also a reduction of the size of specialised personnel at courts for dealing with gender-based violence due to health-related issues, including quarantine, sickness, absences and even death by COVID-19, as well as adjustments to their work due to the health measures that were put in place (UNODC 2021).

3.1.2 Inadequate Skills to Handle Gender-Based Violence

Whilst there are dedicated police units to handle gender-based violence (for instance, the Family Violence Unit and the Child Protection and Sexual Offences Unit in South Africa, and the Victim Friendly Unit in Zimbabwe), there have been reports that the police lack the necessary skills to handle gender-based violence (Committee on the Elimination of Discrimination against Women [CEDAW] 2021; Tracey-Temba 2020). This scenario is confirmed in other studies (e.g., Kholofelo and Tirivangasi 2022; Thobane et al. 2020), which also revealed a gap in training and skills by members of the SAPS as one of the major impediments to policing gender-based violence. Most police stations lack dedicated and trained personnel to attend to gender-based violence and to give victims legally correct information and support (Tracey-Temba 2020). The lack of training and knowledge on how to handle gender-based violence cases is one of the reasons why most victims experience secondary victimisation (an aspect which we will later discuss) when they report their cases at police stations (Thobane et al. 2020). Another important aspect that was noted in a Zimbabwean study by Mashiri and Mawire (2013) relates to the location of the Victim Friendly Unit offices at various police stations. In most cases, the victims have to pass through the charge office to get to the Victim Friendly Unit for reporting gender-based violence, yet those who will be manning the charge offices may not be experienced in handling gender-based violence cases (Mashiri and Mawire 2013). In South Africa, CEDAW (2021) notes that the mandatory five-day training courses on domestic violence do not give them the capacity to apply the Domestic Violence Act and the Sexual Offences Act, conduct gender-sensitive interrogations or collect forensic evidence. A Zimbabwe based nongovernmental organisation noted that the police do not take gender-based violence victims seriously enough when they file cases (Kubatana.net 2021) and this could be a possible result of inadequate training on handling gender-based violence cases.

3.1.3 Attitude Towards Gender-Based Violence by the Police

Closely related to the skills gap is the negative attitude towards gender-based violence by the police officers. While there are clear laws to deal with cases of gender-based violence, police at times choose to administer mediatory efforts, which at times lead to worse outcomes (International Federation of Red Cross and Red Crescent Society [IFRC] 2017). At times female domestic violence victims are turned away by the police, who advise them that their cases should be settled within family circles (Minisini 2021; IFRC 2017). Oftentimes, the police blame the victims of gender-based violence. Instead of taking on the men responsible for the violence and abuse, police always blame women for being victims of sexual violence (Kubatana.net 2021). The attitude towards victims by some of the police officers is not surprising as there are reports that police officers have also been implicated as perpetrators of gender-based violence. After noting a rise in the number of police officers who abuse women in South Africa, a non-governmental organisation [People Opposing Women

Abuse (POWA)] called for the police to rehabilitate officers who abuse women (Govender 2022). Highlighting the impacts of abuse by police officers, POWA had this to say, "If policemen are abusive themselves and measures are not taken to rehabilitate them or get them out of the policing system, it will be difficult for them to deal with cases of gender-based violence and femicide" (Govender 2022). Another worrying trend that possibly shapes the police officers' attitude towards gender-based violence is the murder of police officers who will be responding to domestic violence, with Kholofelo and Tirivangasi (2022) noting that police officers are murdered more in responding to domestic violence incidents than any other type of police incident. Thus, for their own safety, some police officers will try to find ways of avoiding response to domestic violence cases.

3.1.4 Limited Resources for Investigations and Victim Support

Investigations of gender-based violence is resource intensive and without adequate resources, the police will find it difficult to finalise the investigations. The challenge of investigative resource constraints has been more pronounced in sexual violence cases. For instance, there have been concerns over the delays in the finalisation of the cases due to the DNA backlog in South Africa (Govender 2022). It was also reported that 76% of South African police stations did not have adult rape kits as of September 2019, while 69% did not have child rape kits (Mile 2020: 7). With most police stations not having enough rape kits, there have also been concerns over inadequate expertise in the use rape kits within the SAPS (Stoltz 2022). In Zimbabwe, Mushayavanhu et al. (2021) note the centralised processing of gender-based violence forensic services and the absence of rape kits due to lack of funding as impediments to the criminal justice response to gender-based violence. Rape kits and other forensic services are essential when gathering evidence of rape or other sexual crimes and in their absence, criminal proceedings will be negatively impacted. There have also been concerns over limited police vehicles in South Africa (Thobane et al. 2020) and absence of motor vehicles at some police stations in Zimbabwe (Mushayavanhu et al. 2021). A lack of police vehicles hampers the coordination of gender-based violence response efforts. In Zimbabwe, the shortage of vehicles is so dire that police officers at times have to resort to the use of public transport even for docket movement. This creates a risk of compromising sensitive information, losing it or possibilities of fuelling corruption due to lack of accountability, check and balances on docket movements (Mushayavanhu and Phiri 2018: 12).

The Southern African Development Community (SADC) Secretariat (2019) also notes the limited financial and human resources for implementation and monitoring of gender-based violence interventions in the region. While the police also have a duty to ensure that victims get suitable accommodation, the CEDAW report (2021) noted the absence of State-run shelters for women survivors and their children in South Africa. Instead, the government has delegated the provision of such services to non-governmental organisations-run shelters without adequately funding them (CEDAW 2021). The shelters serve the very important role of providing temporary accommodation and support for survivors of gender-based violence. They are places where survivors can be safe, access healthcare services, access psycho-social support, obtain knowledge of the law and access legal support services to obtain remedies. In Zimbabwe, a report by the Zimbabwe Lawyers for Human Rights (ZLHR) (2022) noted that government does not have any shelters for gender-based violence survivors and the Department of Social Welfare is not resourced to assist survivors of gender-based violence. As is the case with South Africa, most of the shelters are run by civil society organisations (CSOs) and these CSOs do not have capacity to sustain the running of these shelters (ZLHR 2022). In the absence of these shelters, survivors have nowhere to go and may end up returning to the only home they know, which is where their perpetrator is. Victims from poor backgrounds also struggle to meet transportation costs for reporting their cases and attending courts, while some do not have the financial means for legal aid (Kubatana.net 2021). Another aspect of victim support relates to communication between the investigating officers and the victims, with a study by Thobane et al (2020) noting poor communication by investigating officers as a challenge that caused frustration to victims as they were not regularly informed about the status of their cases. Shortage of motor vehicles could be the reason for the break in communication between the investigating offers and the victims. Constant communication between the investigating officers and the victims is crucial in building confidence with the whole criminal justice system.

3.1.5 High Rates of Withdrawal of Cases

The effectiveness of a criminal justice process ordinarily ends with the victims getting justice and high incidents of withdrawal of cases will be an affront to justice. A high rate of withdrawal of gender-based violence was cited by the SADC Secretariat (2019) as one of the major challenges of responding to gender-based violence. For example, of the 21,755 gender-based violence that were lodged with the Zimbabwe Republic Police in 2016, a total of 9903 cases were withdrawn at the police stations at the instigation of the survivor, while 1944 cases were withdrawn at Court at the instance of the survivors (CEDAW 2019). In South Africa, an average of 24% of the cases were withdrawn during the 2019/2020 financial year, while 11% were withdrawn during the 2020/2021 financial year (Stoltz 2022). Notwithstanding the fact that most of the withdrawals are instigated by the victims, there are also incidents where the cases are just struck of the court role, with poor investigations and lack of evidence as the primary reasons (Thobane et al. 2020).

Withdrawal of gender-based violence cases is prompted by a number of reasons. The victims may decide to withdraw cases where their abuser is a breadwinner in the home or a provider for the victim and they may find themselves or their families stranded, should a conviction occur (Mile 2020). Victims also withdraw cases when they have less confidence in the criminal justice system and hence wish to carry on with their lives (Machisa et al. 2017). Many victims also experience social pressure from family members, the community and those known to the accused, which can render the cost of pursuing cases very high for the victims (Machisa et al. 2017).

Ultimately, community attitudes of tolerance towards gender-based violence within families creates social barriers to accessing support services and the justice system, prompting survivors to discontinue with their reported cases. Notwithstanding these various reasons, the rise in the withdrawal of gender-based violence cases paints a grim picture on the efficacy of the criminal justice system to tame the scourge.

3.1.6 Lower Conviction Rates and Lenient Sentences

In addition to high withdrawal of cases, there have been low levels of prosecution and conviction in gender-based violence cases. For example, between April and June 2022, the SAPS opened a total of 9516 rape cases but only 286 were convicted (South African Government 2022). Mile (2020) also notes that only 4% of reported cases of rape lead to convictions in South Africa. There has also been concern over lenient sentences for convicted gender-based violence perpetrators, with reports in Zimbabwe showing that some perpetrators are getting away with fines and very lenient sentences (Tshuma 2021). Gender-based violence has often been characterised by ad hoc sentencing, with some perpetrators committing the crimes knowing fully well that they would walk away with lighter sentences (Butaumocho 2017). Many a time, gender-based violence perpetrators are also granted bail and they return to the same community where they would have committed the offence (Mashiri and Mawire 2013). As a result, survivors will live in fear of reporting their abusers as they fear that they will be let loose or even retaliate with more violence. It thus sends a wrong signal to survivors of gender-based violence and the general population if sexual perverts and other gender-based violence perpetrators are allowed to roam the streets or get away with lenient sentences.

In a study by the International Federation of Red Cross and Red Crescent Society (IFRC) in Zimbabwe, it was established that even where processes at the Victim Friendly Unit might start well, sometimes when cases go to court the dockets are lost or cases are withdrawn, with corruption being cited as the major cause of such occurrences (IFRC 2017). This implies that prosecution may fail to take place despite the formal recording of the reports at police stations. At times, the low conviction rates may be associated with lack of evidence. The main challenges faced by majority of survivors include absence of evidence of rape because they would have washed themselves together with their clothes; while some survivors would have been sexually active such that injuries may not be identified, resulting in absence of definitive evidence (Mushayavanhu et al. 2021). In other instances, important documentary evidence disappears due to corruption, and this results in either the ending of the case or gross miscarriage of justice (Mushayavanhu and Phiri 2018). This challenge with evidence has a negative impact on the prosecution and subsequent conviction in rape trials. Citizens expect to see justice happening and if those cases that go through the criminal justice system do not end up with convictions, they will lose trust in the whole criminal justice process. Because of the mistrust of the criminal justice system, gender-based violence survivors will end up afraid to report as there will be no assurance that the perpetrators will be arrested, and there will also be a fear that the abuser will return to harm them again.

3.1.7 Secondary Victimisation During Investigations and the Trial Process

The unguided and sometimes insensitive line of questioning from law enforcement officials, lawyers and judges who are not trained in women's rights issues often leads to secondary victimisation of women who endure the ordeal of sexual gender-based violence (Mushayavanhu et al. 2021). At times, the prosecutors neither have skills to deal with cases involving children and sexual violence, especially on vetting of dockets, nor give adequate orientation of court processes to the survivors (Mushayavanhu et al. 2021). Victims can be asked to recount their ordeals several times during investigations and during trial proceedings, a phenomenon which will compound the pain and suffering they would have already experienced (International Commission of Jurists (ICJ) 2021). Sometimes, the judiciary questions the authenticity of the rape claims and the evidence that is submitted, especially if the victim is a prostitute, or has a "questionable social background" (Butaumocho 2017). Moreover, rape victims are often re-victimised in the courtroom in the form of attacks on their credibility and past sexual history (Butaumocho 2017). Because of this secondary victimisation, it is not surprising to see survivors opting not to pursue justice in future gender-based violence incidents.

3.1.8 Delays in the Finalisation of Gender-Based Violence Cases

Gender-based violence cases often take long to finalise, resulting in delayed justice for victims. Continued postponements of cases often result in most survivors and witnesses abandoning the cases they had initiated because of the lack of adequate financial means to meet the continued delays (Mushayavanhu et al. 2021). One of the factors leading to the delays is the high staff turnover in the judiciary. In Zimbabwe, 28 of the 46 public prosecutors that were recruited in 2022 had resigned by April 2023 (Sunday Mail 2023). Due to high staff turnover, some matters fail to be completed as the prosecutor would have moved without adequate paper trail of proceedings in court records for new staff or other colleagues to take over, or without adequate handover of dockets and files (Mushayavanhu and Phiri 2018). Moreover, high caseloads may result in the prosecutor's inability to understand the gendered nature of crimes faced by women and girls. The old adage that "justice delayed is justice denied" perfectly explains the current situation, as gender-based violence survivors struggle to get timely justice.

In the first of its kind within the Zimbabwe legal fraternity, a woman who was gang-raped resulting in the birth of a child sued the Ministers responsible for Police, Health and Justice for failing to provide timely service in order to prevent pregnancy (*Mildred Mapingure v. Minister of Home Affairs and 2 Others, ZWSC22/2014*). It was held that the police (first respondent) failed in their duty to assist the Appellant in accessing timely services in order to prevent pregnancy. The doctor (second respondent) also failed to carry out his professional duty to avert the pregnancy when it could have been reasonably prevented. These unlawful omissions took place within the course and scope of their employment, and therefore the first and second respondents were vicariously liable to compensate the Appellant for the harm resulting from the failure to enable her to prevent pregnancy (*Supra*). The *Mildred Mapingure* case clearly shows the agony that some survivors of gender-based violence have to go through due to delays in getting help from the criminal justice players.

4 Addressing the Impediments to the Criminal Justice System' Response to Gender-Based Violence

Having discussed the various challenges that impede the criminal justice system's response to gender-based violence, we look at ways to overcome these challenges. First, there is need for the governments to address the spike in gender-based violence during public health and other emergencies. Gender-based violence services should always be regarded as essential services during emergencies (Roy et al 2022; Tracey-Temba 2020), with the governments creating financial reserves for responding to gender-based violence during such emergencies. There should be emergency measures to support women and girls experiencing gender-based violence, and who are planning to escape the violent environment during regulated lockdown curfew periods (Ndlovu et al. 2022).

The skills gap among police officers and court officials, as well as attitude problems by police officers can be addressed through continuous training. As averred by Kholofelo and Tirivangasi (2022), training should be premised on the "know-what", the "know-how" and the "know-who". For *know-what*, the players in the criminal justice system should be aware of all the laws, as well as policies that govern gender-based violence. With the *know-how*, the criminal justice system players should know the procedures and how to accomplish complex tasks as regards responding to gender-based violence. The necessary skills required include communication skills for effective communication with survivors, analytical skills for solving complex cases, and conflict management skills for managing conflicts arising from gender-based violence environments. The *know-who* provides a platform for the criminal justice players to be aware of whom to contact when cases are reported. Thus, they need to know the health facilities, medical evacuation service providers, location of safe houses, and various non-governmental organisations that can assist victims. CEDAW (2021) reiterates the need for further mandatory, recurrent and effective training on the diverse forms of gender-based violence, as well as gender-sensitive questioning and proper case management and evidence collection. Proper training will also reduce secondary victimisation, as police officers, prosecutors and trial officers will be equipped with the requisite gender-sensitive investigations and questioning techniques.

Government funding for all gender-based violence efforts is also crucial. Given the problem of non-availability of sate-run safe houses for gender-based violence survivors as noted in previous reports (e.g., ZLHR 2022; CEDAW 2021; SADC Secretariat 2019), governments need to urgently channel financial resources towards construction of these safe houses. Delegating the role of providing shelter for survivors to non-governmental organisations will be tantamount to dereliction of duty by the government. While it will be noble to partner these civil society organisations, governments need to take the leading role. Adequate funding should also be channelled towards resources such as motor vehicles, rape kits, and other consumables in the forensic laboratories. There is also need for investment in DNA testing machines or scientific advances that allow for testing of tissue samples, as this will ensure that in cases of sexual gender-based violence, evidence provided is more reliable (Mushayavanhu et al. 2021). Investment in resources and technologies for evidence collection will help to increase the chances of conviction and reduce the withdrawal of cases at courts for lack of evidence.

There is also need for stringent punitive measures for perpetrators of gender-based violence. CEDAW (2021) also recommends the establishment of penalties that are commensurate with all forms of gender-based violence, as well as passing necessary statutory provisions that make it difficult for perpetrators of gender-based violence to be released on bail. For heinous crimes such as rape or other sexual related crimes involving minors and the disabled, there should be mandatory sentences to send a clear message that such actions are not tolerated within societies (Butaumocho 2017). These punitive sentences should be coupled with prompt justice for victims of gender-based violence. With adequate resources and capacitation of the criminal justice officers as recommended in this study, there is need for speedy investigations and trial proceedings. This will build society's confidence in the criminal justice system and reduce non-reporting of gender-based violence cases.

Lastly, multi-stakeholder awareness campaigns are crucial in addressing some of the challenges that the criminal justice system faces. There should be community ownership of the gender-based violence problem, coupled with community mobilisation involving all members of the community, health and legal service providers, teachers and community leaders (Mashiri and Mawire 2013). Citizens also need to be educated about their rights, as well as the criminal justice routes that are available to them when they fall victim to gender-based violence. There should be raised awareness of hidden forms of violence against women and attitudes which condone them should be challenged through media activities, training events and community engagement (Mushayavanhu et al. 2021). Importantly awareness campaigns should also focus on encouraging communities to report all incidents of gender-based violence, as well as dealing with harmful societal practices that promote gender-based violence.

5 Conclusion

Notwithstanding the significant role that the criminal justice system plays in ensuring that survivors of gender-based violence get justice, the chapter has revealed that the system faces a myriad of challenges. Apart from being overwhelmed during public health emergencies such as COVID-19, the police services in both countries have been impacted by a skills gap in handling gender-based violence cases, and shortage of resources such as safe houses, motor vehicles and rape kits. Because of some of the police officers' attitude towards gender-based violence cases, they have sometimes turned away victims of gender-based violence. Despite opening of dockets at police stations, there have been high rates of withdrawal of cases at police stations and courts, with majority of the withdrawals being instigated by the victims. For cases that make it to trial, the conviction rates have been worryingly low, and perpetrators have often received lenient sentences. Secondary victimisation during investigations and trial proceedings, as well as delays in the finalisation of gender-based violence cases have also impeded the criminal justice response. Overall, these challenges result in reduced confidence in the criminal justice system, with multiplier effects such as non-reporting of gender-based violence and continued withdrawal of cases at the behest of victims. Continuous training of police officers and judicial officials, government funding for safe shelter and other resources, stringent punitive measures and multi-sectoral awareness campaigns are the recommended strategies to deal with the criminal justice response challenges.

References

Butaumocho R (2017). Honeymoon over for rapists. The Herald, July 20. https://www.herald.co.zw/hoenymoon-over-for-rapists/

Centre for the Study of Violence and Reconciliation (CSVR) (2017) Violence against women in South Africa: a country in crisis. CSVR, Pretoria

Centre for the Study of Violence and Reconciliation (CSVR) (2019).What drives violence in South Africa? Pretoria, CSVR

Chiweshe MK, Bhatasara S (2022) Intervention—sexual and gender based violence and COVID-19 in urban Zimbabwe. Antipode Online, October 20. https://antipodeonline.org/2022/10/20/sgbv-and-covid-19-in-zimbabwe/

Committee on the Elimination of Discrimination against Women (CEDAW) (2019) Sixth periodic report submitted by Zimbabwe under article 18 of the Convention. United Nations, CEDAW, New York

Committee on the Elimination of Discrimination against Women (CEDAW) (2021) Inquiry concerning South Africa conducted under article 8 of the Optional Protocol to the Convention. CEDAW, New York, United Nations

Dube T (2022) 22 women raped daily as Zimbabwe intensifies fight against GBV. Chronicle, November 28. https://www.chronicle.co.zw/22-women-raped-daily-as-zimbabwe-intensifies-fight-against-gbv/

Dryding D, Mpako A (2021) South Africans say gender-based violence worsening, blame substance abuse. Afrobarometer No. 494, December 7

Govender S (2022) Latest GBV and femicide crime states not accurate, say Powa. Sunday Times, February 21. https://www.timeslive.co.za/news/south-africa/2022-02-21-latest-gbv-and-femicide-crime-stats-not-accurate-says-powa/
International Commission of Jurists (ICJ) (2021) Sexual and gender-based violence in Zimbabwe: Women human rights defenders' experiences and legal challenges. ICJ, Geneva
International Federation of Red Cross and Red Crescent Society (IFRC) (2017) Zimbabwe country case study: Effective law and policy on gender equality and protection from sexual and gender-based violence in disasters. IFRC, Geneva
Jewkes R, Hilker LM, Khan S, Busiello F, Fraser E (2015) What works to prevent violence against women and girls—Evidence reviews: Response mechanisms to prevent violence against women and girls. What Works to Prevent Violence, September
Kholofelo MA, Tirivangasi M (2022) Police capacity building in dealing with domestic violence cases in South Africa: An entry point to women's access to justice. In Lubaale EC, Budoo-Scholtz A (eds) Violence against women and criminal justice in Africa, Sustainable Development Goals Series. Switzerland, Springer Nature
Kubatana.net (2021) Barriers to justice for victims and survivors of GBV in the wake of Covid-19. Kubatana.net, May 24. https://kubatana.net/2021/05/24/barriers-to-justice-for-victims-of-gbv-in-the-wake-of-covid-19/
Legalwise (2022) The role of the SAPS in the context of gender-based violence. Legalwise. https://legalwise.co.za/help-yourself/legal-articles/role-saps-context-gender-based-violence-gbv
Machisa M, Jina R, Labuschagne G, Vetten L, Loots L, Swemmer S, Meyersfeld B, Jewkes R (2017) Rape justice in South Africa: Retrospective study of the investigation, prosecution and adjudication of reported rape cases from 2012. https://www.samrc.ac.za/sites/default/files/files/2017-10-30/RAPSSAreport.pdf
Mashiri L, Mawire PR (2013) An assessment of the effectiveness of interventions against gender-based violence in Zimbabwe: a case study of Gweru Urban District. IOSR J Human Soc Sci 14:13–25
Matzopoulos R, Abrahams N, Bowman B, Shai N, Prinsloo M, Salau S, Bradshaw D, Gray G (2019) Utility of crime surveys for sustainable development goals monitoring and violence prevention using a public health approach. S Afr Med J 109:382–386. https://doi.org/10.7196/SAMJ.2019.v109i6.13806
Mhishi V (2021) South Africa's secondary pandemic: a crisis of gender based violence. Global Risk Insights, March 28. https://globalinsights.com/2021/03/south-africas-secondary-pandemic-a-crisis-of-gender-based-violence/
Mile K (2020) Gender based violence: A South African plague. Rebecca Oppenheimer Internship, South Africa
Minisini V (2021) South Africa's secondary pandemic: A crisis of gender-based violence. Global Risk Insights, March 28. https://creativecommons.org/publicdomain/mark/1.0/
Mlaba N (2022) What's it like on the front lines of fighting violence against women in South Africa. Global Citizen, December 9. https://www.globalcitzen.org/en/content/south-africa-gender-based-violence-frontlines-gbvf/
Moyo-Nyede S (2022) Zimbabweans see gender-based violence as most important women's rights issue to address. Afrobarometer No. 557, October 3
Mugari I, Obioha E (2021) Covid-19 and the restrictive measures: The national security conundrum for Zimbabwe. African Security Rev 30:1–13. https://doi.org/10.1080/10246029.2021.1972015
Mushayavanhu D, Phiri P (2018) Report on development of case management system for the National Prosecuting Authority (NPA). Harare, NPA
Mushayavanhu D, Chiweshe M, Bhatasara S (2021) An assessment of the formal justice system in responding to sexual and gender-based violence (SGBV), harmful practices and sexual reproductive health rights in Zimbabwe. Bulawayo, The Spotlight Initiative, Women and Law in Southern Africa & the Legal Resources Foundation
Mutingwende B (2022) Children account for 58% of sexual abuse cases in 2022. Spiked, December. https://spikedmedia.co.zw/children-account-58-of-sexaul-abuse-cases-in-2022/.

Ndlovu S, Mulondo M, Tsoka N, Gwegweni J, Ndirangu J (2022) COVID-19 impact on gender-based violence among women in South Africa during lockdown: a narrative review. Afr J Reprod Heal 26(7):59–71

Obioha EE, Mugari I (2022) Policing COVID-19 restrictive regulations in Zimbabwe: The shifting crime trends and human rights implications. African Security Rev 31(4):415–428. https://doi.org/10.1080/10246029.2022.2132872

Oparinde K, Matsha RM (2021) Powerful discourse: Gender-based violence and counter-discourse in South Africa. Cogent Soc Sci 8:1–16. https://doi.org/10.1080/23311983.2021.1911035

Oyewale D (2021) Delivering justice to survivors of sexual and gender-based violence through DNA evidence. Harare, UNICEF. https://www.unicef.org/zimbabwe/stories/delivering-justice-survivors-sexual-and-gender-based-violence-through-dna-evidence.

Raditloaneng WN (2013) An analysis of gender-based domestic violence and reactions in Southern Africa. Wudpecker J Sociol Anthropol 1:60–71

Southern African Development Community (SADC) Secretariat (2019) Regional Strategy and framework of Action for addressing gender-based violence 2018–2030. Gaborone, SADC Secretariat

Retief R, Green S (2015) Some challenges of policing domestic violence. Social Work 50:135–147

Roy CM, Bukuluki P, Casey SE, Jagun MO, John NA, Mabhena N, Mwangi M, McGovern T (2022) Impact of COVID-19 on gender-based violence prevention and response services in Kenya, Uganda, Nigeria, and South Africa: a cross-sectional survey. Front Global Women's Heal 2:780771. https://doi.org/10.3389/fgwh.2021.780771

South African Government (2022) Minister Bheki Cele: Quarter Crime statistics 2022/2023. South African Government, August 19. https://www.gov.za/speeches/minister-bheki-cele-quarter-one-crime-statistics-20222023-19-aug-2022/

Stoltz E (2022) South African police are failing victims of gender-based violence, report shows. Mail & Guardian, July 13. https://mg.co.za/news/2022-07-13-south-african-police-are-failing-victims-of-gender-based-violence-report-shows/

Sunday Mail (2023) Massive staff turnover hits NPA. Sunday Mail, April, 16. https://www.sundaymail.co.zw/massive-staff-turnover-hits-npa.

Thobane M, Artz L, Ngubane M, Maksudi K, Haji M (2020) Collaboration in gender-based violence response, access to justice and prevention. Gender, Health and Justice Research Unit, University of cape Town, Cape Town

Tshuma A (2021) Stiffer penalties needed for GBV perpetrators. Chronicle, February 23. https://www.chronicle.co.zw/stiffer-penalties-needed-for-gbv-perpetrators/

Tracey-Temba L (2020) Police and courts must do more to reduce gender-based violence. Reliefweb, July 13. https://reliefweb.int/report/south-africa/police-and-courts-must-do-more-reduce-gender-based-violence

UNODC (2021) The impact of COVID-19 on criminal justice system responses to gender-based violence against women: a global review of emerging evidence. UNODC, Vienna

UNOCHA (2020) Zimbabwe. Cluster status: protection (gender based violence). Situation Report, June 11. https://reports.unocha.org/en/country/zimbabwe/card/2XxB9GOV93/.

Women's Coalition of Zimbabwe (WCOZ) (2020) Strengthening police responsiveness to address violence against women and girls: TROCAIRE. Harare: WCOZ, June 28. https://www.wcoz.org/strengthening-police-responsiveness-to-address-violence-against-women-and-girls-trocaire.

Zimbabwe Lawyers for Human Rights (2022) ZLHR advocates for safe shelters for survivors of gender-based violence. Harare, ZLHR, December 22. https://www.zlhr.org.zw/?p=2929.

Zimfact (2021) Factsheet: gender-based cases. Zimfact, November 22. https://zimfact.org/facts-gender-based-violence-cases/.

Emeka E. Obioha is a Professor of Sociology in the Department of Social Sciences at Walter Sisulu University. His research interests and areas where he has published extensively include:

Social problems, deviance, social control, policing, conflicts, urban ecosystems, development capabilities and systems equilibrium analysis.

Ishmael Mugari holds a Doctorate in Police Science and his research focuses on criminology, police accountability, police strategy and national security issues.

Women Before the Law in Italy: A Picture from the CEDAW Committee's View in the Case A. F. v. Italy

Ilaria Boiano

Abstract This chapter delves into the pervasive influence of stereotypes on legal reasoning and justice systems, particularly regarding gender-based discrimination and violence against women. It examines the feminist critique of patriarchal legal frameworks, highlighting the systemic sexist stereotypes perpetuated within them from the perspective of the Italian legal system as scrutinized by the CEDAW Committee in the case A.F. v. Italy, delving into the positive and negative obligations arising from due diligence by states in cases of gender-based and sexual violence against women.

Keywords Gender · Stereotypes · Sexism · Sexual violence · Legal feminism

1 The Feminist Critique of Law and the Unraveling of 'Rape Myths'

As extensively explored in this volume, stereotypes, i.e., opinions about people or social groups, mostly having to do with sex and gender, nationality, geographical origin, religion, or specific personal conditions (e.g. migrant), rigidly pre-constituted and generalized, i.e., not acquired based on direct experience and evaluation of individual cases but based on simplifications of a different matrix,[1] can influence logical-legal reasoning, with violation of the principle of equality before the law and denial of justice, since the ascertainment of facts, rights, and responsibilities of the subjects involved in litigation can be compromised by 'epistemic violence.'[2]

Between the 1960s and 1970s, the international women's movement, engaged everywhere, albeit from different positions, in a radical critique of legal systems that were profoundly patriarchal and sexist for women, and thus historically declined

[1] See Taruffo (2009), p. 59.
[2] Fricker (2007).

I. Boiano (✉)
Rome, Italy
e-mail: ilariaboiano@me.com

A. Condello and A. Wagner (eds.), *Gender Stereotypes*, Gender, Justice and Legal Feminism 2, https://doi.org/10.1007/978-3-031-63905-0_15

through law, denounced the limits of positive law and judicial practice, revealing the spread of sexist narrative patterns that systemically invalidated judicial ascertainment concerning women.[3]

This feminist critique of the law was articulated in the early stages, starting with the incriminating norms that punished specific conduct of women (such as adultery, abortion, or infanticide) and about rape, a recurring *topos* in feminist literature and a symbolic paradigm of reference used for the reflection conducted on power by the international women's movement.[4] Rape, in fact, along with the issues about its meaning on the cultural level, its legal definition, and the opportunity and modalities of criminal intervention, constitutes a total social fact, as Tamar Pitch clarifies, because it encompasses the structure and shape of social relations in their complexity, proving to be an instrument through which to resolve and interpret distant dynamics of a different nature[5]: rape is thus valuable for social inquiry because it constitutes a persistent sign, albeit in its mutability, of the underlying web of relationships between sexes, generations, classes, and territorial roots.

Consequently, rephrasing the criminal provision sanctioning rape in many legal systems, including the Italian one, has involved a long journey through multiple levels of conflict.[6] Often, the rewriting of the crime has not been sufficient to overcome simplifications and generalizations about women's behavior based on knowledge, beliefs, and expectations accrued based on gender and the 'gender regimes' that structure social relations.[7] However acceptable a law could be written, there was the problem of the 'machinery of justice,' which is an entirely different matter, as Lia Cigarini points out:

> [...] In a court of law, in a trial, which some even consider one political instrument among many possible ones, determined power relations unfavorable to women are reproduced.

---

[3] While the experience of a part of feminism, such as the Italian one, matured in the informal context of the political mobilization of groups of women who 'separated' from the general political movement of contestation to 'start from themselves' and unveil the oppression of visible and invisible patriarchy on women's lives, in other contexts such as the United States and the United Kingdom the mobilization took its start mainly in the academic sphere. For a reconstruction on legal feminism in Italy, see Simoneet al. (2019).

[4] See Bourke (2008) and Feci and Schettini (2017).

[5] Pitch (1998), p. 149.

[6] The popular initiative law deposited in 1979 by the Women's Liberation Movement, the Italian Women's Union and the Roman Collective of Via Pompeo Magno proposed to provoke a first strong symbolic shift: to eliminate the rules that sanction the 'appropriation' of women outside the permitted terrain of negotiation (marriage) and to relocate sexual violence in Title XII among crimes against the person, within Chapter III, dedicated to the protection of individual freedom. The move could not, however, take place with unchanged norms. Still, the crimes had to be reformulated: the code distinguished between rape (rape/rape), which occurred when there had been carnal union because of coercion by violence or threat, and violent acts of lechery. This distinction modulated the seriousness of the offence caused concerning the parts of the body involved in the assault, leading to 'absurd distinctions between the different parts of the woman's body', and in terms of the trial imposed a particularly humiliating investigation on the woman victim of the offence. Finally, the 1979 proposal called for making it possible for associations and movements to be admitted as civil parties, while renouncing any influence on punishment. For a reconstruction, see Virgilio (1997).

[7] Connell (2002).

> When I find myself in a trial, who gives me the possibility to react to the symbolic rape of the judge, the lawyer, and the law that despises women? If one pays attention to physical rape, a law and a trial may perhaps suffice. Still, those who pay attention to symbolic rape ask themselves what practice and what policy allows women to stop being symbolically raped.[8]

Just as the law regulates an internal contradiction in the world of men, so in the process, the regulation of the same contradiction takes shape through the rules of trial, and not infrequently, women seeking redress find themselves confronted with denigrating mechanisms and practices that disqualify them as subjects of law and undermine their credibility. In light of this, Carol Smart, among the various scholars engaged in the critique of law, arrived at the end of the 1980s to encourage the maturation of the awareness of law as an instrument constructed according to a sexist, masculine, and gendered scheme, still incapable of posing 'the woman's question,' since it is blind to the gendered implications of rules and procedures presented as general, neutral and abstract.[9]

In Italy, these contradictions have been documented by the women's movement through mass participation in the hearings of ongoing criminal trials, first in the trials that women were subjected to as defendants for the crime of abortion, then in cases of women who were victims of rape, thus outlining a political practice useful both in not leaving women to the social solitude generally resulting from denouncing sexist and gender-based violence, and in documenting the practices of denigration and stigmatization, not only social but also legal, resulting from the sexist legal arguments transposed by the judicial measures.[10]

In the meantime, within the academic sphere, Britain and American feminists were investigating the social and judicial treatment of women who decided to denounce the sexist violence they had suffered, particularly rape.[11] From the survey of cases, it emerged that women victims of rape were considered responsible for the rape they had suffered, which was often minimized in terms of the consequent damage because it was considered less traumatic than other crimes from a psychological point of view.[12]

Female rape victims were constantly exposed to the risk of not being believed because they never matched what was thought to be the 'real' rape victim, a parameter informed by so-called 'rape myths,' which Burt in 1980 defined as a set of 'prejudiced, stereotyped or false beliefs about rape, rape victims and rapists.'[13]

Some feminist analyses explored not only their impact on the judicial outcome of rape complaints but also how rape myths and the resulting fear of not being believed kept women in a state of awe in personal relationships.[14]

---

[8] Cigarini (2022), p. 52.

[9] Smart (1992), pp. 29–44; (1989).

[10] Filippini (2022).

[11] Calhoun et al. (1976) and Hockett et al. (2016), pp. 139–167.

[12] Simonson and Subich (1999).

[13] Burt (1980). See also Brownmiller (1975) and Lonsway and Fitzgerald (1994).

[14] Herman (1984), Allen (1998), pp. 66–83, Sanday (2003), pp. 337–362, and Buchwald et al. (2005).

2 From Political Condemnation to the Codification of International Obligations Against Sexist Stereotypes

The unraveling of rape myths has had a considerable impact on the debate within the negotiating forums of international law, where feminist scholars and activists have mobilized to overcome the silence of/about women, which has underlined as an integral part of the structure of the international legal order, a 'crucial element of its stability.'[15]

Even in the legal discourse on human rights, the reference subject has been neutral and abstract, coinciding with the male dimension. At the same time, women have been configured as the paradigm of the 'alien [subject] of international law.'[16]

In particular, the critique of the separation of the public and private spheres as a social organization and political model ideologically aiming at perpetuating women's substantive inequality has led internationally to the definition of a renewed theoretical framework to inscribe the full recognition of women's human rights.[17] The primary frame of reference produced thanks to international feminist mobilization was the Convention on the Elimination of All Forms of Discrimination against Women (hereafter CEDAW), adopted by the UN General Assembly on 18 December 1979 and ratified by Italy in 1985.[18]

The preamble opens with the recognition of the inadequacy of the international human rights treaties in force at the time to combat discrimination against women, reconstructing the fundamental stages of the political debate that had developed in the previous years, starting from the conference of the International Year of Women held in Mexico City in 1975, the objective of the CEDAW is clarified as the definition of the obligation of States to adopt and implement specific measures to combat the multiple forms of discrimination that women suffer both in the public and private sphere. The language of the preamble was considered particularly innovative in its entirety and offered essential propelling elements for the interpretation of the treaty by the Monitoring Committee (hereafter CEDAW Committee): repeatedly, in fact, there is the warning to ensure "the maximum participation of women," there is the call for a change in the traditional roles attributed to women and men and the role of women in society.

The most innovative aspect of the CEDAW is to be found in the express prohibition of discrimination against women 'on the grounds of their gender,' thus referring not only to discrimination on the grounds of gender but also to discrimination on the grounds of the roles traditionally attributed to women, providing as a consequent obligation of states the adoption of concrete and practical measures (Articles 2 and 24 CEDAW). It affirms the structural nature of discrimination against women that finds its root, as Article 5 CEDAW specifies, in the patriarchal model of society, roles,

---

[15] Charlesworth (1999), p. 380.

[16] MacKinnon (1983).

[17] Pateman (1988), and Olsen (1993), p. 157.

[18] Freeman et al. (2012).

customs, and practices translated into sexist and gender stereotypes and prejudices that influenced the normative and jurisprudential production of States.

At the time of its adoption, the CEDAW was the only international instrument requiring states to take concrete action on such substantive aspects of discrimination against women, expressly mentioning sexist stereotypes and prejudices as causes of discrimination against women in all spheres of society. Another novelty in the CEDAW is the perspective of the relationship between the state and individuals. While traditionally, international human rights acts have focused on protecting individuals against the acts of the state, in a vertical dimension, the CEDAW recognizes that the threat to women's full enjoyment of human rights also comes from non-state actors. Therefore, the CEDAW has set itself as an operational instrument applicable, through the instrumental role of the State, also to the horizontal dimension of relations between private individuals, in particular thanks to the entry into force of the Optional Protocol to the CEDAW (CEDAW-OP), adopted on 6 October 1999 and in force since 22 December 2000, which has regulated the mechanisms of denunciation and investigation of violations of the CEDAW.[19]

Starting with the actions of documenting institutionalized sexist violence and feminist writings on rape myths and critique of law, the women's movement embarked on an in-depth reflection on sexual and gender-based violence from new political practices: in the United States, South America and Europe, women's organizations were springing up in support of women victims of male violence based on the practice of self-awareness as a method of investigating the causes and dynamics of gendered violence against women, and on the practice of women's relationships as a model for devising support strategies that would enhance the individual resources of women involved in experiences of violence.

In a context so animated by political mobilization and feminist research, General Recommendation No. 19 of 1992 was drafted to expressly address the issue of male violence against women as a specific form of discrimination against women prohibited by CEDAW and outlined the obligations of states to take specific measures under Article 3 CEDAW, which requires states to take positive action to overcome sexist cultural attitudes that view women as subordinate to men.

The issue of stereotypes, furthermore, is taken up in General Recommendation No. 25 in which, again referring to Article 3, in conjunction with Articles 1, 2, 4, and 5, the recommendation to States Parties to take measures in all fields "to address prevailing gender relations and the persistence of gender-based stereotypes" is reinforced.

Judicial' stereotypes are the subject of specific analysis and guidance in General Recommendation No. 33 on women's access to justice: by 'judicial stereotyping,' the Committee refers to the practice of legal practitioners, in particular the judiciary, of attributing specific characteristics or roles to an individual because of their membership in a particular social group or by specific characteristics (e.g., sex and gender roles for women). Sexual, sexist, and gender stereotypes and prejudices in the justice system have been identified as severe obstacles to women's full enjoyment of human

[19] Connors (2012), pp. 607–679.

rights because they "impede women's access to justice in all areas of law and can have a particular impact on women victims and survivors of violence" (§26).

The CEDAW Committee points out that judicial stereotypes distort perceptions and lead to decisions based on preconceived beliefs and myths rather than relevant facts.

Judges often adopt rigid standards on what they consider appropriate behavior for women and penalize those who do not conform to these stereotypes. Stereotypes also affect, the Committee points out, the credibility of women's statements, arguments, and testimony as parties and witnesses with far-reaching consequences, for example, in criminal law, where a culture of impunity for crimes committed against women takes root. In all areas of law, stereotypes undermine the impartiality and integrity of the justice system, which in turn can lead to miscarriages of justice and expose women to secondary victimization, i.e., that resulting from the procedural rules themselves (§26).

General Recommendation No. 35 on gender-based violence against women, updating General Recommendation No. 19 of 1992, reaffirmed that in the face of the pervasiveness of gender-based violence against women, which appears to have "high levels of impunity" (§6), the general obligations of States include "by articles 2 (f) and 5 (a) of the Convention, the adoption and implementation of measures to eradicate the prejudices, stereotypes and practices that underlie gender-based violence against women" (§26). In particular,

> According to articles 2 (d) and (f) and 5 (a), all judicial bodies are required to refrain from engaging in any act or practice of discrimination or gender-based violence against women and to strictly apply all criminal law provisions punishing such violence, ensuring that all legal procedures in cases involving allegations of gender-based violence against women are impartial, fair and unaffected by gender stereotypes or the discriminatory interpretation of legal provisions, including international law. The application of preconceived and stereotypical notions of what constitutes gender-based violence against women, what women's responses to such violence should be and the standard of proof required to substantiate its occurrence can affect women's rights to equality before the law, a fair trial and effective remedy, as established in articles 2 and 15 of the Convention (§26 lit. c).

3 From Negative Obligations of States to Positive Obligations: The Transformative Approach of the CEDAW Committee

International human rights law establishes two orders of obligations for States: the main one is negative, to abstain States from directly violating human rights through its agents and apparatus. The negative obligation is complemented by the positive obligation to take concrete action and adopt specific legislative, political, and cultural measures aimed at non-State actors who violate the human rights of individuals.[20]

[20] Benninger-Bude (2009), p. 11.

All these obligations form the core of the due diligence with which States must operate in the area of fundamental rights, which is deepened by the prevention of violence against women and protection measures both in the context of the United Nations, by the CEDAW Committee and the Special Rapporteur on violence against women, its causes and consequences,[21] and in the context of the Council of Europe, in particular by the European Court of Human Rights, in a constant circularity between the various bodies, thus consolidating due diligence as a principle of customary international law, which then found codification in Article 5 of the Council of Europe Convention on Preventing and Combating Violence against Women and Domestic Violence (henceforth the Istanbul Convention).[22]

On the subject of stereotypes and sexist prejudices, the CEDAW Committee, in interpreting the Convention, has promoted the transformative approach inherent in the Convention's provisions, which codified the positive obligation to intervene to eradicate generalizations and simplifications based on sex- and gender-stereotyped models; naming and identifying sexual, sexist and gender stereotypes and prejudices; rejecting sexist generalizations as parameters for interpreting the law with a commitment to articulate reasons that take into account women's experiences and represent them in a dignified and law-based manner.[23]

In its 2010 view in the case of Karen Tayag Vertido versus Philippines,[24] the CEDAW Committee addressed for the first time in an individual communication the sexist stereotypes that vitiated the judicial finding made in the criminal trial of the rape reported by the author against her hierarchical superior in the work context. The accused was acquitted by the national judicial authority based on arguments that ratified generalizations of the expected behavior of the 'real' victim and a rapist inferred from the judicial practice, putting them as the basis, as expressly indicated by the judge of the case on the merits, of 'guiding principles' underlying the cognition of the facts in the case at hand, consequently read in the light of behavioral patterns coinciding precisely with some of the most widespread rape myths documented in feminist literature. According to the home court, rape accusations were a widespread mode of retaliation by women against men who rejected them after sexual intercourse; the applicant was not credible because she did not take advantage of the available escape routes during the assault; the man was particularly older than the applicant, and a sexual assault with the reported dynamics could not be considered likely.

Karen Tayag Vertido complained to the CEDAW Committee that she had suffered discrimination relevant to Article 1 of the Convention about General Recommendation No. 19 due to the violation of her positive obligations under Articles 2 (c), (d), (f), 5 (a) of the Convention.

Simone Cusack and Alexandra Timmer, in commenting on the view rendered by the CEDAW Committee in the Vertido case, highlighted as a distinctive feature of the communication the rigorous naming of sexual stereotypes, enumerating the rape

---

[21] Ertürk (2006).

[22] Aziz and Moussa (2016).

[23] Cusack and Pusey (2013), pp. 54–92.

[24] CEDAW Committee, *Karen Tayag Vertido c. Filippine,* CEDAW/C/46/D/18/2008.

myths that influenced the logical-legal process of the judicial decision, elaborating on the meaning and importance of each ascription as well as the harm produced by the sexual stereotypes used.

This allowed the CEDAW Committee to understand the nature, forms, causes, and effects of the stereotypes that influenced the domestic judicial authority and to identify concrete measures to remedy the harm caused.

As pointed out by Cusack and Timmer, the CEDAW Committee must undoubtedly be credited with placing the in-depth analysis of the grievances, specifically the reported stereotypes and their impact on the author's access to justice, at the heart of the decision. Still, despite the in-depth contextual analysis offered in the communication, the Committee missed the opportunity to delve into the systemic impact of sexism on law enforcement and to make explicit the content of the State's general positive obligation. Indeed, the decision contains only a generic call to "ensure that all legal procedures in cases of rape and other sexual offenses are impartial and fair and not biased by prejudice or stereotypical notions of gender" (§8.9 lett. b).

These obligations, however, as Cusack and Timmer note, could have been deepened in their nature and scope under Articles 2 (f) and 5 (a) CEDAW had the Committee examined the broader context in which sexual and sexist stereotypes operate in the Philippine justice system and how the same have been perpetuated through the rape cases (and not just the Vertido case).

The scholars advocated, therefore, that the CEDAW Committee take the next step by deepening the scope and content of obligations by indicating specific and consistent measures and initiatives to prevent sexual, sexist, and gender stereotypes from distorting law enforcement and having discriminatory effects against women.

4 The Case of A. F. v. Italy

In the wake of Cusack and Timmer's indications, the CEDAW Committee seems to place itself in the view adopted against Italy on 18 July 2022 about the communication introduced by the writer together with Teresa Manente as lawyers of the Differenza Donna association,[25] on behalf of a woman identified in the decision with the initials A. F., who reported for rape an officer of the Carabinieri.

[25] Differenza Donna is a non-governmental organisation and social promotion association that has been active since 1989 on a national and international level in the prevention of all forms of gender-based violence against women. It currently manages the national anti-violence number 1522 (www.differenzadonna.it).

4.1 The Facts

On 2 December 2008, A. F. was assaulted by her ex-husband and requested the intervention of the police, who found her at home with injuries to her hands. The two officers of the Carabinieri invited the woman to go to the hospital to be treated and to lodge a formal complaint against her ex-husband for domestic violence. One of the intervening officers, identified in the act with the initials C.C., was exceptionally attentive and repeatedly telephoned her under the pretext of asking for an update and referring her to a colleague given the complaint to be filed. The telephone calls continued until late in the evening, although A.F. did not answer at some point. On 3 December 2008, at noon, the carabiniere contacted the woman again, asking her to meet him at his home to share some information he had obtained concerning the proceedings against her ex-husband. The woman, trusting him, accepted the meeting the same day at his home, where he was on sick leave to recover from the previous day's assault. Once he arrived at the woman's home, she immediately realized that C.C. had no information to share and had used the circumstance as a pretext to see her again. The man started talking about his private life, forced the woman into continuous physical contact, and then hid in the kitchen when the doctor arrived for a check-up.

Despite her discomfort at the inappropriate behavior of the carabiniere, A.F. did not ask the doctor for help, relying on the fact that the carabiniere, due to his role, could not be dangerous for her. As soon as the doctor left, C.C. forcibly grabbed F. and raped her twice, then left the house, making sure neighbors did not see him. Once outside the home, A.F., although shocked, collected the sheets, pillowcases, and handkerchiefs used by C.C. and put them in a plastic bag. At the suggestion of a friend overheard on the phone, she tried to lure C.C. into her flat to have him arrested at the scene of the crime, but the carabiniere replied by ordering her not to disturb him at work, so A. F. ceased from all her intentions to entrap him, breaking off all contacts for fear of retaliation against her and her daughters, with whom she cohabited, as known to the military officer.

On 4 December 2008, A. F. confided the sexual assault she had suffered to a friend who accompanied her to a gynecological examination at the emergency of the local hospital, and injuries consistent with non-consensual sexual intercourse were documented. Given the amount of blood she had lost and her psychological condition, A. F. was admitted to the hospital. On 5 December 2008, the woman asked her lawyer for advice to consider filing a complaint against the officer for the rape she had suffered.

The carabiniere insistently telephoned the woman for about a month using an unknown telephone number until he asked her to meet him in person. Although frightened, A.F. agreed to meet him in a bar on 4 January 2009 to understand his intentions. During the meeting, C.C. intimidated the woman to make her desist from any legal action against him, boasting high-ranking, influential connections and retaliation in case of a complaint. After the meeting, C.C. continued to harass F., who, frightened by the police officer's behavior, decided to report him for rape and harassment.

At the outcome of the criminal trial resulting from the complaint lodged by Mrs. A.F., the Tribunal of Cagliari sentenced the soldier to six years imprisonment for sexual violence and to pay compensation for the damage caused. At the same time, the offense of harassment was statute-barred. The motivation highlights the inconsistency and lack of credibility of the defendant's defense, who, in the face of statements made by the victim of the crime that was considered credible and confirmed by further evidence acquired during the trial, had defended himself against the charges by first claiming that the victim was a 'crazy' woman who acted to take revenge on him who 'had left her.' He then claimed that the criminal trial was a plot against him hatched by his colleagues, an argument he then revised again by accusing A.F. of retaliatory intent because he did not reciprocate the woman's interest in him. The defendant claimed that the woman had been paid by one of his colleagues to slander him.

At the end of the hearing, the Court of Cagliari not only failed to find the slightest probative support for the defense's argument but ascertained that the defendant had taken advantage of the woman's vulnerable situation and had abused his position as a carabiniere to sexually assault the victim, whose statements were fully reliable.

C.C. appealed against the conviction, arguing that: (a) the biological analysis had shown amino acids compatible with the use of a condom, which the complainant had never mentioned; (b) the author's credibility was undermined by the documentary evidence (c) the hospital report of 4 December 2008 could not unequivocally prove sexual assault, (d) the author had invented the rape story to protect her reputation (e) the author's behavior was not consistent with that of a raped woman (f) the defendant was a respected police officer with a bright future and therefore would not have risked his career in this way.

On 16 November 2015, the Court of Appeal of Cagliari upheld the defendant's grounds of appeal, acquitting him of all charges. According to the panel of judges, A.F. had enjoyed 'an afternoon of levity or even joy' with him but then felt offended by C.C.'s lack of interest in continuing the relationship. The woman would then contact her friend by telephone to corroborate a narrative that would "protect her reputation and pride and avenge C.C.'s rejection" (§2.15).

The woman's credibility was then undermined by the fact that the accused put on a condom, never mentioned before and this resulted to be a circumstance not compatible with a sexual assault, and by the telephone exchanges with two people just after the rape, which gave the impression of 'banal friendship at a time when she should have been burdened with upset.'

The Cagliari Court of Appeal also found it not credible that the carabiniere had asked the woman to watch the street, since only the woman, according to the panel, would have had a concrete interest in preventing her neighbors, including her relatives, from seeing the man leave her house. It was held to be unreasonable that the woman had not asked the doctor for help during the fiscal examination carried out. At the same time, C.C. was present, concluding that she must have been 'pleased with the defendant's presence.' The Court held that, overall, the author's lucid choices and behavior could not be considered consistent with the fact that she had been raped.

According to the Court of Appeal, the woman, offended by C.C.'s lack of interest after consensual sexual intercourse, had felt cheated and exploited 'as a disposable object of pleasure' and had complained to protect her reputation and obtain priority access to health services, to take revenge on the defendant who she believed had 'abused her surrender to erotic passion at a time in her life when she was troubled.' The Court also held that the medical findings could be interpreted as evidence of the defendant's 'exuberance' and his 'capacity for seduction' and that the author's accusations were motivated by an artfully created drama to compensate for the fact that she had been 'seduced by the defendant and then abandoned.'

A. F. appealed against the judgment before the Court of Cassation, claiming a violation of criminal law and procedural law for manifest illogicality of the motivation and distortion of evidence.

On 19 May 2017, the Supreme Court declared A.F.'s recourse inadmissible, ignoring the legitimacy complaints made against the acquittal verdict and stating generically that the woman had invoked a new judgment on the merits, which was not allowed by law.

4.2 The Complaints

A.F. complained to the CEDAW Committee that she had been the victim of discrimination under Article 1 CEDAW since the reasons supporting the acquittal of the defendant were based solely on sexist stereotypes, which also included an expected behavioral pattern befitting "real" rape victims.

Consequently, A.F. complains that the principle of equality before the law has been violated against her.

The communication expressly named the stereotypes that guided the reasoning of the decision, as indicated by the scholarship,[26] taking as a model the communication Vertido v. Philippines: (a) rape has standardized dynamics and can be ruled out when a condom is used; (b) a real rape victim would not have interacted with third persons through phone calls or; (c) a woman must anticipate that insistent advances could be preliminary to rape; (d) while a rape victim must try to resist and escape by all possible means, she must be suspected of fabricating rape charges if she has the presence of mind to gather evidence after the assault; (e) a single and 'not very young' woman is inherently concerned that a casual sexual relationship will compromise her reputation with a younger man.

These arguments compromised access to justice and the protection of fundamental rights, not only denying justice to the woman and causing a miscarriage of justice but also exposing the woman to secondary and ongoing victimization.

Furthermore, the right to an effective remedy, guaranteed by Article 2 (b) and (c) of the Convention, has been violated because Italy has not adopted legislative and other measures prohibiting all discrimination against women, protecting women's rights on an equal basis with men and ensuring, through competent national courts

[26] Cook and Cusack (2011).

and other public institutions, the adequate protection of women against all acts of discrimination.

It has also complained that Article 2 (d) of the Convention has been violated, as gender stereotypes have compromised the impartiality of the judges of the Cagliari Court of Appeal, which allowed sexist stereotypes to influence their understanding of the facts.

Italy, therefore, failed to ensure that its authorities and public institutions refrained from carrying out any act or practice of sexist discrimination and caused damage due to the excessive duration of the trial, resulting in the statute of limitations for the crime of harassment, and judicial practices, including stereotypical motivations, that exposed women to secondary victimization.

It was pointed out that, on the whole, Italy violated the multiple levels of due diligence obligations on sexual and gender-based violence against women, which requires not only respectful and dignified trial treatment but also adequate criminal legislation to ensure the punishment of violence against women: the incriminatory case provided by Article 609 *bis* of the Italian Criminal Code, which defines sexual violence as coercion to perform or be subjected to sexual acts using violence or threats, use of force and abuse of authority, implies, from the point of view of material conduct, extensive elements that are necessarily subject to an open interpretation in the absence of a homogeneous and stable formation of the judicial authority.

4.3 The View of the CEDAW Committee

The CEDAW Committee was therefore called upon to determine whether the judicial bodies of the State party (Italy), in particular the Court of Appeal of Cagliari and the Court of Cassation, relied on myths and gender stereotypes about rape, on rape victims and women in general, and whether this has resulted in discriminatory treatment of the author of the communication as well as a distorted reading of the evidence acquired in the criminal trial, with a consequent violation of the author's rights and a failure by the State party to fulfill its obligations under Articles 2 (b), (c) and (f) and 5 (a) of the Convention.

The Committee emphasizes in the preamble that its decision does not replace the national authorities in the assessment of the facts, nor does it decide, of course, on the criminal liability of the person accused of the offense, and takes as its starting point the verification of the merits of the complaint of lack of adequate domestic remedy, which is found, in the present case, in the excessive duration of the criminal trial that led to the statute of limitations for the offense of harassment (from 2009 to 2014 for the first instance only).

The Committee then dwells on the reasoning behind the Court of Appeal's decision to annul the rape conviction, pointing out that in the second instance, judges examined the accusatory evidence looking for alternative justifications not anchored in the evidence acquired but based on 'standard' behavior that a 'real' rape victim would have had to adopt.

Even the medical evidence attesting to the presence of bruises on the inside of the woman's knees and further injuries were ignored by the Court of Appeal, which found insufficient the woman's statements on the violent manner in which she had been raped, preferring, therefore, the defendant's explanation that the marks on the woman's body depended on 'exuberance in a consensual encounter,' also because in a non-consensual situation, it would not have been possible to achieve, in the view of the lower court judges, the deeper penetration that these injuries confirm. Moreover, according to the Court, the fact that the woman had not mentioned that she was going to the emergency room in her telephone messages also confirmed that she was not in distress.

The Court further argued that a single and not very young woman' would generally be inherently concerned about her reputation, which a casual sexual relationship could compromise with a younger man, with whom she should be flattered, and that it is to be expected that such a woman would become vindictive in the event of rejection.

The Court deduced that while the author had enjoyed "an afternoon of levity or even joy," she had then felt cheated by the fact that C.C. had exploited her as a "disposable object of pleasure," abusing "her surrender to erotic passion at a stage of life when she was troubled" (§7.11).

The Court also held that a woman could invent the rape allegations to retaliate or to gain priority access to health services and found this to be the most likely narrative in this case.

The Supreme Court held that these arguments were exempt from the legitimacy challenges complained of in the appeal.

The Committee notes that the State party's defense before the CEDAW Committee echoes the Supreme Court's approval of the reasoning of the Court of Appeal of Cagliari.

The first macroscopic disparity of treatment noted by the CEDAW Committee concerns the evaluation of evidence acquired at the request of the prosecution and the offended person as opposed to that introduced by the accused: the victim's statements were repeatedly stigmatized in terms of a "radical" and "absurd" account, in which she had "lied," pointing out a "profound contradiction" of the victim in her reconstruction of the facts, the defendant, on the contrary, according to the Court of Appeal "cannot be blamed for his divergent explanations, as he had become aware of the charges against him and therefore had a pressing need to defend himself against criminal and disciplinary proceedings." The Committee also notes that even the diagnosis of post-traumatic stress disorder presented by a psychologist heard as a witness was read simplistically and as 'natural consequences of the drama in the life of a woman who was already exhausted by a turbulent marital separation' and who had 'succumbed, in a moment of weakness, to the seduction of the carabiniere.'

The reasons that led to the acquittal of the defendant, according to the CEDAW Committee, were the outcome of logical-legal reasoning vitiated by deeply ingrained gender stereotypes that led to the attribution of greater probative weight to the defendant's account, which was preferred, without any critical examination of the defense's arguments, without any re-examination or revision of the evidence to allow the witnesses to explain any perceived inconsistencies, thus fueling a differential credibility regime that disregards procedural rules but is based on generalizations and preconceptions.

Indeed, the Committee considers that the reasoning underlying the acquittal of the accused from rape charges does not follow a logical line of reasoning when measured against any objective criteria and does not meet the procedural obligations of the State party. It further notes that the Court of Cassation limited itself to a superficial assessment that all the evidence was cited logically without considering flaws in the analysis and weighing of the evidence.

The Committee concludes that the treatment of A.F. first by the Court of Appeal, then aggravated at the Supreme Court, violated the principle of equality before the law between the woman victim of sexual and gender-based violence and the defendant and implies the lack of understanding of the gendered constructs of violence against women, of the concept of coercive control the implications and complexities of the abuse of authority, including the use and abuse of trust, the impact of exposure to consecutive trauma, the complex post-traumatic symptoms, including dissociation and memory loss, and the specific vulnerabilities and needs of victims of domestic violence.

In the present case, according to the CEDAW Committee, the acquittal sentence and its confirmation by the Court of Cassation were based on "distorted perceptions, beliefs, and preconceived myths rather than on relevant facts, which led the Regional Court and the Court of Cassation to misinterpret or misapply the laws, thus undermining the impartiality and integrity of the judicial system and producing a miscarriage of justice and the re-victimization of the perpetrator" (§7.18).

Italy's reported efforts in defense concerning legislative and policy initiatives on gender equality and the prevention of violence are thwarted, in the Committee's view, by the failure to acknowledge the existence of these harmful sexist stereotypes and the absence of decisive action to remedy the prejudices.

The laws introduced in Italy, in fact, according to the CEDAW Committee, are not enough and do not allow, in the absence of systemic action, to be relied upon "to change the reality for women, who are disproportionately victims of violence and abuse, which can leave scars (sometimes invisible) for life and intergenerationally" (§7.18).

In closing, in recognizing the violations complained of, the CEDAW Committee agrees with the grievance that stereotypes are fueled by the very wording of the criminal code of the crime of sexual violence, where the criminal offense does not identify consent as the central and determining element. Otherwise, the perpetrator's life, morals, communications, injuries, marital and relationship status, age, and numerous other factors were repeatedly scrutinized to the point where she faced a level of scrutiny that was not applied to C.C., leaving the proceedings vulnerable to conflicting and harmful interpretations based on cultural norms and preconceptions that denied her equal access to justice and not only failed to protect her but repeatedly subjected her to discrimination and traumatization (§7.19).

4.4 Remedies and Recommendations

The Committee recalls that in most jurisdictions women still face many difficulties in accessing justice due to direct and indirect discrimination, as defined in paragraph 16 of General Recommendation No. 28 on the core obligations of States parties under article 2 of the Convention.[27]

This inequality manifests not only in the content and discriminatory impact of laws, regulations, procedures, customs, and practices but also in the lack of capacity of judicial and quasi-judicial institutions to recognize the harmfulness of certain practices and adequately address violations of women's human rights.

Article 15 CEDAW places an obligation on States parties to ensure women's substantive equality with men in all areas of the law, and this implies recognizing and overcoming sexual, sexist, and gender stereotypes that, in the CEDAW Committee's reading, distort understanding of the facts and lead to decisions based on beliefs and myths rather than relevant facts and evidence and affect the assessment of the credibility of women's statements:

> This has far-reaching consequences, for example, in criminal law, where it results in perpetrators not being held legally accountable for violations of women 's rights, thereby upholding a culture of impunity. In all areas of law, stereotyping compromises the impartiality and integrity of the justice system, which can, in turn, lead to miscarriages of justice, including the revictimization of complainants. Judges, magistrates and adjudicators are not the only actors in the justice system who apply, reinforce and perpetuate stereotypes. Prosecutors, law enforcement officials and other actors often allow stereotypes to influence investigations and trials, especially in cases of gender-based violence, with stereotypes undermining the claims of the victim/survivor and simultaneously supporting the defence advanced by the alleged perpetrator. Stereotyping can, therefore, permeate both the investigation and trial phases and shape the final judgment (§7.5).[28]

The Committee recalls that, under Article 2 (a) of the Convention, States Parties are obliged to ensure the practical realization of the principle of equality between men and women and that, under Articles 2 (f) and 5, States Parties are obliged to take all appropriate measures to modify or abolish not only existing laws and regulations but also customs and practices that constitute discrimination against women.

According to Articles 2 (d) (f) and 5 (a), all judicial bodies are obliged to refrain from engaging in any act or practice of discrimination or gender-based violence against women and to strictly enforce all provisions of criminal law that punish such violence, ensuring that all legal proceedings in cases involving allegations of gender-based violence against women are impartial, fair and not influenced by

[27] CEDAW Committee, *General recommendation No. 28 on the core obligations of States parties under article 2 of the Convention on the Elimination of All Forms of Discrimination against Women*, 2010.

[28] CEDAW Committee, *General recommendation No. 33 on women's access to justice*, §§ 22, 26 e 27.

gender stereotyping or discriminatory interpretation of legal provisions, including international law (§7.4).[29]

The application of preconceived and stereotypical notions about what constitutes gender-based violence against women, what women's responses to such violence should be, and the standard of proof required to prove its existence can affect women's rights to equality before the law, a fair trial, and an effective remedy, as set out in Articles 2 and 15 of the Convention.

Recalling that under Article 5 (a) of the Convention, States parties must expose and remove the underlying social and cultural barriers, including gender stereotypes, that prevent women from exercising and claiming their rights and hinder their access to effective remedies, the Committee recommends that Italy repair the moral and social harm caused to A. F. because of the excessive duration of the trial and for being subjected to re-victimization due to the gender-based stereotypes and myths invoked in the judgment of the Court of Appeal of Cagliari, as well as for the acceptance of such stereotypes by the Court of Cassation.

In general, and this is the main novelty of the Committee's decision concerning the Vertido case, Italy is obliged to adopt specific and compelling measures as reparations for the violations ascertained to ensure that legal proceedings concerning sexual offenses are carried out without unjustified delays and that all legal proceedings relating to sexual crimes are impartial, fair, and not influenced by gender bias or stereotypes.

These aims are to be pursued, as the Committee suggests, by adopting a wide range of remedial measures, which the Committee identifies in detail: from general training on CEDAW, Optional Protocol, and the Committee's General Recommendations No. 19, 35, and 33, for judges, lawyers and law enforcement personnel, to specific training programs for judges, lawyers, law enforcement officials, medical personnel and all other relevant stakeholders to explain the legal, cultural and social dimensions of violence against women and gender discrimination.

The Committee also suggests developing strategies to eliminate gender stereotypes in cases of gender-based violence. These strategies include knowledge of the harms produced through evidence-based research and identification of best practices; legal reforms and structural policies; monitoring and analysis of case law to account for trends in judicial reasoning; and mechanisms for reporting gender stereotyping cases in the judiciary.

The CEDAW Committee also recommended the adoption of concrete legislative measures to ensure that the burden of proof is not overly burdensome or vague, leading to an excessively broad or far-reaching interpretation, including the amendment of sexual offenses to redesign the criminal offenses by emphasizing consent as the material element to be ascertained, overcoming the regulatory structure that still requires to prove penetration, use of force or violence, unless these elements constitute other offenses or aggravating circumstances.

[29] View Vertido v. Filippine (CEDAW/C/46/D/18/2008), par 8.9 (b); R.P.B. v. Filippine (CEDAW/C/57/D/34/2011), par 8.3; General Recommendation No. 33, parr. 18 (e), 26 e 29.

By article 7 (4) of the Optional Protocol, the State Party shall give due consideration to the views of the Committee, together with its recommendations, and submit to the Committee, within six months, a written response that includes information on any action taken considering those views and recommendations. The State party is also requested to publish the opinions and recommendations of the Committee and to have them translated into Italian and distributed widely to reach all relevant sectors of society.

5 Concluding Remarks

The view issued by the CEDAW Committee in the case of A.F. versus Italy with its recommendations indicates measures to remedy the gaps and problematic aspects of the cases introduced by Law no. 66/1996 and their procedural application, "closing the circle" of a social and legal policy issue that began with the proposal of the famous initiative law against sexual violence, promoted by a committee set up at the International Feminist Conference on Sexual Violence against Women held in March 1978 at the Governo Vecchio by Mld, Udi, Roman Feminist Movement of Via Pompeo Magno, effe, Noi Donne, Quotidiano donna, and Radio Lilith.

More than a year has passed since the decision was published, and only one of the recommendations was fulfilled: the decision was published and translated on the Ministry of Foreign Affairs page at the initiative of the Interministerial Committee for Human Rights (CIDU).

The specific reparation measures indicated in favor of the author of the communication, Ms. A.F., recognized as a victim of moral and social, as well as financial, damage, have not yet been adopted, nor have the general measures been implemented, even though they were in line with the specific censures repeatedly made by the CEDAW Committee, the European Court of Human Rights and the Council of Europe's Group of Experts on Violence against Women (GREVIO), which monitors the implementation of the Istanbul Convention.

The stratification of sexist stereotypes and prejudices found in case law in disputes concerning women, both in criminal cases, regardless of the position of victim or defendant, and in civil cases in judgments concerning parental responsibility and child custody, appears unscathed by the censure of supranational bodies and courts, and no concrete initiative has been taken in this regard by Italy.[30]

This is not surprising, especially regarding implementing the CEDAW in the Italian legal system, which has been constantly refractory to the obligations arising from its ratification over the years.[31] This has little impact on domestic legislation, which has been amended mostly because of EU law obligations and case law. As far

[30] Alsalem (2023).

[31] Donà (2018), pp. 221–241.

as the higher courts are concerned, the CEDAW is almost completely ignored as a legal reference for decisions.[32]

Judicial decisions reinforce the dynamic of sexist and gender-based violence against women in a spiral that, from being a descriptive model of violence in intimate relationships, becomes a valuable image for also understanding the pervasive mechanisms of institutional violence, i.e., that attributable to subjects attributable to the State, including the judiciary.[33]

The issue has returned to the center of public discourse following the acquittal sentence handed down by the Tribunal of Rome on 7 July 2023 against a school employee accused of sexual violence because 'inside the school premises, with a sudden and unpredictable move, he slipped his hands inside the trousers and briefs of the pupil [...] groping her vagina and bottom. With the aggravating circumstance of the act committed against a minor. With the aggravating circumstance of the act being committed inside a school'.[34]

The offended person, a minor, stated that while she was on the stairs in the school, 'she felt hands entering her trousers from behind, under her panties, which first touched her buttocks and then grabbed her by the panties and pulled her up about two centimeters; the whole thing lasted about five/ten seconds.'

According to the Tribunal, the girl was to be considered fully reliable because her statements were 'detailed, free of contradictions, logical, coherent, as well as devoid of any slanderous intent towards the defendant, with whom the girl also had a cordial relationship and in respect of whom she had no reason to harbor resentment or rancor.'

The man tried to make the young woman desist from actions against him, 'you ruin me,' he shouted, banging his head on the bar counter. Following the man's behavior, the girl found it difficult to go to school for fear of meeting her aggressor again; however, with the support of her parents, teachers, and schoolmates, the facts were brought to the attention of the judicial authorities who subjected the man to the precautionary measure of suspension from public service. A social shift certainly took place as the social scandal shifted from the victim of the sexual assault to the conduct invading the sexual freedom of others and was channeled in the direction of collective support of access to justice.

During the criminal trial held before Section V of the Tribunal of Rome, evidence of the defendant's material conduct emerged, mainly based on the girl's statement, which was deemed reliable: even the usual judicial 'hunt' for the 'humoral' motive (resentment, retaliation, revenge, etc.) of the false accusations that women/girls make against the men around them failed.

---

[32] The Italian Constitutional Court has mentioned the CEDAW only in 5 decisions: sentence No. 422/1995; No. 49/2003, No. 4/2010; No. 286/2016; and ordinance No. 306/2011.

[33] Vaccaro (2021).

[34] Tribunal of Rome, sez. V, 6 July 2023, No. 10917, available at https://www.giurisprudenzapenale.com/2023/07/12/toccamento-dei-glutei-di-una-studentessa-da-parte-di-un-operatore-scolastico-la-sentenza-di-assoluzione-del-tribunale-di-roma/.

However, in the Tribunal's view, the defendant's defense of the playful act, 'certainly inappropriate in the context in which it was carried out due to the nature of the place and the relationship between pupil and auxiliary,' prevailed. The account is taken on the grounds of the acquittal sentence of the jurisprudence of legitimacy, according to which 'on the subject of sexual violence, the gesture made loci causa or to mock qualified as a sexual act punishable under Article 609 bis of the Criminal Code when, due to the intrinsic characteristics of the action, it represents a violent intrusion into the sexual sphere of the victim', however, the girl's trustworthiness is not sufficient to dispel the doubt as to the voluntary nature of the violation of the girl's sexual freedom, considering precisely the nature of the grazing of the buttocks, for an undoubtedly minimal time, given that the entire action is concentrated in a handful of seconds, without any delay in touching. Moreover, it appears likely that the grazing of the buttocks was caused by a clumsy maneuver of the defendant, who, because of the dynamics of the action, carried out. At the same time, the subjects were in motion and at a distance from each other. They could have accidentally and fortuitously activated a further movement that did not align with the initial intent.

And so, according to the Tribunal, the fact does not constitute a crime because there is doubt as to the subjective element, read in terms of voluntariness and awareness of the action and as the pursuit, through the action, of a sexual lust: the defendant was joking, he did not want to attack sexual freedom, a legal good of which, according to the Tribunal of Rome, any violation is measured in the light of the lack or subsistence of the sexual intent of the accused, ignoring the subject whose sexual freedom is violated.

Here, however, the problem of the equality of women before the law emerges, as it was already noted by the CEDAW Committee in the case A. F. v. Italy, and of the overall tightness of the principles of the rule of law: freedom in judging is a safeguard of the independence of the judiciary, but if it is exercised in the strict furrow traced by the law (article 101 Italian Constitution), otherwise it is arbitrariness and institutional violence that the legislation about gender-based violence of the last twenty years has not undermined: if it is true that today women take the public floor, even attempting to access justice, they not infrequently find themselves put 'face to the wall,' both symbolically and materially, recalling a 'protection' measure suggested some time ago by a judge, again of the Tribunal of Rome, to a woman victim of severe abuse and called to testify in court.

In addition to secondary victimization, which is part of a framework of violation of rules of primary rank, one cannot also ignore the epistemological violence produced by such reasoned judgments: the reality of the facts, although ascertained directly from a woman's word' that has come, after centuries, to have the value of proof, is bent and distorted in the light of a sexist perspective of application of criminal law and vision of the world and social relations.[35]

This epistemic injustice can take the form, according to scholar Miranda Fricker,[36] of testimonial injustice, which indicates an (unjustified) prejudice on the credibility

---

[35] Graziosi (1993).

[36] Fricker (2007).

of a person's testimony based on stereotypes and biases, and hermeneutic injustice, which refers to injustice in the accessibility and adequacy of collective resources for the creation of meaning, which ignores individual experiences depriving subjects of the very possibility of knowing and producing knowledge.[37]

The crime of sexual violence, even in its less severe form that punishes groping, as well as any form of gender-based violence against women, is still constructed by the judicial authority by disregarding the meaning given to it by the person who sees his sovereignty over his own body violated, favoring a defensive thesis that is detached from any evidentiary evidence, and based on the belief that the male subject and his perception of facts, relationships, and the world are universal parameters.

Well, in this context, the judgment of the Tribunal of Rome offers us the opportunity to subvert a sexist prejudice that has persecuted women for centuries, right up to the present day, constantly attacked in their credibility: we must take note of the fact that the words of law lie, not the women who seek justice, producing what has been called epistemic injustice, that is, that damage done to someone in particular in their capacity to know.

References

Abdul Aziz Z, Moussa J (2016) Due diligence framework state accountability framework for eliminating violence against women. Malaysia, International Human Rights Initiative, Inc. (IHRI)

Allen PG (1998) Father god and rape culture. In Hooks T (ed) Off the reservation: reflections on boundary-busting, border-crossing loose cannons. Beacon, Boston

Alsalem R (2023) Custody, violence against women and violence against children—report of the Special Rapporteur on violence against women and girls, its causes and consequences. https://www.ohchr.org/en/documents/thematic-reports/ahrc5336-custody-violence-against-women-and-violence-against-children

Benninger-Bude C (2009) Due diligence and its application to protect women from violence. Nijhoff, Leiden, Brill

Bourke J (2008) Rape: a history from 1860 to the present. Virago, London

Brownmiller S (1975) Against our will: men, women and rape. Simon & Schuster, New York

Buchwald E, Fletcher PR, Roth M (eds) (2005) Transforming a rape culture. Milkweed Editions, Minneapolis

Burt MR (1980) Cultural myths and supports for rape. J Pers Soc Psychol 38:217–230

Calhoun LG, Selby JW, Warring LJ (1976) Social perception of the victims' causal role in rape: an exploratory examination of four factors. Human Relat 29:517–526

Charlesworth H (1999) Feminist methods in international law. American J Int Law 93(2):380

Cigarini L (2022) La politica del desiderio e altri scritti. Napoli-Salerno, Orthotes

Connell R (2002) Gender. Polity Press, Cambridge

Connors J (2012) Article 28. In: edited by Freeman M, Chinkin C, Rudolf B, (eds) The UN convention on the elimination of all forms of discrimination against women: a commentary. Oxford University Press, Oxford

Cook RJ, Cusack S (2011) Gender stereotyping: transnational legal perspectives. University of Pennsylvania Press, Philadelphia

[37] Pemberton and Mulder (2023).

Cusack S, Pusey L (2013) CEDAW and the rights to non-discrimination and equality. Melbourne Journal of International Law 14(1):54–92
Donà A (2018) How do international norms matter? the impact of the convention on the elimination of all forms of discrimination against women in Italy. Italian Political Sci Rev/Rivista Italiana di Scienza Politica 48(2):221–241
Ertürk Y (2006) The due diligence standard as a tool for the elimination of violence against women: report of the Special Rapporteur on Violence against Women, Its Causes and Consequences. UN Commission on Human Rights. Special Rapporteur on Violence against Women
Feci S, Schettini L (eds) (2017) La violenza contro le donne nella storia. Contesti, linguaggi, politiche del diritto (secoli XV–XXI). Collana "Storia delle donne e di genere"
Filippini N (2022) Mai più sole contro la violenza sessuale. Una pagina storica del femminismo degli anni Settanta. Roma, Viella
Freeman MA, Chinkin C, Rudolf B (eds) (2012) The UN convention on the elimination of all forms of discrimination against women: a commentary. Oxford University Press, Oxford
Fricker M (2007) Epistemic injustice: power and the ethics of knowing. Oxford University Press, Oxford
Graziosi M (1993) Infirmitas sexus. La donna nell'immaginario penalistico. Democrazia e diritto 33(2):99–143
Herman DF (1984) The rape culture. In Freeman J (Ed) Women: a feminist perspective. Mayfield, Mountain View
Hockett JM, Smith SJ, Klausing CD, Saucier DA (2016) Rape myth consistency and gender differences in perceiving rape victims: a meta-analysis. Viol Against Women 22(2):139–167
Lonsway KA, Fitzgerald LF (1994) Rape myths: in review. Psychol Women Q 18:133–164
MacKinnon C (1983) Feminism, Marxism, method and the state: toward a feminist jurisprudence. Signs 8:96–116
Olsen F (1993) International law: feminist critiques of the public/private distinction. Stud Transnat Legal Pol 25:157
Pateman C (1988) The sexual contract. Stanford University Press, Redwood City
Pemberton A, Mulder E, 2023 Bringing injustice back in: Secondary victimization as epistemic injustice. Criminol Criminal Just
Pitch T (1998) Un diritto per due. La costruzione giuridica di genere, sesso e sessualità. Milano, Il Saggiatore
Sanday PR (2003) Rape-free versus rape-prone: How culture makes a difference. In: Travis CB, (ed) Evolution, gender, and rape, pp 337–361. Boston Review
Simone A, Boiano I, Condello A (eds) (2019) Femminismo giuridico. Theories and Problems. Mondadori Universities, Milan
Simonson K, Subich LM (1999) Rape perceptions as a function of gender-role traditionality and victim-perpetrator association. Sex Roles 40:617–634
Smart C (1989) Feminism and the power of law. Routledge, New York and London
Smart C (1992) The woman of the legal discourse. Soc Leg Stud 1:29–44
Taruffo M (2009) La semplice verità. Il giudice e la costruzione dei fatti. Bari, Laterza
Vaccaro SE (2021) Estudio sobre el análisis de datos de casos de violencia vicaria extrema violencia vicaria: un golpe irreversible contra las madres. Ogíjares – Granada Gráficas Alhambra
Virgilio M (1997) Violenza sessuale e norma. Legislazioni penali a confronto. Quaderni di critica del diritto 5:139

Ilaria Boiano is a feminist lawyer and jurist, specializing in women's rights, gender-based violence, and discrimination. She has extensive experience in national and international human rights litigation focused on women's rights and has represented significant cases before bodies such as the European Court of Human Rights and the CEDAW Committee. Together with attorney Teresa Manente, she coordinates the legal office at Differenza Donna, advocating for victims of violence and promoting policies to combat gender-based violence. An author and speaker at seminars and conferences, her current research explores the influence of gender stereotypes in the legal and social systems and legal policy practices to overcome their discriminatory impact on women.

The Intersectionality Between Cultural Factors and Post-partum Psychosis: A Critical Exploration from the Indian Legal Scenario

Reshma Suresh

Abstract Post-Partum depression is a stage of non-psychotic depression that triggers sadness, anxiety and despair, found in women post child birth. Pregnancy and conditions related to it constitute a significant biological difference that is not based on social status or any power quotient. When women suffering from post-partum depression cause the homicide of their children, the mainstream media and society often view them as 'mothers who kill/murderous mothers'. A parallel is always drawn with the pre-set notions of the society which impose unrealistic responsibility standards on women irrespective of their physical, mental and socio- cultural standards after childbirth. The critical studies pertaining to various cultures have emphasized the notion that post-partum depression could be fully understood completely when the cultural factors are also considered along with the psychological, biomedical and social perspectives. Cultural beliefs and practices play an important role in transitions such as pregnancy and birth. Violence against women in sexual, emotional and physical forms serves as a trigger for Post-Partum Psychosis. The absence of a generic partial responsibility doctrine under the Indian Penal Code makes it difficult to give exceptions to women who commit crimes under situations triggered by social and cultural-violence. The courts in India have constantly failed to understand the pertinent connection between culture, violence, and the emotional state of women in cases that comes before them. The decisions of Indian courts in *Savita Manish Chaudhary* v. *State of Maharashtra* (2017) and *State of Maharashtra v. X* (2022) has sparked much controversy for its understanding of post-partum depression of woman offenders in question during the commission of the offence. The chapter seeks to explore the interplay between culture, violence and emotional state of women and how the courts in India have approached such instances over the years and the way forward.

Keywords Post-partum depression · Gender and cultural factors · Criminal responsibility · India

---

R. Suresh (✉)
VIT School of Law, Vellore Institute of Technology, Chennai, India
e-mail: reshma.suresh@vit.ac.in

A. Condello and A. Wagner (eds.), *Gender Stereotypes*, Gender, Justice and Legal Feminism 2, https://doi.org/10.1007/978-3-031-63905-0_16

1 Introduction

The ideas and perceptions of individuals are shaped by their lived experiences. The cultural environment deeply influences norms and behavioural patterns.[1] Cultural violence can be defined as any aspect of culture that is used to legitimise violence in its direct or structural form.[2] The use of violence and the legitimisation of the violence remains the core of the problem. Internalisation is the psychological mechanism behind cultural violence. How women are viewed in the society is also guided by these internalised perceptions. The cultural construct associated with gender and sexuality often make it difficult for women to come out of their assigned roles set by the society. Cultural violence results in violent gendering where women are often seen as second order beings required to follow the orders and instructions of men, who are considered as first order beings. Charlotte Bunch in their work describes that the culturally embedded practice and assumption of domination is present in almost all societies.[3] She makes the argument that violence against women is supported by cultural attitudes and it is a universal problem associated primarily with the societal perceptions of women and their assigned roles.

Like all societies, India is also deeply influenced by the patriarchal narratives surrounding gender, which often fails to view women outside their of gender specific roles, through an individualistic lens. Culture has often constructed their roles as 'mothers', 'daughters', 'wives' and 'sisters'. Any woman who tries to come out of these pre-set ideological roles are often seen as rebellious. Cultural forces play a significant role in forming societal perceptions as to what 'womanhood' and 'motherhood' means. A 'good mother' is constructed as someone who is selfless. The discourse requires that mothers only present themselves at their best, in a socially recognisable and acceptable manner. A 'good mother' is supposed to be happy all the time and if she remains sad or upset or confused, she is seen as a 'bad mother' not capable of fulfilling her duties. Motherhood in India is mostly seen as a 'duty' and not as a 'choice'.

Culture views a good mother as someone who is 'female, fertile and heterosexual', who remains monogamous in a committed marital relationship. The social construction of motherhood in India was deeply influenced by customs and practices where motherhood was given a sacred space and identity that becomes crucial to a woman's standing in the society. The glorification of the motherhood is evident in the surrounding discourse—from history to present. Mother in Sanskrit is etymologically referred as 'mātṛ' (माता), 'mātā' or 'ammā' or 'ambā', 'janani', which defines mother as the divine form or personified energy of the supreme force. Living mother is considered equivalent to god and motherhood is associated with the fulfilment of a woman. The vedas (sacred texts of Hinduism)—Devī Sūkta, Rātrī Sukta, and Ṛig Veda gives mother the most esteemed status.[4]

---

[1] See Tatar (2022), pp. 40–53.

[2] See Galtung (1990), pp. 291–305.

[3] See Bunch (1990), pp. 486–493.

[4] See Bhat (1987), pp. 471–489.

The celebrated view of motherhood is often associated with maternal love, nurturance, fertility and maternal instincts. Motherhood as an institution is critiqued by feminists for its overpowering patriarchal narrative that makes it difficult for women to have an enriching experience. Traditionally, motherhood in India is viewed within the institution of marriage, keeping outside its ambit adoptive mothers and queer couples. Assigned gender roles forces women to confirm to their social identity, overwhelming their personal identity which results in an alienation from their own mental and physical requirements so as to perform the 'idealised' woman role.[5]

Cultural factors have been found to positive and negatively impact the experiences of women. Culture remains a universal influential factor for posing risk of postpartum depression in women. Culturally women suffering from postpartum depression is not considered as 'sick' or as someone who needs 'medical assistance'. It is understood as a social experience and not as a physical or mental condition. Stigmatization of the condition forces women to deny their experiences or not seek help. Gendered socialization imbibes woman with the idea that birth of a child is the highest state of femininity and the focus is shifted from mother to the new born.[6]

If an offender with mental health compromise commits a crime, he/she can set up a plea of insanity and get total exculpation under section 84 of the Indian Penal Code (now reiterated in section 22 of Bharatiya Nyaya Sanhita, 2023).[7] The said section is the only defence which could be set up by a women with postpartum depression. However, the cultural perceptions makes it difficult for women to successfully defend the cases and get total exculpation under the code. This chapter carefully examines cases of Postpartum depression in India and analyse how cultural perceptions has shaped the judgment of courts.

2 Postpartum Depression, Gender and Cultural Factors

A close observation of the history of psychiatry reveals that women were more prone to affective disorders than men. The pervasive influence of sex roles has a significant impact on the mental health of women. Feminist theorists argue that women specific conditions (like Pre-menstrual stress syndrome and Postpartum Depression) are influenced by socio-cultural factors to a certain extent. It is argued that these socially constructed disorders leads to pathologizing emotions of women and their experience into the set categories of mental health disorders. The factors which lead to these conditions are rarely a subject of analysis and interpretation. Gove, in his work argues that the depressive symptoms exhibited by women are the only coping mechanism which were available to women to break free from their traditional roles in

[5] See Tanupriya and Pannikot (2022), pp. 1–13.

[6] See Bhattacharya (2021), p. 11.

[7] Section 84 of IPC: "Act of a person of unsound mind—Nothing is an offence which is done by a person who, at the time of doing it, by reason of unsoundness of mind, is incapable of knowing the nature of the act, or that he is doing what is either wrong or contrary to law."

the patriarchal society.[8] Taking cue from social constructionist theory, law, medicine and politics has shaped our views of women and their distress. However, the narratives surrounding post-partum depression takes a purely medical standpoint at times, which conveniently discards the socio-cultural factors at play.

Postpartum depression is a disorder that affects significant number of women across the world every year. It can occur from multiple reasons ranging from—hormonal, biological, familial, social as well as cultural factors. Culture is defined as "the learned, shared, and transmitted values, beliefs, norms, and lifeways of a particular group that guides their thinking, decisions, and actions in patterned ways" Stern and Kruckman in their work claims that postpartum depression is a culturally bound affective disorder and lack of organised social support contributes to postpartum depression.[9] Women while embracing motherhood are expected to behave and function in a certain way by the society which puts on additional pressure on them.

The perceptions of 'ideal mother' and unreasonable societal expectations has troubled women throughout history. Postpartum conditions were first addressed as a mental health condition requiring attention by Hippocrates in fourth century BC.[10] Infanticide is the most prevalent crime committed by women in history. The reasons for this ranges from adultery, shame, eugenics and birth control to social pressure. In her work on infanticide, Lallia Williamson points out that "it has been practiced on every continent and by people on every level of cultural complexity, from hunters and gatherers to high civilizations, including our own ancestors. Rather than being an exception, then, it has been the rule"[11] During upper palaeolithic times also, tribal cultures allowed the killing of infants who were disabled, ill or without parental support.[12] In Rome and ancient Greece, killing of new born infants were allowed so that the weak children do not become a burden on the state. Historical evidence from Asian continent also proves that the practice was rampant in countries including India and China.[13]

American Psychiatric Association first recognised Postpartum Mood Disorder in the Diagnostic and Statistical manual of Mental Disorder in 1994. The correlation between infanticide and symptoms of mental illness exhibited by women after delivery were analyzed to note that[14]:

[8] See Fox (1980), pp. 260–267.

[9] See Stern and Kruckman (1983), p. 1027.

[10] See Pearson (1999).

[11] See Williamson (1978), p. 98.

[12] See Carr-Saunders (2018), p. 168.

[13] See Meyer (2001).

[14] In new born mothers, when hallucinations are present, it is often regarding the child. The delusions mainly concern the safety of the child—how the child is possessed and how the mothers are not in a position to protect them. Postpartum depression results in delusions and hallucinations that puts the mothers in a troubles emotional stage thereby putting them in a position where they are driven into killing children.

> When delusions are present, they often concern the newborn infant (e.g., the newborn is possessed by the devil, has special powers, or is destined for a terrible fate). In both the psychotic and non-psychotic presentations, there may be suicidal ideation, obsessional thoughts regarding violence to the child, lack of concentration, and psychomotor agitation.... Infanticide is most often associated with postpartum psychotic episodes that are characterized by command hallucinations to kill the infant or delusions that the infant is possessed, but it can occur in severe postpartum mood episodes without such specific delusions or hallucinations.

Even after DSM categorisation, mental health experts continue deliberations over considering the condition under a separate and distinct category. Postpartum disorders generally start as minor mood disorder that is generally called 'baby blues' which eventually gets elevated into depression and psychosis if left untreated. Social expectations and pressure on the new mother is one of the contributing factors for postpartum depression. The anxiety and adequacy regarding the abilities to take care of the new child is often discarded by the society as 'baby blues'. The fatigue and guilt about not performing the societal expectations of a 'good mother' triggers suicidal as well as homicidal thoughts in new mothers.[15] A mother who suffers from Postpartum Depression finds it extremely difficult to complete regular tasks for herself as well as the child. Women with PPD also exhibit feelings of exhaustion as well as sadness. They also feel withdrawn from family or friends and have serious trouble bonding with the baby. Sandler notes that the reasons for postpartum psychosis are wider in range and notes[16]:

> Some cases cannot be separated clearly from an initial intense episode of maternity blues, but may begin later and seem more clearly related to the psychological adjustments of motherhood and the burden of bringing up the new baby... The balance of evidence points to social and psychological causes for these states

3 Postpartum Depression and Criminal Responsibility

Criminal law aims to assign criminal responsibility based on the actions of the individuals. Traditionally, criminal law takes the view that individuals shall not be considered criminally responsible unless they have the intellectual capacity to understand and control their actions. Deliberations regarding the acknowledgment of women specific conditions has been prominent since long. However, critiques argue that such a recognition may oversimplify criminal behaviour of women to purely biological factors. Postpartum mental illnesses, nature of the condition and the limitations in bringing it under the ambit of insanity laws adds a gendered complexity to the already complex legal arena. Cases generally involves mothers acting in psychotic states or due to a combination of factors including their fragile mental condition and challenging social and economic circumstance.

---

[15] See Oberman (2001), p. 33.

[16] See Pereira et al. (2012), p. 20.

Insanity laws across jurisdictions vary significantly and medical jurisprudence is considered in a limited manner only. Cases involving women with postpartum depression often focuses on gender roles, social constructions, offender's actions and motives, leaving aside questions of *mens rea* and culpability for legal determination. Even when expert opinion in sought in cases, defining categorical symptomology and timelines to assess the offender's mental state remains challenging, considering the transient nature of mental states and its correlation with socio-cultural factors. Postpartum conditions are often disregarded in legal and social discussions, due to entrenched gender narratives surrounding 'ideal motherhood'. Michael Perlin, a researcher focusing on the insanity defence, summarizes the reasons for the inconsistency and incompleteness of jurisprudence regarding postpartum illnesses[17]:

> We are morbidly fascinated with neonaticide cases. Here, our stereotypes of motherhood, of mental illness, of 'good girls' and 'bad girls', and of madness and badness all commingle in a dissonant melange of conflicting images. Until we confront the extent of this dissonance, we can never hope to extract any meaningful doctrinal strands from this counterintuitive legal jumble.

4 Postpartum Depression—Indian Perspective

Postpartum depression is a transient condition involving many stages. It fluctuates from slow and steady onset to stages of rapid psychosis within a matter of months. The extent and pace of progression depends on intertwined social, cultural and economic factors. Hence, granting/framing/drafting a uniform defence that covers everyone who suffers from postpartum depression is not a practical solution. It is pertinent to note that mental illness or disability alone is not the sole reason for infanticide by mothers. It is rather a combination of the vulnerable mental health status of the mother and the social isolation and exclusion she has to face after childbirth.[18] S. 84 of the Indian Penal code (S.22 of Bharatiya Nyaya Sanhita) does not bring under its ambit depression cases unless it leads to complete cognitive faculty compromise. The section mandates that the exception will be available to an offender who is not in a position to understand the nature, wrongfulness or consequence of their act. Insanity defence under the code does not cover cases of mere abnormality of mind, partial delusion, compulsive behaviour or irresistible impulse arising out of existing mental health conditions.

Conversations surrounding Postpartum conditions has seen a leap in recent times because of rapid scientific advancements and research in the area. Societal expectation from a woman embracing motherhood is driven by a lot of cultural factors. A mother is expected to be available emotionally and physically for her child despite of the physical and mental trouble she is in. As soon as the woman becomes a mother, the focus is shifted to the child and the needs and wants of the mother becomes sidelined. This social expectation has reflected in the judicial analysis of cases involving

---

[17] Perlin (2016), p. 1.

[18] Kumar and Marks (1992), p. 257.

mothers who've murdered their children. The stark difference exhibited by courts while dealing with mothers suffering from postpartum depression is an example for the same.

The court delved into the mental position of the offender and contemplated her mental situation during the commission of the offence in the case of *Siddheswari Bora* v. *The State of Assam.*[19] Victim in this case was the three-year-old female child of Siddheswari. She killed her three-year-old child by hacking her on the neck with a dao. The counsel who appeared for Siddheswari argued that her mental faculties were significantly compromised during the commission of the offence. Statement of witnesses in the case also pointed towards this. The court had to determine whether the mental derangement she was suffering from comes within the scope of s. 84 of the Indian Penal Code and she can get an exception under the section.

Confessional statement of Siddheswari stated that she killed her child because of the constant illness the child was suffering from and she was not able to see her child in constant pain. Court explained the offence as impulsive insanity and noted that she committed 'mercy killing' because of the physically weak situation of the child. However, while elaborating on this aspect, court noted that Indian laws are ill-equipped to deal with the same. It was noted that the defence of diminished responsibility was used under English Law to deal with mercy killings like the one committed by Siddheswari Bora where she knew what she was doing, but her intention was colored by the sufferings of the child. The court recognised that under English law, the case was an apt fit for Diminished Responsibility,[20] but held that mercy killing due to mental impairment is not an exception under Indian Law. The woman committed the offence under impulsive insanity. However, her cognitive faculties were not impaired to the extent that she was unable to understand the nature and consequences of her actions. For this reason, an exception under s. 84 was not granted to her.

Court in this case, also referred an earlier judgment given by the Calcutta High Court in 1932, in the case of *Mabajjan Bibi* v. *Emperor.*[21] The accused in this case had killed her 6 months old baby because of desperation that arose from starvation. The offender in this case did not have the financial means to take care of the child. The woman was in an emotionally disturbed situation because of starvation of the child that led to desperation. However, the court did not give the woman an exception under s. 84 citing that she knew the outcome of her actions and still decided to go ahead with it. The impulse was not irresistible and only unresisted for being treated as impulsive insanity. In both of these cases, the offence were committed by mothers, out of a feeling of desperation and helplessness. The courts in these cases fails to look into the emotional burden on mothers and how society expects her to

[19] 1981 SCC OnLine Gau 39.

[20] In Criminal law, the doctrine of diminished responsibility refers to a potential defence or excuse that is raised by offenders to claim that, eventhough their action was wrong, they shall not be held totally responsible criminally since their mental faculties were substantially compromised during the commission of the offence.

[21] AIR 1932 Cal 658.

be perfect in fulfilling her duties as a mother. English law recognises such cases and brings them under the ambit of diminished responsibility, a state of partial cognitive faculty compromise where offenders are not able to comprehend their actions or consequences because of a compromised mental state. The court while elaborating on why it could not consider the offence as 'culpable homicide' noted:

> Had it been permissible to us to treat the offence as one of culpable homicide only under Section 304 of the Penal Code, we would have perhaps done so as we are satisfied that the appellant having been deserted by her husband, living at her father's house and being mother of three female children in succession must have taken the life of her own flesh and blood due to strong impulse only and would have perhaps, awarded as sentence the imprisonment already undergone. But that seems to be out of our reach. The result is that we uphold the conviction though with a heavy heart. The punishment being the minimum contemplated by Section 302 cannot also be interfered with. The appeal therefore stands dismissed. The appellant is however not without a remedy. We think that this is a fit case where the Government could exercise its power of remission specially because it is about 7 years that the appellant is in jail.

The court is fixated on the idea of a 'good mother'. Court notes that a good mother cannot kill their child unless they have a compromised mental health condition. This approach is visible in the cases of postpartum depression that came before the court even after deliberations on postpartum depression and mental health started gaining momentum.

In *Savita Manish Chaudhari* v. *State of Maharashtra*,[22] the Aurangabad Bench of the Bombay High Court has quashed a First Information Report that was registered against a 25-year-old woman named Savita who hailed from Osmanabad who attempted to murder her 3-month-old son in 2015 when she was suffering from postpartum depression. According to the prosecution case, Savita, a married woman with two children, made a call to her husband while he was away for work, informing him that their two-month-old son had been poisoned by an unknown individual and was in critical condition. The husband, believing this information to be true, reported it to the police, attributing the poisoning to an unidentified person. Several days later, Savita attempted to abandon the baby near a garbage dump adjacent to the hospital, and she made an attempt to kill the child with a large stone. Eyewitnesses corroborated this event, and Savita fled the scene afterwards. Consequently, an FIR was lodged against Savita based on the eyewitness testimony, charging her under section 307 of the Indian Penal Code for attempted murder.

While the case was pending for trial in the sessions court, the applicant approached the court for quashing FIR invoking the remedy available under s. 482 of Cr.P.C.[23] Savita contended that, during the commission of the offence she was in an emotionally disturbed state of mind because of postpartum depression. Savita pointed out that she did not commit the act with any sort of ill intention and the attempt to kill her own

---

[22] 2017 SCC OnLine Bom 369.

[23] S. 482 CrPC—Saving of inherent powers of High Court. Nothing in this Code shall be deemed to limit or affect the inherent powers of the High Court to make such orders as may be necessary to give effect to any order under this Code, or to prevent abuse of the process of any Court or otherwise to secure the ends of justice.

son was under the attack of a psychiatric disorder. Her family members as well as the doctor who examined her pointed towards her psychiatric history. She approached the court to quash the FIR after recovering from postpartum depression. The entire family gave the undertaking that they will take care of the woman and her minor child. The bench held that the mental state of the woman during the commission of the offence qualifies her for the general exception mentioned under s. 84 of IPC. The court observed that the evidence presented indicates that the woman lacked comprehension of the gravity of her actions at the time of the offence. Based on this, the court ruled that her actions do not meet the criteria for an offence under Section 84 of the Indian Penal Code. Instead of solely focusing on her compromised cognitive state during the offence, the court emphasized societal expectations of motherhood to explain why she did not commit the crime with full awareness. Consequently, the court decided to dismiss the proceedings against her with the following conclusion:

> It is also the fact that victim was the minor newly born baby of three months old son of the applicant herself. Obviously, being, a sucking child each and every mother including the applicant - Savita would have love and affection towards own newly born child. The applicant being mother of child must have taken care and precaution for his wellbeing and safety. Therefore, she being in such state of mind, could not have thought of committing such gruesome act to snuff out the life of her own sucking child. Taking into consideration the love and affection of the mother towards her own newly born child/baby it would cumbersome to appreciate that the applicant -Savita, mother of newly born baby would intentionally and with ulterior motivation attempt to kill her own baby without any reasonable cause. These circumstances are also sufficient to draw inference that the applicant - Savita must have committed alleged offence under the influence of psychiatric disease i.e., mental disorder. Therefore, it would be unjust and improper to fasten the guilt on the applicant/accused.

A close scrutiny of the judgment makes it clear that the court focuses on the emotional bond between a mother and her child, suggesting that a 'good mother' would not harm her offspring. Section 84 of the Indian Penal Code provides exemption only in cases where the offender is incapable of comprehending the nature, consequences, and repercussions of their actions. In this instance, the mother understood the nature and consequences of her actions but was emotionally distressed due to postpartum depression. Nonetheless, the court acquitted her under Section 84 as there exists no other legal defence in the Indian Penal Code that considers the degree to which an individual's cognitive abilities were impaired during the commission of the offense. Had the acquittal been on the ground that her cognitive faculties were compromised substantially as warranted by s. 84 of the code, it would have been a rational decision. But the court is trying to exempt her from liability by giving the reason that a 'good mother' would never do what she did unless for her compromised mental state. This brings us to the understanding that the judgments of courts are still guided by cultural perceptions.

A contrast judgment was pronounced by Bombay sessions court in *The State of Maharashtra* v. *X*.[24] The defendant in this case was on trial for offences outlined in

[24] Sessions Case No. 508 of 2011.

sections 302 and 317[25,26] of the Indian Penal Code. According to the prosecution, the accused allegedly killed her infant daughter by tossing her out of the washroom window. The accused, along with her fraternal twins, was hospitalized due to premature birth. Security personnel were alerted by a call from the hospital ward where the accused and her babies were staying, reporting the girl child missing. The security officer, accompanied by the accused's husband, conducted a search and heard the cries of the child emanating from the ward's washroom. Upon investigation, they found the girl child lying on a piece of cloth with a broken ear and multiple injuries on her body. The security guard asked the woman what happened to the baby and after questioning her a few times she confessed that she threw the baby out of the window. From the CCTV footage, it was evident that the woman committed the crime. She went inside the washroom with the girl and came out empty handed. As per the statement of the husband, relatives and the doctors, the woman was behaving differently since the birth of the children. The twins were born pre-term and were underweight and had severe breathing issues for which they were kept under treatment in the hospital. The doctor testified that the woman exhibited depressive symptoms since the birth of her twins. She had lost two children in the past and this had caused recurring emotional disturbances in her.

Besides suffering from postpartum disorder, the woman was also distressed by the family's financial struggles. The twins critical condition necessitated advanced medical treatment, adding to the family's burden. Moreover, the accused was informed of the slim chances of the girl child surviving the situation, which deeply troubled her. The woman's argument was that her mental state prevented her from comprehending the gravity, repercussions, and moral wrongdoing of her actions at the time, thus warranting exemption under Section 84. Section 84 of the penal code addresses situations where cognitive faculties completely shut down. However, it does not provide exemption for mental health conditions that only partially compromise cognitive faculties. Postpartum depression, for instance, is a condition with varying degrees of severity according to DSM V standards recognized by the American Psychiatric Association. This severity can be influenced by cultural, social, and economic factors. Not all stages of postpartum depression fit within the legal definition of insanity outlined in Section 84 of the IPC. Additionally, the degree of cognitive impairment differs among individuals. When an offender claims exemption under Section 84, the court must assess whether they comprehended the nature of their actions or if their mental state rendered the act contrary to existing laws. The conduct of the accused from the time of the offence to the commencement of court proceedings is crucial in determining the authenticity of an insanity plea—whether it is genuine, an afterthought, or fabricated.

---

[25] Section 302: Punishment for murder —Whoever commits murder shall be punished with death, or imprisonment for life, and shall also be liable to fine.

[26] Section 317—Exposure and abandonment of child under twelve years, by parent or person having care of it: Whoever being the father or mother of a child under the age of twelve years, or having the care of such child, shall expose or leave such child in any place with the intention of wholly abandoning such child, shall be punished with imprisonment of either description for a term which may extend to seven years, or with fine, or with both.

The doctor who examined the woman testified that she was exhibiting depressive symptoms because of the loss of her two children. But the statement was recorded after the incident. The court noted that there is nothing on record to prove her emotionally disturbed state of mind when she was admitted in the hospital. The woman was under treatment for postpartum care and not for depression. It was noted that there is no available evidence to prove that she was suffering from unsoundness of mind when she committed the act. As per the facts of the case, after throwing her child through the washroom window, she came back and started shouting at the staff to create the impression that her child was missing. Taking into accounts these facts, the court held that the woman had the intention to abandon the girl child. The court noted that she selectively chose the girl child leaving the boy child in the cot with the *malafide* intention to kill the girl child considering her economic condition and the social expectations that comes up with raising a girl child. The woman was convicted under s. 302 of the Indian Penal Code and was directed to undergo imprisonment for life and pay a fine of 5000 Rs. She was also convicted under s. 317 of the Indian Penal Code and directed to undergo imprisonment for three years.

The court while deciding the case observed the factual situations closely to hold the woman responsible. The woman had lost two children previously and she was in a constant state of dilemma since years. She expressed symptoms of depression and insomnia. The doctor who examined her had testified this in the statement. However, the court was of the view that it is insufficient to prove her troubled state of mind during the commission of the offence. Postpartum depression is a condition that slowly but steadily progresses from mild to severe symptoms. As the Assistant Public Prosecutor in the case argued, the accused would have been in a conscious state of mind when she picked up the girl child and decided to throw the child off the window. But her decision would have been triggered by her emotionally disturbed state of mind. The medical reports suggested that the babies had less chances of recovery and the girl child was in a serious condition. The decision to kill the girl child would have stemmed from the less chances of survival of the baby as suggested by the doctors also. The court, however was not ready to consider any of these aspects. The judgment makes it evident that the court considered postpartum depression as a one-stage condition and failed to understand the transitory elements existing in the condition. The court was not able to exculpate her because her postpartum depression does not satisfy the requirements highlighted under s. 84 of the code. The narrow construction of insanity defence when it comes to women offenders is also because of the inherent patriarchal ideas that paints a mother as a 'selfless' individual willing to make any sacrifice for their children.

In Reshma R Nair v. *State of Kerala*[27], Postpartum depression was cited to claim the defence under s. 84. The sessions case proceedings are still ongoing, but the Kerala High Court took a favorable stance toward the petitioner's bail application, acknowledging her struggle with postpartum depression. According to the case details, the woman experienced postpartum depression following the birth of her child. Her

[27] In CRMC 80/2023, District Court & Sessions Court, Thodupuzha, E-Filing No.—Ef-Hck-2023-014318.

health condition prevented her body from producing enough breast milk for the baby, resulting in the baby's weakened state. Both her husband and relatives attested to her persistent feelings of guilt and ongoing depression. On the day of the fateful incident, she was feeding the baby and the baby accidentally slipped from her hands. The child's head hit the floor and was severely injured. The child was rushed to the hospital and was admitted in the Intensive Care Unit. However, the baby succumbed to the injuries a day after the incident. The woman's mental health condition deteriorated because of the guilt and trauma from the incident. She was diagnosed with severe postpartum depression symptoms and the doctor advised her to continue the treatment for two years. The contention of the woman was that, s. 302 was charged on her wrongly since she did not intend to cause any harm to the child and it was an accident. The bench decided upon the petition favourably and granted her bail.

5 Conclusion

Postpartum depression like any other mental health condition could excuse a person's action only if it satisfies the jurisdictional test for insanity. The act of a mother killing her child is always seen from a pedestal guided by cultural perceptions and patriarchal notions. Law often falls into the 'bad/mad' categorisation of women while deciding such cases. But it is important to note that not every case of infanticide falls within the definition of legal insanity. Not every case of postpartum depression is qualified enough to get an exception under s. 84 of the IPC. The criminal justice system in India has only two approaches regarding capacity- either the accused person has the capacity to commit the act or he doesn't have the capacity to commit the act. The gradations that exist in mental health conditions are not taken into consideration. Cultural perceptions and social factors that drive offenders into commission of offences, are not looked into. Traditional criminal law scholarship in India often views culpability from a 'guilt' or 'innocence' realm. The system is ill-equipped to deal with these nuances which leads to inappropriate responses denying offenders the care and consideration they deserve. Adoption of a partial generic responsibility into Indian Penal Code (Bharatiya Nyaya Sanhita) could be a way forward to recognise transient mental conditions of offenders triggered by social, cultural and biological factors.

References

Bhat GK (1987) Mother in Vedic literature [Brāhmaṇas and Āraṇyakas]. Annal Bhandarkar Oriental Rese Inst 68:471–489

Bunch C (1990) Women's rights as human rights: toward a re-vision of human rights. Human Rights Quart 12:486–498

Carr-Saunders A (2018) The population problem: a study in human evolution. Sagwan Press, California, p 168

Fox JW (1980) Gove's specific sex-role theory of mental illness: a research note. J Heal Soc Behav 21:260–267
Galtung J (1990) J Peace Res 27:291–305
Kumar R, Marks M (1992) Infanticide and the law in England and Wales. In Alexander J (ed) Postpartum psychiatric illness: a picture puzzle, p 257
Meyer C (2001) Mothers who kill their children: understanding the acts of moms from Susan Smith to the "prom mom." New York University Press, New York
Oberman M (2001) Lady Madonna, children at your feet: tragedies at the intersection of motherhood, mental illness and the law. William and Mary J Women Law 10:33
Pearson P (1999) When she was bad: how women get away with murder. Virago Press, United Kingdom
Pereira PK et al (2012) Maternal mental disorders in pregnancy and the puerperium and risks to infant health. World J Clinical Paed 1:20–23
Stern G, Kruckman (1983) Multi-disciplinary perspectives on post-partum depression: an anthropological critique. Soc Sci Med 17:1027–1041
Tanupriya, Pannikot D (2022) Cultural violence, violent gendering, and abjection: discourses on sites of violence through trans women's narratives from India. J Int Women's Stud 24:44 (On violence and resistance: narratives of women in South Asia)
Tatar M (2022) The cultural basis of the violence against woman. Shanlax Int J Educ 10:40–53
Williamson L (1978) Infanticide: an anthropological analysis. In Kohl M (ed) Infanticide and the value of life. Prometheus Books, New York

Dr. Reshma Suresh currently serves as an Assistant Professor at the School of Law, Vellore Institute of Technology, Chennai.She obtained her PhD from the Indian Law Institute, New Delhi. Her thesis was titled "Doctrine of Diminished Responsibility: A study of its absence in the Indian Penal Code (Bharathiya Nyaya Sanhita)" and it investigated conditions that result in partial cognitive faculty compromise in individuals and it critically explored why an offence committed by them should be seen distinctly from a situation where an autonomous, rational actor commits a proscribed act. She completed her BA LLB (Hons) degree from the National University of Advanced Legal Studies, Kochi and LLM in Criminal Law with a first rank in her specialization from the Indian Law Institute, New Delhi. Her areas of interest includes Criminal Law and Feminist Jurisprudence. She has served as the Senior Student Editor of the coveted Indian Law Institute Law Review, Peer Review Board of CLEB blog run by DSNLU and Student Coordinator of the NUALS Law Journal. In furtherance of her research, she has presented her work at University of Guelph, Canada, University of British Columbia and the University of Indonesia. She wish to spend her working life in academia.

The *Bildungsroman* of Consent and Its Impact on the Adjudication of Sexual Violence

Honni van Rijswijk

Abstract This chapter critically explores how consent is constructed within cultural and legal frameworks through the lens of the figure of the girl. It posits that, while consent remains fundamental in evaluating sexual violence in law and culture, the concept obscures systemic power imbalances and injustices. The genre of the *bildungsroman* historically shapes narratives around young women's development through sexual violence and consent, positioning them as subjects of violation. The chapter critiques the didactic approaches in consent education and recent legal reforms that mirror the genre of the *bildungsroman*, revealing their limitations and the persistence of gender stereotypes in legal practices. Drawing from contemporary texts such as *My Dark Vanessa* (Russell, My Dark Vanessa, HarperCollins, New York, 2020) and *I May Destroy You* (Coel, HBC and BBC One, 2020) HBO and BBC One. Produced by Michaela Coel, Simon Meyers, and Simon Maloney. London, England and Ostia, Italy), the chapter examines how these works question and resist traditional narratives of consent. It also considers what genres like horror reveal about consent, focusing on *It Follows* (2014) and *Dogville* (2003). Ultimately, it advocates moving beyond individualistic frameworks of consent to address larger structural issues, emphasizing a need for radical rethinking of justice and responsibility in addressing sexual violence.

Keywords Consent · Cultural frameworks · Legal frameworks · Sexual violence · Figure of the girl · *Bildungsroman* · Power imbalances · Gender stereotypes · Structural injustice

1 Introduction: The Continuing Dominance of Consent

Consent is conceptualized at the crossroads of legal and cultural discourses, with the law relying on it as a core element for assessing sexual violence, despite indications that this framework may be flawed. In cultural portrayals, consent and the related

H. van Rijswijk (✉)
University of Technology Sydney, Sydney, Australia
e-mail: honni.vanrijswijk@uts.edu.au

A. Condello and A. Wagner (eds.), *Gender Stereotypes*, Gender, Justice and Legal Feminism 2, https://doi.org/10.1007/978-3-031-63905-0_17

idea of contract significantly shape representations of sexual violence, creating a *bildungsroman*-like narrative for young women. This chapter argues that the figure of the girl is essential for understanding contemporary cultural and legal perspectives on consent. Historically and today, this figure embodies complex socio-legal dynamics and cultural narratives, positioning her as a subject of both consent and violation frameworks. Yet, the girl's figure also holds potential for reimagining accountability in sexual violence. This chapter explores how some radical creators challenge and critique established discourses, offering new perspectives on responsibility.

The *bildungsroman* for girls has historically centered on their sexual development, often portraying young women's moral and existential growth through narratives of desire, sexual violence, and "seduction," frequently linked to consent. Since the inception of the English novel, the figure of the girl has been defined by themes of innocence, vulnerability, and victimhood. In Samuel Richardson's *Pamela* (1740) and *Clarissa* (1748), the protagonists face seduction and rape attempts that shape their psychological and ethical development. These novels not only reflected societal norms but also established the enduring trope of sexual violence as pivotal to the girl's maturation, a theme still echoed in modern legal and cultural discourses.

This chapter begins by tracing the cultural history of consent, then critically assesses contemporary didactic approaches that span cultural, policy, and quasi-legal spheres. The didactic model, recently popularized in Australia, is reflected in legal reforms clarifying consent definitions and educational programs teaching young people about it. This approach appears in Jess Hill's documentary *Asking for It: Creating Consent Culture* (2023) and Chanel Contos's book *Consent Laid Bare* (2023). While these works focus on young women advocating for change, their experiences reveal deeper issues of power imbalance and structural injustice beyond the didactic consent narrative. The chapter argues that law and culture are intertwined with a didactic framework that centers the girl's sexuality, framing her developmental journey around consent as a core concept.

The persistently high rates of sexual violence against girls highlight the limitations of the cultural and legal focus on consent, which often masks underlying power structures and systemic inequalities, especially for marginalized groups like First Nations girls and women who experience disproportionately high rates of such violence in contexts shaped by ongoing colonialism (Behrendt 2000, p. 355). Given the centrality of the girl figure in consent discourses, contemporary cultural forms frequently critique this narrative. For instance, Kate Elizabeth Russell's *My Dark Vanessa* (2020) and Michaela Coel's television series *I May Destroy You* (HBO 2020) interrogate the consent framework, revealing its inadequacy in safeguarding against abuse and its role in concealing power imbalances. These works ultimately stress the significance of knowledge and awareness in sexual negotiations while demonstrating the limits of focusing solely on individual agency, as the consent framework often prescribes. I then turn to genres that, in a stark manner, reveal the ineffectiveness and harm of consent narratives, conveying an intense sense of hopelessness. Yet, this bleakness can serve as a foundation for hope—by dismantling both legal and cultural narratives around consent, we can build new frameworks grounded in structural, decolonizing approaches to sexual violence. The first example is David

Robert Mitchell's *It Follows* (2014), which employs horror to dismantle the concept of individual agency as a defense against sexual violence, portraying the ongoing threat of violation to expose consent's limitations as a safeguard. The second critique of consent narratives appears in Lars von Trier's *Dogville* (2003), which offers an aesthetic and affective exploration of subordination under liberal law and democracy. Through the character of Grace, a young woman who seeks shelter in a small town but faces escalating violence and exploitation, the film critiques the social contract and consent. It illustrates how these ideals not only fail to protect the vulnerable but also perversely justify violence under the guise of mutual obligation, revealing the material realities masked by abstract justice. In *Dogville*, Grace's subjugation becomes essential to the town's cohesion, demonstrating the limits of individual agency in combating sexual violence and highlighting the need for collective resistance as a starting point for meaningful change.

2 The Legal Framing of Consent

Many feminist legal scholars are sceptical of reforming sexual assault law solely through the lens of consent, yet this framework still dominates legal and cultural responses to rising rates of sexual violence. Recent changes in Australian law reflect this focus, particularly with the introduction of "affirmative consent" in the *Crimes Legislation Amendment (Sexual Consent Reforms) Act 2021* (NSW), which amended the Crimes Act 1900 (NSW). This reform specifies that consent must be a freely given agreement and includes a positive obligation for the accused to actively consider the issue of consent:

> A belief in consent is not reasonable if the accused person did not, within a reasonable time before or at the time of the sexual activity, say or do anything to find out whether the other person was consenting. (Pt 3, Div 10, Sub-div 1A (ss 61HF–61HK)

Despite formal amendments in Australian law, Julia Quilter contends that, in practice, the legal system still relies on outdated expectations that victims must demonstrate resistance to prove non-consent (Quilter 2020). Similarly, Elisabeth McDonald argues that requiring affirmative consent does not address cultural biases that influence trial outcomes, as gender stereotypes and misconceptions about sexual assault often overshadow legal definitions of consent (McDonald 2020). Janet Halley critiques affirmative consent as a "conservative" approach that reinforces traditional gender norms, positioning women as passive subjects of violation (Halley 2016, pp. 258–259). Halley also notes that affirmative consent frameworks permit verbal consent to acts that may not be genuinely desired (Halley 2016, p. 277). Nonetheless, discourse around consent, particularly concerning young women, has expanded across political, policy, and legal reform arenas.

3 The Cultural Framework of Consent and the *Bildungsroman* of the Girl

When a coming-of-age narrative centres on a girl protagonist, it often foregrounds trauma, particularly sexual violence, as central to her psychological, moral, and existential development. This trope, foundational to the early English novel, appears in works like Samuel Richardson's *Pamela* (1740) and *Clarissa* (1748). In *Pamela*, a young servant resists her master's advances, leading to her "reward" in marriage. In *Clarissa*, a young woman's abduction and brutal assault reveal how sexual violence permeates her moral journey, framing her personhood within trauma and underscoring themes of consent and resistance. Such narratives have established sexual violence as a recurring element in the bildungsroman of girls, forming the basis of their moral growth. This motif extends into historical novels like *Evelina* (Burney 1778), *Tess of the D'Urbervilles* (Hardy 1891), and *Lolita* (Nabokov 1955), as well as contemporary works like *The Girl with the Dragon Tattoo* (2008), *Fifty Shades of Grey* (2011), and *The Virgin Suicides* (1993). Fiona Nelson further identifies a "dead girl genre" in Young Adult literature, where the girl's lack of agency is fetishized within a culture that limits her autonomy (Nelson 2017, p. 39).

4 The Didactic Turn and the Limits of Consent Education

The didactic approach to tackling sexual violence, which emphasizes consent education, has become prominent in Australia. This approach includes two main elements: legal reforms that clarify consent guidelines—such as affirming that silence or lack of resistance does not imply consent—and educational programs aimed at teaching young people about consent, addressing cultural attitudes tied to masculinity, sexuality, and gender (Henry and Powell 2014, p. 3). School-based programs are a primary prevention strategy, as noted in a report by the National Association of Services Against Sexual Violence (Carmody et al. 2009, p. 14). The *Women NSW* strategy further supports educational initiatives to deepen understanding of domestic violence causes and foster attitudinal change (Women NSW 2016, p. 3). This focus is reinforced through funding for 'Respectful Relationships' educational initiatives (Walden and Wall 2014, p. 11).

In 2021, Australian student Chanel Contos sparked a viral movement by inviting others on Instagram to share their experiences of sexual assault during school, gathering nearly 7000 testimonies, primarily from girls and young women. In *Consent Laid Bare* (MacMillan, 2021), Contos critiques how entrenched gender norms shape sexuality, questioning whether genuine consent is possible within a culture driven by porn, patriarchy, and entitlement. Through Teach Us Consent, she advocates for mandatory consent education in Australia, earning several honors, including the Australian Human Rights Commission Young People's Medal in 2021 and the NSW Young Woman of the Year in 2023. Consent Laid Bare recounts Contos's own teenage years, shaping a bildungsroman narrative where her turning point is the moment she learns the concept of consent. This knowledge allows her to reframe past actions against herself and her peers as sexual assault, positioning both sexual violence and consent as pivotal to their adolescent development. Contos presents this journey as follows:

> I'm 15 years old and my school has booked a speaker for the Year 10 students. I am excited because it means I get to miss science and spend the day with two friends I don't normally see in class. … We are told sexual assault means sexual intercourse with another person without that person's consent. We are taught that this includes genital penetration with any part of the body of another person or a foreign object, including digitally, and placing a penis into the mouth of another person, or cunnilingus – without consent. The most surprising thing this man says to us is that if someone is intoxicated, consent is void. Hearing these definitions is how my friends and I re-label acts of unpleasant/painful/awkward/embarrassing/drunk sexual experiences to date as criminal acts. … As we continue to listen to the speaker, we mouth the names of various boys, wide-eyed with shock but also with an overwhelming sense of validation. Behaviours that we have regarded as completely normal, like arse-grabbing or groping, are suddenly being labelled as 'indecent assault.' Surely not. (Contos 2023, p. 25)

In Contos's framework, consent and awareness empower her and her peers to reinterpret previously dismissed or uncomfortable sexual experiences as criminal acts (Contos 2023, p. 25). While these insights offer individual empowerment, emphasizing consent and personal agency risks overshadowing the systemic issues that enable sexual violence. Contos describes this as the start of her advocacy for consent education, reflecting on how her life might have changed had she received a consent talk at age 13 instead of 15:

> When I found out that the guy who sexually assaulted me had also sexually assaulted another girl, my first thought was: 'If I had known what consent was, I could have reported him and stopped him from doing the same thing to her'. (Contos 2023, p. 28)

I think this is especially problematic when the didactic approach is seen as a solution for managing perpetrators or potential perpetrators of sexual violence, as though the narrative of a girl understanding the nature of violence can be used as a structure to understand perpetration of that violence—that both perpetrators and victim/survivors inhabit the same *bildungsroman* framed by consent. Contos continues:

> Now I think: 'If he had known what consent was, maybe he would have never done it to me, or anyone else.' … In order to process the magnitude of boys who have committed sexual assault, I've adopted the view that the vast majority of these instances were perpetrated without the perpetrator understanding the weight of their actions because they lacked any education in consent. Again, the type of sexual assault that I am talking about here is one where the confusion comes from the absence of understanding the nature of consent. (Contos 2023, p. 29)

Although Contos's book is framed as an argument for consent education, there are many times when Contos acknowledges deeper structural issues of power:

> We end up teaching men 'how not to rape' when we should actually be striving for a world where healthy intimacy is the standard, and rape would be a bizarre thing to do if you

> were operating within a social contract based on equality. This is especially difficult in a world that's structured to cater to male satisfaction and is saddled with taboos around female sexuality. (Contos 2023, p. 53)

Contos distinguishes types of sexual violence, categorizing it as arising from misunderstandings versus structural issues. However, this distinction can overlook how consent's ambiguity and sexual violence are part of a continuum of gender violence. She highlights the "entitled opportunist"—often viewed as a "good guy"—who benefits from privilege and social norms, especially within elite institutions like the private schools in Sydney, which intersect with power and privilege. Contos suggests these offenders may change with education, but argues that focusing solely on consent education risks concealing the systemic patriarchy at play. Her research, including a Master's thesis, links colonial history with Australia's elite boys' schools, underscoring that sexual violence is structural. Australia's high rate of sexual violence, as seen today, is shaped by its colonial legacy (SBS 2023, ep. 3). Consent, Contos notes, serves as a stand-in for complex structural issues, yet mainstream discourse often limits itself to this narrow view, overshadowing broader social contexts.

The didactic approach, rooted in 1970s and 1980s radical feminism, initially used "rape culture" to highlight the structural nature of sexual violence. However, the modern paradigm shifts this approach to focus primarily on culture, diverting attention from foundational issues like patriarchy, colonialism, and capitalism. This shift risks reducing sexual violence to personal and cultural narratives, overlooking institutional and material causes. As Anna Hush notes, while changing cultural norms is vital, we must also address material conditions, including ongoing colonial structures and the intersecting hierarchies that produce sexual violence (Hush 2023, p. 10). Grace Kyungwon Hong critiques this "culture-focused" model, arguing it flattens distinct power hierarchies—such as racism and queerphobia—that contribute to sexual violence (Hong 2018).

The focus on "culture" and didacticism in addressing sexual violence often distorts the structural issues at its root, shifting the responsibility to individuals who supposedly lack the knowledge of "healthy relationships" (Messner 2016, p. 60). This approach, known as the "good man/bystander" model (Messner et al. 2015, pp. 121–123), frames men as either ethical or unethical based on their understanding of consent, as exemplified by the U.S. campaign *My Strength Is Not for Hurting* (Murphy 2009). While promoting respectful masculinity is beneficial, viewing sexual violence as solely an ethical lapse overlooks systemic patriarchal influences. Messner argues that this framework reinforces dominant masculinity rather than challenging it (Messner 2016, p. 62). Tanya Serisier critiques this approach as classed and racialized, casting middle-class white men as knowledgeable and positioning others as lacking (Serisier 2021, p. 15). Salter links this to neoliberal interpretations of social issues as individual failings, which can drift into xenophobic generalizations about "other cultures" in conservative discourse (Salter 2016a, p. 466; Phipps 2020, pp. 12–34). The idea of 'rape culture' is also integral to some of the feminist literature around how law frames sexual violence through scholarship that asserts that the law has reached a 'best practice plateau' and justice for victims is now being held back primarily by the aberrant 'attitudes' of criminal justice actors charged with implementing that law (Russell 2017, p. 274). But it is the law itself that is the problem, Russel argues, not an inchoate 'culture' that attends it: instead of looking at culture, we should look at structural issues, including courtroom processes, and law's complicity in its own failures, since 'it relies, for its own survival and coherence, on the erasure of woman as a subject' (Russell 2017, p. 275).

While consent education is an important component in the fight against sexual violence, it must be part of a broader strategy that addresses deep-rooted power dynamics and structural inequalities. The instrumentalisation of girls and young women within the consent discourse must be avoided by paying attention to their observations about how structural inequalities and power imbalances have also determined their experiences of sexual violence. We also need to more deeply investigate the nature of 'rape culture' and how it relates to the consent framework.

5 Taking on Rape Culture in the Cultural Domain

Since the 1970s and 1980s, popular culture has seen a reclamation of the figure of the girl, with contemporary films and novels critically re-examining representations that once perpetuated rape culture. These recent narratives foreground issues like consent, power dynamics, and systemic structures behind sexual violence, reflecting a shift away from simplistic consent frameworks towards a deeper engagement with structural issues.

Popular culture has long faced criticism for normalizing rape culture, presenting sexual harassment and assault as social norms and even as mainstream fantasies (Projansky 2001, p. 3). Reflecting on the 1980s films that defined her career, actor Molly Ringwald recalls in *The New Yorker* how her characters were frequently subjected to harassment presented as romantic or comedic moments. For example, in *The Breakfast Club* (1985), her character Claire becomes involved with Bender, who has spent the film harassing her, and in *Sixteen Candles* (1984), Samantha, also played by Ringwald, faces repeated harassment (Ringwald 2018). These films, along with others like *Porky's* (1981), *Revenge of the Nerds* (1984), and *Weird Science* (1985), often depicted teenage boys coercing, deceiving, or spying on girls, reinforcing rape culture (Meek 2021a, p. 101).

This normalization of sexual violence reached a broader societal reflection when Brett Kavanaugh, under scrutiny for allegations of sexual assault, referenced 1980s teen movies to downplay his actions as "goofy or stupid things" from high school (Paschal 2018). Sarah Projansky argues that such depictions embed rape within the cultural landscape, portraying it as an entrenched and acceptable part of media narratives (Projansky 2001, p. 2).

Recent films, TV series, and novels critically examine the limitations of consent in discussions of sexual violence. Works like *Baby Reindeer* (2024), *Consent* (2023), *Cat Person* (2023), *Queenie* (2024), *Tomorrow Sex Will Be Good Again* (Angel

2023), and *Boys and Sex* (Orenstein 2020) question the applicability of consent and explore hidden power dynamics, probing the conditions for genuine autonomy. Two key examples, Kate Elizabeth Russell's *My Dark Vanessa* (2020) and HBO's *I May Destroy You* (2020), examine whether consent can effectively address the complexities of sexual violence or if deeper questions of power, coercion, patriarchy, and capitalism are more appropriate.

My Dark Vanessa follows Vanessa Wye, a 15-year-old boarding school student, in her "relationship" with Jacob Strane, her 42-year-old teacher. The narrative alternates between 2001 and 2017, showing Vanessa's shifting perspective, from viewing Strane as a "first love" to recognizing him as an abuser. This dual narrative invites readers to experience her teenage viewpoint—imbued with a sense of seductive power—contrasted with her adult self's recognition of manipulation and grooming. The novel thus reframes their "relationship" from romance to abuse, as Vanessa, even years later, remains psychologically bound to Strane's influence. Russell's work critiques the cultural fetishization of young girls, using Vanessa's story to highlight how society often places responsibility for men's actions on girls, a culpability that victims internalize. Strane manipulates Vanessa through literature, gifting her Nabokov's *Lolita* to reinforce this power dynamic. *My Dark Vanessa* serves as a didactic narrative, encouraging readers to understand the dynamics of grooming and abuse, contextualized by the #MeToo movement's growing awareness.

In the 2020 HBO TV series *I May Destroy You*, Michaela Coel presents the story of a working-class English black woman named Arabella who is drugged and then sexually assaulted at a bar by an unknown man. The series, inspired by Coel's own experiences with sexual assault, explores the nuanced terrain of ambiguous sexual encounters, which Coel has termed 'blurry thefts of consent,' and the profound impact of these events (*Dazed Digital*, 21 September 2021). *I May Destroy You* explores the challenging healing process of a character grappling with the reality of multiple types of assaults inflicted on herself and her close friends in the course of everyday life. While she attempts the process of healing from a stranger rape through the support of her friends, Bella again finds herself in the position of victim as she is violated by a seemingly-consensual sexual act in the episode 'That Was Fun.' While having sex with Zain, a fellow writer helping Bella finish her book, Zain removes the condom without Bella's consent and then later pleads ignorance at her lack of approval. While she is shocked when she finds out what happened, she accepts his explanation of 'I thought you knew' as miscommunication in the moment. Later, Bella becomes aware of the violation as two women on a podcast she is listening to describe the act of removing the condom without consent as 'stealthing,' using Zain's words verbatim as a common excuse used to deceive sexual partners. Two police investigators inform Bella that Zain's actions are considered rape, even if the sex started with consent. 'The problem is when people don't know what is a crime, and what isn't a crime they don't report it. And then people get away with it,' the investigator tells Bella, this didactic moment inspiring Bella to take matters into her own hands (*I May Destroy You* 2021). Armed with the knowledge that Zain's actions are a crime, Bella decides to 'out' him in front of his mother, his publishers, and an audience gathered to hear each of them read from their respective upcoming books. Bella calmly and coolly tells the audience of her assault: 'Zain Sareen is a rapist. ... He is a rapist, not rape-adjacent, or a bit rapey. He's a rapist under UK law' (*I May Destroy You* 2021). Here, knowledge is thematised as the key to culpability: it is only when Bella understands the nature of the act that she can pursue justice, both through the criminal system and by extra-legal means. And yet, it is only when power relations are in Bella's favour that there are consequences for Zain's assault. The police inform Bella that Zain's actions were criminal, but this is not only a transfer of knowledge—in doing so, the institutional power of the police (and state law) also supports Bella. Similarly, when Bella 'outs' Zain, it is in the context of a supportive community of allies, friends and family: her re-framing of the act is important, but also important are the social and power relations involved.

Kate Elizabeth Russell's *My Dark Vanessa* and Michaela Coel's *I May Destroy You* challenge the notion that consent alone can address the complexities of sexual violence. Through the figure of the girl, these stories demand a more comprehensive standard that addresses both individual experiences and the broader social and political contexts in which they occur. By doing so, they emphasise that autonomy and justice require challenging not just interpersonal dynamics but the political structures. However, the fact that consent is still thematised, even to be complicated or rejected, shows its power in mainstream culture—it's as though sexual violence cannot be represented without it.

6 The Political Economy of Consent

Consent is a foundational concept in modern understandings of sexual violence and legal frameworks, shaping not only cultural narratives but also our social, economic, and political lives. As Moira Gatens emphasizes, consent and contract are central to legitimizing social and political relations (Gatens 2008, p. 31). This trope spans both public and private law (Drakopoulou 2007), with a distinctly gendered dimension that impacts the construction of the legal and political subject. Legal theories of consent derive from social contract theories, especially John Locke's, which propose that individuals consent to governance in exchange for its benefits (Locke 1952, p. 119). Carole Pateman critiques this view, arguing that liberal consent is more akin to submission, inherently legitimizing domination, particularly patriarchal structures (Pateman 1980, pp. 150–151). In *The Sexual Contract*, Pateman contends that liberal contracts uphold male power, embedding hierarchical structures under the guise of equality (Pateman 1980). In *Contract and Domination*, Pateman and Charles W. Mills discuss contract theory's limitations, with Mills suggesting that the concept could serve as a "diagnostic device" to highlight injustices in race, gender, and class, introducing the "domination contract" to reveal inherent power imbalances and challenge these constructs (Pateman and Mills 2007, pp. 79–105). This theoretical approach repositions contract theory as a tool to diagnose and dismantle systemic inequalities.

The contract operates as an abstract construct, presenting parties as equals while concealing underlying power dynamics related to race, class, and gender. Wendy Brown argues that consent simultaneously produces and legitimates authority and subordination (Brown 2015, p. 163). Consequently, reforming consent to achieve social justice is challenging. Modern interpretations of consent often mask structural inequalities, particularly in settler colonial contexts where, as Maria Giannacopoulos notes, state legitimacy is undermined by the lack of Indigenous consent at its foundation. She introduces *nomocide*, the "genocide of law," as a term to describe law's role in sustaining colonial power (Giannacopoulos 2020, p. 250). This view parallels Carole Pateman's critique of "hypothetical voluntarism," underscoring that after-the-fact consent cannot address foundational legitimacy issues in settler states. The ongoing colonial assumption of consent effectively erases coercion faced by Indigenous people, especially Indigenous women, whose autonomy is persistently constrained by colonial power structures. Megan Davis highlights how this erasure perpetuates violence against Indigenous women, rendering "consent" a redundant term in this context (Ryan 2023, p. 103).

7 The Aesthetics of Subordination Through Consent

Aesthetics and affect play crucial roles in reinforcing the notion of consent as foundational to the social contract, impacting both legal and cultural understandings. This section examines films that utilize extreme genres, like horror, to interrogate consent and subordination through the figure of the girl. For example, *It Follows* (David Robert Mitchell) uses horror to symbolize the relentless nature of sexual violence, critiquing the limitations of consent as a defense against it. Similarly, Lars von Trier's *Dogville* uses the figure of Grace to critique liberal law and democracy; as she endures escalating abuse justified by the townspeople as lawful, the film exposes how cultural narratives around consent can obscure the realities of exploitation. Both *Dogville* and *It Follows* explore how aesthetic and emotional elements shape consent narratives, suggesting that these frameworks often mask deeper systems of power. Through the figure of the girl, these films prompt audiences to move beyond abstract ideas of consent and confront the material conditions of power, control, and subjugation embedded in society.

8 *It Follows:* Unwanted Sex as a Force-Field

It Follows (dir. David Robert Mitchell 2014) is a horror film that has not been widely considered a film about sexual violence and consent, but very clearly thematises anxiety, even horror, about these concepts. The film begins on an archetypal suburban American street. It's dusk, and quiet, apart from birdsong. The camera pans to an average house and, in the continuing silence, a teenaged girl, Annie, runs out the front door. Annie runs along the street in underclothes and high-heels—she has probably been getting ready for bed when something happened. Annie suddenly stops in the street and stares at something that the audience can't see. Her neighbour, then her father, each call out to her, but she ignores them, transfixed by something that nobody else can see, but which nevertheless terrifies her. She runs back inside her home to get her car keys, then comes outside again and drives away. In the next shot, Annie is sitting on the edge of a body of water in the light of her car's headlights, fearful but despondent, as she leaves a final message for her parents. The last shot of Annie is her dismembered and grotesquely re-arranged body on the shoreline—her legs are torn and twisted. Whatever Annie was fearing has caught up with her.

The next scene shifts back to suburbia, and back to apparent happy normality, focusing on a different teenage girl, Jay (Maika Monroe). We first see Jay floating, relaxed, in an above-ground swimming pool, listening to the sound of children playing nearby. Jay then goes inside her house to get ready for a date with an apparently nice guy called Hugh (Jake Weary). They go on a date to the movies, where Hugh is scared by something that Jay can't see. They then have sex in Hugh's car, and Hugh chloroforms Jay. Once she is unconscious, Hugh ties Jay to a wheelchair in an abandoned building and explains to her the nature of the demon that is now pursuing her, thereby explaining to the viewer the rules of the monster that are an essential part of the horror genre. Hugh explains that because Jay has had sex with him, she will be followed, at a zombie's walking-pace, by a demon that only she and other cursed people can see, and which will pursue her relentlessly until it kills her. Then the demon will come after Hugh, and back through the chain of people who have had sex with each other. The only way Jay put some distance between herself and the demon is to have sex with someone else—whether consensual or not is not specified—and so pass the curse on to them. Hugh says:

> This thing ... it's going to follow you. Somebody gave it to me, and I passed it to you ... It could look like someone you know, or it could be a stranger in a crowd. Whatever it helps to get close to you. It could look like anyone. (Mitchell 2014, n.p.)

He encourages her to sleep with someone else and 'pass it along' as soon as she can:

> You can get rid of it, okay? Just sleep with someone as soon as you can. Just pass it along. If it kills you, it'll come after me. ... Never go into a place that doesn't have more than one exit. It's very slow but it's not dumb. (Mitchell 2014, n.p.)

As evidence of Hugh's speech, the demon emerges from the darkness at the edge of the building in the form of a naked woman, walking directly towards Jay. Hugh takes Jay home and places her on the nature strip, dressed only in her bra and underpants. Her sister Kelly (Lili Sepe), and friends Yara (Olivia Luccardi) and Paul (Keir Gilchrist) rush up to her and call the police, assuming that she has been sexually assaulted. The police ask, 'It was consensual?' 'Yeah,' Jay replies—meaning the sex, but not the chloroform or false imprisonment, and not the curse she has been assigned (Mitchell 2014, n.p.). The demon relentlessly follows Jay, walking slowly but persistently towards her, and only she and others who have been cursed can see it.

As Jay tries to cope with the terror and the growing sense of dread, she enlists the help of her friends, including her sister Kelly, her friend Paul and their neighbour Greg (Daniel Zovatto). Together, they attempt various strategies to evade and understand the entity, including trying to track its origin and figuring out if there is a way to destroy it.

The great advantage of the genre of horror is that it can provide new visual, linguistic, affective and aural frameworks to represent and explain sexual violence. Horror is particularly effective at giving language to the more extreme elements of human experience, exploring death and suffering in excessive and often nasty ways; and foregrounding that which society normalises and makes invisible. Horror does this through innovative tropes including haunting and monstrosity, and through figures such as the vampire, the demon and the zombie.[1] In *Zombie Capitalism*, the political scientist McNally justifies a turn to horror as an antidote to our obliviousness, since 'capitalism – and the work that is integral to it – are so naturalised that we do not see the harms, or we accept them as natural, part of the routine and everyday' (McNally 2011, p. 9). We draw upon horror to render the familiar strange. Elsewhere, Penny Crofts and I have developed the idea of *routine horror*, which encapsulates the horror of the everyday (Crofts and van Rijswijk 2024). This idea builds upon Hannah Arendt's idea of the banality of evil, which she developed in response to the horrific events of the Holocaust and Eichmann's trial (Arendt 1994). Arendt's use of the term *banality* can be interpreted in a number of ways, including an intention to break from traditional representations of evil as exceptional. For Arendt, Eichmann was a bureaucrat, who followed rules and simply wanted to be good at his job, and yet this seemingly anodyne thoughtlessness resulted in the brutal deaths of millions of people.[2] Here, we propose the concept of *routine horror* to develop Arendt's idea of banal evil further—going beyond an exploration of limit-events such as the Holocaust to explore how horror shapes the everyday laws and politics of our lives (Crofts and van Rijswijk 2024). Routine horror provides an account of the slow violence that is structural and, more specifically, bound up in our institutions. For Rob Nixon, slow violence is 'a violence occur[ing] gradually and out of sight, a violence of delayed destruction… dispersed across time and space, an attritional violence that is typically not viewed as violence at all' (Nixon 2011, p. 2). *It Follows* represents the routine horror of sexual violence: it represents sexual violence as a relentless, slow force, generating trauma that radiates beyond each victim-survivor. Almost nobody can escape this contagion of experiencing and producing harm. Throughout this horrific violence, the monotonous world of suburban normality continues. Scared for her life, Jay nevertheless continues with school, friends, the mall and movies, her terror revealed to be part of the routine, violent normality of suburban life. There are no safe places—all are potential or actual sites of violence and nobody else is able to see the

[1] There has recently been an explosion in innovative scholarship using the horror lens to provide new frameworks for culpability and suffering. See eg., Linnemann (2022), Crofts (2022a, b, 2024); Crofts and van Rijswijk (2024).

[2] Arendt's representation of Eichmann as a bureaucrat motivated by promotion rather than any malice towards Jews has been challenged (Stangneth, 2016).

demons who stalk the suburbs. The film's analogy to the high rates of sexual violence in our society, especially against teenage girls, is clear. Joshua Grimm argues that Jay's experience 'is that of a sexual assault victim' (Grimm 2018, p. 62). Clearly, Jay has not given consent: while Jay was happy to have sex (she suggested to Hugh that they return to the car), consent was not given with full knowledge: she would likely not have consented to sex if she had known that Hugh was transferring a demon to her. Grimm says: 'In a film where the word 'yes' is spoken just five times, while the word 'no' is spoken 42 times, consent is a constant discussion' (Grimm 2018, p. 63). Jay is initially met with incredulity when she explains her experience to her friends—nobody can see the entity besides her. The police take her statement but don't even track Hugh down, despite the fact that he has chloroformed and tied Jay up, and Jay has given the police his address. Further, the film is saturated by the imagery of sexual violence, representing its pervasiveness, which nobody besides Jay can see. The first time Jay sees the entity in her home, it takes the form of an assault victim: a young woman bruised and bloodied, her shirt torn and her hands tied behind her back. The entity takes the form of her friend Greg's mother, who then violently sexually assaults Greg until he is dead. For Grimm, 'Jay is battling a brutal sexual injustice only she can see' (Grimm 2018, p. 64). This is obviously sex under a domain of force—consent is meaningless for both parties, in different ways. The perpetrator is in a moral and legal grey zone, at best, and the victim has no awareness of what's going on.

The film blends horror and psychological suspense, with a pervasive sense of paranoia and inevitability. The slow, inevitable approach of the entity creates a constant state of tension and fear, as Jay and her friends realise that the demon will never stop following its target. The ending of *It Follows* is intentionally left open to interpretation, contributing to the film's unsettling effect. After a series of failed attempts to evade the entity, Jay and her friends devise a plan to lure it into a swimming pool at a local high school. They hope to electrocute it using electrical appliances, but the plan goes awry. The entity, which has taken the form of Jay's father, attacks her in the pool. Eventually, Paul shoots the entity in the head, causing it to sink into the water. However, it remains unclear whether the entity is truly dead.

In the final scenes, Jay and Paul have sex. The film concludes with Jay and Paul walking hand-in-hand down a suburban street, with a figure walking behind them in the distance. The camera lingers on this figure, leaving viewers to wonder whether it is the entity or simply someone passing by—the entity may still be following them, implying that the curse might be inescapable. *It Follows* posits sexual violence as an operating force field: it has rules, it has power dynamics, it has a logic that can be navigated but not, at present, be defeated. The affect it produces is a sense of hopelessness, even horror, at individual and collective efforts to thwart sexual violence. Since this violence and trauma cannot be resolved, people have to pass it along to others in order to survive. The demon's relentless pursuit of Jay symbolises the pervasive and inescapable nature of sexual violence, emphasising that the issue extends beyond individual agency to include societal and structural forces. The film portrays sexual violence as an unstoppable force, with consent raised as a question but demonstrated to be essentially irrelevant. It demonstrates that not only consent, but any framework based on the ideology of individual agency is ineffective in combating sexual violence; rather, collective action in fighting back and treating trauma are the baseline starting points. By setting the horror within the backdrop of suburban normality—where people go to work, wash their cars and attend classes in a routine manner, unable to see the horror as it unfolds in the foreground—the film underscores how sexual violence is embedded in everyday life, so quotidian and normalised that it has become invisible. Even though it is demonically powerful, it is invisible to everyone apart from the victim/survivor and the perpetrator/the one who passes it along.

9 *Dogville*: Consent in the Social Contract as a Tool of Subordination

Dogville serves as an aesthetic and affective critique of liberal law and democracy, centered on the figure of the degraded girl/woman. As the first film in von Trier's USA: Land of Opportunity trilogy (followed by *Manderlay* (2005) and the planned *Washington*), it follows Grace Margaret Mulligan, a fugitive subjected to increasing violence and degradation by the townspeople, who justify their actions as lawful. *Dogville* critiques the social contract and consent, showing how these concepts can mask violence and subjugation. The film encourages viewers to question the role of consent and justice within a liberal framework by exposing the material realities beneath these abstract ideals, ultimately challenging the relationship between consent and subordination in contemporary society.

Dogville effectively represents subjugation, allowing for a radical critique of consent. The film thematises and diagnoses the aestheticisation of subordination and material violation as intrinsic to liberal political and legal practice. By staging community-building, *Dogville* exposes the hidden dynamics of the social contract, making them painfully visible to viewers. The gendered and racialised nature of contracts and law in liberal democracies is disturbingly highlighted through the sexual and physical violence inflicted on Grace's body. Rancière argues that the film centres on suffering caused by evil rather than on a 'system of domination that could be understood and destroyed' (Rancière 2006, p. 5). However, I contend that *Dogville* critiques the norm rather than the exception. My analysis reveals how the film critiques the legal, social, and cultural concept of consent, emphasising its disproportionate influence in legal and extra-legal judgments about sexual violence. Consent not only fails to aid in making these judgments but also disguises the actual operating logics and material power relations at play, creating an illusion of justice.

Dogville illustrates how women, non-white people, and other "outsiders" to dominant groups are subjected to violence that is rationalized by abstract principles within political and legal liberalism. The film methodically exposes how constructs like justice, judgment, contract, and debt not only disguise violence but actively produce it. Here, the concept of a "consensual contract" transcends a literal exchange, serving instead as a metaphor for exploitative and sadistic violence. The townspeople abandon even the appearance of Grace's autonomy, highlighting how discourses of consent and equality can mask subordination, humiliation, and collective legitimization of violence. Grace's degradation becomes essential to Dogville's communal identity, with her character symbolizing the structural violence rooted in gender, race, and class dynamics, underscoring how individual suffering reinforces a broader social contract.

Dogville, set in 1933 Depression-era America, centers on Grace, a fugitive seeking refuge from her mafia-affiliated father. She is persuaded by Thomas Edison Jr., a local philosopher, to offer her labor to the struggling town, establishing a contract that rapidly devolves into exploitation. Initially framed as mutual benefit, Grace's role soon shifts to forced labor, abuse, and eventual enslavement under the townspeople's collective authority. Despite the neutral language of "fairness" and "exchange," her work is undervalued, and she is subjected to escalating violence and betrayal, highlighting her subordination through a veneer of contractual obligation. When falsely accused of a crime, Dogville's residents justify full sadistic control over her, chaining her under the pretext of communal protection and systematically exploiting her, ultimately betraying her to her father and the mafia.

Dogville demonstrates that a logic of power based on the 'will of the people,' said to instantiate morality and justice, is in fact arbitrary and violent. *Dogville* thereby thematises a narrative frequently used to justify subjugation of those who are said to lie outside community's boundaries. In a film about genocide and slavery, contract is thematised as the key to social and political interaction, thereby exploring the relationship between suffering, contract and authority. The townspeople's justification of their violence towards Grace as contractually fair underscores the manipulative use of contractual language to mask exploitation and brutality. *Dogville* serves as a diagnostic tool, illustrating how the notion of fair exchange is exploited to create an authoritative collective or 'sovereignty' that falsely claims to represent the 'will of the people,' despite evident oppression. Grace's ordeal, involving forced labour, mockery, and sexual violence, is a collective act of subjugation, witnessed and tacitly approved by the entire community. The film's stark set design, with buildings simply outlined in chalk, amplifies the collective visibility of Grace's abuse, implicating the whole town in her exploitation. In Dogville, then, it is not freedom, equality, or the rule of law that founds and sustains the democratic order: rather, Dogville's social contract is bound together through its violent subordination of an outsider. Material and specific violence underpins and sustains the democratic way of life that Dogvillians defend through their town meetings and voting procedures, such as the collective decision to not only harbour Grace, but also to enslave and exchange her for money.

The film *Dogville* challenges viewers to consider what constitutes a just response to the town's atrocities. When Grace is freed by her father and his mafia associates, she hesitates to judge the townspeople, initially justifying their actions as driven by hardship. However, after reflecting on their cruelty, she rejects this view, concluding that their behavior exceeds mere human weakness. In a decisive act of retribution, Grace enforces justice upon the entire town, including the children, holding them collectively accountable. Her actions signal a shift from victimhood to avenger, rejecting traditional justice in favor of raw authority, underscoring a critique of societal laws as instruments of power.

Dogville examines the theme of exceptionalism, ambiguously exploring how violence intersects with legal norms. The townspeople exploit Grace, justifying their actions with claims of poverty and hardship, which they frame as "exceptional circumstances" that validate their behavior under a self-constructed legal and moral code. This rationalization, based on ideas of contract and exchange, legitimizes acts of violence against Grace, including slavery and rape. As Grace exacts revenge, the audience is confronted with their own complicit pleasure in her retaliation, navigating both empathy for her and a critique of her excessive response. The film ultimately challenges viewers' passive roles as jurists, complicating our identification with liberal ideals and exposing an unsettling satisfaction in the narrative's destructive conclusion, where judgment becomes voyeuristic and ethically fraught.

Dogville examines subjection to highlight how modern liberal logics link individual subjectivity with subjection, particularly within a political economy that instrumentalizes individuals through constructs like contract. While not focused explicitly on law, *Dogville* reflects on the foundational role of contract in enabling Grace's exploitation and on how individual contracts relate to the wider social contract of the town. It critiques liberalism's promises of equality and justice, revealing these concepts as abstracted and complicit in systemic violence. The film presents contract as not merely an exchange but as an aesthetic vehicle for subjugation, showing how affect and aesthetics are central to understanding legality (Olson 2022).

By embodying various perspectives—Grace's, the townspeople's, and even that of the viewer—the film encourages a move from detached logic toward empathy, horror, and disgust, suggesting new critical approaches that challenge the abstract fairness traditionally celebrated by liberalism. While the townspeople claim Grace's formal consent, her suffering unifies Dogville, transforming her violent subjection into the town's very identity. This portrayal complicates traditional concepts of consent, suggesting that the appearance of autonomy often masks deeper material realities of power and control, upheld by liberal aesthetics of subordination.

The hope offered by the seemingly hopeless films *It Follows* and *Dogville* is that they point to what we have ignored and not seen; in their bleak diagnoses, they indicate the much more radical frameworks we need to embrace to remedy the pervasiveness of sexual violence. We need to move beyond the liberal social contract and its abstractions; we need to move beyond colonialism, patriarchy and capitalism and their structural subjugations. We need to move beyond the framework of individual agency towards collective action.

10 Conclusion: Where is the *Bildungsroman* of the Sexual Perpetrator?

In this chapter, I have explored how the figure, voice, and experiences of girls have been instrumentalised for legal change based on the concept of consent, despite the inherent problems with this framework. The legal system's reliance on better consent laws falls into the trap of a linear, teleological narrative, promising that rape law will inevitably and incrementally improve over time. This framework is matched by the societal belief that a better cultural response to rape will also develop incrementally. However, such promises are misleading and ultimately insufficient. The recent emphasis on the girl as an apparent agent for cultural change through the consent framework should not be seen as a sign of progress but rather as a symptom of structural resistance to substantive change.

Society, including the legal system, often shows little genuine concern for addressing sexual violence. Young men aged 15–19 years are the demographic most likely to perpetrate sexual violence, and young women of that age group are the most likely to be victims of sexual violence (Australian Institute of Health and Welfare 2020). Further, one quarter of young men aged 18–30 have used physical violence against an intimate partner, and one-fifth have used sexual violence against an intimate partner; both behaviours are more likely among the young men who more strongly endorse more traditional stereotypes of masculinity (Flood 2024). While stories of violation have long been central to the young girl's *bildungsroman*, the narrative of boys as perpetrators is generally absent from their coming-of-age stories. Recent foregrounding of the consent-didactic approach suggests that we can merely map the consent experience of girls' *bildungsroman* onto the experience of boys, even though they occupy different structural positions. If we are going to take a didactic approach, it would be better to focus on structural power systems (patriarchy, colonialism, capitalism) and instruction on how *not* to become a sexual violence perpetrator, stalker, or coercive controller. Instead of an appeal to boys and men to understand, we could communicate a public safety message of zero tolerance, as has been done with legal reform based on harm reduction including the so-called 'coward punch' laws (Schreiber et al. 2016), and for drink-driving offences.

We still fail to fully recognise the systemic violence inflicted upon women and children as an everyday occurrence. These failures are evident not only in the legal system but also in mainstream social and cultural life. To truly address sexual violence, which is occurring on an epidemic scale, we must adopt a materialist, political approach that dismantles colonialism, capitalism, and patriarchy. Only by recognising and addressing the systemic violence inflicted upon women and children as a matter of everyday life can we hope to create meaningful change. This requires not only reforming laws and cultural practices but also fundamentally challenging the underlying power structures that perpetuate inequality and exploitation.

References

Bibliography

ABC Television (2018) I am that girl. 4Corners, May 7. Available at: https://www.abc.net.au/news/2018-05-07/kings-cross-rape-case-that-put-consent-on-trial/9695858

Adalian J (2018) Inside the binge factory. Vulture, June 11. Available at: https://www.vulture.com/2018/06/how-netflix-swallowed-tv-industry.html

Amrani N (2023) Consent. BBC Channel 4, UK

Angel K (2023) Tomorrow sex will be good again. Verso, New York

Arendt H (1994) Eichmann in Jerusalem: a report on the banality of evil. Penguin, London

Australian Institute of Health and Welfare (2020) Contributions from young people: Australia's youth. https://www.aihw.gov.au/reports/children-youth/contributions-from-young-people

Behrendt L (2000) Consent in a (neo)colonial society: aboriginal women as sexual and legal "other." Aust Fem Stud 15(33):353–355

Beres M (2020) Perspectives of rape-prevention educators on the role of consent in sexual violence prevention. Sex Educ: Sexual, Soc Learn 20(2):227–238

Brown W (2015) Undoing the demos: Neoliberalism's stealth revolution. Zone Books, New York

Burney F (1778) Evelina, or the history of a young lady's entrance into the world. Thomas Lowndes, London

Carly-Williams C (2024) Queenie. BBC Channel 4, UK

Carmody M, Ovenden G, Hoffmann A (2009) Sex & ethics: the sexual ethics education programme for young people—Developing ethical behaviour in sexual relationships. NSW Rape Crisis Centre and University of Western Sydney

Chambliss WJ (ed) (2011) Crime and criminal behavior. SAGE Publications Inc., Thousand Oaks, California

Contos C (2023) Consent Laid Bare. Macmillan

Cooper L (2018) Luke Lazarus breaks silence over 2013 Kings Cross rape after being acquitted. 9 News, May 17. Available at: https://www.9news.com.au/national/kings-cross-rape-case-luke-lazarus-acquitted-breaks-silence-saxon-mullins-story/b62cd7ce-ba73-4d36-910a-d45133454123

Cowdrey K (2018) "Milkman" by Anna Burns wins Man Booker Prize. The Bookseller, October 16. Available at: https://www.thebookseller.com/news/anna-burns-named-first-northern-irish-writer-win-man-booker-876051

Crofts P (2022a) The corporate monster metaphor. Law Text Cult 26:73–96

Crofts P (2022b) The horror of corporate harms. Australian J Corporate Law 38(1):23–45

Crofts P (2024) Evil corporations, 1st edn, Vol. 1. Routledge, London

Crofts P, van Rijswijk H (2024) The horror of corporate harms. Routledge, London

Dawson B (2021) Michaela Coel dedicates her Emmy win to sexual assault survivors, 20th September. Available at: https://www.dazeddigital.com/film-tv/article/54221/1/michaela-coel-dedicates-emmy-win-to-sexual-assault-survivors-i-may-destroy-you

Drakopoulou M (2007) Feminism and consent: a genealogical inquiry. In: Hunter R, Cowan S (eds) Choice and consent: feminist engagements with law and subjectivity. Routledge-Cavendish, London, pp 9–30

Eugenides J (1993) The virgin suicides. Farrar, Straus and Giroux, New York

Fischel JJ (2019) Screw consent: a better politics of sexual justice. University of California Press, Oakland

Flowers RB (2006) Sex crimes: perpetrators, predators, prostitutes, and victims, 2nd edn. Charles C. Thomas, Springfield, IL

Flood M (2024) The man box 2024: re-examining what it means to be a man in Australia. Jesuit Social Services, Melbourne

Fogei S (dir) (2023). Cat Person. Studio Canal, UK

Gatens M (2008) Paradoxes of liberal politics: contracts rights and consent. In O'Neill DI, Shanley ML, Young IM (eds) Illusion of consent: engaging with Carole Pateman. Pennsylvania State University Press, pp 31–47

Giannacopoulos M (2020) White law/black deaths: nomocide and the foundational absence of consent in Australian Law. Aust Fem Law J 46(2):249–268

Grimm J (2018) The horror of consent: David Robert Mitchell's it follows. J Horror Stud 2(1):60–64

Halley J (2016) The move to affirmative consent. Signs: J Women Cult Soc 42(1):257–280

Hardy T (1891) Tess of the D'Urbervilles. James R. Osgood, McIlvaine and Co., London

Henry N, Powell A (2014) Preventing sexual violence: interdisciplinary approaches to overcoming a rape culture. Palgrave Macmillan, New York

Hill J (2023) Asking for it: creating consent culture series 1, Ep 1–3. SBS

Hush A (2023) Thinking beyond "cultural change": towards a materialist theory of sexual violence prevention. In New directions in sexual violence scholarship, 1st edn, Vol. 1. Routledge, pp. 9–26. https://doi.org/10.4324/9781003379331-3

I May Destroy You (2020) HBO and BBC One. Produced by Michaela Coel, Simon Meyers, and Simon Maloney. London, England and Ostia, Italy

James EL (2011) Fifty shades of grey. Vintage Books, New York

Lamm K (2015) Texting girls: images, sounds, and words in neoliberal cultures of femininity. Women Perform 25(2):111–127

Larsson S (2008) The girl with the dragon tattoo. Translated from Swedish by R. Keeland. MacLehose Press, London

Linnemann T (2022) The horror of police. University of Minnesota Press

Locke J (1952) The second treatise of government. Liberal Arts Press, New York

Lübecker N (2011) The politics of the imagination: aesthetics and cultural exchange between France and Denmark. Museum Tusculanum Press, Copenhagen

MacKinnon CA (1989) Toward a feminist theory of a state. Harvard University Press, Cambridge, MA

Malone P (2022) Measures of obliviousness and disarming obliqueness in Anna Burns' Milkman. Text Pract 36(7):1143–1174

McDonald E (2020) Communicating absence of consent is not enough: the results of an examination of contemporary rape trials. Aust Fem Law J 46(2):205–224

McNally D (2011) Monsters of the market: zombies, vampires and global capitalism. Brill.

Mills CW (1997) The racial contract built upon the sexual contract, extending Pateman's critique to racial exclusion. Cornell University Press, Ithaca, NY

Meek M (2021a) Exposing flaws of affirmative consent through contemporary American teen films. Girlhood Stud 14(1):101–116

Meek J (2021b) Teenage rape culture in 1980s cinema: Porky's, revenge of the Nerds, and weird science. Springer, New York

Messner M (2016) Getting consent "right": sexual assault law reform in New South Wales. Aust Fem Law J 42(1):58–70

Messner M, Greenberg MA, Peretz T (2015) Some men: feminist allies and the movement to end violence against women. Oxford University Press, New York

Miller F, Wertheimer A (2009) The ethics of consent: theory and practice. Oxford University Press, New York

Mills C (2007) The domination contract. In: Pateman C, Mills C (eds) Contract and domination. Polity Press, Cambridge, pp 79–105

Mitchell DR (2014) It follows (Film). Directed by David Robert Mitchell. Northern Lights Films, USA

Murphy J (2009) My strength is not for hurting: men's anti-rape websites and their construction of masculinity and male sexuality. J Media Cult Stud 23(2):137–151

Nabokov V (1955) Lolita. Olympia Press, Paris

Nelson F (2017) The girl: dead. Young Adult Literat Quart 5(1):38–45

Nixon N (2011) Slow violence and the environmentalism of the poor. Harvard University Press, Boston

O'Keeffe A (2014) A girl is a half-formed thing review—Eimear McBride's daring and dazzling novel. The Observer, May 18. Available at: https://www.theguardian.com/books/2014/may/18/girl-is-a-half-formed-thing-review-daring-dazzling-eimear-mcbride

Olson G (2022) From law and literature to legality and affect. Oxford University Press, Oxford

Orenstein P (2020) Boys and sex. Profile Books, New York

Oriel J (2019) We still need to decide who comes here and how. The Australian, July 22, 2018, 12

Paschal O (2018) Read Brett Kavanaugh's defiant statement to the senate judiciary committee. The Atlantic, September 27. Available at: https://www.theatlantic.com/politics/archive/2018/09/brett-kavanaugh-delivers-fiery-opening-statement/571570/

Pateman C (1980) Women and consent. Polit Theory 8(2):149–168

Phipps A (2020) Me, not you: the trouble with mainstream feminism. Manchester University Press, Manchester

Projansky S (2001) Watching rape: film and television in postfeminist culture. New York University Press, New York

Quilter J (2020) Getting consent "right": sexual assault law reform in New South Wales. Aust Fem Law J 46(2):225–246

Rancière J (2006) The ethical turn of aesthetics and politics. Crit Horiz 7(1):5–20

Richardson S (1740) Pamela, or virtue rewarded. Samuel Richardson, London

Richardson S (1748) Clarissa, or the history of a young lady. Samuel Richardson, London

Ringwald M (2018) Reflections on John Hughes films. The New Yorker, 6 April

Russell Y (2017) Woman's voice/law's logos: the rape trial and the limits of liberal reform. Aust Fem Law J 42(2):273–296

Russell KE (2020) My dark Vanessa. HarperCollins, New York

Ryan T (2023) No consent and no disclosure. In: Black Australian women and sexual violence. https://doi.org/10.4324/9781003379331-8

Salter M (2012) Organised sexual abuse. Available at: https://doi.org/10.4324/9780203082188

Salter M (2016a) "Real men don't hit women": constructing masculinity in the prevention of violence against women. Austral New Zealand J Criminol 49:463–479. https://doi.org/10.1177/0004865815587031

Salter M (2016b) Real men do hit women. MEANJIN 75:97–104. Available at: https://www.webofscience.com/api/gateway?GWVersion=2&SrcApp=PARTNER_APP&SrcAuth=LinksAMR&KeyUT=WOS:000371845300028&DestLinkType=FullRecord&DestApp=ALL_WOS&UsrCustomerID=891bb5ab6ba270e68a29b250adbe88d1

Salter M (2016c) Men's rights or men's needs? anti-feminism in Australian men's health promotion. Canadian J Women Law 28:69–90. Available at: https://doi.org/10.3138/cjwl.28.1.69

Schreiber J et al (2016) Kings to cowards: one-punch assaults. J Law Med Ethics 44(2):332–341

Serisier T (2021) Speaking out: feminism, rape and narrative politics. Palgrave Macmillan, New York

Seuffert N (2020) The law and politics of consent: legal and political subjectivity. Aust Fem Law J 46(2):153–168

Stangneth B (2016) Eichmann before Jerusalem: the unexamined life of a mass murderer. Vintage, London

Tofilska W, Bornebusch J (2024) Baby reindeer (TV series). Clerkenwell Films, UK

Tully J (2011) Consent, hegemony, and dissent in treaty negotiations. In: Webber J, Macleod CM (eds) Between consenting peoples: political community and the meaning of consent. UBC Press, Vancouver, pp 233–256

von Trier L (2003) Dogville (Film). Zentropa Entertainments, Denmark

Walden V, Wall L (2014) Respectful relationships education: violence prevention and respectful relationships education in Victorian secondary schools. Department of Education and Early Childhood Development, Melbourne

Women NSW (2016) NSW domestic and family violence blueprint for reform 2016–2021: safer lives for women, men and children. NSW Government, Sydney
Wood J (2014) Useless prayers. The New Yorker, September 22. Available at: https://www.newyorker.com/magazine/2014/09/29/useless-prayers

Legislation

Crimes Act 1900 (NSW)
Crimes Legislation Amendment (Sexual Consent Reforms) Act 2021 (NSW)

Honni van Rijswijk is a graduate of Sydney Law School and received her Ph.D. from the University of Washington, where she was a Fellow in the Society of Scholars at the Simpson Center for the Humanities. Her research is interdisciplinary, and she writes primarily at the intersections of law, literature and critical theory. She has published on feminist theories of harm, formulations of responsibility in law and literature, the role of history in the common law, and on questions of justice relating to the Stolen Generations. Honni's book Law, Culture and the Figure of the Girl: Genre and Gender Violence is published with Routledge.

Criminal Law and Gender Stereotypes in the Prosecution of Cult-Based Sexual Violence in South Korea

Sou Hee Yang

Abstract Sexual violence within South Korean cults has emerged as a persistent and highly complex criminal justice issue. Cult leaders' near-absolute authority, the insular nature of these groups, and victims' lack of social support impede disclosure and investigation. These difficulties are further intensified by deeply rooted gender stereotypes and rape myths within Korean society and the criminal justice system, which distort assessments of victim credibility and limit the effectiveness of existing sex crime laws. This chapter examines the structural and doctrinal barriers to prosecuting cult-based sexual violence and evaluates two key legislative options: creating offenses that target the abuse of religious authority and reforming sex crime statutes toward a consent-based framework. While criminal law reform is essential, meaningful progress also requires improved victim protection, public education to counter rape myths, and training for legal professionals to ensure that cult-based sexual violence is properly recognized and prosecuted.

Keywords Gender stereotypes · Rape myth · Cult · Religion · Sexual violence · South Korea

1 Introduction

Sexual violence can be a prevalent issue within religious groups, largely because of the influential status of religious leaders and the rigid hierarchy within the groups. In South Korea, several sex crime scandals in cult religions ensued. While sexual violence in cult organizations shares certain features with sexual violence occurring in traditional or mainstream religious groups, the distinctive characteristics of cults—such as the absolute authority of the leader, rigid hierarchical structures, and the clandestine nature of the community—significantly contribute to the problem. Moreover, sexual violence within cults is particularly difficult to penalize due to the

S. H. Yang (✉)
Takasaki City University of Economics, Takasaki, Japan
e-mail: ssophiey@toki.waseda.jp

A. Condello and A. Wagner (eds.), *Gender Stereotypes*, Gender, Justice and Legal Feminism 2, https://doi.org/10.1007/978-3-031-63905-0_18

group's insular structure and the frequent unwillingness of community members, including victims, to cooperate with authorities.

As later illustrated through the South Korean case, these cult characteristics, combined with pervasive gender stereotypes, further impede the prevention and prosecution of sexual violence within such groups. Examining cult-based sexual violence in South Korea is therefore essential to understanding how religion, gender norms, and legal responses intersect.

Therefore, this chapter explores sexual violence in South Korean cult religions, analyzing its characteristics, and the challenges associated with prosecuting such cases. Additionally, the role of gender stereotypes in perpetuating these offenses is examined. The chapter also evaluates two potential legal reforms for prosecuting sexual violence in cult settings and examines the key factors that must be considered when assessing these options. It concludes by recommending a multifaceted approach that combines targeted criminal law amendments, enhanced support systems for victims, broader public efforts to challenge rape myths, and specialized training for legal professionals to more effectively respond to sexual violence within cult religions.

2 Characteristics of Sexual Violence in Cult Religions

Cults can be defined in various ways; however, in this chapter, they refer to religious groups that "breaks with accepted religious traditions and composed of individuals seeking some type of mystical experience" (Feldmann and Johnson 1995, p. 240). "Members of cults are recruited and controlled with what Hochman describes as the concepts of 'miracle, mystery, and authority'" (Feldmann and Johnson 1995, p. 240)."

Within a cult, acts of sexual violence may be committed not only by the cult leader but also by other individuals in positions of authority. Nevertheless, because a substantial proportion of cases involve the cult leader, the analysis in this chapter will focus primarily on this category. Although cult-based sexual violence manifests in multiple forms, its underlying causes are rooted in the belief systems and organizational structures of these groups. Most fundamentally, the near-absolute authority of the cult leader enables the leader to commit sexual violence with ease. Religious communities that combine strong leadership authority with hierarchical structures that discourage dissent or criticism create environments where sexual violence by religious leaders can readily occur (Cho 2015). The long history of sexual abuse within the Catholic Church illustrates this dynamic (Boer 2019).

In many cults, the leader is regarded as a god or a godlike figure, and his or her directives are treated as sacred and unquestionable. This dynamic creates an environment in which sexual violence can be easily perpetrated and concealed within the group. For example, the leader of a cult known as JMS, Myung Suk Jung, raped and sexually assaulted victims of various nationalities and ages, including those in elementary school, by claiming that his sexual acts were the act of a god (Jung 2002,

p. 146–147). He subjected his female followers to rape and assault by deceitfully presenting the sexual acts as a form of "health examination" (Jung 2002, p. 147).

Cult followers' perception of a cult leader as a god or divine representative makes it hard for them to reject the leader's sexual advances or question his actions. For example, one victim recalled a feeling of extreme confusion when her cult leader sexually assaulted her, thinking "Is he testing my faith? Is this an act of God forgiving my sins?" (Jung 2002, p. 147). In another case, he made the victim undress by telling her, "A person who is saved has nothing to feel shame about, so you should undress in front of Messiah (referring to himself)" or "I need to examine you (using my god-given power) to make sure you don't have gynecological diseases." He raped her by saying, "God allowed every women in the world to me. Jesus rejoices through my body. If you refuse me, you will get into a lot of trouble" (Jung 2002, p. 147–148). Despite the seeming incredulity that a cult leader's words could wield such unyielding power over so many individuals, the influence these leaders exert over their followers is often nearly absolute. A striking example is found in the case of the Manmin Central Church, where approximately ten male followers castrated themselves in obedience to leader Jae Rok Lee's directive that they must abstain from all sexual desire (Yang 2023b).

Additionally, in a cult, the follower's other social support systems are quickly removed to increase reliance on the cult. For example, one cult group known as Aga Dong-san requires believers to renounce their three desires: sexual, material, and relational (Lee 2009). Therefore, followers are required to sever all social relationships, including one's own family members (Lee 2009). Especially, followers of cult religions are often required to sever relationships with individuals outside the group. This creates an isolated society where followers of cults do not have any social resources except for those provided by the cult. The limited supply of social resources means that followers who experience sexual violence often have no support system to help them leave the cult or report the abuse to the authorities.

Brainwashing and gaslighting also cause victims to submit to the cult leader's directives and refrain from reporting instances of sexual violence. As in the case of Jung, cult leaders often brainwash sexual violence victims by claiming that the leaders' actions are those of God, and gaslight them by telling them that if they feel upset about the cult leaders' sexual advances, it is because of their lack of faith. Through indoctrination that frames the leader's sexual acts as a path to heaven, victims may come to believe that they are supposed to welcome or feel gratitude for their own victimization. This belief system also discourages victims from speaking about the abuse or reporting it, as leaders often warn that doing so would amount to betraying God. This dynamic is further reinforced by the reactions of the cult community when a victim experiences sexual violence by the leader. Friends and family within the group often tell the victim that "you are blessed" or "you should be grateful," leading the victim to believe that the abuse was a privilege that granted them special attention from the leader (Lee 2023a).

Brainwashing and gaslighting within the cult often occur in an organized manner. In the case of JMS, there were members of the cult who specialized in selecting, monitoring, and managing sexual violence victims (Lee 2023a). Jo Eun Jung (pseudonym), a female follower and Myung Suk Jung's second-in-command, was arrested as an accomplice to Jung's crimes (Choi 2023a). In addition to recruiting victims, she helped create an environment that enabled Jung's sexual assaults. She instructed the victim to sleep in an isolated area near Jung's bedroom and, after the victim was raped, dismissed her pleas for help by saying, "it is the proactive expression of the love of God" (Choi 2023b). The facilitation of sexual violence by other group members underscores the deeply coercive and exploitative dynamics of cult-based sexual violence.

Lastly, it is difficult for sex crime victims in cult groups to identify themselves as victims because they are often compelled to participate in the further commission of sexual violence by the cult leader, blurring the lines between victim and aider and abettor. In the case of Jo Eun Jung, it is clear that she acted as a willful accomplice to Myung Suk Jung's sexual violence. However, in other cases, distinguishing victims from aiders and abettors is far more complex. Within JMS, victims were often compelled after their own victimization to facilitate Jung's assaults on others—for example, by directing another follower to sleep near Jung's bedroom or by persuading newly victimized women that they should not doubt the leader and that what they experienced was an act of God. This coerced participation exacerbates the difficulty of reporting, as victims experience profound cognitive dissonance: acknowledging their own sexual victimization would require them to confront the fact that they also helped expose other female followers—often close friends or trusted community members—to the same abuse.

As demonstrated in the foregoing discussion, various characteristics of cult groups—such as the leader's godlike authority and the restriction of victims' access to social resources—create conditions that impede victims from seeking assistance. Furthermore, the use of manipulative tactics such as brainwashing and gaslighting, together with the challenges victims face in recognizing their experiences as sexual violence, collectively cultivate an environment in which sexual abuse by the cult leader can be readily perpetrated and perpetuated.

3 Gender Stereotypes, Rape Myths, and the Victim-Blaming Culture in Korean Society

The prevalence of gender stereotypes in Korean society, including rape myths, contributes to the perpetuation of sexual violence within cults by fostering an environment that enables victim blaming and the concealment of abuse. While female rights have advanced significantly, stereotypes about traditional female gender roles remain deeply entrenched (Shim and Endo 2013, p. 366). Moreover, rape myths and other misguided beliefs about sexual violence play a substantial role in sustaining conditions under which sexual violence continues to occur.

Rape myths refer to misinformed beliefs and stereotypes about sexual violence, sex crime victims, and sex crime perpetrators (Huh 2019, p. 2). They include beliefs that the sex crime perpetrators would be of low social status and strangers to the victims, and victims would strongly resist (Huh 2019, p. 2–3). It includes other misguided beliefs that blame victims for their own victimization, such as that if the victim dressed inappropriately, invited the perpetrator into their home, or allowed other forms of physical contact, then the victim was "asking for" it. Rape myths also reinforce the belief that cases that do not adhere to these stereotypes and misbeliefs are not sexual violence (Huh 2019, p. 3).

According to the Sexual Violence Survey Research Report published by the Korean Women's Development Institute (2022), more than 40% of the Korean public continues to endorse rape myths and gender stereotypes. Out of 10,020 respondents, 52.6% reported that they believe "a person who has been a victim of sexual violence would report to the police right away" (p. ix). In addition, 39.7% believed that "many people falsely report sexual violence out of financial incentives or a feeling of resentment or vengefulness toward the other" (p. ix). In addition, 31.9% believed "letting the other person to kiss you or making out means that the person is also allowing sexual intercourse" (p. ix).

Male respondents tended to agree more with the rape myth statements than female respondents (p. x). For example, 52.1% of male respondents and 39.7% of female respondents agreed with the statement, "sexual violence is caused by revealing clothes" (p. x). Overall, 36.2% of male respondents and 27.9% of female respondents agreed with the statement that "when a person experienced sexual violence while drunk, then the person is also responsible" (p. x). In addition, 29.4% of male respondents and 21.8% of female respondents agreed with the statement that "when two persons are in a relationship, there is no need to ask for permission for physical contact" (p. x). While belief in rape myths and misconceptions about sexual violence generally increased with age, male respondents in their 20s and 30s showed the strongest agreement with several of the statements such as "many people falsely report sexual violence out of financial incentives or a feeling of resentment or vengefulness toward the other" (the highest rate of "somewhat agrees" and "strongly agrees" responses coming from male respondents in their 30 s [43. 5%]) and "it is impossible to rape someone when the victim persistently resists" (the highest rate of "somewhat agrees" and "strongly agrees" responses coming from male respondents in their 20 s [27.7%]) (p. x-xi).

The survey demonstrates that a large proportion of the Korean public still believes in gender stereotypes and rape myths. The pervasiveness of gender role stereotypes in society promotes an environment that facilitates the perpetration of sexual violence. The stronger one's belief in gender-role stereotypes, the more permissive one's attitudes toward sexual violence tend to be, which in turn increases the likelihood of being exposed to sexual violence (Kang and Park 2016, p. 277). Another research conducted on Korean college students supports the idea that higher awareness about sexual assault and gender equality can lead to a less permissive attitude toward sexual violence (Kang et al. 2016, p. 557).

Additionally, gender stereotypes and rape myths embedded within the Korean justice system hinder the proper prosecution of sex crimes. Public outrage followed a case in which a court acquitted a man of rape based on unreasonable assumptions about women's behavior. In that case, the court found the defendant not guilty by concluding that it could not rule out the possibility that he genuinely believed the victim had consented to the sexual act (의정부지방법원 2019. 11.12. 선고 2019 고합 129 판결). In reaching this conclusion, the court cited several factors, including that the victim—who met the defendant for the first time on the day of the incident—had served food onto his plate at a restaurant and had stated during the police investigation that she anticipated some physical contact, though not sexual intercourse. The court also noted that the defendant had asked her whether she wanted to spend the night with him and had initiated other physical contact, such as holding her hand. Regarding the victim's testimony that she clearly expressed refusal by saying no and that she could not further resist because she felt afraid, the court acknowledged that the defendant had ignored her verbal refusal and proceeded with sexual intercourse. Nevertheless, the court reasoned that the victim's fear arose from her own thoughts and that there had been no use of force or threat sufficient to render resistance difficult. The verdict was later overturned on appeal, and the defendant was ultimately found guilty of rape (Ahn 2020). Nevertheless, the case illustrates how deeply ingrained rape myths—both about how a "real" victim is expected to behave and how rape is assumed to occur—can influence judicial decision-making in South Korea.

Another case also well demonstrates the rape myth inherent in the Korean justice system. In this case, a 13-year-old girl with an intellectual disability, with an IQ of a seven-year-old, broke the screen of her cell phone (Kim 2018). Fearing that her mom would get mad at her, she left home and went to meet a 25-year-old man who offered her a place to sleep on a mobile chatting application (Kim 2018). He put her in a motel room and sexually assaulted her (Kim 2018). On the next day, another man in his 20 s contacted her and had sexual intercourse with her using the same method (Kim 2018). During the next five days, the girl had sexual intercourse with seven male adults (Kim 2018). Finally, she was found in a park, suffering from illusions and auditory hallucinations (Kim 2018). However, during the trial for her medical bill and mental suffering, the court found that because she set up the chatroom herself and was able to stay in the motel room in return, she voluntarily engaged in prostitution (Kim 2018). Although the decision was also overturned on appeal (Ahn 2016), the case underscores the extent to which rape myths influence judicial determinations in sex crime cases in South Korea, revealing how readily victims—including minors with intellectual disabilities—can be blamed for the sexual violence committed against them.

In Korea, there is still a pervasive culture that questions sex crime victims and suspects them of being "꽃뱀(*Kot-baem*)," which literally translates to "flower snake" but refers to women who lie that they are victims of sex crimes for monetary gains. Huh explains that hermeneutical injustice, which is the inability to properly understand marginalized groups due to a limitation to words that can properly explain their experiences (Huh 2017, p. 4), is at play in the social phenomenon that women's experience (of sexual violence) is neither properly understood nor their testimony trusted (Huh 2017, p. 4). "The reason why women's voices are not properly heard or their voices are distorted is the lack of trust in women" (Huh 2017, p. 4).

Indeed, the broader societal tendency to distrust victims of sexual violence has, in some cases, led to victims being transformed into criminal defendants merely for reporting their experiences. In one notable example, a victim referred to as Cha (pseudonym) endured a legal battle for 32 months defending herself against a charge of false accusation under Article 156 of the Criminal Act, brought simply because she had reported an incident of sexual harassment to the police (Huh 2017, p. 5). Cha was sexually molested by the director of a learning center she attended during a drinking gathering with the director and other members of the center. Although she initially sought to address the harm directly with the director rather than involving the police, she reported the incident after he reversed his earlier agreement and refused to pay for her treatment (Huh 2017, p. 6–7). During the police investigation, Cha felt as if the investigator did not trust her words, as the investigator said that he had "never seen a victim like you" (Huh 2017, p.10). The investigator doubted her report due to "the most common bias about sex crimes," namely the assumption that a victim who does not immediately report the incident or physically resist during the assault is not credible, although delayed reporting and an inability to resist are well-documented, typical responses among victims assaulted by someone they know (Huh 2017, pp. 10–11).

The investigator also told Cha that her attitude during the investigation was different from that of a typical victim, as she was too coherent, adamant, and clear about her answers (Huh 2017, p. 12). Huh, analyzing Cha's case, suggested that "the proactive, intelligent, and assertive attitude of Cha seems to have caused hostility against her" (Huh 2017, p. 22). "The stronger one's belief in gender stereotypes, the stronger their hostility towards 'women who raises her voice' and 'assertive women'" (Huh 2017, p.23). Her case illustrates testimonial injustice, a phenomenon in which stereotypes of the listener cause distrust in the person testifying (Huh 2017, p. 24). Due to the investigator forming preconceptions about Cha and refusing to believe her accounts of the event, the perpetrator was not thoroughly investigated, leading to rumors that she was fabricating the incident for financial settlement. (Huh 2017, p. 14). Cha's case illustrates the harsh realities of sex-crime investigations in South Korea, where police distrust of victims can lead to inadequate investigations and incomplete evidence collection—and, in the worst cases, even expose victims to criminal charges themselves (Huh 2017, p.14).

Within a religious framework, stereotypes hold even greater influence due to the rigid hierarchy and emphasis on traditional gender roles. Choi (2015) explains that the social stereotype that "defines men and women in a dichotomic sense, male as leaders and females as submissive followers of the leadership" is even more deeply rooted in churches than in the broader Korean society, as it is considered to be the order provided by God (p. 17). This streotype, however, leaves women powerless to resist male violence and often drives them toward self-blame (Choi 2015, p. 17). Moreover, the cultural ideal of women as inherently submissive to men, once internalized, hinders female followers from understanding that they have the right and ability to resist sexual violence by religious leaders (Choi 2015, p. 18). One victim, for example, explained that the reason why she did not tell anyone about sexual assault by her clergy is that "because I should not judge or condemn the clergy, but only pray that he could be healed, as he was still my clergy and a respected leader who influences a lot of people" (Choi 2015, p. 19). Moreover, in religious environments, a broader culture of distrusting victims of sexual violence makes it easy to portray them as "temptresses" who challenged the leader or as malicious liars seeking to destroy the religion for personal gain. As a result, gender stereotypes and rape myths not only facilitate the perpetration of sexual violence within cults but also make it significantly more difficult for such cases to be disclosed and properly prosecuted.

4 Sex Crime Laws in South Korea

This section introduces the relevant provisions of the South Korean Criminal Act applicable to sexual violence committed within cult groups[1]:

> Article 297 (Rape): A person who, by means of force (폭행) or threat (협박), has sexual intercourse (강간) with another shall be punished by imprisonment for a limited term of at least three years.
>
> Article 297–2 (Imitative Rape): A person, by means of force or threat, inserts his or her genitals into another's bodily part (excluding genitals), such as mouth or anus, or inserts his or her finger or other bodily part (excluding genitals) or any instrument into another's genitals or anus shall be punished by imprisonment for a limited term of at least two years.
>
> Article 298 (Indecent Act by Compulsion): A person who, through force or threat, commits an indecent act (추행) on another shall be punished by imprisonment for not more than 10 years or by a fine not exceeding 15 million won.
>
> Article 299 (Quasi-rape, Quasi-Indecent Act by Compulsion): A person who has sexual intercourse (간음) with another or commits an indecent act on another by taking advantage of the other's state of non compos mentis or inability to resist shall be punished in accordance with Articles 297, 297-2, or 298.
>
> Article 303 (Sexual Intercourse by Abuse of Occupational Authority, etc.): A person who, by means of deception or by the abuse of power,[2] has sexual intercourse with another who is under his or her protection or supervision for his or her business, employment, or other

[1] The translations are largely based on the English version of the Criminal Act, provided by the Korean Law Information Center under the Ministry of Government Legislation, Korea Legislation Research Institute (https://elaw.klri.re.kr/eng_service/lawViewMultiContent.do?hseq=28627). However, for certain terms that are not accurately interpreted, alternative words have been employed in the translation. For example, under Article 297, instead of "violence or intimidation," force or threat has been used as it better conveys the meaning of the Korean words used in the statutes. Additionally, instead of "condition of unconsciousness," noncompos mentis is used, as the original word, "심신상실," refers to not only the state where the person is unconscious but also the state where the person lacks the ability to make rational decisions. Moreover, as the English translation provided is based on criminal law as of 2013, the translation has been modified to reflect recent amendments since 2013.

[2] There are various translations for deception (위계) and abuse of power (위력). In the English version of the Criminal Act, provided by the Korean Law Information Center under the Ministry of Government Legislation, the Korea Legislation Research Institute translates deception as fraud and abuse of power as the threat of authority (https://www.law.go.kr/LSW/lsInfoP.do?lsiSeq=138767&viewCls=engLsInfoR&urlMode=engLsInfoR&chrClsCd=010203#0000). Alternatively, Kim (2019) translates abuse of power as "threat of force" (p. 154).

> relationship shall be punished by imprisonment for not more than seven years or by a fine not exceeding 30 million won.

Additionally, under the Act on Special Provisions for Punishment, etc. of Sexual Violence Crimes, article 10, paragraph 1, can be relevant to punishing sexual violence in a cult religion.

> Article 10 (Indecent Act by Abuse of Occupational Authority, etc.): (1) A person who, by means of deception or by the abuse of power, has sexual intercourse with another who is under his or her protection or supervision for his or her business, employment, or other relationship shall be punished by imprisonment for not more than three years, or by a fine not exceeding 15 million won.

Under the Criminal Act of South Korea, various sexual acts committed using (1) force or threat (Article 297, Article 297–2, Article 298) or (2) taking advantage of the other's state of noncompos mentis or inability to resist (Article 299) can be punished. Force or threat is not limited to those related to the use of physical force, and it is sufficient if there has been the use of some kind of force that made resistance by the victim difficult.

Courts determine whether there has been sufficient force or threat to make a victim's resistance difficult by considering the totality of circumstances, including how the force or threat has been used, the relationship between the defendant and the victim, and the circumstances surrounding the alleged case (대법원 2012. 7. 26. 선고 2011도8805 판결). In assessing whether an indecent act by force or threat has occurred, the Supreme Court of Korea has held that the force involved need not reach a level that overcomes the victim's will, and that the indecent act itself may be regarded as an exercise of force (대법원 2015. 9. 10. 선고 2015도6980 판결). Conversely, in a case where the defendant exposed his genitals to a victim on the road, the Court found that Article 298 was not applicable, as no force or threat had been employed. Notably, the Court determined that no force or threat was present because the defendant kept a distance from the victim, made no physical contact, and the victim was able to seek assistance from others passing by. Furthermore, although the defendant verbally confronted the victim, the Court held that this did not amount to force, as the language used was not sexual in nature and bore no relation to an indecent act. Given the absence of any circumstances that could be understood as infringing the victim's sexual liberty—a legally protected interest under Korean sex crime laws—the Court found the defendant not guilty (대법원 2012. 7. 26. 선고 2011도8805 판결).

Inability to resist refers to when mental or physical resistance is absolutely impossible or conspicuously difficult (대법원 2000. 5. 26. 선고 98도3257 판결, 대법원 2000. 5. 26. 선고 98도3257 판결, 대법원 2009. 4. 23. 선고 2009도2001 판결, 대법원 2012. 6. 28. 선고 2012도2631 판결). Non compos mentis refers to a state where the victim lacks the ability to make rational decisions about sexual acts as a result of mental incapability (대법원 2006. 2. 23. 선고 2005도9422 판결, 대법원 2012. 6. 28. 선고 2012도2631 판결).

Alternatively, sexual intercourse (Article 303) and indecent acts (Article 10 of the Act on Special Provisions for Punishment, etc.) by deception or abuse of power by a person with (occupational or other types of) authority can be used to punish sexual violence in cult religions. In addition to the fact that relationships between cult leaders and followers are grounded in absolute authority, many cults form self-contained communities and often "hire" their followers to perform work, compensating them with food and shelter. In determining the applicability of this provision, what is crucial is whether a de facto relationship of protection or supervision exists. Abuse of power refers to "power sufficient to overcome the victim's free will, including the use of physical or other force or threat or the use of social, economic, and political position or authority, and it is not required that the victim's free will be actually overcome" (대법원 2020. 7. 9. 선고 2020도5646 판결). Courts determine whether there has been abuse of power by considering the totality of circumstances, including the type of power or authority abused, the position and authority of the defendant, the age of the victim, prior relationship between the victim and the defendant, and circumstances that led up to the facts alleged in the case (대법원 1998. 1. 23. 선고 97도2506 판결, 대법원 2019. 9. 9. 선고 2019도2562 판결).

While there are several laws penalizing sexual acts in various circumstances under the law of South Korea, sexual violence in cult religions is still not properly punished in practice. In the next section, the challenges of prosecuting cult-based sexual violence in South Korea are introduced.

5 Challenges in Prosecuting Cult-Based Sexual Violence

Proper prosecution of cult-based sexual violence in South Korea is hindered by several challenges. First, even when victims manage to report their experiences of sexual abuse to the police, witnesses often do not cooperate. In sex crime cases, the only evidence available is often the testimony of witnesses. Moreover, in cult-based sexual violence cases, key evidence—such as security camera recordings—is often in the possession of the cult community itself. Believing that their leader is a god who is being wrongfully persecuted, followers frequently refuse to cooperate with the police and may even pressure or threaten victims not to cooperate with the investigation.

The followers often work together as a community to defend the cult leader and destroy the credibility of the victims. Followers of JMS, for example, raised money to prepare settlement funds, some even by selling their houses (Lee 2023b). In one case, a follower of the Manmin Central Church inflicted secondary harm on the victims by disclosing their personal information and scheduled testimony dates, circulating this information in a followers' group chat under the label "witness list of lying women expected to participate in the trial" (Witch: Anti-Sexual Violence Activist 2023). Followers often even commit perjury to protect their leaders. In the case of Manmin Central Church, three followers of the cult were convicted of committing organized perjury during their leader Jae Rok Lee's trial (Kim 2021). Similarly, in the JMS case, one of the six followers arrested in 2023 as accomplices to the sexual crimes committed by Jung stated that Jung, or lawyers affiliated with JMS, frequently instructed followers on what to say in their testimony (Yang 2023a). Therefore, evidence gets lost, and witnesses lie and disappear, making it challenging to prosecute cult-based sexual violence.

Second, there are practical legal difficulties associated with prosecuting these cases.

Sexual violence in religions rarely occurs by using force or threat; rather, it often occurs through deceptive practices or through the religious leader's exercise of authoritative power. Jeung Shin Cho (2015), director of the Korea Gender Violence Crisis Center, explains that in cases of sexual violence committed by clergy, the social respect they command and their influence over congregants often lead to situations in which sexual acts appear to result from the believers' voluntary submission and compliance. This, in turn, makes it difficult to prove that victimization occurred (p. 6).

Sexual violence in cult religions is the same or worse. For example, when a cult leader claims that sexual relations with him or her are a path to salvation, followers may appear to engage in such acts voluntarily. Consequently, legally establishing that victims were under the cult leader's influence and therefore unable to resist the leader's sexual advances is highly challenging, even in cases where the victims clearly did not provide meaningful consent.

Moreover, because the exercise of authority or deception leading to sexual violence typically occurs in private settings, the victim's testimony is often the only available evidence when determining whether a sex crime occurred (Park 2018, p. 94). As a result, these cases frequently turn on the credibility of the victim's versus the defendant's testimony (Park 2018, p. 94). In the context of cults, however, followers frequently support and reinforce the defendant's account while undermining the victim's credibility, leading to heightened skepticism toward the victim's testimony.

Cho (2015) points out that in cults; sex is often used as a means to solidify the group: female followers, having been religiously indoctrinated by Jung, were raped and sexually assaulted without the ability to logically perceive or assess the situation (p. 7). While it is evident that these sexual acts were committed without the victims' meaningful consent, prosecuting such cases under current South Korean law remains difficult. In the case of JMS, when a missionary learned of the rapes committed by Myung-suk Jung, he extorted money from JMS by threatening to disclose the assaults to the media, and he himself raped the victims by threatening to reveal their victimization to their fiancés or by exploiting his authority as a missionary (Jung 2002, p. 149). He was arrested in 2000 but was only convicted of making threats, not of rape, as the police found: "Although his actions are morally condemnable for causing confusion among the victims through the irrational beliefs of the cult religion, it is difficult to establish rape because the victims are adults, were not in a state of non compos mentis, and did not actively resist" (Jung 2002, p. 149).

Proving an inability to resist, deception, or abuse of power is especially challenging when believers grow up being taught to be sexually submissive to their leaders and therefore offer no outward signs of resistance to their sexual advances. In cases where parents are believers in a cult, their children often get raised within the cult without any interaction with the outside world. For example, in a cult called

Dolnara, all female believers are considered wives of its leader, Myung Ho Park. Park propagated that he needed to have sexual relations with female followers for the salvation and prosperity of humanity (Baek 2023). What was even more troubling was that the female children within the group were brought up being taught that the leader in his 70 s is their future husband, preparing performances for him singing how much they love their "husband" (Lim 2022). When these children grow up and the leader tries to rape them, it is difficult for them to even conceive that they can refuse his sexual advances, as lifelong brainwashing has deprived them of the ability to resist. When such indoctrination causes believers to appear to welcome the leader's sexual advances, it becomes extremely difficult to pursue criminal charges.

In the case of JMS, Jung was not able to escape all liability. In 2009, he was convicted after four victims who came forward, found guilty of inflicting bodily injury by quasi-rape (Article 301), and later released after serving ten years in prison. While other victims have attempted to report their cases, they have been unsuccessful because of threats and interference by followers. As of December 2023, he was arrested and tried again as two victims of foreign nationalities reported their cases to the police (Shin 2022). On December 22, 2023, the trial court sentenced him to 23 years' imprisonment on charges of quasi-rape, quasi-imitative rape, quasi-indecent acts, indecent acts by compulsion, and false accusation (Shin 2023). His sentence was reduced to 17 years on appeal, and the Court subsequently affirmed the judgment (대법원 2025. 1. 9. 선고 2024도16761, 2024전도172(병합) 판결).

However, legal repercussions for Jung have been restricted to only a small proportion of his victims. Myung Suk Jung has claimed that he will "provide sexual salvation to 10,000 women and make them into lovers of heaven," and Do Hyung Kim, an activist opposing JMS, claimed that he has already reached his target number of victims (Kim 2023). Therefore, legal accountability has fallen significantly short of addressing the sexual violence he committed against countless victims not only in Korea but also across the world. His case illustrates how investigatory and legal challenges—compounded by a culture of victim blaming and pervasive rape myths in Korean society—create substantial obstacles to properly addressing and punishing sexual violence within cults.

6 Penalizing Sexual Violence in Cult Religions

To ensure the effective punishment of sexual violence in cult religions, this section considers two possible approaches to criminal law reform and discusses the problems and challenges each presents, especially when viewed against the backdrop of the gender stereotypes previously examined.

6.1 Approaches in Criminal Law

The criminal law responses to such cases can be broadly grouped into four categories. The first approach is to apply general sex crime laws—for example, in the Korean context, provisions that criminalize sexual intercourse or indecent acts committed through means such as force or threat, states of non compos mentis, or inability to resist. While these broadly framed provisions can technically encompass cult-based sexual violence, they are less suited than other approaches to accounting for the unique dynamics and characteristics of such cases.

The second approach is to apply sex crime laws that focus on the power disparity inherent in the relationship between the parties. This involves creating a distinct sexual offense that captures situations in which the perpetrator exploits a position of authority or trust. Such laws often use terms like "using one's position or authority over the other." For example, Article 303 of the Criminal Act and Article 10 of the Act on Special Provisions for the Punishment of Sexual Violence Crimes penalize sexual conduct committed through occupational authority or other forms of power disparity, with an additional requirement to prove deception or abuse of power. In cases of cult-based sexual violence, provisions that more generally address sexual violence arising from relationships characterized by inherent power imbalances—such as those between clergy and parishioners, or teachers and students—could also be introduced with an additional requirement of abuse of power. Although this approach may be more effective than relying solely on general sex crime laws, it still falls short in many cult-based cases, particularly when the cult leader exploits his or her authority implicitly rather than through explicit acts of coercion or abuse. At the same time, if such provisions are applied too broadly without an additional requirement of abuse of power, they risk criminalizing a wide range of sexual relationships that simply involve some degree of power disparity.

The third approach is the application of sex crime laws that specifically apply to individuals in religious positions. This involves enacting provisions that prohibit leaders in designated religious roles from engaging in sexual relationships with members of their congregations—for example, statutes that bar clergy from having sexual relations with parishioners. Such laws are highly effective in penalizing cult-based sexual violence because they do not require proof of lack of consent or other coercive elements. However, this approach raises serious legal concerns. First, there is the potential for constitutional rights violations, including possible infringement of the right to pursue happiness under Article 10 of the Constitution of Korea, as it restricts the ability of religious leaders to engage in consensual sexual relationships. Additionally, this approach raises fairness concerns, as it prompts the question of whether imposing a blanket criminal prohibition on the sexual activities of an entire category of individuals is a just and equitable method of addressing the problem.

Finally, a fourth approach is the application of sex crime laws that specifically target individuals in religious positions with the added requirement that the perpetrator has taken advantage of the nature of the relationship. It involves enacting provisions that penalize sexual acts committed by "using one's influence and authoritative position in a religion." Although its effectiveness may resemble that of the second approach, it allows such cases to be assessed within the specific context of religion, ensuring that the unique dynamics of religious authority are considered. At the same time, by requiring proof that the perpetrator used his or her religious influence and position, this approach alleviates the constitutional and fairness concerns associated with the third approach, which imposes a blanket prohibition on the sexual activities of certain religious leaders. An example of this model can be found in the law of the state of Arkansas in the United States.

> Arkansas Code §5-14-126 (2020) (sexual assault in the third degree)
>
> (a) A person commits sexual assault in the third degree if the person:
>
> (1) Engages in sexual intercourse or deviate sexual activity with another person who is not the actor's spouse, and the actor is:
>
> (A)-(C) Omitted
>
> (D) A mandated reporter under § 12-18-402(b) or a member of the clergy and is in a position of trust or authority over the victim and uses the position of trust or authority to engage in sexual intercourse or deviate sexual activity (underline added);
>
> [omitted]

In *Talbert v. State*, 367 Ark. 262 (2006), a pastor was convicted of sexually assaulting two victims who attended and worked at his church. The Arkansas Supreme Court rejected the defendant's argument that the law violated the U.S. and the Arkansas Constitution, and upheld that there was sufficient evidence to convict Talbert based on the victim's testimony that "she was afraid of what he might do if she refused…[and] that Talbert was a father figure to her and she viewed him as her preacher" (at 268). While Talbert contended that the testimony of the two victims demonstrated nothing more than that there was a consensual relationship, the court disagreed, emphasizing that "(the victim) … told Talbert regarding sex, 'No, you're a preacher. It's not proper. It's not right.' This testimony does not indicate a consensual relationship. It indicates that Talbert, as a minister, used his position of trust and authority over these two victims to engage in unwanted sexual activity with them" (At 268–9). The court additionally held that "[b]ecause the clergy is held in such a high regard, there is a legitimate reason for the State to criminalize a clergyman's abuse of this trust and authority to procure sex." (at 270). The Talbert decision demonstrates how a statute tailored to religious authority can withstand constitutional scrutiny while effectively addressing abuses of religious influence, offering insight into how similar legislation could function in South Korea.

6.2 Amendment Based on the Fourth Approach

Based on an evaluation of the four categories, there are two primary ways to improve Korean law to better address cult-based sexual violence. First, to enact a criminal law that can effectively penalize cult-based sexual violence while mitigating concerns such as over-prosecution or potential constitutional rights violations, the fourth approach appears to offer a pragmatic solution. In South Korea, for instance, Kim (2016) has proposed adding new paragraphs 3–5 of Article 10 of the Act on Special Provisions for Punishment, etc. of Sexual Violence Crimes (Obscene Acts Due to Business Power, etc.). The proposed provisions are as follows:

1. If a person in a religious position engages in sexual intercourse with an individual who receives his or her protection, supervision, guidance, or education by means of deception or abuse of power, the person shall be sentenced to a minimum of three years of imprisonment.
2. If a person in a religious position engages in an indecent act against an individual who receives his or her protection, supervision, guidance, or education by means of deception or abuse of power, the person shall be sentenced to imprisonment for up to ten years or a fine not exceeding 15 million won.
3. If the head of, or any person working in, a religious facility or religious organization becomes aware, in the course of performing his or her duties, of the occurrence of a sex crime against a believer, the person shall immediately report the matter to law enforcement authorities (Kim 2016, p. 38).

While the enactment of such paragraphs will enhance the clarity of legal penalties for cult-based sexual violence, several challenges remain. The first challenge concerns the potential redundancy of such legislation. Article 303 of the Criminal Act and Article 10 of the Act on Special Provisions for Punishment, etc. already criminalize sexual acts committed through deception or abuse of power in occupational and other relationships, some of which may arise in religious contexts. On this point, Byung Kyu Kim argues that "because a religious leader's power over followers is much stronger than other social relationships, and more strict ethical standards should be required for religious leaders, it is crucial to distinguish between sexual violence by religious leaders from other sex crimes using occupational authority" (p. 39). Kim also legitimately points out that the inability of the current law to properly punish religion-based sex crimes proves the need for a specific law addressing religion-based sexual violence (p. 39).

Additionally, such enactment may not provide a complete solution for the proper punishment of cult-based sexual violence, as difficulties may also arise from the burden of proof and from judicial interpretations that construe deception and abuse of power too narrowly. Nonetheless, adopting new legislation under the fourth approach may encourage courts to interpret deception and abuse of power in a manner that better reflects the power dynamics and distinctive characteristics of cults and other religious groups.

Another challenge is the persistence of rape myths and a culture of victim blaming, both of which make it difficult to garner public support for such legislation. Yet religion-based sexual violence is particularly condemnable because it exploits individuals' religious beliefs—often central to their identity—to facilitate acts of sexual abuse. Therefore, as the *Talbert* court recognized, there is a valid and legitimate governmental interest in enacting criminal laws that enable the proper prosecution of such cases. Moreover, such legislation can, in turn, help cultivate broader public recognition that sexual acts committed through the abuse of religious authority constitute blameworthy forms of sexual violence.

6.3 Amendment Toward a Consent-Based Sex Crime Law

The second way is to consider amending the sex crime laws in South Korea so that elements of the law are consent-based instead of force or threat. Courts in Korea are supposed to interpret force or threat in a broad sense so that force or threat can serve as objective standards for whether a victim has consented to the act. However, the persistence of rape myths and gender stereotypes in Korean society complicates their use as genuinely objective criteria. Judicial assessments of surrounding circumstances are frequently influenced by misconceptions about sexual violence and its victims. In addition, the broad interpretation of force or threat has shifted these terms far from their ordinary meaning, creating public confusion about what conduct is subject to criminal punishment. The requirement that force or threat be of a degree that makes a victim's resistance difficult has also been criticized for reinforcing assumptions about women's physical vulnerability while overlooking other forms of coercion—such as exploitation of vulnerability or trust, deception, and the misuse of social or religious authority (Huh 2019, p. 5–24). For these reasons, amending the statutory elements from force or threat to standards grounded in consent—such as "lack of consent" or conduct "against one's will"—would clarify the scope of criminal liability and help ensure that all forms of nonconsensual sexual intercourse, including cult-based sexual violence, are punishable under Korean law.

Despite several past attempts to amend South Korea's sex crime laws to adopt a consent-based framework, these efforts have repeatedly failed due to strong opposition. One major source of resistance is the concern that consent is too subjective to serve as a sufficiently objective legal element. Critics argue that, particularly in the context of sexual offenses, proving a lack of consent is uniquely challenging. Some even contend that shifting to a consent-based standard may produce outcomes opposite to those intended—making prosecutions more difficult if courts continue to require clear, overt signs of non-consent, such as physical resistance or the perpetrator's use of violence. This concern is especially salient in Korea, where, as earlier cases demonstrate, judicial reasoning has often been influenced by rape myths and stereotypical assumptions about how "real" victims behave.

The police also seem to share concerns regarding a potential shift to a consent-based sex crime framework. To assess law-enforcement perspectives on such an amendment, a survey was conducted among 32 police officers stationed in Seoul, Korea. While 24 respondents agreed with the statement "rape can occur without the use of force or threat," 26 agreed with the statement that "the element of force or threat is necessary for proper legal enforcement (for sex crimes)" (with one officer declining to answer). Among all respondents, 19 officers agreed with the statement that "if the current law based on force or threat is amended to be based on consent, it will lead to a serious increase in the number of cases of false accusation." Additionally, 13 respondents agreed with the statement that "if a victim did not resist even in the absence of force or threat during the sexual act, then the victim has in fact consented to the sexual act," and 11 agreed with the statement "unless the perpetrator is using severe violence, sexual violence can be avoided if the victim tries."

A minority of respondents agreed with the following statements: Eight respondents agreed with the statement that "it does not make sense that the victim could not actively resist rape just because the defendant is the victim's boss or of a high social position." Nine respondents agreed with the statement that "even if the perpetrator made the victim comply with the sexual act by lying, there has been no commission of sexual violence if the victim has consented to the act." One respondent further commented, with respect to sex crime investigations, that "it is difficult to obtain objective evidence in sex crimes as it takes place in the context of private relationship of the two persons, man and woman." The survey, while limited in sample size, indicates that while the police officers in South Korea generally acknowledge that rape can occur without the use of force or threat, many nevertheless believe that these elements are necessary for the proper prosecution of sex crimes.

Therefore, amending sex crime laws to adopt a consent-based standard remains challenging, as consent is still widely perceived as a less clear and more subjective element than force or threat. Moreover, even if a consent-based framework would allow more cases of sexual violence to be prosecuted, proving the absence of consent may remain difficult in situations where victims appear to outwardly comply with the cult leader's sexual advances. A victim may act in a friendly or accommodating manner toward the leader despite experiencing fear and distress during coerced sexual intercourse, and such behavior may later be used against her to undermine the claim of non-consent. Additionally, as with the first approach of enacting laws specifically targeting religion-based sexual violence, a consent-based model does not overcome the evidentiary obstacles inherent in cult-based sexual violence, where obtaining corroborating evidence is often exceptionally difficult.

7 Discussions

Cult-based sexual violence is a serious problem that can produce numerous victims if not addressed effectively. Yet significant challenges impede the proper prosecution of such offenses. Witnesses—often believers themselves—may refuse to testify, provide false statements, intimidate victims, or destroy evidence. Prosecution also becomes difficult when victims appear to consent outwardly as a result of the cult leader's deception, manipulation, or religious coercion, which can obscure the absence of meaningful consent. To confront these obstacles, two legislative pathways have been proposed: enacting a specific law targeting the abuse of authority by religious leaders, and amending sex crime laws to adopt a consent-based standard. Although neither approach offers a complete solution to all aspects of cult-based sexual violence, legal reform can nonetheless deliver an essential societal message that the sexual exploitation perpetrated by religious authorities is unequivocally condemnable and that any sexual act lacking meaningful consent must be subject to criminal sanction. By doing so, the enactment of appropriate sex crime legislation can also help challenge and dismantle entrenched gender stereotypes and rape myths. Accordingly, legal reform represents a pivotal step toward ensuring the proper prosecution of sex crimes in Korea.

When amending penal laws to properly address cult-based sexual violence, the following factors must be taken into account. First, because cult-based sexual violence occurs within a religious context, any newly created offense will necessarily apply to all forms of religion-based sexual violence, not only those committed within cults. This necessitates careful calibration to ensure that legislation intended to regulate or deter harmful conduct in cults does not inadvertently infringe upon the constitutionally protected freedom of religion guaranteed under Article 20 of the Constitution of South Korea. Such scrutiny is particularly important given that many cults originate from deviations within traditional religious communities—such as splinter groups formed by ministers who diverge from established Christian doctrines—raising concerns about how broadly such laws may apply and how they may affect legitimate religious practices.

Next, while establishing specific offenses for religion-based sexual violence is important, it is equally critical to address the pervasive influence of rape myths and victim-blaming attitudes on investigative and judicial processes. To mitigate these effects, legal professionals must receive comprehensive training on the dynamics of sexual violence to ensure that investigations are conducted with sensitivity and that victims are not subjected to secondary harm through the application of misguided stereotypes. Equipping investigators, prosecutors, and judges with a nuanced understanding of sex crimes is essential for the law to function as intended. In addition, broader efforts are needed to dismantle harmful societal beliefs through public education and awareness initiatives. Only by confronting and transforming these entrenched social attitudes can the proper punishment of cult-based sexual violence be effectively achieved.

Moreover, to address the challenges associated with investigating cult-based sexual violence, it can be beneficial to legally mandate employees of churches and religious organizations to report incidents and preserve evidence when they become aware of sexual violence within the group. Finally, government resources and support services should be made available to victims. For example, making safe houses available would help ensure the safety of individuals leaving a cult or seeking to report their victimization to the police. As demonstrated in this section, addressing cult-based sexual violence requires a multifaceted approach that extends beyond amendments to criminal law. Only by confronting broader social attitudes toward sexual violence in South Korea and providing adequate resources and protection for victims can proper accountability for cult-based sexual violence be achieved.

8 Conclusion

Cult-based sexual violence in South Korea is not an issue that can be easily disregarded. It occurs in various religious groups, and the number of victims within a cult can escalate rapidly when the problem is not promptly and properly addressed. In this regard, amendments to criminal law constitute an essential step toward securing the proper prosecution of sex crimes in Korea. A decision to amend sex crime laws must be made with holistic consideration of multiple factors, including the feasibility of applying the law in practice, the moral blameworthiness of cult-based and religion-based sexual violence, and the potential risks of over-prosecution or infringement of constitutional rights.

Yet criminal law reform alone is insufficient. Meaningful progress also requires a broader set of measures, including training for legal professionals, public education, and awareness campaigns aimed at dismantling harmful gender stereotypes and rape myths that undermine the fair and effective prosecution of sexual violence. Equally important is the provision of support for victims of cult-based sexual violence, who often lack social resources outside the cult community. Cult-based abuse inflicts severe and lasting psychological harm, as victims not only experience sexual victimization but also suffer the profound betrayal of trust by spiritual leaders and fellow believers whom they regarded as family and friends. To prevent such harm and to hold perpetrators accountable for exploiting their authority, comprehensive and effective measures against cult-based sexual violence must be established.

References

Ahn HS (2016) "하은이 사건" 뒤집혀…"지적장애아 성매수 남성 1천만원 배상". Yonhap News https://www.yna.co.kr/view/AKR20161028065051004

Ahn SY (2020) 호의를 성관계 암묵적 동의라 여겼던 "감자탕 사건", 2심에선 성폭행 인정돼 구속. Law Talk News. https://lawtalknews.co.kr/article/A2KIN0WGJWJ5

Baek AY (2023) '블랙2' 사이비 종교 '돌나라', '강간면허증'으로 신도 성 착취·정관 수술 강요. iMBC. https://enews.imbc.com/News/ViewAmp/379886

Boer W (2019) The Catholic Church and sexual abuse, then and now. Origins. https://origins.osu.edu/article/catholic-church-sexual-abuse-pope-confession-priests-nuns?language_content_entity=en

Cho JS (2015) 교회 성폭력 무엇이 문제인가? -교회 내 성폭력 실태 및 피해자의 고통-. '교회 성폭력의 현실과 과제' 포럼. pp. 3–13

Choi SY (2015) 교회, 성폭력 피해에 왜 취약한가? -교회 성폭력에 대한 사회 구조적 접근-. '교회 성폭력의 현실과 과제' 포럼. pp. 14–21

Choi YR (2023a) JMS 2인자 '제이 언니' 정조은 구속…여성 유인 '성범죄 공범' 혐의. Hankyoreh. https://www.hani.co.kr/arti/area/chungcheong/1088295.html

Choi YR (2023b) 정명석 공범 JMS 2인자 '제이 언니' 징역 7년 선고. Hankyoreh. https://www.hani.co.kr/arti/area/chungcheong/1112976.html

Feldmann TB, Johnson PW (1995) Cult membership as a source of self-cohesion: forensic implications. J Am Acad Psychiatry Law Online 23:239–248

Huh MS (2017) "너 같은 피해자를 본 적이 없다": 성폭력 피해자 무고죄 기소를 통해 본 수사과정의 비합리성과 피해자다움의 신화. Korean Assoc Women's Stud 33:1–31

Huh MS (2019) 보통의 강간: 폭행·협박 없는 성폭력: - 상담일지 분석을 중심으로 -. Korean Assoc Women's Stud 35:1–30. https://doi.org/10.30719/JKWS.2019.12.35.4.1
Jung JH (2002) JMS 정명석 전 총재의 성추문-하나님이 나에게 세상의 모든 여자를 허락하셨다. 월간말 198:146–150
Kang CS, Jung M, Yeom SJ, Park JH (2016) 대학생의 성폭력 인식도가 성폭력 피해경험에 미치는 영향: 성폭력 허용도의 매개효과. J Korea Acad Ind Coop Soc 17:551–560
Kang CS, Park JH (2016) 대학생의 성역할 고정관념과 성폭력피해경험과의 관계에서 성폭력 허용도의 매개효과: 제주지역 중심으로대학생의 성역할 고정관념과 성폭력피해경험과의 관계에서 성폭력 허용도의 매개효과: 제주지역 중심으로. J Korea Acad Ind Coop Soc 17:273–279
Kim BK (2016) 종교인의 성폭력범죄의 가중처벌에 대한 검토. 늘어나는 종교인의 성폭력 범죄 어떻게 할 것인가?. pp 30-39
Kim GI (2018) 지적장애 13세 하은이, "성매매女" 낙인찍힌 사연. No Cut News. https://www.nocutnews.co.kr/news/4591834
Kim SD (2019) 형법상 위력개념의 해석과 업무상 위력간음죄의 위력. Korean Criminol Rev 117:123–155
Kim JH (2021) "이재록, 집단 성관계 없었다" 허위 증언한 신도들. 檢 실형 구형. Financial News https://www.fnnews.com/news/202104121344397398
Kim JA (2023) "정명석, 오로지 성폭행에 매진…1만명 목표 초과 달성했을 것." Chosun Ilbo. https://www.chosun.com/national/national_general/2023/03/15/42OZPXPWN5COBKSDFE527U3ZGU/
Korean Women's Development Institute (2022) 2022년 성폭력 안전실태조사 연구
Lee H (2009) [사이비종교/아가동산 教理 실체]물질-인륜-정욕 단절. Donga News https://www.donga.com/news/Society/article/all/19961211/7214474/1
Lee HJ (2023a) 2인자 등이 신도들 세뇌하고 성범죄 도와…JMS의 조직적 범행. Yonhap News. https://m.yonhapnewstv.co.kr/news/MYH20230503012000641
Lee SG (2023b) 성폭행 안했다더니…6억원 현금다발 준비했다는 JMS 정명석, 왜? Maeil Business. https://www.mk.co.kr/news/society/10864611
Lim MS (2022) '돌나라 오아시스' 70대 교주를 "여보" "낭군님" 이라 부르는 아이들…농장 실태도 충격. Segye Ilbo. https://www.segye.com/newsView/20220907524635
Park CG (2018) 업무상 위력에 의한 성범죄의 적용상 한계 및 개선방안에 대한 비판적 검토. Korean Criminol Rev 29:87–115
Shim MH, Endo Y (2013) 한국인의 성역할고정관념과 성차별의식 및 군복무에 대한 태도. Korean J Woman Psychol 18:365–385
Shin JH (2022) 외국 국적 여신도 "성폭행 당했다"…JMS 정명석 사전 구속영장. Joongang Ilbo. https://www.joongang.co.kr/article/25105895#home
Shin JH (2023) 여신도 상대 성범죄 JMS 정명석, 징역 23년 선고받아. Chosun Ilbo https://www.chosun.com/national/court_law/2023/12/22/7J57GWGDAJAOHNUHNOQMWSGZ7M/
Witch: Anti-Sexual Violence Activist (2023) JMS·만민중앙교회 성폭력, 교주 문제로 축소하지 마라. Hankyoreh. https://www.hani.co.kr/arti/society/society_general/1084167.html
Yang DH (2023a) JMS 2인자'도 구속되나… "조직적으로 허위 진술 강요". YTN. https://www.ytn.co.kr/_ln/0115_202304172050445687
Yang SH (2023b) JMS 판박이, 이재록은 어떻게 '만민'의 신이 되었나[사이비 격파]. No Cut News. https://www.nocutnews.co.kr/news/5922855

Sou Hee Yang is a lecturer at Takasaki City University of Economics in Japan. Specializing in a comparative analysis of sex crime laws across jurisdictions, such as the United States, Japan, and Korea, her research critically examines the role of criminal law in addressing diverse forms of gender-based violence.

Holding a JD degree from Columbia University and licensed to practice law in New York, Yang focuses her expertise on the interaction between culture and sex crime prosecution. She adopts an interdisciplinary approach to her research, incorporating perspectives from diverse fields such as philosophy, psychology, and public health to enrich her scholarly investigations.

Reflections on Slavery, Christianity and Gender in Barbados

Jill St George

Abstract This chapter interrogates two key aspects of slavery in Barbados. The first is a consideration of the roles of sex and gender during enslavement, with focus on recognised experiences of slave women. The second is a consideration of the role Christianity has played throughout Barbados's history, from initial colonial settlement in 1627 to its role in nation building. These two aspects, sex and gender and Christianity, merit individualised attention owing to their unique presentation and/or operation in Barbadian history and highlight the increasing recognition of need for a more nuanced analysis of slave societies to avoid essentialising enslavement.

Keywords Slavery · Barbados · Christianity · Sex · Gender

1 Introduction

Barbados is an island situated in the Winward island chain, bordering the Atlantic ocean and Caribbean sea. It is 166 square miles and holds a majority Christian population which is comprised of 92.4% black, with 2% white.[1] Barbados was (re)discovered, uninhabited by the English in 1625, settled in 1627, became independent from the United Kingdom in 1966, and a Republic in 2022. Slavery operated in Barbados for over 200 years, from 1627–1834/38, and the system of dehumanisation which it enabled was instrumental in the creation of the state. In turn, it has been instrumental in the development of many societal and cultural norms which Barbados exhibits, rendering an understanding of its individualised function, as opposed to an essentialised analysis of enslavement, integral to any understanding of Barbados today.

[1] Barbados Integrated Government Statistics, Census 2010.

J. S. George (✉)
Open University, Milton Keynes, UK
e-mail: jill.stgeorge@open.ac.uk

A. Condello and A. Wagner (eds.), *Gender Stereotypes*, Gender, Justice and Legal Feminism 2, https://doi.org/10.1007/978-3-031-63905-0_19

Describing plantation slavery in the *Black Atlantic,* Gilroy states, "plantation slavery was more than just a system of labour and a distinct mode of racial domination (...) it provided the foundations for a distinctive network of economic, social and political relations".[2] To term slavery a historic event in Barbados's history appears reductive and dismissive, failing to recognise the monumental impact which enslavement had and continues to have. Networks of economic, social and political relations in Barbados were created through enslavement onto a population with distinctive features, those absent from other slave societies, influencing their impact. For the purposes of this chapter, three have been selected. The first, integral to understanding the remaining, is the absence of an indigenous population—a cultural, social, religious foundation on which to rely or revert. The second is the creation of a slave population which was self-sustaining, therefore developing Barbadian cultural and societal norms through enslavement as opposed to ones interrupted through constant population movement and the introduction/reintroduction of varying cultural and societal norms. The third is the intentional withholding of religion, of Christianity in Barbados from the enslaved, dispelling the traditionally held notions of colonisation seeking conversion and dissemination of religious beliefs and structures.

There are multiple themes available for extrapolation and analysis when reflecting on Barbadian slave history which account for its unique features, two of which are the roles of sex and gender, and the role of Christianity.

2 The History of Barbados

In the early 1500s, Barbados was discovered,[3] uninhabited, and named by the Portuguese, though it was never settled. Caribs, Arawaks and Amerindians had been present on the island during the preceding centuries, however by the late fifteenth century, all had been either killed or relocated.[4] In 1625, Barbados was 're-discovered', uninhabited, by the English. They took ownership of and settled on the island under the doctrine of discovery, with "James, K of E and this island" inscribed on a tree to successfully claim the land for the English Monarch.[5] The earliest settlers began carrying out crop experimentation in cotton and tobacco, however both proved unsuccessful. Following advice and guidance from the Dutch, the early settlers to Barbados began cultivating and harvesting sugar cane. During this initial period, the land was divided into many smallholdings, owned by varying landowners. Labour was supplied predominantly through indentured servants, both forced and voluntary. An indentureship was a contract which served to bind an employee to their employer for a defined period, often between five and ten years. In exchange for

[2] P Gilroy, *The Black Atlantic* (Verso, 1993) 54–55

[3] Discovered in this context is intended to convey its discovery by colonisers, as opposed to its initial habitation.

[4] FA Hoyos, *Barbados, A History from Amerindians to Independence* (Macmillan Publishers, 1978)

[5] Ibid 14

their labour, at the end of the prescribed period, indentured servants were promised a small piece of land (often 3–5 acres)[6] and tools.[7] The island possessed an ideal environment in which to grow sugar and it began operating as a plantation economy from 1640 onwards.[8] Plantation economy here is used to mean large scale operations, specialising in one form of crop, employing a substantial workforce with the aim of producing commodities for export.[9]

The success of sugar was immense, creating what has been termed the Sugar Revolution. This revolution occurred in the Caribbean during the mid-seventeenth century,[10] typically dated 1640–1660, and saw significant changes take place, to the land, population demographics, wealth and economy. According to White, the six core features of this transition from the pre-sugar revolution to sugar revolution time period included:

> (…) a swift shift from diversified agriculture to sugar monoculture, from production on small farms to large plantations, from free to slave labour, from sparse to dense settlement, from white to black populations, and from low to high value per caput output.[11]

The fortunes of Barbadian landowners increased dramatically as sugar became a much-desired commodity internationally.[12] Smallholdings disappeared as large plantations needed for sugar cultivation overtook the landscape, with landowners numbering between 8300–11,200 in the mid-1640's declining to 2638 in 1679.[13] This success thrust Barbados into a period of great economic prosperity, with white landowners alongside the metropole[14] reaping the rewards. Being uninhabited upon discovery, the trajectory of the island was to be determined by those with interest in it, and that interest was centred not in cultural, societal or religious intentions, but the furtherance of economic interests and wealth acquisition.

---

[6] Ibid 34

[7] See S O'Callaghan *To Hell or Barbados: The Ethnic Cleansing of Ireland* (Brandon Publishing, 2016) 6670

[8] K Knorr, British Colonial Theories 1570–1850 (University of Toronto Press, 1944) 12; W Nicholls 'Barbados: A Case Study of the Plantation Economy' (Master of Arts, McGill University, 1969)

[9] C Petley, Plantations in the Atlantic World (Oxford Biographies, 2018)

[10] Typically dated 1640–1660, BW Higman, 'The Sugar Revolution' Economic History Review LIII (2000) 3213) 220

[11] Ibid 220

[12] S Dwyer, *Caribbean Exchanges: Slavery and the Transformation of English Society, 1640–1700* (University Of North Carolina Press, 2007)29

[13] S Dwyer, *Caribbean Exchanges: Slavery and the Transformation of English Society, 1640–1700* (University Of North Carolina Press, 2007)29

[14] Metropole here is concerned only with the British following Boaventura de Sousa Santos analysis of abyssal thinking that "divided the world sharply between metropolitan and colonial societies", B Santos, *If God were a Human Rights Activist* (Stanford University Press, 2015) 2.

3 History: Slavery

The most impactful decision in Barbadian history was the decision to use slaves, a decision made from the earliest point in its (re)discovery by the English. En-route to their inaugural visit to the island in 1627, the settlers intercepted a Portuguese ship and captured the ten slaves which the ship was carrying.[15] The stolen slaves, alongside the settlers, were the first to arrive on the island following the initial 1625 claim for the Crown. Initially, slaves and indentured servants worked side-by-side, however the exponential growth in demand for sugar during the Sugar Revolution significantly influenced the preferred labour source of landowners. Land was no longer a reasonable trade for work under indentureship, as the success of sugar rendered the price of land increasing dramatically. During this time, 500 acres is reported to have increased in value to 35 times higher than its pre-sugar price.[16]

As the sugar industry began to boom between 1640–1660, the Dutch took over slave barracoons from the Portuguese in West Africa, positioning them as able to fill the labour shortage left by indentured servants in Barbados.[17] This enabled an increase in available slave labour, with slave numbers steadily increasing from 1627 onwards. Barbados had a black majority population by 1660 which comprised of over 75% of the population by 1700.[18] Over 181,000 slaves were estimated to have been imported into Barbados between 1627–1700, over 304,000 between 1701 and 1800 and over 7000 from 1801 until emancipation in 1834/38.[19] By the end of the seventeenth century, slave numbers exceeded free persons by such numbers that Barbados transitioned from being a society with slaves to a slave society, the first society to make such a transition.[20] Dunn notes:

> Once the Barbadians took the plunge and began importing Negroes from Africa by the boat-load, they never looked back. Nor did they pause to consider whether these black laborers had to be enslaved, whether they might not be organized as indentured servants or wageworkers. The African was only attractive to the Englishman as a fixed possession, like a horse or a cow[21]

As time progressed, the importation of slaves from Africa became less important for the continued exploitation of Barbadian land. Slaves were reproducing on plantations, and under *partus sequitur ventrem,* a Roman maxim adopted in Barbados, those born to a slave mother inherited slave status. The status of the father, enslaved or free, was irrelevant. The once culturally diverse slave society became a self-sustaining slave

---

[15] H Prasier *The Adventure Guide to Barbados, Caribbean Guide Series* (Hunter Publications, 1990)

[16] Hoyos 38.

[17] Hoyos 40

[18] D Galenson, 'The Atlantic Slave Trade and the Barbados Market, 1673–1723' The Journal of Economic History (1982) 42, 3, 492

[19] A O'Neill, *Slave Arrivals to the British Caribbean by Region and Century 1606–1842*, published via Statista Research Service (2022).

[20] H Beckles 'On Barbados, The First Black Slave Society' Black Perspectives, AAIHS (2017)

[21] R Dunn, *Sugar and Slaves: The Rise of the Planter Class in the English West Indies, 1624–1713* (Chapel Hill, University of North Carolina Press, 2000)

population that coalesced around a mutual history of exploitation and oppression.[22] A reduction in slaves transported into Barbados from Africa owing to the increase in Barbadian born slaves saw the slave identity became intergenerational, passed down from parents, who were first generation slaves, to their children. As the slave population grew organically through birth, a slave identity and culture solidified. By 1817, only 7% of the slaves in Barbados were not born in the Caribbean, leaving 93% born either in Barbados or the wider region.[23]

Although seemingly with similarities, slavery and indentureship are highly distinguishable. Slavery was for life, inheritable by children and designation was determined by race. Indentureship was for a defined period of time, and, in the main, operated as an exchange—for passage, for land etc. Indentureship was not inheritable, and designation as an indentured servant was not dependent on race.

A further distinguishing feature of slavery was its legal basis, found in the laws of property. Slavery had been condemned in England from as early as 1102,[24] (although no law explicitly prohibited it) and the closest anyone in England came to being treated as a slave was through the operation of the Vagrancy Act 1547, under which two years servitude could be prescribed. However, the Act was repealed two years after coming into force due to it being "unenforceable on account of its severity."[25] In the case of *Cartwright*,[26] decided in 1569, the English courts condemned the whipping of Russian slaves, and concluding that England was "too pure an air for slaves to breathe in."[27] As no express legal provisions existed in the metropole permitting slavery, the early settlers instead utilised English norms and customs concerning property rights to recognise their legal ownership of slaves. These norms then served to govern slave/slave owner relations in the years of Barbados prior to the enactment of the first slave legislation, the *Act for the Better Ordering and Governing Negroes* (1661), termed the Slave Code 1661. Slaves were the property of their masters, and in being designated as such, their status was transformed from human subject to propertied object, from human to chattel. The preamble of the Slave Code 1661, expressly acknowledged the lack of laws in England available to provide guidance on the governance of slaves,[28] and used the term 'Negro' and 'Slave' interchangeably (whilst the clauses within the Act stated 'Negro' only). As the first piece of codified law governing slavery, the 1661 *Slave Code* formalised and institutionalised racism in Barbados.

---

[22] J Handler and J Jacoby, 'Slave Names and Naming in Barbados, 1650–1830' (1996) The William and Mary Quarterly, Third Series, 689

[23] B Higman, 'The Slave Family and Household in the British West Indies 1800–1834' The Journal of Interdisciplinary History (1975) 6, 2, 261–287, 236

[24] R Bartlett *England Under The Norman and Angevin Kings: 1075–1255 (New Oxford History of England)* (Oxford University Press, 2002)

[25] D Eltis 'Europeans and the Rise and Fall of African Slavery in the Americas: An Interpretation' The American Historical Review (2000) 98, 5, 1408

[26] J Rushworth, *Hearsay Report: Historical Collections* (London, 1686) 468–69

[27] D Browne *Historical Collections Of Private Passages Of State: Volume 2, 1629–3* (London, 1721)

[28] Ibid

The propertied nature of slaves was extended through the 1668 *Slave Code*, which classified Negros as real estate instead of chattel if their owner died intestate,[29] attaching slaves to a plantation. This meant that whomever inherited the deceased's plantation would also inherit their slaves preventing executors from disassembling plantations in the event that a plantation owner died in testate.

Being an uninhabited island on the arrival of the English, swiftly populated with a majority enslaved population, wholly owned as property by individual owners, enabled Barbadian society to be constructed from scratch—without consideration to existing norms, customs or societal and cultural foundations. Designating slaves as property enabled owners to disregard and deny agency and history from their existence, which in turn enabled a new society to be created in the economically focused image required by landowners.

4 History: Christianity

The religion of the early settlers to Barbados, of the metropole, and eventually of Barbados was Christianity. The first Church in Barbados built in 1628 close to the original landing site.[30] However, Christianity operated differently in Barbados as a slave society than it did in other British colonies. The majority of colonising missions were proselytising missions which concerned the spread of Christianity, many of which were characterised by forceful conversion or death. However, in Barbados, those with power withheld the Christian religion from slaves. Worthington Smith suggests justification for detaching slaves from religion included: the time spent receiving religious instruction could be better used for economic gains; fear of uprisings due to large congregations; increase in status due to learning to read and write; the breakdown of the inferior/superior dynamic in the minds of slaves through introducing the notion that all are equal before God; reduced dependency on their master; and introduction of a spiritual master, serving to reduce the power held by the slave master.[31]

Some of the earliest evidence of the withholding of Christianity is provided by Richard Ligon. Ligon was a royalist who left England to seek fortune in Barbados in 1647, and in 1657, he published a narrative of life on the island, detailing the landscape, flora and fauna, plantations and their inhabitants, alongside a newly created map. Within the narrative, Ligon recounts a conversation with a slave master, wherein a slave requested to be converted to Christianity.[32] Ligon spoke to the master, who replied "The people of that island were governed by the Laws of England, and by

[29] J Handler *The Unappropriated People, Freedman in the Slave Society of Barbados* (University of the West Indies Press, 2009) 15

[30] Hoyos

[31] R Worthington Smith, 'Slavery and Christianity in the British West Indies' Church History (1950) 171–186

[32] R Ligon, *A True & Exact History Of Barbados* (First Published 1657, Routledge, 2011) 101

those Laws, we could not make a Christian a Slave." Ligon informed the master that he wished the converse, to make a slave a Christian. The master responded: "being once a Christian, he could no more account him a Slave, and so lose the hold they had of them as Slaves, by making them Christians; and by that means should open such a gap, as all the Planters in the Island would curse him."[33] By this reasoning, Christians could not be slaves, nor slaves Christians.

This distinction, occurring through custom, was then codified in 1661through the *Slave Code*. The 1661 *Slave Code* explicitly linked race and religion throughout, with the terms 'Negro' and 'Christian' used to distinguish between slaves and free men. As 'Negro' were described as commodities and thus non-human, in juxtaposition those that were referred to as Christian were not only free, but also 'human' under the law, rendering them worthy of legal protection, rights and political recognition. The preamble of the *Slave Code* called for the protection of slaves "as we do many other goods and chattels, and also somewhat further as being created Men though without the knowledge of God in the world."[34] In doing so, it spoke to the lack of religious knowledge of slaves—noting their absent religious awareness and acknowledging the religious responsibility of those who were not slaves.

In contrast to other Caribbean islands, and despite calls from London from as early as 1661 to introduce slaves to Christianity,[35] the elite, those holding power, succeeded in keeping missionary movements and Quakers at bay throughout the period of slavery.[36]

5 The Role of Sex and Gender during Slavery

The unique set of relations formed through the economy of slavery in Barbados was not limited to race and religion, and extended into gender and family roles within the slave society.

5.1 Female Majority

Females comprised the majority of the population during slavery in Barbados, both with regards free white women,[37] enslaved black and mixed (termed mulatto in the

[33] Ibid

[34] Engerman, Drescher and Paquette *Slavery* (Oxford University Press, 2001) 105

[35] <https://tif.ssrc.org/2018/06/26/conversion-and-race-in-colonial-slavery/>

[36] K Gerbner, 'The Ultimate Sin: Christianising Slaves in Barbados in the Seventeenth Century' *Slavery & Abolition: A Journal of Slave and Post-Slave Studies* (2010) 59, 69–70

[37] C Jones 'Contesting the boundaries of gender, race and sexuality in Barbadian plantation society' Women's History Review (2003) 12:2, 195–232, 198

literature) race women.[38] This was unique, and in "marked contrast to the rest of the Caribbean".[39] Figures held from 1817 report the male to female ratio in Barbados as 86 males per 100 females.[40] Explaining the imbalance in slave numbers, Beckles posits a number of potential factors: indentured servants had carried out much of the land clearance, owner expectations with regards tasks did not distinguish male/female, and limits were yet to exist on the number of female slaves.

The data held comparing slave purchase price evidences female slaves consistently valued lower than male slaves:

> Ligon noted that males in Barbados were valued at £30, women at £25-27. By 1789 male and female field slaves were priced at £80-100, imported slaves, £50. Galenson found that from 1673 to 1723 female slaves were valued at about 85 percent of male slaves at auction markets in Barbados.[41]

These links, between demographic ratio in Barbados and cost are of particular interest when explored in relation to the natural increase in slave population which occurred in Barbados, a phenomenon unique to Barbados.[42] By 1800, 90% of the black population of Barbados was "island born".[43]

Research of enslavement in the US and Caribbean has recognised and explained the consistent failure of slave societies to successfully reproduce themselves, and has done so through consideration of "plantation work regimens, slaves' nutrition and disease incidence, gender imbalances, and women's intentionality" despite encouragement by owners and colonial authorities.[44] The distinctive position in which Barbados found itself, with both a female majority and the ability to reproduce, impacted Barbadian slave society, and in turn, aspects of developing Barbadian cultural and societal norms. This is, in part, attributable to the early creation of an identity forged through the experience of enslavement, producing unique kinds of cultural communities built around their shared experiences of slavery and exploitation.

---

[38] H Beckles, *Natural Rebels: A Social History of Enslaved Black Women in Barbados* (1989, Rutgers University Press, USA)

[39] C Johnson-Odim, 'Review: H Beckles, *Natural Rebels: A Social History of Enslaved Black Women in Barbados* (1989, Rutgers University Press, USA)' Ethnohistroy (1991) 38, 3, 347–349

[40] C.O. 28/86, Conrade Howell to Lord Combermere, 31 Oct. I817 (Public Record Office, London); Parliamentary Papers, 1832, XX (721), 521; C.O. 295/66, Folio 300; Parliamentary Papers, 1833, XXVI (539), 473–477.

[41] M Morrissey, *Slave Women in the New World: Gender Stratification in the Caribbean* (University Press of Kansas, 1989, 2021) 37

[42] Ibid xi

[43] J Morgan, *Reproduction and Creolization Among Slave Women* (University of Pennsylvania Press, USA 2004) 108

[44] M Morrissey, *Slave Women in the New World: Gender Stratification in the Caribbean* (University Press of Kansas, 1989, 2021) xi

5.2 *Interpretation of Sex*

Female slaves in Barbados inhabited a liminal space, straddling a European gendered order and an economic agenda whilst possessing reproductive capabilities essential for the continuation of slavery, ensuring the production of commodities and wealth.

On the one hand, evidence suggests their sex was irrelevant when measured against males for the purposes of their contribution to the production of sugar. In the provision of labour, female slaves were considered equal to their male counterpart in terms of work expected to be carried out.[45] Morrissey notes:

> There is virtually no task in Caribbean commodity production not at some time carried out by female slaves. Indeed, in the declining years of sugar production women generally outnumbered men and sometimes, with older slaves and children, achieved at least as high levels of per capita labor productivity as earlier generations of young, robust males.[46]

Barbados was established from a base of capitalist ideals, with unpaid labour exampling individualist economic goals. This was not only through the lack of exchange for labour (be that in the form of land, goods or money), but through its fundamental reduction of humans to property, enabling an expansion of individual wealth and capital through the commodification of human beings. Women, as men, were an asset, and as history, agency and autonomy were disregarded, so too were European gendered roles and behaviours with regards the roles, expectations and punishments of such assets. Bush notes "The labour regime ensured that women shared the same backbreaking work, miseries and punishments as men".[47]

However, whilst irrelevance and/or insignificance of sex was adopted for work directly concerning the production of sugar, research indicates that it did not apply with regards cost of slaves (female slaves were consistently valued lower than male), nor did it apply with regards domestic tasks. In their research analysing gender, race and sexuality in Barbadian plantation society, Jones details the instrumental role which white women played in the reconfiguration of gender identity within the enslaved population. A transfer of a European gendered order, behaviours, roles and ideals onto female slaves took place, and responsibility for the transference was held by white women. Jones notes:

> In the formative years of slavery, for instance, it is highly likely that such household tasks as instructing newly enslaved women in European methods and standards of food preparation, or in the care and cleaning of perhaps unfamiliar household items, would have fallen into the domain of 'woman's work', and thus the province of the plantation mistress, or in the absence of a mistress, to a white female servant/housekeeper.[48]

---

[45] P Downes, 'More Than Objects: Understanding Female Slaves in the Early Modern Period' MA Thesis (2015) CUNYC, 21

[46] Morrissey, citing Higman 1976a; Klein 1978, 33

[47] B Bush-Slimani 'Hard Labour: Women, Childbirth, Resistance in British Caribbean Slaves Societies' Colonial and Post-Colonial History (1993)36, 83–99

[48] C Jones 'Contesting the boundaries of gender, race and sexuality in Barbadian plantation society' Women's History Review (2003) 12:2, 195–232

Jones cites a letter, sent to Ireland in 1675 by a Barbadian planter, noting that 'washing, starching, making of drink, keeping the house in order' was 'no small task to undergoe', but he remained helpless without the assistance of a reliable white woman to instruct a recently purchased female slave in her new household duties.[49] Female slaves were expected to labour as male slaves, whilst also labouring in line with European gendered roles—assigned domestic tasks and behaviours.

Labour of female slaves was not confined to domestic and physical labour but included sexual and reproductive labour. Despite the adoption of banal language, sexual labour in this context is synonymous with rape and sexual assault. The sexual exploitation of slave women is well documented,[50] with its perpetration not restricted to, although primarily conducted by, white males. Seventeenth century plantation records indicate "the master enjoyed commandeering his prettiest slave girl and exacting his presumed rights from her."[51] Hilary Beckles cites John Oldmixon in 1708, reporting on the domestic lives of slave owners, noting that "the handsomest, cleanest black maidens are bred to menial services in order to satisfy their masters in divers ways".[52] Sexual exploitation was also carried out by slave-owning white females who would profit from the sale of sexual services by their female slaves.[53]

The participation of female slaves in reproductive labour is also well documented, in particular in the latter half of Barbados as a slave society.[54] Reproduction of slaves utilising the existing Barbadian slave population became preferable to reliance on the importation of slaves from Africa or elsewhere in the region. This extended the labour responsibilities of female slaves from domestic and physical labour to include the literal production of labour, termed the 'dual-burden' by Barbara Bush-Slimani.[55] As noted above, the status of a child born to a slave followed that of their mother[56] adhering to the Roman Law concept of *partus sequitur ventrem*,[57] a maxim traditionally used in relation to ownership of animals.[58] Early reasoning for adoption of the

---

[49] C Jones 'Contesting the boundaries of gender, race and sexuality in Barbadian plantation society' Women's History Review (2003) 12:2, 206

[50] S LaFont, 'Very Straight Sex: The Development of Sexual Morés in Jamaica' Journal of Colonialism and Colonial History (2001) 2 11

[51] R Dunn, *Sugar and Slaves: The Rise Of The Planter Class In The English West Indies, 1624–1713* (University of South Carolina Press, 2000) 253

[52] H Beckles *Centring Woman* (Ian Randle, 2012) 24

[53] H Beckles, *Natural Rebels: A Social History of Enslaved Black Women in Barbados* (1989, Rutgers University Press, USA)

[54] J Morgan *Laboring Women: Reproduction and Gender in New World Slavery* (University of Pennsylvania Press, 2004) and H Beckles *Centring Woman* (Ian Randle, 2012)

[55] B Bush-Slimani 'Hard Labour: Women, Childbirth, Resistance in British Caribbean Slaves Societies' Colonial and Post-Colonial History (1993)36, 83–99

[56] D J Cowles, 'Barbados' in Paul Joseph (Eds), *The SAGE Encyclopaedia of War: Social Science Perspectives* (SAGE Publications, 2016) 151

[57] R Tyree, 'On Slavery 9—Partus Sequitur Ventrem' <wigwags.wordpress.com/2008/12/01/On-Slavery-9-Partus-Sequitur-Ventrem/>

[58] J Handler, 'Custom and Law: The Status of Enslaved Africans in Seventeenth-Century Barbados' Slavery & Abolition (2016) 240

maxim was centred in the economic loss suffered during pregnancy and the likely unknown male. Application of the maxim compensated the owner of the female slave during pregnancy with a future slave, whilst ensuring the continued repopulation of slaves and simultaneously exploiting and commodifying female slaves not only for their contribution via physical and domestic labour, but also in reproductive labour through the provision of a supply of labour. Jones notes:

> Black women's bodies belonged neither to themselves, nor to their partners and husbands, but ultimately to white masters and mistresses. Perceptions of black women as sexually libidinous creatures also enabled white males to justify the routine sexual exploitation and abuse of black women.[59]

English authors perpetuated this perception of black bodies, manipulating representations of female slaves to focus on nudity, shamelessness and sexual availability, alongside painless childbirth and breast-feeding.[60] Focus on such aspects assisted in demonstrating their suitability for enslavement, dehumanising slave women and assigning characteristics which conformed to the propertied legal status under which they were enslaved.

The juxtaposition of irrelevance of sex with exploitation of sex is evident in the treatment of female slaves during pregnancy, the very period in which the maxim *partus sequitur ventrem* sought to compensate for. A pregnant slave produces one or more slaves for the slave owner, producing economic value, whilst they were in fact mandated to work throughout pregnancy with return required within weeks of childbirth.[61] The capital held in slaves was realised through reproduction, but not limited to it, as physical, domestic and reproductive labour operated almost simultaneously—economic value was duplicated, achieved through production of slave and continuing to be a slave, through a female slave creating future labour whilst operating as labour themselves.

Space does not permit an extensive discussion of the impact of *partus sequitur ventrem* and the operation of enslavement on slave/child relations, in particular the potential for or reality of removal of child or parent from the union. Being mindful not to essentialise the slave experience, motherhood and maternal feelings towards children are individualistic, and whilst assumptions may be made based on likelihood, evidence appears scant. Furthermore, despite the control held by owners regarding primary aspects of reproduction, from sex to motherhood, Morgan argues that slaves "understood themselves to be members of a community in the process of reproducing itself."[62]

---

[59] C Jones 'Contesting the boundaries of gender, race and sexuality in Barbadian plantation society' Women's History Review (2003) 12, 2, 216 citing B Bush 'Hard Labour: women, childbirth and resistance in British Caribbean slave societies' in D Barry Gaspar & Darlene Clark Hine (Eds) *More than Chattel: black women and slavery in the Americas* (Indiana University Press, 1996) 17–18.

[60] J Morgan *Laboring Women: Reproduction and Gender in New World Slavery* (University of Pennsylvania Press, 2004) 41

[61] B Bush-Slimani 'Hard Labour: Women, Childbirth, Resistance in British Caribbean Slaves Societies' Colonial and Post-Colonial History (1993)36, 83–99, 86

[62] J Morgan *Laboring Women: Reproduction and Gender in New World Slavery* (University of Pennsylvania Press, 2004) 139

5.3 Social Hierarchy

In *Slave Women in the New World*[63] Morrissey discusses two opposing critiques of slave relations and the gender hierarchy, evidencing tension between the structuralist, the traditional route of research and analysis, and the class analysis of culture. For the structuralist, cultural expression was constrained by the slavery, whereas the class analysis recognises levels of autonomy in "constructing kinship and other forms of culture."[64] Within the structuralist approach, perceived gender equality existed amongst slaves, achieved through the propertied nature of both enabling owner authority of each. Morrissey notes "Males' and females' equality was hence achieved by males' social decline rather than by females' social ascent."[65] Both male and female slaves held equal position under the law, both could be bought and sold, and suffer equal punishment. Neither had increased opportunities for resource acquisition or social mobility over and above the other (although some argue women were more likely to receive manumission than males).[66] Within the social hierarchy, they were situated in the same position in the order. Morrissey notes:

> The common perception that males and females were interchangeable to slaveholders derives from Caribbean slave women's unusually high level of participation in commodity export agriculture (Mathurin 1975, p.S; Patterson 1969, p. 167; 1982, pp. 173-174). Conceptions of gender equity based on slaves' nearly gender-free identities form an elegant notion and separate slavery from all other labor systems. Slave men and women were so fully subjugated, it is argued, that all marks of individuality and comparison except perhaps physical strength-were obliterated.[67]

However, this equality would have been disturbed by the operation of slavery, the role of slave owners in their dealings with each and with owners (and white women as noted above) possessing and transferring European gendered orders and/or stereotypes leading to distinction in treatment. Despite their equal propertied status under the law, women typically occupied unskilled agricultural tasks in field labour and work in domestic service, whilst males undertook more skilled tasks, such as carpentry, driving, fishing and as watchmen.[68]

[63] M Morrissey, *Slave Women in the New World: Gender Stratification in the Caribbean* (University Press of Kansas, 1989, 2021)

[64] Ibid 81

[65] Ibid 83

[66] B Bush, 'White 'Ladies,' Coloured 'Favourites' and Black 'Wenches': Some Considerations on Sex, Race and Class Factors in Social Relations in White Creole Society in the British Caribbean' Slavery & Abolition (1981) 2, 245–262.

[67] M Morrissey, *Slave Women in the New World: Gender Stratification in the Caribbean* (University Press of Kansas, 1989, 2021) 79

[68] Ibid 67

5.4 Slave Families

The legalised commodification of slaves as chattels, as property belonging to another, served to undermine traditional family structures. The proprietary rights of slave owners superseded that of parents of spouses, leaving families vulnerable to separation through the movement of members, be that by sale, bequeathment, use as security on loans etc. This disruption, or destruction, to family structure affected not only parenthood and marriage, but all familial relationships, including siblings, grandparents, aunts and uncles, cousins. Greenfield notes ""the slaves mated, but the plantation system denied them any family life."[69]

There is however evidence that this changed somewhat alongside the population changes in Barbados. As noted above, as slavery progressed, reliance transferred from the importation of slaves to a self-sustaining population, which in turn affected the stability of familial units. The following data is from Newton plantation, a sugar plantation in the south of Barbados, from 1796 which details whether mothers, fathers, wives husbands and children were residing on the same plantation (see Table 1).[70]

Table 1 Newton plantation.

Categories	Slaves with no family ties	Total slaves
Men	20	51
Women	13	59
Grown boys	1	7
Grown girls	3	16
Old women	3	14
Boys	4	35
Girls	3	45
Diseased	7	7
Doll's family	0	21
Total	54	255

For context, evidencing the self-sustaining population in Barbados, all but six of the slaves included in the above data had been born at Newton, three of those came from other parts of Barbados and three were born in Africa. None of those listed as 'diseased' had family ties, and the majority of those without family ties were male.

Broadly speaking, slave marriages were rare, with commentators arguing their incompatibility with the absolute ownership held by slave owners. Between 1827

[69] SM Greenfield *English Rustics in Black Skin* (College and University Press, 1966) as cited in B Higman, 'The Slave Family and Household in the British West Indies 1800–1834' The Journal of Interdisciplinary History (1975) 6, 2, 261–287, 261

[70] Newton Estate Papers, 523/288 'Report on where born, ages, employments, families, sexes' (1796, University of London Library

and 1834, available data for, Barbados lists 19 slave marriages having taken place.[71] Davis notes "marriage leads to a contractual relationship of authority and obedience, of reciprocal rights and obligations within a family, which is clearly incompatible with the concept of a master's absolute ownership of slaves."[72] However, there is evidence in Barbados that it was encouraged by some plantation owners/managers owing to its economic benefit in the anticipated production of slaves:

> I endeavour to lead them likewise into intermarriages at home, for a Negro man will run after his wife to the other end of the island and be back next morning to his work (…) I encourage their breeding as much as I can (…) I, therefore, when any marry in the estates give them a couple of dollars to set up house-keeping, and buy a young goat and a pig-if they agree for a twelve-month a couple more [dollars].[73]

For some slave owners, encouraging marriage encouraged reproduction, which when successful increased commodity ownership, increasing wealth and labour force, whilst operating under law providing the ability to disrupt such unions as required and/or desired.

Commentators have sought to explain the relatively low marriage rates between slaves through consideration of economic obligations, with their removal removing the role of slave men when compared to a non-enslaved partnership. Goveia notes:

> The "husband" was not an essential part of the slave family. It made little difference whether he was a free man or the slave of the same or another plantation. As long as his "wife" and children were the property of another, he had no legal rights over them, and they were not even dependent on him for their maintenance, since they received their allowances directly from the master.[74]

In addition to economic obligations, traditional aspects of marriage, such as monogamy and protection, may have been absent within slave unions. The propertied nature of slaves under law left both males and females without the ability to protect each other from the cruelties of slavery. Cruelty here concerns the core operation of slavery in itself, in addition to the physical, emotional and psychological cruelty slaves were subjected to. Further, sexual exploitation and rape was commonplace, disrupting the potential monogamy expected through third party intimacy, be that consensual or non-consensual.

---

[71] List of Marriages at Fairfield, Manchester, 1829–40; Carmel Church Book, 1813–37; List of the Members of the Congregation at Fairfield arranged according to the estates on which they reside, October 12, 1824 (Moravian Church Archives, Malvem, Jamaica); Church Book of the Mission of the United Brethren among the Negroes in the Island Barbadoes since the year I767, and particularly of the Negro-Congregation belonging to Sharon, St. Thomas Parish; Mount Tabor Moravian Church: List of Marriages

[72] D Davis *The Problem of Slavery in Western Culture* (Cornell University Press, USA, 1966) 104

[73] Newton Estate Papers, 523/381 'Report on where born, ages, employments, families, sexes' (1796, University of London Library, Sampson Wood to Thomas Lane 19th October 1798, as cited in B Higman, 'The Slave Family and Household in the British West Indies 1800–1834' The Journal of Interdisciplinary History (1975) 6, 2, 261–287, 270

[74] E Goveia, *Slave Society in the British Leeward Islands at the End of the Eighteenth Century* (Yale University Press, 1965) 235

The capacity of owners to disrupt and destroy familial units, alongside female capacity to feed, and the juxtaposing removal of gendered expectations with regards labour but imposition of European orders of gender are all pertinent in understanding the family structures which emerged, defined by many as matrifocal.

> It was the influence of slavery which insured that the matrifocal family would become the dominant family type among the Negro slaves.[75]

The term matrifocality was coined by Raymond Smith in 1966 following a study of families in Guyana (then British Guiana). The definition includes (but is not exclusive to) female headed households, wherein "women in their role as mothers (…) come to be the focus of relationships, rather than head of household as such",[76] focusing on the significance of women in a variety of roles, including of mothers and grandmothers in the Caribbean.

The gendered order established during enslavement saw multiple forms of exploitation imposed upon and endured by female slaves. An interrogation of the roles played by sex and gender in Barbados during enslavement produces a web of exceptional features, all of which have influenced the development of norms in Barbados. Further, any analysis of Barbados must be contextualised through consideration of one integral feature—a lacking indigenous population, contrasting to many colonised states.

6 The Role of Christianity

The role of Christianity in Barbados was unique, with slave owners actively preventing the access of slaves to Christianity. Christianity was used as a tool to both control and distinguish between groups within a slave society, identifying through law who was to be recognised as chattels and treated as property belonging to another. Contrasting to many colonised states, no pre-existing framework of faith existed, as no indigenous population existed. This enabled Christianity to move freely across the Atlantic with the early settlers, permitting selected implementation of religion to take place with consideration centred in the maintenance of an economy created through, held up and enabled by slavery.

Only those in society who were free, which included indentured servants[77] were permitted access to the faith. Such a rigid exclusion laid the foundations for a relationship between humanity, freedom, and Christianity. Contextualised within a framework of time, rejection of slave's access to the Christian faith started with the initial settlement of Barbados in 1625 and continued until 1834/8, when slavery was abolished.

---

[75] Ibid 237

[76] R Smith *The Matrifocal Family* (New York, Routledge, 1996)

[77] See Slave Code 1661 which separated Negroes and Christians

6.1 Enslavement

Christianity was reserved for free persons in Barbados during enslavement, in contrast to the manner in which religion was enforced on both colonised[78] and other slave states.[79] Slaves were, in the main, refused access, enabling Christianity to become synonymous with humanity. It acted as an identifier of "Anglo-Barbadians as both English and free".[80] As noted by Katherine Gerbner "[t]he planter elite believed that their status as Protestants was inseparable from their identity as free Englishmen"[81] and in discussing church inscriptions in Barbados noted "these monumental inscriptions were a testament to the social and political power of the planter elite, who saw the church as central to their personal and public lives."[82] Christianity was synonymous with "being human", or at least not being the property of another. The baptism of slaves was described as "the ultimate sin" and was vehemently opposed by the Barbadian elite.[83] Those against any religious instruction of slaves argued that religion:

> had the effect of producing in the minds of the slaves a belief that they could not serve both a spiritual and a temporal master; thereby occasioning themselves to resist the lawful authority of their temporal master, under the delusion of rendering themselves more acceptable to a spiritual master[84]

This continued throughout slavery, with the 1795 "Instructions Issued to Missionaries of the Established Church," warning:

> never to attempt to instruct, or to educate the Negro slaves of any plantation without the consent and approbation of the proprietor of that plantation (and to) dwell most strongly and frequently on the great practical duties of piety, and obedience to their masters, contentment, patience, and resignation to the will of heaven.[85]

This warning placed the slave owner as their God, using religious language to define the relationship between slave owner and slave.

As the legal abolition of slavery drew closer, the metropole encouraged improvements in the treatment of slaves, which was done through linking Christianity and

---

[78] *The philosophy of colonialism: civilization, Christianity, and commerce* available at: <https://scholarblogs.emory.edu/violenceinafrica/sample-page/the-philosophy-of-colonialism-civilization-christianity-and-commerce/>

[79] R Dunn, *Sugar and Slaves: The Rise Of The Planter Class In The English West Indies, 1624–1713* (University of South Carolina Press, 2000) 249

[80] K Gerbner, 'Christian Slavery: Protestant Missions and Slave Conversion in the Atlantic World, 1660–1760' (Doctoral dissertation, Harvard University 2013) 38

[81] Ibid 1

[82] Ibid 35

[83] K Gerbner 'Conversion and Race in Colonial Slavery', 2018, blog post (https://tif.ssrc.org/2018/06/26/conversion-and-race-in-colonial-slavery/) 57–73

[84] S Gordon, *A Century of West Indian Education-A Source Book* (Longmans, 1963) 10

[85] R Proctor, 'Early Developments in Barbadian Education' The Journal of Negro Education (1980) 49, 2 citing J Latimer, 'The Foundation of Religious Education in the British West Indies' The Journal of Negro Education (1965) 436–437

one's access to it to legal rights and recognition. This is exampled in the *Consolidated Slave Law 1825*, which admitted 'Negroes' to give evidence in court[86] provided several conditions were met. Conditions included the production of records of baptism along with a declaration certifying instruction in the Christian religion, their knowledge of a Deity and their acquaintance with the Christian doctrine, signed by a clergyman of the Established Church.[87] Prior to giving evidence, "the slave was to be first examined by the court as to his proficiency in the knowledge of the Christian doctrine".[88] Analysing the restrictions, Claude Levy noted "(...) the terms of the law virtually excluded the servile population from giving evidence"[89] as they had been denied access to such knowledge. Law aligning Christian knowledge and practice to the recognition rights reaffirmed the relationship between Christianity and freedom, humanity and capacity.

6.2 Abolition

During the campaign for abolition, Christianity was used as a method to save those who were enslaved, the same slaves whom it had previously rejected, and it was the language of the abolitionists. The withholding of Christianity throughout slavery angered abolitionists, who utilised the lack of religious exposure in their arguments for abolishing slavery. As noted by Gerbner:

> (b)y the late eighteenth century, it was easy for abolitionists to claim that the sugar islands were islands of depravity and to evoke the deep well of criticism focusing on the planters' refusal to convert their slaves. Planters' failure to even pay lip service to the missionary movement enraged abolitionists in Europe who made strong and successful arguments against the slave trade on moral and religious grounds.[90]

The arguments for abolition were both moral and religious—slavery is immoral and this is in part due to slaves lack of religious exposure; therefore, non-exposure to religion is immoral, and conversely, religion determines morality.

This use of Christianity is demonstrated through the acts of William Wilberforce, one of the most familiar anti-slavery campaigners of the 18th and nineteenth century. In a quest to spread Christianity, in 1791, William Wilberforce was instrumental in the establishment of the Sierra Leone Company, an initiative which sought to "provide

[86] C Levy, 'Barbados: The Last Years of Slavery 1823–1833' The Journal of Negro History (1959) 44, 4, 317

[87] House of Commons Debate, State of Slavery in the Colonies Hose of Commons debate 19 May 1826 (15 cc1284–3,661,306)

[88] Ibid

[89] C Levy, 'Barbados: The Last Years of Slavery 1823–1833' The Journal of Negro History (1959) 44, 4

[90] K Gerbner, *Christian Slavery, Conversion and Race in the Protestant Atlantic World* (University of Pennsylvania Press, 2018) 224

a basis for legitimate commerce and the spread of Christianity in West Africa".[91] In 1860, the link between Christianity and commerce was described as necessary, as:

> there is little hope of promoting commerce in Africa, unless Christianity is planted in it; and, in the next place, there is very little ground for hoping that Christianity will be able to make its proper way unless we can establish a lawful commerce in the country (...) (Christianity has the) effect of training the human race to a degree of excellence which it could never attain in non-Christian countries', giving 'value to life', 'dignity to labour' and 'security to possession', with the result that a Christian people would tend to be 'a wealth-producing people, an exporting people and so a commercial people[92]

The desire to disseminate Christianity manifested itself in Wilberforce's abolitionist campaigns, wherein Wilberforce's arguments for abolition included the expansion of commerce and that slaves themselves should have the opportunity to hear and respond to the Christian Gospel.[93] Professor Wolffe cites this desire to spread Christianity as central to Wilberforce's campaign:

> In relation to slavery, while he was happy to deploy an extensive armoury of rational argument, his underlying preoccupations were that the British nation should be true to its Christian identity, and that the slaves themselves should have the opportunity to hear and respond to the Christian Gospel.[94]

The above continues: "Herein for him lay the path not only of religious duty but of national self-interest, because in the West Indies, as in Britain, a Christian people would also be an orderly one."[95]

As noted by Michael Cranton:

> Humanising the slave system was imperative, but "civilising" the slaves was of more primary importance even than granting them freedom (...) Even the Quakers, abolitionist pioneers, seem to have wanted to free the slaves only into social and economic responsibility; to bring them from the status of outcasts into a society with God-determined "unequal stations"; free to enjoy the "burdens and coercions of the Protestant work ethic"; Sunday schools and savings banks.[96]

The abolitionists succeeded, and slavery was abolished between 1834–1838. The period 1834–1838, or 1834/38 has been used throughout this chapter, as despite 1834 representing when the Emancipation Act 1833 came into force, with the Act came an apprenticeship system. Apprenticeship was mandated for all slaves, presented as a

---

[91] J Wolffe 'Wilberforce', Open University available at: <https://www.open.edu/openlearn/ocw/mod/oucontent/view.php?id=1698&printable=1 para 5.2>

[92] S Wilberforce, *Speeches on missions* (ed. Rev. Henry Rowley) (London, I874), as cited in A Potter, 'Commerce and Christianity': The Rise and Fall of a Nineteenth-Century Missionary Slogan' The Historical Journal (1985) 28, 3597–598

[93] Ibid

[94] Ibid

[95] Ibid

[96] D Davis, *The Problem of Slavery in the Age of Revolution, 1770–1823* (Cornell University Press, 1975) 254 as cited in M Craton, 'Christianity, and Slavery in the British West Indies 1750–1865', Historical Reflections (1978) 5, 2, 146

plan to prepare the once enslaved for freedom through "instruction and conversion"[97] as "the great mass of them had remained non-Christian and illiterate"[98] whilst maintaining a labour force providing costless labour to ensure plantation productivity. Despite the original intention of six years apprenticeship for field slaves, the system was abolished in 1838. Through the mandating of apprenticeship, the labour conditions of enslavement were preserved with the introduction of Christian instruction, meaning that whilst this period is not enslavement, as persons were no longer propertised by law, it is also not easily distinguishable from enslavement as the law continue to mandate ex-slaves work without pay for a defined period, albeit whilst recognising their humanity.

With the abolition of slavery, Christianity and freedom were further integrated, amplifying the already established norm of religion evidencing humanity and freedom.

6.3 Postenslavement

After freeing slaves, Christianity served as the primary tool used to educate those who it had originally refused and then saved. As education was denied to slaves, after emancipation educational institutions and curriculum became increasingly bound up with Christianity. As Blouet notes:

> (i)t was felt, especially in missionary circles, that a religious moral educational policy should accompany emancipation. The development of mass education for the population offered a way in which to effect a reformation of the blacks—a way in which to (C)hristianize, civilize, humanize and, in the final analysis, Anglicize.[99]

The entrenchment of Christianity was cemented by recommendations of the Committee of the Council on Education, who in their report of 1846–1847 recommended "that the curriculum of the primary schools should include, first, as the backbone, religious education (…) The Bible was the principal textbook".[100] Once slaves were permitted to become Christians and to exercise the faith freely, they benefitted from the privileges that came with being recognised as human—education, equality of status, rights, freedom and liberties, serving to highlight the paradox of the saviour narrative.[101]

These unique historical conditions provided the context whereby newly freed men and women drew on the Christian narrative that was associated with becoming human

---

[97] J Latimer, 'The Apprenticeship System in the British West Indies' The Journal of Negro Education (1964) 33, 1, 52–57

[98] Ibid

[99] O M Blouet 'Education and Emancipation in Barbados, 1833–1846: A Study in Cultural Transference' Ethnic and Racial Studies, (1981) 4,2, 232

[100] Ibid 192

[101] F Vergès, 'The White Saviour or Racism Without Race', Unmaking Colonial History, (2020) Roxa Luxemburg Stiftung, Brussels

in the development of new laws—those who were "freed" as a result of Christian beliefs felt it necessary to include Christian beliefs, practices, and doctrines into the development of their own legal system. Christian language, imagery and doctrine remain present in case law and demonstrates how the relationship between Christianity, slavery and the law remains.[102] The situating of analysis of Christianity in Barbados should be contextualised against a backdrop of its use with regards slavery, recognising the humanising, freeing, organising and educating roles which it played during enslavement, abolition, postenslavement and nation building. Christianity serves as a constant thread which runs throughout Barbadian history, used as an indicator of humanity and freedom.

7 Conclusion

The impact of slavery on Barbados cannot be overstated, and warrants extensive investigation and analysis to continue producing an understanding of how it has influenced Barbados and continues to do so. The roles of sex and gender during enslavement, and the role of Christianity during and post enslavement are but two themes which serve to distinguish slavery in Barbados, and echo the call for increased understanding through nuanced inquiry.

References

Bibliography

Barbados Integrated Government Statistics, 2010 Census

Bartlett R (2002) England under the Norman and Angevin kings: 1075–1255 (new Oxford history of England). Oxford University Press, UK

Beckles H Natural rebels: a social history of enslaved black women in Barbados (Rutgers University Press, USA, 1989)

Beckles H centring woman (Ian Randle, 2012)

Beckles H (2017) On Barbados, the first black slave society, Black Perspectives, AAIHS

Blouet OM (1981) Education and emancipation in Barbados, 1833–1846: a study in cultural transference. Ethn Racial Stud 4:2

Browne D (1721) Historical collections of private passages of state, vol 2, London, pp 1629–1623

Bush B (1981) White 'ladies,' coloured 'favourites' and black 'wenches': some considerations on sex, race and class factors in social relations in white creole Society in the British Caribbean. Slavery & Abolition 2:245–262

[102] See case authorities listed in the references; L Lazarus 'The Church and the Law: Examining the Role of Christianity in Shaping Sexual Politics in Jamaica' (PhD dissertation, York University, 2013) citing J Soares, 'Eden After Eve: Christian Fundamentalism and Women in Barbados' in *Nation Dance: Religion, Identity, and Cultural Difference in the Caribbean*, (eds P Taylor) (Indiana University Press, 2001) 108. See various weblinks listed in the references.

Bush B (1996) Hard Labour: women, childbirth and resistance in British Caribbean slave societies. In: Barry Gaspar D, Hine DC (eds) More than chattel: black women and slavery in the Americas. Indiana University Press
Bush-Slimani B (1993) 'Hard Labour: women, childbirth, resistance in British Caribbean slaves societies' colonial and post-colonial. History 36:83–99
C.O. 28/86, Conrade Howell to Lord Combermere, 31 Oct. I817 (Public Record Office, London); Parliamentary Papers, 1832, XX (721), 521; C.O. 295/66, Folio 300; Parliamentary Papers, 1833, XXVI (539), 473-477C Petley, Plantations in the Atlantic World (Oxford Biographies, 2018)
Cowles D J 'Barbados' In Paul Joseph (Eds), The SAGE encyclopaedia of war: social science perspectives (SAGE Publications, 2016)
Craton M (1978) Christianity, and slavery in the British West Indies 1750-1865. Historical Reflections 5:2
Davis D (1966) The problem of slavery in Western culture. Cornell University Press, USA
Davis D (1975) The problem of slavery in the age of revolution, 1770–1823. Cornell University Press, USA
Downes P (2015) 'More than objects: understanding female slaves in the early modern period' MA thesis. CUNYC:21
Dunn Sugar R (2000) Slaves: the rise of the planter class in the English West Indies, 1624–1713. Chapel Hill, University of North Carolina Press, USA
Dwyer S (2007) Caribbean exchanges: slavery and the transformation of English society, 1640–1700. University Of North Carolina Press, USA
Eltis D (2000) Europeans and the rise and fall of African slavery in the Americas: an interpretation. Am Hist Rev 98:5
Engerman (2001) Drescher and Paquette slavery. Oxford University Press, UK
FA Hoyos Barbados (1978) A history from Amerindians to Independence. Macmillan Publishers
Galenson D (1982) The Atlantic slave trade and the Barbados market, 1673-1723. J Econ Hist 42:3
Gerbner K (2013) Christian slavery: Protestant missions and slave conversion in the Atlantic world, 1660–1760.' (Doctoral dissertation,. Harvard University
Gerbner K (2018a) Christian slavery, conversion and race in the Protestant Atlantic world. University of Pennsylvania Press, USA
Gordon S (1963) A century of west Indian education-a source book, Longmans
Goveia E Slave Society in the British Leeward Islands at the end of the eighteenth century (Yale University Press, 1965)
Handler J (2016) Custom and law: the status of enslaved Africans in seventeenth-century Barbados. Slavery & Abolition:240
Handler J, Jacoby J (1996) Slave names and naming in Barbados, 1650-1830. The William and Mary Quarterly, Third Series 689
Handler J, The Unappropriated People (2009) Freedman in the slave Society of Barbados. University of the West Indies Press
Higman B (1975) The slave family and household in the British West Indies 1800-1834. J Interdiscip Hist 6:2
Higman B (2000) The Sugar revolution. Economic History Review LIII:3 213
House of Commons Debate, State of Slavery in the Colonies Hose of Commons debate 19 May 1826 (15 cc1284–366 1306)
C Johnson-Odim 'Review: H Beckles, Natural Rebels: A Social History of Enslaved Black Women in Barbados (1989, Rutgers University Press, USA)' Ethnohistroy (1991) 38, 3
Jones C (2003) Contesting the boundaries of gender, race and sexuality in Barbadian plantation society. Women's Hist Rev 12:2
Knorr K (1944) British colonial theories 1570–1850. University of Toronto Press, Canada
LaFont S (2001) Very straight sex: the development of sexual Morés in Jamaica. J Colon Colon Hist 2:11
Latimer J (1964) 'The apprenticeship system in the British West Indies' the. J Negro Educ 33:1

Lazarus L (2013) Thc church and thc law: examining the role of Christianity in shaping sexual politics in Jamaica.' (PhD dissertation,. York University
Levy C (1959) Barbados: the last years of slavery 1823-1833. The Journal of Negro History 44:4
Ligon R A True & exact history of Barbados (first published 1657, Routledge, 2011)
Marriage records: List of Marriages at Fairfield, Manchester, 1829–40; Carmel Church Book, 1813–37; List of the Members of the Congregation at Fairfield arranged according to the estates on which thcy rcside, October 12, 1824 (Moravian Church Archives, Malvem, Jamaica); Church Book of the Mission of the United Brethren among the Negroes in the Island Barbadoes since the year I767, and particularly of the Negro-Congregation belonging to Sharon, St. Thomas Parish; Mount Tabor Moravian Church: List of Marriages
Morgan J (2004a) Laboring women: reproduction and gender in New World slavery. University of Pennsylvania Press, USA
Morgan J (2004b) Reproduction and creolization among slave women. University of Pennsylvania Press, USA
M Morrissey, Slave women in the New World: gender stratification in the Caribbean (University Press of Kansas, 1989, 2021)
Newton Estate Papers, 523/288 'Report on where born, ages, employments, families, sexes' (1796, University of London Library)
Newton Estate Papers, 523/381 'Report on where born, ages, employments, families, sexes' (1796, University of London Library, Sampson Wood to Thomas Lane 19th October 1798)
Nicholls W (1969) Barbados: a case study of the plantation economy. Master of Arts, McGill University
S O'Callaghan To hell or Barbados: the ethnic cleansing of Ireland (Brandon Publishing, 2016)
O'Neill A (2022) Slave arrivals to the British Caribbean by region and century 1606–1842. published via Statista Research Service
P Gilroy The Black Atlantic (Verso, 1993)
H Prasier The adventure guide to Barbados, Caribbean guide series (Hunter Publications, 1990)
R Proctor 'Early Developments in Barbadian Education' The Journal of Negro Education (1980) 49, 2 citing J Latimer, 'The Foundation of Religious Education in the British West Indies' The Journal of Negro Education (1965)
Rushworth J (1686) Hearsay report: historical collections, London, pp 468–469
Santos B (2015) If god were a human rights activist. Stanford University Press, USA
Slave Code 1661 (Barbados)
(2010) K Gerbner 'the ultimate sin: Christianising slaves in Barbados in the seventeenth century'. Slavery & Abolition: A Journal of Slave and Post-Slave Studies 59:69–70
SM greenfield English rustics in black skin (College and University Press, 1966)
Smith RW (1950) Slavery and Christianity in the British West Indies. Church History
Smith R (1996) The matrifocal family. Routledge, New York
Soares J (2001) Eden After Eve: Christian Fundamentalism and Women in Barbados. In: Taylor P (ed) Nation dance: religion, identity, and cultural difference in the Caribbean. Indiana University Press
Vergès F 'The White Saviour or Racism Without Race', Unmaking Colonial History (2020) Roxa Luxemburg Stiftung, Brussels
Wilberforce S, Speeches on missions (ed. Rev. Henry Rowley) (London, I874), as cited in A Potter, 'Commerce and Christianity': The Rise and Fall of a Nineteenth-Century Missionary Slogan' The Historical Journal (1985) 28, 3

Weblinks

Gerbner K 'Conversion and Race in Colonial Slavery', 2018b, blog post https://tif.ssrc.org/2018/06/26/conversion-and-race-in-colonial-slavery/

The philosophy of colonialism: civilization, Christianity, and commerce. https://scholarblogs.emory.edu/violenceinafrica/sample-page/the-philosophy-of-colonialism-civilization-christianity-and-commerce/
Tyree R, 'On Slavery 9—Partus Sequitur Ventrem'. wigwags.wordpress.com/2008/12/01/On-Slavery-9-Partus-Sequitur-Ventrem/
Wolffe J 'Wilberforce', Open University. https://www.open.edu/openlearn/ocw/mod/oucontent/view.php?id=1698&printable=1 para 5.2

Case Authorities

Re Griffith, Tennyson, Harris et al, BB 2005 HC 21
v D (2010a) The Queen BB. CA:23
v M (2010b) The queen BB. CA:8
v S (2015) The queen BB. CA:3
v S (2016) Clarke BB. HC:36

Jill St George is a lecturer in law at the Open University, UK. Jill's research interests are in gender, sexuality and slavery in the Commonwealth Caribbean.

Orthodox Religious Tradition and Gender 'Distinctiveness': Mary's Iconology and Its Transformative Projections on Female Imagery

Simona Fabiola Girneata

Abstract The Christian Orthodox thought, when structuring the roles of men and women in society, pursues the values of justice and equity among human beings. This approach to gender equality results in a binary view of women and men with respect to their roles. This means that equality is declined according to aspects of justice relying on Christian moral standards and corresponding personal icons. The prime example that structures the role of women in the community is above all that of Mary, the mother of God. But the relationship of the Orthodox Church with this example is not always as linear as it might appear from a superficial reading of the personal and global history of this character. Indeed, on the one hand Mary represents the icon of the mother and wife, but on the other hand she also represents the image of a strong female self-determination, of an independence from the male figure that is ahistorical if we think of the context in which she lived. For this reason, the reflection to be made on the Orthodox Church's contribution in shaping 'gender roles' is profound and should not be limited to criticism alone, but to an in-depth study of the symbolic universe that, although it may seem anchored to a monolithic and static traditionalism, creatively transforms itself over the years and adapts to new contexts such as the diaspora. The Orthodox diaspora represents a privileged laboratory where anthropology associated with the study of human rights can investigate these new phenomena, allowing and supporting intersectional feminisms to focus on the complexity of this reality. Pausing in doubt can be a good practice to find new tools co-constructed with and for communities, so that feminisms can inhabit these spaces and defuse mechanisms of gender violence that are structural and structured over time by incomplete narratives.

Keywords Gender · Mary · Feminism · Christian Orthodoxy · Human Rights · Legal Anthropology

S. F. Girneata (✉)
University of Rome La Sapienza, Rome, Italy

A. Condello and A. Wagner (eds.), *Gender Stereotypes*, Gender, Justice and Legal Feminism 2, https://doi.org/10.1007/978-3-031-63905-0_20

1 Introduction

This article aims to develop an in-depth analysis of the figure of Mary, Mother of God, within Romanian Orthodox Christian communities, adopting an anthropological approach that engages both an anthropological-theological perspective and an investigation of contemporary social dynamics. The first part of the article provides a historical reconstruction of the figure of Mary, examining her development within Orthodox theology and her role as mediatrix, as well as the symbolism associated with divine motherhood. Through a reading of sacred texts and patristic tradition, I will investigate how the figure of Mary has progressively assumed a central position in Orthodox devotion, becoming an important key to understanding both the theological dimension and discourse over the years, as well as the individual and collective faith and spirituality of the communities I will be analysing.

In the second part, the result of fieldwork reveals how the figure of Mary influences Orthodox women today within their communities. It will examine how her image shapes women's imagery, religious practices and their social roles. Mary, while representing an ideal of humility and obedience, can also be interpreted as a subversive figure, as she offers an example of spiritual capacity, toughness and autonomy. She also demonstrates strong creative agency, capable of rethinking the world around her. Orthodox women can find in Mary a source of empowerment and identification, seeing her not only as a submissive mother, but as a woman who wields significant spiritual power. Through the analysis of testimonies and personal experiences, an attempt will be made to understand how Orthodox women have reinterpreted the Marian model within their lives, often in contrast with the traditional idea of their roles.

Moreover, by interweaving the biblical experience of Mary with the everyday experiences of these women, the essay will explore how her figure can represent a model capable of deconstructing stereotypical narratives, offering a new key to understanding forms of female subordination. It will analyse if and how the figure of Mary can be reinterpreted as an icon of resistance and transformation, stimulating a debate on feminist demands within orthodox Christianity.

Finally, the article will attempt to show how Mary, while often represented through ideals of obedience, can be reinterpreted as a figure who challenges patriarchal structures, allowing for a more inclusive and equal reinterpretation and future writing of human history within the Orthodox Church and society. This re-reading will explore how religion - considered in this paper not only in denominational terms but as a meaning-making agency, a kind of unremitting source of world-production, can be compatible with modern claims for gender equality, providing fertile ground for a dialogue between theology, anthropology and human rights.

2 Mary in Theological Interpretations: A Silent Revolution of the Gender Category

During a fieldwork in Romania, I happen to be in one a very amazing (and somewhat unusual) bar in Timisoara, a place for gathering and discussion. On the ground floor one enters a sort of museum of communist consumerism, full of objects typical of the regime period. On the upper floor there is an amphitheatre managed by a feminist collective that stages performances by street artists. Whitin this ambience I am surprised to find a small statuette of the Praying Madonna, covered with coins, flowers and banknotes offered by customers. In a 'revolutionary' context linked to an apparently secularised symbolic dimension, completely at odds with conservative Romania and linked to the Christian Orthodox religion, the 'mascot', the 'centrepiece of the collection', was precisely a depiction of the mother of God, a symbol seemingly completely out of place.

I sit at the table in front of this statuette, and to each person I see approaching it and leaving a donation, I ask why they to that. Many answer that they are not practising Orthodox, but that they pray to Mary because she represents a maternal symbol, the great mother, the one who rewrote the fate of humanity. When I ask the manager of the place why she had chosen that statuette as a symbol, she replies: 'anyone who dreams of change is inspired by the story of Mary, after all, her choice was revolutionary'.

Understanding how Mary's choice was 'revolutionary' in that particular ambience requires in-depth analysis from a theological, historical and anthropological perspective, areas in which relevant symbolic and social dimensions are intertwined. In this context, I will limit myself to providing some insights into the significance of this figure and its impact on culture and gender dynamics.

The presence of the mother of God in the Christian Orthodox economy of salvation appears to be fundamental. In fact, studying the sources it emerges that 'one of the indispensable conditions' of the incarnation was precisely the appearance of a woman in the world, a virgin, from whom God would become man[1]. Mary, however, is not presented as an ordinary character on a historical level. She belonged to the royal lineage of David, for the Virgin Mary's father, Joachim, was descended from Nathan, son of David. Her mother, Anne, belonged to the lineage of Aaron, hence Mary was, on her father's side, of royal lineage and, on her mother's side, of priestly lineage. St Nicodemus the Hagiorite reminds us that Mary's birth itself was a very special and unique event in the Old Testament.[2] Although other women miraculously conceived children after years of infertility, such as Sarah, Rachel or Samson's mother, all of them gave birth to sons. The only one to give birth to a daughter was Anne, the barren one: who was Mary's mother. The exception in the sequence of sons, is interpreted as evidence that Mary was the chosen one to bring the Son of God to earth.

[1] In particular, this pertains to the reflections of Athanasios (2012).

[2] Cfr. Sfântul Nicodim Aghioritul (2022).

Mary spent a life, described by the Church Fathers, as 'most pure'. She dwelled for 15 years of her life in the Temple in Jerusalem, in the Holy of Holies[3]. According to the teaching of St Gregory Palamas, when she was brought to the Temple at the age of three, "not only did she enter the Holy of Holies, but she also found a dwelling place there, for she was consecrated to God for more than a few years, and through her the heavens will open at the proper time and be given as an eternal dwelling place to those who believe in her miraculous birth".[4]

In many patristic writings, the Church Fathers state that the Son of God delayed his coming for a long time, and the timing of the birth and life of the mother of God constituted an element of that divine 'Kairos' of the Incarnation[5]. However, as Lossky points out, the entire Christic revolution, the history of humanity, and every realisation of the divine plan depended on Mary's choice and free will[6]. Although predestined, she could oppose such a task, especially given the repercussions this choice could have on her life. If we retrospectively consider the historical conditions in which she lived, we find a profoundly misogynistic and violent environment, in which pregnancy out of wedlock would have been a death sentence. Yet her faith not only saved her, but she herself attained salvation in profound terms, bringing into the world the one who 'is' predestined to save humanity. Woman and man, one through and in the other, erased the boundaries between them, Christ having come through his mother's womb, together in a *unicum* that revolutionised the known world. This event was made possible respectively by the act of humility of Christ who became man and came into the world by being born from his mother's womb, and, on the other hand, by Mary's act of humility, according to which she said "Behold, I am the handmaid of the Lord; let it be to me according to your word. And the angel departed from her".[7]

In the Byzantine tradition, Orthodox theologians tend represent Mary as the antithesis of Eve[8], as the one who washed away the original sin produced by the first woman. I, however, am aligned to an opposing current of interpretation[9]. I find a strong continuity between the two. Eve is the mother of humanity, without her action

[3] In order to reconstruct the life history of Mary, I specifically relied on the writings of Maximus the Confessor. I utilized translated and adapted sources from Romanian publishers to gain a deeper understanding of the framework of the Romanian Orthodox Church, see: Epifanie Monahul et al. (2007).

[4] Sfântul Grigorie Palama (2007).

[5] Numerous Romanian authors have examined the question of incarnation within patristic writings; specifically, I refer to the works of Petroaia (2005).

[6] Cfr. Lossky (1984).

[7] Luke 1:38

[8] In Origen's reflection, structured in his three levels of biblical interpretation: body, soul, and spirit; Mary emerges as the antithesis of Eve. This framework suggests that while Eve, in her disobedience, embodies the fallibility of humanity and the introduction of sin, Mary, through her obedience and acceptance of God's will, symbolizes redemption and the restoration of humanity's relationship with the divine. Thus, Origen positions Mary not only as a pivotal figure in salvation history but also as a model for spiritual ascent, contrasting sharply with the narrative of Eve, Origen (1902).

[9] In this regard, feminist theologian Harrison proposes very interesting remarks: (2008).

there would have been no beginning and no Revelation of the project of Salvation, which is in turn re-actualized through the apparent non-action, the non-sin of Mary, the mother of God. The 'second Eve' or the 'New Eve', in analogy with the title 'New Adam' attributed to Christ, becomes the protagonist of the salvation of mankind. It is no coincidence that, similarly to Christ, the Virgin Mary is commemorated for both her birth and death in the liturgical calendar. Indeed, her figure occupies a prominent position in the temporal and symbolic structure of the Orthodox Church, remaining a mirror-like presence to Christ not only on a theological level, but also in the construction of sacred time. The numerous festivities dedicated to Mary highlight her central role in the Christian narrative of salvation and contribute to the configuration of liturgical time as a continuum in which Mother and Son coexist and interact. This chronological symmetry between Christ and Mary underlines how Orthodox time is built around a system of sacred relationships that integrate divine and human space. Mary thus becomes not only a spiritual, but also a cosmological reference point, contributing to the creation of a sacred time that represents the harmony between heaven and earth. A harmony that is broken with the expulsion from Eden and is recomposed in the forgiveness of Christ on the Cross.

The analysis of the sacred texts shows a clear distinction between the destiny of Eve and that of the Virgin Mary: while Eve receives the curse of bearing children in pain and being subordinate to man, Mary is exalted through the Archangel Gabriel's proclamation: "Rejoice, full of grace!"[10]. Here, an essential paradigm shift becomes evident. If we were to reason in terms of the patriarchal cultural norms of the time, Mary should be considered the 'most sinful' of women, having conceived a child outside her marriage. But through her choice, to welcome the Son of Man, she defies the customary social and biological order. However, this choice would have meant much less if it did not complement Eve's decision to disobey God and eat of the fruit of knowledge. Mary disobeys the system, and listens to herself, her faith. But Eve too disobeys the system, the economy of the Garden of Eden, to fulfil her destiny. The reverse orientation of self-determination exerted by these two figures is rarely portrayed in a mirror-image fashion, but in my view each becomes a projection of the other. Mary's capacity for self-assertion invests her with extraordinary authority. The worship reserved for the Virgin Mary, in fact, exceeds the veneration accorded to any human being, without however violating the theological principle of the distinction between the worship due exclusively to God and the veneration directed to the saints. In a nutshell, the importance of the Virgin Mary in the Orthodox context cannot be underestimated. Her centrality in theology and worship is a significant example of the discrepancies that sometimes emerge between formal representations of religion and concrete practices. The veneration of Mary takes on not only a theological, but also a juridical-social dimension, as her figure is legitimised and reinforced within community and ritual dynamics.

Mary is not just a woman. She is first of all God, before both man and woman. It is God who makes Himself a gift, a womb, a hospitable emptiness from which being germinates. By accepting to host Jesus, Mary accepts becoming the very principle of

---

[10] Luke 1:28

creation. If in the Genesis passage 'In the beginning God created...'[11], Christ is 'the beginning', Mary is the 'in'. She humbly becomes Chora[12], renouncing determination to arise indeterminate, infinite, beyond all determination. Chora receives everything, without ever taking the form of the objects that become part of it. She is made to be a model for all things, moving and taking the form of what she receives; and that is why she seems different every time.

In accepting to become the mother of God, Mary assumes a fundamental role in Orthodox theology. In restoration anthropology, in fact, when traditionalist theologians refer to deification (theosis), they mean the whole of human nature, not just a part of it, whether female or male. The theological cornerstone lies in the fact that human nature is not a static autonomous entity, but a dynamic reality whose essential determination is its relationship with God, its Creator and source of life. An integral part of this anthropology is Mariology, which states that 'woman is realised in spiritual motherhood, in the power she has when she is truly a new creature, the power to conceive God in ravaged souls'. Paul Evdokimov emphasises that the female condition is neither isolated nor inferior to the male condition[13], but the truth is that the Marian case teaches us precisely how to break out of this dichotomy. Mary takes a revolutionary position in that she challenges and transcends the traditional gender role assigned to her by the society of her time. Her figure overcome the social and cultural expectations associated with femininity, redefining her identity in autonomous terms that do not conform to gender stereotypes and established roles. In this way, Mary subverts traditional sexual binarism, overcoming rigid dichotomies between masculinity and femininity. If we analyse the Mary-Joseph couple through the lens of social constructions of gender, Mary embodies a form of acting that is historically associated with masculinity. Her choices are characterised by autonomy, determination and a fight for her ideals, signs of a strong personal agency. Joseph, on the contrary, represents an alternative masculinity, historically defined as feminine, based on listening, trust and support. His role is configured as complementary and supportive of Mary's mission, highlighting a gender dynamic that deconstructs the traditional patriarchal model.

In this sense, Mary not only challenges the social rules of the time, but together with Joseph embodies a prototypical relationship in which gender categories are suspended and even transcended. Mary's character is multifaceted and of great interest precisely because she faces different contextual conditions that influenced her life. On the one hand, Mary was subject to strict social and cultural patterns, such as the obligation to marry an older man, conforming to the traditional expectations reserved for women of the time. On the other hand, however, she also enjoyed a privileged status: she came from a family of prominent lineage and had received an education, both elements that provided her with relevant social and cultural tools[14].

---

[11] Genesis 1:1.

[12] For a deeper exploration of the concept of Chora from a philosophical perspective, I refer to: Sallis (1999) and more recently, Heritier (2023).

[13] Cfr. Evdokimov (1983).

[14] For a socio-theological analysis of Mary's condition, see: Anderson (1987).

Mary was able to exploit these resources to make conscious choices, interpreting her position of advantage to act in an unconventional way within the context that surrounded her. Her figure, therefore, is not reducible to a model of mere submission, but stands out for its ability to make decisions that, when set within the framework of the social norms and expectations of the time, shows elements of rupture and revolutionary instances. The complexity of the figure of Mary makes her an extraordinarily powerful symbol, capable of representing the possibility of transformation and innovation within an established social system. This symbolic power is particularly relevant for the Orthodox faithful, for whom Mary is not only a model of a mother in a profound spiritual sense, but also embodies the power of faith and the struggle for goodness. Her icon, with all its theological and symbolic implications, plays a decisive role in shaping the collective imagination, offering a source of inspiration that transcends the traditional boundaries of gender and social function.

As I will try to illustrate in the second part of this article, the cult of Mary is central to Orthodox religious practice, with hundreds of prayers, acathists, chants and orations dedicated to her, written by the Church fathers. These liturgical texts, recited daily by the faithful, either as a collective canon or as individual prayers, reveal not only her role as a symbol of hope, but also her representation as a figure of power. Mary is worshipped as Queen, Empress, Mother of all[15]—roles that also find expression on an iconographic level, as in the Byzantine icons depicting her with sceptre and crown. In this sense, Mary is not simply a moral example or a spiritual model to be imitated, but a true leader, a guiding figure with authority and power. She is someone to be actively followed, capable of exerting a significant influence on a spiritual as well as a social and symbolic level. Mary thus is endowed with a transcendent force, able to guide and inspire human beings through the power of her faith and kingship, and thereby reinforcing her status as a spiritual leader within the Orthodox community.

3 Some Methodological Remarks

This paper relies on an experimental and interdisciplinary work that intermingles anthropological and historical-theological methodologies. The aim is to outline a phenomenological background against which to carry out a critical analysis of gender and human rights policies, with specific reference to the role of women within Orthodox communities. In my view, taking such an interdisciplinary approach is crucial to grasping the multifaceted interaction between secular law and religious law underlying the narratives that concur to perpetuate forms of violence on both sides. I believe that this kind of critical and comparative perspective can be useful in trying to understand how to defuse the mechanisms of discrimination that contribute to triggering gender-based violence in everyday life.

---

[15] Cfr. Athanasios (1857)

The Romanian Orthodox Church is certainly to be configured as a strictly patriarchal and male chauvinist space—just think of the dimension of power management, and the question of the priesthood. Nevertheless, it is possible to find within it some internal experiences of female agentivity that relativize the apparent absolute rigidity of such a monolithic system. On the contrary and almost symmetrically, the claims of modern feminism tend to ossify the experiences of religious women, Orthodox Christian in this case, and label them as 'scripts of subalternity'. However, this merely contrastive secular view risks fuelling a narrative that fails to recognize the full dignity of positions and experiences, which instead deserve to have a voice of their own. The polarisation of the debate, either in one sense or the other, proves to be a short-sighted exercise. Conversely, it is necessary to develop elements of dialogue and translation that can support the construction of truly polyphonic and inclusive policies, precisely to avoid a partial and ultimately misleading understanding of the 'experiential landscape' to be interpreted. In this sense, precisely the role of Mary and its anthropological reception can be used as an interface of translation. Actually, the fieldwork data suggest that the cultural icon of Mary functions as a catalyst for renewing the potential of the multiple subjectivities at play. Somehow, it seems to have the power to regenerate seemingly atrophied systems, transforming them into active/creative spaces for the political and social implementation of human rights.

In the first part of my contribution I tried to proffer a theoretical approach, a hermeneutic investigation that leverages traditional sources to reconstruct the figure of Mary in all its facets. Conversely, this second part results from my ethnographic fieldwork carried out in the Romanian Orthodox communities of the Emilia-Romagna[16] and Lazio regions between 2017 and 2024. Here, I specifically refer to 15 semi-structured interviews and 10 free interviews, which are the ethnographic outcome of encounters with women from these communities. Of these, eight were wives of the religious leaders of the parishes I attended.

A relevant element that almost immediately gushed out from my fieldwork concerns the composition of these communities, about 65% of which are women, with an average age between 35-50 years. Most of these women are migrants from Romania, with medium to low levels of schooling, working in Italy in jobs related to handicrafts, catering and social assistance jobs.

The third part of my paper weaves together theoretical interdisciplinary patterns with the qualitative data that emerged in the field. The specific goal is to offer insights for future reflections that can open a fertile avenue for dialogue and mutual understanding between two seemingly distant worlds as such assumed as unable to communicate and interplay.

[16] My initial field research among the Romanian Orthodox communities in Italy started in 2017, simultaneously with the first mapping project of Orthodox realities in the Emilia-Romagna region. The insights and corpus of data gathered during this preliminary investigation have culminated in the following publication: Carnevale (2018).

4 Mary as a Horizon of Meaning in The Experiences of Gender and Religious Freedom Among Migrant Women of The Romanian Orthodox Diaspora

I would now like to present an account of the experiences of several women I had the opportunity to interview during my fieldwork. However, it is essential to introduce some essential epistemological assumptions that will guide my analysis and understanding of these testimonies. The experiences of the women interviewed convey an emic and privileged glimpse into the subject. They show how gender and religious identities are not static, but evolve over time, in response to changing contexts. The testimonies of the interviewees will be interpreted with this dynamism in mind, that is, recognising their capacity to adapt and transform in the face of challenges and opportunities. In this regard, the concluding example of the first section, concerning Mary's ability to transcend gender categories, could be taken as a useful theoretical tool to highlight the dialectical/epistemological biases that connote some expressions of modern feminism and to suggest the adoption of a renew hermeneutical perspective. As observed, Mary, in her symbolic and theological role, challenges rigid gender classifications and proposes a model of agency that transcends divisions between male and female. The experiential icon she embodies can help reconsider the theoretical foundations of contemporary feminism, which, while aspiring to overcome binary categorisation, runs the risk of remaining anchored in a logic of classification so ingrained in traditional culture and its discriminatory pitfalls that it already seems outdated. For example, the risk of even extraordinarily innovative interpretive models such as intersectionality is to think that they can fully capture the multiple facets of human experience. However, even intersectionality, while extremely useful in highlighting the interplay between different forms of oppression, could fall prey to the danger of becoming yet another tool for categorising and crystallising the experiences of subjectivity, rather than enabling the exploration of the generative potential of human beings more broadly.[17]

The categorisation of 'women's roles' in religious institutions, as well as in modern debates, is complex and requires a multi-perspectival critical analysis of

---

[17] The concept of 'intersectionality', introduced by Crenshaw (1989) marked a crucial turning point in feminist discourse, paving the way for the analysis of the intersections between multiple forms of oppression. However, as noted by Azzurra and Cirillo (2017), for example the dimension of social class was initially overlooked in intersectional theory. It was only later that feminism incorporated analyses of class dynamics, previously explored by thinkers such as Marx, Engels, Babel, Kollontaj, and Zetkin, highlighting that while women are oppressed as women, the nature and intensity of this oppression vary depending on their class background. This demonstrates that intersectionality, although a significant advancement, cannot be considered a final endpoint. Posthumanism, in fact, calls for rethinking the transcendence of categories not through their total elimination, but by promoting their critical and conscious use, free from ideological assumptions and aimed at a more nuanced and complex understanding of power and oppression dynamics. A recent collection of essays collection based on the implication of posthumanism examine the extent to which we can still engage with dichotomous categories, such as man/woman, us/them, and others. This discussion is meticulously summarized in the well-articulated introduction of Taylor (2019).

existing social norms and hierarchical structures. According to Goffman's theory, 'role' refers to a set of behaviours that conform to the normative expectations associated with a specific status[18], in this case the status of 'woman'. The adoption of such hermeneutic pattern, however, could end up caging female subjectivity within established and limiting stereotypes, which reduce the plurality of individual experiences and expressions to a single normative dimension gauged on the biological sex they belong to. The reference to the status of woman, as opposed to man, raises relevant and intricate anthropological questions, as gender categories cannot be treated in a static or universally applicable manner. According to physical anthropologists and primatologists' studies—including those by Frans de Waal in the case of our close cousins the primates—social roles are not necessarily or exclusively based on biological sex[19], and these studies challenge the common assumption that such divisions are inevitable because they are 'natural'. The division of roles is not rigidly determined by biological sex but can be negotiated and transformed according to the needs and characteristics of communities.

Evolutionary psychology and sociobiology suggest that human adaptation functions according to flexible and porous conjectures, not rigid patterns. Talking about 'experiences of humanity' in a pluralistic sense, and not of a 'woman's role', allows to explore different forms of manifestation, which are not limited to compliance with pre-established social and religious norms, but include a creative and regenerative dimension.

In the above perspective, overcoming the rigid normative view of the role of women within religions becomes crucial to enhancing the potential inherent in the concrete practices and experiences of the interviewees. It is therefore necessary to shift the focus away from the formal prescriptions about what a woman 'should' do or be to the recognition of her actual conduct and contribution as a human being, as becomes clear by analyzing the figure of Mary, not only for what is remembered of her as a distant symbolic icon, but for what she really represented in her human and spiritual dimension.

This perspective makes it possible to explore, also at a legal and institutional level, new forms of participation and recognition for women, enhancing their agency and transformative potential within social structures, without binding them to predetermined roles or rigid gender patterns.

---

[18] Cfr.Goffman (2013).

[19] Recent research on primates has prompted physical anthropologists and primatologists to critically reconsider the longstanding dichotomous frameworks through which we have categorized animals based on sex. Observations of primate communities reveal a more intricate social landscape, characterized by fluidity and complexity, wherein divisions do not always conform to rigid binaries. It is crucial to acknowledge that our understanding of the natural world is significantly influenced by our projections and expectations regarding animal behavior. Therefore, these studies are indispensable for elucidating the intricate relationship between the natural and the cultural realms, highlighting how cultural constructs can shape our perceptions of nature and viceversa. De Waal (2022).

During the first field approaches geared towards getting to know communities, mapping them and beginning ethnographic analysis[20], it soon became apparent that priests' wives do not play a marginal role in Romanian Orthodox Communities, but rather are endowed with a pivotal role in managing community dynamics. Initially, the methodological approach I adopted was to collect data through direct interviews with the priest, who is considered the formal leader of the community. However, it soon became evident that in order to fully understand the functioning and internal dynamics of the communities, it was essential to interact also and above all with the priests' wives, as they were key figures in the social organisation.

During the first interviews, the wives were often present, although they initially maintained an apparently passive role, engaging in secondary activities such as preparing food or handling small practical tasks. Nevertheless, they frequently intervened to correct or complete relevant information, e.g. the number of worshippers, children's participation, or activities organised by the community. In some cases, they took control of the conversation, interrupting the husband when they felt he was revealing details that were inappropriate or too specific for an interview with a researcher.

The power dynamics between the priest and his wife proved to be balanced in most cases, with the community leadership role oscillating between the two. In many circumstances, the wife exerted more influence in the day-to-day running of the community than the priest. This turned out to be one of the most significant aspects that emerged during the fieldwork, underlining the centrality of the female role within the Romanian Orthodox communities, often not formally recognised but ultimately decisive. From a legal point of view, this role can be traced back to the category of 'informal authority' or 'tacit leadership', insofar as it is not formally sanctioned by ecclesiastical or state norms but consolidated through customary and social practices.

The interviews made clear that around half of the priests' wives interviewed have a medium-high level of education, often higher than that of their spouses. This educational discrepancy affects the distribution of responsibilities within the community: while the priest is mainly concerned with spiritual care, the wives tend to take on functions that fall within the scope of the administration and management of the material and immaterial patrimony of the religious community. From the point of view of denominational (orthodox) and civil law, while not formally holding any official religious or administrative function, these women act as 'de facto administrators' of community resources. Their contribution falls within the framework of private law, particularly regarding the management of religious associations or bodies of worship, where they play a non-codified, but essential, external representative role in relations with civil authorities and dioceses. It is interesting to note that, for example, in the Romanian Orthodox diocese in Italy, there is a predominance of women in administrative positions, although it is important to remember that the hierarchical structure is headed by the bishop, vice-bishop, protopapes, priests and deacons, all

[20] For a deeper insight into the collected data and mapping work, refer to Carnevale and Girneata (2018); Carnevale and Girneata (2023).

male figures who manage, control, design and structure the diocese. However, it is to be underscored how in real life, the wives' greater familiarity with the language of the host country and their skill in interpersonal relations place them in a privileged position to manage cultural and diplomatic aspects, configuring them as subjects who exert a relevant social and community influence, even if not formally recognised by the ecclesiastical order. Women organise gathering spaces, interface with civil and religious institutions, and create networks of solidarity and mutual assistance, acting as promoters of economic and social activities within the community. Among other activities, they maintain notice boards in many of the mapped parishes, as well as create and manage groups on social networks where this information continues to circulate.

This is the case of Nela[21], who arrived in Italy with her husband in the late 1990s when she was only 20 years old and has now become one of the key figures in the management of the youth policies of the Romanian Orthodox Diocese in Italy. During the interview, Nela tells me that, at least at first, taking on the role of a priest's wife was not easy at all. Unlike the theological schools and universities, where men are taught how to become priests, there is no institutional structure that teaches women how to fulfil their role within the community. That is why taking on that role often becomes a personal challenge: "it is up to you, to understand what you can and wish to do for the community. Since I had studied to become an educator in Romania, I immediately thought of directing my efforts towards educating the youngest children. But I didn't want to do it in the traditional way, so I started to explore different methods, and schools of thought. I didn't want to simply do catechism with the children of the diaspora, I wanted to offer them tools for growth, first and foremost".

Nela started by managing the group of children, who attended the celebration every Sunday in the small church in the Roman suburbs. Then, as a result of her successful practices, she was called by the bishop to manage the summer centres of the diocese, and the various activities aimed at educating and bringing young people closer to the Orthodox Church.

Nela tells me that it was not easy to gain a voice within the diocese. It is not enough to be competent; one must also know how to make oneself heard, and fight if one has an idea and is sure of its possible success. I point out to her the similarity of her experience to Mary's action, in choosing to defy all the rules for what she had faith in, and she immediately pulls out from the cover of her phone a small icon with Mary and the Child. "The Mother of God is my protector, she has always inspired me, not only as a model of faith, because I think no one in the world had more than her... But because of how she loved God. Even when her son was on the cross, she did not lose hope, she knew that God's love would be stronger than human hatred, because she experienced it herself. Here I am inspired by this model of love, which surpasses even that of a mother. I personally am not a mother, but I feel that I love

[21] All names presented in this paper are fictitious in order to preserve the anonymity of the individuals interviewed. This choise is due to ethical research standards that prioritize the confidentiality and privacy of the informants.

all these children, and that I have a strong hope in what God, through me, does for them".

Veronica is the wife of another priest of a small community on the outskirts of Bologna. She is a very elegant woman, loves fashion, and almost never wears a veil during the celebration. This aspect intrigues me, since in the Orthodox church women are formally required to cover their heads during the celebration, and many of the priests' wives in the communities I have visited do not seem to follow this practice. I ask her why she does not wear a veil: "Covering one's head is just a consequence of covering one's ego, giving up a little, bowing one's head to see what is going on around us. But if we are not able to do this in the first place, it is useless to pose as charismatic people, humble only in appearance. Personally, I consider myself a person who is still a long way from that ideal of humility, and I do not like to give an impression of myself, far from the truth, just because I am the priest's wife! There are Sundays when this gesture comes from my heart, and I do it, but there are Sundays when I feel I want to express myself differently. At the beginning this choice weighed heavily on me, especially because other women within the church criticised me, gossiping about how inappropriate it was for me, who held a certain role, to present myself in that way. The curious thing is that I have never received any criticism from men on this aspect... Perhaps because they do not feel the same pressure as us women to wear the veil during the liturgy, and so they are less attentive to who does or does not do it. But it made me smile that it is always women, who go against other women, even in a sacred context... in church, where our attention should be focused elsewhere".

In the province of Latina, I met Lucia, a migrant of Romanian origin who upon her arrival in Italy started working as a tomato and strawberry picker in the fields. She lived in a shack with other Romanian migrants. Her husband had remained in Romania with their children aged ten and fifteen. Lucia took on the role of provider in the family; everything she earned was put aside to send to her children and husband. Thanks to Lucia, the children were able to attend a school in the city, better than the one they had in the small village in the country where they lived. In this regard, Lucia tearfully tells me: "They had clean clothes, and plenty of food, but they did not have me beside them. Yes, there was my husband, who was always an attentive, good father, but not very strict. The one with the strongest character was always me, to tell you the truth, they listened to me who was here 2000 km away, and not their father who was in the other room at home. I always worked because I didn't want them to lack anything, but things became difficult when they grew up. The older one started having gambling debts, he beat his father. When I returned to Romania I found a desperate situation, I went back to work here to be able to pay my son's debts. I was in a deep depression until I discovered the Romanian church here. From that point on, I went every Sunday. Prayer saved me, took me out of depression, and gave me back my dignity. I started to understand that besides money, I had to offer more to my children, in a human sense [...] I gave them faith in something, hope. They saw me reborn, and they were reborn with me. We have been miraculously blessed by the mother of God, I pray to her every night to protect me and my children, she has compassion for everyone, no one excluded, and it is said that she alone has the power to intercede before God, to bring our prayers instantly before Him".

In addition to the role of the community leader assumed by the priest's wife as exemplified above, there are other female figures, women who take care of the churches in spatial, logistical and social terms, who very often become and remain the figures of reference for the community, especially when a priest has to transfer to another community. This is the case of one of the communities in Rome, where Doinita, a migrant woman in her fifties who arrived in Italy in 2006, has been looking after the church where the Romanian community has celebrated since 2008, and has seen as many as three priests change over time. It is precisely the religious leader who points Doinita out to me when I ask for some information on the history of the place, telling me she is the history of the place. Smiling, she tells me about when she first came to the community in Rome to replace the second priest. Doinita explained everything to him, not only the history of the place and the community, but also how to relate to the various members of the community, how to interact with local institutions, how to develop projects for the youngest but also intercultural projects between the Orthodox community and the Catholic community that hosts them in this old neighbourhood parish. Doinita was the priest's teacher but remains—as he confirms in the interview—the 'mistress' of the place. "I don't allow myself to move a single plant without Doinita knowing about it. She also manages a part of our finances, destined for the care and organisation of the place, as well as the funds for the agape or the feast of the patron saint of the church".

During the interview with Doinita she is often moved, telling me how she escaped from a marriage to an abusive man in Romania, how her family never supported her as the last of ten children. Doinita was not a religious person in Romania and had never studied, but once she started to frequent the Orthodox community, she started to read all the books on sale at the 'pangar', partly because it was the only place where she could find books in Romanian, as she had difficulty reading in Italian. Doinita tells me how on her journey as a migrant she had invested a lot of hope, but when she arrived in Italy, she was often the victim of discrimination and violence. In the house where she worked as a caregiver, the son of the elderly woman she was caring for began to make increasingly intrusive advances, until in the face of Doinita's continuous refusals he began to threaten her, and she was forced to flee. With nowhere to go, no knowledge of the language, and no money, Doinita, who heard about the parish where the Romanians celebrated, felt it would be the only safe place to take refuge at that time. And so, it was.

Doinita's story had a happy ending, but surely there are many stories of migrant women who have suffered violence, discrimination, poor job opportunities, and even poorer economic resources. It is easy to understand how the sacred space in the diaspora also represents a safe space for these women, who are certainly not literate in the use of safe spaces in the city such as counselling centres, associations, or civic place of complaint such as police and *carabinieri*. In the religious community they build not only a space for emergency refuge, but also an existential/experiential circuit within which they can stay, live, put down roots and develop subjective empowerment dynamics.

Approaching the church means developing powerful inter-subjective relationships, talking to other women who speak their language, finding the courage to talk about one's own situation, interacting with each other, finding solutions, but also relying on a solid assistance network in finding a job, renting an apartment, learning how to obtain documentation such as *ISEE- Indicatore Situazione Economica Equivalente*[22] and receiving governmental economic aid. But it is also the space where they rediscover their passions: many of them discover reading, theological study, or Byzantine psaltic music by singing in the choir. Others engage the educational and cultural dimension by taking care of activities for children, studying the Romanian language and culture, or creating plays, Romanian folk dances, poetry. The community environment allows these women to find a social step up, to the point of elevating them to roles close to leadership, acquiring new skills for the workplace, referrals, but also a powerful mutual aid network, which allows all the women of the community to increase their social and economic capital. This unprecedented potential for self-determination translates into changes in lifestyle, future expectations, and a new awareness of one's rights.

In the Orthodox diaspora communities, new spaces of agency and self-reflection are thus opening up for migrant women that go beyond the mere theological dimension, but which, as we have seen, are semantically oriented by powerful icons such as those of Mary. These changes redefine gender roles in the orthodox religious context of the diaspora, creating a significant impact also in the secular communities where migrants arrive, where a translation of religious empowerment into socio-economic empowerment can be observed more and more clearly. Incorporating the experience of these women into feminist studies through ethnographic research becomes, in my opinion, crucial not only to ensure increasingly representative, polyphonic as well as critical discourses, but also to highlight the pervasively relational, porous and therefore continuously transformative nature of the interplay between women, religions, society and rights. As Veena Das points out, the restorative work done by women cannot be underestimated, since the condition of vulnerability does not necessarily coincide with that of victimisation[23]. One cannot automatically assume that social or religious norms or cultural expectations and stereotypes translate directly into forms of oppression. In fact, it is necessary to carefully ponder the gap between the abstract existence of a social rule and its concrete application, as well as its translation into the politics of everyday human experience.

Had Mary merely passively conformed to the impositions of the socio-cultural context of the time, rigidly adhering to the role assigned to women, Western history would most likely have taken a different course. However, while individual lives are shaped by historical and social conditions, they are also capable of generating new contexts. Mary is a paradigmatic example of this capacity for agency. For this reason, her role is fundamental in reconsidering the image of the 'femina religiosa', not in

[22] A calculation tool used in the Italian economic system to assess the economic conditions of households applying for subsidised social benefits or facilitated access to public utility services, i.e. those services that depend on the applicant's economic condition.

[23] Cfr. Das (2005).

opposition or subordination to ‘homo religiosus’[24], but as an integral part of fluid, interchangeable and interconnected realities.

5 Concluding Insights: Mary as a Critical Lens for Rethinking Human Rights Beyond Sex Categories

To reach the final conclusions here, it is crucial to understand how the experiences of these women do not follow a binary logic. Instead, they demonstrate that the religious terrain, though often associated with the irrational and subjective dimension, has become, especially in diaspora migrant communities, a fertile space for transformation. This terrain allows for the rethinking of instances seen as fixed and defined, which instead prove to be increasingly malleable and adaptable to the new contextual needs experienced daily. This element of creativity and freedom is not accidental, but has deep anthropological roots, linked to the forms of exposure of the body and mind to the sacred[25] to which these women have been subjected over time. Upon entering an Orthodox church, the faithful are immediately confronted with icons of Christ and the mother of God, Mary, placed at the same height and equal in size. This choice is not only aesthetic, but conveys a profound message, since in the Orthodox tradition icons are not mere representations, but participate in divine reality, shaping earthly reality. They are ‘places’ of encounter with the sacred, as also suggested by Pavel Florensky, who defines the icon as a window onto divine light, where materiality becomes a vehicle for transcendent reality[26].

The visual balance between Christ and Mary in the Orthodox iconographic tradition thus speaks of a complementarity and reciprocity, which is also part of the behavioural codes of the faithful. Interestingly, from childhood, the Orthodox are taught to relate to these sacred figures not in terms of subordination, but in terms of symbolic equality. Christ and Mary, man and woman, share a common iconographic space and are venerated with equal intensity and respect. This constant visual impact arouses and gives shape to a perception of the divine that challenges the dominant patriarchal structures, opening up a space for a vision that is completely inverse to the dominant one. Despite the patriarchal structure of Orthodox ecclesiastical power, the visual dimension of Orthodox worship suggests that men and women can share a sacred space of equal dignity. This symbolic parallelism cognitively influences perception within the community, showing spaces of implicit, if not explicit, equality. In short, the Orthodox tradition, through its icons and liturgical codes, seems to suggest a gender balance that, although not present in formal hierarchies, profoundly influences the perception of the ‘sacred’, which is by no means only a

[24] Cfr. Eliade (1995).

[25] The research conducted within the field of cognitive sciences regarding the embodiment of religion holds significant relevance for understanding the interplay between cognition and physical experience in the religious phenomenon, Soliman et al. (2015).

[26] Cfr. Florensky (2006).

masculine and patriarchal one, as one may be led to think. This phenomenon invites exploring how visual representation and ritual behaviour can subvert or at least mitigate apparent patriarchal structures, introducing a dialogue between genders that is anything but marginal.

Analysing the content posted online, and attending religious communities moreover, it is possible to see how it is women who are increasingly attending both the liturgical and secular activities of the community in greater numbers. The presence of men is decreasing in a space that seems to be frequented, understood and desired more and more by women, and consequently also constructed or reconstructed by them. This becomes possible precisely because what is intended to be a masculine and androcentric space begins to be experienced as a semantically neutral space. Such phenomenon is echoed in the interviews with religious leaders that show how their mission is to emphasise the relationship between the human being and God, regardless of gender. In the same vein, it is relevant to note that the liturgy does not include moments reserved exclusively for women or men. Conversely, the priest addresses the community of the faithful as a single, undivided entity. Through participation in the rite, the community shares Christ's sacrifice for the salvation of humanity, culminating in the consummation of the Eucharist, that is, the body and blood of Christ. And if this aspect could seem secondary if compared with the differentiations enunciated above, it turns out instead to be the most important one. The reason is that it is precisely in this potential space that the diaphragm of encounter and intersubjective relationship takes shaped: an experiental circuit where gender roles are constructed, but also where they are deconstructed and transformed, claiming new forms of agency. From this perspective, there seems to be an abysmal zone of freedom in the Christic message that surpasses all human categorisations, and at the same time makes such categorisations both conceivable and surmountable, at least if one approaches such a message with '*smerenie*', or humility. In this case, the verse Galatians 3:28 "There is neither Jew nor Greek; there is neither slave nor free; there is neither male nor female, for you are all one in Christ Jesus" looks emblematic.

In light of the above analysis, symbolic orthodoxy seems to embody a contradiction that is nevertheless to be considered part of human experience itself, of the relativism of multiple worlds and 'natures' that cannot be reduced to fixed cultures.

Religion, as we have seen, is a powerful agent in shaping reality, and the Marian icon represents for orthodox women a horizon of meaning that legitimises and inspires their actions. Through the figure of Mary, the sacred dimension is transformed into a dynamic field, capable of influencing everyday life and offering new tools for interpreting and adapting to life's challenges. This process of identity reworking, which takes place in a religious context, highlights the ability of these communities to use religion not as a conservative element, but as a resource for the construction of new subjectivities and for overcoming traditional social and gender rigidities.

The question, however, remains as to how to use these local paradigms as translation tools in secular orders[27]. In my view, the points made so far are part of that debate concerning the redefinition of legal subjectivity in the age of globalising and globalised capitalism. In her essay 'Antropologia del soggetto di diritto',[28] Marella describes the dynamics of transformation of this particular legal category over the centuries. She states that the idea of a 'weak' subjectivity, proposed in the context of the commons project, reflects a model in which the individual no longer constitutes the centre of the legal system, but is reconceived as a function of collective access to resources, from a non-anthropocentric perspective. This notion introduces the concept of a 'non-subject', characterised by the dissolution of individual identity and the emergence of an impersonal subjectivity. This approach contrasts with the traditional models of subjectivity characteristic of contemporary globalisation, proposing a deconstruction of particular identities and a social reconstruction beyond identity paradigms.

Marella goes on to explain how the concept is further articulated in the notion of the 'whatever singularity', theorised by Giorgio Agamben, which draws a subject without rigid and universal identities, belonging to a non-essential community and located outside the traditional legal categories of liberalism. This subjective figure is part of a context of crisis in modern legal structures and represents a response to the aporias of universalism and identitarianism. Within this framework, biopower becomes an object of critique. The non-subject takes the form of a strategy to oppose such forms of biopolitical control, which are also expressed through contemporary legal grammar. The latter, based on human rights and anti-discrimination, is seen as a legal technique that conceals underlying power relations, obscuring the political implications of its application.

From an anti-identitarian perspective, Marella takes up the queer perspective and explains how it questions the role of law in consolidating identity-based social hierarchies. Legal institutions, through the recognition and protection of identities, not only perpetuate such hierarchies, but risk reducing identity to a normative issue, which becomes both an object of protection and control. This engenders a paradox: identity, while central to legal reform projects, remains part of the structural problem. Queer critique emphasises the potential coercive effects of the legal recognition of identities, since such recognition may imply the imposition of codes of conduct associated with identity itself.

In my view, the argument about overcoming categorisation, and the Marian example, become central to this debate. Imagining a 'sexually absurd' world, like the one described by H.G. Wells in his 'Country of the Blind'[29], could offer a new paradigm of thought. In a context where gender categories do not exist or are perceived differently, we could perhaps begin to understand how to decolonise

---

[27] In this context, to gain a comprehensive understanding of the methodology and theoretical foundations that inform these proposed approaches to translation work, refer to: Ricca (2023) and Ricca (2022).

[28] Cfr. Marella (2021).

[29] Cfr. Wells, H. G. (1977). The Country of the Blind, And Other Stories.

our collective imagination and overcome the rigid divisions that lead to violence. In this sense, the figure of Mary as we have analysed so far not only transcends traditional gender categorisations, but actively deconstructs pre-established roles, demonstrating through her actions the possibility of an existence not limited by gender norms. Nonetheless, a critical and simultaneously prospective question must conclude this essay: to what extent do contemporary liberal-democratic legal systems provide adequate protection for 'contemporary Marys'?

References

Anderson JC (1987) Mary's Difference: Gender and Patriarchy in the Birth Narratives. J Relig 67(2):183–202

Athanasios. (1857) Sermo in annuntiationem sanctissimae Dominae nostrae Deiparae. In: PG vol. 28, cols. 955–95

Athanasios (2012) De Incarnatione, trans. John Behr. St. Vladimir's Seminary Press, Crestwood, NY

Azzurra C, Cirillo L (2017) Storia delle storie del femminismo. Alegre, Roma

Biblia sau Sfânta Scriptură. (2013) Editura Institutului Biblic şi de Misiune Ortodoxă, Bucureşti

Carnevale DN (2018) I cristianesimi ortodossi in Emilia Romagna: una mappatura. In: I Monoteismi in Emilia Romagna: Ebraismo, Cristianesimo ortodosso e Islam, a cura dell'Osservatorio sul pluralismo religioso e dell'Assemblea Legislativa Regione Emilia Romagna Servizio Diritti dei Cittadini, Centro Stampa Regionale, Bologna

Carnevale DN, and Girneata SF (2018) Le chiese ortodosse. In: Aspettative e bisogni delle comunità religiose a Bologna

Carnevale DN, and Girneata SF (2023) Case in chiesa. Pratiche, discorsi e spazi dell'integrazione fra i migranti ortodossi in Italia. In: Fuccillo A (ed) Pluralismo confessionale e dinamiche interculturali. Le best practices per una società inclusive

Crenshaw K (1989) Demarginalizing the Intersection of Race and Sex: A Black Feminist Critique of Antidiscrimination Doctrine, Feminist Theory and Antiracist Politics. University of Chicago Legal Forum 1:139–167

Das V (2005) L'atto del testimoniare. Violenza, conoscenza avvelenata e soggettività. In: Antropologia della violenza, pp 215–246

De Waal F (2022) Different: Gender through the eyes of a primatologist. WW Norton & Company, New York

Eliade M. (1995) Sacrul şi profanul. Ed. Humanitas, Bucureşti

Monahul E, Metafrastul S, Mărturisitorul M (2007) Trei Vieţi bizantine ale Maicii Domnului. Editura Deisis, Sibiu

Evdokimov P (1983) La femme et le salut du monde. Desclée de Brouwer, Paris

Florensky P (2006) Beyond vision: Essays on the perception of art. Reaktion Books, London

Goffman E (2013) Frame Analysis. L'organizzazione dell'esperienza, Armando editore, Roma

Harrison NV (2008) Eve, the Mother of God, and other women. Ecumen Rev 60(1–2):71–81

Heritier P (2023) Understanding Legal Semiotics. In: Wagner A, Marusek S, Elgar E (eds) Research Handbook on Legal Semiotics. Publishing, Cheltenham, pp 11–31

Lossky V (1984) Orthodox Theology. SVS Press, Crestwood, NY

Marella MR (2021) Antropologia del soggetto di diritto. Note sulle trasformazioni di una categoria giuridica. Osservatorio dir civ e comm 10(1):71–104

Origen. (1857) Fragmenta in Lucam, Ex Macabii Chrysocephali Orationibus in Lucam, III. In: PG vol. 13, col. 1902. J.-P. Migne, Paris

Petroaia LV (2005) Învățătura despre Maica Domnului în cântările Octoihului. Teologie şi Educaţie la Dunărea de Jos 4(4):319–366

Ricca M (2022) Perpetually astride Eden's boundaries: the limits to the 'limits of law' and the semiotic inconsistency of 'legal enclosures'. Int J Semiot Law 35:179–229. https://doi.org/10.1007/s11196-020-09771-0

Ricca M (2023) Intercultural Spaces of Law: Translating Invisibilities, vol 10. Springer, Cham

Sallis J (1999) Chorology: on beginning in Platos Timaeus. Indiana University Press, Bloomington

Sfântul Grigorie Palama (2007) Omilia 52. Predică la Intrarea în Sfânta Sfintelor a Preasfintei Stăpânei noastre, Născătoarea de Dumnezeu. In: Omilii vol. III, traducere de Parascheva Grigoriu, Editura Anastasia, Bucureşti

Sfântul Nicodim Aghioritul. (2022) Maica Domnului şi Intrările ei în Templu în tâlcuiri mistagogice—cuvinte şi poeme. Editura Deisis, Sibiu

Soliman TM, Johnson KA, Song H (2015) Its not all in your head understanding religion from an embodied cognition perspective. Perspect Psychol Sci 10(6):852–864

St. Athanasius the Great (2020). (PG vol. 28) Sermo in annuntiationem sanctissimae Dominae nostrae Deiparae, 13–14, col 955, 958. J-P. Migne, Paris;

Taylor CA, Bayley A (eds) (2019) Posthumanism and higher education: Reimagining pedagogy, practice and research. Springer, Cham

Wells HG (1977) The Country of the Blind. Penguin Books, Harmondsworth, And Other Stories

Simona Fabiola Girneata is a doctoral candidate in Legal Anthropology at the University of Rome La Sapienza. In 2017, she participated in the first project mapping Orthodox Christian communities in Italy, and since then, she has been actively engaged with Romanian and Moldovan migrant communities in the region. Her academic training at the University of Bologna and the University Pantheon Sorbonne 1 in Paris has shaped her research, which is grounded in a legal anthropological methodology. Her work focuses on various areas, including human rights, religious pluralism, environmental justice, and cultural heritage.

GPSR Compliance

The European Union's (EU) General Product Safety Regulation (GPSR) is a set of rules that requires consumer products to be safe and our obligations to ensure this.

If you have any concerns about our products, you can contact us on ProductSafety@springernature.com

In case Publisher is established outside the EU, the EU authorized representative is:

Springer Nature Customer Service Center GmbH
Europaplatz 3
69115 Heidelberg, Germany

Batch number: 10755222

Printed by Printforce, the Netherlands